The Chartist General

General Charles James Napier was sent to confront the tens of thousands of Chartist protesters marching through the cities of the North of England in the late 1830s. A well-known leftist who agreed with the Chartist demands for democracy, Napier managed to keep the peace. In South Asia, the same man would later provoke a war and conquer Sind. In this first-ever scholarly biography of Napier, Edward Beasley asks how the conventional depictions of the man as a peacemaker in England and a warmonger in Asia can be reconciled. Employing deep archival research and close readings of Napier's published books (ignored by prior scholars), this well-written volume demonstrates that Napier was a liberal imperialist who believed that if freedom was right for the people of England it was right for the people of Sind – even if "freedom" had to be imposed by military force. Napier also confronted the messy aftermath of Western conquest, carrying out nation-building with mixed success, trying to end the honour killing of women, and eventually discovering the limits of imperial interference.

Edward Beasley is Professor of History at San Diego State University. He is author of *The Victorian Reinvention of Race, Empire as the Triumph of Theory* and *Mid-Victorian Imperialists*, all available from Routledge.

Routledge Studies in Modern British History

For a full list of titles in this series, please visit www.routledge.com

4 The Victorian Reinvention of Race
New racisms and the problem of grouping in the human sciences
Edward Beasley

5 Origins of Pan-Africanism
Henry Sylvester Williams, Africa, and the African diaspora
Marika Sherwood

6 Statistics and the Public Sphere
Numbers and the people in Modern Britain, c. 1800–2000
Edited by Tom Crook and Glen O'Hara

7 Public Health in the British Empire
Intermediaries, subordinates, and the practice of public health, 1850–1960
Edited by Ryan Johnson and Amna Khalid

8 Disability in Eighteenth-Century England
Imagining physical impairment
David M. Turner

9 British Student Activism in the Long Sixties
Caroline M. Hoefferle

10 Philanthropy and Voluntary Action in the First World War
Mobilizing charity
Peter Grant

11 The British Army Regular Mounted Infantry 1880–1913
Andrew Winrow

12 The Chartist General
Charles James Napier, the conquest of Sind, and imperial liberalism
Edward Beasley

The Chartist General

Charles James Napier, the conquest of Sind, and imperial liberalism

Edward Beasley

LONDON AND NEW YORK

First published 2017
by Routledge
2 Park Square, Milton Park, Abingdon, Oxon OX14 4RN

and by Routledge
711 Third Avenue, New York, NY 10017

Routledge is an imprint of the Taylor & Francis Group, an informa business

© 2017 Edward Beasley

The right of Edward Beasley to be identified as author of this work has been asserted by him in accordance with sections 77 and 78 of the Copyright, Designs and Patents Act 1988.

All rights reserved. No part of this book may be reprinted or reproduced or utilised in any form or by any electronic, mechanical, or other means, now known or hereafter invented, including photocopying and recording, or in any information storage or retrieval system, without permission in writing from the publishers.

Trademark notice: Product or corporate names may be trademarks or registered trademarks, and are used only for identification and explanation without intent to infringe.

British Library Cataloguing in Publication Data
A catalogue record for this book is available from the British Library

Library of Congress Cataloging in Publication Data
Names: Beasley, Edward, 1964– author.
Title: The Chartist general : Charles James Napier, the conquest of Sind, and imperial liberalism / Edward Beasley, San Diego State University.
Description: Abingdon, Oxon ; New York, NY : Routledge, 2016. | Series: Routledge studies in modern British history ; 12 | Includes bibliographical references.
Identifiers: LCCN 2016025010 | ISBN 9781138699267 (hardback : alk. paper) | ISBN 9781315517292 (ebook)
Subjects: LCSH: Napier, Charles James, 1782–1853. | Generals—Great Britain—Biography. | Great Britain—History, Military—19th century. | Sindh (Pakistan)—History, Military—19th century. | India—History—British occupation, 1765–1947. | Chartism.
Classification: LCC DA68.12.N2 B43 2016 | DDC 359.0092 [B]—dc23
LC record available at https://lccn.loc.gov/2016025010

ISBN: 9781138699267 (hbk)
ISBN: 9781315517292 (ebk)

Typeset in Bembo
by Apex CoVantage, LLC

Printed and bound by CPI Group (UK) Ltd, Croydon, CR0 4YY

Contents

List of figures	vii
List of maps	viii
Acknowledgements	ix
Introduction: liberalism and Napier	1

PART I
Boyhood and war — 13

1 Early days	15
2 A soldier	26
3 In America and France	40

PART II
The radical abroad and at home — 51

4 Greece and the Greeks	53
5 Cephalonia and the Greek Revolution	64
6 Social reform for Cephalonia	76
7 Departure and bereavement	93
8 Australia and idealism	103
9 Flogging and politics	114

PART III
The north of England — 127

10 The coming of Chartism	129

vi *Contents*

11	Command in the north	136
12	The long-term threat	151
13	Newport and after	160

PART IV
The conquest of Sind   177

14	To India and Sind	179
15	Napier's motivations	194
16	To and from the battle of Miani	209
17	The battle of Dubba	223

PART V
'In Scinde as in Cephalonia . . .'   235

18	Victory in the sun	237
19	'To protect the poor from Barbarian Tyranny!'	253
20	Conflict and decline	265

PART VI
Commander-in-Chief   275

21	Home and back	277
22	Reforming the army	291
23	The Kohat expedition	299
24	The mutinies of Charles James Napier	314
	Conclusion: Napier, liberalism, and imperialism	328

| *Bibliography* | 343 |
| *Index* | 365 |

Figures

1.1	Background to Napier's youth: 'Massacre at Scullabogue', by George Cruickshank	21
1.2	Napier in 1798, at age sixteen	23
5.1	Argostoli	66
6.1	The St. Theodore Lighthouse, Argostoli	85
12.1	The factory chimneys of Manchester as seen from Kersal Moor in 1857	152
13.1	A notable Chartist demonstration: 'Procession Attending the Great National Petition of 3,317,702, to the House of Commons, 1842'	171
16.1	Miani, 17 February 1843, with Napier on horseback	216
16.2	'Hyderabad on the Indus', showing the fort. Drawn by William Purser and engraved by Edward Finden, from a sketch by Captain Robert Melville Grindlay, 1808	218
17.1	Wellington and Peel attempting to guide or restrain Ellenborough in 1830: 'A Wild Elephant led Between Two Tame Ones'	230
20.1	Napier at Truckee in 1845: 'Lieutenant General Sir Charles James Napier, G.C.B. Governor of Scinde. In the costume he wore during his campaign against the Hill Tribes. The rocky fastness of Truckee with walls 1000 feet high, where he forced them to surrender, forms the background'	268
21.1	Self-representation: Napier's *carte de visite*	278
21.2	Self-representation represented: Napier writing	279
21.3	Representation by others: Napier's bust in a contemporary engraving	280
22.1	Napier as Commander-in-Chief of the Indian Army: *Illustrated London News*, 2 March 1850	291

Maps

4.1	The Ionian Islands	54
11.1	The Northern District: selected cities and towns mentioned in the text	140
14.1	Sind and Punjab in the 1840s	185

Acknowledgements

For her encouragement and her editing I thank my best friend, Rebecca Hartmann.

For their support, assistance, and suggestions, my thanks to my goddaughter Sarah Wyer; her husband Joseph Wyer; my housemate Ronald Zavala; Pablo Ben, Norma Bouchard, Bruce Castleman, Elizabeth Cobbs, Joanne Ferraro, Annika Frieberg, David McClintock, Walter Penrose, and Maria Rybakova; at Routledge, Rob Langham, Tom Gray, Michael Bourne, Jennifer Morrow, and the anonymous reviewers; at Apex CoVantage, Sheri Sipka and her team; Geoffrey Foaud for drawing the maps; at Bridgeman Images, Melissa Goldstein; at the San Diego State University Library, Edward DiBella, Joan Goodwin, Laurel Bliss, and the Interlibrary Loan staff; the librarians and library staffs at the British Library, the Bodleian Library, the National Archives (Kew), the National Army Museum (Chelsea), Senate House Library, the San Diego Public Library, and the libraries of University College, London, the University of California, San Diego, and the University of Oregon; the staff and owners of the Adams Avenue Bookstore, Fifth Avenue Books, and Bluestocking Books in San Diego, Maxwell's House of Books in La Mesa, Powell's Books in Portland, Oregon, the Smith Family Bookstore (both locations) in Eugene, Oregon; and in London, Skoob Books and the booksellers of Charing Cross Road. For their peacefulness, civility, and bustle, I owe a great deal to the locations where most of this book was written, namely about sixty-four coffeehouses and cafes in San Diego, London, Oxford, Paris, Portland, Eugene, Seattle, Mexico City, and San Miguel de Allende, Guanajuato, not to mention the airports, train stations, and public parks. My thanks (once again) to my department chair, Joanne Ferraro, and the San Diego State University History Department for the travel monies which allowed me to carry out archival research over the last six years. And for making possible my longest visit to the archives for this project, I thank San Diego State University for my Spring 2013 Sabbatical and an associated University Research Grant. I dedicate this book to my late father.

Introduction

Liberalism and Napier

There is a saying that one writes the book one wants to read. In preparing a chapter for an academic book a few years ago, I read the classic works old and new on Chartism and the Chartists. I kept running into references to General Charles Napier. The consensus in what I read was that he did a surprisingly humane job as the commander of the army that faced the Chartist protesters in the north of England at the beginning of the 1840s. He may have saved England from revolution, and at the very least he saved some of the members of the working class from massacre. The key to his success in the north of England seemed to be that he agreed with the Chartists about most things. When he was waiting to take over his command he wrote a book accusing the factory owners of the systematic murder of children – the very factory owners he was about to defend from the Chartists.

But the more I learned, the larger did the question of Napier's radicalism grow. Most of the Chartists were working class and proudly so. I wanted to know more about how this upper-class general came to sympathize with the Chartist demands. The best account, a page long, suggested that Charles James Napier derived his political opinions from his namesake, Charles James Fox, the great Whig politician of the late eighteenth and very early nineteenth centuries.[1] Yet Napier came from such a large extended family that it seemed tenuous at best to ascribe the vehemence of his political opinions in the 1830s and 1840s to the influence of a relative who died in 1806. Were the Foxites still an important faction thirty years later?[2] Surely Napier's own education and experiences must have played a greater role in making him who he was.

And then there was the looming question of his imperial activities. Immediately after his Chartist years, Napier conquered Sind (which now makes up much of southern Pakistan) in a war that he seemed to provoke. His name has served as a byword for cynical imperialism ever since. So how did a man with his strange leftist opinions end up going off to conquer a country to add to the British Empire? The books and articles that I was reading never seemed to address this disparity.

As I went further, the mystery kept deepening. Napier conquered Sind in 1843. Soon after, he seemed to recall his leftism. From 1849 until his death in 1853, Napier – for a time the commander-in-chief of the Indian Army and

2 Introduction

then in retirement – began to agitate against the new British practice of burning villages in the hills of Punjab, a campaign of destruction being carried out under the auspices of the governor-general, Lord Dalhousie. Napier believed that spreading destruction in this way was hardly the best way to bring tranquillity to the area or to make the people of the region cooperate with the West. And it looks like he was right. The villages were being burned in the Kohat Valley, south of Peshawar – only seventy miles south of Malakand, where the young Winston Churchill would one day recommend the same policy of setting villages alight. In the 1930s, George Orwell noted that burning these villages and others nearby from the air was being called 'pacification'. More recently, American drones have been exploding in the same region. Yet around 1850 Napier insisted that destroying homes and villages was neither an effective nor a morally acceptable policy for bringing long-term peace. On his deathbed he wrote a book excoriating what he believed were the crimes of British authorities in the area and of the whole British regime in India. British rule was nothing more than organized violence designed to steal money and resources from the Indian people, wrote the conqueror of Sind.

***

I soon learned that just as the historians of Chartism barely mention Napier's later activities in India – or cover them in no more than a few sentences – the specialists on Indian history usually omit his activities in the Chartist period and pay scant attention to his protests over the village-burnings. Nothing matters till he arrived in Sind and nothing matters once he left it. H. T. Lambrick in 1952 and M. E. Yapp in 1980 have done the most detailed work on Napier's time in Sind.[3] Yet neither author says much about Napier's previous life. Neither tries to address the basic question of how Napier could be the Saint in the north of England and the Devil in Sind.

Lambrick's is the most exhaustive scholarly treatment of Napier's conquest. Yet Lambrick was a mid-twentieth-century imperial official, and he shows that focus and that mindset. He discusses Napier's Chartist period in only one page, and he fails to explore Napier's radicalism or read Napier's many books with sustained attention. He dismisses what Napier said about politics as 'the common clap-trap of radicalism'.[4] Lambrick does set out the humane and in some degree successful way Napier administered Sind once he conquered it.[5] But the final impression that one takes from Lambrick's book is that of Napier as conqueror and little else. Minimizing the Chartist part of Napier's life and – more than that – leaving out both Napier's political position and what the man himself had to say in the books he wrote can give nothing but a distorted view.

Later writers mentioning Napier's time in Sind derive their accounts ultimately from Lambrick. Unfortunately they seldom explore the complexities that his volume offers. The newer authors glance at Lambrick, take what they want, and then twist the picture unrecognizably. For them, Napier was a notorious sadist, a man whom no one could ever try to defend.[6] He has been called 'an eccentric swashbuckler', even a 'fascist'.[7] One author has announced that

Napier suffered from unadulterated, lifelong bloodthirstiness.[8] Another says that 'Napier's sadism was matched only by the mystic fervour of his religious zeal, for he believed himself to be a divinity incarnate.'[9] In reading the massive amount of prose that makes up Napier's books, journals, and letters, as I have now done, I can find no hint that Napier confused himself with any part of the Christian Trinity.

My first goal in this book is to reconcile the Good Napier with the Bad. The Good Napier gets very high praise from the scholars of English history – G. M. Young called Charles Napier a 'wise and sympathetic choice' to lead the army in the Chartist period for the way he avoided bloodshed; and more recently Malcolm Chase has commented on Napier's 'shrewd and humane handling of events' – 'partly for humanitarian reasons and partly because he was genuinely sympathetic to the core objectives of the Charter'.[10] Meanwhile according to scholars of imperialism Napier is the 'fascist' who conquered Sind. Perhaps by looking at all the sources, by reading the books that Napier wrote (which really none of the scholars or biographers has done[11]), and by examining both the Chartist and the Indian sides of his career in one volume, I can do the man justice, whether he might be angel or devil.[12] In reality he was, like most of us, something in between.

I have to acknowledge at the outset that the differences between the Good Napier and the Bad can seem very extreme. Napier castigated himself within his own journals for succumbing to the temptations of conquest. Scholars can cite Napier's own agonized testimony in making out a case that his actions in India were indeed immoral and base.[13] But I think we need to tread more carefully and employ more historical imagination to recapture the spirit of the time. To take Napier's anguished confessions literally, as proof of how vicious, how sinful, even how self-absorbed he was is more than a bit misleading.[14] Religious self-loathing may have lost some of its sparkle and appeal in our own lives, but Napier was living in a different era, when the dark night of the soul was a semi-regular occurrence for many people. The early nineteenth century is replete with their private anguishings. Napier's journals reflect that fact.[15] But they also record that he truly believed in what he was doing – conquering people to set them free and then administering them for their own good.

What Napier believed in was not conquest for its own sake, but conquest followed by good government at the hands of administrators like himself. In his view he was removing a despotic foreign regime but also replacing it with something better. The starting point of his thinking on this matter was that no competent nor activist state could be run by the victimized or the ignorant. Napier did not want the poor themselves seizing power, and he certainly did not want them to get killed trying to do so. What he *did* want was a well-meaning government of experts who would look after the poor and create a better society.[16] This meant right-thinking (or in Napier's case *left*-thinking) administrators like himself working hard to build change on the ground.

This active and caring government that Napier envisioned stood in sharp contrast to the inefficiency and immorality of the British government of the

4   *Introduction*

late eighteenth and early nineteenth centuries – or so Napier and like-minded thinkers saw the matter. During his lifetime there was a strong movement away from the corruption that typified eighteenth-century government and towards new models of honest and competent bureaucratic activity.[17] There were also great advances in empirical social research and statistics (which originally meant the knowledge needed to run a state).[18] Napier was himself part of the intellectual movement towards upright rulership and statistical measurement, and his administrative career provides examples of these principles in action, not least in his use of questionnaires.

But the key point is that for Napier, honesty and the new model of administrative competence were the means of turning radicalism into action and social change. In his view, a *military* that was honest and well run could honour the common soldiers, taking proper measures to safeguard their lives. A *government* that was honest would be less of a burden upon the starving poor.

Nor was Napier afraid to take on the hard work of good government himself. When he was sent to deal with the Chartists, he set himself the task of rushing about the north of England, engaging in the kind of on-the-ground politics that the aristocratic politicians of the day would not enter into. He raised money to feed the starving; he worked hard to talk to both rich and poor, going down coal mines to talk to the miners; he calmed panicked dukes and gatherings of frightened, trigger-happy magistrates; he helped everyone understand what they could and could not safely do in their struggles against each other. He *actively* kept the peace. On one occasion Napier explained to the Chartists how much damage to the human body his artillery could inflict, and on another he made sure that they saw how good his men were at handling their weapons. And yet the Chartists knew he was on their side. He may have been commanding the army sent to repress them, but he also attended their meetings. And his presence was no secret to the Chartists. Napier was a small man who wore a huge beard. It spread well down his chest at a time when few English gentlemen sported anything of the kind. (He originally grew it in sympathy with the Greek Revolutionaries of the 1820s, who were bearded.) He had a huge nose and thick glasses, and he was nothing if not recognizable. As he stood listening approvingly to the Chartist orators, everyone knew who he was: the commander of the army that was waiting over the hill, discouraging any outbreak of violence by its looming presence.

But what about the Napier who governed Sind? We need to explore that Charles Napier, too, and the way his work in Cephalonia in earlier years and in the north of England led him to pursue policies that would make enduring changes in Sindhi society, and not of the kind he had in mind.

My assumption is that the two sides of Napier had – at very least – a great deal in common. The Napier of the north of England and the Napier of Sind were the same man, only a year or two apart. Some scholars say that the biographical form may impose an artificial unity on a subject's life, or lends itself to a growth-and-redemption story.[19] So, am I trying to make coherent a life that was in some sense incoherent? I think not. Napier did have several periods when he indulged himself with a kind of prolix depression, writing huge obsessive letters and journal entries for hours every day. He seemed a very different person then. Nonetheless I believe a real unity is apparent in the evidence which he has left us. The radicalism of his youth, when seen alongside what he wrote in his middle years on the need to free Islamic peoples from the despotism of their rulers, does seem relevant to what he did later on. The liberal imperialism that runs through my biographical account of him was something that he himself continually discussed.

The liberal dilemma

I do have a larger goal for this volume, too – above and beyond trying to show how Napier the Angel and Napier the Devil were in fact the same man. I want to address the growing body of scholarship concerning what I think is an important problem: the self-appointed mission of Western powers to extend their own ideas of justice and political order to those living outside the West, and what can happen when they try to do so. The original goal of liberal imperial intervention might be to free a people from the tyranny of its rulers or it might be to feed the starving. Both of these objectives were present in Napier's mind when he conquered Sind.

As we will see, Napier for most of his life wanted to overturn the corrupt elite of England and Ireland, and eventually he turned his attention to corrupt elites abroad. His universalism – his belief that liberal values ought to apply to everyone – turned him into a liberal imperialist. Napier's desire was to bring freedom to the British Isles and to foreign countries alike, and this in my view is the real key to putting him together – above and beyond the abounding faith he had in his own administrative competence.

This actively imperialist side of liberal universalism, this desire to conquer people in order to set them free, is something that many scholars have noted in modern Western thought.[20] Jennifer Pitts and others have examined liberal imperialism in the writings of James Mill, John Stuart Mill, and Alexis de Tocqueville.[21] Certainly there is a substantial literature on the imperial strain in Tocqueville's thinking, a subject upon which I have written elsewhere.[22] And the liberal imperialism of J. S. Mill has drawn special attention from Lynn Zastoupil, Don Habibi, Uday Singh Mehta, Karuna Mantena, and Michael W. Doyle. They have explored Mill's apparent belief that outside the countries of the West freedom has to be established in the first instance by an imperial power exercising a well-intentioned despotism over the non-Western people concerned. But as Duncan Bell has pointed out, the way in which imperialism arose in the mind of J. S. Mill may not have been *exactly* how it arose in the minds of other, less intellectually exalted liberals.[23]

In any case, moral universalism predates the canonical thinkers of the nineteenth century. The idea of rescuing non-Westerners from cannibalism or human sacrifice stretches from Francisco de Vitoria in the sixteenth century to modern human rights treaties.[24] The fact that liberal universalism and the

6   *Introduction*

imperialism that goes with it have a long history seems clear – although, as Andrew Sartori has argued, we need to be mindful of the danger of projecting onto earlier thinkers the imperialist logic of a later period.[25]

In looking in some depth at Napier's life and writings, we can get a better sense of how the desire to conquer foreign peoples for their own good could arise out of a wish for the radical reform of one's own society – in Napier's time and perhaps in our own. In his own lifetime, certainly, Napier was hardly the only person whose ideas were running in this direction. The leaders of revolutionary France wanted to bring freedom to others by force of arms.[26] Napier was a generation younger than most of these figures and he grew up in the shadow of the French Revolution. But it is also significant that he was more than two decades *older* than Tocqueville and John Stuart Mill. So his ideas were shaped instead by some of the older generation of political and economic writers, chiefly William Cobbett and Jean Charles Léonard Simonde de Sismondi. And Napier may have liked these thinkers because he already agreed with them. So it is best to approach how ideas so similar to theirs might arise over the course of Napier's career rather than trying to grasp his thoughts in too intellectual a context. I believe that a biographical element is needed to understand Napier above and beyond the analytical element. Napier can serve as a test case, an applied case, for what a Western conqueror during the 'turn to empire' that Jennifer Pitts discusses really thought he was doing; and for how much in the way of liberal imperialism such a man could work out in the course of his own busy life rather than in a quiet study. The ideas about the spread of universalized Western values which (as I will show) suffused Napier's thinking from an early age turned on the same underlying logic that would work itself out, too, in the minds of the intellectual figures whom Pitts and others have examined. That is, if you have become free and enlightened, and you think the peoples of the rest of the world are as good as you are, shouldn't you help them to become free and enlightened as well? and shouldn't you help rid them of their despotic governments as a first step?

Indeed, what is it that is wrong with this view – save that making the world free by force would cost too much blood and treasure? One answer comes from the Venezuelan sociologist Edgardo Lander. He explains that European liberal thought usually defines progress in terms of the growing political rights of the individual, and in doing so it excludes any examination of communal life and customs. So liberalism has a hard time accounting for the community life it ignores. Yet liberalism's supposedly autonomous individuals, especially if they are living in a colonized society, may belong to poor and marginalized groups whose traditions shape their conception of the world – as with the many indigenous *campesinos* in Latin America. Given economic realities, it is hard for them to achieve equality as autonomous fellow citizens alongside the educated and the well-to-do of their country, whatever the theoretical equality of everyone under a liberal or neoliberal regime. Lander thinks these *campesinos* ought to be listened to rather than always being preached at and modernized.

Introduction 7

This line of reasoning makes for a more complex way of looking at the matter than the strictly liberal view – the view that extra-European countries and communities ought to be made to conform to intra-European individualist politics and economic life. In the last analysis, the indigenous groups who stand outside the liberal tradition may not *want* to conform to it. As Lander asks: All other things being equal, what kind of culture with any choice in the matter rejects its own identity in order to assume a supposedly better one?[27] We will see that in Sind Napier failed to bridge the cultural gap and open any productive dialogue with the people he conquered and ruled.

But for the moment we can leave aside the possible range of views in Sind. We can return to the world of the liberal imperialist discourse in which Napier himself operated. Even within liberalism there may arise – or there should arise – a nagging question. Can a conqueror really bring freedom? On occasion Napier himself entertained some doubts on that point, as we will see. In any case no less a figure than Napoleon I admitted that in his conquests he did *not* impose liberty but a universal order. To do something for the common people he first had to wipe away their traditional rulers and make the laws everywhere the same: 'The annexed territories must be just like France,' the emperor explained, 'and if you went on annexing everything as far as Gibraltar and Kamchatka, the laws of France would have to spread there, too. I am pleading the cause of the humble folk; the others would never lack good dinners and brilliant drawing rooms that will plead for them.'[28] But with Napoleon to plead the cause of the plebeians there was no reason why they should be allowed to plead it themselves: 'Liberty is a need felt by a small class of people whom nature has endowed with nobler minds than the mass of men. Consequently, it may be repressed with impunity. Equality, on the other hand, pleases the masses.'[29] When Napier was rescuing Sind and replacing its traditional rulers for his own ends, he too tried to bring social improvements to please the masses – and not any form of self-rule above the local level.

To find other examples of how this policy of conquest in the name of universal rights, however nobly intended, might wind up diminishing rather than increasing the freedom of the conquered, we do not need to go all the way back to Napoleon. More recent illustrations are not far to seek. Many of the 'neoconservatives' of the United States in the later twentieth and early twenty-first centuries were leftists during the 1960s. Their radical focus on human rights would turn them thirty or forty years later into advocates of American intervention in Afghanistan and Iraq.[30] So was Napier something like them?

And when and how did he become like that? How did he become a liberal imperialist? To do a decent job of answering this question we will need to review the whole of his life in scholarly depth. Charles Napier saw the Irish Rebellion of 1798 when he was a boy, and it taught him something about the consequences of civil unrest. His idea of the importance of keeping the peace was further conditioned by what he experienced on the battlefields of the Peninsular War. He knew and worked with Lord Byron in Greece. And he wrote an historical romance novel in which an eleventh-century Druid predicted a

8 *Introduction*

socialist revolution eight hundred years later.[31] The different parts of Napier's life, and especially his time in the north of England and South Asia, need to be seen in proportion to the whole if we are to form a decent judgement of any one aspect.

Yet I hope I can avoid simply rewriting the great tomes of family biography produced about Charles Napier in the nineteenth century.[32] Nor do I want to recreate the chatty and unsourced volumes written about Napier more recently.[33] These works give short shrift to the Chartist period when they include it at all. They concentrate on Napier's early years in the Napoleonic Wars and his time in India three decades later.

And while many of these books tell amusing stories, they have no footnotes or endnotes. Their authors seldom take the trouble of getting their sources set down just right, and their books are riddled with inaccuracies great and small.[34] I think the problem is this: the writers of these books have stopped with just enough sources to create their well-turned sentences and a continuous story, without casting a wider net for still the other sources they would need to put their conclusions to a real test. One might as well say that Odysseus left Troy, sailed across the beautiful Aegean, and went home. But that makes an epic journey into a weekend excursion. Looking harder for sources will make a more complicated but a more worthwhile and at the same time a more believable story, informed at the appropriate points by the perspectives worked out by modern historians, political scientists, and other scholars.

The factual errors and scholarly omissions in the family histories do matter. So do the errors in judgement and sympathy – when so little attention is paid to what Napier himself could have known in the thick of events, and so little care is shown for the human agency or the sufferings of the people he conquered, killed, or indeed protected.

***

Further, I will strive to resist going too deeply into the war of charges and countercharges that Napier's friends and enemies made in the many volumes they wrote on his time in Sind.[35] I have no desire to take the reader through every last twist and turn in Lambrick's account of what Napier's brother William said about the two main nineteenth-century critics (John Jacob and James Outram), nor what they in turn said about William Napier. The focus will remain on what *Charles* Napier himself thought of all this, and mercifully he did not publish anything on the matter. We need to look at his actions and his letters in depth, but we do not need to look at *everything* that everyone else said about him.

Besides, presenting all that sprawling antiquarian controversy would take another volume at least. And I am afraid that such a volume would not be very worthy as an academic work. For neither side – neither William Napier, who wrote reams of paper in his brother's defence, nor the volumes that Outram and Jacob produced in turn – told the truth quite all the time.[36] One nineteenth-century reviewer described the four-volume biography that William wrote

Introduction 9

about his late brother as 'one of the most indiscrete publications which has ever come from the press' and 'a tissue of gross misrepresentations and abuse'.[37] To spend another hundred pages correcting these men in their squabbles would be a very unattractive prospect. There are more important matters to discuss.

All this does not mean that I will ignore William Napier completely. In his four-volume biography of his brother he gives us many of Charles's letters, as well as large extracts from his journals. Much of this material is not available elsewhere. When it is, the only substantive changes I have found are when William suppresses the comments Charles made about his own – William's own – physical suffering.[38] (For most of his life William Napier's judgement would be poisoned by the opiates he took for his war injuries.[39]) So while most of the present book is constructed from the immense archival sources on Charles Napier himself and on the man's own published works, and while I will be ignoring the eccentric judgements and diatribes of William Napier unless they helped to shape what his brother was thinking at the time, nonetheless on many occasions I will use Charles's journals as William presents them, as well as some of the letters that William incorporates. I do not believe that suppressing Charles Napier's journal would help us toward a deeper understanding of his liberal Imperialism. But I shall use such material in tandem with what may be given elsewhere, not least in the many books that Charles Napier himself wrote.

Notes

1 F. C. Mather, *Public Order in the Age of the Chartists* (1959; New York: Augustus M. Kelley, 1967), 154. Another brief account along these lines: Stanley H. Palmer, *Police and Protest in England and Ireland, 1780–1850* (Cambridge: Cambridge UP, 1988), 432–33. Mather later decided that it was Napier's Irish upbringing which made him a radical – Palmer, 'Charles Napier: Irishman, Chartist, and Commander of the Northern District in England, 1839–41', *The Irish Sword: The Journal of the Military History Society of Ireland* 15 (1982), 89–100.

2 See the review article by Abraham D. Kriegel, 'Whiggery in the Age of Reform', *Journal of British Studies* 32, 3 (July 1993), 290–98 at 295–96.

3 H. T. Lambrick, *Sir Charles Napier and Sind* (Oxford: Clarendon Press, 1952), 35; M. E. Yapp, *Strategies of British India: Britain, Ireland, and Afghanistan, 1798–1850* (Oxford: Clarendon Press, 1980).

4 LNS, 1–6, 32–36, quotation 33; cf. Yapp, *Strategies*, 484–85.

5 LNS, 318, 340–44. Lambrick's positive judgement of Napier's administration of the land he conquered underlines the views of P. N. Khera, *British Policy towards Sindh up to the Annexation, 1843* (1941; Delhi: Ranjit Printers & Publishers, 1963).

6 Piers Brendon, *The Decline and Fall of the British Empire, 1783–1997* (2007; New York: Alfred A. Knopf, 2008), 117; N. Jayapalan, *History of India*, vol. 3, *From 1773 to Lord Minto, Including Constitutional Development* (New Delhi: Atlantic Publishers and Distributors, 2001), 3:124.

7 Vincent A. Smith, *The Oxford History of India*, 4th edn, Percival Spear (ed.) (Delhi: Oxford UP, 1981), 609.

8 William St. Clair, *That Greece Might Still Be Free: The Philhellenes in the War of Independence* (London: Oxford UP, 1972), 167–68, 302–03; see also Alice Albinia, *Empires of the Indus: The Story of a River* (London: John Murray, 2008), 43–44.

10   *Introduction*

9 Stanley Wolpert, *A New History of India*, 3rd edn (New York: Oxford UP, 1989), 222.

10 G. M. Young, *Early Victorian England: 1830–1865*, 2 vols (Oxford: Clarendon Press, 1934), 2:444; H. Palmer, *Police and Protest*, 432; Malcolm Chase, *Chartism: A New History* (Manchester: Manchester UP, 2007), 62, 71.

11 Uniquely, Priscilla Napier seems to have read a few of these books, but it does not seem that she read all of them – Priscilla Napier, *Revolution and the Napier Brothers, 1820–1840* (London: Michael Joseph, 1973), 209.

12 Briefer accounts in popular works on imperialism tend to give short shrift to Napier's radicalism. See Jan Morris, *Heaven's Command: An Imperial Progress* (1972; New York: Harcourt, Brace, Jovanovich, 1974), 176–80, 254–55; Byron Farwell, *Eminent Victorian Soldiers* (New York: Norton, 1985), 62–101. And for Morris the British had yet to abolish *sati* in India (179). The best short account of Napier is in Rodney Mace, *Trafalgar Square: Emblem of an Empire* (London: Lawrence and Wishart, 1976), 113–17. But even Mace says the army Napier defeated in Sind had no guns at all. In fact they did, along with heavy artillery.

13 Robert A. Huttenback, *British Relations with Sind, 1799–1843: An Anatomy of Imperialism* (Berkeley and Los Angeles: University of California Press, 1962), 70–71.

14 Napier to Frederick Robertson, late August 1840, NP, BL Add. MS 49107, fols 37–44 at 41–42, and 20 November 1846, fols 89–91. On another occasion Napier said that while he had a duty to judge the Amirs of Sind on behalf of his own country, and end their tyranny over the people, nonetheless he felt he was a 'worm', full of the 'consciousness of his own guilt in the eyes of God', like a judge who had to condemn criminals rather than letting them all go free – Napier to Robertson, 19 April 1843, fols 68–69.

15 For another example: Napier's journal, 21 January 1846, NP, BL Add. MS 49140, 111–12. Lambrick sees the moral seriousness of Napier's self-examination: H. T. Lambrick, *John Jacob of Jacobabad*, 2nd edn (Karachi: Oxford UP, 1975), 70. For religious self-questioning, see Standish Meacham, 'The Evangelical Inheritance', *Journal of British Studies* 3, 1 (November 1963), 88–104 at 90–91; Ian Bradley, *The Call to Seriousness: The Evangelical Impact on the Victorians* (New York: Macmillan, 1976), 23–24; Elizabeth Jay, *The Religion of the Heart: Anglican Evangelicalism and the Nineteenth-Century Novel* (Oxford: Clarendon Press, 1979), 148–50.

16 Other imperial careerists thought in the same way, wanting (as Napier did) to protect colonized peoples, institute jury trials, and reduce the gap between rich and poor – in Ireland and in the colonies in question. See Zöe Laidlaw, 'Richard Bourke: Irish Liberalism Tempered by Empire', in David Lambert and Alan Lester (eds), *Colonial Lives Across the British Empire: Imperial Careering in the Long Nineteenth Century* (Cambridge: Cambridge UP, 2006), 113–44 at 118–21, 135. However, Napier as a self-described radical who wanted to break up large farms was not one of the much more moderate Irish liberals whom Laidlaw discusses.

17 W. D. Rubinstein, 'The End of the "Old Corruption in Britain", 1780–1860', in Rubinstein (ed.), *Elites and the Wealthy in Modern British History: Essays in Social and Economic History* (Brighton: Harvester; New York: St. Martin's, 1987), 265–303; Philip Harling, *The Waning of 'Old Corruption': The Politics of Economical Reform in Britain, 1779–1846* (Oxford: Clarendon Press, 1996).

18 See Gillian Sutherland (ed.), *Studies in the Growth of Nineteenth-Century Government* (Totowa, NJ: Rowman and Littlefeld, 1972); John W. Osborne, *The Silent Revolution: The Industrial Revolution in England as a Source of Cultural Change* (New York: Charles Scribner's Sons, 1970); Michael J. Cullen, *The Statistical Movement in Early Victorian Britain: The Foundations of Empirical Social Research* (Hassocks, Sussex: Harvester, 1975); Zöe Laidlaw, *Colonial Connections, 1815–1845: Patronage, the Information Revolution, and Colonial Government* (Manchester: Manchester University Press, 2005), chapter 7; Tom Crook and Glen O'Hara (eds), *Statistics in the Public Sphere: Numbers and the People in Modern Britain, c. 1800–2000* (London: Routledge, 2011).

19 For a review of these, see David Lambert and Alan Lester, 'Introduction: Imperial Spaces, Imperial Subjects', in Lambert and Lester (eds), *Colonial Lives Across the British Empire*,

Introduction   11

1–31 at 18–24. See also James Clifford, ' "Hanging up Looking Glasses at Odd Corners" ', in Daniel Aaron (ed.), *Studies in Biography* (Cambridge, MA: Harvard UP, 1978), 41–56; Mary Evans, *Missing Persons: The Impossibility of Auto/Biography* (London: Routledge, 1999); Miranda Seymour, 'Shaping the Truth', in Peter France and William St. Clair (eds), *Mapping Lives: The Uses of Biography* (Oxford: Oxford UP, 2002), 253–66 at 254–55, 263–64; and in the same volume, James Walter, ' "The Solace of Doubt"?: Biographical Writing after the Short Twentieth Century', 321–35.

20 William Appleman Williams, *Empire as a Way of Life: An Essay on the Causes and Character of America's Present Predicament, along with a Few Thoughts about an Alternative* (New York: Oxford UP, 1980), 37–41, 53–54, 87–88, 113–15; Michael C. Desch, 'America's Illiberal Liberalism: The Ideological Origins of Overreaction in U.S. Foreign Policy', *International Security* 32, 3 (Winter 2007/8), 7–43; Martin J. Wiener, *An Empire on Trial: Race, Murder, and Justice under British Rule, 1870–1935* (Cambridge: Cambridge UP, 2009), 1–5, 231–33; Brett Bowden, *The Empire of Civilization: The Evolution of an Imperial Idea* (Chicago: University of Chicago Press, 2009), chapters 4, 8; Georg Sørenson, *A Liberal World Order in Crisis: Choosing between Imposition and Restraint* (Ithaca and London: Cornell UP, 2011); and the 'English School' of International Relations theory, as discussed in Christian Reus-Smit, 'Human Rights in a Global Ecumene', *International Affairs* 87, 5 (2011), 1205–18.

21 Jennifer Pitts, *A Turn to Empire: The Rise of Imperial Liberalism in Britain and France* (Princeton, NJ: Princeton UP, 2005); Bart Schulz and Georgios Varouxakis (eds), *Utilitarianism and Empire* (Lanham, MD: Lexington Books, 2005).

22 Cheryl B. Welch, 'Colonial Violence and the Rhetoric of Evasion: Tocqueville on Algeria', *Political Theory* 31, 2 (April 2003), 235–64; Roger Boesche, 'The Dark Side of Tocqueville: On War and Empire', *Review of Politics* 67, 4 (Fall 2005), 737–52; Edward Beasley, *The Victorian Reinvention of Race: New Racisms and the Problem of Grouping in the Human Sciences* (New York: Routledge, 2010), 34–43; Shanti Singham, 'From Cosmopolitan Anticolonialism to Liberal Imperialism: French Intellectuals and Muslim North Africa in the Late Eighteenth and Early Nineteenth Centuries', in Charles Walton (ed.), *Into Print: Essays in Honor of Robert Darnton* (University Park: Pennsylvania State UP, 2011), 198–215.

23 Lynn Zastoupil, *John Stuart Mill and India* (Stanford, CA: Stanford UP, 1994); Don A. Habibi, 'The Moral Dimensions of J. S. Mill's Colonialism', *Journal of Social Philosophy* 30, 1 (Spring 1999), 125–46; Uday Singh Mehta, *Liberalism and Empire: A Study in Nineteenth-Century British Liberal Thought* (Chicago: University of Chicago Press, 1999); Karuna Mantena, 'Mill's Imperial Predicament', in Nadia Urbananti and Alex Zakarias (eds), *J. S. Mill's Political Thought: A Bicentennial Reassessment* (Cambridge: Cambridge UP, 2007), 298–318; Michael W. Doyle, *The Question of Intervention: John Stuart Mill and the Responsibility to Protect* (New Haven, CT: Yale UP, 2015); Duncan Bell, 'Victorian Visions of Global Order: An Introduction', in Bell (ed.), *Victorian Visions of Global Order: Empire and International Relations in Nineteenth-century Political Thought* (Cambridge: Cambridge UP, 2007), 1–25 at 4.

24 Anthony Pagden, 'Human Rights, Natural Rights, and Europe's Imperial Legacy', *Political Theory* 31, 2 (April 2003), 171–99.

25 Andrew Sartori, 'The British Empire and Its Liberal Mission', *Journal of Modern History* 78, 3 (September 2006), 623–42.

26 For Tocqueville, the French Revolution had the universalist character of a religious crusade – Alexis de Tocqueville, *The Old Régime and the French Revolution, Vol. 1: The Complete Text*, François Furet and Françoise Mélonio (eds), (trans.) Alan S. Kahan (Chicago: University of Chicago Press, 1998), 99–101 (book 1, chapter 3), and the editorial notes at 324–29. See also Naomi Schor, 'The Crisis of French Universalism', *Yale French Studies* 100 (2001), 43–64 at 43–48; Tzvetan Todorov, *On Human Diversity: Nationalism, Racism, and Exoticism in French Thought*, (trans.) Catherine Porter (Cambridge, MA: Harvard UP, 1993), 187–89.

27 Edgardo Lander, *Neoliberalismo, sociedad civil y democracia: ensayos sobre América Latina y Venezuela* (Caracas: Universidad Central de Venezuela, Consejo de Desarrollo Científico y

12   *Introduction*

Humanístico, 2000), 180–83, 187–88. My thanks to Norma Bouchard for pointing me in the direction of Lander.

28   Ibid, 72.

29   Napoleon quoted in J. Christopher Herold (ed. and trans.), *The Mind of Napoleon: A Selection from His Written and Spoken Words* (1955; New York: Columbia UP, 1961), 73.

30   See Richard Seymour, *The Liberal Defence of Murder* (London: Verso, 2008); and Thomas McCarthy, *Race, Empire, and the Idea of Human Development* (Cambridge: Cambridge UP, 2009), 214–19. And see the thirty-one-page table of Western interventions since 1815 in Doyle, *The Question of Intervention*, 228–59.

31   Charles James Napier, *William the Conqueror: A Historical Romance*, William Napier (ed.) (London: G. Routledge & Co., 1858), 383, 407–8.

32   Most notably William Napier's *The Life and Opinions of General Sir Charles James Napier, G.C.B.* Two early biographies from outside the family are William F. Butler, *Sir Charles Napier* (London: Macmillan, 1890) and Thomas Rice Holmes, *Sir Charles Napier* (Cambridge: Cambridge UP, 1925). Butler wrote to entertain, but Holmes was a reasonably careful historian, although he focusses mostly on military affairs in India. He had written an earlier life of Napier – in his *Four Famous Soldiers: Sir Charles Napier; Hodson of Hodson's Horse; Sir William Napier, Sir Herbert Edwardes* (London: W.H. Allen, 1889). Holmes rewrote the Napier section when new military memoirs became available, and the result was his 1925 book. By then Holmes also had the benefit of major figures in Napier's life reading and vetting his first account.

33   Rosamund Lawrence, *Charles Napier: Friend and Fighter* (London: John Murray, 1952); and four books by Priscilla Napier, *The Sword Dance: Lady Sarah Lennox and the Napiers* (London: Michael Joseph, 1971); *Revolution and the Napier Brothers*; and *Raven Castle: Sir Charles Napier in India, 1844–1851* (London: Michael Joseph, 1991).

34   I will allow myself one example only: Priscilla Napier's *Revolution and the Napier Brothers* invents a mass march of the Chartists on London in 1839 to present their 'ten points'; when their ideas go unheard, they march back disappointedly to the North of England – 252, 259.

35   William Napier, *The History of General Sir Charles Napier's Conquest of Scinde* (London: T. & W. Boone, 1845); James Outram, *The Conquest of Scinde: A Commentary* (Edinburgh and London: William Blackwood and Sons, 1846); Richard Napier, *Remarks on Lieut.-Colonel Outram's Work, Entitled 'The Conquest of Sindh, a Commentary'* (London: James Ridgway, 1847); William Napier, *The History of General Sir Charles Napier's Administration of Scinde and Campaign in the Cutchee Hills* (London: Chapman and Hall, 1851); John Jacob, *Notes on Sir W. Napier's Administration of Sinde* (privately printed, no date).

36   For this judgement: LNS, 56–57, 264–65, 295–96; F. J. Goldsmid, *James Outram: A Biography*, 2nd edn, 2 vols (London: Smith, Elder & Co., 1881), 1:277–78; Lionel J. Trotter, *The Bayard of India: A Life of General Sir James Outram, Bart.* (Edinburgh and London: William Blackwood and Sons, 1903), 139.

37   [John William Kaye], 'The Life and Opinions of Gen. Charles James Napier, G.C.B.', *Edinburgh Review* 106 (October 1857), 322–55 at 322, 324, 348–50, 355. The latest scholar to point out that William Napier's books cannot be mined uncritically is Thomas Rodger in his undergraduate thesis at Leeds University: '*The Life and Opinions of General Sir Charles James Napier, G.C.B.* and Chartism', 2009. My thanks to Mr Rodger for providing me with a copy of his thesis as this book was about to go to press.

38   There were also the minor changes to correct punctuation errors and the informal language of the manuscript. Nineteenth-century typesetters often rewrote what they wished with no reference to the author in order to make a paragraph fit a page. See Allan C. Dooley, *Author and Printer in Victorian England* (Charlottesville: University Press of Virginia, 1992).

39   J. W. Fortescue, *Historical and Military Essays* (London: Macmillan, 1928), 224–29.

Part I

Boyhood and war

1   Early days

Charles Napier, who was raised in Ireland in the era of the 1798 rebellion, was the product of a time and place that would shape his ideas about poverty and civil unrest.

He was also very well connected. His mother was Lady Sarah Lennox. Born in 1745, she was the daughter of Charles Lennox, 2nd Duke of Richmond and Lennox, and the great-granddaughter of Charles II and his mistress Louise de Kéroualle. Lady Sarah, too, was able to turn the royal eye. In 1759 the Prince of Wales fell in love with her, but his advisers made the future George III acknowledge that she was a 'country woman' rather than a foreign princess, and so he could not marry her. But he did not forget Lady Sarah, and when he ascended the throne in 1760 he proposed marriage after all.[1]

He was king. She was in her mid-teens. She did not give him a clear answer. When she heard of his engagement to Princess Charlotte of Mecklenburg-Strelitz she tried to get him to repeat his offer, but it was too late.[2]

When Lady Sarah Napier, as she eventually became, looked back on how she had spent her life, she said she would not have enjoyed being queen.[3] Indeed, playing the role of consort would have required a certain steadiness in her romantic life that at first she was not prepared for – and it was her adventurous romantic career that explains how the daughter of a duke wound up marrying a poor army officer and bringing Charles Napier into the world.

For when the king married Princess Charlotte, Lady Sarah rushed into a marriage herself, to one Sir Charles Bunbury. Theirs was not a natural match, and after at least two dalliances on her part – one with the earl of Carlisle, an affair which may not have been consummated, and the other with the French duc de Lauzun, which certainly was consummated – in 1768 she became pregnant by her cousin, Lord William Gordon. Their child Louisa Bunbury was born in the new year. But then Lady Sarah decided to tell everyone the child was not her husband's, and she ran away to live with Lord William.[4]

Bunbury divorced her. The divorce stretched over several years and required an Act of Parliament, as divorces did in that era. When it finally came in 1776 Lady Sarah had made herself notorious. Meanwhile her affections continued to ebb and flow, and she was no longer attached to her cousin Lord William.[5]

For some time Lady Sarah lived quietly in a cottage that her brother the duke built for her on his Sussex estate.[6] But there was an army camp nearby,

16 *Boyhood and war*

and it was not long after the divorce that Lady Sarah met the tall and attractive Captain the Hon. George Napier. He was already married, but that was of little concern. After his wife died Lady Sarah married him herself.

At the time of this second marriage Lady Sarah was thirty-six. She said that with her new husband she was happy for the first time. She and Captain Napier went on to have eight children together.

But George III would never forget her. Years later in his illness he called Lady Sarah his first love. When Captain Napier died in 1804 and Lady Sarah brought herself to the king's attention, George III granted her a pension – almost half a century after he proposed marriage.[7]

***

Lady Sarah had many brothers and sisters who shaped the family world in which Charles Napier would grow up. Her brother Charles Lennox, 3rd Duke of Richmond, took in Lady Sarah when she had made herself notorious. But for a time he was notorious himself. Although a duke, he was a left-wing agitator detested by the king. A friend of the radical Major John Cartwright, the duke gave left-wing speeches and wrote pamphlets of the same ilk in the early to mid-1780s, advocating universal manhood suffrage and annual parliaments.[8] But the excesses of the French Revolution eventually turned him into a moderate and he went to work for the government. He was the founder of the Ordnance Survey.

Through one of Lady Sarah's sisters, Lady Emilia Lennox, there was another connection to left-wing politics. Lady Emilia married the Earl of Kildare, later created Duke of Leinster. The earl was the leader of the radical Patriot (or Popular) wing in Ireland, and he controlled twelve seats in the Irish House of Commons. But Charles Napier would never know him. The duke died young and left Lady Emilia a widow.

She was a radical herself, trying to hire Jean-Jacques Rousseau as tutor for her children. When he turned her down, she hired a certain William Ogilvie, whom the dowager duchess went on to marry.[9]

Over the course of her two marriages Lady Emilia had *twenty-two* children – twenty-two cousins for Charles Napier. Among them was Lord Edward Fitzgerald, a main leader of the 1798 rebellion of the United Irishmen. He was wounded while resisting arrest; charged with treason, he died before trial. Another of Lady Sarah's sisters, Lady Louisa, visited her doomed nephew in Newgate Prison. She pleaded with the authorities on his behalf, and then on his death she helped arrange the funeral.[10]

Lady Louisa also deserves a few words in her own right, for she too was sympathetic to the cause of Irish freedom. She married the wealthy reform politician Thomas Conolly, and they kept the largest house in Ireland, Castletown, which they made a centre of Irish political and cultural life. They had no children but they raised one of Lady Sarah's daughters, Emily Napier, as their own child. Emily was Charles Napier's eldest full sister and the only full sister he had who would survive to adulthood. She would become one of his main confidantes in later years.[11]

Early days 17

There are only a few more of his mother's relations for us to look at in weighing Napier's political antecedents – namely, the family of Lady Sarah's much older sister Lady Caroline. At twenty-one Lady Caroline Lennox had defied her parents to secretly marry Henry Fox, age thirty-nine.[12] Their London home was Holland House, which together they made a seat of Whig politics; Lady Caroline would be created Baroness Holland in her own right. Their son was Charles James Fox, the great leader of the Whig party who opposed the Younger Pitt and helped to shape British politics for a generation.

Again, Lady Caroline was much older than Lady Sarah, who in any case had married Captain Napier when she was in her thirties. Charles James Napier was fully thirty-three years younger than his cousin Charles James Fox, and as we have now seen, Fox was not the only politically involved person in the family. Several of Napier's uncles and aunts were as radical as Charles James Fox or more radical yet. But it is true that Charles James Napier was named for the politician, for Charles James Fox was especially dear to Lady Sarah. She was among the youngest of her brothers and sisters, and she was only four years older than her nephew. Indeed they grew up together, because Lady Sarah spent part of her childhood living with the Foxes after her parents died. Charles James Fox and Lady Sarah were boon companions, putting on plays and discussing in their chatty letters each other's various romantic attachments. And down through the years Lady Sarah would always remain devoted to Fox. She was convinced of his supreme patriotism, the unalloyed wisdom of his policies, and as her biographer puts it, the ideal of 'disinterested service to the nation' for which he stood.[13]

The Napiers and Celbridge

While the Lennoxes gave the world large families and radical politicians, the Napiers gave the world logarithms and soldiers.

Charles's father and Lady Sarah's husband was the Hon. George Napier, the penniless sixth son of Scottish peer Lord Napier of Merchistoun. The family descended from John Napier, who invented logarithms in the sixteenth century. Charles Napier's father George, born in 1751, was educated in Edinburgh under David Hume.

Six-foot-two and rather impressive looking although short-sighted, he went into the army. After he met the recently divorced Lady Sarah, his military career took him to America during the Revolution. And then in New York in 1780 George Napier and his young family contracted yellow fever. He lost his wife and all but one child. The Honourable George himself was not expected to live, and so as he lay unconscious a brother officer sold his commission so that his one surviving daughter would not be left destitute. No longer in the army, George Napier was put on a ship for England.

And then despite all this he recovered – no longer employed and with a child to raise. It was then, in 1781, that he married Napier's mother Lady Sarah and became a part of Ireland's Protestant Ascendancy.[14] Yet this marriage did not solve the problem of money, and in 1782 George Napier managed to get himself

18   *Boyhood and war*

reappointed to the army as an ensign, beginning his second military career as an officer of the lowest possible rank. He did receive some assistance from his new brother-in-law the Duke of Richmond, Master-General of the Ordnance. The thirty-one-year-old ensign took up a junior position created for him at the laboratory at the Royal Arsenal, Woolwich. He would assist in the rocket experiments carried out by the man in charge, William Congreve, a relative of the playwright. It was while Ensign the Honourable George Napier and Lady Sarah were living in London that Charles Napier was born in August 1782.

After a posting in Wolverhampton in 1785 the family settled in County Kildare. This was when Charles Napier was three. For a time they lived with the Conollys in their vast house of Castletown. Then in 1787 they moved only a mile away to the town of Celbridge, on the River Liffey ten miles from Dublin. Celbridge sat just outside Castletown's gates. Tom Conolly bought the house for them and they paid him annually. It was a substantial home on about seventy acres of land, but it was not a mansion, and it had only two more bedrooms than the Napiers required with their growing family and the two Louisas – Louisa Napier, who was the Honourable George's surviving daughter from his first marriage, and Louisa Bunbury, who was Lady Sarah's daughter by her cousin.[15]

The town of Celbridge, in addition to sitting outside the Conolly's front gate, was also very close to Carton House, the seat of the Leinsters – the second Duke of Leinster was the premier peer of Ireland and another of Charles Napier's (much older) cousins through his aunt Lady Emilia, the dowager duchess. Yet despite these grand connections to the greatest houses in the neighbourhood, the Napier children attended the local day school in Celbridge, and there was very little money in their home. Charles Napier's early years were far from sheltered. Many of the children with whom he attended school were of modest means, and many were Roman Catholics. Young Charles did see some of the world, visiting not only Castletown House but also the Isle of Wight, Bristol, and Southampton, when his father was on his way to or from one of his postings abroad.[16]

George Napier had a number of staff positions in Ireland, and he was able to rise once again through the ranks after the outbreak of war with France in 1793. In 1799 he became comptroller of army accounts in Ireland, where apparently he broke with precedent and refused to divert any money to himself or his family.[17] He died in 1804, still comptroller, still honest, still poor, and a brevet colonel. We know that he hated the British establishment for its abuse of power, but he hated the idea of a republican revolution even more: 'Our king sends millions to slaughter, and yet we cannot, in common sense, wish his crown to fall and to belong to a republic of tyrants, as all republics are', he once commented.[18] That is why he was willing to fight against the republican revolutionaries of America and France. As he explained on another occasion,

> I hold Mr. Pitt to be the bane of his country, and of course could never utter a falsehood and praise him; but never did I for a moment hesitate to

follow the duties of my profession, which I hold too high by far ever to subject them to political opinions.[19]

So while he would complain about the politicians he would loyally serve the king. His son would do much the same thing.

But first things first. When Charles Napier was all of eleven his parents decided that he ought to go into the army and secure his future. They found a free commission for him, and soon they were able to exchange it for a better one that would seem before all the world indeed to have cost money. As the military historian Byron Farwell points out, childhood commissions were not unknown in the eighteenth century; one young man received an army commission at age two and another on the day of his birth.[20] Charles's commission at the comparatively ripe age of eleven was in the 33rd regiment, and then he was transferred to the 89th, where his father was assistant quartermaster. Charles met the regiment at Netley, Hampshire and strapped on his father's sword, an incident that he would remember for the rest of his life.

When 89th broke camp and was shipped overseas, Charles did not go with them. He transferred into the 4th regiment, but in fact he went back to school as a dayboy in Celbridge.[21]

Irish conditions and Napier the radical

The historian C. A. Bayly has argued that the British elite of the second half of the eighteenth century adopted a creed which he calls 'agrarian patriotism'. They wanted to improve the lives of the people by improving farming and reducing poverty in the countryside. This focus on rural progress was in Bayly's view the dominant faith of this 'laicized' period, and it was as important in English life as evangelicalism came to be after 1780. Further Bayly writes that Charles James Napier was a man imbued with exactly this 'agrarian patriotism'.

I agree that on his occasional visits to the *English* countryside the young Charles may have seen something of this spirit of rural improvement put into effect. And Bayly is right to argue that Napier would always remain concerned with the well-being of the rural population. Napier did carry this concern with him from his Irish youth.[22] But what shaped Charles Napier's thinking on rural life was what he saw in Ireland, where he spent most of his time as a child and a young man. And in the Irish countryside there was nothing like the semi-religious programme of rural improvement that Bayly describes in England. If most of the landowners in the Ireland of Napier's youth believed in improving their farms and bettering the living conditions of the rural population, they kept this belief well hidden. By and large, the Irish landlords did not improve their land. They left the majority of the Irish people to suffer misery and bloody oppression. So what Napier saw in Ireland could not have inspired in him much of what Bayly had in mind: a sense that social betterment was ramifying out across the land because of the work of earnest Tory squires.

20 Boyhood and war

Bayly is right in pointing out that rural improvement and social amelioration were matters of faith to Napier, but I think it is important to be clear that Napier's faith in improving the land was always *oppositional* in its orientation. Napier would forever rail against the utter indifference to improvement, the hardheartedness, and the greed of the capitalist farmers in Ireland and in England, too. In his mind they cared not a bit about the suffering of the rural poor. And later he would rail against – and overthrow – the Muslim leaders of Sind for the same reasons.

Rather than Bayly's term 'agrarian patriotism', I think we should call Napier's views 'agrarian radicalism'. As we will see, Charles Napier wanted to liquidate the class of comfortable Irish and English farmers and build a working-class rural culture in its place. At the centre he wanted to create an activist state on the Napoleonic model. He wrote despairingly of the hundreds of years – up through the nineteenth century itself – when the landlords of the Protestant Ascendancy had never bothered to improve their farms, had never built roads, and had never founded schools. We might recall that as late as the 1830s Alexis de Tocqueville would argue that the huts of the Iroquois were of a better quality than the squalid constructions lacking all furniture he had seen in Ireland. For one thing, the Iroquois shelters had holes in the roof for the smoke to escape.[23]

***

The young Napier saw this squalor in the Irish countryside, and he also saw what civil unrest could look like. For in response to the long-term neglect of the Irish people came the uprising of the United Irishmen. It began in May 1798 when Napier was fifteen (see Figure 1.1). By the beginning of the year 280,000 people had pledged to fight for Ireland's freedom. Even before the uprising broke out, the Orangemen who organized to oppose it were burning the houses of Roman Catholics – United Irishmen and uninvolved bystanders alike. The British commander in Ireland, Sir Ralph Abercromby, tried to stop all of that, but to most of the Protestant Ascendancy he seemed to be more concerned with ending loyalist violence than with heading off the rebellion itself. Abercromby resigned. His attempts to contain loyalist anger were quickly forgotten. It was open season on the Irish until the arrival of Lord Cornwallis as the new commander in June 1798, and the atrocities continued for another year or more before Cornwallis could fully exert his authority.[24]

The young Charles Napier was not sheltered from all this. In late May, a force of two hundred United Irishmen broke through the gates of Castletown to make a shortcut across the grounds. The Lennox clan worked all their powers of persuasion to redirect the armed men away from Celbridge and save the town. They were able to point out that nearby Carton House was Lord Edward Fitzgerald's childhood home. But they could not keep the town safe forever. Part of a Scottish regiment was soon quartered in Celbridge itself. Some of the population refused to give up their pikes. The Scottish soldiers threatened to burn the town, and in fact they did set fire to five houses.[25] There is also a story that

Figure 1.1 Background to Napier's youth: 'Massacre at Scullabogue', by George Cruickshank. From William Hamilton Maxwell, *History of the Irish Rebellion in 1798; with Memoirs of the Union, and Emmett's Insurrection in 1803* (London: H. G. Bohn, 1854), opposite 125.

© The British Library Board 12/03/2016

William Napier tells of how the boys were given guns and put to work defending their besieged house. Yet William, her third son, was only twelve then, and his mother's account of that day was rather different. She was afraid that her house might be burnt, so she packed up her children and went to Castletown. She does not mention any shooting or any siege – much less her husband arming all five of their sons (the youngest of whom was only nine) and putting them in harm's way, as William claimed more than half a century later.[26]

While there was no reason for arming nine year olds, there was ample reason to be afraid. All across County Kildare, loyalist soldiers and bandits spread destruction and terror until the end of June.[27] What lesson did Charles Napier or his parents draw from all this? Writing of the predicament of her nephew the Duke of Leinster after the capture and death of Lord Edward – the duke's own brother – Lady Sarah pointed out how

> [t]he county of Kildare, in which is all his property, is almost desolate, and growing worse every day. The peculiar marked object has been to ruin

22   *Boyhood and war*

his tenants, and the insurgents will now finish it; for although personal attachment to him makes them anxious to avoid it, yet necessity forces them to take what they can get. The cruel hardship put on his tenants, preferably to all others, has driven them to despair, and they join the insurgents, saying, 'It's better to die with a pike in my hand than be shot like a dog at my work, or see my children faint for want of food before my eyes.'[28]

By then, Wexford, to the south, had been retaken by government forces under General Sir John Moore, who in a few years was to be Charles Napier's commanding officer. In Lady Sarah's view, General Moore had little to be proud of: 'The victory, as it is called, in Wexford, has only secured the town, and killed five thousand, – a lamentable victory; yet, if it tends to save more lives, it is success; but how far it *does* do that no mortal can yet decide.'[29]

According to modern sources, closer to a thousand died at Wexford than the five thousand she said, even if one adds in the battles of Foulkesmills and Vinegar Hill; Moore's forces entered Wexford itself unopposed. But Lady Sarah was right about the climate of violence. In County Kildare, hundreds of Irish prisoners were slaughtered at Gibbet Rath on 29 May 1798. Even more killing took place in smaller incidents. As she noted in October, a court-martial carried out after Lord Cornwallis took command revealed how the Orange Order militias had sent out their members in small groups without their officers to commit murder, and they were none too careful about who they killed.[30]

Charles Napier, schoolboy in Celbridge and already for some years an army officer, turned sixteen in August (Figure 1.2). As the trouble brewed and various corps of yeomen were organized – or so runs William's account – Charles convinced his father to allow him to organize his own corps of yeomanry among his schoolmates. Charles was able to win the consent of their parents because most of his schoolfellows were indeed Roman Catholics, so this little troop of yeomen could never be mistaken for Orangemen.[31] Charles Napier's little militia marched about under arms, and when they were attacked and pelted with dirt by a mob of boys from another and more posh school, they levelled their bayonets and stood their ground, with Charles telling the group to stay in formation and refrain from attacking the unarmed. Charles's force, many of whom were not far shy of twenty years of age, won the day without bloodshed.

There were worse days. Someone burst into Charles's schoolroom with the news that an informer had been murdered in his home along with his eighty-year-old mother. Charles Napier ran out and saw the corpse of the old lady with blood matting her hair. It was on that day that he may have begun to develop his lifelong abhorrence of civil war, or so his brother William tells us, rather sensibly.[32]

Figure 1.2 Napier in 1798, at age sixteen. Engraving by William Henry Egleton after a miniature. Published by John Murray, 1857. NPG Number D38461.

© National Portrait Gallery, London

24 *Boyhood and war*

Notes

1 George Prince of Wales to Lord Bute, four letters, winter 1759–1760, given in Romney Sedgwick (ed.), *Letters from George III to Lord Bute* (London: Macmillan, 1939), 37–40.

2 Lord Holland's memoir, given in the Countess of Ilchester and Lord Stavordale, *The Life and Letters of Lady Sarah Lennox, 1745–1826*, 2 vols (London: John Murray, 1901), 1:3–81 at 26–30, 47–51; Sarah Lennox to Susan Fox Strangeways, 19 June 1761, 7 July 1761, 1:102–06; Henry Napier's statement, from his journal of 28 April 1837, 1:85–96 at 89–95; Stella Tillyard, *Aristocrats: Caroline, Emily, Louisa, and Sarah Lennox, 1740–1832* (New York: Farrar, Straus, and Giroux, 1994), 112–19.

3 Sarah Napier to Susan O'Brien, 29 May 1798 and 10 September 1804, postscript, given in ISSL, 2:67–69 and 2:169–71.

4 Armand Louis de Gontaut, duc de Lauzun, duc de Biron, *Memoirs of the duc de Lauzun (Armand Louis de Gontaut, duc de Biron), 1747–1783*, (trans.) E. Jules Méras (New York: Sturgis & Walton, 1912), 43–47, 54–70, 96–97; Lady Holland to the Duchess of Leinster, 13 March 1769, given in Brian Fitzgerald (ed.), *Correspondence of Emily, Duchess of Leinster (1731–1814)*, 3 vols (Dublin: Stationery Office, 1953), 1:567–70; Tillyard, *Aristocrats*, 229–48, 251–57. Lord William Gordon, the natural father of Louisa Bunbury, was the brother of the Lord George Gordon of the anti-Catholic Gordon Riots of 1780.

5 Lady Holland to the Duchess of Leinster, 13 March 1769, given in Fitzgerald (ed.), *Correspondence*, 1:567–70; Tillyard, *Aristocrats*, 124–32, 231–48, 251–57.

6 Alison Gilbert Olson, *The Radical Duke: Career and Correspondence of Charles Lennox, Third Duke of Richmond* (London: Oxford UP, 1961), 10; ISSL, 1:224.

7 Sarah Napier to Susan O'Brien, 25 February 1783, 20 August and 2 December 1805, given in ISSL, 2:31–33, 199–201; Tillyard, *Aristocrats*, 257–62, 295–300, 315.

8 Anthony Page, *John Jebb and the Enlightenment Origins of British Radicalism* (Westport, CT: Praeger, 2003), 241, 246–48.

9 Henry Steele Commager, *The Empire of Reason: How Europe Imagined and America Realized the Enlightenment* (London: Weidenfeld and Nicolson, 1978), 137; Fitzgerald (ed.), *Correspondence*, 2:40n; Brian Fitzgerald, *Emily Duchess of Leinster, 1731–1814: A Study of Her Life and Times* (London: Staples Press, 1949), 117.

10 Brian Fitzgerald, *Lady Louisa Conolly, 1743–1821: An Anglo-Irish Biography* (London: Staples Press, 1950), 174–75; Stella Tillyard, *Citizen Lord: The Life of Edward Fitzgerald, Irish Revolutionary* (New York: Farrar, Straus and Giroux, 1997), 292–95.

11 Fitzgerald (ed.), *Correspondence*, 3:ix–xi; R. B. McDowell, *Ireland in the Age of Imperialism and Revolution, 1760–1801* (Oxford: Clarendon Press, 1979), 122, 430, 447; Sarah Napier to Susan O'Brien, 8 September 1784, given in ISSL, 2:48–49.

12 Stanley Ayling, *Fox: The Life of Charles James Fox* (London: John Murray, 1991), 6–7. A book has been written about the sisters: Tillyard, *Aristocrats*. It became a five-hour television series in 1999.

13 Countess of Kildare to Earl of Kildare (later Duchess and Duke of Leinster), given in Fitzgerald (ed.), *Correspondence*, 20 May 1757, 7 July 1757, 1:37, 57–59; Marquis of Kildare to Marchioness of Kildare, 20 April, 22 April 1762, 1:118–20, 120–22; Ayling, *Fox*, 16–18, 23–24, 41–42, 48, 226; quotation from Tillyard, *Aristocrats*, 305.

14 William Napier, *The Life and Opinions of General Sir Charles James Napier, G.C.B.*, 2nd edn, 4 vols (London: John Murray, 1857), 1:48.

15 Sarah Napier to Susan O'Brien, 15 September 1787 and 26 October 1804, given in ISSL, 2:65–66, 174–78 at 176.

16 Fitzgerald, *Louisa Conolly*, 154; November 1793, given in ISSL, 2:80–82 and 92–94; Sarah Napier to the Duchess of Leinster, 6 February 1794, given in Fitzgerald (ed.), *Correspondence*, 2:342–43.

17 Sarah Napier to Susan O'Brien, 6 July 1794, 23 December 1794, and 25 March 1799, given in ISSL, 2:103–03, 120–21, 135–42.

Early days 25

18 Sarah Napier (in fact George Napier) to Charles James Fox [c. 1796], given in Thomas Moore and Martin MacDermott, *Memoirs of Lord Edward Fitzgerald* (London: Downey and Co., 1897), 470–76 at 473–74.

19 Reported in Sarah Napier to the Duke of Richmond [c. 1796], given in ibid, 476–79.

20 Sarah Napier to the Duchess of Leinster, 8 January 1794 and [April 1794], given in Fitzgerald (ed.), *Correspondence*, 2:338–42 at 340 and 2:354–59 at 358; Byron Farwell, *Queen Victoria's Little Wars* (New York: W.W. Norton, 1972), 25. The commission came from a different family friend than the man young Charles had written to.

21 WN, 1:5; Charles Napier's journal, 8 October 1850, given in ibid, 4:296–97.

22 C. A. Bayly, *Imperial Meridian: The British Empire and the World, 1780–1830* (London and New York: Longman, 1989), 80–81, 157–58.

23 Charles James Napier, *An Essay on the Present State of Ireland, Showing the Chief Cause of, and the Remedy for, the Existing Distress of that Country* (London: Ridgway, 1839), 57–59; Emmet Larkin, 'Introduction', in Emmet Larkin (ed. and trans.), *Alexis de Tocqueville's Journey to Ireland, July-August, 1835* (Washington, DC: Catholic University of America Press, 1990), 1–15 at 7.

24 Tony Gaynor, 'The Abercromby Affair', in Bartlett, Dickson, Keogh, and Whelan (eds), *1798: A Bicentenary Perspective* (Dublin: Four Courts Press, 2003), 401–03.

25 Sarah Napier to the Duke of Richmond, 27 June 1798, given in Moore and MacDermott, *Memoirs of Lord Edward Fitzgerald*, 451–55 at 454; Fitzgerald, *Louisa Conolly*, 172.

26 WN, 1:10; Sarah Napier to Susan O'Brien, 20 July 1798, given in ISSL, 132–35.

27 General Moore's diary, 4 July 1798, given in J. F. Maurice (ed.), *The Diary of Sir John Moore*, 2 vols (London: Edward Arnold, 1904), 1:303–04; Kevin O'Neill, ' "Woe to the Oppressor of the Poor": Post-rebellion Violence in Ballitore, County Kildare', in Bartlett, Dickson, Keogh, and Whelan (eds), *1798: A Bicentenary Perspective*, 363–67.

28 Sarah Napier to the Duke of Richmond, 27 June 1798, given in Moore and MacDermott, *Memoirs of Lord Edward Fitzgerald*, 451–55 at 453.

29 Sarah Napier to the Duke of Richmond, 27 October 1798, given in ibid, 468–69.

30 Daniel Gahan, *The People's Rising: Wexford, 1798* (Dublin: Gill & Macmillan, 1995), 199–202, 210–24; Thomas Pakenham, *The Year of Liberty: The Story of the Great Irish Rebellion of 1798* (1969; Englewood Cliffs, NJ: Prentice-Hall, 1970), 162–64; Sarah Napier to the Duke of Richmond, 27 October 1798, given in Moore and MacDermott, *Memoirs of Lord Edward Fitzgerald*, 468–69.

31 WN, 1:6.

32 Ibid, 1:6–8.

2 A soldier

There are other sources for this period, too, besides the sometimes exaggerated William – such as a set of letters in the National Army Museum. From these we know that Charles Napier's life as a schoolboy in Celbridge came to an end not long after the rebellion of the United Irishmen. His military career commenced in earnest in the latter part of 1799, when, as a favour to the family, their friend Sir James Duff accepted the seventeen-year-old sight unseen as his aide-de-camp at Limerick. Off Napier went on his own for the first time. By June 1800, he was the senior lieutenant and aide-de-camp in his unit, the 60th Regiment 2nd Battalion, which was scheduled to go to the West Indies for seven years. It was not expected to see combat against the French, so Napier transferred to the Rifles so that he might see fighting. He then broke his leg, but he was able to rejoin the unit at the end of the year, reporting to Blatchington Barracks in Sussex. There Napier came under the command of Sir John Moore for the first time.[1]

Napier was to serve for much of the rest of the Napoleonic Wars under General Moore, and he always had great respect for him. As we have seen, John Moore took Wexford in 1798 with minimal loss of life. The general was shocked by the violence of the loyalists. He worked to control it and to maintain a professional restraint among his own forces. Whenever the common people of Ireland handed in their arms he protected them and their property. When they did not give up their arms, Moore engaged in selective house-burning – 'to excite terror' and bring about a quicker disarmament, as he wrote. By these means on a single campaign in Western Cork he seized 800 pikes and 3,400 guns. Moore *did* order his men to impose themselves on the population and live on whatever food they could find ('free quartering').[2] He thought it necessary. Yet in the context of the Irish atrocities all this was moderate behaviour. Moore behaved with relative decency when faced with an insurgent population, something that Napier would remember in more than one part of the world.

At the personal level, too, John Moore became for Napier the model, the hero, the beau ideal of proper military bearing – humorous and unaffected and never haughty to those under his command. He would roughhouse with his young officers and suddenly challenge them to foot races.[3] But for now Napier was only one of many young men setting out to learn their profession, and as yet he had little to do with General Moore personally. Although Blatchington came under Moore's overall responsibility, the camp itself was under the command of Colonel Coote Manningham. Manningham's orders were to organize the rifle detachments into a light infantry force. The Commander-in-Chief of the Forces at the time, the Duke of York, wanted to create a light infantry in response to Napoleon's highly mobile rifle corps. Instead of fighting in close lines, the men were to move quickly and in pairs, covering each other. Or alternately they could become entirely detached and act as scouts. They fired their weapons at particular targets such as the enemy artillery rather than aiming straight ahead as the line regiments usually did. This was the kind of military work that Napier was learning. He remained at Blatchington until 1802, save for some recruiting duty in Ireland. He next went to Shorncliffe, near Folkestone in Kent, serving again under Manningham. Shorncliffe now became the main centre of the light infantry – and fighting in this way became known as the Shorncliffe system.[4]

After being posted to Chatham, in 1803 Napier joined the staff of General Henry Edward Fox (another of his many much older maternal cousins), the new commander in Ireland, in time to see more civil unrest, although it was less extensive than what he had already seen. Napier arrived in Dublin in time to witness Emmet's Rebellion on 23 July. During these disturbances fifty rebels appeared at the Napier house in Celbridge and frightened a servant into giving them the weapons, but they took nothing else. The rebels seem to have been particularly well behaved and they did not burn any houses. The rebellion collapsed the day after it broke out, but it was enough to get General Fox recalled to London. Napier and the rest of the staff returned with him.[5]

So much for the Irish posting. Now in London for some time, Napier had little but routine staff duties to occupy him. It was during this lull in his military career that he sometimes went to stay with the most prominent of his cousins, Charles James Fox himself, who lived at St. Anne's Hill in Surrey. Napier got to know Fox for the first time, and he enjoyed Fox's humour and spontaneity. But in his many books and his voluminous letters he would never say anything else about his visits to St. Anne's hill.[6]

***

Charles Napier disliked London. For one thing, he found it expensive.[7] The emptiness of the days he spent on General Fox's staff even began to affect his nerves. He told his mother that he was given to late-night spasms of resentment against anyone who might have wronged him. By morning he would feel better. As he wrote in December 1803, in a letter that William gives us,

> Last night I sat up till two o'clock, writing on the old subject of grievances, and lashing myself into a fury with everything. Abusing the army, pulling off my breeches, cursing creditors, and putting out the candle all in a minute I jumped into bed and lay there blaspheming, praying and

28   *Boyhood and war*

perspiring for two hours, when sleep came. What I wrote is not worth sending however, being full of jokes, politics and blue devils.[8]

On the day after Christmas he confessed to his mother that he wanted to be in William's regiment –

but no more of what you call my madness. What a curse to have a turn of mind similar to mine! Misery to oneself, and teazing [*sic*] to others, unless disguised, which can only be with those not really loved. Great exertion or perfect tranquillity is necessary to me, who have not that superior intellect which can regulate itself: there is more of Cassius than of Brutus in me.[9]

Much of the problem was that at the ripe age of twenty-one he was impatient for professional advancement and a better assignment. But his prospects would soon improve – indeed, they improved literally the day after he wrote this letter, when he found that he had been promoted to captain and attached to the recently formed Staff Corps.[10]

This was a very desirable commission. Almost immediately another officer wanted to buy it from Napier for a thousand guineas and on top of that a commission in the dragoons – where Napier would immediately become captain of a whole company. But as Napier explained, his professional frustrations and all his dark self-doubts would hardly be cured if he became a captain and a company commander at twenty-one. With all the pretentious but perhaps not entirely inaccurate self-discernment of a twenty-one year old, he recorded that having his own company so early might 'create in a warm imagination ideas of future honours, of hopes, and wishes to rise to the head of my profession, and all the deuce knows what, which such reveries lead to'.[11] He had a vision of what decades later he might become:

I see the wizened face of a general grinning over the parapet of a fine frill, and telling extraordinary lies, while his claret, if he can afford claret, is going down the throats of his wondering or quizzing aides-de-camp. . . . Yet people wonder I don't like the army!

And the worst of the vision:

To me military life is like dancing up a long room with a mirror at the end, against which we cut our faces, and so the deception ends. It is thus gaily men follow their *trade of blood*, thinking it glitters, but to me it appears without brightness or reflection, a dirty red!

Yet he had no prospect of another career.

***

In the new year of 1804 this newly minted officer in the Staff Corps – for indeed he did not trade out his new commission – thought that he might make

A soldier 29

himself more useful were he to return to Chatham and study engineering.[12] Besides its obvious role in providing staff officers, in this period the Staff Corps had light engineering duties as well.[13] Napier found the course at Chatham reasonably interesting, and he discovered that he already knew more about drill and military procedure than most of the other students did.

Having completed his training as an engineer, in 1805 Charles Napier went to Hythe (only half a mile from his former camp at Shorncliffe) to help in the cutting of the Royal Military Canal and in the other defences which were being erected against the danger of a cross-Channel invasion. Here Napier came back under the command of John Moore.[14]

At this point, Napier asked his mother to send him his father's military and medical books, and especially the military books in French – better than most anything available in English, he said, and the volumes were expensive and hard to find.[15] He was taking charge of his own education in a number of other ways, too. He believed that he had learned more than enough engineering for an officer of the line, so now he wanted to spend six months on the continent to work on his languages before war came again – and not least he wanted to see Napoleon once in his lifetime. For – and here he did reflect Charles James Fox's opinions, it would seem – Napier decided that the emperor was no 'scourge', and the same number of men would die with Napoleon's intervention in history as without.[16]

Napier's six months on the continent were not to be – not yet. In 1806 Moore and the 52nd were ordered to Sicily to serve under General Fox. But Napier did not go with the 52nd, for through a final influence of Charles James Fox, now on his last legs, Napier was promoted to major in a unit about to leave for the Cape of Good Hope.[17]

But he did not go there, either. As William Napier tells the story, Charles was in Portsmouth with his new unit awaiting favourable winds for the Cape. There he fell in with the men of the 50th regiment, and he transferred into it. This was in November 1806. Stationed at Bognor, Charles Napier would now spend a period with the 50th organizing the defences of Sussex, and he paid some visits to his uncle, the 3rd Duke of Richmond, at Goodwood. He was also visiting a number of young ladies. As he had done for years, he described the targets of his ardour in long letters to his mother.[18] The historian Lawrence Stone writes that Lady Sarah Napier was a good example of the kind of companionate mothering notable in this era – in her own words, she was her children's friend as much as their tutor.[19] Napier's candid letters to her would seem to back this up.

***

Napier's promotion to brevet major had become effective in May 1806, but his permanent rank was still captain and he still drew a captain's pay.[20] He had no money to buy a higher rank and so he had to bide his time. Early in 1807, his company went to Guernsey in preparation for joining the rest of Sir John Moore's force on the expedition to Copenhagen. Napier hoped to lead a brigade in battle or to be allowed to join the naval expedition, but to his disappointment he and his men never went beyond Guernsey itself. Brother

30 Boyhood and war

William saw action in Copenhagen. So did their naval brother Henry, who was in the flotilla. But Charles had little to do but attend the parties and balls of the island. And he joined the Masons.[21]

Napier's regiment also missed out on duty in Ireland at this time because it contained too many Irish volunteers. Some regiments deliberately excluded the Irish for this reason – simply to keep themselves available for Irish duty. In one of his letters Napier reminded his mother about what all this said about the injustice of British rule – that regiments which excluded Irish soldiers were necessary for keeping down the country.[22] Increasingly he was becoming troubled about other aspects of British policy, too. The attack on Copenhagen which he had once hoped to join was an attack against a city, he now reflected; it was an attack on civilians rather than an army. Further, Denmark was a neutral country:

> England has been unjust! Was not our high honour worth the danger we should *perhaps* risk by maintaining it inviolate[?]; by this action we countenance every action of Buonaparte, by a single action to banish justice among nations, in a crime too great for pardon. I think it would have been both more honorable and more politick to have hazarded an invasion and lost whole armies in Ireland than to have stamped *power* as right *forever*. England has lost her honor in the history of nations, and I cannot believe Mr. Fox would have allowed it in his administration.[23]

As he expected to be sent into harm's way, in September 1807 he made out a will. Napier now had some resources, namely the £1200 (Irish) due to him on the death of his uncle Mr Conolly, and the £300 sterling due to his mother. He left the money in trust to his younger brother Richard, then at Oriel, who was to pay £10 a year to their nurse Susan Frost. But Napier also wanted to pay £70 per year to a certain Mrs. Elizabeth Kelly – to whom he left his watch, his ring, and his other personal effects as well. In the event of Elizabeth Kelly's death, the capital would go to his sister Caroline.[24]

We know from his letters to Lady Sarah that Napier was maintaining an active and varied romantic life with the young women who came his way. Yet from this period forward he would always return to Mrs. Kelly for peace and companionship. Born Elizabeth Oakley, and fifteen years Napier's senior, she was married to a naval officer, Captain Francis John Kelly, the Barrack Master at Hythe when Napier was stationed there. Sometime later Captain Kelly left his wife and died many years later in Sierra Leone.[25] Napier visited Mrs. Kelly constantly. She was to be an important part of his life for the next quarter-century.

The Peninsular War

In 1807 Napoleon invaded Portugal and in 1808 he seized control of Spain, installing his brother on the throne in Madrid. Both the Spanish and Portuguese rose up against the French in May 1808, and in August the British Army

A soldier 31

came to the assistance of Portugal. Now Napier, like so many others, would see all the combat he wanted and more.

Napier was twenty-six. He and his men were ordered to Lisbon after the Battle of Vimeiro in August 1808, and from there they went to join Moore's forces. General Moore was carrying out an improvised retreat through north-western Spain to draw off Napoleon's army and give the Spanish insurgents time to regroup. But the British retreat was hard going and the army starved.[26]

Napier saw the first real fighting of his army career at the port town of La Coruña on 16 January 1809. Moore's army was attempting to embark to avoid destruction by the forces of Marshal Soult. Soult arrived and fighting broke out before the British could get away. Brother George Napier was there, too, and he fought courageously,[27] but it was Charles who played the most notable part in the events of the day.[28] With his friend Major Charles Stanhope, he led a movement towards the village of Elviña. Moore looked on, revising his battle plans in light of the fortunes of the advancing party. But then as Napier and Stanhope pressed forward their advance, Moore was hit by a cannonball. It tore off his left shoulder and part of his collarbone, exposing his lung. The general was taken off the battlefield. He composed some final messages for his friends and family and then died. Command passed to General Sir John Hope, but Hope did not send the expected reinforcements after Napier.

Meanwhile Napier did not know that Moore had fallen, and he continued to advance towards Elviña. With no support coming from behind, he found himself cut off among the French. Then he lost his sabre when he grabbed for the musket of a French soldier who was trying to bayonet him.[29]

Years later in the House of Commons, Napier's Scottish cousin, also named Charles Napier and referred to in the family as 'Black Charlie', described some of what happened that day:

> [I]t was the first time he had seen an action, or heard the fire of an enemy in his life – he advanced at the head of his men, leading them on with the greatest possible coolness. Something occurred to impede them – he was surrounded by French troops – received a cut on the head with a sabre – was stabbed in the back with a bayonet – a bullet went through his leg, and two of his ribs were broken by a cannon-ball. 'I think (said the gallant Officer) that was a dose enough to settle any man.'[30]

Charles Napier's own written account of these events filled seventeen pages when it was printed – and as he told his sister he left all he might have said about the depression he suffered, covered in the blood of his men in addition to his own.[31] Black Charlie was right in his catalogue of the wounds: Napier had been shot, hit with a cannonball, and stabbed, and then he suffered a sabre cut to the head. The Italian wielding the sabre was ready to strike again and finish the job when his hand was stayed by a French drummer named Guibert. At Guibert's insistence the Italian helped Napier towards the lines. Soon Guibert started to move away. The Italian began pulling out his sword, but now Napier

32 *Boyhood and war*

was able to cry out to Guibert – in French – that brave Frenchmen do not kill their prisoners. Guibert turned, swearing at the Italian and saving Napier's life a second time. He then helped Napier off the battlefield. When they finally reached the main French force, Napier was questioned. There he received his first medical attention.

But Napier and Guibert had not yet reached the French headquarters, and for some time Napier, now finally separated from the drummer, would continue to endure kicks and rough handling from the French soldiers, being saved on each occasion by some passing officer. Abandoned, he spent a cold and horrible night and day and then all of night and day wandering the battlefield half-undressed, finding shelter where he could. A number of Frenchmen saw him and took no notice. Eventually, in increasing agony from his wounds and with ever less awareness of what was happening, he was conducted to the French commanders and thus to safety. Marshal Soult sent his personal surgeon. When Soult finally heard Napier's story he arranged for the drummer Guibert to get the Cross of the Legion of Honour.[32]

At last Napier was properly attended to and cleaned up. He found that he still had the ring his mother had given him, and he never took it off for the rest of his life. Years later he recalled that his hand was so caked with blood that no one had seen it.[33]

But there was still one more shock. In the care of the French, Napier could only sit and watch as the British forces sailed away. What could have happened? He was sure that the only reason his brother George had not come under a white flag to arrange his immediate release was that George himself had been killed. In fact George was very much alive, but on his part he thought Charles had died. He had seen the bodies of other friends and John Moore himself all within a few hours. Then when he set off to look for Charles, several men told him that his brother had expired from the staggering number of wounds they saw him receive. Convinced of the worst, George did not think of going under the white flag to ask for his brother in the French camp, although doing so would have been ordinary enough in those days. Visits to the enemy were routine. British officers would share a pleasant conversation with the French commanders after a battle, or have a nice dinner with them. Englishmen and Frenchmen would talk about who had been especially courteous or brave on the battlefield hours before.[34]

This spirit of chivalry extended also to the exchange of prisoners. Captured officers would be released to go home to England or France, as the case might be, on a 'parole of honour' – giving their word that they would not fight again or resume their duties with the army until they were officially exchanged. The exchange could take months. To break such a parole and return to the war in the meantime was considered ungentlemanly; one would become a social pariah.[35]

But on this occasion Napier was left behind as a long-term prisoner. What was to be done with him? At the behest of Marshal Ney (for Soult had left the area) he was nursed back to health in the home of the American consul. Then when Ney heard that Napier's mother was a widow, and blind, as she had become, Ney gave him a parole himself.[36]

Meanwhile Napier's family believed he was dead. They even proved his will – so if they did not know about Elizabeth Kelly before, now they did. Yet eventually they heard a rumour that he might be alive after all, and in captivity.[37] The Admiralty decided to send a ship to La Coruña under a flag of truce to make official inquiries. Because of Ney's parole the ship was able to bring Napier back, but they sent no word ahead. So no solid evidence that Napier was still alive had reached England before the ship carrying him docked at Plymouth.

Therefore Napier was able to bring the good news himself. He wrote to his mother at the end of March; the letter ended 'Huidibras, you lie – "For I have been in battle slain, / And yet I live to fight again"'. His brother George and his sisters Louisa and Emily then hurried to meet him at Exeter, from where they escorted him to London to see Lady Sarah.[38]

Charles Napier was twenty-six when he came back from the dead. He spent much of 1809 recovering at the house of his blind mother in Cadogan Place, and indeed his presence helped to alleviate her financial troubles for a time; she had her pension from the king but she also had a number of grown children with their own expenses.

Eventually Napier healed and he was well enough to take in the London scene during George III's Jubilee in October. He wandered through the crowds and watched the illuminations. Late at night he came home to his mother – she who might have been George III's queen – to tell her all about the festivities as she sat writing her letters in the dark. Although blind, she still could write, and in a neat hand, using a moving frame devised by one of her sisters and made up by a carpenter.[39]

***

In December 1809 Napier was exchanged and released from his parole. He rejoined his regiment when it returned from Walcheren.[40] But there had been some changes in the army in the eleven months he had been away. The Duke of York had resigned as Commander-in-Chief of the Forces; there had been a scandal. Yet while personally the duke was debauched and pleasure-seeking, these vices did not make him a bad Commander-in-Chief. As a royal duke he was above party, and he had spent many years improving training and morale. He was kind and he was popular with the soldiers. The duke's replacement as Commander-in-Chief was the very old, very thin, very laconic Sir David Dundas. Dundas was the author of most of the army drill manuals then in use, and he had been an important reformer in his day. But he was now in his mid-seventies. He was still respected for his mind and his expertise, but as Commander-in-Chief, Dundas gave the impression of an old Scotch miser who did not want to spend the smallest amount of money or promote anyone. Charles Napier's experience with Dundas was typical. The other majors who distinguished themselves at La Coruña were promoted to lieutenant-colonel. Charles Napier missed the promotion only because he was he was thought to be dead. Now once again very much alive, he went to see the Commander-in-Chief in London to ask for his advancement. All that Dundas would say again

34   Boyhood and war

and again was wear flannel – *Major* Napier should always wear flannel. Napier did not get his promotion.[41]

And when Major Napier returned to the Peninsula, he found that things had changed for the army in the field, as well. The warmth and openness of John Moore were sorely missed by the junior officers. The new commander was Arthur Wellesley, recently ennobled as the Viscount Wellington. He was a very different man than John Moore, cold and distant to his subordinates. Moreover, he was carrying out a policy of continual retreat that he refused to explain. (He once sent his reasoning to Whitehall only to read about it in the newspapers. Wellington knew that the French could read the newspapers, too. He did not repeat the experiment.) While in fact the general was at the beginning of a multi-year campaign to exhaust Napoleon's forces, all the apparent blunders and evacuations along the way hardly inspired confidence among the officers carrying them out. And Napier himself began on an especially bad footing with the new commander. He was trying to get his promotion to colonel by other means – by arranging a transfer – and in the meantime he wanted to avoid rejoining his own unit. With that in mind he went on three-months leave, although he remained with the army. He was given permission to fight as a volunteer, serving wherever he wished until his leave expired. This was an odd arrangement. When Napier asked to extend his leave still further, Wellington agreed – but only until Napier could receive from the Horse Guards (the headquarters of the British Army in Whitehall) a final answer about the promotion. And Wellington added that Napier's orders from the Horse Guards when they came ought to be a reprimand and an order to go home.[42]

While technically on leave, Napier saw action at the Battle of Coa on 24 July 1810. He had gone to the area to tend his brother George, who was ill. George pulled through and like Charles saw action when the battle came. Brother William also fought at Coa and he was wounded there. Coa was another of the rearguard actions carried out by the light troops with whom Napier had trained. The object was to defend the Portuguese border from the advancing French. In command was Brigadier Robert Craufurd; on the day of the battle Napier served on Craufurd's staff relaying orders. In the aftermath of Coa, Charles Napier continued for a time to serve as Craufurd's aide-de-camp. Craufurd was a great flogger of his men, and Napier found that this was not to his taste.[43] He would one day write a book on this subject. Napier remained under Craufurd as the light troops continued to resist the French advance in August and September.

Wounded again

Charles James Napier's cousin, the Scottish Charles James Napier – who was a wandering naval officer – happened to be serving beside our Charles Napier at his next major engagement. This was the Battle of Busaco on 27 September 1810. Busaco was a much larger affair than Coa. Sixty-five thousand French troops repeatedly tried and failed to dislodge the fifty thousand British and Portuguese troops of Wellington's army. Wellington had deployed his forces

A soldier   35

along a ten-mile ridge, or rather just under the crest of the ridge, so the attacking Frenchmen could neither see nor shell them very effectively. George and William Napier both led troops that day as the French advanced out of the mist of the valley and tried to come up over the hill. Charles served on Wellington's staff. As the three brothers were preparing for battle they were told that their sister Caroline had died at age twenty-two.[44]

As before, we could do worse than look at the reminiscences of Black Charlie (Commodore Napier, as by then he had become) in the House of Commons in 1844:

> At the battle of Busaco [Charles James Napier] . . . was shot through the nose, and the ball fell into his jaw. . . . Napier was dressed in the red uniform of his regiment – the coat of his staff was blue – he was with the staff – and he (Commodore Napier) cautioned him that he was in a bad position. "Either you or I shall be shot; put on your cloak," he said. 'No', was the answer, 'I am in the uniform of my regiment, and in it I will stand or fall.' He had hardly uttered these words before he was struck. When going off the field, he met the Duke of Wellington; and, though the body was weak, the soldier's mind was firm. He took off his hat, cheered the Duke as he passed, and said, 'I cannot die at a better moment.' [The future Commodore] held him whilst the ball was extracted from his jaw, and though he kicked, he uttered not a word.[45]

The bullet passed diagonally through Napier's face and he began to suffocate. The bullet was extracted, but he lost part of his jaw and some of his teeth. He would feel the pain of the wound every day until his death forty-two years later.[46] He was twenty-eight. He recovered in Lisbon in the house of a Frenchwoman, Madame Frannalette, whom George Napier (who was often there) remembered as being always full of joy. For a time the swelling was so bad his nose could not be seen.[47]

It seems that Napier recovered with all due speed despite the best medical care of the day, which included electric shocks to restore feeling. In March 1811 he was able to go back to the war although his face had yet to fully heal. When he caught up with the army he found that both George and William had been wounded, William with a flesh wound in the back and George with a broken arm. Now it was his turn to visit them as they recuperated at Coimbra. Back with the army, in this period Napier once again would know the real privations of troops on the march, the real hunger of the British forces as they moved through the parts of Portugal and Spain devastated by Marshal Masséna – this was the blasted landscape that would be depicted by Goya. Napier and his brothers-in-arms were in pursuit of Masséna's forces.[48]

***

At about this time Charles Napier began to think more about his profession and his country. He read the memoirs of Prince Eugene in French. Far more

36 *Boyhood and war*

important for his intellectual development in the long run, he now for the first time confessed a fondness for the writings of William Cobbett, the journalist who founded parliamentary reporting and what became Hansard. Cobbett was a famous radical. And it is no anachronism to use the word 'radical' to describe him, despite the assertion by one scholar that there could be no radicalism in the United Kingdom until well after the Napoleonic period.[49] Against the views of this scholar we can set the authority of the *Oxford English Dictionary*, which dates 'radical' in the political sense to 1783. And Napier would certainly use the word 'radical' to describe himself many times over the years.[50]

William Cobbett emphasized peace, sound money, and a conservative and nostalgic vision of a healthy rural life. So how is his agenda properly described as a radical one? Cobbett was a radical because in the name of the freedom of the people he brutally excoriated what we might now call the Establishment. In his amazing output of journalism (he may have published more words than anyone one else in the history of the English language[51]), he denounced the 'Old Corruption', that system under which sinecurists and jobbers in the British government ran up the national debt, which the bankers then serviced for their own profit. In Cobbett's view, England suffered under the dominance of a parliamentary and financial clique that promoted urban, commercial interests over rural welfare, and that favoured colonial and foreign wars with their profits for the few over the interests of the broad mass of English taxpayers.

All of these views would become Napier's own, and he would spend much of his life hammering them home in his letters and published writings. But for the moment a more personal question seemed to concern the young officer above all else. He had been writing letter after letter to the Commander-in-Chief and the Prince Regent, still trying to get his promotion from major to lieutenant-colonel. And he pursued the matter perhaps more rigorously than wisely, for he admitted that his letters to the Royal Princes on the subject were not always polite.[52]

In fact he did not have long to wait. Dundas soon left the scene, so Napier's desire for promotion at last could be fulfilled. In May 1811 the Duke of York came back as Commander-in-Chief. Napier received a letter from the Horse Guards in July saying that even before reading the latest of his pleas for promotion the duke had already decided to make him lieutenant-colonel of the 102nd Regiment, then in Guernsey.

This took Charles Napier out of the Peninsular War. And so it took him away from a theatre where the role of the British Army was, at least in theory, to protect the civilian population from a foreign invader. Soon the increasingly radical young officer would have to come to terms with seeing the British Army carrying out a very different task.

Notes

1 Col. George Napier to Lieutenant Hewitt, June 1800, NP, NAM 1991–04–188 (typescript), fols 15–16; Charles Napier to Hewitt, 8 December 1800, NP, NAM 1991–04–188

(typescript), fol. 16; Charles Napier to Emily Napier, 26 November 1800, Bodleian MS Eng. lett. c. 241, fol. 112.

2 R. B. McDowell, *Ireland in the Age of Imperialism and Revolution* (Oxford: Clarendon Press, 1979), 632–33; David Dickson, 'Smoke without Fire?: Munster and the 1798 Rebellion', in Bartlett, Dickson, Keogh, and Whelan (eds), *1798: A Bicentenary Perspective* (Dublin: Four Courts Press, 2003), 147–73 at 168; Tony Gaynor, 'The Abercromby Affair', in Bartlett, Dickson, Keogh, and Whelan (eds), *1798: A Bicentenary Perspective* (Dublin: Four Courts Press, 2003), 399; J. F. Maurice (ed.), *The Diary of Sir John Moore*, 2 vols (London: Edward Arnold, 1904), 27 May 1798, 1:290; Paul M. Kerrigan, 'General John Moore in Ireland in 1798', *Irish Sword* 3, 94 (2003), 401–08.

3 Charles Napier, editor's note to Part 1, chapter 3, in Alfred Victor, comte de Vigny, *Lights and Shades of Military Life*, Charles James Napier (ed.), 2 vols. in 1 (London: Henry Colburn, 1840), 1:369–70; 2nd edn (London: Henry Colburn, 1850), 55–56.

4 Stewart to Napier, 18 May [1802], NP, BL Add. MS 54539, fols 1–2; Sarah Napier to Susan O'Brien, 20 April 1801, 20 October 1802, 22 January 1803, given in ISSL, 2:151–53, 2:155–57, 2:157–62 at 161; Napier to Louisa Napier, 2–8 January 1802, Bodleian MS Eng. lett. c. 240, fols 3–5; Richard Glover, *Peninsular Preparation: The Reform of the British Army, 1795–1809* (Cambridge: Cambridge UP, 1963), 127–32, 142; David Gates, *The British Light Infantry Arm, c. 1790–1815: Its Creation, Training, and Operational Role* (London: B.T. Batsford, 1987), 86–109; Coote Manningham, *Military Lectures Delivered to the Officers of the 95th (Rifle) Regiment at Shorn-Cliff Barracks, Kent, during the Spring of 1803* (London: T. Egerton, 1803; reprinted, no publisher, 1897); J. F. Maurice (ed.), *Diary of John Moore*, 2 vols (London: Edward Arnold, 1904), 2:65.

5 Napier to his commanding officer, 11 June 1802, Bodleian MS Eng. lett. c. 241, fols 233–34; Sarah Napier to Mrs. Hewitt, 20 August 1802, NP, NAM 1991–04–188 (typescript), fols 12–14; Charles Napier to Emily Napier, 1 January 1803, Bodleian MS Eng. lett. c. 241, fols 114–15; Rúan O'Donnell, *Robert Emmet and the Rising of 1803* (Dublin: Irish Academic Press, 2003), 113; Rúan O'Donnell, *Aftermath: Post-Rebellion Insurgency in Wicklow, 1799–1803* (Dublin: Irish Academic Press, 2000), 144; George Napier to Lord Hardwicke, 24 July 1803, BL Add. MS 35740, fols 328–29; WN, 1:31.

6 Ibid, 38–39.

7 Napier to his mother, March 1802, given in ibid, 1:25.

8 Napier to his mother, December 1803, given in ibid, 1:36.

9 Napier to his mother, 26 December 1803, given in ibid, 1:36.

10 On 27 December – *London Gazette*, 27 December 1803, 15660 p. 1823. On 6 December he had been promoted to First Lieutenant of Artillery – *London Gazette*, 10 December 1803, 15655 p. 1744.

11 Napier's to his mother, 29 December 1803, given in WN, 1:37–38.

12 WN, 1:40. The army engineering college at Chatham had not yet been founded, but Chatham housed one of the original companies of Royal Engineers, created by the Duke of Richmond in 1787 – T.W.J. Connolly, *The History of the Corps of Royal Sappers and Miners*, 2 vols (London: Longman, Brown, Green, and Longmans, 1855), 1:2–63.

13 J. W. Fortescue, *A History of the British Army*, 13 vols (London: Macmillan, 1910–1930), 10:203–04.

14 WN, 1:58; Sarah Napier to Susan O'Brien, 21 July 1805, given in ISSL, 2:195–97; Carola Oman, *Sir John Moore* (London: Hodder and Stoughton, 1953), 329–30.

15 Napier to his mother, January 1806, given in WN, 1:63–64.

16 Ibid; L. G. Mitchell, *Charles James Fox* (Oxford: Oxford UP, 1992), 166–69.

17 George Thomas Napier, *Passages in the Early Military Life of General George T. Napier, K.C.B., Written by Himself*, W.C.E. Napier (ed.) (London: John Murray, 1884), 23; *London Gazette*, 31 May 1806, 15924 p. 683; WN, 1:67.

18 Sarah Napier to Susan O'Brien, 17 July 1806, given in ISSL, 2:213–15; WN, 1:66–67; *London Gazette*, 8 November 1806, 15972 p. 1449; Napier to his mother, 6 February 1807, given in WN, 1:69.

38 Boyhood and war

19 Lawrence Stone, *The Family, Sex, and Marriage in England, 1500–1800* (New York: Harper & Row, 1977), 456–57. Stone cites some of Sarah's comments on parenting as written down by George Thomas Napier's wife, Margaret; see ISSL, 2:312–13.

20 Napier's notes, 25 September 1809, NP BL Add. MS 49112, fol. 17; Napier to the Prince Regent, 23 April 1811, NP BL Add. MS 49112, fol. 22.

21 Napier to his mother, [?] May, 13 May, 28 May, 3 June, 27 June, 4 July 1807, Bodleian MS Eng. lett. c. 236, fols 106–17; Masonic Certificate of Appointment, 20 June 1807, NP BL Add. MS 49112, fol. 9; Brownrigg to Napier 17 July 1807, NP, BL Add MS 54539, fol. 9.

22 Napier to his mother, September 1807, given in WN, 1:76.

23 Napier to his mother, fragment, September 1807, Bodleian MS Eng. lett. c. 236, fols 134–35.

24 Will, 12 September 1807, NP BL Add. MS 49112, fols 12–4. In the case of Caroline's death the money was to be split between his given-away sister Emily and his half-sister Louisa.

25 Samuel Laing, *The Autobiography of Samuel Laing of Papdale, 1780–1868*, R. P. Fereday (ed.) (Kirkwall, Orkney: Bellavista Publications, 2000), 101, 148–49.

26 Alexander Gordon to Lord Aberdeen, 6 January 1809, given in Rory Muir (ed.), *At Wellington's Right Hand: The Letters of Lieutenant-Colonel Sir Alexander Gordon, 1808–1815*, Publications of the Army Records Society, 21 (Stroud, Gloucestershire: Sutton Publishing Company, 2003), 32–34.

27 G. Napier, *Passages*, 124–26.

28 Bentinck to Napier, 15 February 1810, NP, BL Add. MS 54539, fols 36–37.

29 Maurice (ed.), *Diary of John Moore*, 2:390–93; Napier's journal, 16 January 1851, given in WN, 4:305.

30 HC Deb 12 February 1844 vol 72 cc562–68 at c562.

31 WN, 1:94–112; Napier to Emily Napier, 8 January 1852, Bodleian MS Eng. lett. c. 241, fols 47–48.

32 G. Napier, *Passages*, 69–70.

33 Napier's will, August 1852, TNA PROB 11/2181/182.

34 Gordon to Aberdeen, 5 October 1810, given in Muir (ed.), *At Wellington's Right Hand*, 118; G. Napier, *Passages*, 65–67, 109.

35 G. Napier, *Passages*, 51–52, 70, 126; Manningham, *Military Lectures*, 8–9.

36 W. Napier, 'Letter', *Illustrated London News*, 17 September 1853, 230; G. Napier, *Passages*, 51–52.

37 Major William Clunes to George Napier, 29 January 1809, NP, BL Add. MS 49169, fols 7–8. Louisa Conolly to George Napier, 31 January, 5 February 1809, NP, BL Add. MS 49169, fols 10–15; Caroline Fox to Sarah O'Brien, 25 January 1809, given in ISSL, 2:218–20; Louisa Napier to Susan O'Brien, 21 February 1809, 2:220–22. The will was proved on 10 February 1809: Will, 12 September 1807, NP BL Add. MS 49112, fols 12–14. For the rumours that he was alive: W. Bowers to George Napier, 5 February 1809, NP, BL Add. MS 49169, fol. 16; George Walker to George Napier, 22, March 1809, fol. 30; Louisa Napier to Susan O'Brien, 9 March 1809, 2:222–23; Sarah Napier to Charles Napier, 27 March 1809, NP, BL Add. MS 49089, fols 226–27.

38 George Napier to General LeFevre (copy), 17 March 1809, NP, BL Add. MS 49169, fols 27–28; Richard Napier to William O'Brien, 31 March 1809, 2:223; Sarah Napier to Susan O'Brien, 1 April 1809, given in ISSL, 2:223–24; G. Napier, *Passages*, 81–84; statement by Charles Napier, given in WN, 1:113–14; WN, 1:116; Laing, *Autobiography*, 149.

39 Sarah Napier to Susan O'Brien, 25 October 1809, given in ISSL, 2:224–30 at 225; Tillyard, *Aristocrats: Caroline, Emily, Louisa, and Sarah Lennox, 1740–1832* (New York: Farrar, Straus, and Giroux, 1994), 366–67. Charles Napier once complained that he could no longer read half of what she wrote, and she needed someone to hold her hand and retrain her – Napier to his mother, 14 May 1815, Bodleian MS Eng. lett. c. 236, fols 174–75.

40 Sarah Napier to Susan O'Brien, 18 December 1809, given in ISSL, 2:230–33.

A soldier 39

41 Napier to his mother, April 1810, given in WN, 1:122–23; G. Napier, *Passages*, 72–74.

42 WN, 1:123; Napier to his mother, 1 July 1810, 1:130–31; Godfrey Davies, *Wellington and His Army* (Oxford: Basil Blackwell, 1954), 28–31; Michael Glover, *The Peninsular War, 1807–1814: A Concise Military History* (Newton Abbot: David and Charles, 1974), 72–87; Huw W. Davies, *Wellington's Wars: The Making of a Military Genius* (New Haven, CT and London: Yale UP, 2012), 115–25; G. Napier, *Passages*, 56–57.

43 Napier's journal, 27 September 1849, given in WN, 4:190–91; Gates, *Light Infantry Arm*, 134–35, 158; Alexander H. Craufurd, *General Craufurd and His Light Division* (London: Griffith, Farran, Okeden, and Welsh, 1891), 53–59, 146–49.

44 Gates, *Light Infantry Arm*, 166–67; Fortescue, *History of the British Army*, 7:508–14; Napier's journal, 27 September 1849, given in WN, 4:191–92.

45 HC Deb 12 February 1844 vol 72 cc562–68 at cc562–63. See also Wellington to Sarah Napier, 30 September 1810, NP, NAM 1992–11–131, item 1.

46 G. Napier, *Passages*, 133–36; Napier's journal, 27 September 1849, given in WN, 4:191.

47 G. Napier, *Passages*, 136–38.

48 Napier to his mother, December 1810, 21 March, 24 March, 6 April 1811, given in WN, 1:154, 164–66; Napier's journal, 22 March 1810, 1:159; Wellington to Sarah Napier, 16 March 1811, given in Arthur Wellesley, Duke of Wellington, *The Dispatches of Field Marshall the Duke of Wellington*, new edn, 13 vols, J. Gurwood (ed.) (London: John Murray, 1834–1839), 7:367; G. Napier, *Passages*, 159, 167.

49 For the radical tendency in the second half of the eighteenth century, see John Cannon, 'New Lamps for Old: The End of Hanoverian England', in Cannon (ed.), *The Whig Ascendancy: Colloquies on Hanoverian England* (New York: St. Martin's), 100–18 at 101–02.

50 As in 1837: Charles James Napier, *Remarks on Military Law and the Punishment of Flogging* (London: T. and W. Boone, 1837), 149n. His brother George called Napier's politics 'Radical' in 1828: G. Napier, *Passages*, 11. With the *OED* dating 'radical' in the context of politics to 1783, it is hard to concur with J.C.D. Clark, who insists that political radicalism could not exist before the 1820s. See Clark, 'Religion and the Origins of Radicalism in Nineteenth-Century Britain', in Glenn Burgess and Matthew Festenstein (eds), *English Radicalism 1550–1850* (Cambridge: Cambridge UP, 2007), 241–84 at 241–44.

51 George Spater, *William Cobbett: The Poor Man's Friend*, 2 vols (Cambridge: Cambridge UP, 1982), 1:2, 2:433.

52 Napier to his mother, 6 April 1810, July 1810, given in WN, 1:134–35, 166–69; Napier's Journal, 19 May 1810, 2:170; Napier to Commander-in-Chief Sir David Dundas, January 1811, imperfect copy by Napier, NP BL Add. MS 49112, fol. 20; Napier to the Prince Regent, 23 April 1811, fol. 22; Napier to Dundas, copy, 23 April 1811, fol. 23; fragments of letters to Dundas, fols 24–26.

3 In America and France

In 1811 Napier, finally a lieutenant-colonel, was sent to Guernsey to take command of the 102nd Regiment as soon as he could, for 'the state of discipline of that corps requires that you should join it without loss of time'. The 102nd had the reputation for being the worst regiment in the army. In 1808 it had mutinied against Captain Bligh in New South Wales (this mutiny was nineteen years after Fletcher Christian's more famous rebellion). Napier said he would make the 102nd the best regiment there was. But he was not yet in the best shape himself. His wounds left him feverish and prone to fits.[1]

Napier joined his men in January 1812, and in June they were ordered to Bermuda on their way to take part in the hostilities against the United States. They arrived on the island in September. In addition to commanding the five-hundred-man 102nd, Napier was also made second-in-command of the larger force of Sir Sydney Beckwith, of which the 102nd now formed a part.[2]

The passage across the Atlantic was stormy and prolonged. Bermuda turned out to be unpleasant and it was plagued by yellow fever. Napier noted the horrible rate of tropical disease among his troops, and he began to work with the medical men to see if there might be a solution in hygiene, diet, or exercise.[3] He also found that he had a great deal of work to do in disciplining the men of Beckwith's force for their brawling and fighting. The worst trouble was with the *chasseurs*, two companies of none-too-well-behaved French prisoners and deserters from the Peninsular War. And Napier still had to contend with the disciplinary problems of his own regiment, the horrible 102nd. He took great care over these matters, preparing detailed statements about the legal questions coming before him.[4]

Some discipline he had to mete out more directly. One soldier in Bermuda – fully sober at the time – began to beat his wife. He knocked her down and kicked her, and then he began to jump on her breasts in his heavy boots. He was about to land on her once again, perhaps killing her, when Napier opened his head with a bayonet and knocked him sideways with another blow:

> Had you heard the horrible shrieks of the woman, till her breath was stamped out, and seen the rascal's violence and face, you would have thought, as I did, that her days were numbered. . . . This kind of man it gives me pleasure to flog, and no regiment is without several.[5]

However, in the court-martial this man was *not* ordered flogged, for Napier had hit him and this contravened regulations.

***

In calmer hours Charles Napier continued with his studies of military science, writing essays for himself on different points. He read Arrian and dreamt of Alexander's campaigns in the east.[6] And in his journal he reflected on the larger war against Napoleon in which he had played a part. So much had been wasted and so many men had died; so many opportunities had been lost. Napier wrote that if England could somehow proclaim and act on her own liberal values, then it could save the world.

At the moment, what he had in mind was England improving Portugal. British policy when occupying and defending the country had been far too moderate, too unambitious, he wrote. So much more could have been done:

> We have flattered their vanity and deprived them of no public custom or ornament; we meddled not with their religion, we paid their soldiers when their own prince did not; and we might have done more on a sound system, but we always act on the confined basis of – present expediency. We might have regulated their whole civil government and founded a free nation, entirely and truly regenerating them as a people. . . . I adduce Portugal because I know it, and because it is a proof that conquest may be made easy: for disguise it as we may, we are really the conquerors of the Portuguese in this war.[7]

France had fallen short in its civilizing mission as well, he went on. But the French had failed because they murdered and pillaged in the countries they conquered. Surely England would not wreak havoc in this way? There were moral dangers in imperial conquest, but there were also great opportunities: '[N]o generosity can afterwards wash out the first guilt of unprovoked conquest. Nevertheless, give riches and be poor; give plenty though at your monetary cost: let your chain be golden, or at last gilt, and you may rule the world.'[8]

Coastal raider

The war in which Napier now found himself was very different from the main task of the British Army in this period, which was defending the Spanish and Portuguese from the French. Napier could not understand 'the sacking and burning of towns' along the coast of Virginia: '[I]t is bad employment for British troops.'[9] Years later he looked back on this war in America as one of 'folly and piracy, uniting all that is bad without a redeeming point, not even that of success'.[10]

The lack of success was apparent early on. Operationally he reported to Beckwith, but in fact Beckwith himself did not enjoy full responsibility for the mission. Command was shared between Beckwith from the army and the naval officer George Cockburn. Double leadership did not work very well and

42 *Boyhood and war*

the campaign was shambolic. For Napier, Cockburn trusted too much in luck and did not engage in enough planning and thought. In Napier's view, the habit of absolute obedience on a ship meant that naval officers like Cockburn never learned to 'use their judgment in command' the way every army officer had to do. Officers in the army

> from habitual familiarity have to support themselves against wit and satire, and even impudence at times. A naval officer has only to enforce manual acts of obedience. . . . A regimental commander has to convince those under him that his orders are wise, and to procure obedience to them when he is not present. In fine a soldier's mind is always exercised in the study of mankind, and a seaman's in the theory and practice of manual operations.[11]

On one occasion he was a part of the fifty-boat assault, led by Beckwith, against Craney Island in the Chesapeake. This island formed part of the defensive perimeter for Norfolk harbour. From the beginning the operation went badly. The leading boat ran aground and the Americans began wading towards it. After managing to disembark, Beckwith and the main body of the British force aimlessly wandered the island. When they reached the channel on the other side they found it too deep to ford and too wide for their muskets to hit anything on the far shore. A local guide somehow appeared who promised to lead them towards a bridge that may or may not have existed. Eventually Beckwith grew doubtful and turned the men around. Under (the albeit distant) bombardment of the American heavy guns across the channel in Norfolk, and the deadlier grapeshot fired from the American gunboats and the island's fort, Napier and Beckwith had to get their boats launched while the men inexpertly clambered aboard. Several dozen British soldiers were killed and not one American. Throughout the operation it was apparent that no single mind had worked out how the men and weapons from the army and the boats from the navy were supposed to operate together with one another on the terrain at hand to achieve any reasonable military objective.[12]

Worse was to come a few days later, when Napier was present at the battle of Hampton, Virginia. The town was taken against very light resistance and it was held quietly by the British forces that night. But the next day, long after the fighting had ended, Beckwith's French *chasseurs* began terrorizing the civilian population.[13] A woman was raped and her husband was shot in their home. Napier was horrified. He would later claim that he was too busy keeping the men of the 102nd from joining in the mêlée to shoot the miscreant *chasseurs* on the spot. In his view the whole thing was a 'disgraceful affair' that reflected poorly on Beckwith in particular.[14]

Napier told his sister that this was one of the 'many incidences of [the Frenchmen] killing without any object on Earth but the pleasure of murdering'. But

In America and France 43

that wasn't his only moral complaint about what he saw. British forces were being asked to fight the wrong people:

> I would rather ten Frenchmen shot than one American. It is quite shocking to have men who speak one's own language brought in wounded: one feels as if they are English peasants. . . . There are numbers of officers in the navy in particular whose families are American, and their fathers in one or two instances absolutely being in the towns we are trying to burn. Even Sir Sydney Beckwith has relations in America. It is certainly a most unnatural war, a sort of bastard rebellion. . . . I flatter myself I put a *stop to plunder*, and tho' I assure you the people were treated *too well*[,] being paid nearly *double* for everything and the soldiers kept in perfect order, yet I am told I shall be abused in the American press as a perfect savage the same was as J. W. and Admiral Cockburn were.[15]

He described how one soldier of the 102nd had made 'an atrocious attempt to murder a man' and he could not find out who the soldier was. Therefore Napier and his men took in the injured American civilian, nursed him to health, and set him ashore where he liked, with eight pounds from Admiral Cockburn himself.

His one criticism of the morality of the *American* forces was how they shot nails and jagged pieces of iron out of their cannons:

> [A] man *delights* to be killed according to the law of nations – nothing so pleasant or correct, but to be *doused* against all rule is quite offensive, a man don't kick like a gentlemen. – A 24 lb. shot in the stomach is fine, we die heroically!; but a *brass candlestick* for stuffing, with a garnish of *rusty twopenny nails* make us die as *ungenteelly* as if one had the cholick.'[16]

***

When word spread about the massacre of civilians at Hampton, the British and American publics were aghast. An Admiralty enquiry cleared Cockburn and fixed the blame on the French prisoners. But no one outside the Admiralty believed that this absolved the British commander of his responsibility for preventing crime. Hampton boosted the American resolve to continue fighting the war. Napier himself burned with resentment at the officers and men who he thought responsible for the carnage. These men were never held to account for what they had done to civilians, and this shocked Napier.[17]

Still under Cockburn's direction, in July Napier and his men went along on raids around Ocracoke in the barrier islands of Virginia. Cockburn claimed to be attacking the 'commerce' along the inland waterways around the 'port of Ocracoke' – but how much commerce there was in this small place may be open to question. Very different was Napier's own description of the work that

44   Boyhood and war

he and his men were doing: They were stealing cattle and ruining the poor, and Napier decided that he did not like it one bit.[18] In Bermuda, as we saw, he had devoted some of his private hours to studying and writing long essays on a variety of military questions – touching on everything from cavalry warfare to how the baggage train of different kinds of troops might be reduced. One topic he explored was whether it can ever be right to steal from the enemy. So he had been pondering this topic well before he and his force carried out their first raid on American property.[19]

One point he stressed in Bermuda became especially important in light of the coastal raids. Napier argued that an army should indeed be allowed to live on the resources of the enemy population – but he argued that any large quantity of provisions should be secured only through regularly organized exaction from the enemy authorities. Meanwhile the soldiers could take what they wanted:

> Booty, when taken by the troops, should be divided amongst them; contributions should be taken for the supply of the army. And all towns taken by storm should give prize money, if not sacked; an act which should be punished by abundant executions, as being inconsistent with discipline, with policy; and lastly with humanity, for in war that must come last. Plunder or booty, is absolutely needful in some shape or other, to urge the soldiers to enterprize, because interest is the great stimulant of human nature.[20]

However well organized the raids of Cockburn and Beckwith might have been – and they were not very well organized at all – they could hardly pass this moral bar that Napier had set in Bermuda. For what he had been writing about was how to provision an army *that actually had to operate within hostile territory.* Such an army would need to be fed somehow. Cockburn and Beckwith's activities were of another kind: They were going to the enemy's territory specifically for the purpose of raiding the civilians. Then they would leave, going back to the ships where they already had all the provisions they needed.

This was not the only ethical problem. If the Americans offered no resistance, Cockburn would pay for the livestock and property he took. But Cockburn's own men noted that he only paid a small fraction of the value – a dollar for a sheep when it was worth six. And when he would pay he did so in a promissory note that would become redeemable only after the end of the war. The whole idea was to hurt the American population and get them to pressure their government to make peace; paying promptly and in full would hardly make sense.[21] But raiding individuals in this way was nothing like the policy of requisitioning *necessary* provisions from the enemy authorities that Napier had written about in Bermuda.

Many other officers also disapproved of what was going on, but Napier wrote out his ideas at the time and sent them up the chain of command. He suggested sending provisions officers ashore to take the cattle and other goods without ruining the civilian farmers. He wanted to pay the Americans in vouchers which they would then submit to the American government. If the vouchers were not redeemed, then the coastal population would have only their own authorities to blame. Not only would this new system be more fair to the American civilians, but it would also help to keep the British troops under better discipline, which as Napier had said in his notebook, was so important a goal. On his own copy of the proposal, Napier wrote that he was trying to prevent any repetition of the horrors of Hampton, so 'disgraceful to the British people'.[22]

***

Meanwhile, he thought, perhaps there was a way for Britain to gain a truly decisive victory while righting a great injustice. Where Great Britain had failed to take over and reform the Portuguese, it might take over and reform the Americans. What he now suggested was arming the American slaves, turning them into a fighting force, and then marching with them to the city of Washington to end slavery and dictate the terms of peace. Napier outlined the size of the force he would need (for yes, he would lead it himself), and how he would attract and train the slaves; and he sent these ideas to the new naval commander in the theatre, Vice Admiral Sir George Cochrane. Once again, we see a Napierian *leitmotif*: the possibility of using British power to save a people from injustice and exploitation. As he recalled in 1825:

> My plan was as follows: may it yet be executed! seeing a black population of slaves ruled by a thin population of whites, the blacks thinking the English demi-gods and their Yankee master devils, I said to the authorities Give me two hundred thousand stands of arms, and land me in Virginia with only the officers and non-commissioned officers of three black regiments, that is to say about one hundred persons accustomed to drill black men. Let the ships with store lay off the coast while I strike into the woods with my drill men, my own regiment, and proclamations exciting the blacks to rise for freedom: forbidding them however to commit excesses under penalty of being given up or hanged.[23]

Napier wanted to use the navy to transport his new force to the Delmarva Peninsula, where the black women and children could grow food. Their army could be doubled to two hundred thousand and get proper training until time came to coordinate with a British force coming from Canada. A pincer movement could then be carried out to seize Washington.

Napier never got an answer from his commanders. For his own part, Cochrane was already recruiting blacks in the Chesapeake, and he was as pleased as anyone with the quality of their service in uniform. But he did not think that individually they could be kept in the military for very long, because they were impatient to be settled somewhere and begin their lives of freedom.[24] Whitehall blew hot and cold on the idea of expanding the use of

46 *Boyhood and war*

American blacks in the war effort, finally deciding in mid-1814 to proceed on only a small scale to avoid atrocities (as the historians C. J. Bartlett and G. A Smith have shown[25]). In looking back over the matter a decade later, Napier would argue that an exponentially larger force of blacks should have been raised. He believed that after the war they might have been sent to Canada to help fill up the country and defend it from the Americans. This would answer any question about where they could go after they were free. He did not address a different objection: that his plan might have disturbed the British slave populations of the West Indies.[26]

Yet Napier did consider the possibility that he might have stirred up a race war in America, although he dismissed it. He summed up the matter in words that might serve as a comment on his own actions in Sind in the 1840s. Reflecting on this idea of using the former slaves for a march on Washington, he suggested that a war could be justifiable if its object were to free an oppressed people from the rule of tyrants:

> As to horrors, war is full of horrors. No large army ever did or can move without horrors! Accursed be they who make unjust war! but the blacks could be held in more rigid discipline than our own troops, and there was no reason to think many horrors would have been perpetrated. Some! yes! so much the worse, yet on whom? Slaveholders! Men on whom God's justice would have fallen, through the medium of the poor wretches in whom they had outraged his laws and their own image: they would have reaped as they had sowed![27]

In any case, Napier's active involvement in the American War was soon over. In September, Napier and Beckwith and their forces were moved to Halifax, Nova Scotia, having lived aboard ship since leaving Bermuda and first travelling to the American coast in June.[28] Napier soon transferred back into the 50th Regiment to fight in the Pyrenees. However, Napoleon had been defeated by the time he could return to Europe.

Coming home

Peace brought new challenges. How was Napier to support himself? In 1814 England had been fighting the French for most of the past twenty-two years. Now the military establishment was to be substantially reduced, and Napier and many other officers were put on the half-pay list. He retained his rank but he had no military assignment. He also received a £250 major's pension for his wounds. This was upgraded to the £300 due to his promotion to lieutenant-colonel in February 1815; he began to receive this higher amount in June. By way of compensation for his suffering, he also had a small sinecure as titular governor of the Virgin Islands. But he never went to the colony, and he seems to have given up his sinecure after a few years. He also made some attempt to get a share of the prize money for the seizure of two American ships during the Ocracoke expedition, but little came of this.[29]

Would he try to remain in the army? As a first step he began studying fortification at the military college at Farnham. Then in the spring of 1815 he took a three-month leave to perfect his French in Belgium and Paris, first spending some time with the ailing Mrs. Kelly and then paying a visit to his mother in London. He arrived on the Continent during the Hundred Days. He took lodgings in Ghent, waiting for developments and observing the scene. Napier was excited about the possibility that France might return to Napoleonic rule – putting paid to 'Alexander the fat and all the other crowned butter puddings', as he put it. He had to admit that in getting his *Grande Armée* massacred, Napoleon had made himself terribly unpopular, but he wrote to his mother that the horrible rule of the Bourbons would make the French forget even this. Years later he would tell the story of a dinner he attended with Louis XVIII's officers about a week before Waterloo. He admired their new ribbons and medals, and he asked them what all the new decorations were for. And they told him – these were the awards they had given themselves for their retreat from Paris.[30] Napoleon's rule had to be better than the rule of this group.

Preparing for the inevitable battle, Charles Napier made a new will in Ghent on 16 June 1815. For us, all that matters about the will was its timing and location. For indeed Napier was still in Ghent and the Battle of Waterloo had been the previous day. Napier had missed it. He had managed to get himself reattached to the 50th Regiment in April, but he had not been properly put to work by the regiment, so quickly did Napoleon force the pace of events. He also applied to be on Wellington's staff. In turning him down, the general said the Horse Guards had overstaffed his army.[31]

Although Napier had failed to reach the battle in time, he did arrive at Waterloo before all the wounded could be carried away and he saw their suffering. Then he was put to work in helping to mop up resistance on the outskirts of Paris. As an old man he would recall seeing 'the French Chambers discussing constitutions when we were in Camp in [the] Bois de Boulogne, and Blücher place 6 guns to disperse the scoundrels'.[32]

***

Napier returned to Farnham, where he remained until the end of 1817. But when the course was over, the question of employment once again loomed, and so he took a first step into civilian life. He went to live in France, at St. Omer, and this brought him once again near his brother William. Before the Hundred Days William had planned to join Charles on the course at Farnham, but after Waterloo he remained with the army of occupation, at Bapaume.[33] William was about eighty miles from where Charles now settled at St. Omer.

At this time William was sending to England for a number of books, often the works of Cobbett. Perhaps the two brothers discussed Cobbett. Certainly Charles Napier was inserting disquisitions in praise of Cobbett's radicalism into the letters he wrote to his mother. He told her in 1816 that Cobbett and the other educated leaders of radical opinion were fighting the good fight. The 'starving people' of England were not fools, and they had great men among them. The poor would soon be vindicated, he said. The 'multitude' would rise

48 *Boyhood and war*

up: '[T]he people are in motion, and those who oppose them will be crushed like pebbles under a rolling stone.' But he added that if all went well, the efforts of Cobbett and others to educate the common people about their real interests might lead them to rise up *peacefully*, through petitioning rather than violence. To this end Cobbett's writings might help the poor see who their real enemies were. Then they would be able to target their anger at the right people, rather than lashing out violently against anyone and everyone more privileged than themselves.[34] We have already seen Napier the liberal imperialist dream of bringing freedom to the Portuguese and then to the American slaves. Now the man who would one day confront the Chartists wanted the common people of England to rise up and petition for their rights.

But what of the more practical matter of his career? In 1819 he applied again for active service in the army. This time he was successful. Napier was appointed field inspector of the forces in the British government of the Ionian Islands, which commanded the Adriatic and remained in British hands after the French Wars. For all his radicalism, Napier would now have a role – however modest it might be – in the administration of a British colony.[35]

Notes

1 Napier to his mother, 13 August 1811, given in WN, 1:180–82; Sarah Napier to Susan O'Brien, 17 December 1811, given in ISSL, 2:247–48; quotation from Henry Torrens to Charles Napier, 18 July 1811, BL Add. MS 49112, fol. 27.
2 WN, 1:186–87; Napier to his mother, May 1813, 1:201–03; Fortescue, *History of the British Army*, 13 vols (London: Macmillan, 1910–1930), 9:321 and 321–2n1.
3 Napier's journal, 1 January 1813, [February 1813?], quoted in WN, 1:193–94, 198; Napier, *Memoir on the Roads of Cephalonia* (London: James Ridgway, 1825), 67–69.
4 J. Mackay Hitsman and Alice Sorby, 'Independent Foreigners or Canadian Chasseurs', *Military Affairs* 25, 1 (Spring 1961), 11–17; Napier's papers, April and May 1813, NP Add. MS 49112, fols 40–78ff.
5 Napier's journal, February 1813, given in WN, 1:198–99.
6 Ibid, 24 September 1842, 2:195.
7 Napier's journal in Bermuda, 1812, given in WN, 1:238.
8 Ibid.
9 Ibid, 1 June 1813, given in WN, 1:212.
10 Ibid, April 1825, 1:358. He never changed his mind, making the same point in 1840: Napier, editor's note to Part 1, chapter 1, in Alfred Victor, comte de Vigny, *Lights and Shades of Military Life*, Charles James Napier (ed.), 2 vols. in 1 (London: Henry Colburn, 1840), 1:319; 2nd edn, 12.
11 Napier's journal, 25 and 30 June 1813, given in WN, 1:218–20.
12 WN, 1:213–14; Christopher T. George, *Terror on the Chesapeake: The War of 1812 on the Bay* (Shippensburg, PA: White Mane Books, 2000), 42–47.
13 Henry Adams, *History of the United States of America During the Second Administration of James Madison*, 3 vols (New York: Charles Scribner's Sons, 1890), 1:271–78.
14 Hitsman and Sorby, 'Independent Foreigners or Canadian Chasseurs', 15; Napier's journal, 12 August 1813, given in WN, 222; George, *Terror on the Chesapeake*, 50–51; endorsement on map, NP BL Add. MS 49112, fol. 84.
15 Napier to Emily Napier, 23 July 1813, Bodleian MS Eng. lett. c. 241, fols 116–19.
16 Ibid.
17 Napier's journal, 12 August 1813, September 1825, given in WN, 1:220–22, 1:371; Jeremy Black, *The War of 1812 in the Age of Napoleon* (Norman: University of Oklahoma Press,

2009), 110–13; Donald R. Hickey, *The War of 1812: A Forgotten Conflict: Bicentennial Edition* (Urbana, Chicago, and Springfield: University of Illinois Press, 2012), 155–57.

18 Napier to his sister, 22 August 1813, given in WN, 1:225–26; Cockburn's letter to Admiral Warren, 12 July 1813, extract given in the *Times*, 8 September 1813, 2 col. a.

19 Napier's journal, Bermuda, 1813, given in WN, 1:244–46, 249, 253–55; Napier to his mother, May 1813, quoted in ibid, 1:202–03.

20 Napier's journal, Bermuda, 1813, given in ibid, 1:247. On soldiers plundering if denied their prize money: Napier to Emily Bunbury, 16 March 1844, NP, BL Add. MS 49110, fols 5–7.

21 John Latimer, *1812: War with America* (Cambridge, MA: Harvard UP, 2007), 159–60; C. J. Bartlett and G. A Smith, 'A "Species of Milito-Nautico-Guerilla-Plundering Warfare": Admiral Alexander Cochrane's Naval Campaign against the United States, 1814–1815', in Julie Flavell and Stephen Conway (eds), *Britain and America Go to War: The Impact of War and Warfare in Anglo-America, 1754–1815* (Gainesville: UP of Florida, 2004), 174–204 at 182–86.

22 Napier to Admiral Cochrane, 1813, NP, BL Add. MS 49112, fol. 89.

23 Napier's journal, September 1825, given in WN, 1:369.

24 Frank A. Cassell, 'Slaves of the Chesapeake Bay Area and the War of 1812', *Journal of Negro History* 57, 2 (April 1972), 144–55 at 151–52; Nathaniel Millett, 'Britain's 1814 Occupation of Pensacola and America's Response: An Episode in the War of 1812 in the Southeastern Borderlands', *Florida Historical Quarterly* 84, 2 (Fall 2005), 229–55 at 230–33.

25 Bartlett and Smith, 'Milito-Nautico-Guerilla-Plundering Warfare', 186–89.

26 *The Colonies: Treating of their Value Generally – Of the Ionian Islands in Particular; The Importance of the Latter in War and Commerce – As Regards Russian Policy – Their Finances – Why an Expense to Great Britain – Detailed Proofs that they Need not Be so – Turkish Government – Battle of Navarino – Ali Pacha – Sir Thomas Maitland – Strictures on the Administration of Sir Frederick Adam* (London: Thomas and William Boone, 1833), 461–63.

27 Napier's journal, September 1825, given in WN, 1:371.

28 Napier's journal, 24 September 1813, given in ibid, 1:226.

29 Pension award form, 5 September 1815, NP, BL Add. MS 54539, fol. 47; pension award form, 19 February 1816, fol. 55; Great Britain, Parliament, *An Account, Specifying the Names of the Governors, Lieutenant Governors, and General Officers, Upon the Staff of the Several Foreign Colonies, Settlements, and Governments, Now Belonging to His Majesty . . .* (1814–1815), No. 353, 4–5; Great Britain, Parliament, *Return of the Names of the Officers in the Army Who Receive Pensions for the Loss of Limbs, or for Wounds . . .*, (1818), No. 294, 15–16; *Manchester Mercury*, 25 February 1812, 4s col. e; WN, 1:182, 230.

30 Napier to his mother, 24 March, 12 April, 25 April, 14 May 1815, Bodleian MS Eng. lett. c. 236, fols 165, 168–71, 174–75, quotation from 12 April; Charles James Napier, *Colonization, Particularly in Southern Australia, with some Remarks on Small Farms and Overpopulation* (London: T. and W. Boone, 1835; New York, Augustus M. Kelly, 1969), 16–17.

31 Will, 16 June 1815, NP, BL Add. MS 49112, fol. 96; Napier to his mother, 25 April, 29 April 1815, Bodleian MS Eng. lett. c. 236, fols 170–73.

32 Napier to Emily Bunbury, 22 December 1852, NP, BL Add. MS 49110, fols 144–45.

33 H. A. Bruce, *Life of General Sir William Napier, G.C.B.*, 2 vols (London: John Murray, 1864), 1:188. This work appeared under the name of Napier Bruce (later Lord Aberdare), but while he edited and prepared it, most of the writing seems to have been done by General Patrick MacDougall – see Jay Luvaas, *The Education of an Army: British Military Thought, 1815–1940* (Chicago: University of Chicago Press, 1964), 8n2, 108–09. Both Bruce and MacDougall were sons-in-law of William Napier.

34 Napier to his mother, November 1816, given in WN, 1:271–72.

35 Bruce, *William Napier*, 1:188–98; WN, 1:273–75; Napier to Richard Napier, 11 April 1819, NP, BL Add, MS 49111, fols 59–60.

Part II

The radical abroad and at home

4 Greece and the Greeks

In following Napier to Greece, we can begin to get a better idea of who the man was – and how bringing freedom to the common people was no mere rationalization for the conquest of Sind but a matter of settled principle. The prospect of overthrowing Islamic tyrants was something he had been turning over in his mind for a long time.

He also believed in benevolent despotism. When he first went to Ionia, Napier discussed the glories of the late Napoleonic regime with the peasants of France, Switzerland, and Italy whom he met along the way. He heartily concurred in what he said was their view – that the emperor had achieved great things.[1]

***

Napier's destination was the 'Septinsular Republic' of the seven Ionian Islands (see Map 4.1). In theory they were an independent state but in fact as a result of the French Wars the islands were under British control. The governor – Napier's commander and a man who would shape his career – was Sir Thomas Maitland, or 'king Tom', the Lord High Commissioner of the Ionian Islands, Commander-in-Chief of the Mediterranean (except Gibraltar), and Governor of Malta.

By all accounts Maitland was a man of a soon-to-vanish era, an era of earthiness and flamboyant alcoholism.[2] But Napier came to respect Maitland and from him he would learn much about colonial governance. For like Napier, Maitland combined the roles of military officer and radical. A younger son of the Earl of Lauderdale, he had gone into the army and fought against Haider Ali and Tippoo Sultan (he of Tippoo's Tiger) in Mysore in the 1780s. In and out of Parliament for a family seat from 1790 to 1814, he became a leading Whig critic of the war against Tippoo in which he had fought so hard. And he broadened his criticism to include most aspects of the government's military policy in India and Europe.[3] For one thing, he consistently opposed the building of barracks. He thought they led to military despotism. And yet after he commanded a raid on the French coast in 1800 and re-entered Parliament once again, he turned into a loyal supporter of the government. It seemed to many that he had been bought off. Nonetheless he supported Roman Catholic relief in 1813 – that much of his radicalism remained, at least.[4]

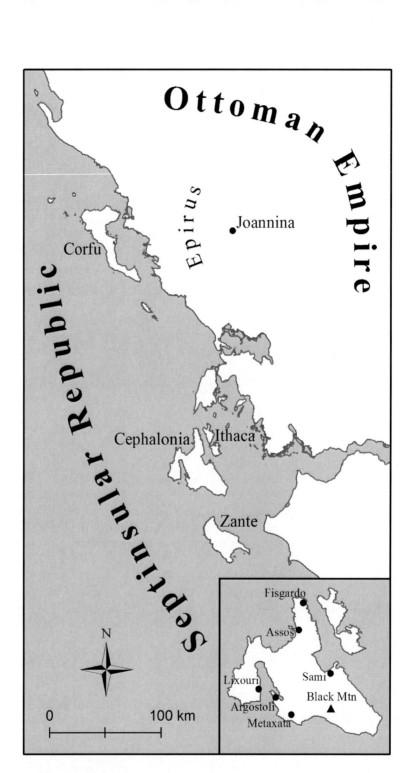

Map 4.1 The Ionian Islands.
Map prepared by Geoffrey Fouad

Maitland had played the radical in the military as well as in politics. In 1798, largely on his own initiative, he evacuated British troops from Haiti, refusing to leave a garrison there or to stake a British claim to the territory. Then from 1805 to 1811, as governor of Ceylon, he ended a protracted and bloody war with the Kingdom of Kandy. Rather than trying to make a formal peace with the alienated Kandyan leaders, Maitland simply stopped fighting them: 'I shall not enter into any foolish expeditions; I will not throw away the Lives of His Majesty's Subjects by Disease in burning and destroying the defenceless huts of the innocent natives.'[5]

Meanwhile he reformed the courts in Ceylon, promoting the interests of the common people over the rich. He improved and expanded agriculture. And he employed quarantines and other public health measures – all the while radiating a sense of brusque and imperious command and indulging in every carnal appetite. Apart from his debauchery, Maitland was the kind of commander *cum* administrator that Napier wanted to be, and the kind of man whom Napier thought especially necessary in Greece.[6] Napier admitted in an early work that Maitland was 'despotic and arbitrary', but he was despotic in the right way. Despotism, Napier explained somewhat dubiously, is no more than being successful. The question he insisted upon was this: despotism to what end? Napier added that like all men, Maitland was sometimes right and sometimes wrong.[7]

And so Napier went to work beside Maitland in the Ionian Islands, striving for radical social reform and 'protecting the labouring class'. But Maitland's and soon enough Napier's activities within local Greek society had to be of the Virgilian kind. They found that they had to humble the proud, the local aristocrats, if they wanted to accomplish anything for the commoners.[8]

Along these lines Maitland rewrote the constitution of the Septinsular Republic to make it far more complex and the government all the easier for him to dominate. He gave the President of the Senate (whom he had appointed) the title of 'His Highness'.[9] The Senators were required to consider all the bills and proposals which the High Commissioner might introduce before them, yet on his own account each Senator could introduce only one bill per session – and the members of the lower house could introduce no bills, ever, unless they were given special permission to do so. The only official who could grant this permission was none other than the High Commissioner himself.[10]

As Napier tells it, all this was very clever, sidelining the rich and allowing Maitland to do good things for the poor. But Maitland's chief error, as Napier explained the matter later on, came when he allowed his arbitrary nature to overpower his own desire for reform. Maitland abolished the ballot in order – or so Maitland said – to give the Greeks 'boldness'. Now they would have to declare their votes in public. For Charles Napier, this could only increase the power of the feudal lords over their dependents, exactly the wrong move.

In Napier's view, what Maitland was really trying to do in abolishing the ballot was to secure government influence. Were ballots so un-English and so corrupting, Napier asked, when they were used in the United Service Club? Are the generals and the admirals and 'the chivalry' of England so un-English,

56 *The radical abroad and at home*

so dishonest when they elect or blackball each other in secret? And yet, he added, English voters were asked to make their choices known in public in front of rich men who could crush them, and upon whose employment or custom they depended. Napier insisted that men sometimes have to put feeding themselves above voting their consciences. On one march in the Peninsular War, he added, he was himself so hungry that he would have voted Tory 'for a biscuit'.[11]

Turkish despotism vs. British despotism

Napier had gone to the Ionian Islands as Inspector of Militia, but the first major task that Maitland gave him was to help the mainland Greeks in their struggle against Ottoman rule. Hope centred on a rebellious Ottoman official, Ali Pasha, and the British government had ordered Maitland to assist him.[12]

Ali Pasha was, in full, the Ali Pasha of Joannina (today's Ioannina, but we will use Napier's version). He was the governor of Epirus, the Ottoman province occupying the northwestern part of the Greek mainland just opposite the Ionian capital of Corfu. Originally an Albanian chieftain, he was born probably around 1750.[13] From the town of his birth he is also known as Ali Pasha Tepelini.

In 1820 and early 1821, Napier paid three visits to Ali Pasha in order to assess his military situation. This was Napier's first experience of an Islamic society. By all accounts Ali Pasha was a colourful character. He had corresponded with Napoleon and he had entertained the deposed king of Sweden. But he also amassed a long record of cruelty and conquest. One English-language biography devoted to him – this was an 1837 book that Napier heartily agreed with when it came out[14] – begins with two quotations from Shakespeare: 'There is no more mercy in him than there is milk in a male tiger'; and 'Go forward and be choked by thy ambition'.[15]

In trying to help Ali Pasha, Napier was at first carrying out his instructions from Maitland, as we have seen, but soon those instructions would change.

For many years the British ministers at Constantinople had done what they could to protect the nearly independent Ali Pasha from the wrath of the Sultan. The Pasha of Epirus was regarded as a loyal ally against the French. In 1820, Maitland was asked to see what could be done. But Maitland worried that Ali Pasha's machinations would draw in the Russians, and he asked for instructions from home. Meanwhile in July Napier offered Ali Pasha more concrete British assistance. In exchange for greater freedom for the Christians in his territories, Maitland secretly supplied arms. But then the instructions that Maitland had requested from the Colonial Secretary finally arrived – stay out of it.[16]

Yet now that he had begun conspiring with Ali Pasha on how to fight the Ottoman Turks, this was a hard order for Napier to accept. Greece was on the cusp of its 1821 revolution against the Ottomans. Discontent was in the air and so was hope. Napier made a private tour of southern Greece, scouting defensive positions for a possible Greek revolt. He imagined what he could do at the head of 200,000 Greeks in arms. Romantic nationalism called him.

So did other kinds of romance. He tells us that on this journey he visited Byron's 'Maid of Athens'. She was a half-English young lady whom the poet had celebrated only a few years before.[17] In his journal Napier hinted that as one should not kiss and tell, there were things about this visit to Athens that he could not record. He does note that English travellers tended to break hearts. They refused to marry the young women who deserved it; they married on the other hand those whom they would betray.

Napier's visit to the Greek mainland closed when he left Patras in March 1821, only five days before the outbreak of the Greek Revolution in that very city, and that is all that is known about the matter.[18]

***

Now thirty-eight, Napier returned to England. There he wrote his first short book, less than fifty pages long. This was a modest beginning for his writing career. In time he would produce thick volumes extolling his own abilities, criticizing his superiors, and justifying his conduct in every affair. He would justify his idea of rulership in the Ionian Islands, in Ireland, and in India – a vision of rulership under men like himself, unfettered by mere laws, free to combat the desires of corrupt local elites by whatever means they saw fit, ruling in the larger interests of the poor – efficient rulers triumphing over the Old Corruption in England, too.

But for now, in this first anonymous work, *War in Greece* [1821], the question was not how to rule over or reengineer a society over which one had control, but how the Greeks might win control of their society in the first place. Weren't they so quarrelsome and so impractical that any British help would simply be wasted on them?[19]

Napier tried to address the objection head on. There was nothing wrong with the Greek character, he said. It was true that the Greeks *did* seem to have some problems working together, but there was no flaw in their basic nature. Instead the difficulty arose from their historical experiences. For if indeed there was any underlying Greek character, Napier insisted, it consisted of nothing more than changeability itself. The Greeks had undergone constant adjustments in their national personality because they had lived under governments of so many different kinds.[20]

This idea that there is no in-born collective character, and that a people's various national characteristics derive only from the collective experiences of each new generation, was the natural opening position for Napier to take on the age-old question of nature versus nurture. The idea of in-born or biological race-nature was on the rise both in France and in the United States in the first half of the nineteenth century as these countries struggled to establish their post-revolutionary identities.[21] But Napier belonged to a very different and more British school of thought. We should remember the mental universe of the Romantics, grounded upon the assumptions of associationalist psychology: The human personality was nothing more than a blank slate on which various sense impressions had left their mark, each associated with the pleasure

58 *The radical abroad and at home*

or the pain it had produced. The mind was the resulting pattern of connections and associations.

At birth the blank slate was blank for everyone; it did not come in different colours. Given this idea of the mind, there was at least in theory no room for in-born racial character. It is true that by the end of the eighteenth century and the early nineteenth, the Romantic movement had thrown a special light upon any mental associations that might be connected to one's own origins, to one's childhood, to the folk traditions of the people among whom one was raised, and to one's formative language, landscape, and nation. And this Romantic view of personal or national character could indeed be reconciled with an idea of the biological inheritance of acquired cultural characteristics, as it was in the growing Continental and North American schools of racist thinking. Ideas like this might appeal to colonial landowners in the British Empire, who were already committed to racial oppression or maintaining the stratification of a creole society.

But in the British Isles themselves, there were memories of so many waves of conquerors and settlers, and there was a pride in the national mongrelhood.[22] In Great Britain the idea of biologically inherited races was rejected by most people well into the nineteenth century. Theories about the inbred inferiority of some groups seemed too much like the special pleading of colonial slave-owners. More important, the idea that there were separate, unequal species of humanity contradicted the plainer, monogenetic interpretation of the book of Genesis. That was no small thing in England after the Evangelical Revival of the eighteenth century. The key figure in British anthropology for the greatest part of Napier's life was James Cowles Prichard, for whom there were no human colour-races. For Prichard, the different groups within the single human species had diverged under the influence of different climates from – as Prichard believed at one point – a black Adam and Eve.

Napier's thinking about human groups would always fit within this same mental universe. He very much believed in mutability, in nurture rather than nature. He rejected any idea of racial distinction.[23] Only on the basis of a nonracist world view does his desire to spread what he thought were universal human rights to Eastern populations make any sense, and his liberal universalism was predicated upon it. In 1813 in the Chesapeake, Napier did not think the American blacks belonged in slavery, and in 1821 in Greece and back in England he did not think the Greeks or anyone else deserved to languish under subjection to the pashas. There were no human races – there were only peoples who had become corrupted by history and oppression and who could be saved by better governance. The social injustices against which he would fight had a special sting because of what they did to people whose apparent differences were in fact purely cultural. That is, the vast crowd of the poor would become *better* people, their minds developing along better channels of association and sympathy, if only they were treated less horribly – if only they were freed from the tyranny of their social superiors and a state that served the interests of the rich. In the current instance, if the Greeks won their independence they would be able to work together much better than they seemed capable of at present.

In the early pamphlet on supporting the Greek revolutionaries that we are reviewing, Napier argued that the character of the Greeks he met did show the effects of ancient provincialism and, later on, of centuries of fanaticism and enslavement. And yet Greek patriotism, piety, and learning thrived nonetheless. There were Greek students across Europe. The Greek nation itself was wakening. Napier admitted that the Greeks do lie, they do cheat, they do keep assassinating one another. But such is the kind of people they become when the Turks steal their wives and children, take their money, or kill many of them outright. For none of their many sins could the Greeks be reproached under these conditions. One could find fault with them for one thing only – for not standing up for themselves and driving out the Turks long ago. And now at last they were doing just that. The struggle between the Greeks and the Turks showed 'a contrast between the light of the nineteenth century and the remnant of the dark ages'. Success was inevitable.[24] 'God only knows' why England kept propping up the Turks, Napier said, and he added that England might one day fight Russia over the issue. (Napier would die only two months before the outbreak of the Crimean War.) Whoever might win in such a contest, he feared that Turkey would disappear in the process. But if the Russian Emperor were to act like a good Christian and hold back from the conflict, then the Greeks and the Turks could fight it out between themselves.[25]

The man who could save Greece under these conditions, in Napier's view, was none other than Ali Pasha. The governor of Epirus might make himself into the monarch of a Greek nation strong enough to keep the country together and keep out the European powers. It was well known that the language of administration under Ali Pasha was Greek. He presided over a blossoming of Greek publishing in his territory and over a long period of cultural and economic growth. So in this 1821 pamphlet Napier suggested that Ali Pasha could indeed make a good king for Greece if he ruled constitutionally. Ali already had his decades of experience as a ruler. And within a unified Greece, the five million armed Greeks would be able to confine him to the role of a limited monarch, for he could never overawe them if they worked together.[26]

For Napier, that might be the best the Greeks could hope for, a kingdom under Ali Pasha. The European powers would not allow the Greeks to have a republic. 'The world' was divided, Napier said, on the merits of republics. But one's personal views of democracy did not matter, he said; the great monarchs would never allow a republic in Greece. Nor could the Greeks simply pick a European prince for their king, as no other European power besides the man's own would accept the choice. And neither could the Greeks make one of their own men king, for none of the other Greeks would accept any fellow national who was set up over them. Only Ali would work, as he had already been exalted under the Turks.[27]

***

Whomever they chose, the Greeks would have to defend themselves. So more or less on the assumption that Ali Pasha would be able to form a government, Napier proceeded to lay out an operational plan under which the Greek

60   *The radical abroad and at home*

revolutionaries could maintain and extend the territory they controlled. Their base would be the Isthmus of Corinth. With proper defensive emplacements, as well as a canal the Greeks themselves could cut, they could successfully fend off the Austrians, the Russians, and the Turks.

Meanwhile for Napier it was inconceivable that the new Greek state would *not* take Constantinople as its own capital unless the Russians took it first.[28] The romantic hope of undoing 1453, reclaiming Constantinople for Christendom, and removing the main toehold of Islam in Europe seems part and parcel, in Napier's mind, with the more limited dream of a modern Greece freed from Turkish control and ruled as a constitutional monarchy.

Indeed, Napier allowed himself to get rather worked up over this. England was giving aid to the very 'Mahometans' who were oppressing the Christians, he complained. Christians were merely trying to save their women and children. So England was going to the aid of the fifteenth century struggling against the nineteenth! England was siding with the barbarians who were fighting against civilization! England was taking the part of Asiatic slavery, despite campaigning so strongly against slavery in Africa! And England was working against the feelings of her own Ionian subjects, whom she had undertaken to protect.[29] Where, he demanded, was the indignation of the English people at the way their own government thwarted – not so much Greek nationalism, but the larger struggle of Christian against Muslim civilization? Where were Wilberforce and the Bible societies?

By now Napier was throwing every argument he could against the Turks. And he had one more – universalism. Much did England complain, Napier said, of 'the enormities of the French Revolution' and the Terror, and the denial of people's most basic rights. What was going on in Greece under Turkish rule was worse. Europe once went on a crusade 'for a few silly pilgrims', he says. What about now? Where was the crusade to save five million Christians? The medieval crusades were justly condemned as mad, he says. The current apathy when faced with the slaughter of the Greeks was a worse madness.[30]

Napier then concludes this first of his published writings with one of his ugliest ideas. As I have said before, over most of his life (*all* of the rest of his life, in fact) Napier would propound a non-racialist theory of the mutability of national characteristics – as indeed he began doing earlier in this very pamphlet, when discussing what had made the Greeks what they were. But now he was so worked up against the Turks that he began to racialize them.

Great Britain, he explained, had interceded with the Porte on behalf of the Greeks. But when, he asks, did a Mahometan ever show mercy on a Christian? The Ottoman Emperor, 'an ignorant barbarian, shut up in a seraglio . . . rejoices in the excesses' of the massacres of the Greeks. Napier concludes with a picture of lying, mischievous Turks, an Eastern people critically different from the Europeans. If you pass a Turk in the street he will insult you. And so in *all* one's dealing with the Turks, you should take any opportunity to throw them into the mud before they can do the same to you.[31]

This was not a biological racialization of Eastern peoples, but it certainly was an essentializing, Orientalizing racialization. Most Western writers of the

Greece and the Greeks 61

period, and Napier no less than Lord Byron,[32] were quick to tar Islamic rulers with a broad brush. All that these Westerners could see in any Oriental society was the seemingly arbitrary power at the top. They failed to grasp the local traditions of mutual adjustment or accommodation between the Eastern rulers and their peoples. So for them there was no principle of *legitimate* rule in the Islamic East. Eastern rulers were nothing more than predators and the people were their prey.[33] Indeed the main principle of the Turkish government, as Napier would discuss it some years later when he turned again to his experiences in Epirus, was to rob the people as much as possible without pushing them into open rebellion.[34] In the name of spreading freedom he was becoming a crusader.

***

As it happened, the Greek fighters were soon on the verge of extermination – or so Napier would claim in an even shorter work three years later. Also anonymous, *Greece in 1824* ('by the author of *War in Greece*') insisted that the Greeks had shown tremendous courage and resourcefulness. They had nothing like the kind of government they needed to fight a war against an organized enemy. So it was not surprising that everything the Greeks had done had been confused and blundering, except for their one good battle on land and several of their small naval engagements. They had no plan. They only survived because of their challenging geography, their spirit, and the nobility of their cause.

If the Greeks had a strong central authority to organize things they *should* be able to beat the Turks, who were led by a monarch so base that he had ordered his own best commander to commit suicide. That commander carried out the order and took his own life.[35] Meanwhile Ali Pasha was no longer in the picture as a possible leader, as he had been executed in Constantinople.

Napier suggested another solution to all the Greeks' problems: If the Russians were to attack Constantinople, then England could intervene to save both the Greeks and the Turks. The Turks and the independent Greeks could become allies against the Russian threat, although he admitted that the Greek and Turkish armies could never be brought into personal contact.[36]

This view of a more or less peaceful coexistence between Greek and Turkish states living under British protection seems different in emphasis – not only less Orientalist but altogether sunnier – than what he had said about the Turks in his earlier pamphlet.

What had changed? For one thing, in the three years that separated these two pamphlets, Napier had entered into a golden period.

Notes

1 Napier's journal, 30 May 12 June 1819, WN, 1:278–79, 281–82.
2 Viscount Kirkwall [George William Hamilton Fitzmaurice Orkney], *Four Years in the Ionian Islands*, 2 vols (London: Chapman and Hall, 1864), 1:85–86.
3 Maitland's opposition to armaments, see William Pitt to George III, 13 April 1791, given in A. Aspinall (ed.), *The Later Correspondence of George III*, 5 vols (Cambridge: Cambridge UP, 1966), 1:527. Maitland's antiwar and anti-imperialist opinions: Pitt to the king:

62   The radical abroad and at home

31 January 1792, 1:582; 16 March 1792, 1:586; Pitt to George III, 17 February 1793, 2:8; 11 April 1794, 2:193; 19 June 1804, 4:195. Maitland's support for parliamentary reform opposed by Pitt – Pitt to the king, 30 April 1792, 590.

4 H. M. Chichester, 'Maitland, Sir Thomas (1760–1824)', revised by Roger T. Stearn, in H.C.G. Matthew and Brian Harrison (eds), *Oxford Dictionary of National Biography* (Oxford: Oxford UP, 2004), online edn, edited by Lawrence Goldman, May 2006, http:// www.oxforddnb.com/view/article/17835, accessed 25 April 2016.

5 Maitland to Camden, 19 October 1805, quoted in Geoffrey Powell, *The Kandyan Wars: The British Army in Ceylon, 1803–1818* (London: Leo Cooper, 1973), 184.

6 Walter Frewen Lord, *Sir Thomas Maitland: The Mastery of the Mediterranean* (London: T. Fisher Unwin, 1897), 240; Powell, *The Kandyan Wars*, 178–84; Lennox A. Mills, *Ceylon under British Rule, 1795–1932* [1933] (London: Frank Cass, 1964); Napier, *Colonies*, ix–x; see also 52–56, 72.

7 Ibid, 139–41. A French view of Maitland's despotism: Édouard Driault, *Histoire Diplomatique de la Grèce de 1821 a nos Jours*, vol. 1, *L'Insurrection et l'Independence (1821–1830)* (Paris: Les Presses Universitaires de France, 1925), 71–77. For John Capodistrias's very different but also highly critical opinion: C. M. Woodhouse, *Capodistria: The Founder of Greek Independence* (London: Oxford UP, 1973), 203–09, 213–14.

8 Napier, *Colonies*, 51–52, 56–59, 64, 97–100, quotation at 97.

9 C. Willis Dixon, *The Colonial Administrations of Sir Thomas Maitland* (London: Longmans, Green, and Co., 1939), 182–93; Walter Frewen Lord, *Sir Thomas Maitland: The Mastery of the Mediterranean* (London: T. Fisher Unwin, 1897), 194–98; William Miller, *The Ottoman Empire and Its Successors, 1801–1827, with an Appendix, 1927–1936* (Cambridge: Cambridge UP, 1936), 58–61.

10 W. D. Wrigley, *The Diplomatic Significance of Ionian Neutrality, 1821–1831*, American University Studies 9, History, vol. 41 (New York: Peter Lang, 1988), 77.

11 Napier, *Colonies*, 356–59.

12 Dennis N. Skiotis, 'The Greek Revolution: Ali Pasha's Last Gamble', in Nikiforos P. Diamandouros, John P. Anton, John A. Petropulos and Peter Topping (eds), *Hellenism and the First Greek War of Liberation (1821–1830), Continuity and Change* (Thessaloniki: Institute for Balkan Studies, 1976), 98–109 at 101–03.

13 Dennis N. Skiotis, 'From Bandit to Pasha: First Steps in the Rise to Power of Ali of Tepelen, 1750–1784', *International Journal of Middle East Studies* 2, 3 (July 1971), 219–44 at 228–29.

14 Napier to R. A. Davenport, 18 September 1837, NP, BL Add. MS 49128, fols 34–35.

15 R. A. Davenport, *The Life of Ali Pasha, of Tepelini, Vizier of Epirus: Surnamed Aslan, or the Lion* (London: Thomas Tegg and Son, 1837), title page quotations from *Coriolanus* and *Henry VI, Part I*.

16 Stanley Lane-Poole, *The Life of the Right-Honourable Stratford Canning, Viscount Stratford de Redcliffe*, 2 vols (London: Longmans, Green, and Co., 1888), 1:105, 152; John W. Baggally, *Ali Pasha and Great Britain* (Oxford: Basil Blackwell, 1938), 78–80; William Meyer to Frederick Adam, 27 July 1820, given in E. Prevelakis and K. Kalliataki Merticopoulou (eds), *Epirus, Ali Pasha, and the Greek Revolution: Consular Reports of William Meyer from Preveza*, 2 vols, Academy of Athens Monuments of Greek History 12 (Athens: Research Centre for the Study of Modern Greek History, 1996), 1:152–56, reference at 156; WN, 1:292.

17 Theresa Macri, who later married an English vice-consul named Black – Napier, *Colonies*, 371. See 'Maid of Athens, Ere We Part' [1810], published 1812, in *The Complete Poetical Works of Lord Byron*, Leslie Stephen (ed.) (London: Macmillan, 1909), 294–95.

18 WN, 1:286–87, 293–97, 300, 302, 356.

19 [Charles James Napier], *War in Greece* (London: James Ridgway, 1821), 3. Byron too believed that Greek quarrels would alienate English donors. Translation of Byron to the Greek Government, [?] November 1823, TNA CO 136/1090, fols 286–8.

20 [Napier], *War in Greece*, 5.

21 Edward Beasley, *Victorian Reinvention of Race: New Racisms and the Problem of Grouping in the Human Sciences* (New York: Routledge, 2010), 13–14, 25–27; Martin S. Staum, *Labeling*

People: French Scholars on Society, Race, and Empire, 1815–1848 (Montreal and Kingston: McGill-Queen's University Press, 2003); Michael O'Brien, *Conjectures of Order: Intellectual Life in the American South, 1810–1860*, 2 vols (Chapel Hill: University of North Carolina Press, 2004), 1:221–52.

22 See Peter Mandler, *The English National Character: The History of an Idea from Edmund Burke to Tony Blair* (New Haven and London: Yale University Press, 2006), 14–16.

23 For example, see his views on the blacks that he had seen in the new world: Napier's draft on abolition, 1837, NP, BL Add. MS 54544, fols 161–62.

24 [Napier], *War in Greece*, 8–9.

25 Ibid, 9.

26 Davenport, *The Life of Ali Pasha*, 304, 368–69; K. E. Fleming, *The Muslim Bonaparte: Diplomacy and Orientalism in Ali Pasha's Greece* (Princeton, NJ: Princeton UP, 1999), 24, 63–66; David Brewer, *Greece, the Hidden Centuries: Turkish Rule from the Fall of Constantinople to Greek Independence* (London: I.B. Tauris, 2010), 214–15; K. W. Arafat, 'A Legacy of Islam in Greece: Ali Pasha and Ioannina', *Bulletin (British Society for Middle Eastern Studies)* 14, 2 (1987), 172–82 at 176–78; [Napier], *War in Greece*, 26–27.

27 [Napier], *War in Greece*, 28–29.

28 Ibid, 31–39.

29 Ibid, 40.

30 Ibid, 42.

31 Ibid, 43–45.

32 'Childe Harold's Pilgrimage', Canto II, LXIII, *Complete Poetical Works*, 202–03.

33 Talal Asad, 'Two European Images of Non-European Rule', in Asad (ed.), *Anthropology and the Colonial Encounter* (Atlantic Highlands, NJ: Humanities Press International; Reading, UK: Ithaca Press, 1973), 103–18; Norman Daniel, *Islam, Europe, and Empire* (Edinburgh: Edinburgh UP, 1966), 11, 72; Ranajit Guha, *A Rule of Property for Bengal: An Essay on the Idea of Permanent Settlement* (1963; Durham, NC: Duke UP, 1996), 17–24; Shanti Singham, 'From Cosmopolitan Anticolonialism to Liberal Imperialism: French Intellectuals and Muslim North Africa in the Late Eighteenth and Early Nineteenth Centuries'. In Charles Walton (ed.), *Into Print: Essays in Honor of Robert Darnton* (University Park: Pennsylvania State UP, 2011)', 203–04; Chen Tzoref-Ashkenazi, 'Romantic Attitudes toward Oriental Despotism', *Journal of Modern History* 85, 2 (June 2013), 280–320.

34 Napier, *Colonies*, 134–37.

35 [Charles James Napier], *Greece in 1824* (London: James Ridgway, 1824), 3–5.

36 Ibid, 10–14, 16–23.

5 Cephalonia and the Greek Revolution

In March 1822, at age thirty-nine, Napier went back to the Adriatic as Resident of the island of Cephalonia. Although he remained subject to Maitland's overall supervision, he was the *de facto* governor of the island.[1] Maitland ran Corfu directly, but he appointed Residents like Napier to govern the other islands making up the Septinsular Republic. Within Cephalonia Napier had full civil and military authority. But his appointment came with a warning. Maitland's deputy, Frederick Adam, told him that his impetuousness and the violence of his temper might cause trouble now that he was in a responsible position. This Napier chose to read not as a complaint about his personality but about his opinions. As he wrote to his mother, 'This is the first time I ever heard of my violence in politics except from Tories, who call everyone violent who don't agree with them.'[2]

As Resident of Cephalonia Napier made no secret of his political views. He even grew his beard down to his chest and left it wild in the fashion of the Greek revolutionaries. This was hardly a style of grooming that his superiors in Corfu could accept for a uniformed British officer, and the Deputy Adjutant told Napier to shave. Napier did so, but he sent the man his whiskers in an envelope. It seems that the whiskers covered his scars, and he would return to the hirsute look later in life. His example may have inspired the mid-Victorian beard movement.[3]

***

Charles Napier was to spend eight years – 'the happiest part of my life', he would recall[4] – as Cephalonia's energetic and impassioned autocrat. So we should pay more attention than we have so far to the exact location of the Ionian Islands and the place of Cephalonia among them.

Cephalonia, the largest of the group, sits with most of the other Ionian islands at the entrance to the Gulf of Corinth, the narrow body of water dividing mainland Greece from the Peloponnesian Peninsula (called at the time 'the Morea'). While the mainland of Greece was under the rule of the Ottoman Empire, the Ionian Islands had been governed for two hundred years by Venice until Napoleon extinguished the Venetian Republic in 1797.

In the years that followed, Cephalonia was ruled first by the French and then by a joint Russo-Turkish force. Under this Russo-Turkish rule, the 'Septinsular

Cephalonia and the Greek Revolution   65

Republic' was created in 1800. It is said that this was the only time the Ottoman Empire ever granted a free constitution. France retook the islands in 1807, and Great Britain captured most of them two years later. The Congress of Vienna placed the 'United States of the Ionian Islands' under British protection, although the Septinsular Republic remained theoretically independent and all its institutions remained in place.

Meanwhile the Turks sat close by on the mainland. They did not recognize the Septinsular flag when the British took control, and for a long time they seized Ionian ships and sailors.

The political situation within the Septinsular Republic was equally complex even before Maitland took over. There was the Senate that Maitland treated with disdain, and there was also a substantial corps of Republican officeholders, many from the Italian-speaking elite.[5] Most of the other officeholders were foreigners rather than Greeks. Meanwhile there were several parties among the Greek population of villagers and fishermen: a pan-Orthodox, pro-Russian faction; a pro-French faction; a faction that favoured Greek independence; and even a faction that favoured the English, mostly for economic reasons. Cephalonia, along with Zante (another of the Septinsular islands), produced much of Great Britain's supply of currants. The currants were indeed Cephalonia's only export crop. Much of the island's arable land had been replanted in currant bushes for the British market, and by Napier's time much of the grain to feed the island had to be purchased abroad. If the currants failed, the island would have little money for importing food.[6]

Cephalonia had two major towns, Argostoli and Lixouri. They stood across from each other on either side of a long bay in the south. In the north of the island, there were several smaller ports, such as Assos, Sami, and at the extreme northern tip of the island at the end of its own peninsula, Fisgardo. The towns and settlements were cut off from each other by chains of mountains that were only passable, if at all, by treacherous paths. A few roads had been constructed across the mountains by the first British officer to command the island, Major de Bosset, who as a Swiss national seems to have understood mountain conditions. De Bosset had also built a causeway linking Argostoli with the mainland of the island across an inlet of the bay.

Lying only two miles off the northern peninsula of Cephalonia was Odysseus' island of Ithaca, unless Homer really meant Cephalonia itself.[7] Ithaca had its own Resident and it was not Napier's responsibility. From Ithaca, Odysseus would seem to have ruled the much larger island of Cephalonia as well, and evocative ancient remains could be found on both islands.

More recent remains existed, too. On a mountaintop commanding the coast of southern Cephalonia stood an abandoned Venetian fort. Control of the island had once seemed vital to the defence of the Adriatic and thus of Venice itself. But in Napier's opinion Cephalonia had lost any strategic significance when the whole of the Mediterranean came under the dominance of the Royal Navy.[8]

The Venetian era had left its mark nonetheless. The Italian-derived elite still owned the great estates, and they continued to send their children to school

Figure 5.1 Argostoli. Engraving by Edward Finden from a picture by J.M.W. Turner, after a sketch by William Page, early 1830s, prepared for *Finden's Illustrations of the Life and Works of Lord Byron*, vol. 3 (London: John Murray, 1834).

Cephalonia (engraving), Turner, Joseph Mallord William (1775–1851) (after) / Private Collection / © Look and Learn / Bridgeman Images

Cephalonia and the Greek Revolution   67

in Italy. The greatest of these Italian noble families each had its hard-to-reach and seldom-visited country seat in some isolated tract, plus its commodious town home. And each of the great families had its phalanx of lawyers on call in Cephalonia and at the capital in Corfu and its dependents among the Greek peasantry in the countryside and in the towns. It was among this Italian aristocracy that the small corps of British officials lived and entertained.

There was also a substantial contingent of British troops stationed in Cephalonia. Catering to them was a network of taverns and wine-merchants approved by the British authorities.[9]

In the wilder stretches of the countryside the Greeks lived mostly on their own. And when circumstances drove them to it, they benefited from an unusual system of ecclesiastical poor relief. Much of the best land belonged to the Orthodox monasteries, which also owned vast areas in more desolate countryside. Travellers would have to make their way over the emptier parts if they wanted to cross the island. And so the poor were taken care of in this way: Destitute families were put into a monastic building in some remote location where they would live for months or even years. There they would 'help', as it were, any lost or isolated travellers – helping them anonymously, at night, out in the open, at gunpoint. Eventually the family, having recovered its finances or even having founded a fortune, would be ready to leave the church lands and rejoin society.[10]

The Greek population remained the social inferiors of the Italians, trading, fishing, and growing the currants. Napier had to deal with both groups, and soon he could speak both Italian and Modern Greek, even writing letters in Modern Greek.[11]

It was a rich life for Napier to bask in – the towns, the sun, the sea, the church-sponsored bandits, the wooded 'Black Mountain' presiding over the south of the island; and not least the ruins of the ancient city of Sami, Homer's Samos. And Napier did drink it in, writing again and again how much he enjoyed the landscape and the people, and the mountain meadows with their cool breezes.

In Cephalonia Napier would found his somewhat unconventional family. Early on he took as his mistress a Greek nationalist named Anastasia. With her he would have two daughters, Sarah Susan and Emily Cephalonia – English names, or English enough. Napier, devoted and doting, would set out to give them an English life. They left Cephalonia with him and accompanied him on his military campaigns in India even when they were in their twenties. Although illegitimate, they became great Victorian ladies. Emily Cephalonia would marry one of her Napier cousins, a man who became governor of the Royal Military College, Sandhurst. She would have seven children, naming one of them Margaret Cephalonia. She lived until 1908. Sarah Susan, Napier's elder daughter, would marry her father's adjutant in India, William Montagu Scott McMurdo, whose military career would prosper as well. As her sister did, Sarah Susan ended up a general's wife as well as a general's daughter. She was still alive in 1894.

68 *The radical abroad and at home*

But the family that Napier acquired in Cephalonia was not yet complete. In 1827, he visited England to settle the affairs of his mother, who had recently died, and while he was there he was at last able to marry Elizabeth Kelly. Her husband had died the year before, but she asked Napier to wait for a time to consider whether he might want the children which at her age she could not give him.[12] In fact Napier had recently become a father for the first time with the birth of Sarah Susan – although this fact went unmentioned in Napier's letters home to England.

Certainly it was true that Elizabeth could give Napier no children herself. She was sixty to his forty-five in the year they wed. She had two grown sons and a married daughter. Her son-in-law Samuel Laing, an army friend of Napier's from Hythe and two years his senior, was not at all pleased at the marriage of his mother-in-law to a man his own age. After a few years he demanded money from Napier for the gambling debts he once had to pay for his late father-in-law, Captain Kelly. Napier refused.[13]

After their marriage in England, Napier brought Elizabeth to Cephalonia and installed her as the head of his household. Her reaction on learning of Napier's daughters is unrecorded. Nor do we know what Anastasia thought of all this – the sudden appearance of a sixty-year-old Mrs Napier must have been something of a surprise. Anastasia had recently given birth to Napier's second daughter; she had learned she was pregnant only after Napier had left for England.[14] (Emily Cephalonia Napier, the younger daughter, was born on 20 June 1827.[15])

When Charles Napier and Elizabeth Kelly had been married for about three years, they left Cephalonia for what was intended to be a short stay in England. But as we will see, their stay stretched far longer than they could have imagined, and so they sent for Sarah Susan and Emily Cephalonia to be brought along after them. Anastasia did not accompany the little girls, who at that point were about four and not quite three years old.[16] A Napier family tradition has it that Anastasia put the girls in a boat and pushed them out to sea to *make* Napier take them along when he left the island. But given how Charles Napier doted on the children this would not have been necessary. And in any case the story does not fit the facts: When he left, Napier and everyone else thought he would be back within a few months. He had arranged for an English family to care for the girls in the interim. He did not have to pluck them from a boat and take them at that instant. As I said, the evidence shows that he sent for them later.[17]

When it finally became clear that Napier would never return, Anastasia married a Greek officer. Napier admitted to feeling some anger at this, but he was the first to confess that in fact he had no right to remain angry, and at that point he increased Anastasia's allowance and made sure that it would continue after his death. He confessed to his sister Louisa that while his best friend in Cephalonia (a brother officer) knew of these arrangements, he wanted Louisa to know about them, too. She needed to keep his letters so that if he and his friend should both die, she could use them as evidence of his intentions.

He wanted to make sure that Anastasia was provided for and that she would always remain financially independent of her husband.

Napier also told his sister that he would have left the girls with Anastasia if she had wanted them, although it would have broken his heart. But he added that in fact Anastasia did *not* want the girls, and furthermore she was a bad mother. He said – in the strictest confidence, for this was something that not even his best friend in Cephalonia was to know – that he had to force Anastasia to nurse Sarah. And she refused ever to nurse Emily, leaving the child small and sickly for the rest of her life.[18]

Anastasia died in 1837. Napier did not learn of this until a year later. She had been recruiting men and collecting materiel for the continuing war of independence. Napier said he felt pangs of love and of melancholy on learning of her death, but he admitted he also felt relief. He had worried over how to tell his growing daughters that their mother was alive – something which they did not know. Now he would be spared having to take them to Greece to see her, as he was sure they would ask him to do. Their mother's death would save the girls from 'much suffering'. And he set up a small pension for Anastasia's mother.[19]

Byron

> The dead have been awakened – shall I sleep?
> The World's at war with tyrant's – shall I crouch?
> The harvest's ripe – and shall I pause to reap?
> I slumber not; the thorn is in my Couch;
> Each day a trumpet sounded in mine ear,
> Its echo in my heart –
> Lord Byron, 'Journal in Cephalonia'[20]

***

There were many wealthy young Europeans who wanted the Greeks to win their freedom from the Ottomans. They were called Philhellenes. A number of them visited Cephalonia while Napier was there, as his tolerance for the friends of Greek independence was well known.

One of these idealistic visitors towers above the rest. George Gordon, Lord Byron, arrived on the island on 3 August 1823. Byron called his mission to Greece a 'kind of bear-taming', for he had his doubts about the military discipline and organization of the Greek rebel force.[21] But he had come nonetheless, 'willing', he said, 'to do what I can'. Byron planned to stay in the Ionian Islands for some time while he considered how he might enter Greece itself without getting shot by the Turks. Napier was away from town when Byron landed, but on his return two days later he greeted the poet and pressed him to take a house in Argostoli.

Some sources say that at first Byron found Napier's manner rather brusque, and so the poet lived for a month on board his hired ship, the *Hercules*, in

70 *The radical abroad and at home*

Argostoli harbour. In fact Byron stayed on board because he had not yet decided where to go and the Greek revolutionaries had failed to send anyone to receive him. It was not due to any brusqueness on Napier's part. Byron told his half-sister and lover Augusta Leigh that Napier 'has been extremely kind and hospitable'.[22]

Byron and Napier had to maintain some official distance, and early on they tried to do so.[23] But soon they became friends and their friendship became a source of complaint. In Maitland's opinion, in the opinion of his deputy Frederick Adam – and not least in the opinion of the Turks – Napier in giving Byron so much freedom seemed to be acting in something other than the strictest conformity with Ionian neutrality. One comment was that Napier was too lax in inspecting Byron's mail and passing on what he discovered. Yet Maitland and Adam seem to have come to appreciate the value of what Napier *did* tell them about the revolutionaries. For his part, Byron noticed that there were some odd delays in getting his letters, but he said he was grateful enough to Napier for providing them in the end.[24]

In any case the poet and the solider came to know each other well, spending a good deal of time together. They shared meals and visited local worthies. More than once they dined in the home of a British doctor who would spend hours over dinner trying to convert Byron to Methodism. Napier could not fathom why Byron would listen for so long to these Methodist speeches. Eventually he took the poet aside to ask why he always refused to turn the conversation in some other direction. Byron said it was because he was doing research. He wanted to make Don Juan a Methodist in the next canto. Napier replied he did not like the idea of mocking the doctor at his own table, and he forced Byron to make a confession to their host. But the Methodist doctor did not mind a bit, and he kept going on about his religion.[25]

Eventually Byron did leave the ship and take a house, although it was in the relative privacy of Metaxata, a high and wooded town of cool breezes four and a half miles from Argostoli. He paid off his ship and moved in with his stores and substantial entourage. Byron was travelling with a variety of missionaries, plus members of the London Greek Committee and several hangers on, who tended to be young men. Byron and company would stay at Metaxata for five months, save for a week of sightseeing on Ithaca.

The little household planned Greek independence, or at least how to get to the mainland without getting killed. Napier visited when he could. He found Byron 'a very good fellow, very pleasant, always laughing and joking'.[26] For his part, Byron discovered that he and Napier had similar views about the position of Greece. Napier's unaffected manner and his habit – which had become plain – of allowing Greek patriots to slip out of Cephalonia and into battle began to grow on the poet. They became close. Still, Byron found Napier's ardour for conquering all the way to Constantinople to be somewhat impractical when the core of Greece had yet to win its independence or organize itself.[27]

But it may have been for this very reason, Napier's ardour and his eagerness for the cause, that Bryon formed a plan to have Napier selected as the

Cephalonia and the Greek Revolution   71

commander of the Greek revolutionary forces. Ardour was no bad thing in a commander. By the end of September 1823 Napier was sending Byron his military plans:

> I can see no better way to save Greece than to collect all the foreigners, and as many Greek fugitives from the north as you can, at Napoli di Romania [Nafplion]: form these people into a regular force, paying them with the money collected by the committee, and your own. When strong enough, which would be very soon, seize the town, and declare it the seat of government, with all parties to assemble there, but allow no armed man to enter.[28]

Nafplion, a port town in the northwestern Peloponnesus, did indeed become the Greek capital later in the revolution (it remained the capital of Greece until 1834). Other elements of the plan were perhaps too romantic. Napier wanted the city to be a civilian preserve where the greatest people from all of Greece could bring their fortunes, construct a bustling civil society, and counterbalance the power of the military chiefs in the war effort. Historically, as Napier reminded Byron, town life had often served to keep the military aristocracy of the countryside 'in order'. It might take centuries to reshape the character of the Greek nation as a whole, but Nafplion could offer refuge to 'thousands' of wealthy people who would come and remake the immediate area at once.

Yet Napier added that the task of creating a civil society in this way should not be allowed to interfere with the more vital and immediate task of setting up a strong central command for the Greek forces. A key part of his military plan was to be the role of Byron himself as the supreme authority in Nafplion. 'In such [a military] enterprise', Napier told the poet, 'there is the advantage, that no one but yourself need know of it, till you were prepared to strike, and then you would be sure of success' with any regular force.[29] To pull it off, Byron

> must hold the purse and the revenue and destroy everyone who masters him without hesitation. Then he must make the people of Morea an enemy [*sic*]. This is the only thing Greeks understand or respect and about which in a state of invasion England herself would be obliged to accommodate to, or the consequences.

In some rough sentences whose handwriting suggests the presence of alcohol, Napier explained that if and only if it were ruled properly – ruthlessly – the Morea could support 10,000 troops conquering all the way to Salonica. With a success like that, the new government would be able to make an alliance with England:

> There are fools who would say that this would not be giving Greece liberty; the answer is, who wants liberty when a foreign army occupies your country? One wants arms, not parliamentary debates.

72 *The radical abroad and at home*

Indeed, despite Napier's early hopes for promoting civil life in Nafplion or elsewhere, he certainly agreed with Byron that the first key task was building an effective military organization and defeating the Turks. On this point Byron and Napier differed sharply from the other English partisans of Greek independence. Colonel Leicester Stanhope and his fellow Philhellenes had come to Greece with a very different idea about how to effect Greek independence – not through creating a military organization but through immediately restoring something of the culture and politics of classical Athens. They wanted to construct an independent Greece that was ruled democratically from the outset, with no strong military commander and no king. To bring this vision closer to reality, Colonel Stanhope went about founding newspapers and various social improvement organizations. He founded so many newspapers that Byron and others began to call him the 'Typographical Colonel'.[30]

A similar vision about a rebirth of the classical Greek mind – rather than any rebirth in Greek military effectiveness – seems to have been uppermost in the thinking of the members of the London Greek Committee in its first days. Or so it would seem from the supplies they chose to send to the Greek fighters. The committee was organized in March 1823 to support the Greek Revolution, and it mounted a public campaign in order to raise money and purchase materials for the cause.[31] Some of the items which the committee dispatched from England, as Byron wrote to its secretary, were

> useful, and all excellent in their kind; but occasionally hardly *practical* enough, in the present state of Greece; for instance, the mathematical instruments are thrown away – none of the Greeks know a problem from a poker – we must conquer first and plan afterwards.

Byron showed Napier some of what had been sent. Even Napier with his engineering training could not identify all of it. One item they thought might be a 'transit instrument'. There were also watercolour paints in a quantity that would be sufficient, in Napier's view, to make plans of all of Greece and then 'paint all their women into the bargain'. Crates of mathematical instruments and watercolours were not what the freedom fighters most needed. Byron told the Greek Committee that '[t]he use of the trumpets, too, may be doubted, unless Constantinople were Jericho'.[32]

Byron wrote that he and Napier were of one mind on all this. They each, 'like men who had seen the country and human life, there and elsewhere', believed that Greece could be improved in many ways, but only '*gradually*' [Byron's emphasis], once the main work of removing the Turks had been accomplished.[33]

***

Byron and his entourage remained at Metaxata until January 1824, before proceeding into the thick of the revolution in Missolonghi on the mainland.

In the meantime, Byron would continue trying to get Napier appointed commander, writing to the members of the London Greek Committee. Byron then sent Napier himself to London. Bearing the poet's letters and instructions, Napier took a leave at the beginning of the year and went home to see the London Committee in person. He arrived in England only a few weeks before the announcement of Byron's death at Missolonghi on 19 April.[34] (During this 1824 visit, in the last days of Byron's life, Napier wrote the second of his – anonymous – short books on Greek independence, a work which we have already examined.)

In London, Napier did not find his superiors in the army very friendly to the idea of a British officer taking employment among foreign freedom fighters. In fact the practice was illegal.[35] Further, Napier was reprimanded by Lord Bathurst, the Colonial Secretary, for the partiality that he had already shown to the Greek partisans.

Still, he had his army commission. Should he sell it and throw in his lot with the Greeks? Napier had every confidence in the Greek forces, as he told the secretary of the Greek Committee – but *only* if the troops were adequately paid. Like all fighting men, they could not be expected to remain loyal if they were not paid properly.[36] The Committee countered with an offer of higher pay for Napier himself if he would no longer ask them for the huge sum for men and equipment that he was demanding. Napier was taken aback by what he saw as their parsimony. In his view, in Byron's absence neither the Greek Committee in London nor the revolutionary fighters within Greece itself were ready to make the sacrifices necessary to carry out the most basic of the defensive measures that Napier had sketched out for Nafplion and the Morea.

So Napier turned down the Committee's offer to become their commander. In a letter of apology to Bathurst, he said that he felt especially loyal as a British officer now that he had seen the unprofessionalism of the Greek Committee, the group for which he might once have given up his army career.[37]

And having reassured Bathurst of his loyalty as a British officer, he went back to Cephalonia. He also refused to take a place on the commission to escort the 'Greek Loan' from the Committee to the fighting forces. He was right to steer clear. As William Cobbett would tirelessly publicize over the next several years, the Committee did not manage its money very well. Not all of the Greek Loan reached Greece. If Napier had become involved, Cobbett – his intellectual hero – would have crusaded against *him*.[38]

Notes

1 Napier, *Colonization*, iii n.
2 Napier to his mother [1822], quoted in WN, 1:304.
3 Napier, *Colonies*, 542–43 and 543n. Wonderfully, scholars have explored the beard movement. See Christopher Oldstone-Moore, 'The Beard Movement in Victorian Britain', *Victorian Studies* 48, 1 (Autumn 2005), 7–34.
4 Napier, *Colonies*, 431; Napier's journal, 6 August 1849, given in WN, 4:181.
5 Dixon, *Maitland*, 225–26.

74   The radical abroad and at home

6 David Hannell, 'The Ionian Islands under the British Protectorate: Social and Economic Problems', *Journal of Modern Greek Studies* 7, 1 (May 1989), 105–32 at 117–18.

7 Nicholas D. Khristof, 'Odysseus Lies Here?', *New York Times*, 11 March 2012, SR11. My thanks to Rebecca Hartmann for this reference.

8 Napier, *Colonies*, 172–75, 234–36.

9 Napier, *Colonies*, 188–93.

10 Ibid, 287–88, 296–98.

11 Kirkwall, *Ionian Islands*, 1:115.

12 Napier to Emily Napier, 22 June 1826, NP, BL Add. MS 49109, fols 90–91.

13 Laing, *Autobiography*, 99–101, 139–40, 148–49.

14 Kennedy to Napier, 1 February 1827, NP, BL Add. MS 54535, fols 21–22.

15 Emily Cephalonia Napier to Napier, 24 June 1843, NP, BL Add. MS 54533, fols 86–87.

16 Sarah Susan seems to have been about one-and-a-half years older than Emily Cephalonia, or perhaps slightly more. See Napier to Robertson, 25 April 1841, NP, BL Add. MS 49107, fols 55–56 – where Napier says one of his daughters 'is past 15. The other 14.' But how far past 15 ? In fact Emily Cephalonia was still only 13, not 14. From the context, it seems that he may have been thinking of how old they would be when he took them to India in the autumn.

17 Lawrence, *Charles Napier*, 68, 76–77; Phillip V. Blake-Hill, 'The Napier Papers', *British Library Journal* 1 (1975), 25–31; P. Napier, *Revolution and the Napier Brothers, 1820–1840* (London: Michael Joseph, 1973), 77, 114; Napier to Captain James Robert Colthorst, 21 June 1831, NP, BL Add. MS 41063, fols 42–43; Kennedy to Napier, 14 July 1830, NP, BL Add. MS 54535, fol. 31.

18 Napier to Louisa Napier, 20 May 1835, Bodleian MS Eng. lett. c. 240, fols 34–35.

19 Napier to Louisa Napier, 3 August 1838, Bodleian MS Eng. lett. c. 240, fols 42–43.

20 George Gordon Byron, Lord Byron, *Letters and Journals*, vol. 6, Rowland E. Prothero (ed.) (London: John Murray, 1901), 238.

21 Byron to Napier, 9 September 1823, given in ibid, 6:257.

22 Roderick Beaton, *Byron's War: Romantic Rebellion, Greek Revolution* (Cambridge: Cambridge UP, 2013), 159; Byron to Augusta Leigh, 12 October 1823, given in Byron, *Letters and Journals*, 6:258–64 at 259–60; Edward John Trelawny, *Recollections of the Last Days of Shelley and Byron* (London: Edward Moxon, 1858), 134–35. Cf. William Parry, *The Last Days of Lord Byron* (Paris: A. and W. Galignani, 1826), 203.

23 Count Peter Gamba, *Lord Byron's Journey to Greece* (London: John Murray, 1825), 38.

24 W. D. Wrigley, *Diplomatic Significance of Ionian Neutrality, 1821–1831*, American University Studies 9, History, vol. 41 (New York: Peter Lang, 1988), 190–91; W. D. Wrigley, 'Dissension in the Ionian Islands: Colonel Charles James Napier and the Commissioners (1819–1833)', *Balkan Studies* 16, 2 (1975), 11–22 at 13n4; Byron's Cephalonian Journal, 1823, in Byron, *Letters and Journals*, 6:243.

25 Joseph Wolff, *Travels and Adventures of the Rev. Joseph Wolff, D.D., LL.D.*, 2 vols (London: Saunders, Otley, and Co., 1860), 1:401–05; Napier to Wolff, 7 February, 14 March, 1 August 1852, given at 2:459–63.

26 Napier to his mother, 13 November 1823, given in WN, 1:329–30.

27 Byron, *Letters and Journals*, 6:238–293 ff. Primary sources for Byron's relations with Napier by Byron's companions: Gamba, *Byron's Journey*, 18–21, 37–38; Parry, *Last Days*, 203, 239; Julius Millingen, *Memoirs of the Affairs of Greece* (London: John Rodwell, 1831), 18–19, 39, 93–94; George Finlay, *History of the Greek Revolution and the Reign of King Otho*, 2 vols (Edinburgh: William Blackwood and Sons, 1861), 2:22–25; and – although confused on matters the author did not himself witness – Leicester Stanhope, *Greece in 1823 and 1824* (Philadelphia: A. Small, E. Parker, Marot & Walter, and E. Littell, 1825), especially 26. See also Douglas Dakin, *British and American Philhellenes during the War of Greek Independence, 1821–1833* (Thessaloniki: Society for Macedonian Studies, 1955), 47–48; C. M. Woodhouse, *The Philhellenes* (London: Hodder and Stoughten, 1969), 98, 102–03; 128–29.

Cephalonia and the Greek Revolution 75

28 Napier to Byron, 21 Sept. 1823, NP, BL Add. MS 49121, fols 96b-99.

29 Ibid.

30 John L. Comstock, *History of the Greek Revolution* (New York: William W. Reed, 1828), 292–93; Thomas Gordon, *History of the Greek Revolution*, 2nd edn, 2 vols (Edinburgh: William Blackwood; London: T. Cadell, 1844), 2:107–10; Samuel Gridley Howe, *An Historical Sketch of the Greek Revolution* [1828], revised and edited by George Georgiades Arnakis (Austin, TX: Center for Neo-Hellenic Studies, 1966), 194–98; F. Rosen, *Bentham, Byron, and Greece: Constitutionalism, Nationalism, and Early Liberal Political Thought* (Oxford: Clarendon Press, 1992), 144–50, 158–62, 179, 199–202; Gary J. Bass, *Freedom's Battle: The Origins of Humanitarian Intervention* (New York: Alfred A. Knopf, 2008), 102–05.

31 Gordon, *Greek Revolution*, 2:79–86.

32 Byron to Bowring, 26 December 1823, given in Byron, *Letters and Journals*, 6:292–94; Napier on Byron's visit, no date, NP, BL Add. MS 54561, fols 32–37 at 32–33.

33 Byron to Bowring, 26 December 1823, given in ibid, 6:292–94.

34 Byron to Bowring, 10 December 1823, given in ibid, 6:282–83; Byron to Bowring, 13 December 1823, 285–87.

35 Napier, extracts of letters and journals, 1825, quoted in WN, 1:372–76.

36 Napier to Bowring, 1 May 1824, given in E. S. de Beer and Walter Seton, 'Byroniana: The Archives of the London Greek Committee', *Nineteenth Century* 100 (September 1926), 396–412 at 410–11.

37 Napier to Bathurst (copy), 26 November 1824, NP, BL Add. MS 49109, fols 54–55; another copy, with an added explanation to his sister Emily, Bodleian MS Eng. lett. c. 241, fols 124–25.

38 Robert E. Zegger, *John Cam Hobhouse: A Political Life, 1819–1852* (Columbia: University of Missouri Press, 1973), 122–29, 135; Dakin, *British and American Philhellenes*, 77, 115–16; Rosen, *Bentham, Byron, and Greece*, 266–70, 285–86.

6 Social reform for Cephalonia

By the middle of the decade one thing seemed clear. The Greek Revolution was hardly surging ahead to victory. Ali Pasha and his forces had been exterminated in February 1822; Byron died in April 1824; and the Greeks were defeated at Missolonghi in April 1826. The dream of freeing all of Greece receded, although there remained a core of independent territory in the Peloponnesus and the southern Greek mainland. Eventually, after the assassination of the Greek head of state John Capodistrias in 1831, the Great Powers intervened to create a new, very small Greek kingdom, and the crown was given to Prince Otto of Bavaria. By then Napier was no longer in the country.

As the Greeks were going from defeat to defeat, Napier had one final opportunity to work for their cause. In the summer of 1825 he was offered command of the Greek forces by Alexandros Mavrocordatos. Napier considered the offer for several months. His demands changed from one letter to the next, but fundamentally he was asking for £12,000 for himself, £1,000 for each of two military engineers, and either £100,000 or £150,000 to pay the troops for the first six months; plus ten to twenty thousand muskets and bayonets and the recruitment of five hundred foreign mercenaries outfitted like British troops. Further, he insisted that he would never fight against the British, and he would answer to no higher commander in Greece. If all these conditions were met, he promised to serve as long as the Greeks needed him, never requesting any other pay beyond his initial £12,000.[1]

These resources would have given him the authority and the material resources that he thought he needed for success. Again nothing came of this, and command of the Greek insurgents went instead to another British officer, R. W. Church. But in the period before Church's arrival, the idea that Napier might be going over to the Greeks was no secret. Frederick Adam in Corfu was told by one of his private sources how the Greek officers in Nafplion said that 'if Napier or Church were to come, they would put their sons under them'.[2]

***

But given the gloomier military situation of the Greeks in the period after Byron's death, Napier began to occupy himself rather less with the old vision of freeing the mainland. Instead he turned his attention to the governance of the part of Greece for which he was actually responsible. In the Ionian Islands there was ample opportunity for officers like himself to accomplish 'liberal and progressive reforms', as he would later explain, reforms which both the Greek revolutionary and the pro-English factions would support. Those who favoured Russian despotism would resist any changes, as would the local feudal party.[3] Such people were obstructionists.

***

Maitland had warned Napier that as he worked for social reform he would need to keep a close eye on the justice system. Here the grip of the feudal barons was strongest. The judges were handed instructions from the feudal chiefs in open court.[4] Often the judge would allow a malefactor to go free for fear of offending his protector and landlord. In such cases the Resident had to intervene in the court system, and despotically, overriding the supposedly independent judges.[5]

When Napier arrived in Cephalonia in 1822 martial law was still in effect after Greek revolutionary riots of the year before. So until martial law ended in June, Napier spent six hours a day hearing cases. Only when civil law returned and his legal duties were reduced did Napier have the time to explore the island rather more, although he would still spend hours at his desk reading the judicial paperwork.[6]

As Resident, Napier instituted a number of improvements in the legal system. He made the constables execute the orders of the court upon everyone equally, no matter who they were or how far from town. And where the interests of the great people impinged too directly upon a particular case, Napier had it tried by 'European' (as distinct from Cephalonian) magistrates. Looking back on this period, he would insist that the punishments imposed by his special judges were generally lighter and less likely to provoke popular resentment than what the local authorities would have ordered. And he stressed that the common people had come to see that the law was fairly administered; it applied equally to rich and poor alike. Making sure that this was the case was especially difficult for a foreigner like himself, Napier admitted. And so, as he tells us, he began his review of each case by assuming that when a poor person stood up to a rich person, the poor person must be in the right. But despite this initial bias, he took great pains to actually review the evidence each time.[7]

Preserving the impression of fairness was especially hard in capital cases, where there was the emotionally fraught situation of a foreign power executing the locals. On one occasion, '[i]t was, unfortunately, necessary to execute a man for the murder of his wife; it seemed to me to be a strong trial upon the people, that a foreign soldier should come among them, and adjudge one of them to die.' He said the practice had been for British soldiers to attend all the executions, but this time he had the murderer executed by the civil authorities of his own remote village, with no soldiers present. The people seemed satisfied and the execution proceeded quietly. (When Ionians were executed, they always died manfully, Napier assures us.[8]) The Cephalonians were not lawless,

78   *The radical abroad and at home*

he believed; they were simply prejudiced against feudal and unevenly applied laws. 'When the laws of a country are weak, the rich soon oppress the poor, and the law becomes the instrument of oppression.' This was all the more true in a small country than in a big one, he thought, for a limited territory could be covered in a densely packed network of personal connection. In a larger country, or so Napier explained the matter, it is possible to have liberal institutions, dispassionate debate, and milder laws; the judges judge strangers. And passions are more violent in hot climates like Cephalonia's 'than with us'.[9]

That said, he did not believe the Cephalonians incapable of trial by jury. He wanted to institute jury trials, or so he claimed in a later book, but Maitland and his successor as High Commissioner (the same Frederick Adam who had been Maitland's deputy) prevented him from doing so. The English community in Cephalonia would scream if trial by jury were introduced, but he insisted that arguments and not popularity should decide the question. Yes, there would be evils and injustices from the jury system when it first came in, given the feudal state of the island. But to this objection he responded that there can be no progress, no 'improvement', if progressive steps are never taken.[10] (Here Napier's line of reasoning anticipates a key theme in John Stuart Mill's later works, such as *Considerations on Representative Government* and *The Subjection of Women*. Napier and Mill both believed that the extension of political rights is by itself the best and indeed the only way to prepare a people for the serious exercise of those very rights. Civilized peoples ought to be given their rights first and prepared for them later.[11]) Jury service increases the dignity and honesty of the jurors, Napier explained. Such was the case in England, and such would be the case among the Greeks. But raising the public tone in this way would take some time. The reforming executive – Napier or his successors – would have to remain in power for the whole of the transitional period.[12]

***

A discordant note: One modern author makes a case that Napier 'loved violence itself'. The nature of British rule in this era, one reads, could be seen well enough in the gibbets looming above the harbour.[13]

There were indeed gibbets standing high above an Ionian port. But as the author I am referring to has to admit, they stood on another island (Zante) and not on Cephalonia. Indeed, this scene of the looming gibbets belongs to the period *before* Napier had returned to the Ionian Islands to become Resident. And the man who set up the gibbets and put them to use was not Charles Napier but Thomas Maitland's deputy, Sir Frederick Adam.[14]

***

The picture that Napier himself gives of Adam, who succeeded Maitland as High Commissioner in 1824, is a highly coloured one, to say the least. Indeed, Napier wrote a six-hundred-page polemic against the man. Following the overly full style of the time, Napier called the book *The Colonies: Treating of their Value Generally – Of the Ionian Islands in Particular; The Importance of the Latter in War and Commerce – As Regards Russian Policy – Their Finances – Why an Expense to Great Britain – Detailed Proofs that they need not be so – Turkish Government – Battle of Navarino – Ali Pacha – Sir Thomas Maitland – Strictures on the Administration of Sir Frederick Adam.* And on the crowded title page the name of the hated Adam at the tail end of all of this appeared in bigger type than Napier's own name as author of the book. One might conclude that the material presented might be out of balance in some way. Indeed, at the outset Napier admits that a reader may very well suspect that the book's material on Adam was 'warped by my indignation'.[15] Quite so. Yet, however strange this tome might appear, it also gives us a wonderful treasury of events, perspectives, and documents from Napier's time on the island. Not only was Napier happy there, but as a reformer he was operating with enough independence and on a large enough stage – the population was 60,000 – that he was able to see many of his plans for colonial government and social justice put into effect. Writing at such length, Napier could be as indiscreet and as funny as he wanted, and many parts of the book work better as self-revelation than as self-justification.

Even so grand a figure as John Stuart Mill himself loved the volume when it came out in 1833. He had to admit that Napier was neither a disciplined philosopher nor a deep political economist. But what Napier had written, Mill said, could stand up to careful analysis on several levels. Not only was it a very engaging portrait of the Cephalonian people and their stage of society, but it was also a valuable guide to colonial governance. It showed how a colonized people might be freed from their feudal chains by a foreign ruler.[16] In other words, Napier had come out in favour of the liberal imperial mission of spreading universal progressive values, and none other than John Stuart Mill saw and approved.

As Napier himself put it,

> [T]he present state of society, all over Europe, is such, that it will no longer, patiently, submit to injustice. The spirit of the age will bear forward in its stern progress, and neither individual talent, nor the force of armies, can arrest its steady course, though it might be roused to great violence by opposition.[17]

And so, it would seem, if progress were resisted the people might take to the streets.

Championing the Greeks and the Irish

However, there is yet another perspective on Napier's rule in Cephalonia. The historian Thomas Gallant has argued that when the British took over the Ionian Islands, they needed to find some reason, some rationale, for colonizing a European people. Therefore British authorities (and Gallant names Napier

80   *The radical abroad and at home*

among them) began to portray the Ionian Greeks the way they portrayed the Irish – as a mendacious population requiring British control.[18]

It must be said that Napier *did* compare the people of Cephalonia to the Irish:

> Now I am once more among the merry Greeks, who are worth all other nations put together. I like to see them, to hear them; I like their fun, their good humour, their Paddy ways, for they are very like Irishmen. As to cleanliness they cannot brag; soap and water, or small-toothed combs are not more used in Greece than in other countries. Yet they are cleaner than the Italians, and don't love dirt like the Venetians; they only suffered it out of politeness when the last were their masters, and are now leaving it off in compliment to us; all their bad habits are Venetian; their wit, their eloquence, their good nature are their own.[19]

But in his mind the rule of the British in Ireland and the rule of the Venetian aristocracy – as well as of the Turks in mainland Greece – was all of it equally unjust and stupid and oppressive, and each regime was destructive to the character of the people. Napier's blood boiled for the oppressed Irish and the oppressed Greeks alike, whoever their oppressors happened to be. Or as he put it in some private notes in 1825, '[T]the Greeks are more like the Irish than any other people; so like, even to the oppression they suffer, that as I could not do good to Ireland the next pleasure was to serve men groaning under similar tyranny.'[20]

Already Napier was pulling no punches when it came to discussing injustice and how it should be vigorously resisted everywhere, including Ireland and Cephalonia. Only those who knew Irish conditions could understand how horribly the rich of Greece oppressed the poor. But in the final analysis, he said the feudal oppression in Ireland remained worse than in Cephalonia. At least in Cephalonia the landlords knew their tenants and could see their suffering.[21] The United States was lucky, he added. It had only the plight of one million slaves to contend with, while England had seven million slaves in Ireland.

So the Irish were slaves. How then did the British retain Ireland? Only by use of the Coercion Bill. Napier drove home the irony: In 1827 the British government had remonstrated with the Sultan over his use of a coercion bill in Greece. Now the Sultan could very well remonstrate to the British about a similar measure within in the British Isles.[22]

And so by no means was Napier grounding the legitimacy of his rule in Cephalonia on the idea that Great Britain ought to do for the Ionian Islands what it had done for Ireland, as Gallant suggests. Rather the opposite. Napier believed that his campaign against the Cephalonian aristocrats was a model for the kind of social revolution that was needed in Ireland itself. It is true that in Napier's estimation, several centuries of tyrannical oppression under the British had harmed the character of the Irish people in the same way that several centuries of oppression under the Turks had harmed the character of the mainland Greeks. And a further two centuries under Venetian rule had

Social reform for Cephalonia 81

left the *Ionian* Greeks dependent and dishonest.[23] But the only way to redeem the character of all these people – the Irish and the Greeks alike – would be to free them from their oppressors. In comparing the Irish and the Ionians, Napier was comparing unjust situations caused by unjust regimes. He was not comparing inferior races that each required – because of their indelible racial character – some beneficial period of British governance. Napier's views were rather different from those of British officials several decades later who racialized every situation.[24]

The road network

A central part of his plan for freeing the people was building roads.

As he detailed in a short book on the subject in 1825, *Memoir on the Roads of Cephalonia*, the mountain ranges of the island were almost impassable. Because of the extreme difficulty of travel, the estate owners all lived together in Argostoli, and they seldom visited their empty and broken-down seats. The rural peasants were left isolated and ignorant. New roads would change all this. Also, a coast road would help to fight smuggling, and it would open up the coast itself to settlement and cultivation. It would help with conservation, too, catching the soil from higher elevations. This would retard the loss of topsoil – a problem to which, as Napier understood the matter, these poorly wooded Mediterranean islands were otherwise prone. So all in all, good roads were vital.[25]

He set out his plan by taking the reader on a tour of the island – the valleys that would be opened up, the towns, the ports, the spine of interior routes he wanted to build, the passes and switchbacks that he would carve through the mountains. He projected a one-hundred-mile road system, not including the coastal route. Some of the mountain passes would be higher than Mt. Vesuvius, and certainly higher than anything in England. And he insisted that building merely a portion of the system would do no good, for then there could be no carriages; his plan for carrying the aristocracy back to their people might fail. When he wrote, he could report that some of his roads were already finished.[26]

Throughout the account, Napier conveys his conviction that a mastery of administrative detail is central if an activist government is to do any real good for the common people. So he explains that there should never be a greater slope for a road than one-in-twelve, or the water could race along and destroy what had been built. The limitation on the grade determined the placement of the switchbacks and indeed the whole layout; for the one thing that could never be changed after the road had been built was the slope, at least not without moving to a wholly new roadbed and wasting all the previous work. Another of his discoveries was that erosion was worse when the cross section of a road was angled in the same direction as the slope of a hill, with the water running off the side of the cut all the way along. Instead, a road running on a hill needed to be angled back into the hill itself to form a shallow V-shaped trough, suitably provided with drains and traps to catch the soil from above the cut.[27]

82 *The radical abroad and at home*

And deforestation made this work of combating erosion all the more important. Goats ran rampant, but they belonged to the peasants, he explained, who loved the animals for the way they lived off the land. Yet the goats hurt the peasants' crops as much as they hurt the wild groundcover. He wanted to tax the goats and encourage the peasants to keep sheep instead.[28]

What we are beginning to see in all this is something of Napier's belief that a government – however activist and reformist – needed to be run by technical experts and not, at least in its details, by the common people themselves. But he was not claiming to embody all that expertise in his own person. Napier never said he had discovered all of this road-building and erosion-fighting wisdom himself, through his own programme of experimentation. Instead he credited the engineers who worked under him. Chief among them – in rank as well as in his personal importance to Napier – was a certain 'Captain Kennedy'.[29]

John Pitt Kennedy was to be Napier's closest friend for the rest of their lives – he was the friend to whom Napier confided the arrangements over Anastasia. An Irish Protestant and an officer in the Royal Engineers, Kennedy had served in Malta under Maitland. In 1820 he began working on docks and canals in the Ionian Islands. When Napier first took up his post in Cephalonia, Kennedy was in England. Napier brought him back as Colonial Secretary and Director of Works.[30]

With Kennedy in place as engineer, road-building began in earnest. The work was funded through voluntary contributions and local taxes until a requirement came from the general government in Corfu that a corvée of one kind or another should be instituted on each of the islands. After the inauguration of the corvée Napier's road-building project accelerated.[31] Soon there was progress all over the island. Already in 1822 Byron could see it, and in an emergency Byron himself once picked up a shovel to help. One day a working party undermined a high embankment and twelve men were buried in a landslide. Napier galloped to Byron's house at Metaxata to summon the medical doctors living there. Byron came back with them, and when the energies of the rescuers seemed to flag before it was fully clear – at least to Byron – that all hands had been unearthed, the poet seized a spade and began digging himself.[32]

Working together in this period, Kennedy and Napier went on to develop an almost military system of controls and procedures to prevent any further accidents. Napier promulgated the final and most elaborate set of his road-building regulations with Kennedy's help in 1824 (these regulations would remain in effect until they were cancelled by Frederick Adam in 1828). They ran to more than two dozen sections and took up five pages of small type. And – or so the preamble says – they were to be read in their entirety to every group of workers at the beginning of *each day's* work. From these regulations we can discern still more about the style of governance that Napier thought appropriate for managing the common people.

So many details were carefully set out, from mealtimes to who was supposed to bring which tools, and whether they were to bring their tools from home

Social reform for Cephalonia   83

or from the stores. Nothing could be done without levels and drop lines to make sure that the slope did not vary above the one-in-twelve ratio. But the most important regulations concerned who had to work and when. A regular schedule was available weeks in advance for when the men of each village were expected to appear. Initially one day of work was required per week,[33] and then once every three weeks with the corvée. When the corvée began, no one was exempted from either working or paying his way out of it – save the Greek priests and the elderly. Not even the richest men escaped, and neither did the English officers, not even Napier himself – although again most of the wealthier people and Napier too bought their way out. Only the masons *had* to work and could not buy their freedom. For everyone else, the buy-out price was set by income band, and it was low enough that everyone of any income group could afford to go to the police station the day before he was scheduled to appear and have himself struck off the rolls on that occasion. The rich paid more than the poor, and Napier himself paid most of all.[34]

When the men did turn up to work, according to these long regulations they had to carry out their tasks exactly as they were told. They must not change or get ahead of the plans. Only an engineer could lay a foundation, and only an engineer could direct anyone about where to start digging.[35] If a property line had to be infringed upon, or if a pile of stones had to be taken from someone's field, it all went into a book and proper compensation was paid. This record-keeping would stand Napier in good stead in the 1830s, when Adam laid seventy charges against him, many of them connected to the road-building project. When challenged, Adam reduced the number of charges to nineteen. John Kennedy, who was still in Cephalonia at the time, was able to consult the records and refute almost all the charges at once. Compensation had indeed been paid in nearly every case of encroachment, and in some cases no encroachment had occurred. In a small number of instances the government had indeed been at fault – but no compensation had been asked for until years later, when Adam let it be known that he would look favourably upon anyone reporting irregularities from before 1828, when he substituted his own road-building system for Napier's.[36]

Yet if we ought to try to remain mindful of the disparities in power between Frederick Adam and the Greek peasant landowners from whom he was soliciting complaints, we should be mindful as well of the disparity in power between Napier and Kennedy, taken together, and the Greek villagers whom they compelled to go out in the sun and break rocks every three weeks. The British and the Greek views of the fairness of the corvée may well have differed; and the spirit of complaint that Adam detected – even though in the end he could not back up many of the specifics – may have been very real.

The work that was done made a substantial impact upon the land and its people. In his 1825 pamphlet, Napier projected that finishing the road system would take eight more years. Maitland had been supportive of the road project, and Adam as Maitland's deputy had more than once told Napier what good work he was doing on the island. So Napier sketched out additional projects.

84 *The radical abroad and at home*

He had his eye on improving harbour defences, and – along with Adam, who had already bought the land required – he wanted to build a new courthouse and prison. Napier's plan for the prison followed the American model of spokes radiating from a central observation point, or perhaps James Mill's panopticon, although in Cephalonia only half the spokes were built.[37]

We get more detail about what happened next from Napier's *Colonies* book than from the road-building pamphlet: Adam eventually imposed his own road-building scheme in place of Napier's. But according to Charles Napier, the price which Adam set for buying out of the corvée for the day was too high and so a culture of shirking developed. Further, the main funding for the scheme was to come from a tax on the import of cattle – yet Cephalonia did not import cattle, and so road-building there wound down.[38]

Most of Napier's criticisms of Adam are of this kind. Napier's picture of the High Commissioner is of a man who did not have a sufficient grasp of the detail needed to implement major policies. He could not recognize what measures were fit for purpose and what measures were not. We read that Adam completely changed the Ionian legal system three times in two years. The results were bewildering and frustrating to all but those who would benefit from the confusion – namely the local aristocrats and their lawyers.

And then there was the matter of the new palace and the money Adam was wasting. Adam was running up the Ionian public debt mainly for a ceremonial robe and a state coach and, yes, a new palace for himself.[39] The palace was poorly sited, and Adam's successor as High Commissioner, Lord Nugent, declined to live in it. In the 1833 book, Napier gleefully added that it had been turned into a hospital for idiots.[40]

Moral economy

Much of the construction that Napier and Kennedy undertook on Cephalonia – and what Adam was building on Corfu, if his governance of the island is looked at more charitably than Napier might be inclined to do – formed a part of a broader move among British authorities to clean up and 'Westernize' Ionian public spaces. This is a subject that historian Thomas Gallant has explored. In addition to the marketplaces and the lighthouse (Figure 6.1), certain sanitary reforms that Napier and Kennedy made may be seen in the same light. However, on another of the Ionian Islands, Zante, the Greeks *themselves* contributed to the clean-up effort through the regulations they passed through their town councils. Napier would allow no such local initiatives on the part of the Cephalonians. He joked to his sister Emily that the lighthouse was begun 'in the fourth year of my reign and the 44th of my age'.[41]

In trying to clean up the island, Napier was trying to reform social behaviour and create a public sphere in exactly the way Gallant suggests. When he arrived in Cephalonia, the residents of the two main towns, Argostoli and Lixouri, had nowhere to buy vegetables save for 'a few onions', as he tells us. The leading citizens let some of the houses for informal shops, but there was no

Figure 6.1 The St. Theodore Lighthouse, Argostoli. Designed and built by John Pitt Kennedy, rebuilt after the 1953 earthquake.

© David Kilpatrick / Alamy Stock Photo

regular trade, and all the best produce and the best fish was taken as a matter of course to the kitchen of one's feudal patron. Not only did Napier and Kennedy's new market buildings change all that, but the same markets – built in the form of open porticoes that could not be locked at night – gave the country people who were bringing their produce to town a place to repair out of the noonday sun, and at night they could sleep among the porticoes.

Viscount Kirkwall, who would serve in the Ionian islands several decades later, said that a traveller in Cephalonia would find that Napier was responsible for everything, like the Marquis de Carabas in *Puss in Boots*. If one asked the people, Napier built the moles, the roads, the courthouses, the gaols, and everything else, and reformed every aspect of life. This is not far from the truth. Napier went so far as to require the butchers to display a sign in the shape of the animal whose flesh they were selling, with a number of dots giving the price in half-pence. That way the illiterate and the innumerate could shop more effectively. Kirkwall said that if more British administrators had been like Napier, the Ionian Islanders of his own day would not be trying to rejoin Greece. Local opinion was that the rulers ought to 'do everything' as Napier had done, or they should go home to England.[42] 'A man-of-war must take care of the slowest-sailing merchant ships', Napier wrote, and the poor

> are like slow-sailing vessels, they are deeply laden with the heavy cargo of poverty. The countryman who comes to market, finds a sort of

86 *The radical abroad and at home*

town-house in a public edifice of this description, and establishes his stall under the shelter of its stately portico.

Napier's was an activist administration. But because he was careful and he refused to spend much money on himself, he reduced taxes in Cephalonia by a quarter.[43]

Life and death

The most important area in which Napier intervened was agriculture. As Resident he worked out an activist, sometimes even frenetic policy of extending government control over the production and distribution of food, and he strongly defended this policy against the idea of *laissez-faire*. All the free market could do, he thought, was bring starvation the way it had in Ireland.

Napier's first major intervention involved the currant crop. As the year's currants came in, he and Kennedy suddenly realized that many of the merchants were guilty of sharp practice. They would dump a farmer's crop into the bin and once the currants were mixed in with others and could no longer be reweighed or revalued, they would pay much less than agreed. The farmer could hardly overpower the merchant and the merchant's men and take from them the money originally promised. So Napier and his deputy spent an almost frantic twenty-four hours creating regulations out of whole cloth, setting up scales and a government currant market. The farmers were to weigh their crops only on the government-approved scales and sell their crop only to the government-approved wholesalers according to the official weights and grades, with all of this taking place only within the government-approved market buildings.[44] This was exactly the kind of detail-oriented administrative activism that Napier thought Adam was incapable of – but Napier set up the system in a mad dash of rule-making before all of that years' currants had been sold.

And there were other examples of this scramble for intervention, as with the public bakery that Napier called into being in the wake of a bakers' strike. To make sure there would be enough bread for the people, Napier ordered the bakers back to their ovens, and to protect them from the mob he brought in soldiers. Each baker had a soldier as his personal bodyguard, twenty-four hours a day. The bakers found this sufficiently annoying, as they were meant to do, and so they reached a settlement to mollify their customers. Napier then founded a public bakery so they would no longer have a monopoly. Adam found Napier's behaviour in this matter high-handed. To him it smelled of military intimidation.[45]

***

And then in 1829, late in Napier's tenure, there was a famine in Cephalonia. Already Napier had spent much of his eight years as Resident trying to get the island's food production back up to a level that would assure self-sufficiency.

Social reform for Cephalonia   87

He tried to increase the sale and thus the cultivation of vegetables, and he ran pilot projects to demonstrate crop rotation. He brought in experts and even settlers from Malta to show the farmers new practices, such as planting the crops in rows and tilling them properly to keep the weeds down. These practices had not been customary on the island.[46]

But still there was not enough food for hard times. In 1829, bad weather came, leaving snow on the ground and killing the dandelions and wild greens on which the poorer people depended. *Lackana*, the dish they cooked out of this greenery that appeared of its own accord, was a key staple, eaten along with bread and oil.

The snows built up, rather than melting in a few days as they normally would. Snow filled the valleys, even collapsing houses. There would be no *lackana* for some time. 'The local government', as Napier recalled, 'felt that it was its duty to intervene. It had no idea of allowing so disgraceful a scene, as the people being dependent on private charity for subsistence.'[47] Not for Napier the idea that a people ought to take care of each other out of Christian feeling and a sense of self-reliance; not for him the idea that the people ought to be weaned off their dependence on the government.

So as Resident he directed the government officers to buy up any cheap food, secure mules, and fan out over the countryside, feeding everyone. Magistrates were to visit the 'largest, or most accessible village in each district'. The primates or overseers of the smaller settlements were to bring all the inhabitants to the larger villages. Three days' food would be given out, with a receipt issued for how much each settlement or parish had received; the receipts were to be kept by the magistrate. There was also a receipt given for each individual parcel of food. Those receipts were kept by the local primates. Each receipt listed the day, the quantity, and the kind of food ('wheat, or peas, or corn, or bread, etc.'). And it stated that the food was a loan and not a gift: a 'loan from the Government, to be repaid in money, or in kind, or in labour, within a certain period, and by entailments'.[48]

After three days, when the snow had subsided, anyone needing food was instructed to come to Argostoli for a second loan in kind. Napier's roads had made these visits to Argostoli possible. Indeed Napier tells us that he might have directed that the hungry people should come into Argostoli for their *first* instalment of food – but then the magistrates would not have had the occasion to move through the countryside to assess the real needs, and the whole of the population would have found themselves in Argostoli in the worst of the weather, without adequate shelter.

Four or five thousand people got relief out in the countryside in the first round, and in Argostoli three days later the villagers appeared in an orderly fashion for the second instalment. A number of people were put on public works. Napier says the whole effort lasted a month, until the *lackana* reappeared. It cost the government only £400. No more food had been provided than what was needed 'to prevent starvation', and most all the loans were repaid save where the local governments were lax. Only children and the old

88   *The radical abroad and at home*

were excused from repayment, and the cost of their food made up only a small part of the £400. Napier wanted the sum for the food for the old and the very young to be taken out of the convent funds, since the convents existed for this very purpose of supporting the poor. But he says he did not press the point.

He loved describing the larger significance of what he achieved by his intervention in the economy. As the snow fell, there were rumours that private loans were being offered to the poor so they could buy food, loans that would probably have to be repaid in hard work the following summer. But in stepped Napier with his magistrates and his food depots, saving the people from the predations of private enterprise:

> [W]ithout the greatest care, some hundreds of peasants would have been enslaved by tricks of all kinds, for villainy is ingenious, and among the Cephalonians there were men not more scrupulous than among the Irish, some of whom, it is said, turned the subscription made for the starving poor, into personal gain, by paying their own labourers therewith. The mass of Cephalonians felt every possible desire to relieve their countrymen, and many instances of great generosity took place; but times of distress are times of harvest for knaves.[49]

Note the phrasing – for 'among the Cephalonians' as 'among the Irish' there was a dishonest minority, while the great mass of the people were generous and patriotic. But the middlemen who exaggerated the amount of suffering wanted only to profit from a government-*subsidized* rather than a government-*run* system of grain distribution. Napier's government-run system had frustrated their plans, or so he thought.[50]

***

He painted a very different picture of Adam's role as the crisis played out. As usual, his theme is that Adam lacked acumen. In this case, Adam wasn't smart enough to outwit the speculators.

At bottom, the High Commissioner had misunderstood the very nature of the crisis, Napier tells us. Adam did send grain to the island. But the Cephalonians already had plenty of grain, says Napier. The problem was that the common people did not have the money to buy it. To add injury to insult, not only was this grain sent from Corfu completely unnecessary, it came with a bill to be paid by the Cephalonian government, and thus as Napier stresses '*ultimately by the poor*'. And worse yet, the price charged by Corfu was *higher* than the open market price in Cephalonia.[51]

On top of all that, moreover, Adam's government had defrauded the people. Napier explained that two kinds of wheat were grown in the Ionian Islands, hard and soft, and they differed in price. The grain Adam sent from Corfu was of both kinds, but all of it was charged at the higher rate. Napier cried, he remonstrated, he wrote to Adam and others, but in vain. The Cephalonian taxpayer had to pay for the grain. So Napier tells us that his final option was to write this book that he was placing before the educated public. All he could do was publish his account of the matter, with its voluminous appendices to prove his case. Indeed, one quarter of the book's six hundred pages is made up of letters and other documents marshalled to prove Napier's various claims.[52]

But Napier also says that in laying out all this detail about food and famine, he had a larger purpose than merely damning the High Commissioner. If he, Charles Napier, could save four thousand people from starving for £400 – and with most of the money soon repaid to the treasury – then there was 'no reason why an extension of the same system, when Ireland suffers famine, may not have the same results'. Napier admitted that Cephalonia had 60,000 people while Ireland had eight million, but he did not see this as much of an objection. It was more of an opportunity. While four thousand starved in Cephalonia, 'it is said that three hundred thousand were starving in Ireland':

> Therefore, where one magistrate was employed at Cephalonia, the Irish government ought to employ sixty, or a hundred; and where we lend the people four hundred pounds, there would be, perhaps, thirty thousand pounds required in Ireland, a sum much less than the amount of private subscriptions.[53]

And now Napier explained more fully *why* he so strongly preferred government relief to private charity. For the role played by private charity in the recent Irish famine did the government there no credit at all, he said. In his view, the problem with relying on private charity was not that it failed. Indeed, private charity had not failed. He believed that the Irish people certainly had provided charity to one another. Nor was the problem with what happened in Ireland the fact that speculators came out of the woodwork to prey upon the poor. They would do that anywhere, he said. Instead the problem with charity in Napier's opinion was simply this: It is not a legitimate principle or instrument of the state. Private subscriptions for relieving the hunger of Ireland 'were discreditable to government. Is a whole nation to be treated as a mass of paupers, dependent upon private charity, and that charity from another country?' Napier had a higher idea of the dignity of the state than all that.

And the state should arrange the matter so that it got its money back: '[T]his sum of thirty thousand pounds would not have been charity, either public or private,' he says of the Irish relief fund that he was proposing; it would be 'repaid in money or in labour. It would only have been a loan' – just as the food he gave out on Cephalonia had to be paid for later on by those who had received it.[54] Here Napier seems to have shared at least some part of the nineteenth-century British fixation on individual responsibility. The usual idea was that the hungry should not be turned into dependents. Even if they were starving, they should be put to work to earn their bread – for if the poor were simply given food they might become irresponsible and no longer willing to work in the way they should.[55]

90 *The radical abroad and at home*

The British were special in thinking in this way. As my colleague Kathryn Edgerton-Tarpley has argued, in China it was the government's responsibility pure and simple to save lives during a time of dearth.[56] It would seem that in this sense Napier's own opinions came somewhere in between the British and Chinese views. For Charles Napier, famine was a test of the government's willingness to fulfil its responsibilities to the starving poor; and in the present case the Cephalonian famine was a test of his own abilities as the governor of the island. Could he use the resources of government to save the people, even while he showed that he could conform to the expectations of his countrymen and combat the famine through loans instead of gifts? If he could, great things might result:

> By such an arrangement as I have now stated [the scaling up of his Cephalonian system of famine relief], the [Irish] horrors of 1831, and other periods, might have been prevented; though it is hoped that the establishment of poor laws will prevent our ever again seeing the infamous exhibition of a population, starving in the midst of abundance of food.[57]

He ended his famine discussion with a flourish:

> I have done; but a man may be pardoned for being carried away by such a subject; a subject which must fill everyone with horror when reflected upon. We hear people rave against war; but surely war is not so horrible as the scenes witnessed in Ireland! It is the fashion to cry out against war, and war is, no doubt, a great evil; but it is not such an evil as bad government. The bloodshed, the destruction, the miseries of war, are produced by bad statesmen, who do not suffer the hardships and meet the danger! and yet war is, perhaps, the least of the evils that such men inflict upon their fellow creatures.[58]

Notes

1 Mavrocordatos to Napier, 13 June 1825, NP, TNA PRO 30/64/3, fols 8–9; Napier's demands, 1825, NP, TNA PRO 30/64/3, fol. 10; Napier to Henry Napier, 20 September, 6 October, and [?] October 1825, NP, TNA PRO 30/64/3, fols 11, 18–21.
2 G. W. Hamilton to Adam, 16 March 1826, CO 537/148, fols 56–67 at 62.
3 Napier, *Colonies*, 19–20.
4 Ibid, 58. Maitland strove to prevent crime and leave the gaols 'shut for want of business'. See Maitland to Bathurst, 22 December 1823, TNA CO 136/1090, fol. 292.
5 Napier, *Colonies*, 51–53.
6 Ibid, 56–57; Napier to his mother, 18 March, 2 June, 10 June 1822, given in WN, 1:307–11; W. D. Wrigley, *Diplomatic Significance of Ionian Neutrality, 1821–1831*, American University Studies 9, History, vol. 41 (New York: Peter Lang, 1988), 116–20. After the riots, one British officer in Cephalonia went out of his way to flog and shave Greek Orthodox priests. This took place in late 1821, before Napier's arrival, and Maitland tried to stop it.
7 Napier, *Colonies*, 92–94.
8 Ibid, 14.

9 Ibid, 59–60.

10 Ibid, 64–65.

11 John Stuart Mill, *Considerations on Representative Government* (1861), chapters VIII and XVIII; John Stuart Mill, *The Subjection of Women* (1869) – in Mill, *Collected Works*, Ann M. Robson and John Robson (eds), 33 vols (Toronto: University of Toronto Press, 1963–1991), vols. 19 and 21.

12 Napier argued that because the British had such an overwhelming military force in Cephalonia they could afford to try a measure of social experimentation, even at the cost of initial unrest. Napier, *Colonies*, 67, 98–100.

13 William St. Clair, *That Greece Might Still Be Free: The Philhellenes in the War of Independence* (London: Oxford UP, 1972), 167–68, 302–03, quotation at 303.

14 For these hangings, see John L. Comstock, *History of the Greek Revolution* (New York: William W. Reed, 1828), 209–10; Wrigley, *Diplomatic Significance of Ionian Neutrality*, 112. And for doubts about the accuracy of the story: Gordon, *Greek Revolution*, 1:320.

15 Napier, *Colonies*, viii.

16 [John Stuart Mill], 'Napier's *The Colonies*', *Literary Examiner* (24 November 1833), 740–41; given in *Collected Works*, 23:647–56. See also [John Stuart Mill], 'The Marvelous Ministry', *Literary Examiner* (29 September 1833), 23:608–17 at 615. Mill as editor ran a piece making similar points two years later: [Charles Buller], 'Napier on the Ionian Islands', *London Review* 25 (July 1835), 295–316.

17 Napier, *Colonies*, 67. For a statement by Mill along these lines, see the concluding chapter of *Utilitarianism* (1863), in Mill, *Collected Works*, 10:259.

18 Thomas W. Gallant, *Experiencing Dominion: Culture, Identity, and Power in the British Mediterranean* (Notre Dame, IN: University of Notre Dame Press, 2002), 15–19, 25, 35–45.

19 Napier's private notes, March 1825, given in WN, 1:357.

20 Given in WN, 1:366.

21 Napier, *Colonies*, 241–42, 299.

22 Ibid, 463, 475.

23 Ibid, 6. On the Venetian-influenced aristocracy and its control over a more or less feudal peasantry, see David Hannell, 'The Ionian Islands under the British Protectorate: Social and Economic Problems', *Journal of Modern Greek Studies* 7, 1 (May 1989), 109–12, 124–26.

24 For later racial views, see Edward Beasley, *Victorian Reinvention of Race: New Racisms and the Problem of Grouping in the Human Sciences* (New York: Routledge, 2010), 18–21, 66–68, 88–94, 105–09; Douglas A. Lorimer, *Colour, Class, and the Victorians: English Attitudes to the Negro in the Mid-Nineteenth Century* (Leicester: Leicester UP, 1978), 12–17, 87–89, 131–53; Nancy Stepan, *The Idea of Race in Science: Great Britain, 1800–1960* (Hamden, CT: Archon Books, 1982), 20–46; George Stocking, 'Introduction to James Cowles Prichard', in George Stocking (ed.), *Researches into the Physical History of Man* [1813] (Chicago: University of Chicago Press, 1973), lxxix–lxxxiii, lxxxviii–lxxxix; Catherine Hall, *Civilising Subjects: Metropole and Colony in the English Imagination, 1830–1867* (Chicago: University of Chicago Press, 2002), 211–21, 274–82, 398–400; Catherine Hall, 'The Nation Within and Without', in Catherine Hall, Keith McClelland, and Jane Rendall (eds), *Defining the Victorian Nation: Class, Race, Gender, and the Reform Act of 1867* (Cambridge: Cambridge UP, 2000), 179–233.

25 Charles James Napier, *Roads of Cephalonia*, 1–7.

26 Ibid, 13–14, 24.

27 Ibid, 16.

28 Ibid, 19–21.

29 Ibid, iv.

30 R.H. Vetch, 'Kennedy, John Pitt (1796–1879)', revised by Roger T. Stearn, in H.C.G. Matthew and Brian Harrison (eds), *Oxford Dictionary of National Biography* (Oxford: Oxford UP, 2004), online edn, edited by Lawrence Goldman, May 2010, http://www.oxforddnb.com/view/article/15387, accessed 25 April 2016; Napier, *Colonies*, v, 6;

92 The radical abroad and at home

Anonymous, 'John Pitt Kennedy', *Minutes of the Proceedings of the Institution of Civil Engineers* 59, 1 (1879–80), 293–98.

31 Napier, *Colonies*, 219.

32 Count Peter Gamba, *A Narrative of Lord Byron's Journey to Greece* (London: John Murray, 1825), 19, 293–94.

33 Napier to his mother, 2 June 1822, given in WN, 1:308–09.

34 WN, 1:408; Napier to his mother, 27 June 1822, 1:311; Napier, *Colonies*, 404, 415, and Napier to Adam, 22 June 1822, 540–42.

35 Napier, *Colonies*, 537n20.

36 Ibid, 431–32, 591–92.

37 Adam to Napier, 18 November 1822, 7 March 1823, NP, BL Add. MS 54540, fols 30, 57–58; Napier, *Roads of Cephalonia*, 45–51; Kirkwall, *Ionian Islands*, 2: 104–05.

38 Napier, *Colonies*, 222–26.

39 Ibid, 84–89, 211–12, 213n. On how Adam wasted money on palaces and fortifications, see Peter Prineas, *Britain's Greek Islands: Kythera and the Ionian Islands, 1809–1864* (Darlington, New South Wales: Plateia, 2009), 117. Later High Commissioners cut the bureaucracy substantially – Hannell, 'The Ionian Islands under the British Protectorate', 122.

40 Napier, *Colonies*, 170, 211–12, 213n.

41 Gallant, *Experiencing Dominion*, 62–63; Napier to Emily Napier, 14 August 1826, NP, BL Add. MS 49109, fols 94–95.

42 Napier, *Colonies*, 317–25, 329–30; Kirkwall, *Ionian Islands*, 2:68, 144.

43 Napier, *Colonies*, 329.

44 Ibid, 341–44; Gallant, *Experiencing Dominion*, 106–09; Hannell, 'The Ionian Islands under the British Protectorate', 114–15.

45 Napier, *Colonies*, 361–64.

46 Napier's private notes, 1825, given in WN, 1:359; Napier to his mother, 1 January 1826, 380–81; Napier, *Colonies*, 260–86.

47 Napier, *Colonies*, 349; see also Napier to his brother, July 1832, in WN, 1:438–39.

48 Napier, *Colonies*, 350.

49 Ibid, 349.

50 Ibid.

51 Ibid, 351.

52 Ibid, 352–55, 565–69.

53 Ibid, 353–54.

54 Ibid, 354.

55 A classic statement is David Ricardo, *On Protection to Agriculture* (London: John Murray, 1822). For examples in practice: Sanjay Sharma, *Famine, Philanthropy, and the Colonial State: North India in the Early Nineteenth Century* (New Delhi: Oxford UP, 2001).

56 Kathryn Edgerton-Tarpley, *Tears from Iron: Cultural Responses to Famine in Nineteenth-Century China* (Berkeley and Los Angeles: University of California Press, 2008), chapter 4; R. Bin Wong, chapters 1, 13, and 14, in Pierre-Étienne Will and R. Bin Wong (eds), *Nourish the People: The State Granary System in China*, Michigan Monographs in Chinese Studies 60 (Ann Arbor: Center for Chinese Studies Publications, University of Michigan, 1991).

57 Napier, *Colonies*, 354.

58 Ibid, 354–56.

7 Departure and bereavement

When the famine of 1829 had passed and another winter had come and gone, Elizabeth Napier found herself in failing health. She was now well into her sixties. In the spring of 1830 she had a health crisis and Napier took her back to England, leaving the children behind. The couple travelled by way of Corfu, setting sail from there on 20 May.[1] It is best for the moment to let Napier himself tell the next part of the story. At the outset of the eighty-page chapter on his departure with which he closed the anti-Adam book, he recalls that on Corfu he

> received the most marked kindness from Sir Frederick Adam; he received my sick wife on the beach, lodged us in the palace, and gave us a passage on board a public vessel. . . . [H]e accompanied us on board, and his last words to me, were (I believe I quote his exact words, certainly I quote their meaning): – *'Well Napier, good bye. Stay in England as long as Mrs. Napier's health requires it, but remember, that the longer you stay away, the worse for us here.'* How could I imagine, that this man was, at the moment, trying to prevent my return, and that his apparent kindness arose from his desire to get rid of me? I had not been long in England, when I heard that he had already begun to overturn my plans at Cephalonia, plans sanctioned by himself; and I saw, with regret, that he was the dupe, and (by his situation) the powerful agent, of a faction, to calumniate an absent man.[2]

In other words, when Napier thought he was on leave Adam replaced him. There was no misunderstanding on Adam's part over whether Napier wanted to return. Adam wrote a letter saying that Napier was going on leave and would come back. Also, he sent Napier an officer named Colonel Pitt to serve 'during your absense' and as 'your locum tenens'. Napier trained Pitt.[3]

In England in July Napier still had no idea that he was unemployed. He did hear from Cephalonia that Adam had criticized him. What he did not hear was that Adam had appointed a new Resident to succeed him (not Colonel Pitt as *locum tenens* but another man). And then in the latter part of August it became clear to Napier that indeed he had been replaced. He sent for his children at once. They were brought to England by his kinsman Edward Curling,

94   *The radical abroad and at home*

who had been in Cephalonia working on agricultural improvements. And in December Napier made his arrangements for supporting Anastasia.[4]

Charles Napier would never see the Ionian Islands again. But for the rest of his life he would continue to correspond with his Cephalonian friends and to look after them the best he could. Today he is fondly remembered on the island for his good roads and his good works and is commemorated in gardens and exhibits.[5]

Adam's side

What was in Adam's mind initially is not clear. But after he had once begun to criticize Napier publicly, several events transpired which convinced him that he needed to make sure that Napier did not return.

Adam's initial criticisms of Napier came in the wake of trouble that broke out soon after Napier left. George IV had died in late June, and oddly this led to unrest in Cephalonia. When the accession of William IV was proclaimed on the island in the autumn, some of the leading citizens refused to sign the statement of congratulations. An anti-British whispering campaign followed and satirical pamphlets appeared. According to one rumour, the British were going to force the islanders to give up the Orthodox religion and become Protestants.

Adam chose to regard all the disloyal talk and the nasty pamphlets as a form of open rebellion, although there had been no violence and there had been no interference with British officials. He came to Cephalonia in October and arrested the four leading pamphleteers. He also seized Napier's official papers. Only Kennedy's quick efforts saved Napier's private papers from a similar fate.[6]

The crisis passed when Adam gave a public address to the so-called trouble-makers. He told them there had never been any danger to their religion and that it was the duty of any good citizen to congratulate the king.[7]

Napier would not hear about this speech for some time, but when he did he found a sting in the tail. Adam had gone on to explain to the Cephalonians what he thought was the real reason for their petty rebellion, namely the injustice under which Cephalonia had long suffered: '[T]here have been grievances, I am sorry to say, but these grievances I did not know of, or I should have immediately remedied them. . . . I am surprised that you have not reported them to me', he told the assembled Cephalonians.[8]

Napier would argue in his book that the High Commissioner had been in Cephalonia many times over the years, meeting privately with people of all kinds. He would have known about any real discontent.[9]

Napier's assessment on this point seems true enough. But in October there *was* something which Adam heard about Napier's administration that gave him a sudden start. Adam's source on this occasion was none other than John Kennedy. In an unguarded moment, Kennedy told the High Commissioner about that incident four years before (when Adam was visiting England) when Napier had quartered troops on the bakers – even if it was only for the several hours (as Kennedy remembered) that it took for the bakers to give in and resume baking.[10]

This at least was a new discovery for Adam. And it was later in the very month of October when he found out about the bakery affair that Adam wrote to Napier's temporary replacement, Colonel Pitt, to say that an officer named Travers would shortly be arriving as the new permanent Resident of Cephalonia and that Colonel Pitt and John Kennedy as well should show him everything he needed to know. Adam went on to say that Kennedy's successor as Engineer would be arriving soon after. Indeed, Kennedy had already requested leave after a misunderstanding that he had with a local magistrate. Given the terms Kennedy had used, Adam might well have thought that he had resigned his position as Engineer, even if he knew that Napier had not in fact resigned as Resident.[11]

Either way, Adam was ending the Napier regime. But he did say this to the people of Cephalonia:

> I have the highest esteem and affection for Colonel Napier, and have the honor of being a friend of his; and perhaps my feelings of friendship have induced me to think too favourably of some of his measures, but I certainly feel, and everyone must see, that if the good which he has rendered to Cephalonia were put in a balance against the evils, the good would infinitely, most infinitely override them. The system of administration of justice which he has established, seconded, ably seconded, by the administrators, will at once shew the good that has been done by Colonel Napier. Now, the poor man can get justice against the Signori, who cannot, as in former times, oppress and injure him.[12]

William, and the attempt to return to the garden

In England William Napier now began fanning the flames of his brother's resentment. Early in 1831, he asked Charles whether Frederick Adam's seizure of his papers would mean that the 'means of exposing [Adam would] be cramped'. 'Adam', William added, 'is an infamous scoundrel, as I always suspected him to be. You must be cautious or he will ruin you.'[13] William also mentioned that the Colonial Secretary, Lord Goderich – who three years before had resigned as Prime Minister after only five months – was too weak to help Napier and reign in Adam.

When Charles Napier left Cephalonia he fell into a correspondence with his brother that in later years would become voluminous. Eventually they would spend hours almost every day writing several-thousand-word letters to each other. Even when Charles was too busy with public affairs he would make the time to dash off a hasty complaint to William, and perhaps a few expletives about the government ministers responsible for any perceived slight. Charles Napier was a garrulous man. Many of his letters were written to tease or amuse. But they were not without their consequences. A decade or more

96   *The radical abroad and at home*

later, William would still be keeping alive all the resentments that Charles had once expressed in a passing moment. Whenever Charles Napier needed the wise, calming counsel of a brother, William poured petrol on the flames. And William *published* his screeds against anyone he thought might be his own and Charles's enemies in a slough of letters-to-the-editor and newspaper articles, plus seventeen volumes of biography and military history (if we count his long work on the Peninsular War).[14] Some of these tomes were published while his brother Charles was still alive.

Charles Napier re-echoed the resentments in his own huge letters to William. But even Charles would sometimes implore William to suspend judgement rather than going off half-cocked at some supposed enemy. As he wrote in India:

> [M]y dear Bill be cautious for this reason for the things I tell you and you only, I get from others and there may be errors. . . . For example, I told you (and *thought*) that the Bombay government had stopped the great pier at Kurrachee. No such thing! It was Dalhousie. He told me so yesterday. He was *ill-informed*; it was no fault of his, but weakness and want of head! Now if quarrel with him I should be unjust, for he does his *best* to support me. So be very careful because things may *change* and may lead you wrong which in print would do mischief.[15]

But Charles was too loyal to his brother and too fond of him to discount everything William said. Some of the feuds that William promoted – if 'feuds' is even the right word, for Adam for one never chose never to waste any time by responding – some of these *resentments* seemed to take over William's life and Charles's as well.

Goaded by William, Charles Napier now spent several years trying to get back to Cephalonia. He campaigned to have Adam *ordered* to reappoint him as Resident. When Adam moved on to become governor of Madras, Charles Napier tried to get the next High Commissioner ordered to bring him back to Cephalonia in his old capacity. Napier's single fixed idea was that his return to the island as Resident was the one and only way to show the world that there was no reason to remove him in the first place.

It seems that he had taken leave of his senses. More than one actor in this three-year drama pointed out how Napier's demand that he *must* be reappointed Resident and that his reappointment *must* be seen by the world really meant that he wanted to turn the privilege of governing the people of the island into a species of private property owed to him personally, purely to assuage a slight that was perceptible chiefly to himself. Apparently the new High Commissioner in Corfu should see his right of appointment taken away so that Napier could be reinstalled; and the new Resident in Cephalonia itself, equally innocent, should be turned out of a job – all so that Charles Napier would have his record on the island vindicated before an indifferent globe. For

Departure and bereavement   97

perhaps the world was not paying such keen attention as he and his brother were to the vital question of why he had moved on after eight successful years.

Napier's attempt to get his job back proceeded though more intricate steps than we need to follow, mainly in various letters to Adam and the Colonial Secretary, Lord Goderich. When Goderich finally saw Napier in 1832, to Napier's shock the Colonial Secretary did not seem to think that Adam's speech in Cephalonia had been so very insulting. Goderich then offered what even Napier himself had to agree was a promotion, the Residency of the island of Zante. But Napier said that taking this new position would mean admitting before the world that Adam had been right to remove him from Cephalonia in the first place. He refused the appointment. So Goderich acquiesced this far: He sent Napier's latest complaint on to Adam, and he reluctantly agreed to arbitrate between Napier and Adam on the question of who was at fault in their quarrel. What concrete result the arbitration might have, and what the real use of it was, never became entirely clear.[16]

Responding to Goderich's request, Adam duly provided his long list of accusations against Napier. Napier responded in turn with his own set of terribly lengthy refutations and commentaries. He had this new material ready for Goderich in March 1832. As printed in the back of the anti-Adam book, it takes up fifty pages of small type.[17] In reality Goderich was blessed with the handwritten version, complete with long, paragraph-like lists of the contents of each chapter – these are written in especially tiny handwriting, to mimic the headings in a printed book.[18]

One can imagine Goderich's reaction on being given all this paperwork. With the attachments it took up four bundles of foolscap.[19] Four bundles!

While Napier was preparing this material for Goderich, wiser counsel suggested to him that he should reconsider what he was doing. As one experienced officer explained to John Kennedy, what Napier ought to send instead was a normal letter and nothing else:

> The form and great detail of Napier's vindication are not well chosen with a view to what must be the great object, viz, to ensure Lord Goderich's attention [to] a direct and prompt decision on the merits of the case. There ought to be a letter in an official form, concise, pointed, and confident; referring to the other papers . . . as *proofs* and *vouchers*; and expressing a firm expectation that Lord Goderich must see how utterly frivolous the charges are and that he will render Napier ready justice.[20]

Kennedy passed this advice on to Napier, adding that 'everyone appears to agree' that Goderich simply would not read all that Napier wanted him to.[21]

Napier ignored these concerns. He asked Kennedy, who was then in London, to send Goderich all four bundles of paper and a summary on top of that. Kennedy, who at this point was also trying to secure for himself a disability pension over a knee injury, now presented a similarly huge stack of his own

98   *The radical abroad and at home*

papers to the permanent secretary at the War Office, who simply put them in a drawer. Did Kennedy expect that anything else would happen? Napier's four bundles got slightly better treatment. Goderich gave them to an M.P. by the name of Sir James MacDonald, who was to be the next High Commissioner in Corfu. When MacDonald first began to work through them, he was sympathetic to Napier. He became far less so as Napier's sarcastic tone and the sheer length of what Napier provided began to grate on him. After several weeks MacDonald had finished reading the last of the bundles. A few days later he died, never having gone to Greece.[22] Napier was responsible for this one death at least.

But even this was not the end of Napier's complaining. For soon he developed a theory, and yes with some assistance from his brother William, that what Adam had said to the people of Cephalonia was part of a carefully worked out campaign by the High Commissioner to impoverish and humiliate him. It was all an intricate plot, Napier believed. For Adam *had* to know how he, Charles Napier, would react to the charges. And Adam *had* to know, Napier insisted, that as his leave expired and he went on the half-pay list, he would have no choice but to come out to Corfu to defend himself. This would mean a second expensive journey for Napier and his sick family from one end of Europe to the other. The expenses of that journey were also part of Adam's plot to break him. And furthermore Adam *had* to know – Adam *had* to have worked out what would happen still further in the future – that Charles Napier, once he was back in Corfu to organize his defence, his 'finances exhausted', would *have* to take an inferior post as a favour from Adam, 'acknowledging my dismissal from Cephalonia to be a well-merited punishment'. 'So was the cup of bitterness prepared for me by Sir Frederick Adam.'[23] One wonders how much of the plot to bat his family back and forth across Europe and ruin them financially Napier tried to explain to Goderich during their various meetings.

It took Napier three years to accept that in the end there would be no *deus ex machina* in the form of the Colonial Secretary to make everything better. He finally began to understand that he would never be going back to Cephalonia. Now he only wanted a hearing on who had been right. By July 1832 Goderich stopped responding to Napier's letters at all. One can hardly blame poor Goderich. As the historian and media theorist Ben Kafka reminds us, petitioners who write letter after letter and report after report, pursuing a seemingly endless campaign to get the bureaucracy to set aside its own procedures and make everything right in their own individual case, are asking for a degree of personal attention and emotional fulfilment that bureaucracies are not set up to provide.[24]

Nonetheless, to clear his name of charges that probably no one but himself, his brother, and John Kennedy ever willingly paid attention to, Napier now wrote his great tome of self-justification and remonstrance. He did have some practical concerns to engage his attention as well. He set up a home with his family and his ailing wife, at first in Berkshire, then Hampshire, and finally in Bath. He did some gardening and he worked with the poor, or so his brother tells us.[25] But mostly he poured his passion for social justice and combating the lordly elite entirely into the pages of his anti-Adam book – or rather into the better parts of it.

***

In January 1833 both Charles Napier and his wife Elizabeth contracted cholera. The disease had appeared in India in 1817 and it was only now reaching Europe. Napier himself would survive, but after much struggle and suffering, Elizabeth died on 31 July.[26]

He was devastated. We have already seen that he felt things deeply as he walked back and forth in the night – he would make himself upset over little things, as he told his mother years before. The death of his wife was on another level. He described his feelings in a letter to a friend:

> 29 years ago I fell in love with her beauty and her powerful mind. I dared to tell her so and received such a lecture as probably no man has ever before received – treating me as a boy for I was but 22 and she was near 40, she forgave me . . . but on forgiving me and granting me her friendship she excited in me a force of love and admiration which ever died in my breast. . . . When her husband died she was left without means, unless as the pensioner of her son-in-law, a Mr. Laing. I had never married (though often strongly pressed by her to do so) because I felt such unshaken friendship and affection for her that, however pure, would not be justifiable in the eyes of any woman of feeling that I might marry. I was in love with no one. Why then give up the friendship of years for the risk which attend matrimony? I was therefore single when she became a widow. I was at my ease. The person I most esteemed and most valued for her great virtues was single, was poor, was sick. I had not an instant's doubt. My heart she had had for 23 years; I had by my undeviating friendship completely won hers. It is true she was sixty but if I did not mind that whom did it concern? We married and I found the wife all that I expected such a woman would be; my long-smothered love blazed out and I adored her. . . . In all that depended on her I was as happy as I could be; on the 16th of July she was taken ill, and died on the 31st, leaving me in a state of wretchedness. . . . [M]y feelings are numbed and dead.[27]

But he had two daughters to think about. The girls were seven (or recently eight) and six. What could he do? He had to think of them – he had to think of something other than himself, something other than all he had lost, something other than Cephalonia and Lord Goderich.

Napier's anti-Adam book was now (very recently) in print and the events it recounted could begin to recede into the past. By Christmas Napier had taken his girls to settle in Normandy, at Caen, hoping they would be happy but fearing that they would not.[28] He had decided to raise them abroad for

100 *The radical abroad and at home*

a time, and after perhaps a year to come back and settle in County Wicklow near John Kennedy.[29]

He soon published another book – a thin volume which he said his late wife had written for the girls in her last days. But in fact this work was not addressed to the girls but to their caregiver. Elizabeth wrote the book as a guide for her younger husband after she was gone. One hears a loving voice in it, and a voice from her era. She discussed how anyone taking care of children has to make sure they grow independent and strong, and raise them so they are ready to educate themselves. The girls – the girls whose mother she had become in the place of her husband's mistress – should be brought up with love and regular habits, and they should never to be allowed to be idle when they could be sewing. And they should often be taken out in the sun and shown the beauty of nature so they will come to feel the glory of their Creator.[30]

To this Charles Napier added an affecting preface. *His* focus was on how children need to develop their ready presence of mind so they can act with resolution and alacrity. The model he held up for his daughters was Napoleon. He wanted to make them like Napoleon.

***

Thomas Gordon, an historian of the Greek Revolution and a one-time member of the London Greek Committee,[31] wrote to Napier at about this time. Gordon told Napier his view's about the huge anti-Adam volume which was now before the public. Years earlier he had passed through Cephalonia in researching his history. Napier thought he had passed through too quickly – Gordon did not see all that Maitland had accomplished, and Napier made just this complaint about Gordon in his anti-Adam book. But still Gordon was appreciative, and he thought Napier ought to pursue his writing career:

> I have just read your astonishing book remarkable alike for its nervous style and terse reasoning. You seem to me to have turned Phoenix inside out, demolishing and pulverizing him. To me you have given a vast deal of light on subjects I did not understand and have changed my opinions on many things. It is a pity you do not employ your leisure in writing an extended series of military and political essays after the manner of Marshal Saxe – showing how troops ought to be treated and decayed countries improved: I do not think there is a man in Europe able to do it as well as yourself.[32]

Gordon was on his way to the new Kingdom of Greece which the Great Powers had imposed on the Turks. He was colonel and aide-de-camp to the new king, Otho. 'O that we had you in Hellas!' he told Napier. '[A]t least your work shall go there, and I hope our rulers will read it.' Perhaps this was some comfort to Napier – that his ideas on the balance between the social classes in Greece, on the justice system, on public works, on agricultural reform, and on so many other things were carefully studied by at least one official of the new Greek court. But it did not get Napier back to Cephalonia.

Departure and bereavement 101

Notes

1 WN, 1:428, 439; Adam to Col. Pitt, Acting Resident of Cephalonia, 21 May 1830, TNA CO 136/1275, fol. 610.
2 Napier, *Colonies*, 377.
3 Adam to Napier, 7 April 1830, TNA CO 136/1275, fols 631–32.
4 Napier to Captain J. R. Colthorst, 21 June, 26 August, 2 December 1831, NP, BL Add. MS 41063, fols 42–47; Kennedy to Napier, 23 July 1830, NP. BL Add. MS 54535, fols 33–34.
5 Napier, *Colonies*, 433; Napier's copies of Napier to Sir Howard Douglas, 6 July and 17 November 1835, NP, BL Add. MS 49127, fols 20–22, 46–48; Napier to Montferrato, transcribed by Susan Napier, March or April 1836, NP, BL Add. MS 49128, fols 4–6; Lord Edward Howard in Downing Street to Napier, 21 February 1841, NLB, fol. 13; Napier to Count Metaxa, 26 August 1850, Bodleian MS Eng. lett. c. 241, fols 235–38. For Napier's more recent reputation in Cephalonia, see Jim Potts, *The Ionian Islands and Epirus: A Cultural History* (Oxford: Oxford UP, 2010), 44–45, 64, 129, 136–37, 151; Lawrence Durrell, *The Greek Islands* (New York: Viking Press, 1978), 48.
6 Kennedy to Napier, 7 July 1832, NP, BL Add. MS 54535, fols 96–97.
7 Napier, *Colonies*, 395, 423; Kennedy to Napier, 30 October, 12 November 1830, 15 January 1831, NP, BL Add. MS 54535, fols 41, 43–44, 49.
8 Napier to Goderich, 25 December 1831, enclosure, TNA CO 136/63/5027; Napier, *Colonies*, 572. Kennedy appears to have told Napier about the speech in England the following spring. Previously he wrote Napier that he was too upset to set down a detailed account when very soon they would talk in person: Kennedy to Napier, 15 January 1831, NP, BL Add. MS 54535, fol. 49.
9 Napier, *Colonies*, 441–42.
10 Kennedy to Napier, 9 October 1830, NP, BL Add. MS 54535, fols 39–40.
11 Adam to Pitt, TNA CO 136/1275, 21 October 1830, fols 452–53; for the misunderstanding, Kennedy to Napier, 30 October, 12 November 1830, NP, BL Add. MS 54535, fols 41, 43–44.
12 Napier to Goderich, 25 December 1831, enclosure, TNA CO 136/63/5027.
13 W. Napier to Charles Napier, 19 March 1831, NP, BL Add. MS 54525, fol. 1. See also W. Napier to Charles Napier, [?] May 1831, fols 2–3.
14 William's main work was his *History of the War in the Peninsula and in the South of France, from the Year 1807 to the Year 1814*, 6 vols (London: Thomas and William Boone, 1828–1840). Napier's great successor, Charles Oman, said that Napier's was 'the one military classic whom most Englishmen have read'; further, '[e]very student of the Peninsular War, in short, must read Napier: but he must not think that, when the reading is finished, he has mastered the whole importance or meaning of the great struggle' – Oman, *A History of the Peninsular War*, 6 vols (Oxford: Oxford University Press, 1902–1930), 1:89, xii. Others argue that William's habit of picking favourites led him to distort history in order to sing their praises: David Gates, *The British Light Infantry Arm, c. 1790–1815: Its Creation, Training, and Operational Role* (London: B.T. Batsford, 1987), 112–17.
15 Napier to W. Napier, 7 December 1849, Bodleian MS Eng. lett. c. 243, fols 168–69.
16 Napier, *Colonies*, 379–80, 386–89.
17 Ibid, 396–446. He had worked through this hurried memorandum several times: Napier to Goderich, drafts, 18 March 1832, NP, TNA PRO 30/64/5, fols 14–19.
18 'Col. Napier's Reply to Sir F. Adam's Letter', TNA CO 136/64/1107, fols 433–87.
19 Kennedy to Napier, 27 March 1832, NP, BL Add. MS 54535, fols 73–74.
20 Quoted in Kennedy to Napier, 17 March 1832, NP, BL Add. MS 54535, fols 69–70.
21 Ibid. Kennedy underscored this advice a few days later: Kennedy to Napier, 22 March 1832, NP. BL Add. MS 54535, fols 71–72.
22 Kennedy to Napier, 22 May, 7, 26 June, [1 July] 1832, NP, BL Add. MS 54535, fols 83, 90–95.

102   *The radical abroad and at home*

23 Napier, *Colonies*, 379.
24 Ben Kafka, *The Demon of Writing: Powers and Failures of Paperwork* (New York: Zone Books, 2012), 78–79.
25 WN, 1:443.
26 Elizabeth Napier and Charles Napier to Louisa Napier, 17 March 1833, Bodleian MS Eng. lett. c. 240, fols 6–7; WN, 1:443; Mark Harrison, *Climates and Constitutions: Health, Race, Environment, and British Imperialism in India, 1600–1850* (Oxford: Oxford UP, 1999), 177–78, 183–85; Michael Durey, *The Return of the Plague: British Society and Cholera, 1831–32* (Dublin: Gill and Macmillan, 1979); David Arnold, *Colonizing the Body: State Medicine and Epidemic Disease in Nineteenth-Century India* (Berkeley and Los Angeles: University of California Press, 1993), 159–71.
27 Napier to Robertson, 10 August 1833, NP, BL Add. MS 49107, fols 1–2.
28 WN, 1:444.
29 Napier to Louisa Napier, 14 September 1833, Bodleian MS Eng. lett. c. 240, fols 9–10.
30 Elizabeth Napier, *The Nursery Governess* (London: T. & W. Boone, 1834). Also, children should not eat with their parents so they do not learn about dessert – 42.
31 Napier, *Colonies*, 54.
32 Thomas Gordon to Napier, 21 July 1833, NP, BL Add. MS 49114, fol. 73.

8   Australia and idealism

Now we must turn our attention back to England, as Napier himself finally began to do. What could be done about the poor? One particular solution to the great question of social injustice seemed to present itself to a few English thinkers in this period. Why not send the poor abroad and then send men like Napier to rule them? Rather than acceding to the rigours of the New Poor Law of 1834 – being locked up, separated from their families, set to backbreaking work, and given the least and worst – the English poor could simply depart. Emigration was the key, said Edward Gibbon Wakefield, who recently had burst upon the English scene as the next great prophet of social reform.

And now that he had finished his anti-Adam book, for a time it seemed that Charles Napier would be running the first of Wakefield's new colonies. He was selected as the founding governor of South Australia.

Napier had already considered taking his family to the Antipodes. When he left Cephalonia he thought of going to New South Wales, where he could 'rear young kangaroos to play with Susan and Emily'. But his wife was too old, he said.[1] Then in August 1834, Napier (now a widower) was contacted by the newly chartered South Australia Company. They asked him to found a colony on the southern coast of the Australian continent and serve as governor.[2] Napier's record in Cephalonia – including his six-hundred-page diatribe against Adam – showed enough ability and good sense that a party of strangers approached him to run their colony.

Wakefield, the man who had inspired the project, was tending his ailing daughter and so he did not become so directly involved in the daily business of this first colonial scheme as he would be in other colonization efforts later on. But it was Wakefield's presence that loomed above the South Australia scheme nonetheless. He had already begun to earn a measure of fame for his efforts to reform the empire, and he has since been called 'the builder of the British Commonwealth'.[3]

A few words on Wakefield and his plans are in order. Edward Gibbon Wakefield wanted to fight poverty in England by shipping to the colonies not so much the poorest of the poor, but rather a good number of respectable young couples from straitened circumstances. They would go to a new world and start a new life. But he did not want them to fan out across the

104 *The radical abroad and at home*

virgin countryside and become backwoodsmen. His middle-class emigrants would stay in the newly built towns, run shops, and ply their trades. Moreover, because of the vitality of these new towns, the rich would go out to the colonies, too. They would find the middle-class tradesmen to take care of them and the shops to shop in. And they would employ the *very* poor as their servants, which was the only trade which those at the bottom of society knew or were fit for. This would remove some of the poorest people from England.

What would keep the middle-class emigrants living in town instead of homesteading in the countryside? The open lands would be owned by the government and only sold to people who could afford them – the landowning class lured to the colony by town life and the presence of a decent number of tradesmen and servants. The money which the colonial government would raise from selling land would pay for still more middle-class immigrants. In this way the colonization effort would be financially self-sustaining. Wakefield called the system 'Colonial Reform'.

In 1834, only five years had passed since Wakefield had published his first book, *A Letter from Sydney*,[4] which set out his vision; most of his many colonization efforts still lay in the future. But what was already clear was that the main thrust of the Wakefieldian enterprise was to take the English class system at home and export it abroad.

Napier was walking into a Wakefieldian project but he would soon discover that he did not share Wakefield's opinions about politics and class. Napier's view was that British society should in the first instance be made *just*; if it were, there would be no 'surplus' of downtrodden people for the political economist to expel from their heartless native land. So while Napier very much liked the idea of administering and governing a new colony, his radicalism would soon run up against the more capitalistic, more conservative vision that Wakefield had in mind.[5] For Edward Gibbon Wakefield the basic problem in England was the poor. For Charles Napier, England's problem was the rich. And this was a point that Napier soon set out to explain.

Napier's most important book

And the words poured out of him. Yet before he could publish his book on the colony, he told the South Australia Commissioners in May 1835 that he would go there after all. In a dispute reminiscent of his contretemps with the Greek Committee, the Commissioners had refused Napier's repeated entreaties to send more money or more troops than what they had originally offered. The secretary of the South Australia Commissioners, Rowland Hill (who would soon reform the Post Office and invent the Penny Postage) told Napier that the Commissioners simply could not afford all the troops he had in mind. And nor were these troops necessary. Hill explained: 'The most flourishing British colonies in North America were founded without pecuniary aid from the mother country, and without the aid of a military force, though planted in the immediate neighbourhood of warlike Indian nations.'[6]

Australia and idealism 105

Napier's response was interesting. Many of the North American colonies had been destroyed by the Indians, he claimed, or in any case they had undergone long periods of hardship. He also saw problems with the Wakefieldian scheme itself and its self-financing mechanism. As Napier recognized, the backers at the very outset of the enterprise might not have enough money to employ everyone. The poor would be left to starve, or to plunder the better off. Order would have to be kept and soldiers were necessary. And to Rowland Hill's argument that no such body of soldiers had been required at the founding of some of the American colonies: Napier responded that William Penn was leading a party of Quakers, while the governor of South Australia would have no such advantage. So Napier did the sums for how much a police force (which would be hard to recruit) or more likely a sufficient body of soldiers would have to be paid. First Adam and now the South Australia Commissioners seemed to be innocent of important details and calculations like these.[7]

***

So Napier was not going. But in preparing for the journey he had already remarried.

He chose another widow, Frances Philips Alcock. The new Mrs Napier had been brought up by Napier's cousin Lady Lucy Foley. Her first husband was a navy captain, Richard Alcock (little more is known of him). Napier wanted his children to have a mother when they left the country. 'Tell your mama', Napier wrote to one of his girls very soon after the marriage, 'to order the *Penny Magazine* and make you put your spectacles on and read it to her!'[8]

When it was clear that there would be no move to Australia after all, Napier thought he would settle with his family in Bath. He certainly had his pangs of regret at not going to the Antipodes and at not having the active work that going there would have meant. But his new wife, Fanny, told him that she did not want to go anyway.[9] She seems to have been a good match, helping to calm him.

Napier on colonization

Napier was not going to South Australia but the woman he married to take there was still his wife and the book that he wrote on colonization was still his book. The woman he remained married to, and the book he went ahead and published. It was the most powerful and the most passionate statement he would ever write of his political views and of the assumptions and emotions from which they sprang.

Colonization, Particularly in Southern Australia, with some Remarks on Small Farms and Overpopulation poses questions of greater import than the fate of one small colony. Napier asks: '1st. Are we not the most *scientific*, and most wealthy nation in the world?' and '2nd. Are we not so miserable, so starving, that no one can say that the poor will not rise up upon, and destroy the rich?'[10]

From the very outset Napier attacks the cogency of the Wakefieldian programme. He examines four reasons people usually gave for founding a colony:

106   *The radical abroad and at home*

As an outlet for overpopulation; as a market 'for our over produce'; as a way of enlarging 'the field for employing capital'; and as 'a model by which to correct our system of Colonial Government'.[11] Napier spends a good deal of time ranging back and forth through politics and history to *correct* each of these impressions about any good that a colony could do. For one thing, there was no real overpopulation – no need for the United Kingdom to send anyone abroad. Further, to fight poverty it made no sense telling the poor to lead thriftier lives or trying to get them to have fewer children. The political economists who were most closely associated with these positions – Harriet Martineau and Thomas Malthus – Napier criticizes by name. To inveigle the poor as Martineau and Malthus did, trying to prevent them from spending their time or having their families as they might see fit, was something that Napier found insulting, when the real trouble lay in the inequitable distribution of wealth in society.

The proper solution was reforming agriculture and putting waste lands to use. Ireland alone could support *thirty million people* in comfort rather than eight million people in poverty, and it would not have to send families into exile.[12]

And yet Napier marvelled that the rich always seemed to be more concerned with their own shallow sense of oppression than with the real suffering of the poor at home or the emigrants sent abroad. Comfortable people complain very loudly about having to pay the poor rates and having to see paupers in the streets, Napier says. But when the rich men ask 'are we to be devoured by poor rates and by paupers!', Napier replies (as he puts it): 'I hope so with all my heart.'[13]

> When I hear of great farmers groaning under the weight of the poor laws, I think of Hannibal's scornful smile when the Carthaginian Senate wept. Reproached for his mirth, he answered, '*ye weep for the loss of your money, but ye wept not for the miseries of your country; scorn for you, is sorrow for Carthage!*'[14]

The writer Simonde de Sismondi had made a similar point, he adds. Napier then quotes Sismondi for extra emphasis. But he claims that he did not really *need* to quote Sismondi, for he – Charles Napier – has no need to seek support in the work of any political economist, so sure is he of his own views.[15]

In other words, in this discussion of how the rich had robbed the poor not only of money, but also of a chance for emotional fulfilment in their native landscape, Napier has taken so much from Sismondi's work, or he has found so many of his own opinions more fully developed in the pages of Sismondi, that he – Charles Napier – has begun to worry that his own book might not seem very original. And well he might worry about this point. All through the rest of Napier's life, Sismondi's work was to be the touchstone of his thinking.

Who was this Sismondi? A native of Geneva, Jean-Charles Léonard Simonde was driven by the French Revolution first to England and then to Italy. He was originally an historian, but on his travels he began to observe what rapid economic change was doing to the poor. Eventually he came to admire Napoleon's attempt to create a politically and economically balanced society, especially in the constitution around which the Emperor rallied the nation during the Hundred Days. Under this new constitution, each of the different social classes would have its say in the state and its own share in national economic life.[16]

Sismondi went on to write a number of works in which he attacked the principle of *laissez-faire* so prevalent in Scotland and England. The British had removed all obstacles to the increase of wealth, and so the wealth of Great Britain had wonderfully increased! But so had poverty, degradation, and – even for the rich – insecurity. That was not all. Paper money and the Corn Laws had led to an overconcentration of wealth in one class, and one effect of this was the moral corruption of those who enjoyed the wealth. Meanwhile, speculative overproduction by those who were trying to maximize their income at all costs – farmers and manufacturers alike – had created a cycle of boom and bust that hurt everyone. The attempt to maximize income with machinery and every manner of cost-cutting had ground the workers and the farmhands into the dust, turning them into mere 'operatives'.

Sismondi argued that what had been forgotten was that maximizing wealth was *not* the proper goal for social science or public policy; social investigation should centre instead on how to maximize happiness. If wealth is not to corrupt those who possess it, it should come to them only through work, and each class in society should have its appropriate share of both the work that has to be done and the fruits of that work. 'Social science' was misguided when it ignored its highest goal – increasing happiness. It was equally misguided when it tried to maximize some abstract measure of national wealth rather than paying attention to how that wealth was distributed. Ideas like these would become bread and butter for Napier too. So would Sismondi's most basic assumption: that in analyzing the political and economic health of a country, one should look first at whether the agricultural workers had the secure possession of their land.[17]

***

Sismondi has been criticized for diagnosing society's ills without prescribing any cure. So Napier would seem to have been following in his master's footsteps when in his *Colonization* book he simply rejected many of the reform proposals that were in the air at the time – whether Martineau's program of preaching to the poor and making them thriftier and harder working, Malthus' belief in restraining the growth of the population, or Wakefield's desire to ship the poor abroad. But if we look more carefully at Sismondi's ideas and Napier's, too, we can appreciate why both men stood aloof from these modest reforms. For them, economic growth had been allowed to proceed *too quickly*, so that in the interests of maximizing the wealth of the rich, the poor had been left behind. But if the *speed* of social change was the problem, then quick solutions to reform the behaviour of the poor or reduce their number was not the answer. As a very perceptive reading of Sismondi that was published in the 1920s nicely points

108   *The radical abroad and at home*

out, Sismondi stressed slow evolutionary change; so the prescriptions that he had in mind would have to be just as slow in their effects.[18]

For Sismondi, then, revolution was not the answer and neither was violence, even if as a matter of justice the rich deserved anything they might get.[19] Violence would not bring back the balance between classes and the slow social and economic improvement that had been lost. It would do nothing to alleviate the human misery of the operatives in the fields and the factories.[20] Competent, detail-oriented government on behalf of the poor – Napoleon's kind of government – was the answer to social ills. Government *by* the poor, who had not been educated to it, would do no good.

Sismondi's main prescription, therefore – like Napier's – was a competent and activist state, working on behalf of everyone and not merely the rich. Sismondi wanted the state authorities to impose a number of innovations to bring back balance and fairness and to put a brake on runaway growth. He wanted a limitation on work hours. He wanted a minimum wage; an end to child labour; the introduction of old-age pensions, health insurance, and profit-sharing for workers; and the reform of inheritance law and landholding.[21] The idea of competent administration we can see here – an activist government, state compassion rather than private charity, and a distrust by the authorities of the prescriptions of the wealthy, for the rich do tend to be self-serving – also echo the views in Napier's anti-Adam book. In Cephalonia, Napier had rejected on principle any private measures during the famine, and he created a system of state famine relief instead. As we have seen, he intervened in the cases before the Cephalonian courts to bring balance back to the justice system, always assuming that when the weak complained against the rich and powerful, the weak were in the right. In each court case he nonetheless went on to check the facts, working carefully through the evidence rather than accepting any ideological shortcut around the hard and detailed work of governance and administration.

The writings of Sismondi, with their rejection of the policies of *laissez-faire*, their rejection of the fetish of economic growth, and their idealization of an activist administrative state working for the poor rather than the rich, appealed deeply to Napier. Yet it must be said that Napier was no committed intellectual. In later years Sismondi would go on to write about several other subjects. He would describe the pleasure-seeking and the cupidity of British officials in India, as well as the aloofness with which the British community kept itself separate from the Indian people.[22] Napier would complain about these things as well. But there is no evidence that Napier ever read what Sismondi had to say about the Raj. He had taken what he wanted from the Genevan and it seems that he felt no need to explore further.

British farmers and why they should be liquidated

Although Napier would never depart from Sismondi's general way of looking at things, he was broader and bloodier in his criticism of the rich than Sismondi was. In the new Australian book, Napier claimed that the rich were

Australia and idealism 109

no more than a polished mob, a mob that smelled good. Their opinions should count for no more than anyone else's. Yet they had the right to hang those who disagreed with them. Colonization is 'grand', Napier wrote, but it will not solve the problem of a society dominated by the rich. Colonization should not distract us from real social questions.[23]

Napier stressed that unlike Wakefield he wanted to see a world of small farmers on small landholdings. This was the system of happy, self-sufficient peasants that he had grown accustomed to in Normandy. Owning their own small farms, the French peasants knew farming in all its aspects and took pride in them. The French system of independent small farms contrasted with the pattern dominant in England, where farm labourers were employed as hired hands on large estates. Their employers were large-scale farmer-capitalists who did none of the physical work. The farmer-capitalists did not own the land they managed. Instead they leased it from the ground landlords, the aristocrats. So the English farmer-capitalists were middlemen standing between the owners of the land and those who truly worked it. They provided management, tools, and liquid capital. By contrast, the labourers underneath them were deskilled and demoralized.[24]

The existence of this system of labour in the English countryside would hardly have been news to Napier's readers. What he added was that the farmers and their families alike were simply a drain on the countryside and the British nation. They were extra mouths to feed, and they wasted the country's treasure in trying to maintain a false cultural and emotional position, for they accustomed themselves to fine houses and fine furniture. Napier says that the whole class of English farmers were an unnecessary burden carried by those who actually did the labour. Or in his words: 'I speak of large farmers as a *class*, when I say they are injurious. But, as individuals, I am sure there are among them, *many* talented, and excellent men.'[25] It was the false consciousness of this class that was the great challenge. The small farmers who *ought* to occupy the land, working it themselves if the French system were adopted, would never raise their children to think they were too good to get their hands dirty. Their children might never learn 'the history of the Grand Chartreuse, or the Vatican', Napier says, and they might never see the *Penny Magazine*, which he wanted his own daughters to read. But the farm children would learn the habits of industry and self-reliance: 'The *farm is a school*, and a noble school, too' (emphasis original).[26]

With his vision of small farmers who were little schooled in the history of the Grand Chartreuse or the *Penny Magazine* but who could take pride in doing all the work of the farm with their own hands, Napier was looking forward to a wholesale removal from the countryside of the middle class, its values, its big houses and styles of furnishing, its claret, and its refined children brought up to read fine literature but never to till the soil themselves. Napier wanted to replace all of that with a sturdy working-class culture, one like he saw among the Norman peasants who were so learned in the land and the practical knowledge that it takes to run a farm. In a private letter in 1835, Napier predicted that when some people have five times the land they need to

110   *The radical abroad and at home*

support themselves, and others have none and thus starve, then '*physical force*' (his emphasis) will eventually right the wrongs. If the landlords do not of their own accord 'give up the grasping avarice described by Jesus Christ as inherent in the rich' and rent the land out as small farms, then the common people will rise up and take the land they need. He did not want violence, he stressed, but he added: 'I would rather see Civil War, than see the people of England treated as they now are.' The common people might indeed be driven to civil conflict and republicanism (Napier adds that he hated both) if the Whig Party did not stop withholding any real reform when they were in office and stirring up violent dreams of change when they were out.[27]

Napier wanted the rich to divide up their estates of their own accord and rent them out as small farms, but nonetheless as a good Sismondian he did not want them to do it *immediately*. There would be danger if the new yeomanry – that is to say, the new class of small farmers with land they could manage with their own labour[28] – were to be established in the English countryside too quickly. Napier explains in *Colonization* that if this productive new class, working for itself and living more abundantly and with the greater self-respect that comes from honest work, were to spread too rapidly through the land – if their physical and psychological comfort came too soon – then certain other very necessary reforms in the British state might never come to pass. So if the Duke of Devonshire's estates were broken into several thousand twenty-acre farms, there would soon be ten or twelve thousand 'staunch . . . retainers' on his land. The duke could use them to prevent any future reform. Political progress would stop short:

> Talk of democratic principles indeed! I should like to see what progress such principles could make among a nation of *well-fed*, industrious small farmers? . . . [S]uch men might not bestir themselves sufficiently to enforce the reforms that are so necessary, in some of the departments of state; . . . they might not take the part of an individual opposed by some great man.[29]

Napier said he found exactly this species of premature conservatism among the well-fed yeomanry of Caen whom he had spoken to. And as members of the National Guard they helped put down the republicans in Paris.[30]

It is significant, too, that although in Napier's vision the middle class of the countryside would be replaced by his stable, culturally working-class yeomanry, nonetheless the landowning aristocrats would be able to maintain their own level of culture (which was the culture in which Napier was at home). It is only the farmers who would have to give up their pretensions and join the working class.

***

Much of the rest of the book Napier took from Australian articles and guidebooks written by others, adding only the occasional comment himself. But

Australia and idealism   111

a few of Napier's comments in the balance of the book need to be reviewed if we are to complete our picture of his radicalism.

One recurrent theme: He was no more fond of the Whigs' Factory Acts than he was of their Poor Law. Under the new legislation, Napier says, a child is never made to work more than ten hours a day, nor ever beaten with a stick '*much* thicker than a man's thumb'.[31]

He also says something about human nature and social relations across the colour line. In South Australia, he tells his readers, only a strong enlightened kind of leadership like his own could keep colonist from killing native. We see one of the main reasons he wanted to go out with extra troops: so the natives might be saved from the kind of 'horrid cruelties' and outright extermination wrought by the supposedly civilized colonists.[32]

For everyone has the right to be happy, Napier explains. He can 'see no reason why the savage should not choose his own way, as well as other people'. They are not some lower order of humanity, unable to work, although some people assert as much. The natives of Australia are as 'highly gifted' as anyone else. He thinks they might well form part of the rural workforce in twenty years if the distrust they feel towards the murderous white settlers can ever be overcome. And interbreeding might further unite the two peoples.[33]

Socially the natives have a different '*degree* of *progress*' and 'great nobleness of mind and talents'.[34] 'Their practices are in many instances horrible; so are ours but in a different way.'[35] Insisting that they should move off the land and settle near the Europeans is robbery; and as it deprives them of their food and brings them into contact with disease, it is an act of 'progressive extermination'.[36] The natives of Australia cannot change their way of life quickly enough (Napier is ever the Sismondian) to cope with these policies. Soon they would be huddled together like British themselves, and – again like the British of Napier's day – they would be 'crazy' and immoral from the overcrowding of the cities, cowering under gaslights, and trying to recover their health with blue bottles of patent medicine.[37] The British people have made 'National Wealth . . . our God'. They 'make large mercantile fortunes by the wholesale murder of infants, in our manufactures, while all around is misery, despair, and famine!' In the colonies, too, we 'civilized' and 'religious' and 'moral' people have inflicted 'every sort of torture, mental and bodily', shooting the natives' food (the kangaroos) to protect ours (the sheep), and calling the natives uncivilized 'because they do not love us'. As governor, Napier says he will impose capital punishment upon those who murder the natives.[38]

Meanwhile the European settlers had made Australia a hell, he explained. They insisted on treating the natives as an inferior group instead of as individuals. The natives of Australia, he insists, cannot all of them be lumped together into one or another civilizational or psychological stage of humanity: 'I repeat it; this "gradatory scale" is one composed of individuals, not nations.' Many Aboriginals are smarter and better than many of the European officials. For individuals are always different, he says, and he spends a good deal of space on the matter.[39] He demonstrates still more clearly than he was able to do in

112   *The radical abroad and at home*

his Cephalonian book that he includes the non-whites in his overall vision of everyone living as free people on their own land and doing as they please. Napier sees them as diverse and rational adults, not as some sub-European stage in the development of humanity towards a European or English standard.

Charles Napier's concern here is with the colonies of white settlement and the crimes the settlers commit; nowhere in this book does he re-examine the idea of freeing Oriental peoples from Islamic rule. But we should note that even in these pages he wanted to enforce an idea of universal morality upon the white settlers, just as he would later try to enforce an idea of universal morality by removing the rulers of Sind and taking control of their country. For him, the question in each case was what would it take to bring freedom to the lower classes and the oppressed?

Notes

1 Napier to his sister, 1832, given in WN, 1:441–43. Sarah Susan eventually became Susan.
2 Napier, *Colonization*, iii; South Australian Literary and Scientific Association, *Laws of the South Australian Literary and Scientific Association* (London: privately printed, 1834); Douglas Pike, *Paradise of Dissent* (London: Longmans, Green, and Co., 1957), 102–03.
3 Philip Temple, *A Sort of Conscience: The Wakefields* (Auckland, New Zealand: Auckland UP, 2002), 160; Paul Bloomfield, *Edward Gibbon Wakefield: Builder of the British Commonwealth* (London: Longmans, Green, & Co., 1961).
4 [Edward Gibbon Wakefield], 'A Letter from Sydney, the Principal Town of Australasia [1829]', in *A Letter from Sydney and Other Writings* (London: J.M. Dent, 1929), 3–106.
5 While Wakefield was well to the right of Napier, an argument exists that he retained much of his early radicalism, sympathized with the Chartists, and wanted a more equal society in the colonies than in England – John E. Martin, ' "A Small Nation on the Move": Wakefield's Theory of Colonisation and Relationship between State and Labour in the Mid-Nineteenth Century', in Friends of the Turnbull Library (eds), *Edward Gibbon Wakefield and the Colonial Dream: A Reconsideration* (Wellington, New Zealand: GP Publications, 1997), 106–22 at 108–12.
6 Napier, *Colonization*, ix, xii–xxx. Napier's quotation from Hill is word perfect – see Hill to Napier, 22 May 1835, given in Great Britain, Parliament, *Copies of any Correspondence in the Colonial Department Relative to the Establishment of the Settlement of South Australia, since the Year 1831, and its Present Financial Difficulties* (1841 session 1), No. 129, 53.
7 Ibid, xxi–xxiii.
8 Napier to Robertson, 9 March 1837, NP, BL Add. MS 49107, fol. 3; Napier to W. Napier, 30 November 1834, given in WN, 1:454–57; Napier to Tristram Kennedy (in Frances Napier's deposition of 25 September 1835), NP, BL Add. MS 49127, fols 44–45; Napier to his daughter Emily Cephalonia, by July 1835, NP, BL Add. MS 49148, fol. 3.
9 Napier to his sister Louisa, 29 July 1835, Bodleian MS Eng. lett. c. 240, fols 40–41.
10 Napier, *Colonization*, 101.
11 Ibid, 2.
12 Ibid, 8, 10.
13 Ibid, 12. For the view Napier complained of: Nassau William Senior, *Three Lectures on the Rate of Wages*, 2nd edn (London: John Murray 1831; New York: Augustus M. Kelley, 1966), xi–xiv.
14 Napier, *Colonization*, 12.
15 Ibid, 13.
16 Jean-Charles Léonard Simonde de Sismondi, 'Interview with Napoleon', in Sismondi, *Political Economy and the Philosophy of Government: A Series of Essays Selected from the Works*

of M. de Sismondi (London: John Chapman, 1847; New York: Augustus M. Kelley, 1966), 53–61. Some English radicals took the same view: Stuart Semmel, 'English Radicals and "Legitimacy": Napoleon in the Mirror of History', *Past & Present* 167 (May 2000), 140–75.

17 Jean-Charles Léonard Simonde de Sismondi, 'Preface to the New Principles of Political Economy', *Révue Encyclopéique* (September 1826), given in Sismondi, *Political Economy and the Philosophy of Government*, 113–22.

18 Mao-Lan Tuan, *Simonde de Sismondi as an Economist*, Columbia University Studies in the Social Sciences 298 (New York: Columbia UP, 1927; New York: AMS Press, 1968), 112–14.

19 Gareth Stedman Jones postulates that Sismondi left most British radicals cold because they blamed the Old Corruption for Britain's ills, while for Sismondi social inequality and inefficiency grew instead out of overproduction. In Napier's view, the workers were impoverished by *both* phenomena. See Gareth Stedman Jones, *An End to Poverty?: An Historical Debate* (New York: Columbia UP, 2004), 154–55, 182, 185–87.

20 Tuan, *Simonde de Sismondi as an Economist*, 119.

21 Ibid, 114–15, 118–29.

22 Jean-Charles Léonard Simonde de Sismondi, 'The Colonies of the Ancients Compared with Those of the Moderns, as Regards their Influence on the Happiness of Mankind', *Tiré de la Bibliothèque universelle de Genève* (January 1837), given in Sismondi, *Political Economy and the Philosophy of Government*, 245–85 at 277; C. A. Bayly, *Recovering Liberties: Indian Thought in the Age of Liberalism and Empire* (Cambridge: Cambridge UP, 2012), 47, 85.

23 Napier, *Colonization*, 10–11.

24 Ibid, 14–15, 17–22.

25 Ibid, 25n.

26 Ibid, 23–25, quotations at 25. For how *Penny Magazine* showed the world to the British people in a new way, see Patricia Anderson, *The Printed Image and the Transformation of Popular Culture, 1790–1860* (Oxford: Clarendon Press, 1991).

27 Napier, *Colonization*, 26; Napier to Edward Bunbury [1835], NP, BL Add. MS 49127, fols 32–44 at 38–39, 42–43.

28 Some would define yeomen as those having at least sixty acres, not the twenty Napier had in mind. See Kathryn Beresford, '"Witnesses for the Defence": The Yeomen of Old England and the Land Question, *c.* 1815–1837', in Matthew Cragoe and Paul Readman (eds), *The Land Question in Britain, 1750–1850* (Basingstoke: Palgrave Macmillan, 2010), 37–56 at 37–39.

29 Napier, *Colonization*, 27.

30 Ibid; for the Parisian events Napier refers to, see the *Annual Register* for 1834, 350–53.

31 Napier, *Colonization*, 97n–98n.

32 Ibid, 94–97, quotation at 94–95.

33 Ibid, 104–05, 123, 125, quotations at 99 and 169.

34 Ibid, 94.

35 Ibid, 125.

36 The idea that civilization meant extermination would occur to other nineteenth-century figures as well – see Edward Wilson, *Rambles at the Antipodes: A Series of Sketches of Moreton Bay, New Zealand, the Murray River, and South Australia, and the Overland Route* (London: W.H. Smith and Son, 1859), 25–26. Very different was the idea that it was the primitivism or behaviour of the subject peoples themselves that caused their decline – a view amply documented by Patrick Brantlinger, *Dark Vanishings: Discourse on the Extinction of Primitive Races, 1800–1930* (Ithaca, NY: Cornell UP, 2003).

37 Napier, *Colonization*, 102–03.

38 Ibid, 96–97, 97n, 178–79.

39 Ibid, 144–47, 150–51, 155–56, 169–70, quotation at 151.

9 Flogging and politics

When the Australian project fell through, Napier threw himself into a new work. On the heels of *Colonization* he wrote a two-hundred-seventy-page book on the abolition of flogging in the army in peacetime. This work needs to be looked at with some care as well. For what he had written about public order in this volume may have been the reason he was posted to the north of England.

***

At this period, military flogging was once again a subject of debate in the British press, as it had been when Napier was a young officer in the first decade of the century.[1] Horror stories had appeared of soldiers being flogged to death at the order of their commander.

But even when flogging was not carried so far, it was horrific. Recent regulations had reduced the number of lashes to which a soldier could be sentenced. After 1836 the limit was two hundred.[2] Previously soldiers could be subjected to *many hundreds* of lashes. These extreme sentences were delivered several hundred lashes at a time. The unfortunate man was sent to the hospital for his skin to re-grow before he could be strung up again for the next instalment. A soldier would sometimes have to recuperate in the hospital three or four times before the whole sentence could be administered. Napier had seen this happen more than once. It disgusted him as it disgusted most everyone else to see the man's pink, newly healed flesh laid bare for the lash.

Napier tells the reader that he always had to turn away from the first few lashes in any flogging. Yet under military regulations he and all the assembled men were expected to watch as the lashes mounted up to three hundred, to four hundred, or more. After three hundred or so, the man would stop his screaming and writhing. All the skin was gone. The drummer – it was the drummers who did the flogging – seemed to be attacking a lump of dead bloody flesh. The assembled soldiers kept looking on with what Napier describes as an almost silent whisper. Indeed, his stirring account of this whisper of horror and the other terrors of flogging made an impression that reverberated across British culture and the growing public debate, being noted in *Punch*.[3]

Flogging and politics   115

For he knew all about what was going on. Having men flogged was a normal part of an officer's life. As Napier tells us, he had ordered men flogged on hundreds of occasions throughout his military career. He had to do so because the crime of desertion had only two legal punishments. One was flogging and the other was death. Flogging was also the only punishment in military law for being drunk on duty. A military unit could not function if drunkenness on duty much less desertion went unpunished. Napier says he never sentenced a man to so many strokes as to require multiple hospitalizations, but he added that *any* flogging left the man in the hospital for weeks on end and scarred for life. He was against the practice for several reasons. It was torture; it was uneven in the pain it caused, and uneven in the risk of death for the recipient; and above all it demoralized and brutalized all concerned – dulling the morals of the soldiers witnessing it and making a hero out of the criminal for having endured it.[4]

The usual argument for flogging, as Napier detailed the matter, is that the majority of the soldiers come from the dregs of society, especially in the radically expanded army of the Napoleonic period. Many were habitual criminals who were accustomed to violence before they ever took the king's shilling. So without the lash they could never be kept from plundering and carrying out rape against the civilian population, *even within England.*

Napier rejected this contention. He insisted that British soldiers were less criminal than the general population, not more so, and in any case they were better than the soldiers of any other army. When the British forces came home after Waterloo and the soldiers fanned out across the land, the people of England prepared themselves for a rise in crime, and a rise in crime there was – as the professional thieves of London went on a spree of robberies in the metropolis and the Home Counties. On each occasion, the real criminals would send the magistrates after the innocent soldiers passing through. The magistrates admitted this afterward; and indeed as we know from sources beyond the writings of Charles Napier, the soldiers had behaved rather well.[5]

Napier admitted that in time of war the criminal soldiers did indeed have to be kept from terrorizing the civilians of whatever foreign country they were operating in. Their good behaviour could be ensured only on pain of death or the lash. But this was not the case in peacetime, he stressed. During peace the men ought to be led as much by rewards as by punishments, and no soldier should be flogged. To make this case more fully, Napier devoted several chapters to a general system of rewards that might be instituted in the army. Briefly: He wanted pensions for soldiers (none existed in the army); and he wanted to give them medals (the common soldiers had earned medals only for Waterloo – no other medals or honours of any kind had been awarded to enlisted men during the whole of the French Revolutionary and Napoleonic Wars). Napier also wanted to give the men access to a savings bank so they might have a safe place to put their money. As things stood, they had to keep all of it in their pockets all of the time. So they had all of their money with

116 *The radical abroad and at home*

them whenever they passed a wine shop with their friends. (Captains could hold money for their men, but this was not a universal practice, and it would hardly remain practical if a large number of the men were to take advantage of it all at once. There was no other physical place where the soldier's money could be kept except on their bodies.)

Having so much cash at hand led to drunkenness. Napier says that even the soldiers who had no particular desire to drink were forced to spend their time in the canteens nonetheless. There they found a 'Pandemonium' of noise where no reading or quiet conversation was possible. The men were indeed forced to be there, because as Napier had discussed in his Cephalonia book, the army signed contracts with some of the canteen owners and the soldiers were forbidden from going anywhere else. When he found soldiers drinking wine out in the open in the Cephalonian countryside (rather than drinking in their canteen, where they were supposed to be), Napier tells us he always contrived not to see them, but whenever they were brought before him he had to ratify their punishments. Meanwhile he had organized games and considered founding libraries.[6] One soldier who served under Napier in Argostoli wrote that General Orders would come out from time to time saying that the men were supposed to be in the canteens – and garrison orders came at the same time saying the opposite. One order began: 'Lt. Colonel Napier does not approve of the system of coddling up British soldiers like a pack of old women.'[7]

In the flogging book Napier suggested several detailed strategies for keeping the soldiers from getting drunk and earning the lash. He also suggested some alternative punishments for when alcohol did get them in trouble. The drunken soldiers might be sent to the hospital to have their backs blistered on the medical fiction that they had a fever. Their blisters would heal in a few days without scarring. This strategy had worked well in Guernsey with a drunken and mutinous regiment, Napier tells us. But after their move to Bermuda there was not enough blistering powder to waste in this way and so flogging resumed. Napier coyly describes the blistering experiment as having been carried out by 'a friend', but he was the man in charge of the regiment being discussed.[8]

***

Although Napier wanted flogging abolished in peacetime, he supported its continuance in time of war: On the battlefield, men had to be flogged or shot on the spot to keep them from killing or pillaging the civilian population of the war zone. Napier described the suffering – the robbery, the murder – that would be inflicted upon the civilians if the soldiers were not flogged. Also, soldiers needed to be hanged or flogged so they would not desert to the other side or flee altogether. Otherwise wars would be lost.

For soldiers had to be made to obey. Napier did not want blind obedience from the men, he tells us, but he explained that he wanted something that did not fall far short of it. To make his point clear he discussed a battlefield emergency: What if men were ordered to shell a private house around the ears

Flogging and politics   117

of the family that occupied it, leaving the father holding the broken bodies of his children? Napier expected the men to obey their orders even in situations like that – or victory might indeed go to the enemy and 'millions' more women and children could be killed. And *that* level of obedience in wartime required enforcing military discipline with the lash and the gallows. But only in wartime were such punishments needed because only in wartime could so daunting but critical a need for obedience arise. (The blame for shelling the house would lie, Napier believed, with the politicians ordering the war and not with the soldiers obeying the order.)[9]

Napier himself would continue to order floggings throughout his military career.[10] And sometimes he wanted the men flogged. When he was in India, the only way to punish a serious infraction even by a good soldier was a full court-martial. But often the court martial could only turn the man out of the army on the spot. This was hardly a practical step when the force was surrounded by enemy tribes near the Afghan border. Napier wanted the offending soldiers flogged and forgiven rather than court-martialled and forever lost to the army.[11] Indeed, while the practice of flogging was abolished in the Indian Army by the time Napier went there, it was brought back to a limited degree by Governor-General Henry Hardinge in 1845. Flogging was reintroduced so it could be applied to the drunken lower-class European conscripts – not to the high-status, Indian volunteers. Napier applauded its reintroduction.[12]

***

In writing the flogging book, Napier could not entirely repress his politics. The book includes some colourful language about the crimes of the Poor Law Guardians and the M.P.s who had passed the Poor Law in the first place – damning the Poor Law Commissioners for tearing families apart, and damning equally 'the horrid child torturing murderers in the manufactories' for killing their child workers. Nor did the British state itself escape Napier's criticism for the high taxes that crushed the poor. He frankly admitted that he was in favour of annual parliaments, universal suffrage, and the secret ballot. But he said that *militarily* he was in favour of a despotic style of governance over the army in the field, and he saw 'no incongruity in these opinions'.[13]

Yet in most of the book Napier showed a more restrained and politic side. He admitted that his overall argument that flogging ought to be kept in wartime but abolished during peace may have pleased no one, whether Whig, Radical, or Tory, who wanted either to abolish flogging or defend it. But intriguingly he said that in this 'age of discussion' he had a more modest ambition for the book than currying favour in whichever corner. Public opinion was turning against the practice of flogging and he wanted to help shape a more intelligent outcome.[14] So in much of the book he takes pains to seem thoughtful and sincere, a wise, even moderate officer with a wealth of practical ideas about how to lead men, how to punish them more humanely and how to reward them creatively. Napier made a convincing case that he knew how to defuse soldiers' resentments rather than magnifying them. Anyone in a high position reading

118   *The radical abroad and at home*

this book and wondering whom to appoint to deal with the Chartists might well consider Napier for the job – as much I think from the tenor and wisdom of most of the text as from the rather short passages that he included on how to deal with civilian rioters.

But indeed Napier covered that subject as well and we ought to examine what he said. He discussed a number of riots going back to the eighteenth century. In his view, a lack of definition on some legal key points often left the soldiers between a rock and a hard place in terms of criminal responsibility. Soldiers had been prosecuted in the civilian courts for what they had been ordered to do under martial law. Napier insists they should never have to fear civil prosecution simply for carrying out their orders. And there was another problem with how martial law had been applied in the case of domestic riot – for there was ample room for the magistrates to exploit the military forces if they wanted to. The local authorities were altogether too cavalier when declaring a state of martial law, and they had used the soldiers as their agents in the oppression of the people.[15]

He suggested a new arrangement. If they were faced with civil unrest, the magistrates should first do their best to quieten things. If some of the magistrates were hotheads, then the calmer magistrates should get them out of the way for a time. And the remaining magistrates might even let some of the guilty rioters escape in the interests of avoiding a broader conflict. Everything should be done to restore the peace while civilian law was still in effect. But after the Riot Act was read, and the magistrates had decided that their constables could no longer control things, then civilian law would be entirely suspended. There should be no period at all – and certainly no extended period – of overlapping civilian and military authority, with each side ready to blame the other for the inevitable confusion and escalation in the level of violence.

On being handed authority – full authority under which all civil law was suspended – the army commander would in essence follow a script: He would announce that he would open fire after a period of time set by law, a period that everyone would understand. And at that point he should indeed open fire with his soldiers coming under no legal risk. They should only shoot at the rioters who had thrown stones.

Napier explained that under the current confused system of joint military/ civilian control, sometimes the magistrates would tell the soldiers *not* to shoot back or not to use their bayonets, while nonetheless they ordered the military to charge and restore the peace with only their swords and pistols. So the soldiers could be taunted and stoned without being able to respond with adequate force. And if they became frustrated and angry in the mêlée, out of their anger might come a tragedy.

Napier wanted a new system where soldiers could defend themselves and yet any casualties that might result from indiscipline or panic would be avoided. Further, the magistrates would not call out the troops unnecessarily, for once they read the Riot Act they would have no power to order the soldiers about. And if there were questions afterwards about the justice of the proceedings, parliament should investigate and punish the magistrates themselves, and punish *only* the magistrates and not the soldiers who had followed their orders. He argues that the civil authorities should be held to account either for calling out the troops needlessly when the threat was not so serious; or if there actually had been a riot that required military intervention, then for so oppressing the citizens as to drive them to violence.[16]

Yes, oppression. Napier stressed that martial law and the Irish Coercion Bill were still thought necessary. Why was this the case? Something 'has made the labouring classes poor and miserable; and consequently increased the number of bad characters among them'.[17] The subtext of this statement – I would argue – is that what poor economic conditions had done to increase the influence of the worst men, better conditions could reverse. Perfect social peace was not to be expected in the foreseeable future, but Napier's words did suggest grounds for hope. Patient work and greater restraint on the part of the magistrates might bring rewards, as patient work had brought rewards with the drunken soldiers. Napier's vision of a clear but restrained use of force in calming civil unrest might well have seemed attractive to a government worried about insurrection.

So while it was clear from all the radicalism in the flogging book what side Napier was on, it was also clear that in the end he believed in order. Indeed, in an historical novel about the Norman conquest that he wrote at this time (it was not published until after his death), Napier explained:

> If the people rebel the king knows that his ministers are bad, and 'tis his duty to remedy the wrong; and holy and kingly it is to do so. Let him punish also: not the people driven to madness, but those who oppress them. To effect this he must be deaf to ministers; for they, being the real culprits, will bewilder him with falsehoods; he must listen to his people. . . . Yet insurgents must be held in check for they will commit wild and horrid excesses; they cannot help it: they rise against wrong, are passionate, and under no control. Do them justice and they will be steadfast.[18]

The politics of the late 1830s

If Napier's ideas about keeping the peace were becoming apparent to a wider audience, so were his radical views in politics. When Napier set up his household in Bath in 1836 his brother William was also living in the city. Soon they were both attending radical meetings – William had been doing so since at least 1833.[19] Charles Napier involved himself in the politics of the town as soon as he arrived. For one thing, he now enjoyed the franchise for the first time. In the houses which he had rented in various places before moving to France, he had always paid the local rates through his landlord rather than directly. This meant he had no vote. Along with six-sevenths of the adult male population of the United Kingdom, he paid too little in taxes to demonstrate that he had a sufficient stake in society, so he was not entrusted with the franchise under the qualifications set forth in the 1832 Reform Act.[20] Napier was a colonel in the

120 *The radical abroad and at home*

Army, he was disfigured by the wounds he sustained in the service of king and country, he was a Companion of the Most Noble The Order of the Bath (as of 1815[21]), he was a former colonial official, governing 60,000 people for the better part of a decade, he was in his fifties, and he had written several books, but as yet he had never been allowed to vote.

Yet now that he was settled into a house under different rental terms, this had changed, and he plunged himself into the campaign against the Whig ministry in January 1837, speaking alongside such radicals and Utilitarians as Sir William Molesworth and the long-time Bath M.P. John Roebuck. Napier helped to organize the local Radical Committee. At the public dinners, the various loyal toasts to the Royal Family were followed by a very different toast, 'The People, the only source of legitimate power' – which was the traditional toast of the Radicals.[22]

John Roebuck was defeated that July. He had the support of the majority of the population, but of course the majority of the population did not enjoy the franchise. It was Charles Napier who drafted the community address of consolation to Roebuck – something which he said he took more pains over than anything else he ever wrote. And in this address he stressed that the secret ballot and the universal franchise were the means by which the people of England might someday be able to express their will.[23]

But was it vital that they should indeed express their will directly if they had a government that would really take care of them? Which was the more important to him: democratic participation or good government by those who knew best?[24] Napier had to decide, and further political controversies in Bath would help him to clarify his views.

The question at hand had to do with Irish politics. In the midst of the 1837 campaign, Napier found himself in a public quarrel with Daniel O'Connell, the crusader for Irish political rights. O'Connell took umbrage with a comment that Napier made about him at a public meeting. The underlying dispute between the two men was an interesting one: whether the people of Ireland had a more urgent need for political power (O'Connell's view) or economic relief (as Napier believed). Napier the leftist-paternalist wanted the alleviation of hunger to come first, before any political reforms – just as he had once believed that Greece needed independence and security before it could pursue internal liberty. In a speech at Bath, Napier made his usual call for universal suffrage, the secret ballot, annual parliaments, reform of the House of Lords, lower taxes on the poor, and the repeal of the New Poor Law that gaoled paupers. But he also made a chance reference to O'Connell. He said he no longer counted himself one of O'Connell's defenders now that the Liberator (as O'Connell was referred to) had rejected a poor law for Ireland. In light of the chronic food shortages, there were many agricultural reformers who were doing more real good for Ireland than O'Connell was doing, Napier added. They were focussed on the real question of feeding the people.

Battle was joined when O'Connell got wind of Napier's comments. He made fun of Napier in a speech in Dublin: 'This Colonel Napier is a comical person',

Flogging and politics   121

O'Connell claimed, who wanted a poor law for Ireland when he admitted how horrible the English poor law had been.[25]

Napier responded with a nasty letter to the *Times*. He brought up how O'Connell was living off money contributed by the poor themselves. (And indeed O'Connell was doing this very thing, if one looked at the issue in a particular way; for O'Connell was the full-time leader of a mass movement funded by much of the Irish population.) Napier held his own record up to the Liberator's: 'I have governed a country for many years without robbing the poor, which is being a better politician than robbing the poor without governing them'.

'Ireland requires a poor law', Napier said in a private letter:

> Mr. O'Connell sets himself against it because the poorest Irishman, such is their generosity, will always divide his last potatoe [*sic*] with a distressed countryman. He is thus willing to sacrifice the poor to the Irish landlords; saying they shall be left to starve, because they are generous enough to give one-half of their potatoes to starving creatures, and the other half – to Mr. O'Connell![26]

Meanwhile '[t]he starving millions of Ireland raise a cry so loud and horrible, that humanity can no longer endure it'.[27]

Soon after, when O'Connell decided to supported the Irish Poor Law after all, the two men traded further insults. Napier sent O'Connell a poisonous letter gloating over how he changed his mind. O'Connell called Napier a 'ridiculous blockhead'. And it did not stop there.[28] What was clear was that in Napier's view, if the poor were to have any comfort, the government needed to help them. Paupers needed to be fed long before the Irish people needed to be made the agents of their own governance.

Meanwhile Napier's experience with the rough and tumble of electoral politics did little to increase his faith in English representative institutions in their current form. In Bath he saw the meetings and the shouting and the jostling of an election season. He described speakers being drowned out on the hustings, and a city bitterly divided between those who patronized the Tory shops and those who patronized the Radical shops.[29] His comments recall Charles Dickens' famous account of the Eatanswill election in *The Pickwick Papers*, published at just this time.[30] Nonetheless these experiences did not shake Napier's basic desire for democratic reform, for he did not think that democracy *had* to look like this. In Bath, Napier saw votes being cast in public amidst scenes of near riot. But he recalled that at Caen he had seen an election passing off with no tumult. The French employed the secret ballot and so all was quiet. Even the poor were allowed to vote, and in doing so they could feel secure that their employers and landlords would never know their choice. They could not be pressured. Bringing in the secret ballot, as Napier had reflected well before the Bath election, would remove any further excuse for excluding the poor from the political nation.[31]

122   *The radical abroad and at home*

Yet after what he had seen of the campaign, he could tease his brother that

> my thoughts are strangely inclined to a good tough despotic government, sufficiently bloody, as the best of all possible forms of ruling. I would rather be cut down by O'Connell's guards in a rage, than be constitutionally strangled after a long speech from 'The Mandarin,' John Russell. Depend upon it Tiberius was a model for all that is good virtuous and useful, to say nothing of pleasure.[32]

Ireland

Charles Napier's time at Bath was only a brief interlude. For again the question arose: Could he find a new career? Napier remained on the army's half-pay list, and he was continuing to look for full-time employment and a place to settle down. In 1838 he lodged for a time by the docks near Milford Haven so he could finish his novel; then he thought of setting himself up in Dublin. Meanwhile he was still writing to Lord Fitzroy Somerset, the Military Secretary at the Horse Guards, about possible preferments in the army. Napier asked for a position on the Irish staff, and he applied for appointment as lieutenant-governor of Jersey. Not all of these importuning letters were polite. He explained to his sister in 1835 that part of his frustration came from how he could never get a '*yes* or a *no*' out of the military authorities, so he could never be sure whether to recommit himself to a military career or leave the army.[33] And he was distracted by affairs in Ireland.

***

Before we follow Napier to the north of England, it is important to note that in everything he wrote during these years he had revealed his strong opinions about recent Irish affairs. In the *Colonization* book, he had gone so far as to claim that the Irish were more severely oppressed than the natives of Australia and South Africa, as we have seen. In Napier's view, the Tories had oppressed the Irish for thirty years and the Whigs had damned them for it. But with their Coercion Bill, the Whigs showed that they were no better than the Tories. In fact they were worse because they were hypocrites.[34]

Change, then, had to come not from the British government but from the Irish land and the Irish people. Through John Pitt Kennedy, Napier now was able to reconnect more deeply with events on the ground in Ireland, thirty years after his widowed mother sold her house in Celbridge.

In 1831, when Kennedy left Cephalonia, he abandoned his military career and bought land in County Donegal. He also became estate manager for Sir Thomas Charles Style, Bart., at Clogher, also in Donegal; and on top of this he began running the estate of one of his own nephews at Lough Ash in County Tyrone. On these three estates Kennedy carried out a variety of improvements, turning them into models of good farming. But Kennedy wanted more – a revolution in Irish agricultural practices, something on the order of what he and Napier had tried to carry into effect in Cephalonia when they brought in crop rotation and the proper spacing of plants. Indeed, Kennedy radically increased the usable area of each estate by reclaiming waste ground, and he divided the land into the small farms that Napier had written about in his book on Australia. Kennedy was soon responsible for eighty tenant families, or four hundred people who had once been paupers. They prospered, and he was able to collect rent on land where none had been collected before.[35] In autumn 1835, he invited Napier to come see the Irish farms for himself. Napier would pay repeated visits.[36]

In 1837 John Kennedy was appointed Irish Inspector-General of Education and given a seat on the Education Commission. (The Whig government had created a national system of education in Ireland in 1831, decades before England would get any such thing.) But the Archbishop of Dublin, Richard Whately, drove poor Kennedy off the Commission within six months. Kennedy said Whately treated him as 'an intruder and a meddler'.[37] Probably he did. For Whately's secret agenda – as he himself privately admitted – was to use the supposedly non-sectarian system of national schools to wean the Irish people off Roman Catholicism. He did not favour teaching *any* of the agricultural or other religiously neutral material in which Kennedy had taken such an interest.[38] So when Kennedy saw what he was faced with, he resigned from the Commission (at the end of 1838) and then from his position as Chief Inspector in 1839.

Loyally, Napier proceeded to publish an attack on the archbishop. He finished the short book in a Dublin hotel in December 1838. It appeared in the very month when he was preparing to take up his command of the Army of the North,[39] and it contained a key passage on the state of his mind at the point in time when he was turning his full attention to the Chartists. In this short work, Napier explains that the rack-rent landlords of Ireland *do* find a few tenants who are desperate enough to agree to their exorbitant rents. These tenants then overfarm and ruin the land. They fall behind on their payments, they get turned off their holdings, they commit acts of violence, and then they are hanged. It is all perfectly understandable. Indeed, the widows and children of the condemned are taken in by other desperately poor families who can ill afford to feed them. They are taken because the justice of what the condemned man has done is so obvious to the local people.[40] Napier concludes, 'No honest man will defend the commission of crime: but, Reader, if thou hast a wife and children, imagine them to be perishing for want of food, and say where, if thou want a rule, untaught peasant, thy forbearance would cease?'[41]

This passage says many things, but one of them is that it is the suffering of the children that can drive one to violence. Napier's feelings would be much the same when he turned his attention towards the suffering children of England, as he was about to do. He told his sister Louisa how horrible it was that

> the damned Bastilles of the new poor law [tore] their infants from them and sent them to perish in another Bastille far away where they can neither

124 *The radical abroad and at home*

know the treatment they receive from strangers nor if they be sick or well. Lord Stanhope has had . . . *proof* sent to him. *I know* that numbers of infants have been killed. I did not send it but I know who did. When I think of these . . . tortures inflicted upon the poor I do feel how fortunate I am in being rich and that God demands that I should labour to save others rather than complain of my own lot.[42]

Now that he was finally to be given an army command – the command of the army that had to contain the Chartists – what would he do? Would he fire upon the poor?

Notes

1 J. R. Dinwiddy, 'The Early Nineteenth-Century Campaign against Flogging in the Army', *English Historical Review* 97, 383 (April 1982), 308–31; Peter Burroughs, 'Crime and Punishment in the British Army, 1815–1870', *English Historical Review* 100, 396 (July 1985), 545–71 at 561–63.
2 Douglas M. Peers, 'Sepoys, Soldiers, and the Lash: Race, Caste, and Army Discipline in India, 1820–1850', *Journal of Imperial and Commonwealth History* 23, 2 (1995), 211–47 at 233; Burroughs, 'Crime and Punishment in the British Army, 1815–1870', 563–64.
3 Charles James Napier, *Remarks on Military Law and the Punishment of Flogging* (London: T. & W. Boone, 1837), vi, 159–64; Anonymous, 'Sons of Glory!: Recruiting at Birmingham', *Punch: or, The London Charivari*, 7 (1844), 233.
4 Napier, *Military Law*, 149–55, 172–73.
5 Richard Glover, *Peninsular Preparation: The Reform of the British Army, 1795–1809* (Cambridge: Cambridge UP, 1963), 174–81; Napier to Powell, 29 December 1842, given in WN, 2:280; Napier, *Military Law*, 38–39, 73–74.
6 Napier, *Military Law*, 122–25, 205–36, 246–47.
7 Letter of William Wheeler, 7 May 1825, given in B. H. Liddell Hart (ed.), *The Letters of Private Wheeler* (Boston: Houghton Mifflin, 1952), 297–99 and 327–29 at 329.
8 Napier, *Military Law*, 178–80.
9 Ibid, 5, 11–17, 136–38.
10 N. M. Billimoria, 'General Orders of Sir Charles Napier (1843–47)', *Journal of Sind Historical Society* 3, 4 (1938), 51.
11 Napier to Ripon, 7 August 1844, RP, BL Add. MS 40869, fols 61–71 at 61–62.
12 Peers, 'Sepoys, Soldiers, and the Lash'; Hardinge to Napier, 7 June, 31 October 1844, NP, BL Add. MS 54517, fols 55–58, 101–06; Hardinge to James, 19 September 1845, quoted in Bawa Satinder Singh (ed.), *The Letters of the First Viscount Hardinge of Lahore to Lady Hardinge and Sir Walter and Lady James, 1844–1847*, Camden Fourth Series 32 (London: Royal Historical Society, 1986), 112–14; Great Britain, Parliament, *Copies of the Special Reports of the Indian Law Commissioners* (1847), No. 14, 509–10.
13 Napier, *Military Law*, 148n and 268.
14 Ibid, vii.
15 Ibid, 22–24, 34–36, 47.
16 Ibid, 23–24, 36–45.
17 Ibid, 7–8, 67, quotation at 67.
18 Charles James Napier, *William the Conqueror: A Historical Romance*, William Napier (ed.) (London: G. Routledge & Co., 1858), 357.
19 Napier to Louisa Napier, 17 March 1833, Bodleian MS Eng. lett. c. 240, fols 6–7.
20 Napier to Mr Child, January 1833, NP, BL Add. MS 49127, fols 8–16 at 10–11.
21 C.B.E. tariffs, 1815, BL Add. MS 54539, fol. 49; the award was dated 4 June 1815 – *London Gazette*, 16 September 1815 17061 p. 1879.

22 Napier to [?], 31 March 1837, NP, BL Add. MS 49128, fol. 17; Announcement of the formation of the Bath radical committee, Napier's draft, 1837, NP, BL Add. MS 54561, fols 93–94. See R. B. Pugh, 'Chartism in Somerset and Wiltshire', in Asa Briggs (ed.), *Chartist Studies* (London: Macmillan, 1959), 174–219 at 174–76; Robert Eadon Leader, *Life and Letters of John Arthur Roebuck, P.C., Q.C., M.P., with Chapters of Autobiography* (London: Edward Arnold, 1897), 88; WN, 1:462; *Bath Chronicle and Weekly Gazette*, 12 January 1837, 4 col. b. For a history of this toast, see James Epstein, *Radical Expression: Political Language, Ritual, and Symbol in England, 1790–1850* (New York: Oxford UP, 1994), 153–54.

23 Napier to Roebuck, drafts, [ca. 15 July?] 1837, NP, BL Add. MS 54544, fols 83–86.

24 Even J. S. Mill would have a hard time making up his mind about this issue. See the rather conflicted arguments in his *Considerations of Representative Government*, chapters VI and VIII.

25 *Bath Chronicle and Weekly Gazette*, 12 January 1837, 4 col. c, and 19 January 1837, 3 col. e; see also Napier to Lady Lucy Foley, 16 January 1837, NP, BL Add. MS 49128. fols 11–14.

26 Napier quoted in WN, 1:464–65.

27 Napier to the *Times*, 24 January 1837, 2 col. f.

28 WN, 1:465–66.

29 Napier to W. Napier, 7 August 1837, given in ibid, 1:466–68.

30 Charles Dickens, *The Posthumous Papers of the Pickwick Club* [1836–1837] (London: Penguin, 1999), chapter 13.

31 Napier to Mr Child, January 1833, NP, BL Add. MS 49127, fols 8–16 at 14–15.

32 Napier to W. Napier, 12 August 1837, given in WN, 1:468–70.

33 Napier to Louisa Napier, 29 July 1835, Bodleian MS Eng. lett. c. 240, fols 40–41; Napier to Somerset, 12 January 1837, 9 March, 3 April 1838, NP, BL Add. MS 49128, fols 11, 40–42, 44–46; Napier to Robertson, 19 March, 18 June, 9 August 1838, NP, BL Add. MS 49107, fols 14–18; Napier to Louisa Napier, 28 June 1837, 24 March 1838, Bodleian MS Eng. lett. c. 240, fols 17–18, 22–23.

34 Napier, *Colonization*, 136, 176–77, 181–82; Napier to Mr Child, January 1833, NP, BL Add. MS 49127, fols 8–16 at 15.

35 Kennedy to Napier, 15 September – 6 October 1831, 20 September 1832, 2, 5 February 1833, NP, BL Add. MS 54535, fols 59–60, 100–01, 105–08; Napier's memorandum called 'Captain Kennedy: A Visionary!' [no date], NP, TNA PRO 30/64/5, fols 11–12.

36 Napier, *Ireland*, 32, 46, 55; Napier to Boone, 18 September 1837, NP, BL Add. MS 49128, fols 36–37; Napier to Mrs. North, March 1838, fol. 43; Kennedy to Napier, 4 September 1835, NP, BL Add. MS 54535, fols 143–44.

37 Donald H. Akenson, *The Irish Education Experiment: The National System of Education in the Nineteenth Century* (London: Routledge & Kegan Paul, 1970), 59, 130–32, and Kennedy to Thomas Spring-Rice, 12 December 1838, quoted at 131; E. Jane Whately, *Life and Correspondence of Richard Whately, D.D., Late Archbishop of Dublin*, 2 vols (London: Longman's, Green, and Co., 1866), 1:138–40, 2:1–5, 40–44, 264–80. Whately was argumentative and personally not very likeable – Owen Chadwick, *The Victorian Church*, 2 vols (New York: Oxford UP, 1970), 1:42–43, 133.

38 Máire M. Kealy, *Dominican Education in Ireland, 1820–1830* (Dublin: Irish Academic Press, 2007), 22–25; Akenson, *Irish Education Experiment*, 234–37. Whately's purpose may have been to avoid fanaticism on both sides, Roman Catholic and Protestant; see Norman Vance, 'Improving Ireland: Richard Whately, Theology, and Political Economy', in Stefan Collini, Richard Whatmore, and Brian Young (eds), *Economy, Polity, and Society: British Intellectual History, 1750–1950* (Cambridge: Cambridge UP, 2000), 181–202.

39 Napier, *Ireland*, 70; Napier to Fitzroy, 16 December 1838, NP, BL Add. 49114, fol. 128.

40 Napier, *Ireland*, 34. For the resistance to rents, see also Kennedy to Napier, 7 September 1835, NP, BL Add. MS 54535, fols 145–46.

41 Napier, *Ireland*, 36.

42 Napier to Louisa Napier, [?] April 1838, Bodleian MS Eng. lett. c. 240, fols 26–27.

Part III

The north of England

Massacre and torture are now confined to manufactories and the colonies; and inflicted upon infants, untutored savages, and animals.[1]

The general must stand by the magistrates of the land, and say to the fifty thousand rioters: "You are not the people of England; your object may be just or unjust – with that, I, as the leader of these troops, have no concern. Petition and remonstrate, as the constitution decrees; but offend not the laws of the land, which the nation has placed me here to protect.[2]

Notes

1 Charles James Napier, *Remarks on Military Law and the Punishment of Flogging* (London: T. and W. Boone, 1837), 4.
2 Napier, editor's note to Part 1, chapter 1, in Alfred Victor, comte de Vigny, *Lights and Shades of Military Life*, Charles James Napier (ed.), 2nd edn (London: Henry Colburn, 1850), 1:331–32; 2nd edn (1850), 20–21.

10 The coming of Chartism

In the 1830s the working classes in England were facing a decline in jobs. At the same time, wages were being driven down by changes in technology and patterns of work. The common people found they had a very different set of concerns than the enfranchised seemed to have.[1] The Reform Bill for which they had campaigned had developed into a reform law that still excluded them from the vote. And the passage of the New Poor Law drove home their powerlessness.

Radicalism, quiescent in the 1820s, now developed in several new directions. Radicals in the Cooperative Movement founded small stores or co-ops so the poor could band together and buy things more cheaply, denying custom to shopkeepers who favoured the rich and powerful.[2] Robert Owen and others tried to found entirely new, ideal communities. But perhaps the most important of the radical movements of the mid-1830s, when Napier began to pay attention to day-to-day politics in England, was the campaign for an unstamped and thus cheaper and more popular press. Despite the best efforts of the Whig government to destroy the unstamped newspapers, they went from strength to strength – indeed all the more so as repression increased. The government prosecuted and imprisoned hundreds of printers and vendors from 1830 to 1836, when the stamp duty was cut from four pence to one penny.[3]

But with all these different facets of radicalism, from cooperatives to Owenites to the unstamped press (which was itself far from homogeneous in its opinions), it is clear that there was no coherent movement for social change to catch Napier's attention when he returned to England after living in Cephalonia and France.[4] He never paid heed to the cooperative movement or the Owenites. Nor with his ready access to publishers and his preference for writing books did he have much use for the unstamped newspapers. Instead he preached mainly agricultural reform as his own alternative to Wakefieldianism and Irish Coercion. But he caught the general mood of dissatisfaction and danger. Napier came to believe ever more firmly that radical change was necessary to stave off a social revolution. He told one friend that it was in order to *preserve* society that he wanted to change it so radically.[5]

As we have seen, Napier did not go into politics himself, although he might well have done so. In 1837 the cotton-spinning and colliery town of Oldham,

130   *The north of England*

near Manchester, was looking for a new M.P. The borough had two seats in Parliament. One was held by the Paine-ite currency reformer John Fielden. The other had been held by none other than William Cobbett himself. Cobbett had died in June 1835. In a by-election that year, he was replaced by a Tory, John Frederick Lees (Feargus O'Connor had stood as well, helping to split the radical vote). In January 1837, with a general election expected after the imminent death of the king, the Liberal Committee of the borough wrote to Charles Napier, asking him to stand as their candidate alongside Fielden.[6]

But they had some questions for him first. Was he in favour of universal suffrage, the ballot, and annual parliaments? And would he vote to repeal the Poor Law? If so, he could stand with Fielden and incur no campaign expenses himself. The committee were sure that if he did stand he would win.

Napier carefully worked through his reply: Yes, he very much believed in universal suffrage, vote by ballot, annual parliaments, and a better poor law for England, and he added a poor law for Ireland. But he mentioned that he had a family and limited means, and so he could not afford to be in London for so much of the year. He declined the offer.[7]

The man the Committee turned to was indeed elected, and most likely Napier would have been elected too. But in the period when he seemed unable to get off the half-pay list or commit himself to a civilian career, Napier had given up his one clear chance to sit in the House of Commons.

***

Meanwhile, entirely new political configurations were arising. The two most compelling and most influential of the campaigns for social change in this era – far eclipsing the cooperative and the unstamped press movements of the early 1830s – were both founded at about this time. In 1838 came one of the first mass political campaigns to be organized in a modern way, the Anti-Corn Law League. This was a mainly urban movement whose goal was to lower the price of food and thus lower wages. The League was middle class in its aims, methods, and leadership. It had a huge headquarters and a professional staff to track marginal political constituencies and intervene in campaigns. And the League was middle class, too, in its conception of the world. Its leaders owned factories and mills. The members of the League wanted to lower wages because they *paid* wages. Napier would hardly identify with *them*.

Very different was the other mass movement founded at this time. Chartism was a working-class effort that united the poor of the towns and the countryside. It united illiterate workers in the fields and on the shop floors with the crusading writers and editors who had been involved with the unstamped press campaign. The Chartists were not from the middle class. They refused to cooperate with the aims or the leadership of the Anti-Corn Law League. This was much to the surprise and consternation of the League itself, especially when the Chartists broke up their meetings. Well might the League be surprised by this hostility. Were not the Chartists also against the Corn Laws? Surely the two groups ought to work together for a common goal?[8]

The coming of Chartism 131

Yes, the Chartists opposed the legal regime that raised the price of food, but they were not primarily focussed on righting an economic wrong. The Chartist movement came from the masses, the very people who suffered most from economic privation – and yet it made no demands for immediate economic change. The Chartists were holding out for constitutional change. That is what had to come first. They wanted power commensurate to their numbers. Once they had that power, they believed that everyone in the nation, whether rich, middle class, or poor, could work together and create the economic policies that might seem best at the time. Whatever those policies turned out to be, they would be in the interest of the whole nation.[9]

So long as the interests of the upper classes continued to dominate the government, the Chartists distrusted all of those above them, not least the comfortable folk working against the Corn Law because it raised prices and impeded trade.[10] The Chartists trusted the rich no more than Napier would trust the Carthaginian Senators – weeping for their own fortunes rather than for the sufferings of their poorer countrymen.

In some ways the Chartists were men after Napier's heart. They hated the rich.

***

It was clear what the Chartists were against. What they stood *for* should also have been clear to everyone. 'The People's Charter' was written in London in 1837 by a cabinet-maker by the name of William Lovett.[11] Lovett was a veteran of the cooperative, Owenite, *and* unstamped press movements. He had also worked in a number of other radical causes. Lovett founded the London Working Men's Association in 1836. In the following year the LWMA decided to petition Parliament for universal suffrage.[12] Lovett drafted a list of specific demands, and this was what became known as the People's Charter. After much discussion, the list was finally published on 8 May 1838, and presented at a public meeting in Glasgow on 21 May.[13] There were six demands in all. Lovett presented them in this order:

1   Equal electoral districts
2   Universal male suffrage
3   Annual elections for Parliament
4   Abolition of the property qualification for M.P.s
5   Votes by secret ballot
6   Payment of M.P.s.[14]

This list overlapped with what Napier had demanded in Bath and what he included in his letter to the Oldham selection committee, although he had never stressed the first, fourth, and sixth points.

These six demands, so near to Napier's own views, made up the People's Charter that energized much of England for the next decade, especially in the north. The Charter was promulgated through committees of correspondence,

132 *The north of England*

and soon enough through a substantial Chartist press. By some distance the most important of the Chartist newspapers was Feargus O'Connor's stamped, legal, and thus relatively expensive *Northern Star*, which had been founded in November 1837; it was published in Leeds. Little knots of Chartists (and in Scotland, whole Chartist Churches) each bought their weekly paper and shared it; the shoemakers and others who ran their own small shops would have it read aloud to them as they worked.[15]

Despite Lovett's early role, the proprietor of the *Northern Star* became the leader of Chartism. Feargus O'Connor, the Irishman and former M.P. who had stood in Oldham in 1835, was born to wealth. Despite his privileged background, he became the leader of the workers, and he tirelessly covered the north of England organizing and giving speeches.[16] Yet apart from his role, Chartism was led mostly by the working-class men and women themselves, out of whom legions of organizers, writers, reporters, editors, publishers, and orators arose. The aim was to circulate the petition and attract signatures. By August and September 1838, Chartist rallies routinely drew up to 70,000 people. On one occasion in early August, 200,000 gathered in Birmingham; 300,000 in Manchester in September. And at some of these meetings shots were heard.[17]

Parades of tens of thousands of men and women in the northern towns continued marching – by torchlight until the torch-lit processions were finally banned at the end of the year. As Malcolm Chase points out in the best modern history of Chartism, the torches were simply necessary. The parades had to be held at night because the men worked all day. So without the torches they could not see where they were going. But practicalities aside, the fact that so many people were marching by firelight in the night brought a certain mood to the proceedings. Speakers would exhort the crowd to arm themselves. Men said they would stand in front of a cannon and 'stand its blasts' rather than live under the current government. Torches or no torches, old soldiers taught drill. Pikes and bombs were stockpiled. The north of England made up a large part of the industrial heartland of the world, and the marchers were – many of them – the metalworkers of the Industrial Revolution. Not a few could make guns, and any village blacksmith could turn out the pikes and bombs. They could make other things, too. Spiked balls could be chained together – the arrangement was called a caltrops, or crowfoot – and these were fabricated in great numbers, ready to be thrown at the legs of the cavalry horses.[18] By the first half of 1839, the question loomed: What would happen if Parliament rejected the great petition with the Six Points? Some Chartists were willing to make the obvious threat, however carefully: If the monster petition demanding the Charter were rejected by Parliament and the common people were left with no legal avenues for pursuing peaceful change, they could win their freedom by other means.[19]

The government had its spies,[20] and some of the spies were even more alarmist than they needed to be; the stockpiling of weapons and the mass meetings were no secret. So, would Parliament receive the great petition when time came and grant the Charter?

Since the time of Thucydides the idea of universal suffrage had been anathema. Would not the democratic element simply demand the property of the rich, as the mobs of Captain Swing had demanded their beer and cash in 1830? In 1839 neither the English Levellers nor the French Jacobites had been forgotten by the propertied classes of England. Under no circumstances was Parliament going to vote for universal suffrage. When the Monster Petition with its 1,280,959 signatures was delivered on 12 July 1839, the House of Commons rejected it. This was by a vote of 235 to 46. Parliament did not even condescend to debate the question of universal suffrage itself.[21]

The Home Secretary, Lord John Russell, explained his view in the Commons a few weeks later:

> My own opinion is, that upon [the Chartists'] own statements there is no remedy which this House can give – that there is no satisfaction which this House can provide which can remove what they suppose to be grievances. It does seem to me, that their complaints in all their placards, and in all their speeches, are complaints against the constitution of society. They complain that society is so constituted that they have not a sufficient quantity of wealth and means of support in that society, and that by a change of the law some new state of society will take place, by which their happiness will be increased and their grievances redressed. I, Sir, do not think that any law can pass that would at all tend to improve their condition. I am not now speaking of any partial law, but of a total change in the society of this country; and my opinion is that, should such a thing occur, it would not decrease the number of the distressed and discontented, but, while it destroyed the property and the means of the rich, it would act still more fatally against the resources and welfare of the people.[22]

But was the government's inevitable rejection of the Charter going to be the end of the matter? What about the People with their pikes and their bombs? Might violence on either side reach the scale of what took place during the Captain Swing, which the army had helped to put down in 1830?[23] Might things be even worse now? How many martyrs might there be?[24] Napier reflected on the matter in August 1839:

> Poor people. They will suffer. They have set all England against them and their physical force – fools! We have the physical force, not they. They talk of their hundred thousands of men. Who is to move them when I am dancing round them with cavalry; and pelting them with cannon-shot? What would their 100,000 men do with my 100 rockets wriggling their fiery tails among them, roaring, scorching, tearing, smashing all they came near? And when in desperation and despair they broke to fly, how would they bear five regiments of cavalry careering through them? Poor men! How little they know of physical force![25]

134   *The north of England*

Notes

1   William Thomas, *The Philosophic Radicals: Nine Studies in Theory and Practice, 1817–1841* (Oxford: Clarendon Press, 1979), 427; John Belchem, *'Orator' Hunt: Henry Hunt and English Working-Class Radicalism* (Oxford: Clarendon Press, 1985), 9–11; Noel W. Thompson, *The People's Science: The Popular Political Economy of Exploitation and Crisis, 1816–34* (Cambridge: Cambridge UP, 1984).

2   William Lovett, *The Life and Struggles of William Lovett in His Pursuit of Bread, Knowledge, and Freedom* [1876] (London: MacGibbon & Kee, 1967), 33–41, 71–72.

3   Joel H. Wiener, *The War of the Unstamped* (Ithaca, NY: Cornell UP, 1969); Patricia Hollis, *The Pauper Press: A Study in Working-Class Radicalism of the 1830s* (Oxford: Oxford UP, 1970); Lovett, *Life and Struggles*, 48–52.

4   E. P. Thompson, *The Making of the English Working Class* (1963; New York: Vintage Books, 1966), 625–27.

5   Napier to Robertson, 19 February 1839, NP, BL Add. MS 49107, fols 22–24.

6   John Halliwell to Napier, 26 January 1837, NP, BL Add. MS 54544, fol. 76; Stewart Angas Weaver, *John Fielden and the Politics of Popular Radicalism, 1832–1847* (Oxford: Clarendon Press, 1987), 133–35, 176–77.

7   Napier, draft, January 1837, NP, BL Add. MS 54544, fol. 77; see also Napier to Halliwell, 20 January 1837, NP, BL Add. MS 49128, fols 15–16.

8   Thomas, *Philosophical Radicals*, 426–30; Wendy Hinde, *Richard Cobden: A Victorian Outsider* (New Haven, CT: Yale UP, 1987), 65–67, 69–71; Nicholas C. Edsall, *Richard Cobden: Independent and Radical* (Cambridge, MA: Harvard UP, 1986), 75–81; Norman McCord, *The Anti-Corn Law League, 1838–1846* (London: George Allen & Unwin, 1958), 45, 48, 51–53, 83–94; Paul A. Pickering and Alex Tyrell, *The People's Bread: A History of the Anti-Corn Law League* (London: Leicester UP, 2000), 17–28, 139–48, 217–18, 228–32, 237; Archibald Prentice, *History of the Anti-Corn Law League*, 2nd edn, 2 vols (1st edn 1853, London: Frank Cass and New York: Augustus M. Kelley, 1968), 1:90–96, 116–19, 127–29.

9   See, for example, the words of George Barker at Huddersfield on 10 August 1839, TNA HO 40/51/455–69 at 457; and the broadside advertising a Chartist meeting to be held in Bolton, 26 November 1839, TNA HO 40/43/222; and Malcolm Chase, *Chartism: A New History* (Manchester: Manchester UP, 2007), 1, 59, 78, 195–98.

10   They were right to distrust Cobden and others in the Anti-Corn Law League, who deliberately worked to marginalize them and the question of further parliamentary reform – see Thomas, *Philosophical Radicals*, 431–34; Hinde, *Cobden*, 111–13. Yet this did not make the government trust the League.

11   Lovett, *Life and Struggles*, 91–95, 136–37.

12   And he meant universal suffrage, not universal *male* suffrage. The enfranchisement of women was an early goal of his, soon left behind as impolitic for the time being – see ibid, 141n; Chase, *Chartism*, 28, 43.

13   Lovett, *Life and Struggles*, 136–42.

14   Ibid, 313–14.

15   Chase, *Chartism*, 44–45; Dorothy Thompson, *The Chartists: Popular Politics in the Industrial Revolution* (New York: Pantheon, 1984), 42–56.

16   Paul A. Pickering, *Feargus O'Connor: A Political Life* (Monmouth: Merlin Press, 2008), 99–100; Humphrey Southall, 'Agitate! Agitate! Organize! Political Travellers and the Construction of a National Politics, 1839–1880', *Transactions of the Institute of British Geographers*, n.s., 21, 1 (1996), 177–93.

17   Chase, *Chartism*, 30–32, 37.

18   Chase, *Chartism*, 37–39, 61–63; Katrina Navickas, *Protest and the Politics of Space and Place, 1789–1848* (Manchester: Manchester UP, 2016), 234–36; Napier to Phillipps, 21/22 May 1839, TNA HO 40/53/474–76. For a town council requiring the Chartists to meet in daylight – although as the Chartists pointed out everyone knew they were at work all day, see Henry Coppock, Town Clerk of Stockport, to Lord John Russell, 11 May 1839,

TNA HO 40/41/52–62 at 54–55. For a call to arms and standing in front of a cannon, see 57–58.

19 James Epstein, *The Lion of Freedom: Feargus O'Connor and the Chartist Movement* (London and Canberra: Croom Helm, 1982), 49–51, 118–25; Pickering, *O'Connor*, 74–75, 96–97; Chase, *Chartism*, 79–81. Some Chartists expected the petition to be rejected; the nation would then have the moral right to revolt – Epstein, *Radical Expression*, 17.

20 See Neil Pye, *The Home Office and the Chartists, 1838–1848: Protest and Repression in the West Riding of Yorkshire* (Pontypool, Wales: Merlin Press, 2013), 51–53, 59.

21 Chase, *Chartism*, 73, 84.

22 Lord John Russell in the House of Commons, 2 August 1839, HC Deb 02 August 1839 vol 49 cc1157–58.

23 Eric Hobsbawm and Georges Rudé, *Captain Swing: A Social History of the Great English Agricultural Uprising of 1830* (New York: W.W. Norton, 1968), chapter 13; Carl J. Griffin, *The Rural War: Captain Swing and the Politics of Protest* (Manchester and New York: Manchester UP, 2012), 242–46.

24 On the possibility of revolution if the government and Napier had not kept their nerve, or if on the contrary they had resorted to bloodshed, see Epstein, *Lion of Freedom*, 164, 176.

25 Napier's journal, 6 August 1839, given in WN, 2:69.

11 Command in the north

In Dublin in December 1838, Napier was polishing his little book on the problems of Ireland. Yet on the very days when he was setting out his view that anti-landlord violence might have some moral justification, he also found himself corresponding with the London authorities over when he was to take command of the army trying to keep order in the north of England.[1]

Napier's appointment had been communicated to him privately by Lord Hill, who succeeded Wellington as Commander-in-Chief of the Forces when Wellington became Prime Minister in 1829. (Lord Hill – Rowland Hill – was only in the slightest degree related to the much younger Rowland Hill whom Napier had known as the Secretary of the South Australia Company.) Napier himself believed that it was Lord Hill who had selected him for the command, although there is no evidence about whether the idea came originally from the Horse Guards or Whitehall.[2] Hill, a Tory, had been one of Wellington's main subordinates at Waterloo, and even as Commander-in-Chief he continued to take his lead from Wellington under a succession of Whig and Tory governments. (Hill would remain Commander-in-Chief for fourteen years, until he was seventy, resigning because of ill health in 1842 and dying a few months later. On Hill's retirement, Wellington returned to the post.)

Another man who may have had a hand in Napier's appointment was Lord Fitzroy Somerset. Under both of the increasingly elderly Commanders-in-Chief in this period, Wellington and Hill, much of the routine work at the Horse Guards was done by Lord Fitzroy, who served for a full quarter century as Military Secretary. Somerset would turn out to be less than efficient in his first and only field command – in the Crimean War, where as Lord Raglan he fell short of covering himself in glory. But he had proved a very efficient and patient administrator throughout his twenty-five years at the Horse Guards. Lord Fitzroy carried on a daily correspondence with the army commander in the north as the Chartists marched.

The officer in charge of the Army of the Northern District in 1838 was Sir Richard Jackson, but the Cabinet wanted to change commanders. Chartism had made the position of commander in the north rather more important. The Cabinet needed someone who would take charge, someone who could work with and sometimes override the local authorities. The local officials sometimes showed great lassitude – or going to the other extreme they might give in to the kind of panic that had led to the bloodshed of Peterloo. Napier was hard-working, and he would delve into administrative details and the lives of the poor. His radicalism would make him congenial to the Chartists. And someone may well have appreciated that in the flogging book Napier had thought deeply about how the military could be used to defuse social unrest rather than to exacerbate it.

Furthermore Napier was a general now. He had been promoted to Major-General in January 1837.[3] Promotion was by seniority, and being on the half-pay list did not interfere with advances in rank. As a general he was qualified for a command of this stature.

For whatever combination of reasons – in fact there is no record of the government's reasoning or where the idea originally came from – Napier was appointed to succeed Jackson.

Waiting

Charles Napier had been visiting John Kennedy in Ireland since early September.[4] On being told of the new command he prepared to leave for his headquarters in Nottingham. But in December, before he had left Ireland, he was told that because of the 'present unrest' Sir Richard was to be retained in command until Easter. Fitzroy Somerset sent Napier a copy of his letter to Jackson explaining the delay. In that letter Somerset underlined the confidence that Lord Hill had in Napier's abilities, but he said that Jackson had to stay on for now. The situation was delicate and Jackson knew the places and the people. As it turned out, Napier's appointment would be announced publicly only in January.[5]

Napier showed some measure of patience and wisdom despite this delay. He did not react to the disappointment with anything like the leftist frustration that he poured into the book on Ireland – a book that Napier dated on its final page on the very day of Hill's letter to Jackson.[6] He wrote: 'A man must have more vanity . . . who could blame the government for not wanting to change coachmen just at the moment when the horse shows signs of restiveness'. So he resolved to remain in Dublin and wait happily. He also wrote directly to Jackson, referring to how the government have 'very wisely resolved to keep you where you are'.[7]

Replacing Jackson just then was difficult because too much of the government's knowledge about events in the north and the location of the troops lay only in Jackson's head. From time to time he had sent Whitehall the minute details about the shifting of detachments back and forth across the north of the country – but there was neither a clear pattern nor an overall plan.[8] As Zoë Laidlaw has shown in her book about colonial governors, British government departments in this period were only beginning to move from a practice of collecting their information through personal letters to collecting it more systematically, requiring standardized reports from officials out in the field.[9]

***

While General Jackson served out the winter, Napier suffered from a seven-week bout of the shingles, recovering in time to pay a visit to his second cousin

138 *The north of England*

the Duke of Leinster.[10] He had ample opportunity to consider what he planned to do.

He reflected on the matter in his journal:

> The northern district embraces eleven counties, and it is said arms are being provided for insurrection: this is a result of bad government, which has produced want, and the people are rather to be pitied than blamed. They are indeed putting themselves in the wrong, but that does not make those right whose misgovernment has produced this terrible feeling, leading them to believe in every demagogue who preaches violence as a remedy for distress. Poor people!

But there remained hope that wiser counsels would be able to prevent a bloodbath, especially if the people were given their rights. He continued:

> It is very painful to those who, like my brother William and myself, have long foreseen the result of Whig and Tory policy, to find now what we feared come to a head: however the Crown and constitution are not to be overset because a portion of the people follow the mad counsel of men like O'Connor, when by a juster course they could gain their rights without convulsion. My hope is that some better advisers will keep them quiet; for though of all misfortunes of this nature the most terrible is to fire on our countrymen there is no shrinking from duty, and mine shall be done at all hazards: but accursed be they who cause or begin civil war.

In other words, he wanted to see the people led to constructive change and not driven to destruction. But would he really fire on them? He reflected further:

> I expect to have very few soldiers and many enemies: hence, if we deal with pikemen my intent is to put cavalry on their flanks, making my infantry retire as the pikemen advance. If they halt to lace the cavalry, the infantry shall resume fire, for if cavalry charge pikemen in order the cavalry will be defeated; the pike must be opposed by the musket and bayonet, in which the soldiers must be taught to have confidence: it is the master weapon. I am inclined to use buckshot, which would seldom kill or wound dangerously; yet with mobs it would hurt so many that fright would cause dispersion. The great point is to defeat without killing. With a foreign foe, who recovers to fight you again, we must kill; but insurgents we should seek to save, not destroy, because the chances are that the rebellion will be over before the wounded can re-assemble.[11]

Regarding his own radical writings, he told his brother William:

> [A]s an officer and a citizen, I am bound on principle, and resolved, to maintain the constitution against Republican innovators. Hence, if it be

my fate to fire on rioters it cannot be said that I excited people to violence and then turned upon them; never did I excite any persons to violence, and I would fire on rioters.[12]

'[M]y radicalism', he reflected to another friend, 'began, continued, and will end, by my belief that it is the only course to prevent the destruction of the Constitution'.[13]

***

At the end of March, as the time at last approached for Napier to take up his post, he was called to London for interviews with the Home Secretary, Lord John Russell, and other officials. These meetings convinced him that ministers were in a quandary over events in the north. As he noted in his journal: 'The government seems to me alarmed, and not yet vigorous.' For himself, he said that his goal was to moderate the civil war if it broke out. He wanted to avoid savagery.[14]

If the irresolution of the London officials surprised him, so too did their good intentions. Napier found that most of the men who received him seemed mild and reasonable. They were anxious to avoid violence, although in Napier's mind they and not the Chartists were to blame for the terrible state of the country. The political classes were responsible for the national debt, the Corn Laws, and the New Poor Law, and he feared a bad outcome. On the Chartists themselves he reflected to his brother, 'Poor men! they are giving vigour to the worst Toryism and the prospect is gloomy: if they fail an oligarch becomes triumphant; if they succeed we shall have carnage. It looks as if the falling of an empire was beginning.'[15]

Meanwhile, the government knew very little about events in the north. Napier hoped he could win the confidence of the common people away from their leaders. Yet no one knew whether they *had* any leaders besides O'Connor. General Jackson wrote that he could tell Napier everything he knew in half an hour. The Home Office seemed to have little more information. Napier decided that when he was finally allowed to tour the north of England he would be – for all he had been able to prise out of Jackson and the Home Office – 'as blind as a new-born puppy'.[16]

Setting to work

When Napier took command in April 1839, he had not been allowed to tour the area (Map 11.1), mainly because of the cost of coaches and inns. And in fact for that very reason, to save money, he was not allowed to make a tour of the district until several months after taking over from General Jackson.[17] But what he could do at once was to commission a current map of where the soldiers were. He also asked each of the local commanders to send him, as soon as possible, their carefully written answers to two questions: (1) Whether their barracks were adequate in number, and easily defensible in case of sudden attack; and (2) what the disposition of the local population seemed to be.[18]

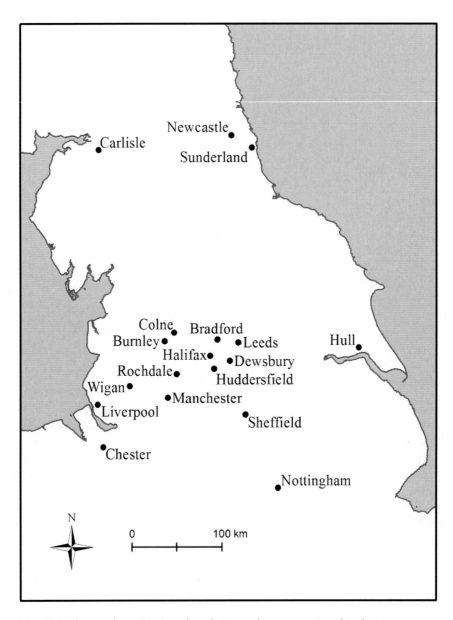

Map 11.1 The Northern District: selected cities and towns mentioned in the text.
Map prepared by Geoffrey Fouad

The answers he received were on the surface reasonable and well composed, and so they struck him at the time. But in fact they represented a near epidemic of wilful blindness. The commander at Rochdale reported that his barracks were adequate and the town was quiet and loyal.[19] What he did not

Command in the north   141

say was that in Rochdale only three months before, on 7 November, Fergus O'Connor or possibly another man (the government informant could not remember which), when he brought up the issue of what might happen if universal suffrage were denied, pointed to the lighted torches, saying 'they speak more than I can tell you'. Later that night, John Fielden, the Oldham M.P., added that if the property of a Poor Law Guardian were on fire, 'I should not advise you to put it out'.[20] Or so in any case said the reports which had reached the Home Office at the beginning of the year. And in early March – only a month before the report to Napier that all was quiet – some of the leading inhabitants of a major town near Rochdale (Heywood, with perhaps fourteen thousand people) petitioned the magistrates for additional protection from the Chartist threat. The large Chartist party there was arming itself with guns and pikes, they said.[21]

But neither the Chartist gatherings nor the arming of the populace figured in the tranquil report to Napier.

Few of the reports which he received were any more accurate than this account, or the equally blithe comments from the commander at Chester.[22] The commander at Sheffield, an officer named Blackley, reassured the general about local opinion. Everything he had been able to learn from speaking to the 'respectable pensioners of artillery', along with all that the police and his own officers had told him, led him to believe that the operatives in the town and 'the labouring classes in the neighbourhood are generally in pretty good employment and are tolerably contented' – although lately there had been some discontent over the Corn Laws. None of his sources had suggested any support for the Chartists or their policy of arming. There had been no Chartist meetings locally, Blackley told his new general. And between 'some of the Respectable Farmers' and his soldiers, he would have heard if there had been.[23]

What he did not say was that in September a rally at Sheffield had drawn 20,000, and that by New Year's, the Sheffield arms industry was selling guns for ten shillings a piece.[24]

So where were the Chartists? Many of Napier's commanders could not seem to find any Chartist activity whatever its size or consequence. The commanding officer at Hull did not himself make a report, assigning the task to Captain Thomas Maitland Edwards. Edwards assured Napier that in that city 'the Chartists are unknown'. Yet he also admitted that 'they have endeavoured in vain to cause excitement, and when the delegates were sent down here, they could not ever call together a sufficient number of persons'.[25] In fact we know from other sources that a Chartist meeting had been held in Hull. In preparation for it, 220 householders had petitioned to use the town hall. They were refused. Another location was found and the meeting seems to have drawn very well.[26] So Captain Edwards' assertion that Chartism was almost unknown in Hull was somewhat wide of the truth.

From Halifax, John Hopton sent Napier a strangely mixed but somewhat more helpful picture. He reported that his troops were quartered not in a barracks but in twenty-one different public houses, where he admitted that in their small groups they could easily be overpowered. As for public

142   *The north of England*

opinion: Yes, Hopton had heard that the Chartists did enjoy support among the labourers, who had armed themselves. So as commander of the troops, he asked the workers in one of the ironworks whether they were Chartists, asking them in front of their overseer, and they had told him they were not. He had repeated the question in another factory. There he received the same answer – again in front of the overseer. But Hopton admitted even then that in the opinion of this very overseer some of the workers were indeed Chartists, although strangely they had denied it in front of him.

Meanwhile Hopton also had to report that the old pensioned soldiers of the town (the Chelsea out-pensioners[27]) were drilling the workers. One of the pensioners said that the sixth of May – when the Chartist petition was to be presented to Parliament – had been set as the day for a general uprising. Hopton's informant had asked what would happen to the soldiers then? The answer was that they would be treated as they had been during the French Revolution.

The common people expected a collision, Hopton explained. The soldiers were hearing 'violent language'

> in the public houses, such as 'they will overthrow the soldiers, who cram the law down their throats at the point of a sword', and that 100 men could easily put down 100 soldiers.
>
> My own thought is that there is more talk than anything else, and that firmness and determination on the part of government will put a stop to any contemplated rising of the misguided people.[28]

He added that the magistrates of the town believed there was nothing to fear.

In the face of all this, only a few officers seemed to be on the alert, as Hopton was. The commander at Blackburn said that his barracks were easily defended. He saw the magistrates regularly and they expected little trouble. But he was sure that the lower orders of the town and country *did* support the Chartists. The night before writing his report, he was told that a general uprising was planned for, yes, 6 May. He added that he wished the magistrates were more given to searching for arms, for he knew that a number of muskets had been sold. And he pointed out that all this activity had occurred *without* any observable Chartist meetings – the apparent lack of meetings that had so comforted the other local commanders. His own soldiers, the Blackburn commander explained, did not mix much with the local population, so they might not know what was going on.[29]

Those commanders who now took the trouble to double-check local conditions after sending Napier their first reports were beginning to hear the most extraordinary things. Would there be a popular uprising on the day the Chartist Petition was to be presented? The commander at Leeds had written to Napier to say that despite the city being O'Connor's headquarters, the Chartists and their 'Field Days' were losing popularity. But he wrote again three days later, on 18 April, to say that he had asked his soldiers to listen after 'the doings and sayings of the people of Leeds when they meet in the Evenings'. Well, his soldiers gave him an earful: 'They tell me that a general rising in May is a thing talked of as a certainty. And the soldiers would not "stand against their brothers".'

So this is what the soldiers were telling their commanding officer: They would fight on the side of the people in a general uprising less than three weeks away.

Meanwhile, at least one northern landowner, the Duke of Portland, was apoplectic. The duke was the son of the earlier Duke of Portland who as Home Secretary had tried to drive English radicalism underground in the 1790s. Our Duke of Portland had undertaken only the briefest of political careers in 1827–8, yet it would seem that as a magistrate in Mansfield he had mixed sufficiently in the local life of Nottinghamshire to know that something was happening even though so many of Napier's local commanders could not see it.[30] Portland said that although he could not fully trust his spies, they had convinced him that something was afoot. By February he was living in fear of a Leveller rebellion. He was especially worried because the lower classes were giving themselves military training. They would be led by the army pensioners if hostilities broke out. So Portland had a suggestion for Napier: to get the War Office to order all the pensioners to appear at headquarters 'under some pretext'.[31]

Portland was very energetic in pressing this matter. The correspondence between the duke, Napier, and the authorities in London flew back and forth. Napier's personal opinion was that the duke was ignorant – strangely ignorant – of the real opinions of his tenants, and that he had been driven to distraction by a malevolent or deluded informant. Yet Napier tried to be as helpful as he could. The local M.P., Launcelot Rolleston, told Napier that he handled Portland very well.[32] And soon Napier agreed to put a troop of cavalry in Mansfield in premises provided by the duke. As for the several hundred out-pensioners about whom the duke was so worried, they were now required to help keep order if they wanted to retain their pensions.[33] Some of these men were put to work as spies in pubs. Napier pointed out that many of the men were Chartists themselves, and that was all to the good. As old soldiers they knew the army could not be easily beaten, and so (Napier imagined) they would tell their Chartist brethren to lie low till a better day, and until then to keep the peace.[34]

***

Military officers at Napier's level are surrounded by conflicting information, and faced with all of it they have to make their plans and convince civilian officials of the need to carry them out. Then they have to monitor the results as a bewildering number of details pour in. Certainly this was the situation in which Napier found himself. To sum up: At first his headquarters did not know where all the troops were, and he had to commission an up-to-date map. Some of the local commanders could not defend their poorly sited barracks – or their soldiers did not have barracks at all, living isolated from each other

144   *The north of England*

in rented rooms in public houses. In Leeds, the soldiers told their officers that they would fight on the side of the people. Commanders elsewhere had the missed preparations for mass unrest three weeks away, and thought nothing was wrong. They could find little support for the Chartists even where large meetings had been held.

Meanwhile, an irate duke was running his own spy network, and it would not be surprising if he were preparing to defend his estates. And the working classes were learning drill under retired soldiers and stockpiling firearms and other war materiel. They had agreed on the date for a revolution – 6 May.

Napier's initial plan

In a letter to his brother in early April, Napier outlined his conclusions from the intelligence gathered so far:

> I drew a plan of the district containing only the towns where any detachments are quartered with the troops and companies in each marked down, so that if I am suddenly turned out of bed by the Chartists I know in a moment where to lay my hand upon the soldiers without fumbling for half an hour through a Brigade Major's distribution returns, smothered in the details of their craft. This was necessary for the troops are in 26 different detachments and extending over half England. Some are above two hundred miles from me. . . . [T]he magistrates are divided into Whigs and Tories [–] and personal enmities[,] every mother's son of them as far as I can yet discover ready to go any length for his sect and creed[,] the town magistrates liberal from fear of the populace. The Country bucks are too old and far gone Tories to have hopes of gaining popularity *now* by being radicals so they are labouring to get troops *near their own houses.*[35]

Operationally, that was the crux of the problem. In their apprehension the leading citizens had asked Jackson to send troops to defend their own little patches and he had complied. But this had left a situation that was militarily untenable. There was 'a foolish dispersion of the troops; because the Magistrates are powerful fellows, that Jackson could not manage them, and probably I shall be also obliged to give way in like manner':

> However I shall nevertheless endeavour to get my people a *little* more together. I do not mind detachments which amount to 100 men well-lodged but I am uneasy at having for example 36 dragoons among the ill-disposed populace at Halifax a man being in billet *here* and his horse *there* so he may get a pike, (or more probably *ten*) into him before he is fairly awake![36]

Napier explained that '[t]he state of the country is bad enough . . . , but it is the distress the people suffer which is the great danger, not their rising to resent it or better their condition'. Indeed, '[t]here appears to be less fear of a rising than of the gradual growth of a *base murderous servile character*'.[37] Indeed, Napier was less concerned about a revolution and more worried about something else – that the common people might become so dispirited they would begin to engage in random yet perhaps widespread acts of violence. That is after all what happened with the better-planned Irish revolution of 1798 that he remembered so well.[38] The assessment that he conveyed to Lord John Russell was that the Chartists were no threat to his troops if met in open combat, so long as his forces were not too thinly dispersed. Meanwhile his officers would provide 'less capricious' intelligence than the magistrates had been producing.[39]

Napier now went to work on several fronts. He pressed the Home Office and the local officials alike for the construction of proper barracks, and he recommended a policy of *not* providing troops to any town that refused to house them properly. If the magistrates stirred up trouble and wanted the army to sort it out, they might try to find decent quarters for the soldiers, and in the meantime they might try to get along with their own people rather better.[40] Meanwhile Napier wanted a new focus on law enforcement. He said that he faced 'many a man who could screw up his courage to a fight but who cannot bear the . . . law preying upon his spirits, and finding it vigorously enforced by the civil authorities.'[41]

Napier remained in frequent contact with the Home Office as well as the Horse Guards. But the Home Secretary, Lord John Russell, himself seemed somewhat distant. One view is that Russell was more interested in managing the House of Commons and the grand strategy of the government than he was in the more detailed work of the Home Office itself; and he was all the more emotionally withdrawn because he had recently lost his wife.[42] Whatever his reasons, Russell only communicated with Napier through the Undersecretary of State, Samuel March Phillipps, with whom Napier maintained an almost daily correspondence.

Meanwhile Napier was unhappy that the distant Lord John had begun to arm the rich. Any of the 'principal Inhabitants' who wished to do so could apply to the Lord Lieutenant of their county for permission to organize yet another local militia. And as soon as it was formed – not trained, for there was no provision for training these new militias – it would be armed *gratis* out of government stockpiles. Hearing of this, at least one group of Chartists wrote to the Home Secretary to ask that he arm *them*. Napier soon came to believe that he had convinced Lord John to back away from this policy of the wholesale arming of civilians, and instead to augment the troops under his command with reinforcements from Ireland. Yet in fact the arms continued to flow to the new militias for some time.[43]

While Napier was engaged in this administrative dance with Russell and Phillipps in the spring of 1839, trying to get the troops and barracks that he needed for his own activities while reining in the reactionary and potentially trigger-happy local elites, he firmed up his military plan.

146 *The north of England*

Operationally he tended to agree with Colonel James Shaw Kennedy, who had written an account of the troubles for the police commissioners. A copy of the report was sent to Napier. Shaw Kennedy made the same point that Napier had made, that the troops were too widely dispersed. But while Napier agreed with Shaw Kennedy about military strategy, he came to a sharply different conclusion politically. For Shaw Kennedy, the Chartists were led by the very same men who were behind the Captain Swing rebellion at the beginning of the decade. Then as now, these individuals were bent on 'plunder and assassination'. And they wanted to bring down the monarchy. Napier summarized Shaw Kennedy's views for the Home Office, adding that '[t]he foregoing observations may not be useless when contrasted with the information sent to the Secretary of State by more able and more competent men'. (Napier's snippiness on this occasion should be set against the bulk of his letters to the Home Office at the time. Often he included apparently sincere expressions of humility, and he frequently expressed a desire to consult with and be advised by Lord John.)

Napier explained that the true state of affairs was very different from the alarmist and conspiratorial picture that Colonel Shaw Kennedy had painted. Napier stressed what the Colonel had failed to see: the distress of the handloom weavers. Even on his full wages a weaver could not feed himself, much less his family. Fully employed single men making the highest rate of wages were starving. If the condition of the people could be ameliorated, then in Napier's view the Chartist danger would pass.[44]

With all this in mind, and drawing as well on the lessons of the Irish rebellions of 1798 and 1803, Napier decided to concentrate his forces and leave many of the towns entirely ungarrisoned.[45] If no soldiers were present when trouble broke out, Napier argued the town could be retaken later. On the other hand, if the troops tried to guard *every* city, and if they were too few in number in any one place – below about one hundred, Napier believed – they could be checked or some of them killed. Then the rumour of a government defeat would spread throughout the British Isles. In the wake of any such rumour, 'rivers of blood would flow' in Ireland.[46]

Napier proceeded to divide his army into three main groups: Nine hundred men under Sir Hew Ross would guard the northern area, including Carlisle, Newcastle, and Sunderland. Under Colonel Thomas Wemyss, two thousand eight hundred men would secure a district stretching between Manchester, Rochdale, Burnley, Wigan, Liverpool, and Chester. And under Napier himself one thousand men would cover the area between Leeds, Hull, and Napier's headquarters in Nottingham. (As new railway lines opened over the next two and a half years, Napier was able to further redeploy and consolidate his units.[47]) If a rebellion broke out in one area, the other two army groups would send assistance. But if the rebellion were a more general one, Napier would select a few positions to defend, and he would use his authority to call in aid from Ireland. In this case Napier said he would make no effort to maintain communications with London. Only if the rebels were moving in that direction would he press them closely to 'protect the country from being widely ravished'.

In developing these plans Napier warmed to the idea of arming the yeomanry and keeping them constantly on duty, so as to overawe the people and prevent trouble. Along the same lines, he wanted to increase the size of his army – not so he could win in a fight, for he was confident of victory if it came to that, but for 'intimidation', so he could prevent a fight from breaking out. And he wanted to have as many Irish troops as he could get for his English theatre of operations. This would help to assure the loyalty of the men. The English troops might be Chartists themselves.[48]

***

It was the 'inordinate avarice' of the employers in not wanting to 'fairly pay their workmen' which had caused all this trouble, Napier told Colonel Wemyss.[49] What was the result? He reflected in his journal:

> These poor people are inclined to rise and if they do what horrid bloodshed! This is dreadful work, would to God I had gone to Australia: however it is now a struggle for existence, a servile war. . . . These people threaten to take arms. If they do they will be crushed by force and then resort to the means which slaves must employ. Mammon has supplanted God: our rulers have worshipped the evil one, and evil are the results.[50]

Now 'Tory injustice and Whig imbecility' in not having granted the suffrage might yet push the people into rebellion:

> Poor fellows, they only want fair play and would then be quiet enough; but they are harassed by taxes till they can bear it no longer. Between five and six thousand men and eighteen guns are under me; we could manage a large force of Chartists, but I trust in God nothing so horrible will happen. . . . The doctrine of slowly reforming while men are starving, is of all silly things the most silly; famishing men cannot wait.[51]

Notes

1 Napier to Fitzroy Somerset, 16 December 1838, NP, BL Add. MS 49114, fol. 128.
2 Napier to Phillipps at the Home Office, 25 August 1839, TNA HO 40/53/737–38.
3 *London Gazette*, 10 January 1837, 19456 p. 64.
4 Emily and Sarah Napier to Napier, 31 August 1837, NP, BL Add. MS 54532, fols 9–10; Napier to Robertson, 26 October 1838, NP, BL Add. MS 49107, fol. 20.
5 Copy of Somerset to Jackson, 16 December 1838, NP, BL Add. MS 49114, fol. 127; John MacDonald to Napier, [December 1838], NP, BL Add. MS 49114, fols 123–24. That year, Easter fell on the last day of March.
6 Napier, *Ireland*, 70.

148 *The north of England*

7 Napier's copies of his letters to Somerset and Jackson, 16 December 1838, NP, BL Add. MS 49114, fol. 128.

8 For some of this, along with Jackson's reports of widespread alarm, see Jackson to Phillipps, 6, 25, 26 February, 9, 16 March 1839, TNA HO 40/53/255–57, 275–57, 283–85, 307–09, 315–17.

9 Zöe Laidlaw, *Colonial Connections, 1815–1845: Patronage, the Information Revolution, and Colonial Government* (Manchester: Manchester University Press, 2005), 169–85, 193–94.

10 Napier to Robertson, 19 January, 19 February 1839, NP, BL Add. MS 49107, fols 21–24.

11 Napier's journal, March 1839, given in WN, 2:4–5.

12 Napier to W. Napier, 9 March 1839, given in WN, 2:2.

13 Napier to Robertson, 19 February 1839, NP, BL Add. MS 49107, fols 22–24.

14 Napier's journal, 29 March 1839, given in WN, 2:4.

15 Napier to W. Napier, 22 March 1839, given in ibid, 2:3.

16 Napier's journal, 30 March 1839, given in ibid, 2:5–7; Napier to W. Napier, 30 March 1830, 2:7. For the difficulty the Home Office had in mastering the volume of information coming in, see Neil Pye, *The Home Office and the Chartists, 1838–1848: Protest and Repression in the West Riding of Yorkshire* (Pontypool, Wales: Merlin Press, 2013), 54–56.

17 Napier to W. Napier, 15 March 1839, given in WN, 2:2–3; Napier to W. Napier, 9 April 1839, NLB, fols 2–4; Napier to Col. Thomas Wemyss, 10 April 1839, NLB, fols 4–7.

18 Map, 18 April 1839, NP, BL Add. MS 54545, fol. 3; on the need for it, see Napier to W. Napier, 9 April 1839, NLB, fols 2–4. Napier's letter to his commanders, 11 April 1839, TNA HO 40/53/341–43. There had already been some attempts to address the inadequacy of the barracks, as with the renting of temporary quarters at Todmorden – John Crossley to Russell, 27 and 29 January 1839, PRO, HO 40/37 fols 64–70. But there does not seem to have been much improvement generally.

19 Napier's journal, 18 April 1839, given in WN, 2:10–11; Louth to Napier, 17 April 1839, NP, BL Add. MS 54545, fols 37–38.

20 Examination of John Tempest, Woollen Manufacturer of Rochdale, 28 December 1838, TNA HO 40/37/24–27.

21 Magistrate Chadwick to Russell, 8 March 1839, with enclosures, TNA HO 40/37/94–102.

22 Major Creagh to Napier, 15 April 1839, NP, BL Add. MS 54545, fols 22–23.

23 Blackley to Napier, 15 April 1839, NP, BL Add. MS 54545, fols 24–25.

24 Chase, *Chartism*, 32, 62.

25 Thomas Maitland Edwards to Napier, 16 April 1839, NP, BL Add. MS 54545, fols 35–36.

26 See R. C. Gammage, *History of the Chartist Movement, 1837–1854* [1854] (1894; reprint, London: Merlin Press, 1969), 117. And Gammage, although a Chartist, was chary of reporting inflated attendance figures for the Chartist meetings. He reported what he thought he knew – Gammage, 113.

27 Soldiers who were medically unfit or whose regiments the state did not want to keep on full pay – Pye, *The Home Office and the Chartists*, 51.

28 John Hopton to Napier, 16 April 1839, NP, BL Add. MS 54545, fols 33–34.

29 Bushe to Napier, 18 April 1839, NP, BL Add. MS 54545, fols 47–49.

30 Scarbrough to Russell, 14 May 1839, TNA HO 40/47/124–29 at 125.

31 Inspector George Martin (who had seen Portland and others in Nottinghamshire) to the Commissioners of Police, 27 February 1839, TNA HO 40/47/1–2; Portland to Napier, 15 April 1839, NP, BL Add. MS 54545, fols 10–11; Somerset to Napier, 16 December 1838, fol. 128. One contemporary noted that the Duke had recently turned Tory and had become an alarmist – copy of Anonymous to General Sir Harold Ferguson, 6 March 1839, HO 40/47/37–40.

32 Napier's journal, 14 April 1839, given in WN, 2:9; Rolleston to Napier, 21 April 1839, NP, BL Add. MS 54545, fols 58–59. Portland seemed to calm down by September – Portland to Normanby, 9 September 1839, TNA HO 40/47/558–59.

Command in the north 149

33 Scarbrough to Russell, 14 May 1839, TNA HO 40/47/124–29; Proclamation to Chelsea Out-Pensioners, 9 May 1839, TNA HO 40/41/360.
34 H. Palmer, *Police and Protest in England and Ireland, 1780–1850* (Cambridge: Cambridge UP, 1988), 431; Napier's Journal, 18 April 1839, given in WN, 2:11.
35 Napier to W. Napier, 9 April 1839, NLB, fols 2–4.
36 Ibid, fol 3. Neil Pye, in his recent book *The Home Office and the Chartists*, has Napier arguing *for* dispersing small detachments away from their officers and *for* putting the barracks in the middle of towns where the troops might be bottled up. Lord Hill resisted Napier on these points, says Pye (90–91). But Pye's argument here is grounded upon a misapprehension of Phillipps to Napier, 9 August 1839, TNA HO 41/14/399–405. Napier had written a memorandum on how the troops should *not* be dispersed into small groups nor put into barracks surrounded by houses. Phillipps is quoting Napier's own views back to him and adding Lord Hill's mostly supportive comments:'You observe,' Phillipps tells Napier,' "that no Detachment should be in barracks situated in the midst of houses in the centre of a town" for the reasons which you assign'. Phillipps added that Lord Hill agreed with what Napier was saying (fols 400–01). Later in his book Pye comes around to my view of Napier's tactics (112–13).
37 Napier to W. Napier, 9 April 1839, NLB, fols 2–4.
38 Ibid, fol. 2; Napier to Wemyss, 10 April 1839, NLB, fols 4–7.
39 Napier to Phillipps at the Home Office, 15 April 1839, TNA HO 40/55/345–47. His first reference to using his men as an intelligence-gathering 'surveillance' network: Napier to Wemyss, 10 April 1839, NLB, fols 4–7.
40 Napier to Phillipps at the Home Office, 1 and 2 May, TNA HO 40/53/401–06. Some magistrates responded by monitoring the Chartists themselves – Huddersfield magistrates to Normanby, 22 January 1840, HO 40/57/255–56. For a hint of the struggles Napier would have with local officials over keeping the promises they made to pay for barracks, see Napier to Fox Maule, 2 October 1839, TNA HO 40/53/797–99.
41 Napier to Phillipps, 3 May 1839, TNA HO 40/53/409–11.
42 F. C. Mather, *Public Order in the Age of the Chartists* (1959; New York: Augustus M. Kelley, 1967), 39–40.
43 Somerset to Napier, 29 April 1839, NP, BL Add. MS 54519, fol. 8; Russell's printed circular, 7 May 1839, TNA HO 40/55/770–72; Russell to Lord Derby as Lord Lieutenant of Lancaster, printed, May 1839, NP, BL Add. MS 54513, fol. 59; Charles Daniel Davies, president of the Stockport Workingmen's Association, to Russell, 25 May 1839, TNA HO 40/41/131; Barnsley magistrates to Russell, 2 August 1839, HO 40/51/315. Sometimes the local authorities were wary of distributing pistols unless a military officer were sent to instruct the inhabitants in their use – Bradford magistrates to Harewood, 6 August 1839, HO 40/51/347–49. Also, the promised arms did not always arrive – Harewood to Russell, 11 August 1839, HO 40/51/387–88. Bronterre O'Brien said that the Chartist request for arms was his idea – O'Brien's speech at Manchester, 20 May 1839, reported in HO 40/43/239–46 at 243.
44 Summarized by Charles Napier, 25 April 1839, TNA HO 40/53/367–70, sent as attachment in Napier to Phillips, 29 April 1839, 40/53/363–65. For Shaw Kennedy, see Palmer, *Police and Protest*, 294–95, 365, 367, 694n10, 712n149.
45 Napier to Wemyss, 10 April 1839, NLB, fols 4–7; Napier to Ross, 11 April 1839, NLB, fol. 7; Napier to Phillipps, 13 April 1839, TNA HO 40/53/345–47.
46 Napier to Wemyss, 22 April 1839, given in WN, 2:13–15. In July Napier more fully explained to the Home Office his views about the unfortunate consequences of the troops even once being defeated: Napier to Phillipps, 24 July 1839, TNA HO 40/53/573–76.
47 Wemyss to Napier, 15, 21 February 1841, NP, BL Add. MS 54512, fols 103–09; Napier to Phillipps, 6 August 1839, TNA HO 40/53/627.
48 Napier's summary of Shaw Kennedy's report, 25 April 1839, TNA HO 40/53/367–70; Napier to de Grey, 8 May 1839, given in WN, 2:30–31; Napier to Phillipps, 9 May 1839,

150   *The north of England*

2:31–32; 'intimidation': Napier to Phillips, 28 April, 29 July 1839, HO 40/53/381–82, 577–79. It would take Napier some time to properly deploy his men (Napier's journal, 27 April 1839, 2:22) although Ross was already in Carlisle – Jackson to Phillipps, 16 March 1839, TNA HO 40/53/315–17.

49 Napier to Wemyss, 22 April 1839, given in WN, 2:13–15.
50 Napier's journal, 23 April 1839, given in WN, 2:12–13.
51 Napier's journal, 27 April 1839, given in ibid, 2:22–23.

12 The long-term threat

Napier kept adjusting his tactics as the danger of a general uprising seemed to recede and the longer-term work of building peace became more important.[1] The rising that was scheduled for 6 May did not come to pass. The idea that violence would break out at the moment the Petition was presented was always more of an assumption among rank-and-file Chartists than a concerted plan by their leaders. When by coincidence Melbourne's government resigned that day, the presentation of the Petition was in any case put off.[2]

Even after 6 May there was danger nonetheless. Before the end of the month there had been a gathering of 100,000 to 150,000 near Huddersfield, and although it passed off peacefully, armed resistance and a redistribution of property were discussed.[3] In Manchester in the middle of the month the Chartist leaders announced a 500,000-person gathering at Kersal Moor. They assured the town authorities that those attending would *not* be armed that day, but they added that their men had weapons nonetheless. And they said that as a body they were numerous enough to enforce their demands and burn and destroy whatever they liked in defiance of the police and the army.[4] One broadside announcing the meeting, brought to Napier, asked the attendees if they had 'plenty of powder and shot', so they could 'nourish the tree of liberty, With The Blood Of Tyrants' (Figure 12.1).[5]

With threats like this, Napier would meet with magistrates in large groups to try to get them to coordinate their efforts in case of crisis. '[N]o doubt there are many really gentlemen [*sic*] and sensible men among them. . . . [W]hen I get acquainted with them all, I shall find out', he had written the month before.[6] He tried to get the local elites to show restraint and not to respond with force merely because they saw flags of protest.[7] He also met with the other side. While he believed that O'Connor merely wanted to prolong the crisis to sell his newspaper,[8] he attempted to reason with other Chartist leaders, and he went to see them in secret:

> I understand you are to have a great meeting on Kersall Moor, with a view to laying your grievances before parliament: you are quite right to do so and I will take care that neither soldier nor policeman shall be within sight to disturb you. But meet peaceably, for if there is the least disturbance I

Figure 12.1 The factory chimneys of Manchester as seen from Kersal Moor in 1857. By Samuel Read, *Illustrated London News*, 4 July 1857. Manchester, from Kersall Moor (engraving), Read, Samuel (1816–83) / Private Collection /

shall be amongst you and at the sacrifice of my life, if necessary, do my duty. Now go and do yours![9]

He also met with 'a gentleman intimate with the Chartist leaders, if not one himself'. He tried to convince the man that if 300,000 people came to Kersal Moor they could not be properly fed or moved around. And if indeed they were armed and starving, violence would break out, they would charge the military, and many of them would wind up dead before the cavalry and the cannons. The gentleman responded that he was not afraid of the troops: 'He said, peace had put us out of practice, and we could not use our artillery; but he was soon convinced that this was nonsense, and reported my observations to the leaders.'[10] Napier continued:

I offered him no abuse, said many Chartists who acted on principle were to be honoured others to be pitied as acting from ignorance, and certain to bitterly repent when they saw the terrible mischief that would ensue. This, I believe, had a good effect, and, saying only what in my conviction was true, it is probable I spoke well, for he seemed struck by the evils pointed out as inevitably attending even a disciplined army.

When the Kersal meeting came, Napier kept his troops out of sight but at the ready, exactly as he said he would do. And he went to the meeting. He was accompanied by Colonel Wemyss, and the colonel managed to argue some of the men and women around him into his own Tory views, or so it seemed to Napier.[11] Napier himself found that he agreed with almost everything he heard from the platform, although he was unimpressed by the size of the crowd:

I attended the meeting yesterday in coloured clothes, and will wager, that if thirty thousand were hanged none would have been left alive! Certainly twenty-five thousand very innocent people, and ten thousand women and children, would have been murdered! The remainder might have been Chartists, expressing orderly, legal political opinions, pretty much – don't tell this! very like my own![12]

So much for the five hundred thousand men who were to have met at Manchester that day. Napier was neither shocked by their ideas nor frightened by their numbers.

***

After what he had seen at Kersal Moor – when the meeting was neither so large nor so unreasonable as he feared it might be – Napier refused to send troops each and every time the local magistrates alarmed themselves over the prospect of a march in the countryside. Sometimes when a Chartist gathering did threaten to become larger than normal and Napier chose to dispatch his forces, he would go out with them, accompanying the magistrates. He did this

154   *The north of England*

on the occasion of the meetings connected to the 'Two or Three Days Holiday' which the Chartist Convention declared across the country that August. Napier recorded that the mere sight of the military would usually defuse the situation.[13] Indeed, defusing situations was his main goal. When the inevitable frictions arose between the soldiers and the civilian authorities, Napier told his officers to be as open and friendly as possible with the local officials and smooth away any areas of contention: '[T]hrow all the good humour you can on the matter,' he told one major, 'for at present we want more oil in our salad than vinegar.'[14]

Napier thought that with his visible and concentrated deployment of the regular army he could control the troublemakers. It was a subtle long-term strategy of using the mere sight of massed soldiers, plus any good will and cooperation which he could maintain among the magistrates, to keep the country at peace until the government should 'consider the Charter in Parliament and cultivate the good-will of the people, or take measures for disarming them: there is no wisdom in letting complaints be rejected and pikes made'.[15]

Napier was on the lookout for any tactics he could find to help keep the peace, such as relying upon his own moral authority as a sympathizer. It happened that one of the riflemen stationed at Nottingham was proving a particularly articulate and influential advocate for Chartism. Napier wanted to talk to the man personally, but Lord John Russell would not agree. The Home Secretary feared the incident would get into the papers, and he wanted Napier to send someone else instead.[16] But as Napier explained to his brother, none of his junior officers could debate the Chartists like he could. They did not understand Chartism the way he did. And nor could they address the dissident rifleman with anything like his authority as a decorated officer who himself had decades of service in the rifle corps and significant combat experience:

> My whole success, or hopes of it, rested on my being known to hold the man's own opinions, and only differing as to the means taken to give them effect: upon the general himself reasoning with him; on my being an old rifleman. Thus I might stop the taint, but if I do as Lord John advises the man will gain a victory and be confirmed in his views.[17]

Napier's radical politics may have helped him in his duties in the north, but as might well be suspected, they were not helpful when it came to maintaining a good relationship with his superiors in London. When Napier told the Horse Guards that real peace would only come when political concessions were made to the Chartists, the Commander-in-Chief of the Forces would not stand for it. As Napier reported the matter to William:

> I fear to write to Lord Fitzroy. A few days ago I merely said that – I saw no way to meet the evil but, to make concessions on the one hand and on the other to organize a strong constabulary, to stand between the troops and the people. His answer was.[sic] 'Lord Hill desires me to point out your

The long-term threat   155

observation, and to suggest that you avoid all remarks having allusion to political questions; and I am to say, without entering into the merits of the question, that it is clear to Lord Hill, that neither he as commander in chief, nor you as the major-general commanding the northern district can have anything to do with the matter; it is therefore better that you should confine yourselves to what is strictly your provinces as military men.'

Napier's reaction:

After this I have no more to say. I gave no advice as to what they ought to do, but merely said that as a matter of fact that discontent was so general I saw no other means to meet it with effect: and that in a confidential letter! You see how fearful they are of looking facts in the face, or involving themselves in difficulty. Perhaps they are right: governed as the country is, if Lord Hill acted otherwise he would be at daggers with the ministry in a week![18]

'[S]oon it will be found that instead of advising me not to allude to political questions', he added, 'it would be better to take my advice. At Hull the soldiers and mob joined to thrash the police.' Indeed, it was apparent at least to Napier that all was not well. In May came word that at Burnley the coal miners had sent a new shaft out under the army barracks so they could blow it up with gunpowder. Elsewhere a soldier wrote to Colonel Wemyss very respectfully, albeit anonymously, to say that he and his comrades would not fire on the people. Their reasoning was that as ex-soldiers they would themselves suffer worst under the Poor Law.[19]

Into the summer

June was relatively quiet all the same, and Napier hoped that his strategy of containment had triumphed. This was not to be.

In July, there were several days of unrest in Birmingham (which was not part of Napier's district), prompted by a baton charge by the police. Then on the fifteenth a mob tried to burn the Bull Ring. They pulled ticking out of the shops to make huge fires, and they set fire to the buildings.[20] Napier was now contemptuous of the government for having used the calm of June as an excuse for ignoring the question of social reform. He told his brother that if he were to confess to his superiors what he really thought about the need for radical change, their only question would be whether to send their commander to Newgate or Bedlam. The people suffered because of the greed of the cotton lords, he said. While he thought he could keep order nevertheless, and the government could maintain the status quo by building up a huge military and police presence, he now despaired of the Whig ministry using any period of quiet in the north as an occasion to effect real social change.[21]

Meanwhile, in the face of a seemingly deteriorating situation that July, he did what he could. He kept imploring the magistrates to show the greatest

156 *The north of England*

restraint in interfering with popular meetings. And he refused to send them troops unless he thought they were really necessary. Yet given all that was happening, the magistrates kept demanding his help. They wore what Napier referred to as their '*asking-for-troops* face', and he wrote that he had grown very tired of seeing it.[22]

***

The violence in the Bull Ring was not the only sign of a deterioration.[23] The very city where Napier maintained his headquarters, Nottingham, was another major focus of Chartist activity. The slums of Nottingham were reputed to be the worst in the British Empire outside India, pushing the lower orders of the town towards radicalism. And few could forget the burning of Nottingham Castle by the Luddites in 1831 – for the building lay in ruins above the town.[24] Napier made extended visits to Wemyss's and Ross's sectors, touring his own district and going on semi-yearly rounds of inspection, so he was not always in Nottingham.[25] But even when he was away from the city he knew of the goings-on there. Spurred on by the Home Office, for months the authorities had made arrests, banned meetings, read the Riot Act, and called for troops – sometimes in Napier's experience (as in the Three Days Holiday in August) reading the Riot Act and demanding soldiers literally every few hours when nothing at all was happening.[26]

Napier tried to find creative ways for offering concessions to the common people where he could. So when the Chartists began filling a Nottingham church each Sunday and leaving no room for anyone else – not least the mass of soldiers who went in parade to the services – Napier had to decide on his response. The simple thing would have been to keep the soldiers away. But Napier worried that a disappearance of the soldiers could signal to the Chartists that the military was somehow offended by their presence. Instead, he told his men to go in last, and any soldiers for whom there was no room would simply not get to attend church that week. Furthermore, he went to the services himself to make clear to both the priests and the magistrates that the army was *not* there with the intention of backing them up or sparking a confrontation. Under Napier's personal supervision, neither the soldiers nor the Chartists would violate the sacredness of the occasion – or so he believed. Napier sought only 'peace and . . . decorum'. And indeed no trouble broke out.[27]

We should not minimize the level of provocation that the beleaguered local authorities were dealing with. Soldiers and magistrates were stoned and they had to face mobs with pikes.[28] At Rochdale on 9 August at one in the morning, after a Chartist demonstration that wound through the town, John Deegan told the crowd – to quote the report of his speech that was sent to Napier –

> Arm yourselves well with pikes and fire arms and get plenty of powder, for the time is near at hand when we must either put down the Government or the Government put down us.
>
>   If Lord John Russell will not give us universal suffrage, we will have universal destruction.[29]

The long-term threat   157

It may be time to stop and take stock of the government reaction to all this. In the House of Commons, Lord John Russell, who over the previous year had repeatedly and publicly expressed his belief in the right of the Chartists to state their grievances peacefully – although not in large meetings or by torchlight – now went on to say that he did not blame them for their mistaken views. He explained that in the 'manufacturing districts', 'very large masses of people' had grown up without the moderating influence of a local aristocracy and without proper religious instruction. But recognizing this state of affairs did not make the government's path in the present moment any easier. Russell complained that prosecutions for sedition were very difficult because the informants could never be called to testify about what they had heard; if they were to testify, they would hardly be allowed to attend another Chartist meeting. And the workingmen could not testify themselves because they would be persecuted by their fellows. Meanwhile, arms were being stockpiled and even displayed.[30] So it seemed that the central government still did not know what to do in the face of the events in the North.

Because of new government fears, over the coming months Napier would be ordered to station troops at Newcastle, Durham, and Cockermouth. This somewhat divided his troops. In his view the safer and the more constitutionally sound measure would have been to found local police forces to uphold the law.[31] Yet despite the interference with the placement of his soldiers, on balance he was given a free hand to carry out his plans. He remained confident that he would prevail.

All the same, by midsummer he could have no further illusions that there would be political change of any kind or that the government would accept the Petition. So for all his confidence of victory, what victory would mean was defeating the poor and destroying any hope for the reforms that he passionately believed in. The irony was not lost on him, but he thought he had an answer for it. As he recorded in his journal near the end of the eventful month of July, he believed as strongly as ever in universal suffrage, vote by ballot, and the reform of the Poor Law. And yet:

> Good government consists in having good laws well obeyed. England has abundance [sic] of bad laws, but is every man to arm against every law he thinks bad? No! Bad laws must be reformed by the concentrated reason of the nation gradually acting on the legislature, not by the pikes of individuals acting on the bodies of the executive. The law, good or bad, is to be obeyed.[32]

Even amidst the fast-moving events of the summer, Napier had not forgotten the teachings of Sismondi[33] – that capitalism changed things too quickly and with no concern for creating a balanced society. One did not simply reform the laws *too quickly* in the other direction, as this passage suggests. In the same journal entry he pointed out that

> [m]anufactures have formed an artificial state of society: a dense polluted population dependent for food on accidental variations of trade, one day

158 *The north of England*

in full work and high wages, the next neither work nor wages, and all willing to break the laws. To meet this you must have a strong police.

But he went on to explain that if Chartism *were* to get out of hand and the monarchy were to be overthrown – this was one of his fears in the night – there was still the hope of Bonapartism:

> Let us suppose the whole people wanted and could force a republic. What would result? A desperate struggle between the manufacturing and the landed interests, ending in a civil war, to be decided finally by a military chief who would not be fool enough to wear a hat when a crown was in his hand. Nor such a rogue either: for what patriotic man would let his country be governed by dozens of squabbling republican fools, when his own good sense and single will could rule and guide her aright?[34]

As he wrote to his sister in September, '[A]n enlightened class of labouring men have left their rulers far behind; the people are weary of them'. If the people were not given their freedom by the self-serving factions of Whigs and Tories, they would take it for themselves. Was there hope? 'With a strong loyal army', the government should declare bankruptcy and bring in immediate universal suffrage. Nothing less would do.[35]

Notes

1 Napier to Phillipps, 14 May 1839, TNA HO 40/53/457–59.
2 Mark Hovell, *The Chartist Movement*, T. F. Tout (ed.), 2nd edn (Manchester: Manchester UP, 1925), 141–44.
3 Napier's journal, 1–6 May 1839, given in WN, 2:23–25; Malcolm Chase, *Chartism: A New History* (Manchester: Manchester UP, 2007), 70–71; deposition of John Brown, labourer, 22 May 1839, TNA HO 40/51/153–59; J. C. Laycock, Clerk of the Huddersfield magistrates, to Lord Harewood, Lord-Lieutenant of the West Riding, 22 May 1839 (copy), HO 40/51/167–68.
4 Thomas Evans, Manchester borough reeve, to Russell, 17 May 1839, TNA HO 40/43/229–31.
5 Given in WN, 2:29–30. For another broadside announcing the Kersal Moor meeting, see TNA HO 40/43/233–35.
6 Napier to W. Napier, 9 April 1839, NLB, fols 2–4. For Napier's attempts to get the magistrates of Manchester to work together, see Napier to Phillipps, 17, 21/22 May 1839, TNA HO 40/53/469–76.
7 Napier to Somerset, 13 May 1839, given in WN, 2:33; Napier to an Undersecretary of State, 14 May 1839, 2:34; Manchester magistrate Foster to Phillipps, 14 May 1839, enclosing a resolution of a meeting of sixteen magistrates on 13 May, TNA HO 40/43/213–17; Napier to Phillipps, 21/22 May 1839, TNA HO 40/53/474–76.
8 Napier to Phillipps, 14 May 1839, TNA HO 40/53/457–59; Napier to W. Napier, 15 May 1839, given in WN, 2:27–28.
9 Quoted in WN, 2:40. Napier alluded to having warned the Chartists towards the end of May about the loss of life that would result from any conflict with his troops: Napier to Robertson, 10 June 1839, NP, BL Add. MS 49107, fols 29–30.
10 Napier's journal, 8 June 1839, given in WN, 2:43–44.

The long-term threat 159

11 Maude to [?] 26 May 1839, TNA HO 40/43/261–62; Napier's journal, April 1839, quoted in William Napier Bruce, *The Life of General Sir Charles Napier, G.C.B.* (London: John Murray, 1885), 135.

12 Napier to Hew Ross, 25 May 1839, given in WN, 2:39–40.

13 Sculthorpe, Clerk of the Nottinghamshire Magistrates, to Russell, 13 August 1839, TNA HO 40/47/388; Nottingham Mayor John Wells to Russell, 14 August 1839, 40/47/410–12; Napier to Robertson, 22 July 1839, NP, BL Add. MS 49107, fol. 31; Napier's journal, 11, 12, and 13 August 1839, given in WN, 2:71–72. The Home Office gave Napier still more discretion about whether or not to post troops where the magistrates wanted them – Napier to Phillipps, 11 August 1839, TNA HO 40/53/643–45.

14 Napier to Major Creagh, July 1839, given in WN, 2:59–60.

15 Napier to Ross, 25 May 1839, given in WN, 2:39–40.

16 Somerset to Napier, 4 July 1839, NP, BL Add. MS 54519, fols 19–20; Napier to Phillipps, 15 July 1839, TNA HO 40/53/545–47.

17 Napier to W. Napier, July 1839, given in WN, 2:53–56.

18 Ibid, 55–56.

19 Napier to Phillipps, 17, 21/22 May 1839, TNA HO 40/53/455–57, 474–76; Napier to Somerset, 17 May 1839, given in WN, 2:35; Napier to Somerset, [late May 1839], 2:38–39.

20 F. C. Mather, *Public Order in the Age of the Chartists* (1959; New York: Augustus M. Kelley, 1967), 13; Napier to W. Napier, July 1839, given in WN, 2:53.

21 Napier to W. Napier, 29 July 1839, given in WN, 2:49–51.

22 Napier to W. Napier, [?] July 1839, given in WN, 2:53–56; see also Napier's journal, 30 July 1839, 2:66.

23 Napier to Somerset, 15 July 1839, given in WN, 2:52–53.

24 Launcelot Rolleston, M.P., to Russell, 29 May 1839, TNA HO 40/47/280–91 at 290.

25 Napier to Phillipps, 28 May 1839, TNA HO 40/53/436–38; Mayor Heysham of Carlisle to Normanby, 26 October 1839, HO 40/41/834–35; Napier's journal, various entries, March 1840, given in WN, 2:118–20; Napier to Phillipps, 11 June 1840, HO 40/58/293–95.

26 Launcelot Rolleston, M.P., to Russell (with quotations from a circular of 7 May 1839 by Russell), 29 May 1839, TNA HO 40/47/280–91; Proclamations of the Nottingham magistrates (unsuccessfully) banning the Whitsuntide meeting, May 1839, HO 40/47/174–80; Napier's journal, 11, 12, and 13 August 1839, given in WN, 2:71–72.

27 Napier to Phillipps, 31 July, 4, 17 August 1839, TNA HO 40/53/593–96, 607, 721–24. For church attendance as Chartist protest, see Katrina Navickas, *Protest and the Politics of Space and Place, 1789–1848* (Manchester: Manchester UP, 2016), 281–85.

28 Cairncross to Napier, August 1839, NP, BL Add. MS 54545, fols 179–82; John Fletcher to Russell, 23 August 1839, HO 40/44/191–97; Chase, *Chartism*, 103–04.

29 Horn at Rochdale to Napier, 10 August 1839, NP, BL Add. MS 54545, fols 140–41; see also *Northern Star*, 17 August 1839, 6 cols c-d. A banner reading 'Universal Suffrage, or Universal Devastation', under a cap of liberty, was seen at Kersal Moor – *Manchester Guardian*, 29 May 1839, 3.

30 Russell in the House of Commons, 2 August 1839, HC Deb 02 August 1839 vol 49 cc1148–60.

31 Napier's journal [December?] 1839, quoted in WN, 2:102.

32 Napier's journal, 26 July 1839, given in WN, 2:63. Later on Napier did wonder whether his desire to enforce the law was a case of the power going to his head – but on balance he thought not. See Napier to W. Napier, 8 September 1839, 2:76–77.

33 See also Napier's long and very Sismondian journal entry of 23 August 1839, given in WN, 2:74–76.

34 Napier's journal, 26 July 1839, given in WN, 2:65.

35 Napier to Emily Bunbury, 21 September 1839, NP, NAM 2005–06–724, item 3.

13 Newport and after

The revolutionary outbreak that Napier half expected when the weather turned cold[1] did indeed take place, but it came outside the area over which he was in command. This was the Newport Rising in Wales on 3–4 November. After long preparation and the stockpiling of weapons, seven thousand or so Chartists marched down the industrial valleys of Monmouthshire in converging columns and took the city. Led by the former magistrate John Frost, they attacked the town officials and thirty-one infantrymen who made a stand in the Westgate Hotel. But when they came under fire themselves they were routed and sent off in a panic. Napier's brother-in-law Henry Bunbury expressed the common view: 'A pretty rascal this . . . Frost must have been! to get a number of poor devils shot, [while] the fellow's only assignable object was that of murdering the magistrates and the handful of soldiers.'[2] Afterwards there were trials and death sentences. (After large protests the death sentences were commuted to transportation for life.) Twenty-two people died at Newport, and perhaps fifty were seriously wounded. Historian Malcolm Chase reminds us that this was 'the largest number of fatalities of any civil disturbance in modern British history'.[3]

Would Napier have to face an open rebellion in his own part of the country after all? Indeed, in September and October some of the Chartist leaders in the north had planned an outbreak of their own – taking place on 3 November in coordination with Frost's attack in Wales. But coordinating the different uprisings proved too difficult and the northern risings were put off. Word of the postponement came too late to prevent the Welsh events.[4]

On hearing of the Newport Rising, Napier himself anticipated only minor outbreaks across the large area of England for which he was responsible. He did not think the Chartists could press forward in any coordinated way.[5] But he and his officers remained on the lookout nonetheless. Some of them expected the worst. The commander at Bradford, George Huband, reported to Napier that the quiet in his city – so strong in Chartism – seemed like the quiet in South Wales before the Rising. In Wales, Chartist activities and the manufacture of weapons had been confined to the countryside until the insurgents were ready to strike. Now Huband believed that despite the apparent quiet of Bradford itself, many of the Chartists of the city were off somewhere in their

Newport and after 161

local hills preparing a violent assault. He knew they were holding their larger meetings outside the town.

Was the threat real? As Huband also reported to Napier:

It would be almost impossible to obtain what would be *in other times* called conclusive evidence of an intention on the part of the Chartists here to turn out. The Welsh magistrates had none until the people actually commenced their march upon Newport and had they not had so far to come they would have entered the place without the knowledge of the civil or military authorities.[6]

Huband was reading the *Northern Star*, the *Northern Liberator*, and the *Western Vindicator* for whatever clues he could find, and he was monitoring the correspondence with Wales that was coming out of the Bradford mills. Meanwhile the Chartists were taking over Bradford church rate meetings, where they told anyone with whom they disagreed: 'Your guts are going to be burned out with vitriol.' Huband's raids had uncovered newly forged musket balls by the bucket load, but their makers always got away. The troublemakers and the mob that supported them could disappear into the many small passages opening off the main streets of the city. The Chartists and their socialist allies, and indeed the whole of Bradford, would never give up the Charter unless they were forced to, Huband believed. He wanted Napier to send more troops.

Napier knew there was trouble in the city, but sending troops there was not a part of his plan.[7] He told Huband that he should not take the overexcitement of the magistrates too seriously, nor worry overmuch about the letters flowing between the Chartists in Bradford and Newport. Bradford was not some special centre of the conspiracy, he said, for the Chartists *everywhere* had been corresponding with their Newport brethren. Huband should not listen to the magistrates but to the more trustworthy of the old soldiers. The general thought the real centre of unrest was Manchester, where Feargus O'Connor had been active.[8]

***

In the weeks after Newport the frequency of Chartist meetings continued to increase. Meanwhile unemployment worsened.[9]

It would seem that Napier had to face the prospect of longer work in the north of England. Fortunately he had subordinates such as Colonel Wemyss, and allies like Sir Charles Shaw, who was the Chief Commissioner of the Police at Manchester and a friend of Napier's brother George (Shaw had also been one of Black Charlie's brothers-in-arms in the Carlist war in Spain a few years before[10]). These men tried to listen to all sides in the social conflict, to do whatever they could to bring reconciliation, and to raise money for the poor.[11] Napier came to rely heavily on Shaw's combination of local knowledge and political independence. As the general was to explain a few years later, Shaw proved himself invaluable even when he was faced with crowds of twenty

162   *The north of England*

thousand or more protesters. Working for the Home Office, Shaw was *not* likely to get caught up in the emotions of the panicked rich, and he had been able to avoid the temptation of using grapeshot. Thus he had prevented 'a second "Peterloo" ', Napier maintained.[12]

In Napier's mind, if Shaw was good, John Pitt Kennedy would have been even better. Napier tried to get Kennedy to come over and join him in the peace-building work of the Northern Command. Perhaps Kennedy could supervise some of the police as Shaw did. But Kennedy declined. He was still engaged in a different kind of peace-building, his agricultural reforms at Lough Ash in Ireland. Kennedy thought he could do more good there as a private citizen than in any official capacity (as we have seen, he had already resigned his position as Chief Inspector of Irish Education). He told Napier that he wondered how long the operation in the north of England would last.[13]

***

By December 1839 economic hardship and conflict in England had become very bad. At Bolton two factories were burned down.[14] In Nottingham, groups several dozen strong wandered the streets begging for food. To try to help them, Napier joined forces with Nottingham's mayor, William Roworth, an Evangelical with a long history of working for social improvement.[15] Roworth agreed with Napier about the evils of the 'thrice-accursed new poor law, its bastilles, and its guardians'.[16] So together Napier and the mayor raised a subscription to relieve the two thousand who were starving in the town.[17] Yet as Napier reported with dismay, not everyone in Nottingham believed the poor were all that deserving. The sum raised in the next few days was £4000, but the Poor Law Guardians played Scrooge, arguing that charity of this kind would 'encourage idleness'.

Napier had hoped that the Guardians would be more generous with their official resources in this the coldest and most straitened part of the year. He wanted them to offer outdoor relief but they would not do so.[18] Napier recorded the case of a pregnant young woman, a stranger in the town, looking around Nottingham on Christmas Day for her husband who had come into the city to find work. She was about to give birth and she could hardly move, but she was refused admission to the poor house. On Christmas night the Guardians left her outside in the heavy rain. In response, Mayor Roworth asked another magistrate to countersign his order to the poor house to take her in after all. The magistrate refused. So the mayor took her in himself and fed her; Napier was with him in the deluge on that Christmas evening when the Guardians were working so hard to discourage her from further idleness.[19]

Some of the better-off citizens of Nottingham felt threatened by the bands of the poor who were roaming the city. There were so many of them. 'The streets of this town are horrible', Napier agreed. But he continued:

> The poor starving people go about by twenties and forties, begging, but
> with the least insolence; and yet some rich villains, and some foolish

Newport and after   163

women, choose to say *they try to extort charity*. It is a lie, and infernal lie, neither more nor less: – nothing can exceed the good behaviour of these poor people, except it be their cruel sufferings.[20]

Privately he did not think the poor were so much of a danger:

> An anonymous letter came with a Chartist plan. Poor creatures, their threats of attack are miserable. With half a cartridge, and half a pike, with no money, no discipline, and no skilful leaders, they would attack men with leaders, money, and discipline, well armed, and having sixty rounds a man. Poor men! A republic! What good did a republic ever do? What good will it ever do?[21]

The most the Chartists could do, he thought, was assassinate *him*. A gunman could easily shoot at him from behind a hedge. But he joked that he did not let himself worry about it very much, for the Chartists would gain nothing by his death. There were 'one hundred sixty-four other major-generals, all anxious to be employed'. Even if all of them were assassinated in turn 'it would only be a godsend to the colonels'.[22]

Local outbreaks would be easy enough to handle if he kept up his guard, he believed, and a widespread rising by well-trained Chartist troops seemed unlikely, for it would require preparatory drilling on a scale that he had seen no sign of. Nonetheless he had his men checking any boats which the Chartists might use for ferrying their men across rivers; and he secured lists of the rooms hired, in case the Chartists were planning to fill them with combustibles and set the towns alight. Napier was taking no chances, travelling to Bradford himself in mid-December to see the position of the eighteen hundred special constables there. He tried to calm the Bradford magistrates, and he urged flexibility and kindness on the part of the Poor Law Guardians in light of the real suffering of the people. Again one gets the impression of Napier's level-headedness when he had real work to do. He patiently explained to the Duke of Portland on Christmas Eve that it was simply 'common sense' that the military pensioners living alone in their 'hamlets' should be Chartists, and that they should be teaching drill. Their lives would be in danger if they did not. But take them away and set them to marching, and remind them of the death penalty for treason, and their opinions would change.

Napier did accept that gunpowder was being sold more widely, but only enough for eight thousand rounds – 'enough for murder and depredation, not open war'. Even when some pot-shots were taken at soldiers in the first days of the new year, Napier was unfazed, and he refused the new Home Secretary Lord Normanby's suggestion that he should advertise a £200 reward for information about the attackers. Napier did not want to publicize such incidents.[23] His focus was on the practical steps he could take to keep the peace, and that was all.

Napier kept talking to the magistrates in this period, but he also kept talking to the Chartists. In November 1839 he went nine hundred feet down a coal

164   *The north of England*

mine to meet the miners.[24] He probably knew the Chartists and their environment better than anyone else in a position of power, and so he was able to keep his head in the face of rumours. When the Chartist Dr Taylor, a proponent of physical force, wrote a letter saying that his French co-conspirators were living with him, and the letter was intercepted by the authorities, Napier did not seem worried. He pointed out to Whitehall that it would be simple enough to check and see whether any Frenchmen were indeed living in Taylor's house. Nor did he attach much importance to the matter if they were.[25]

Still he loved to rail against the comfortable. The rich men of the north of England demanded 'vigorous measures', he reflected – hanging the leaders of the starving poor to make the country quiet. Well, the hangings had taken place and the country was *not* quiet. '*Vigorous measures*', he concluded, were '*idiot measures*', demanded by 'Member John Donkey'.[26] Napier had a growing sense of how well he really understood the situation, far better than John Donkey. A few months before, he had complained that his district was too big for one man to handle.[27] By the new year he seems to have moved past that view.

1840

When word of Frost's conviction for the Newport events spread on the ninth of January, the Chartists set a new date for their rising, on the twelfth.[28] As Napier expected, the civil and military authorities had little trouble in dealing with the outbreaks when they came. At Sheffield two policemen were speared (of all things) but survived, and one man was shot twelve times on his way home to Rotherham. Also in Sheffield, in the wake of skirmishing between several dozen Chartists and the authorities, a preacher was wounded by a wild Chartist shot. But elsewhere in the country things were calmer. At Dewsbury, the Chartists marched through the town and fired guns, but on receiving no word of success from the other centres, they simply went home when the dragoons came – there were only a few broken windows. There was another disturbance at Bradford on the twenty-sixth, but events did not turn out any differently. And in Barnsley on 15 January an attempt was made to set fire to the barracks, but this too came to nothing. The events of January confirmed Napier in his belief that the real danger was not a Chartist uprising, but these isolated outbreaks of violence on the part of out-of-control ruffians. In his view the Chartists needed as much protection from that sort of thing as the propertied classes did.[29]

At Nottingham, Napier met with the magistrates on the eleventh and patrolled all night on the fated twelfth. When he saw 'Chartist sentinels' in the streets, he prevented the magistrates from interfering with them, even though the protesters were armed with pistols. As he explained:

> Seizing these men could do no good: it would not stop Chartism if they were all hanged; and as they offered no violence why starve their wretched families, and worry them with a long imprisonment? I repeat it, Chartism

cannot be stopped, God forbid that it should: what we want is to stop the letting loose of a large body of armed cut-throats upon the public. My wish is to prevent an outbreak, not to provoke one. The magistrates, happily, agreed with me.[30]

***

The January disturbances were followed by a period of sullen, protracted hostility between the rich and poor. The Chartist struggle overlapped with a long set of protests against the New Poor Law.[31] Napier thought the class hatred engendered by the Poor Law might lead to widespread destruction and bloodshed sometime down the road. The country might see incendiarism and assaults on well-dressed individuals. Plans for arson had already begun showing up in the reports of the police spies. One idea was to set a series of fires across the country and make the army dash from one city to another.[32]

Meanwhile there was labour conflict. Strikes continued to break out, so the army had to be on alert against a new source of public disorder – while nonetheless the military refrained from taking sides between employers and workers. For Napier these labour conflicts were private and not political matters, and he did not want to intervene in them without looking at who was right in each particular case.[33] He wrote in the autumn that if he could, he would mediate in these disputes before trouble spread; he would try to make both sides listen to reason. But the mine owners 'seem not only to be unreasonable but somewhat ferocious.'[34]

In the new year, Wemyss reported that some of the mill owners had themselves 'rather encouraged' a strike. The owners who were doing so were those who had not yet lowered their wages. But they had to sell their products at a higher price than the mill owners who had already cut their workers' pay. So because they were being undersold, they did not mind stirring up strikes and bringing the factories of their competitors to a halt.[35] Napier replied that he did not want his troops – any more than the Tory Colonel Wemyss did – to be used to tip the scales of the labour struggle in favour of the employers.[36]

The rich were a problem everywhere. When the 'poor half starving handloom weavers' of Manchester were rumoured to be organizing a march to petition the mayor for relief, Wemyss told Napier he had indeed been trying to organize relief for them for a month, but except for a few 'kind hearts', no one would open their purses. If not for the trouble it might cause, Wemyss (Tory though he may have been) said he would not mind if the poor went and showed their condition to the mayor exactly as they threatened to do.[37] Napier usually wrote a few words of summary on the letters he received. On the back of this letter from Wemyss he noted: 'Manchester all quiet. The vagabond rich starve the poor and make them vagabonds.'

***

A few smaller matters: It was at this time that Napier fought a minor campaign to win compensation for the mileage and hotel bills he incurred for all his

166   *The north of England*

official travel in the district. Travel was costing Napier a tremendous amount of money. The question of compensating him for it became an unpleasantly drawn-out affair, during which Napier came into conflict with the historian Thomas Babington Macaulay, who had been appointed to the War Office in September.[38]

Napier had a number of other concerns in his private life. All along he was as he said 'sufficiently in love'[39] with his daughters. To his sisters he was writing long letters about the various adolescent dilemmas of his girls – a broken-off engagement in the case of the elder; sharpness of tongue, surliness, and frequent ill health in the case of the younger. According to the doctor, they were all supposed to be riding, but this brought up the question of finding horses with the right personalities.

All the while his constant worry over keeping the peace left his stomach in fits, as he confessed to Louisa. He looked forward to when his daughters would settle down a bit; by then he would have moved on to his next posting, probably the command of a regiment or some pleasant colonial appointment, he believed.[40]

***

As yet, there seemed to be little sign of any such period of calm and ease, and his work continued. In the second half of April, there was an outbreak at Colne, when fifteen rather ham-handed policemen were attacked by a mob that had possession of the town, and so the magistrates called in the army. The officer on the spot, Colonel Custance, told Napier how the common people who occupied the streets and footpaths did not mean to be rude or to get in the way of the better sorts; they simply did not know any better. They had no idea of how to behave in public. Policing ought to be a gradual and educative affair to cultivate civility in so remote a town, Custance explained. It should not take the form of a sudden attempt to enforce order – this is what had led to all the trouble. Custance's analysis impressed Napier. The general told the Home Office that gentleness and good sense in policing would go far in getting the new police forces accepted by the as yet hostile populace; and humane policing was in any case a matter of 'doing justice to the poor people who may suffer'.[41]

In the spring, things began to look more hopeful despite the ongoing labour unrest. The expansion of the police forces and at last a general easing of social tensions, especially after the conclusion of the Chartist convention in early April, suggested that the role played by the army in keeping order in the north of England might in time be reduced.[42] Napier gave much of the credit to the more enlightened local officials who had tried to do their duty by the poorer members of society – while the hard-hearted factory owners would try no such thing. He also had to give the government some credit, too. The ministers had avoided the vicious practice of executing people for their political opinions, and this policy had helped to secure the peace.[43]

In April 1840, in the same month as the Colne disturbances, Napier moved his home and headquarters from Nottingham to Chester. He had been seeking permission to take this step since January or perhaps before. A move to Chester had first occurred to him the previous July. Nottingham real estate was too expensive for him to buy a house, and the rent too high for him to continue to live there otherwise. He believed the newly expanded railways made Chester a convenient enough location for communicating with Manchester and almost everywhere else.[44]

And so he moved house. Napier was no longer living in a large city and centre of Chartist activity. He was no recluse, continuing his tours of inspection and attending (for one example) the grand ball in Chester to celebrate the birth of Princess Victoria in November 1840.[45] But rather than being involved in the everyday affairs of one of the main centres of Chartism, such Manchester, Leeds, Bradford, or Nottingham itself, Napier now spent most of his time working on the routine details of administering the army. He devoted hours every day to reviewing courts-martial, even in minor cases. He said he read the report of each case several times before drafting his reply.[46] Meanwhile he was preparing an extensive report for the Home Office on the state of the barracks. The local officials no longer wanted to devote any money at all to housing troops now that things were quieter. Napier recommended spending £160,000 for adequate and healthy quarters for his men.[47]

He would still visit the scene when things went wrong, such as when a landlady was beaten, a policeman stoned senseless, and a special constable (who was a factory owner) was killed in Colne in August.[48] There were other outbreaks. Whether it might be 'begging, pillage, rebellion or what not', something 'evil' had to come from the terrible suffering of the people. Addressing their problems would take years, Napier concluded.[49] But there had been a change in tone. By now many of the leaders had been sentenced to gaol for their activities in the previous year. Chartist meetings continued, but they were mostly in private homes. The meetings in pubs had turned into dances.[50]

How long would he stay in the north of England, and might there be something more exciting for him to do elsewhere? In late summer and autumn 1840, Napier had time to follow Black Charlie's adventures in the Eastern Mediterranean, where the naval Charles Napier was fighting the forces of Mehmet Ali of Egypt. Soon Black Charlie took Acre.[51] With the north of England relatively quiet, our Charles Napier wished that he too could be on the scene in the eastern Mediterranean in command of fighting troops. That way he would be truly earning his bread instead of, as he complained, only carrying out the 'kneading work'. He would like to be a part of any fight against the Ottomans if war came. And he would like to command an army at last, for he had never moved an army in the field against a foreign foe.

But he was not sure. He insisted that it was his hope despite everything that there would be no war, as any war would be bad for England. And there would be other costs: 'A report that the ships have destroyed Beyrout. Sad work! it is great cruelty beating down a town full of women and children and bedridden old people and sick: it is dreadful to fire on any but troops.'[52]

Yet in the last analysis what kind of rule would be best for those suffering Eastern peoples? At this very time the naval Charles Napier was bringing

168 *The north of England*

freedom to a population suffering under an Ottoman tyrant, as our own Charles Napier reminded himself in an excited passage:

> Good news on the taking of Acre! A strong fortress which has stood siege after siege taken in three hours by ships!! The poor Egyptian slaves have been slaughtered by the thousands from the obstinacy of that rascal Mehmet Ali. Poor fellows, their fate is hard, to fall for a tyrant they detest! What a life mine is! drivelled away in reading courts-martial![53]

So in the mind of our Charles Napier, if not of Black Charlie himself, the soldiers of the East were the exploited slaves of rulers they detested. And so in some way the blame for their conquest lay in the hands of those tyrannical rulers and not in the hands of Admiral Napier, their conqueror. We will see this kind of reasoning again.

Wanting a change, Napier now asked Lord Fitzroy Somerset to send him to China so he could take part in the hostilities unfolding there, but Somerset turned him down.[54]

***

In Bradford in November there were some notable acts of incendiarism.[55] The cold weather came and it was a hard time for the people of the north of England. Napier noted the terrible suffering of the poor that winter of 1840–41. He expected that during the period of calm the Chartist leaders had prepared themselves for further action at some future date. He hoped it would not be violent.[56]

Meanwhile the Napiers looked for a permanent home. Napier's wife wanted him to have a garden. Secure in his command, in March 1841 Napier took possession of a house near Chester, Calvelly Hall. It was 'too grand for a poor soldier of fortune without fortune, like me,' he wrote, 'but it is a delight to see my girls running about in this fine air'.[57]

Soon his girls would have farther to run. Lord Fitzroy Somerset came in person to offer Napier a command in India only two weeks after the family settled into Calvelly. 'My scheme of passing some years here is already ended!', the general wrote in a confident moment. But really he was not so sure that he ought to go. He consulted his brother William, his friend John Kennedy, and his old comrade Frederick Robertson about whether he should take the position. He also asked Kennedy to go with him to India in some civil capacity. Kennedy again declined, just as he had declined Napier's offer of a role in controlling the Chartists; he wanted to stay on in Ireland because of his wife and family. His advice was that while Napier might indeed make some money by going to the subcontinent, the climate would not be good for him and he was probably destined for better things.[58]

Napier also wanted his friend Robertson to ask some of the 'old India birds at Cheltenham' about conditions in the east. He wondered – Could he take his family of women safely overland from Alexandria to Bombay by

Newport and after 169

carriage, and what would doing so cost in comparison with a sea voyage? He wondered too whether he could save anything out of his £5000 per year pay while living in India – for if not, there was no point in going. And would the Indian climate harm the health of his daughters?[59] In a more intimate letter to his sister Louisa, Napier worried that he himself would not live long enough to make the move worthwhile. He thought he would need five years to save enough money to leave his daughters secure. Later he thought it would take six.[60]

In the end Napier took two months to think over the matter, not giving his answer until the middle of June.[61] Ultimately he accepted the appointment – although it made for a daunting prospect:'[T]o move my family is fearful! I go overland and shall insure my life for two years. If there is war in the Punjaub, which seems likely, a good command may fall to me.' '[I]t will be sorrowful to leave all of you', as he wrote to William, 'for it is late in life and I am much worn.'[62]

We have a description of Napier from about this time. It was written by his brother Henry, who had come to travel around the north with him for a few days:

> Charles works too much; he is often not in bed till one or two, and always up at five or a little after, and is eternally writing, at an average about four-teen to sixteen hours a day. He has a cough, complains of short breath and weakness, and is allowing his zeal to carry him too far for his own health. I doubt his being able to go on thus. The fatigue of reading and writing is very great, for I see that, as corporal punishment has diminished, courts-martial have increased, and he reads every word of all.[63]

Ever since Busaco, Charles Napier's head and jaws would jerk spasmodically, and he had a frequent tic of jerking his elbows into the sides of his body.[64]

***

While Napier was now set for India, his labours in the North (along with the rheumatism that the climate aggravated) would continue for several months. His coming departure was not announced publicly for some time, and he continued with his tours of inspection.[65] They were not the easiest months for anyone. A downturn in the cotton trade was increasing labour tensions, tensions between Chartists and the Anti-Corn Law League, and tensions between the Chartists and the Irish. According to Wemyss, there was now an ever-greater threat of 'broken heads'.[66] Napier reflected at length in a letter to William in July on what he had or had not accomplished in the north of England:

> [G]ladly shall I get away from this district, for how to deal with violence produced by starvation, by folly, by villainy, and even by a wish to do right, is a hard matter: hard I mean to deal with it conscientiously, for

170   *The north of England*

act as you will it must be with some injustice: honest men on both sides furnish rascals with pretexts, and then blindly follow those rascals as leaders.[67]

He summed up the state of England in a letter to Louisa: 'I am very gloomy . . . and I rejoice in going because I know I can do no good. Nothing can prevent a revolution. I trust in God that Bunbury may be right and Sir R. Peel may overrule the violence of the Tories.'[68] And in a sense that is what happened – when Peel split the Tory Party and repealed the Corn Laws in 1846.

***

In 1842, after Napier left England, there was a resurgence of Chartism as the economy worsened (Figure 13.1). But Napier's successors in this period had learned from his example. They kept their troops together rather than splitting them into the small detachments demanded by the magistrates – as Napier's predecessor General Jackson had found himself doing despite his own inclinations.[69] And so the military commanders in the North were able to do their part over the next few years to keep things under control.[70]

Napier reflected that in keeping the peace, 'some service to the state there I did without bloodshed'.[71] As Mark Hovell put the matter before his career as an historian was cut short in 1916:

> The wisest and most tactful step [of the government] was the appointment of Major-General Sir Charles J. Napier to the command of the Northern District. . . . Napier, the future conqueror of Sind, was perhaps the most brilliant officer of the school of Wellington, but apart from that he was a true gentleman, and a wise and kindly ruler of men. His journal, which forms an important source of information for this troublous period, reveals a man of the most admirable character. His soldierly qualities were only exceeded by his sympathy with he unfortunate men whose wild projects it was his duty to frustrate.[72]

So too the Hammonds, radical contemporaries of Hovell:

> [I]n the North, where provocation was acute, Sir Charles James Napier managed to keep the peace and not just to keep order. Napier, who was not only a very wise man but also more than half a Chartist himself, took infinite trouble to avoid a conflict, and the general respect in which he was held was a powerful influence on the side of peace.[73]

This contrasts with what a modern scholar of Philhellenism says. Having painted for us a Charles Napier who throughout his life was mainly interested in spilling blood, he tells us that Greece (in any case) had been 'fortunate to escape him' as commander.[74]

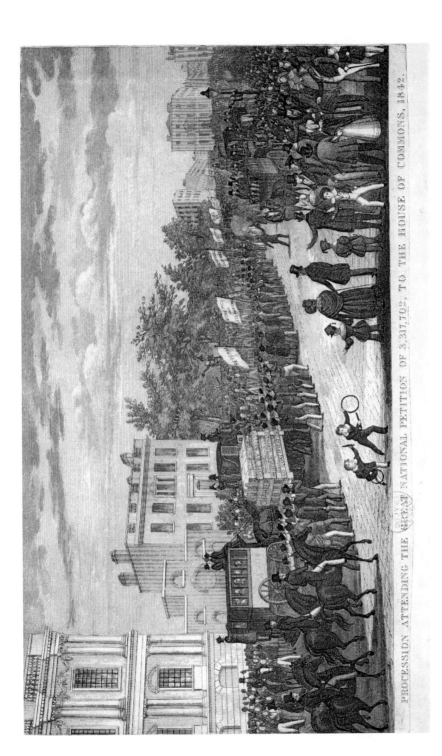

Figure 13.1 A notable Chartist demonstration: 'Procession Attending the Great National Petition of 3,317,702, to the House of Commons, 1842'. From 'A Collection of 226 Engravings, etc., illustrating London and Environs'. British Library Maps C.18.d.6.(81).

© The British Library Board 12/03/2016

172　*The north of England*

Notes

1　Napier to the Master General of the Ordnance, [May or 1839], given in WN, 2:38; Napier's journal, 30 July 1839, 2:66; Napier to Somerset, 25 August 1839, 2:81; Napier to Ross, 1 September 1839, 2:82.
2　H. E. Bunbury to Napier, [8 November 1839], NP, BL Add. MS 54530, fols 72–73.
3　Malcolm Chase, *Chartism: A New History* (Manchester: Manchester UP, 2007), 110–16, 126–27, 139–40, quotation at 109–10.
4　David J. V. Jones, *The Last Rising: The Newport Insurrection of 1839* (Oxford: Clarendon Press, 1985), 99–102, 112–13, 206–07, 213; Ivor Wilks, *South Wales and the Rising of 1839: Class Struggle as Armed Struggle* (London: Croom Helm, 1984), 172–74.
5　Napier's journal, 5, 6, 9, and 15 November 1839, given in WN, 2:91.
6　George Huband to Napier, 24 November 1839, NP, BL Add. MS 54546, fols 63–65.
7　Napier's journal, 20 November 1839, given in WN, 2:92.
8　Napier to Huband, November 1839, given in WN, 2:92.
9　Napier to Phillipps, 15 November 1839, TNA HO 40/53/801–02.
10　Charles Shaw, *Personal Memoirs and Correspondence of Colonel Charles Shaw of the Portuguese Service*, 2 vols (London: Henry Coulburn, 1837), 1:6, 2:44–45, 127–28.
11　Charles Shaw to Phillipps, 3 January 1840, TNA HO 40/54/521–24. Shaw had to overcome deep hostility when he was appointed, as he was seen in the bitterly divided city to be an agent of government oppression. See Paul A. Pickering, *Chartism and the Chartists in Manchester and Salford* (Basingstoke: Macmillan, 1995), 73–74.
12　Napier to Phillipps, 31 May 1841, TNA HO 45/41/25–26.
13　Napier's journal, 23 August 1839, given in WN, 2:76; Kennedy to Napier, 12 December 1839, NP, BL Add. MS 54535, fols 171–72; While Kennedy did not join Napier, Napier's nephew William C. E. Napier (George's son) was Napier's aide-de-camp in this period – *Manchester Guardian*, 18 May 1839, 3.
14　Wemyss to Phillipps, 3 December 1839, TNA HO 40/43/744–45.
15　Malcolm I. Thomis, *Politics and Society in Nottingham, 1785–1835* (New York: Augustus M. Kelly, 1969), 8–9; Roy A. Church, *Economic Change in a Midland Town: Victorian Nottingham, 1815–1900* (London: Frank Cass, 1966), 117–19.
16　Napier's journal, 3 December 1839, given in WN, 2:93–94.
17　Napier to Normanby, 1, 4 December 1839, TNA HO 40/53/813–15, 821–23; Mayor William Roworth to Normanby, 4 January 1840, HO 40/55/710–12; Placard of 5 December 1839 and minutes of the 6 December 1839 public meeting to relieve the poor in Nottingham, HO 52/42/169–71.
18　Napier [to Phillipps], 4 December 1839, TNA HO 40/53/821–23; Napier to Phillipps, 22 December 1839, HO 40/53/865–72 at 871. Nottingham's Poor Law Guardians had consented to putting to work on the roads those destitute men who headed families with two or more children – Nottingham Poor Law Guardians placard, 2 December 1839, H.P. 52/42/198; Roworth to Phillipps, 4 December 1839, HO 52/42/166–67.
19　Napier to W. Napier, 19 January 1840, given in WN, 2:111–14.
20　Napier's journal, 2 December 1839, given in WN, 2:93.
21　Napier's journal, 1 December 1839, given in WN, 2:93.
22　Napier to the Duke of Portland, 8 December 1839, given in WN, 2:95–96.
23　Napier to Emily Bunbury, 2 January 1840, NP, NAM 2005–06–724, item 4; Napier's journal, 1, 2, and 4 January 1840, given in WN, 2:107; Napier to Fox Maule at the Home Office, 5 January 1840, TNA HO 40/58/137–39.
24　Napier to Phillipps, 16 December 1839, TNA HO 40/53/853–54.
25　Napier [to Phillipps], 29 December 1839, TNA HO 40/53/883–84; see also Napier to Normanby, 12 December, HO 40/53/841–44.
26　Napier's journal, [December 1839?], quoted in WN, 2:101–02.
27　Napier's journal, 20 July 1839, given in WN, 2:56.

28 Information from a spy in Dalston, enclosure 2 (nos. 130–31), 28 December 1839, in Napier to Phillipps, 3 January 1840, TNA HO 40/58/121; Wemyss to Napier, 9 January 1840, NP, BL Add. MS 54512, fols 20–21.

29 F. C. Mather, *Public Order in the Age of the Chartists* (1959; New York: Augustus M. Kelley, 1967), 23–25, 206, 213; Neil Pye, *The Home Office and the Chartists, 1838–1848: Protest and Repression in the West Riding of Yorkshire* (Pontypool, Wales: Merlin Press, 2013), 101–07; Napier to the Undersecretary, 12 January 1840, given in WN, 2:110; Napier's journal, 14 and 17 January 1840, 2:110–11; Napier to Phillipps, 12 January 1840, TNA HO 40/58/153–55; Sheffield magistrates to Normanby, 12 January 1840, HO 40/57/173–76; Dewsbury magistrates to Normanby, 15, 16, and 16 January 1840, with enclosed depositions of 13 January, HO 40/57/205–19, 235–37; copies of depositions taken at Dewsbury, 13 February 1840, HO 40/57/325–35 at 325–27; *The Times*, 14 January 1840, 6 col. d; Bradford magistrates to Normanby, 13, 27, 29 January 1840, HO 40/57/193, 273–75, 295–98. In response to these events, the Duke of Portland wanted to arm the pensioners, and indeed the government agreed to send arms for this purpose – copy of Normanby to Portland, 17 January 1840, TNA HO 41/15/286-7.

30 Napier's journal, 12 January 1840, given in WN, 2:109; Mayor Roworth to Normanby, 14 January 1840, TNA HO 40/55/722–24.

31 Shaw to Fax Maule, 12 February 1840, TNA HO 40/54/625–27; Wemyss to Phillipps, 23 August 1839, TNA HO 40/43/600–02; Halifax magistrates to Normanby, 8 August 1840, HO 40/57/486–87.

32 Napier to W. Napier, 19 January, 5 February 1840, given in WN, 2:111–15; deposition of James Harrison, 17 December 1839, TNA HO 40/51/701–03; information from spies, enclosure 2 (nos. 129–31), 28 December 1839, in Napier to Phillipps, 3 January 1840, TNA HO 40/58/121. For how easy it had been for small but disciplined forces at Newport, Sheffield, and Bradford to defeat large groups of protesters, see Napier to Phillipps, 29 January 1839, TNA HO 40/58/193–95.

33 Napier to Phillipps, 29 September 1839, TNA HO 40/53/767–69; Wemyss to Napier, 20 January 1840, NP, BL Add. MS 54512, fols 32–33.

34 Napier to Fox Maule at the Home Office, 2 October 1839, TNA HO 40/53/771–73.

35 Wemyss to Napier, 21 January 1840, NP, BL Add. MS 54512, fol. 34; see also Shaw to Fox Maule, 21 January 1840, TNA HO 40/54/557–59; and for Wemyss's similar suspicions later on, see Wemyss to Napier, 18 February 1841, TNA HO 45/41/11–12.

36 Napier to Phillipps, 15 May 1840, TNA HO 40/58/273–74.

37 Wemyss to Napier, 23 January 1840, NP, BL Add. MS 54512, fols 39–40.

38 Napier to Phillipps, 28 March, 24 May 1840 (copy), and 24 and 27 December 1840, TNA HO 40/58/245–46, 289, 397–404. Napier had first raised the issue in May 1839: Napier to Phillipps, 9 May 1839, HO 40/53/429–30.

39 Napier to Louisa Napier, 18 July 1840, Bodleian MS Eng. lett. c. 240, fols 74–75.

40 Napier to Louisa Napier, 1 May, 22 June, 18 July 1840, Bodleian MS Eng. lett. c. 240, fols 66–68, 71–73, 74–75; Napier to Emily Bunbury, 2, 8 January, 26 August, 4 September 1840, NP, NAM 2005–06–724, items 4, 5, 7, 8. For why he hoped for a new post, more to keep busy than to make money, see Napier to Robertson, 22 December 1847, NP, BL Add. MS 49107, fols 47–48.

41 Napier to Phillipps, 30 April 1840, with enclosure, Colonel Custance to Napier, 29 April 1840, TNA HO 40/58/265–271. For resistance or scepticism toward the newly established police forces of the northern cities, see David Foster, *The Rural Constabulary Act 1839: National Legislation and Problems of Enforcement* (London: Bedford Square Press, 1982), 13–20, 23–30; H. Palmer, *Police and Protest in England and Ireland, 1780–1850* (Cambridge UP, 1988), 422–27; Katrina Navickas, *Protest and the Politics of Space and Place, 1789–1848* (Manchester: Manchester UP, 2016), 141–46. The common people sometimes saw the army as an ally in their conflict with police; early on Napier feared the Chartist leaders might use this good feeling between troops and townspeople as a way to

174 *The north of England*

suborn the army – Napier to Emily Bunbury, 28 July 1839, NP, NAM 2005–06–724, item 2.

42 Napier's journal, 7, 8 April 1840, given in WN, 2:122; Napier to Phillipps, 27 June 1840, TNA HO 40/58/305; Napier to W. Napier, 11 May 1840, given in WN, 2:130. For the founding of the county police forces in 1839 and 1840 and the conditions under which the policemen could be armed, see Palmer, *Police and Protest*, 441–44; Pye, *The Home Office and the Chartists*, 85–86.

43 Napier's journal, 16 April and 13 July 1840, given in WN, 2:125–26, 135.

44 Napier to Louisa Napier, 25 July 1839, Bodleian MS Eng. lett. c. 240, fol. 55; Napier to Somerset, January 1840, given in WN, 2:115; WN, 2:125; Napier to Phillipps, 2 April 1840, HO 40/58/249.

45 *Chester Chronicle*, 4 December 1840, 2 col. c.

46 Napier to W. Napier, 26 March 1840, given in WN, 2:121.

47 Napier to W. Napier, 23 June 1840, given in WN, 2:132–33.

48 Bolton to Normanby, 10, 11 August 1840, TNA HO 40/54/785–97, 801–08; Napier to Phillipps, 10, 15, August 1840, TNA HO 40/58/343, 359–61.

49 Napier to Phillipps, 25 July 1840, TNA HO 40/58/329–32.

50 Napier to Fox Maule, 28 November 1840, TNA HO 40/58/391–92; Shaw to Normanby, 20 December 1840, HO 40/54/889–94; Edward Herford, Prosecuting Solicitor for Manchester, to Normanby, 2 March 1840, TNA HO 40/54/641–44, with the outline of the Home Office answer on fol. 644; Home Office to Herford, 4 March 1840, HO 40/54/667.

51 Napier to Colin Campbell, 20 August 1840, quoted in Lawrence Shadwell, *The Life of Colin Campbell, Lord Clyde*, 2 vols (Edinburgh: William Blackwood and Sons, 1881), 1:96–97.

52 Napier's journal, 8, 12, and 13 September, 5 October 1840, given in WN, 2:139, 141–42.

53 Napier's journal, 29 October 1840, given in WN, 2:142.

54 Napier's journal, 7 January 1841, given in WN, 2:145.

55 Bradford magistrates to Normanby, 17 November 1840, TNA HO 40/51/677–78.

56 Napier to Louisa Napier, 3 November, 1 December 1840, Bodleian MS Eng. lett. c. 240, fols 80–83.

57 Frances Napier to Charles Napier, 8 March 1840, NP, BL Add. MS 54523, fols 37–38; Napier to Louisa Napier, 26 February 1841, Bodleian MS Eng. lett. c. 240, fols 85–87; Napier's journal, 14 March, 5 April 1841, given in WN, 2:146, 151.

58 Napier's journal, 21 April 1841, and a letter to William (no date given), excerpted in WN, 2:151; Kennedy to Napier, 1 May 1841, NP, BL Add. MS 54535, fols 173–74.

59 Napier to Robertson, 25 April 1841, NP, BL Add. MS 49107, fols 55–56.

60 Napier to Louisa Napier, 29 April 1841, Bodleian MS Eng. lett. c. 240, fols 102–03; Napier to Louisa Napier, 26 June, 11 August 1841, Bodleian MS Eng. lett. c. 240, fols 106–07, 110–11.

61 Napier to Louisa Napier, 16 June 1841, Bodleian MS Eng. lett. c. 240, fols 104–05.

62 Napier's journal, 21 April 1841, given in WN, 2:151.

63 Henry Napier to W. Napier, [1840?], quoted in William Napier Bruce, *The Life of General Sir Charles Napier, G.C.B.* (London: John Murray, 1885), 140–41.

64 Bruce, *Charles Napier*, 99, 144; Joseph Wolff, *Travels and Adventures of the Rev. Joseph Wolff, D.D., LL.D.*, 2 vols (London: Saunders, Otley, and Co., 1860), 1:401.

65 Wemyss to Napier, 24 March 1841, NP, BL Add. MS 54512, fols 129–30; Napier to Louisa Napier, 29 April, 20 July 1841, Bodleian MS Eng. lett. c. 240, fols 102–03, 108–09.

66 Wemyss to Napier, 17 March 1841, NP, BL Add. MS 54512, fols 125–26; Napier to [Phillipps?], 6 June 1841, NP, TNA HO 45/41/27–28.

67 Napier to W. Napier, [July 1841?], excerpted in WN, 2:151–53.

68 Napier to Louisa Napier, 11 August 1841, NP, NAM 2005–06–724, item 9.

69 Chase, *Chartism*, 193; 203–05; Mather, *Public Order*, 155–58, 176.

Newport and after   175

70 Pye argues that in the case of the West Riding of Yorkshire, at least, the Home Office would learn by 1848 how better to construct and operate the administrative machinery for ensuring public order – Pye, *The Home Office and the Chartists*, 176–77.
71 Napier's journal, 16 January 1843, given in WN, 2:290.
72 Mark Hovell, *The Chartist Movement*, T. F. Tout (ed.), 2nd edn (Manchester: Manchester UP, 1925), 139–40.
73 J. L. Hammond and Barbara Hammond, *The Age of the Chartists, 1832–1854: A Study of Discontent* (London: Longmans, Green, and Co., 1930), 271. Other scholars have referred to 'Napier's firm but moderate and humane handling' of the Chartists, describing him as 'a kind-hearted man with radical sympathies' – Hinde, *Cobden*, 71. See also J. T. Ward, *Chartism* (London: B.T. Batsford, 1973), 97, 121, 128–29, 138–39.
74 William St. Clair, *That Greece Might Still be Free: The Philhellenes in the War of Independence* (London: Oxford UP, 1972), 167–68, 302–03.

Part IV

The conquest of Sind

[F]rom the standpoint of liberalism, the "Indian Question" was paradigmatically how a body of ideas that professed a universal reach responded to the encounter with the unfamiliar.[1]

Note

1 Uday Singh Mehta, *Liberalism and Empire: A Study in Nineteenth-Century British Liberal Thought* (Chicago: University of Chicago Press, 1999), 8. Also quoted in Sudipta Sen, 'Liberal Empire and Illiberal Trade: The Political Economy of "Responsible Government" in Early British India', in Kathleen Wilson (ed.), *A New Imperial History: Culture, Identity, and Modernity in Britain and the Empire, 1660–1840* (Cambridge: Cambridge UP, 2004), 136–54 at 140.

14 To India and Sind

In September 1841, Napier relinquished command of his army. He joked with one of his sisters that if a war broke out in Punjab, he might come home with enough money to set up a school in Cheltenham. His daughters could run it, and he could spend his time drinking the waters, trying to sooth his conscience over all the people he had murdered.[1] (Indeed he was troubled by the blood spilt on the coast of China by his cousin Black Charlie – 'and through regular robbing, if *only a Chinese*'.[2]) But if there were no war in Punjab he would have a quiet time of it. He had been appointed to a regional command at Poona in the southern part of the Bombay Presidency.

But first he had to get there. Relocating himself and his brood to India was a major undertaking, financially and otherwise. The cost came out of Napier's own pocket and most of it had to be paid in advance. He only barely had enough money to bring it off – and he was able to afford the journey only because his family had spent the last two weeks before their departure in a borrowed house in Bedford Square, so they were able to save on hotel bills. Money was very tight nonetheless. Napier wrote that if anyone in his brood had come down sick and missed the steamer in Marseilles he would have been ruined – 'but my resolution was to risk all for my girls'. He added that 'had I then died, not a farthing was left for them.'

When Napier paid off the ship's bursar on arriving in Bombay, he received £2 in change out of his last £500. He had only that £2 in the world. He did not even have an insurance policy, because with his war wounds no one would sell him one. On top of all this he learned in Poona that his luggage, coming after him, was pilfered on its the way from the port. Among the losses were the mementos of his first wife.[3]

While his girls had enjoyed the trip east, through Alexandria, Cairo, and Aden – constantly taking notes and making watercolours[4] – Charles Napier was more disapproving. He did not like the Ottoman rulers any more in Egypt than he had in Greece. 'A person who has been but a short time in a country has no right to suppose he can trace causes with certainty; he can, however, judge of effects when they are strongly marked.' Egypt had amazing natural resources, he noted, 'a noble people', and easy access to the European market. The Egyptians should be prosperous. But after forty years of the rule of

180 *The conquest of Sind*

Mehmet Ali, whom Black Charlie had defeated but not overthrown, there was still no prosperity. There was only tyranny. Mehmet Ali himself lived a life of luxury.[5] So the Egyptians suffered from the tyranny and rapacity of their rulers – this was a very familiar situation for Napier.

Writing in his journal in the 'very pretty and very stinking' city of Cairo – '[t]his city of caliphs and genii and Arabian Nights' – he gave in to the dream of a benign despotism. What if England had simply kept Egypt after taking it from the French, as he had wanted England to keep Portugal? He let his thoughts run away with the fancy:

> The whole of Egypt is a marvel, and 'tis a sin it is not well governed. Why did we give it up when we were in possession by right of conquest over conquerors? and when it was won by the lives of Abercrombie, and thousands of others! Had it been kept, Alexandria would now be a Liverpool; Cairo would be clean and beautiful, with a full traffic from the interior of Africa, and civilized Abyssinia would be pouring down her produce by the Nile to Cairo. Then the word of God spreading through the *darkness* of Africa! a point so dear to Tories. Think of the bishops! Think of a bishop of Alexandria! another of grand Cairo! a third of Thebes! Deacons of the Delta also! Prebends of the Pyramids! Think of Mahomet floored alongside of Sesostris, and the Pope gibbeted on Pompey's Pillar! Alas! it is no joke to fight battles for nothing when the happiness of a whole country might be created from profiting from the bloody work![6]

For if the blood has already been shed, should not the conqueror take up the reins of power?

***

Napier assumed command in Poona on 28 December. He had to acquaint himself with the sepoy soldiers and the usages of the Bombay Army. The armies of the different presidencies (Bombay, Calcutta, and Madras) each had their own regulations and practices, often rather different from anything Napier was familiar with. As we saw, before leaving England he had heard a rumour that he might be sent to the Indus Frontier if a war broke out in Punjab.[7] In the Bombay Presidency he would have a chance to learn his way about before he took command in a dangerous situation. The prospect of command on the Indus, and of having 'a positive *object* in this life' in being put in charge of an army in the field, now excited him, but there is no clear evidence that at this point he seriously expected to command an army in battle even if a war did come.[8]

Poona was not a strenuous posting. Napier commanded a garrison of about 5,000 troops, and about 3,500 elsewhere in the region.[9] With a population of 60,000, this was the second largest city in the Bombay Presidency. Poona had clean paved streets, a Protestant church, and neighbourhoods of European bungalows. When Sir George Arthur, the governor, returned from a voyage to Europe and made his visit to the city, Poona gave him a lavish welcome. Napier rode in an open carriage with Sir Thomas M'Mahon, the General-in-Chief of the presidency. They went to the house of an Indian who was giving the banquet. As another of the guests tells us, it was a two-storey mansion decorated with flowers and spices on silver salvers, and scented too with attar of roses. The women of the house prepared the meal but they did not appear. They could be glimpsed through wooden screens until they saw they were being observed and withdrew. Dancing girls called bayadères garlanded the guests with flowers.[10] It was all very different from Chartism.

The Napiers themselves did not entertain very much when they were in Poona. Too many of their clothes and possessions had been stolen. Indeed, they had no utensils or dishes except what the M'Mahons gave them. In any case Napier did not like what he saw of European society in the city. He complained about the 'gourmandising' and all the expensive balls costing ten times too much, where the discussions ran to who would marry whom.[11]

There were diversions. As spring and the hot weather approached, Napier's wife and daughters travelled the eighty-four miles to the Bombay Presidency's summer capital at Mahabaleshwar, at four thousand feet. Napier bought a small cottage there for £50. They would camp among the 'tygers', 'cheetas', and scorpions in a pagoda under the tamarind and mango trees, and they watched monkeys steal their food in the night. But in the plains there were rumours of cholera. Napier said he would go and deal with it if the news were confirmed. The cholera among the soldiers was caused, he explained, by the Company having moved them at the wrong time of year; the Company's desire for profit was costing lives. With his love of landscape, his love of family, and his hatred of murderous capitalism, Napier was settling in nicely. His daughters spent their time pressing flowers and classifying them by their scientific names, or – to his horror – tracking a tiger. Napier seemed content. He barely seemed perturbed to learn that his pay would be only £4000 per year. This was £1000 less than what Lord Fitzroy Somerset had promised – Lord Fitzroy had mistaken the exchange rate for rupees.[12]

Yet clouds were gathering. The danger came not from the independent Punjab, as Napier had expected, but from Afghanistan. In January 1842 Napier received the first official word that he might be sent out to Sind to help sort out the mess on India's northwestern frontier. His first thought was that he did not want to leave his girls. Emily and Susan, who were in their teens, and were only now beginning to suspect they were illegitimate. They questioned the soldiers on the matter, and Napier feared that as they learned Hindustani they would question the servants.[13] Nonetheless Napier *did* want to go to the fighting. He noted in his journal that he tried to find quiet time each day to read up on Indian affairs.[14]

***

Indeed, some review of what was happening in the region might be in order for us, too. Lord Auckland had become Governor-General of India in 1836.

182   *The conquest of Sind*

Worried about Russian influence in the northwest, in 1838 Auckland had intervened in Afghanistan to depose one ruler, Dost Mohammed, and replace him with another, Shah Shuja. The invasion was a success. Shah Shuja was put on the throne – a throne from which the Afghans themselves had deposed him almost thirty years before. Yet by 1839 it was apparent that Shah Shuja could not hold the country without the continued presence of a British army of 10,000 men. So Auckland could not withdraw the forces as he had hoped to do. Instead, Afghanistan remained under British occupation, and the country was run as much by the envoy, Sir William Macnaghten, as by the Shah.

In November 1841, as Napier neared India, there was an uprising at Kabul. It was led by Dost Mohammed's son. Macnaghten was killed in December in a parlay that was in fact a trap. Most of the 4,500-man force in Kabul, along with their 12,000 retainers, waited in the cantonment, hoping for permission from the Afghans to leave. Slowly they began to freeze to death. Finally they were allowed to depart on 6 January 1842. They made for the Khyber Pass, and they were harassed and shot at along the way.

Many who were not killed en route died in the snow. The majority of the small band of survivors were slaughtered outright on 13 January. A few were kept alive as prisoners; and one small group escaped at the last moment. Out of that latter number only one European, an assistant surgeon, would reach friendly territory to tell the tale. The death toll since the beginning of the uprising was 16,500, with 63 prisoners and stragglers surviving in various places, plus the assistant surgeon now safe in Jalalabad.[15]

The loss of 16,500 soldiers and dependents was one of the most famous and most complete disasters the British army ever suffered. Lord Auckland was already in the process of being replaced when it happened; the new Governor-General, Edward Law, Lord Ellenborough, had been appointed in October 1841. But Auckland continued to serve until Ellenborough's arrival several months later. In the wake of the disaster, Auckland threw small military units at the Afghans rather than assembling a single army large enough to ensure victory.[16] Most of the units that he sent failed even to break through the Khyber Pass and get into the country. When Ellenborough arrived in Madras on 21 February he framed a very different plan. He wanted to organize a large enough force to enter Afghanistan and muster the retreat of the units that were not in Kabul.

Ever since his arrival, Napier had looked on Afghan events with all due horror, as might well be imagined.[17] He agreed with everything he was hearing in Bombay and Poona, which was that Auckland – who was held in near 'universal contempt' – had all but invited the Afghans to defend 'their country and their independence against our Machiavellian politics, if folly added to villainy can be called [politics]'.[18]

On his way out to India, Ellenborough had taken the southern route, sailing around Africa. At the Cape of Good Hope he was entertained by the governor, who was none other than George Napier, Charles's next oldest brother. Of course they talked about Charles at some point. When Ellenborough arrived in Madras he wrote to Charles to ask for his thoughts on the military situation. And Charles Napier was able to send a full account of his views to the Governor-General in short order. He already had them written out.[19]

Ever the military student, in the wake of the Afghan disaster Napier had drafted a plan for what the East India Company should do next. Napier argued the Company ought to retain the Indus as an easily defensible rampart, even if it also decided to retain territory on the other side of the river. And if the Company were to keep hold of territory on the opposite bank, the Indus would provide the main line of fortifications and communication.

But if the Company were indeed to use the Indus in this way, as the furthest line of defence, should it also take Punjab, which lay along the Indus to the north? The whole of the river system would then serve as a defensible border for India, with no independent Punjabi government on the upper reaches that might attack the British flank: 'If you make conquests, you must do what it takes to support your misdeeds!' Napier wrote. He went on to detail the various key points and the lines of communication that would have to be secured – especially Karachi, which 'will be to India what Calais was to England', and a vital citadel and centre of commerce. Napier also supported – as Ellenborough did – a new mission to Kabul to win some kind of victory there, despite what Napier for one thought was the injustice of the original invasion. Without a victory at Kabul, Britain would suffer even more by its first defeat, opening itself to aggression by enemies large and small in the subcontinent, much less inviting other aggression from the Russians and the Chinese. But with a victory in Kabul, the city itself and several other Afghan bases could be retained as advanced positions beyond the more secure Indus.[20]

Lord Ellenborough was very impressed by all this. Ellenborough would later come to depend on Napier's military advice, eventually mourning Napier as his closest adviser and last true friend.[21] Now at the very beginning of their acquaintance, Ellenborough thought he had his man for getting a punitive expedition into Afghanistan and then back out again – without meeting the same sad fate that had befallen the last British army trying to leave the country. In March 1842, therefore, the Governor-General appointed Napier to command the withdrawal, and if he could, to restore British honour in Afghanistan by winning 'some decisive success'. Yet Ellenborough made it clear that a *total* withdrawal of British forces from the country would take place no matter what Napier did, and no matter what success Napier might have against the Afghan forces.[22]

Privately Napier thought he might win glory in battle but roast in the heat, for the northwest was known to be the hottest part of the subcontinent. He would miss his wife and daughters, and he had no hope of getting any prize money from beating the Afghans. The possible loss of life appalled him, too. A young man whom he had fancied as a prospective son-in-law had recently been killed in Auckland's war. Napier told his sister: 'My God what widespread misery all this folly and injustice of Lord A[uckland] and Hobhouse has

184 *The conquest of Sind*

created!' Auckland and his ignorant commanders ought to be impeached or face charges: 'I came to India for money too,' he admitted, in a profession 'I have spent a life in studying'. Auckland for all his military adventures was not a military man, and neither was Hobhouse – who was the President of the Board of Control (the body that supervised the East India Company in London) when Auckland had launched his invasion. Napier was not happy that soldiers would be killed as a result of their incompetence.[23]

As things turned out, victory at the Khyber Pass speedily came, but it did not come by Napier's hand. In early April, Major-General George Pollock defeated the Afridis and forced the pass. The Governor-General had his victory.

But what was British policy to be in the aftermath? At the end of March, the Duke of Wellington – now once again Commander-in-Chief of the Forces after Lord Hill's resignation – sent a despatch to Ellenborough sketching out a new line of defence for British India. The border would run down the River Sutlej and then along the Indus on its course through Sind. This was much like what Napier had suggested if Punjab remained independent (Map 14.1).

***

And yet for the moment Ellenborough's thinking seemed to be going in another direction. After the victory at the Khyber Pass in April, he at once assured the Prime Minister, Robert Peel, that despite this success he still wanted total withdrawal from the area. Ellenborough then ordered the political officers to show all proper respect to the native princes and uphold their independence.[24] And in a memorandum on 27 April 1842, the Governor-General said that while the East India Company might need to maintain formal relations with Sind, the country that lay on both sides of the lower stretch of the river, no closer tie was required there either. The Company would not stay along the banks of the Indus, for the trade of Sind was not so great as had been thought and the country was not very attractive economically. If Sind were retained – it was the country where British troops had formed up on their way to Afghanistan – the Company could not expect the profits needed to cover the cost of the civil administration and military security.

Sind was hardly the only place that was failing to pay for itself. Ellenborough went on to argue that ever since the Company had achieved the Diwani (the tax-farming contract) of Bengal seventy-seven years before, the profits that India sent to London had remained steady despite the continual annexation of vastly more territory. So the policy of expansion had achieved little. The only winners from the constant growth in the Company's domains were the young officials and military officers employed there, or so Ellenborough reflected.[25] That was not enough to justify this behaviour:

> It is impossible to proceed further in this career of expensive conquest, and further to extend our foreign relations without endangering whatever we now possess, and incurring the certain consequence of being unable to perform the first duty of a government, that of protecting its loyal subjects and punishing the evil doer.[26]

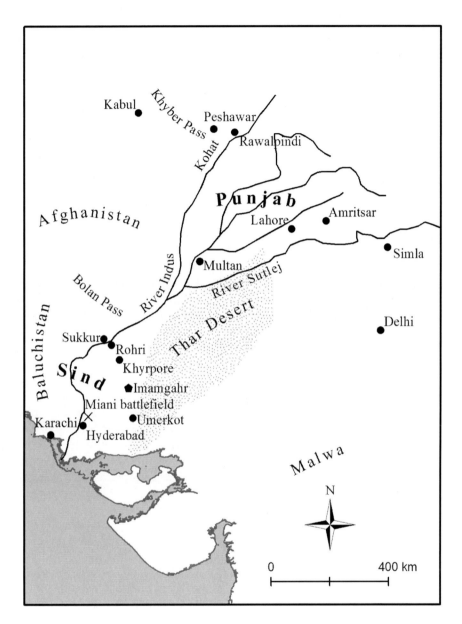

Map 14.1 Sind and Punjab in the 1840s.
Map prepared by Geoffrey Fouad

But resisting *formal* expansion in this way did not mean that the Company would withdraw from trade in the area. Ellenborough had every desire to turn a profit for the East India Company.[27] By June, the Governor-General was ordering new steamers for the Indus. In the northern Sind, Ellenborough

186 *The conquest of Sind*

planned to create a citadel on the river to command trade that he believed would extend to Aden and Suez. To encourage that trade, Ellenborough said he would keep Karachi, near the river's mouth – the city had been occupied during the Afghan affair. In exchange for this territory, he would remit the tribute paid by the forty Amirs who jointly ruled the country.[28] Still, British troops would be leaving the bulk of the independent state of Sind that occupied both banks of the lower Indus.

Or would they?

With Napier to Sind

Charles Napier – as Ellenborough reported to the Queen in September 1842 – 'sailed in the first week of this month for Karachi, to assume the command in the Scinde'. The voyage from Bombay had been nightmarish, with storms and an outbreak of cholera. Dozens died, and Napier was violently seasick.[29]

Karachi was a small and dirty city of 14,000 people, more of them Hindu than Moslem, plus several hundred African slaves brought by the Arabs.[30] The British garrison numbered 2,000. Six miles outside Karachi, on damp ground, lay the European barracks. Napier soon directed that new barracks should be built elsewhere. He also ordered the creation of a government garden, because after four years in the country the British had not yet planted vegetables and the troops had scurvy.[31]

For some time Napier was in no shape to leave the area. In Bombay he had found a stockpile of rockets rotting in a warehouse. They had never been issued to the military and Napier decided to take some of them with him. Two days after he arrived one of the rockets burst very near him during a test. Napier was the only person seriously hurt. He was laid up for the better part of a month with a calf wound that went all the way to the bone.[32]

By the time he was ready to move on, he learned from Ellenborough that he was to establish his headquarters at Sukkur in the northern Sind. There he was to assemble the troops coming out of Afghanistan. And Ellenborough sent Napier European troops from India to add to the sepoys coming across the Afghan frontier.[33]

But what would Napier *do* with those troops once he had them? As we have seen, Ellenborough had a plan for a trading cantonment in northern Sind. But as late as 8 October he still had not told Napier anything about it. So Napier was left to wonder whether he was to move north and join a possible invasion of Punjab.[34] Yet what Ellenborough had in mind was not a secret from everyone. In a letter to the Queen in mid-September Ellenborough explained:

[Napier] will then have together full 10,000 men, and it is to be expected that the Ameers of Scinde, seeing the advance of such forces from different points, will desist from the hostile intentions they have been said to entertain. Their conduct will be maturely considered, and if it should appear that designs have been entertained inconsistent with friendship towards the British Government, the punishment inflicted will be such as to deter all Indian chiefs from similar treachery; but nothing will be done against any one of them without the clearest evidence of guilt.[35]

In this letter, the hostility to widespread annexation that Ellenborough had expressed in April seems perilously close to slipping away. If the Amirs do not behave just right – *and in reference to what?* – they might be attacked.

Napier was not as yet privy to this prospect of punishing the Amirs. In camp as his leg was healing, he for one did not expect that his troops would see any military action.[36]

England and the Amirs of Sind

Napier found himself in control of a growing army occupying much of what was at least in theory an independent state. We should pause for a moment to consider this odd situation and how it came to be.

Sind had once been ruled by the Kalhoras, a crypto-Islamic sect of mendicants to whom the Mughals had assigned the country in the early eighteenth century. The Kalhora rulers employed as their military retainers a tribe of Beluchi warriors, the Talpurs. In turn, the Talpurs conquered the country from their Kalhora masters in the 1780s, when Napier was a child.[37]

Ever since, Sind had been ruled jointly by the forty Talpur Amirs. While the Amirs shared among themselves the government of the country, each had his own territory within it.

For decades the Amirs maintained a policy of isolation. British traders who entered Sind were quickly expelled. Then in 1828, Dr James Burnes was invited to come into the country and treat one of the ruling Amirs, and he wrote a book about what he saw. At the time, the President of the Board of Control, which was (to repeat the fact) the organ of the British government supervising the East India Company in London, was none other than Lord Ellenborough.

Intrigued by Burnes's book on the region, in 1831 Ellenborough arranged for George IV to give a set of English cart-horses to Maharajah Ranjit Singh of Punjab. But how would the horses be delivered? Reluctantly the Amirs agreed to allow the British barge and its attendants to proceed upriver on the way to their more powerful northern neighbour. But they were not happy to see the British examining their country en route. When the foreign ships went by, one *syed* remarked that it marked the end of Sindhi independence. Indeed, the leader of the mission (who was Dr Burnes's brother Alexander) was instructed to use the opportunity to map and sound the river, and to enter into diplomatic discussions with the Amirs. Not long after the journey a commercial treaty was reached to allow for the movement of non-military goods on the river, subject to tariffs being paid to the Amirs.[38]

Between them, James and Alexander Burnes – who published his own book – inaugurated a small genre of British writing on the alleged tyranny and avarice of the Sindhi government. Echoing what a variety of British travellers

188 *The conquest of Sind*

and officials had been saying about the rulers in the rest of India since the 1770s, these books painted the Amirs as sybarites and despots.[39] They were said to be so absorbed in their own pleasures that they refused to cultivate enough of the land, leaving the people to starve. Marianne Postans (the wife of a British officer) recorded at the time of Napier's conquest of Sind in 1843 that the Amirs lived well, drank happily, and lived high at the expense of the poor. Even before Napier arrived, she had set out a case that the Amirs were neglecting to feed their people.[40] All the British observers hated the way the Amirs used the precious watered land along the river for their forested hunting preserves, called *shikargahs*, where wild hogs roamed on what might have been rich farms.[41] Further, Postans and the other British writers said the Amirs persecuted their Hindu subjects. (The Hindu population was substantial.)[42]

The traditional prejudice shared by many of the British observers – not least Charles Napier – was that they could do a much better job ruling an Islamic population than the Islamic rulers could.[43] And indeed while the lands along the river were unstable and subject to being washed away, they had been farmed until the Amirs came, and the country that Napier would see was clearly undergoing depopulation and decline.[44] As he toured Sind for the first time, he began to indulge in at least the fantasy of annexing the country in order to address the problems he was seeing first-hand. Given his engineering background and his experiences in Cephalonia, he filled the long hot hours of travel with dreams of reclaiming the empty land around him. He began to fantasize about how, with John Kennedy at his side, he could leave the country so much better watered and better farmed and so much happier – if only the Amirs could be removed from the picture: 'Did God give a whole people to half a dozen men to torment? I will strive to teach the Amirs a better use of their power, and if they break their treaties the lesson shall be a rough one!'[45] Could his dreams be made real?

The prospect of conquering Sind and removing its allegedly incompetent rulers had arisen in the mind of the very first British visitor to the country, Dr Burnes. Burnes wrote that a British conquest was inevitable, given the way the Company's territory had been growing and the weakness of the Amirs. Conquest when it came would bring the people of Sind 'free institutions and a benignant rule'; economic growth would follow. His brother Alexander wrote only a few years later – in a book which Napier read – that if England conquered Sind, 'I am certain the body of the people will hail the happy day'.[46] These views were not lost on Charles Napier.

Yet already there were those who believed that the best course was, as one of Napier's critics would later put it, to 'preserve and protect the more innocuous of [the Amirs'] institutions, rather than precipitately to subvert them, in order to introduce the systems and usages of Europe in their place'.[47] Thomas Postans (Marianne's husband) held this view. After Sind was taken, he argued that the only hope for stability was to restore the Amirs. While the Amirs were indeed tyrants, and the people their victims, this was the case with all the governments of 'semi-barbarous' countries. It was better to leave the people under a government they knew than to try to give them a better one, he argued.[48]

Ellenborough's plans

In 1839, facing substantial British forces determined to secure the route into Afghanistan, the Amirs had agreed to a set of stringent new treaties with the East India Company. By these treaties the Amirs were made to open the Indus more fully to British navigation. The treaties also granted Sukkur to the British as a crossing point. Further, the East India Company was authorized to establish bases in Sindhi territory, mainly on the route to the Khyber Pass (in Punjab) and the Bolan Pass (in Sind itself).[49]

Sind was now under Company protection. Letters from the Amirs showed that they understood and accepted this, however reluctantly. British power was simply too great for them to resist as the feringhee armies flowed through their territory. Under the new regime the Amirs had to pay tribute to the Company, and they could no longer negotiate with any foreign powers without Company permission. Henry Pottinger, who had helped to impose the new arrangements, predicted that the next time British troops were active in Sind itself – rather than merely moving through the country to get to some other place – they would simply annex it.[50]

There was also a financial motivation to do so. In early October, in a letter carrying the news of Napier's arrival in Karachi, Ellenborough presented to the Duke of Wellington some intriguing details. He said the cost of maintaining the armies across the Indus, including the forces in Sind, was £150,000 per month; while the total revenue of British India was £900,000 per annum, of which £500,000 came from opium.[51] So in one year it would cost more than half again the revenue of India to keep these forces in place!

But what if Sind could make money after all? The improved military picture in Afghanistan left Ellenborough dreaming of making Sukkur not only a base to guard the river trade, as he had planned to do in July, but as an 'emporium of the countries drained by the Indus' further north in Central Asia. He now wanted to annex not only Sind but Punjab as well – a country that was so unstable that he thought it might fall into his lap within a year in any case: 'The state of the Punjab is therefore under my foot'.[52] The former critic of the seventy-seven-year record of unprofitable annexation in India had now worked himself into a very different view. Military victory and a sense of how much money the post-Afghan military establishment across the Indus was costing may have had something to do with the apparent change in Ellenborough's plans. He had come to believe the East India Company might be able to stay in force on the far side of the Indus, make money, and redeem the situation.

And there is another factor to consider that William Napier Bruce, one of Napier's minor biographers, once mentioned. The matter has been discussed as well by the more recent scholars Albert Imlah and Hamida Khuhro, and it has been explored most fully by J. Y. Wong.[53] Sind would never *directly* make money for the East India Company; that much was clear. But annexing Sind would allow the Company to exercise control over an alternate route by

190 *The conquest of Sind*

which opium was being exported to China. The princely states of the Malwa region of north central India had begun shipping opium through Karachi in independent Sind to avoid the British controls on exports through Bombay. As Wong demonstrates, annexing Sind and thus controlling Karachi did indeed allow the East India Company to re-establish monopoly control over opium prices, and thus the Company was able to substantially increase its profits on the crop that was the single biggest source of its revenue. Writing to William Napier ten years after the annexation, in 1853, Ellenborough explained how important taking Sind had been in solving the problem of the Malwa opium and securing higher revenues for India's main export crop; and *Household Words* discussed the same question in 1857.[54]

So while the British government in Sind would always run deficits, nonetheless securing the country was a source of great profit to the East India Company in another way. Before he arrived in India as Governor-General, Ellenborough had served three times as President of the Board of Control. He knew the balance sheet.

But Napier did not. Before he conquered Sind he does *not* seem to have understood how taking the country would shore up the Company's profits from opium. He and his subordinates did become aware of this fact by the time he left Sind several years later. Indeed, by then he was proudly pointing to how the conquest of the country had been profitable in exactly this way.[55]

Notes

1 Napier to Louisa Napier, 11 August 1841, Bodleian MS Eng. lett. c. 240, fols 110–11.
2 Napier to Kennedy, 10 July 1842, NP, TNA PRO 30/64/6, fols 2–3.
3 Napier to W. Napier, [July 1841?], excerpted in WN, 2:151–53; Napier to Louisa Napier, 7 September, 18 December 1841, 14/17 June 1842, Bodleian MS Eng. lett. c. 240, fols 112, 119, 126–28; WN, 2:158.
4 Napier to Louisa Napier, 16 October, 4 November 1841, Bodleian MS Eng. lett. c. 240, Napier to Louisa Napier, 16 October, 4 November 1841, Bodleian MS Eng. lett. c. 240, fols 115–18.
5 WNCS, 6–9.
6 Napier's journal, 7 November 1841, given in WN, 2:157.
7 Napier to Louisa Napier, 20 July, 11 August 1841, Bodleian MS Eng. lett. c. 240, fols 108–11. Further: 'I hear, but not from authority, that I am to be sent off to the Banks of the Indus to command 10,000 men there in the field. If so, I shall leave my women in Bombay and live in a tent.' – Napier to Emily Bunbury, 26 August 1841, NP, NAM 2005–06–724, item 11.
8 Napier to Emily Bunbury, 26 August 1841, NP, NAM 2005–06–724, item 11; Napier's journal, 24 January 1842, 24 July 1842, given in WN, 2:161, 174–75.
9 Napier to Emily Bunbury, 26 January 1842, NP, BL Add. MSS 49109, fols 112–13.
10 Leopold von Orlich, *Travels in India, Including Sinde and the Punjab*, (trans.) H. Evans Lloyd, 2 vols (London: Longman, Brown, Green, and Longmans, 1845), 1:65–68.
11 Napier's journal, [20 June?] and 28 June 1842, given in WN, 2:184–85; Emily Cephalonia Napier to Louisa Napier, [18 August 1842], NP, BL Add. MS 49158, fols 17–18.
12 Napier to Louisa Napier, 27 April, 14/17 June 1842, Bodleian MS Eng. lett. c. 240, fols 123–28; Napier's journal, 3 May and 31 May 1842, given in WN, 2:170–72; Napier to Emily Bunbury, 18–19 December 1841, NP, BL Add. MS 49109, fols 110–11, and

To India and Sind   191

29 April 1842, fols 119–22. Somerset thought the rate was two shillings sixpence. It was two shillings.

13 Napier to Emily Bunbury, 21 March 1842, NP, BL Add. MS 49109, fols 116–18.

14 Napier's journal, 22 November 1842, given in WN, 2:160.

15 J. A. Norris, *The First Afghan War, 1838–1842* (Cambridge: Cambridge UP, 1967), 375–92; John H. Waller, *Beyond the Khyber Pass: The Road to British Disaster in First Afghan War* (Austin: University of Texas Press, 1990), 229–78.

16 Napier to Robertson, 16 March 1849, NP, BL Add. MS 49107, fol. 65.

17 Napier to Emily Bunbury, 18–9 December 1841, NP, BL Add. MS 49109, fols 110–11; Napier to Louisa Napier, 18 December 1841, 24 March 1842, Bodleian MS Eng. lett. c. 240, fols 119–22.

18 Napier to Emily Bunbury, 26 January 1842, NP, BL Add. MS 49109, fols 112–13.

19 Ellenborough to Napier, quoted in Napier's journal, 4 March 1842, as well as the rest of that day's first journal entry, given in WN, 2:161–62.

20 [Charles Napier], 'On the Defense of the Northwestern Frontier of India', EP, TNA PRO 30/12/32/2, quotations at 1–2.

21 Ellenborough to William Napier, 11 September 1852, given in Charles James Napier, *Defects, Civil and Military, of the Indian Government*, W.F.P. Napier (ed.) (London: Charles Westerton, 1853), 357–59.

22 Ellenborough to Napier, 17 March 1842, given in Algernon Law (ed.), *India under Lord Ellenborough, March 1842-June 1844: A Selection from the Hitherto Unpublished Papers and Secret Despatches of Edward Earl of Ellenborough* (London: John Murray, 1926), 23.

23 Napier to Louisa Napier, 27 April 1842, Bodleian MS Eng. lett. c. 240, fols 123–25.

24 Ellenborough to Peel, 21 April 1842; instructions by Ellenborough, 26 April 1842 – both given in ibid, 25–28.

25 Ellenborough, Memorandum on Foreign Policy, 27 April 1842, given in ibid, 28–30.

26 Ibid, 30.

27 Ellenborough to Wellington, 22 April 1843, given in Lord Colchester, *History of the Indian Administration of Lord Ellenborough in His Correspondence with the Duke of Wellington* (London: Richard Bentley and Son, 1874), 359–62.

28 Ellenborough to Outram, 8 May 1842, quoted in Law, *India under Ellenborough*, 179–82; Ellenborough to Wellington, 7 June 1842, given in CEW, 250–56 at 255. Ellenborough's policy is considered in Adrian Duarte, *A History of British Relations with Sind, 1613–1843* (Karachi: National Book Foundation, 1976), 395–446. However there are no reference notes, and as Duarte does not give the date and context of his evidence the argument is difficult to evaluate. One source omitted is Ellenborough's long-published private correspondence.

29 Ellenborough to the Queen, 16 September 1842, given in CEW, 44–47; Napier to Ellenborough, 15 September 1842, EP, TNA 30/12/62 [no folio number]; von Orlich, *Travels*, 1:75–81; WNCS, 16–17; Napier's journal, 9 September 1842, given in WN, 2:190–93.

30 On the substantial slave trade, see S.V.W. Hart, 'Report on the Town and Port of Kurachee [1840]', in R. Hughes Thomas (ed.), *Selections of the Records of the Bombay Government*, new series, 17 (Bombay: Printed for the Government at the Bombay Education Society's Press, 1855), 209–45 at 220–21; R. K. Pringle, 'Report on the Condition and Mode of Administration in Sind', 31 December 1847, in *Selections from the Pre-Mutiny Records of the Commissioner in Sind*, Selection 1 (Sind: Commissioner's Office, n.d.), 1–35 at 2.

31 Napier to Ellenborough, 15 September 1842, EP, TNA 30/12/62 [no folio number]; Edward Archer Langley, *Narrative of a Residence at the Court of Meer Ali Murad, with Wild Sports in the Valley of the Indus*, 2 vols (London: Hurst and Blackett, 1860), 1:68; Napier's journal, 13 September 1842, given in WN, 2:193; Emily Cephalonia Napier to Louisa Napier, 3 July 1845, NP, BL Add. MS 49158, fols 42–44.

32 Napier's journal, 2 and 13 September 1842, given in WN, 2:188–89 and 193.

33 Ellenborough to Wellington, 6 July 1842, 17 August 1842, and 16 September 1842, given in CEW, 256–62 at 259, 280–81, and 281–84.

192   *The conquest of Sind*

34 Napier to Emily Bunbury, 10 August 1841, NP, BL Add. MS 49109, fols 129–31; Napier's journal, 25 August 1842, given in WN, 2:174–75; see also 2 September, 26 September, 2:188, 197; Napier to Louisa Napier, 8 October 1842, Bodleian MS Eng. lett. c. 240, fols 133–34.

35 Ellenborough to the Queen, 16 September 1842, given in ibid, 44–47.

36 von Orlich, *Travels*, 1:123.

37 Suhail Zahir Lari, *History of Sindh* (Karachi: Oxford UP, 1994), 144–45; Hamida Khuhro, *The Making of Modern Sind: British Policy and Social Change in the Nineteenth Century* (Karachi: Oxford UP, 1999), 31–32.

38 James Burnes, *A Visit to the Court of Scinde* (1829; Karachi: Oxford UP, 1974), 9–11, 27–28; Alexander Burnes, *Travels into Bokhara: Being an Account of a Journey from India to Cabool, Tartary, and Persia; also, a Narrative of a Voyage on the Indus, from the Sea to Lahore*, 3 vols (London: John Murray, 1834), 3:1–88, 193–280, with the Syed's remark at 37–38; LNS, 12–13; H. Evan and M. James, 'Introduction in Naomal Hotchand', in (trans.) Alumal Trikamdas Bhojwani, H. Evan, and M. James (eds), *A Forgotten Chapter of Indian History as Described in the Memoirs of Seth Naomal Hotchand, C.S.I., of Karachi, 1804–1878* (Exeter: Printed for private circulation by W. Pollard, 1915), 4–6. See also C. A. Bayly, *Empire and Information: Intelligence Gathering and Social Communication in India, 1780–1870* (Cambridge: Cambridge UP, 1996), 129–30, 136–39.

39 In addition to the sources about to be examined more fully, see James McMurdo, *McMurdo's Account of Sind*, Sarah Ansari (ed.) [1834] (Karachi: Oxford UP, 2007), 20–24, 26–28, 40. For the early history of British ideas about Indian despotism, see Bernard S. Cohn, *Colonialism and Its Forms of Knowledge: The British in India* (Princeton, NJ: Princeton UP, 1996), 62–65; Thomas R. Metcalf, *The New Cambridge History of India*, III.4, *Ideologies of the Raj* [1987] (New Delhi: Oxford UP, 1998), 6–8.

40 Marianne Postans, *Travels, Tales, and Encounters in Sindh and Balochistan, 1840–1843* (Oxford: Oxford UP, 2003), 7, 10–15, 17, 19, 65–68; for her pre-conquest complaints that the Amirs were selfish in the land reserved for their hunts, see 43–44, 52. Postans wrote earlier books on other areas of the subcontinent, also stressing the importance of Western-style agricultural improvements, and excoriating what seemed to her the despotism and rapacity of Indian rulers unconcerned with agricultural reform – Ketaki Kushari Dyson, *A Various Universe: A Study of the Journals and Memoirs of British Men and Women in the Indian Subcontinent, 1765–1856* (New Delhi: Oxford UP, 1978), 16, 261–67.

41 Alexander Burnes said the common people told him in 1831 that taxation under the Amirs was too high to allow for farming – *Travels*, 3:35; see also p. 3:41. Lambrick minimizes the importance of the land sequestered and the villages destroyed, exonerating the Amirs – LNS, 24. But see I. N. Allen, *Diary of a March through Sinde and Afghanistan* (London: J. Hatchard and Son, 1843), 53, 56; J. Burnes, *Scinde*, 79.

42 J. Burnes, *Scinde*, 83–88; Delhoste's Report, 1832, given in Edward Paterson Delhoste, *Observing Sindh*, Matthew A. Cook (ed.) (Oxford: Oxford UP, 2008), 23–24.

43 Sen, 'Liberal Empire and Illiberal Trade', 141; Talal Asad, 'Two European Images of Non-European Rule', in Asad (ed.), *Anthropology and the Colonial Encounter* (Atlantic Highlands, NJ: Humanities Press International; Reading, UK: Ithaca Press, 1973); Norman Daniel, *Islam, Europe, and Empire* (Edinburgh: Edinburgh UP, 1966), 269–70. The competence and probity of non-Islamic rulers further east was distrusted as well: Bayly, *Empire and Information*, 109.

44 Feroz Ahmad, 'Agrarian Change and Class Formation in Sindh', *Economical and Political Weekly* 19, 39 (29 September 1984), A149-A164 at A153-A154. For the widespread economic decline under the Amirs, see S. P. Chablani, *Economic Conditions in Sind, 1592–1843* (Bombay: Orient Longman, 1951), 164–66.

45 Napier's journal, 26 September, 1 October, 3 October, 12 October 1842, given in WN, 2:199, 202, 219; see also 2: 207.

46 J. Burnes, *Scinde*, 120–21; A. Burnes, *Travels*, 3:38 – see also 3:70–71.

47 'Sindh Controversy: Napier and Outram', 572.

48 T. Postans, *Personal Observations on Sindh* (London: Longman, Brown, Green, and Long-mans, 1843), 341–43, 346–55. *The Economist*, in its first number, agreed with Postans – *The Economist*, 9 September 1843, 25–27.

49 C. U. Aitchison, *A Collection of Treaties, Engagements, and Sunnuds Relating to India and Neigh-bouring Countries*, vol. 6, *The Treaties, &c., Relating to the Punjab, Sind, and Beloochistan, and Central Asia*, rev. edn, A. C. Talbot (ed.) (Calcutta: Foreign Office Press, 1876), 6:284–94.

50 Albert H. Imlah, *Lord Ellenborough: A Biography of Edward Law, Earl of Ellenborough, Governor-General of India* (Cambridge, MA: Harvard UP, 1939), 124–27; Law, *India under Ellenborough*, 175–77; Henry Lushington, *A Great Country's Little Wars; or, England, Af-ghanistan, and Sinde* (London: John W. Parker, 1844), 212; Mirza Kalichbeg Fredungbeg (trans.), *History of Sind*, 2 vols, 2 parts (Karachi: Commissioner's Press, 1902), 2:2:179–80; LNS, 40–41; WNCS, 64–65.

51 Ellenborough to Wellington, 4 October 1842, given in CEW, 293–96.

52 Ellenborough to Wellington, 18 October 1842, given in ibid, 297–300. The idea that if the Indus were opened up great amounts of trade would flow from Punjab and Cen-tral Asia had been developed in the writings of Alexander Burnes: A. Burnes, *Travels*, 2:395–412, 3:52.

53 William Napier Bruce, *The Life of General Sir Charles Napier, G.C.B.* (London: John Murray, 1885), 341; Imlah, *Ellenborough*, 146; Hamida Khuhro, *The Making of Modern Sind*, 184–85; J. Y. Wong, 'British Annexation of Sind in 1843: An Economic Perspective', *Modern Asian Studies* 31, 2 (May 1997), 225–44; and J. Y. Wong, *Deadly Dreams: Opium, Imperialism, and the Arrow War (1856–1860) in China* (Cambridge: Cambridge UP, 1998), 417–25. See also J. F. Richards, 'The Indian Empire and Peasant Production of Opium in the Nineteenth Century', *Modern Asian Studies* 15, 1 (1981), 59–82 at 65; and Claude Markovits, 'The Political Economy of Opium Smuggling in Early Nineteenth Century India: Leakage or Resistance?', *Modern Asian Studies* 43, 1 (2009), 89–111. Markovits says the Amirs profited greatly from this trade before the British took Karachi in 1839 (94, 96), but the trade declined so steeply with British occupation that it would not have played a major role in the permanent acquisition of Sind four years later (107–08). Yet this argument depends upon too many contingent factors regarding alternate smuggling routes. In any case, the attempt to control the Malwa trade was a multi-decade effort on the part of the East India Company (96, 105–08), so any decline because of what was intended to be a temporary occupation would hardly factor in. The British became con-fident in the robustness of their opium network only after Sind was annexed – for only then did they raise the taxes on their opium (and substantially so); see Farooqui, *Colo-nialism as Subversion: Colonialism, Indian Merchants, and the Politics of Opium, 1790–1843* (Lanham, MD: Lexington Books, 2005), 200–01, 203.

54 Ellenborough to W. Napier, 11 September 1853, given in Napier, *Defects*, 357–59; and cited in turn in Wong, 'British Annexation of Sind in 1843: An Economic Perspective', 235; Anonymous, 'Opium', *Household Words* 384 (1 August 1857), 104–08 at 107.

55 Napier to Hobhouse, [?] 1846, given in WN, 301–20 at 311. Ellenborough never men-tioned Malwa opium at the time, and he denied that Sind would pay for the costs of its administration: Ellenborough to Napier, copy of second letter of 3 November 1842, PP, BL Add. MS 40522, fols 295–97.

15 Napier's motivations

While Napier wanted to save the Sindhis from oppression, Ellenborough wanted to use Napier to take the country and remove the distribution point for the Malwa opium. Nonetheless for a long time Napier remained ignorant of the aggressive policy which the Governor-General had in mind.[1] But eventually he had his suspicions. When he finally sent Ellenborough his views on 20 October, he told the Governor-General that he could not 'understand how any sane man could contemplate the extension of our Indian territory beyond her Rivers'.[2] Yet Napier himself had already begun to advocate occupying Sukkur – for several reasons: to safeguard it from bandits; to make it a centre of British trade and influence; and to save the Sindhi refugees in the city from having to live once again under the Amirs.[3] So even in Napier's mind it would be a good idea to disattach a section of the Amirs' lands – Sukkur – for the good of the people.

Napier spent the weeks after writing this letter in going about his duties as a prudent army commander. He made detailed military plans against whatever the Amirs might throw at him. If they attacked, he decided that his main response would be to move on Hyderabad.[4] But mostly he contemplated the current behaviour of the Amirs. '[The Amirs] are tyrants', he had recorded in early October, adding that 'so are we, but the poor will have fairer play under our sceptre than under theirs.'[5] And at about this point, it occurred to him that while the Amirs continued to refuse to fix the canal system and to destroy the farms of the poor for the pleasures of the hunt, his own troops were in actual occupation of the country and might stop the madness, as well as taking the opportunity to enforce the Company's treaty rights. But he agonized over the situation in a passage that is worth parsing in some detail:

> These poor foolish Ameers think, that with all those soldiers in possession of the Indus, they can lay out its banks in forests for wild beasts; and with four armed steamers plying the waters can destroy villages and all cultivation, refuse wood for those steamers, and by tolls destroy commerce and the welfare of their wretched people, who are frequently seen to pick the grain from the dung of the officers' horses to eat! *Mene! mene! tekel, upharsin!* How is all this to end? We have no right to seize Scinde, yet we

shall do so, and a very advantageous, useful, humane piece of rascality it will be.[6]

So, now that the British forces were in the country by treaty because of Afghanistan, he did not think them likely to leave. The situation on the ground was too volatile for that to happen. The British would not back away from enforcing the treaty guarantees on the free navigation in the Indus. And it was very tempting to take power and feed the starving.

When this passage from Napier's private notes is quoted by scholars – and it has been quoted many times – it is usually only the last sentence which is included, the sentence with a 'humane piece of rascality'.[7] The rest of what Napier said is seldom discussed – namely his invocation of the biblical writing on the wall, and his belief that annexation would soon come no matter what, given the British troops and British steamers already in possession of the country. Ignoring the rest of what he said makes Napier seem jaunty.[8] And quoting only the one sentence also omits another vital piece of the context: For whom is Napier saying that annexation would be 'useful'? For whom would it be 'humane'?

Perhaps, if a better treaty could be imposed on the Amirs through blithe effrontery, a war with them could be avoided and the government of the country might be improved, or so Napier claims. He goes on to say this:

> But it seems possible so to frighten these Ameers that they would abdicate in our favour if we left them their hunting grounds and revenues, and we might do both. They have usurped their power within sixty years by the sword, but they cannot keep it by the sword, so let it go as it came.[9]

In other words, perhaps the British could take power and save the starving people from having to pick through the dung for their food. And perhaps Napier and his forces might bring this about *without* war, if indeed the Amirs could be inveigled into accepting the new regime and retiring from active rulership. This indeed is the burden of his famous '*Mene!, mene!*' journal entry of 7 October, when it is read in full.

***

And so Napier made his own the mission of getting the Amirs to agree to revise the treaty arrangements of 1839. The brusqueness of his dealings with them, which several observers at the time put down to the general's inexperience with the Indian character, was instead a deliberate strategy to force a political settlement. Even Napier's worst critic at the time, James Outram, did not think that the general was *aiming* for war, only for a general agreement to the new treaty. The war was the result of Napier's brusqueness and how it was received by the Amirs.[10]

Following Ellenborough's lead, Napier decided to hold the Amirs to the current, 1839 treaty structure unforgivingly: '[W]e break treaties', he said, 'but

196   *The conquest of Sind*

that is not a reason for letting others do the same'. He suspected that the Amirs would fail to live up to their commitments somehow, as he wrote on 8 October, and then he would be required to act against them in various ways in order to achieve the settlement: 'I know what would be were I master, and suspect what is likely to be.'[11]

In a long letter to Ellenborough that he composed on 17 October and sent some days later (when he had finished gathering the supporting documents[12]), Napier set out an argument for 'abolishing barbarism and ameliorating the condition of society' in Sind, and accomplishing this 'by obliging the Ameers to do, in compliance with [the] treaties, that which honourable and civilized rulers would do of their own accord'. Napier stressed that this course of action would not justify the British side breaking the treaties in any way, but 'it does sanction . . . exacting a rigid adherence . . . by the Ameers'. 'These things must be kept in mind', he insisted, 'or what I am about to say will appear unjust, which is not the case.'[13] At least he was sensitive to that possibility.

Napier went on to make the dubious point that the British had a treaty right to stay in Sind indefinitely. Yet despite the permanence of the British presence, the situation had become unstable, in his view. The Amirs wanted their independence back and they wanted the British to leave. Meanwhile, the common people were seeking refuge in the British cantonments. In Napier's opinion they had come to escape oppression. Others said they came to escape taxes.

Napier was not alone in foreseeing that events would develop along these lines, with the growth in the number of Sindhis in the cantonments fundamentally destabilizing Sindhi society. Outram, the Political Agent, told Napier that if the area around Shikarpore were declared to be British territory, the land in question would see an immediate influx of population and soon enough a massive upturn in prosperity. The local people would 'flock' to the stretches of land under British control, reclaiming the fertile but unfarmed areas and escaping the 'tyranny' of the Amirs.[14] Outram's answer to this problem of the cantonments, as he reviewed the matter for Napier about a month before hostilities broke out, was that the example of good rule in the British areas would lead the Amirs to treat their 'serfs' better and promote trade.[15]

We know from two other sources that the Amirs themselves were already looking with alarm at the way their subjects were moving to the cantonments, and how their own treasuries were losing revenue. In Hyderabad, Mir Nasir Khan ordered that any merchant setting up a shop in the bazaar of the British camp at Karachi – or who bought anything there, or who sold the British grain – should have all his property seized. If this order had been enforced, it would have impoverished the Hindu merchants, and it threatened to starve out the British population of Karachi and everyone in the cantonment with them.[16]

But the order could not be enforced. As Napier pointed out in his letter, trade with the cantonments would go on anyway. He explained to the Governor-General that with so many Sindhis fleeing to the areas under British control, all the trade on the Indus would soon be monopolized by these British stations, even more seriously impoverishing the rest of the country. Then soon

Napier's motivations   197

enough the government of the Amirs would collapse in degradation – unless in order to prevent this outcome the British troops were to leave the country immediately. But it they were to do so they would leave unprotected the many people who had come to them for safety.[17]

If Britain stayed, then

> the more powerful government will at no distant period swallow up the weaker. Would it not be better to come to the results at once? I think it would be better, *if it can be done with honesty*. Let me then consider how we might go to work on a matter so critical, and whether the facts to which I have called your attention will bear me out in what I propose.
>
> Several Ameers have broken [the] treaty in the various instances stated in the accompanying *'Return of Complaints.'* I have maintained that we only want a fair pretext to coerce the Ameers, and I think these various acts recorded give abundant reason to take Kurachee, Sukkur, Bukkur, Shikarpoor, and Subzulcote for our own, and obliging the Ameers to leave a track way [*sic*] along both banks of the Indus, stipulating for a supply of wood; but at the same time remitting all tribute, in favour of those Ameers whose conduct has been correct; and finally, enter into a fresh treaty with one of those princes alone as chief. I cannot think that such a procedure would be dishonourable or harsh. I am sure that it would be humane. The refractory Ameers break the treaty to gratify their avarice, and we punish that breach. I perceive no injustice.[18]

Keeping Shikarpore, he added, would mean maintaining British rule over a Hindu area perfectly situated for British efforts to repress the nearby hill raiders from whose depredations so much of the northern Sind continually suffered. The Political Agent Outram, Napier said, had read these words and agreed.[19]

In his own mind, Ellenborough had no illusions, no moral qualms, about the likely results of the policy that under his guidance Napier was to pursue. The Governor-General knew that it all would lead to war. After Napier wrote at the beginning of November that force would not be necessary to get the Amirs to agree, Ellenborough replied on 14 November saying that it probably would be.[20] And as Ellenborough wrote to Prime Minister Robert Peel on 15 November, referring to the new arrangements that Napier had now been told to impose on the Amirs,

> I have given instructions to Sir Charles Napier which he thinks he can execute without the use of force. I do not. However, they were necessary. The violations of the Treaty by the Ameers rendered some punishment unavoidable.
>
> I considered well what we ought to demand, and I do not think I have gone beyond what was expedient and just. You should read all my letters to Sir Charles Napier, and all his. If there should be resistance, I shall exact a severe penalty.[21]

198 *The conquest of Sind*

Ellenborough goes on to say that he would exile almost all the Amirs to the right bank of the Indus'. They had not ruled for very long, and '[n]o one will regret their expulsion from India'.

Note that Ellenborough called his behaviour 'expedient and just', in that order. This very letter prompted the current President of the Board of Control, Lord Fitzgerald, to resign over how the Cabinet was continually abetting Ellenborough's aggressiveness, coddling Ellenborough at Wellington's behest. But for the political comfort of the government Peel forbade Fitzgerald from carrying out his resignation.[22] Lord Fitzgerald died four months later, still in office. But in light of mounting criticism, Ellenborough would one day have to defend his aggressive policies or minimize his role in them. The details of getting the Amirs to agree to the new arrangements 'I left . . . in Sir C. Napier's hands', he told Wellington in March 1843.[23]

The new treaty

Ellenborough now told Napier to persuade the Amirs to agree to a new treaty. It was very harsh, underscoring that the Indus was open to trade and reiterating the abolition by the Amirs of all tolls and transit duties and all taxes affecting the British cantonments. The Amirs would also have to yield control to the British of a one-hundred foot-wide strip of land along each bank of the river where trees could be cut to feed the steamships. The crew of the British steamers would not normally cut these trees for themselves if they were provided with the wood they required. But if they were not satisfied they would be able to cut wherever in the one-hundred-foot strips they wished.[24]

Because of this provision alone, the Amirs might well fear for the future of the reforestation and bank-stabilization project that some modern scholars have recognized that they were pursuing.[25] At risk too was their whole style of life – their hunting parks; the sixty- to one hundred-foot 'state pleasure-barges' which they used to travel to their hunts; and indeed the way they saved their discussions with each other for their elaborate hunting blinds. The riverine strips were essential to the way they lived, for away from the river the Upper Sind was desiccated.[26]

But the new treaty went further. The British now would have the sole right to coin money in Sind. In exchange for being released from the obligation to pay tribute to the East India Company, the tribute which had been imposed by Lord Auckland, the Amirs would now be required to cede some of their more profitable territory outright. The treaty guaranteed the permanent British occupation of Karachi, Sukkur, Tatah, Bukkur and Rohri; and still more Sindhi territory would be transferred by certain of the Amirs to the loyal Sultan of Bahawalpore.[27]

In addition, the political situation would be stabilized: The Amir who was the premier sovereign of the north and holder of the Turban of chief authority (he was called the *rais*) would be replaced by his brother, who as the new overlord was to receive one-quarter of the wealth of the other seventeen Amirs of Upper Sind. (The deposed *rais* would retain only his core state of Khyrpore.) The *rais* being deposed was the apparently senile, certainly eighty-five-year-old, Mir Rustam Khan. In his better days he had greeted Alexander Burnes in 1831 with unusual friendship.

On that occasion Mir Rustam himself had foreseen a British conquest of the whole subcontinent, and so he tried to engage Burnes in an alliance.[28] But now in 1842 the British did not want to be his friend. They feared that Mir Rustam would try to divert the succession away from his brother Ali Murad and in favour of his own descendants. Some more explanation is required here. It seems that the normal practice in the country was that one brother would follow another before any of the sons could take control. The difficulty at present – and the reason why Company officials thought they had to intervene and make a special effort to preserve the principle of fraternal succession – was that the two brothers Mir Rustam and Ali Murad were of extraordinarily different ages. Ali Murad was a half-century younger than his brother Mir Rustam. So Mir Rustam was suspected of wanting to leave power to the adult sons to whose interests he had committed himself long before his young brother was ever conceived. Indeed, the two brothers Mir Rustam and Ali Murad had already fought a war over the matter of Ali Murad's birthright. Ali Murad won. The war had concluded with a written promise of land for Ali Murad; this treaty was solemnized just before Napier's arrival in the country.

In trying to impose the treaty that Ellenborough prepared, Napier may have had his suspicions about the justice of this arrangement between the brothers (for after all it had arisen in war), but nonetheless it existed and Mir Rustam seemed to be working against it. For their part, Political Agent James Outram and the other British experts in the country agreed that Mir Rustam should indeed be displaced and that rulership should be passed to a brother before a son. (Later on Outram would change his mind about this, asserting that the question could have been decided either way.[29]) Rather than trying to judge Sindhi inheritance law, Napier simply took the side of Britain's ally Ali Murad, and he went ahead to try to secure agreement to Ellenborough's text. Napier came to see the disunity among the Amirs as a part of the very rationale for imposing the new settlement. Now that Ali Murad would be supreme, the British would have an easier time negotiating with one Amir in the northern part of the country rather than nearly twenty.[30]

So Napier set about in earnest trying to sell the new treaty to the Amirs. He stressed how they would be released from paying tribute to the British. He hoped to convince them that they would come out ahead financially even after the loss of so much of their revenue-producing land. In this way Napier seems to have been trying to convince himself that he was offering a fair settlement. But in fact the specific territorial changes had been framed by Ellenborough with Wellington's defensive line in mind. Many of the Amirs who were losing the territory that Ellenborough had his eye on *were not* the same men who had broken the treaties. And the territory being taken was worth more to them each year than the tribute from which they were being released.[31] In framing

200 *The conquest of Sind*

the new treaty, Ellenborough had taken lands and cities according to his own convenience, and he allowed no substantive modification to the text.[32] But most of the Amirs, now gathered at Hyderabad in the southern Sind, recognized that they had no choice but to accept.

***

By November Charles Napier's plans to either overthrow the Amirs or bring them severely under control had seeped into the public discourse in England, perhaps through the agency of William Napier. The local newspaper in Bath advised that

> the tyranny of the Ameers is proverbial, and the removal of their government would be a blessing to all the inhabitants of the banks of the Indus. It was therefore considered probable that the British Government will, for its own sake, as well as for the advancement of civilization, be speedily induced to control the oppressive acts of those mischievous despots.[33]

The *Times* had said something like this a few days before. Charles Napier had come to the same conclusion. The day before the fateful letter to Ellenborough in October, he wrote in his journal that broader British interests and the real interests of the common people of Sind are 'on this point one':

> Whereof I avow wanting only a just pretext for forcing the Ameers to do right for their people and for themselves. What do they struggle for now? To levy tolls on their own boats while those of other nations go free! . . . The Ameers won't fight, my force is too strong, and this is the moment to do the job; because being strong it could be done without bloodshed, could be done with my pen![34]

What he was saying was that the faster the crisis came, the more peaceful the outcome, but in any case he was determined to use force.

For it may be that in his view the Amirs — or at least some of them — deserved nothing better. When Napier had been in the country for only a few weeks, the officials serving under him started making a case that the native rulers were plotting something. Everything hinged on the authenticity of several intercepted letters. They seemed to prove that none other than Mir Rustam, *rais* of the north, was plotting to bring Sikh troops from Multan in Punjab and to set them against the British. Other correspondence implicated Mir Nasir Khan of Hyderabad — the man who wanted to starve Karachi — in trying to recruit Beebruck Boogtie, the chief of a tribe of hill raiders, to come down in force and fight the British properly. And in addition to these plots, Napier was told of another affront: Mir Rustam (or rather his chief aide) had helped a fugitive to escape.[35]

It was not immediately clear that letters implicating Rustam in the plot to entice the Sikhs to come and fight were indeed authentic. One of the letters

Napier's motivations   201

from Mir Rustam was in the hand of Rustam's minister Futeh Muhammed Ghoree rather than of Rustam himself.[36] Officials disagreed over whether to take the document at face value. Suspicions arose because the letter had come by way of Rustam's brother and rival, Ali Murad, and forged seals were not unknown.[37]

Napier worked carefully through the letters with those who knew the language, and he reasoned his way forward as best he could.[38] Calipers were used to measure the seals on different documents. Not everything matched, but supposedly each Amir had two *almost* identical seals so they could deny a document if necessary. And there were other letters that seemed to confirm Rustam's diplomatic advance to the Sikhs. Eventually Napier became convinced that the threat was genuine, even if historian H. T. Lambrick, who a century later wrote the standard work on Napier's diplomatic and military activities in Sind, professes shock at Napier's certainty. But Napier thought he had proof – 'no question of the fact', as he wrote to Ellenborough in November.[39] And he thought he was in danger. From his journal:

> The Ameers have indeed collected in various places about 20,000 men, who will not however stay long from their homes without money, and their masters are avaricious, like the Greeks, Ali Pacha, and all other barbarians. I am glad to procrastinate for the saving of lives and shall seek to avoid a fight, though to thrash them will be easy and to my worldly advantage: but God preserve me from seeking that at the expense of blood. Lord E. must not lay unnecessary responsibility on me: he is the proper man to decide.[40]

We should take stock of what Napier knew and saw. Every indication is that the people of Sind were starving. There was a three-year drought despite all the water flowing down the Indus. No new land was being brought under cultivation, and the combined taxes and fees paid to the Amirs came in many places to three-quarters of the crop. With taxes that high, there was little incentive for local officials to expand cultivation; nor were the Amirs taking any interest in doing so themselves. The people continued to starve. All of this was well known to British officers in Sind in Napier's first months there.[41] And we should remember that Napier was no mere observer. He was in command of a large army occupying the country. So in terms of physical power, he could do something to save the people's lives if he wished. Napier, who after all was a radical more concerned with establishing justice than respecting tradition, felt a fierce temptation to act against the Amirs in some fashion, under whatever legal excuse he could find. In November he summed up the matter this way:

> My position is difficult. If I thrash these chaps and take their land[,] abuse will follow; if I let them get the better in treating, it will be abandoning the only opportunity their poor subjects have of obtaining a little relief

202   *The conquest of Sind*

from grinding oppression. My mind is however made up: if they fire a shot Scinde shall be annexed to India.[42]

By the end of the month he was sure that the Amirs were biding their time to attack him. In turn he reflected that he had three months of cool weather ahead of him in which he could fight them effectively.[43]

In a sense the course for war was set. And then that autumn James Outram, the Political Agent who actually talked to the Amirs, made a fateful decision to withhold from them a key ultimatum from Lord Ellenborough. The Governor-General had written that if they did not refrain from plotting with foreign powers or interfering with British wishes, they would be deposed. Outram believed that Ellenborough's letter was likely to inflame the situation. He was confident that with his own diplomatic skill he could bring affairs to a happier conclusion with no outside interference from the Governor-General. So he never delivered the ultimatum. It is true that Ellenborough had left Outram free to withhold it if he thought the Amirs innocent of any plot. But Outram did indeed believe that they were plotting and he withheld the letter anyway. (In his own published comments on the matter, Outram elides the 'if' clause in Ellenborough's promise to depose the Amirs *if* they were guilty of intrigue – although it appears in the text of the letter that he quotes.)[44]

From this point on, Outram's views began to undergo a deep transformation. He began to worry that the Amirs might be losing too much land, too high a proportion of their revenues and estates. Now suffering 'depredation and deprivation', the Amirs were fated to rebel, bringing 'rapine and disorder' to the country.[45] Outram's increasingly colourful descriptions of the state of Amirs, alongside his ever more optimistic views of the traditional aristocracy if only it were left to its own devices, meant that his opinions were beginning to diverge markedly from Napier's. For as ever Napier harboured a strong prejudice against the rich of all stripes. In his view, in imposing a new order in Sind he was looking out for the interests of a population oppressed by their illegitimate lords.

As Napier explained to Outram in January, Lord Auckland had started the mess by imposing immoral treaties. But:

> Now what is to be done? That which is best for the advancement of good government and [*sic*] well-being of the population; and we must not sacrifice this to a minute endeavour, utterly hopeless, I may say impossible, to give to these tyrannical, drunken, debauched, cheating, intriguing, contemptible Ameers, a due portion of the plunder they have amassed from the ruined people they conquered sixty years ago. They are fortunate robbers one and all, and though I most decidedly condemn the way we entered this country; just as honest, however, as that by which the Talpoors got it from the Kalloras; I would equally condemn any policy that allowed these rascals to go on plundering the country to supply their debaucheries after we had raised the hopes of every respectable man in the country.[46]

But Napier could not entirely suppress his doubts. He immediately continues:

> If I thought Lord E. was acting on an unjust plan I would of course obey my orders, but should deeply regret my position. But I do no such thing: the whole injustice was committed by Lord Auckland, and such a course of injustice cannot be closed without hardship on some one. It is likely to fall on the Ameers and on a crew more deserving to bear it hardly could it alight.[47]

The Orientalist debate

In a later book, Outram highly commends something the former governor of Bombay, Sir John Malcolm, had said on the subject of how to rule India: British officials should not worry so much about the injustices or tyrannies of Indian life. Instead, they should try to understand society in India as a complicated and intricate structure whose individual elements could never be interfered with without risking the whole building coming down.[48] For Outram and those who agreed with him, the Amirs and their governments were entirely good enough when compared – not with the wonders of European rule – but with any other government run by Asians.[49]

Indeed, there was a long-running debate in the East India Company between the 'Orientalists', who wanted to respect the autonomy of Indian culture, like Malcolm, and the 'Anglicists', who wanted reform, the side Napier found himself agreeing with. For Napier, the 'sticklers for abstract right' who wanted to respect the rights of the Amirs to control the Indus and destroy agriculture were missing the point. The freedom of the Amirs to dominate was not more important than the freedom of the common people to escape domination.[50] The common people of Sind, like the common people everywhere, deserved better. There was no arcane or secret knowledge of the Indian character and Indian institutions that had to be respected, Napier insisted, for people are the same wherever you find them.[51] More than that: Rather than some particular Culture determining who we are, whether Sindhi, Greek, or English, people when taken together show the same range of personalities in one place as they do in any other – the same extremes of good and bad are found wherever you go. In Napier's view, bad governments might leave their people on average more dishonest, while a population living under more fortunate conditions might become more civilized on average, but that is all. A year after he conquered Sind, he told his sister Emily that the '[t]he horrors here are placed to the account of Asiatic *character*! No such thing, Em. The horrors you hear of are the chiefs and *their soldiers*, armed *miscreants* . . . living by robbery and murder'.[52] There was no special Asian character at all. The Sindhis simply deserved freedom, in Napier's opinion.

'Despising and avoiding the society of the natives, "Old Indians" yet pretend to know the character of those natives, and call themselves the statesmen of India!'[53] Napier wrote. He goaded Outram for wanting to respect the local usages when '[y]ou say [the Amirs] are all children and fools'.[54]

204   *The conquest of Sind*

What were Outram's views? The way he looked at the matter, the Amirs were exercising a more or less beneficial patriarchal rule.[55] Western ideas of liberty were not universal, not yet; nor were they something that could be imposed on a country from without if they had not grown in the soil of the place. In his words:

> As in the case with all semi-barbarous nations, there was occasional oppression practiced in Scinde, and appeals were from time to time made to myself and my assistants, against particular acts of individual functionaries. But, beyond friendly intercession, we had no right to interfere with the course of justice, nor with their fiscal arrangements. The systems in force were rooted in, and sprang from, the habits and ideas of the people, and were as much a reflection of the national mind of Scinde, as our own constitution is that of Britain. To improve their habits, to enlarge their minds, and thereby to render them fit for a better system, appeared to me the object we should propose to ourselves.[56]

So in Outram's opinion, Napier was taking a course of action very different from what 'practical' men like himself and Henry Pottinger would countenance. Men who had real experience in the country knew the local people and 'understood the workings of the human mind'. Napier, 'profoundly ignorant' of such things, was by contrast 'a theorist who invented systems, and acted on them as if they were realities'.[57]

What theory had Napier invented? What abstract comparison had Napier insisted upon? For him, the Talpurs were no more than the tyrannical conquerors of sixty years back. They had impoverished Sind, ruining the once-flourishing towns and leaving the people living 'little better than animals . . . in straw sheds, or such wretched mud houses as would *"beggar all Ireland"*'.[58]

The coming of war

As Napier put the matter in a joint letter to his own family and John Kennedy in mid-December 1842 (he explained that he was too busy to correspond with everyone individually),

> I shall do what I am ordered and unless they attack *me* no blood will be spilled. I can produce a war in two hours if I like, but I want to prevent it, and trust in God I shall. I am the only man in Camp who does not wish for war with the Ameers, and their own peasantry detest them and are longing for us. But still they collect great numbers of Beloochees and other warlike tribes of the mountains. All these robbers form their armies, and their deserts are difficult . . . wild deserts, except along the River, there are great jungles in the deserts, so it is necessary to be careful. A very little rashness might involve disaster for my small army; and, as it is, I have nearly 900 sick with fever.[59]

Napier's motivations 205

If he could get his troops in between the forces of the Amirs and the territory he was taking over, and if the Amirs did not attack him in the process, then 'my work will be done without blood – God be thanked for that great mercy'.[60] Or on another occasion, 'I am perfectly prepared, should they resist, to act in a way which I imagine will bring them to reason, without bloodshed, not but that I have troops enough (and ready enough!) to thrash them heartily if they resolve to try their strength'.[61]

Clearly Napier was no pacifist. He kept up a strong front so the Amirs would not think him weak and attack him. Right into December he worried constantly about the withdrawal from Afghanistan, still under way, and the safety and comfort of the troops coming back through the passes – as well as his own safety if the Afghans, the Punjabis, or the Amirs themselves should decide to attack his forces.[62] Again and again he discussed political settlements that might leave the Amirs as princes in the land and enable the quick withdrawal of the bulk of the British troops: '[M]y mind is bent on stopping war, and if left alone I will do so. Barbaric chiefs must be bullied or they think you are afraid. . . . My popularity would be small if the soldiers knew my strong resolution to prevent prize money! What a wretch is man!' Further:

> My ambition is not for a *butcher's bill*. The fear of creating such bloody work is always in my mind; my wish is to save them, and I am likely to success, being so bent on it; but if we come to blows they cannot be saved. . . . Poor people! The Ameers' women have been sent out of the way of danger I hear, which gladdens me; but I must have the poor class of women and children out of mischief also.'[63]

Napier has been called a megalomaniac for some of what he wrote in his journal during this period.[64] But in fact the passage that scholars often quote to make this point was concocted by the mid-twentieth-century historian Robert Huttenback. Huttenback put together some of Napier's journal entries from several months apart. Some of what he used was written in Poona and referred to the battles of Dunbar and Worcester in the seventeenth century, but one important section was written in Sind during one of Napier's dark nights of the soul: 'Get thee behind me Satan!' Napier said. 'My God! how humble I feel when I think! How exalted when I behold! I have worked my way to this great command and am grateful at having it, yet despise myself for being so gratified. . . . He who takes command loves it.'[65] This was not the megalomania of the conqueror.

In fact Napier's journals before the war portray not a lust for blood but perhaps another kind of megalomania. He struggled over a desire to prevent the Amirs from interfering any further with the lives and welfare of the people of Sind. This was the Napier that we have seen earlier – he was still the same man, still looking for an opportunity to save the weak and smash the rich. The poor of Sind were coming to him with their complaints, he tells us. It seems that he felt the justice of those complaints weighing upon him as Outram's negotiations

206 *The conquest of Sind*

with the Amirs dragged on. As Napier travelled about, he kept recording how he saw the flat, fertile, well-watered lands covered in thick brush rather than crops, while nearby the people huddled in poverty in towns, unable to work the land. The land went unfarmed, he noted, because the Amirs could not restrain the marauders who might attack anyone who went out in the fields; and the Amirs themselves demanded too much in the way of taxes and tribute. '[T]hese poor people: they live in a larder and yet starve!', he said.[66]

Notes

1 Napier to Ellenborough, 15 September 1842, EP, TNA 30/12/62 [no folio number].
2 Napier to Ellenborough, 20 October 1842, second letter, EP, TNA 30/12/62 [no folio number].
3 Napier to George Arthur, 18 October 1842, given in WN, 2:214–15; Napier's report of 17 October 1842, 2:229–35 at 232.
4 Napier to Ellenborough, 18 November 1842, EP, TNA 30/12/62 [no folio number].
5 Napier's journal, 27 September 1842, given in WN, 2:200–01. See also 7 October 1842, 2:217.
6 Napier's journal, 7 October 1842, given in WN, 2:218.
7 Some examples: Sidney Low and Lloyd C. Saunders, *The History of England during the Reign of Queen Victoria (1837–1901)* (1907; New York: Haskell House, 1969), 132; G. M. Trevelyan, *British History in the Nineteenth Century (1782–1901)* (London: Longmans, Green, and Co., 1922), 317; Robert A. Huttenback, *British Relations with Sind, 1799–1843: An Anatomy of Imperialism* (Berkeley and Los Angeles: University of California Press, 1962), 77; Byron Farwell, *Queen Victoria's Little Wars* (New York: W.W. Norton, 1972), 27; Jan Morris, *Heaven's Command: An Imperial Progress* (1972; New York: Harcourt, Brace, Jovanovich, 1974), 180; Stanley Wolpert: *Zulfi Bhutto of Pakistan: His Life and Times* (New York: Oxford UP, 1993), 5; N. Jayapalan, *History of India*, vol. 3, *From 1773 to Lord Minto, Including Constitutional Development* (New Delhi: Atlantic Publishers and Distributors, 2001), 3:124; Tarak Barkawi, 'Globalization, Culture, and War: On the Popular Mediation of "Small Wars" ', *Cultural Critique* 58 (Autumn 2004), 115–47 at 139; Piers Brendon, *The Decline and Fall of the British Empire, 1783–1997* (2007; New York: Alfred A. Knopf, 2008), 117; Alice Albinia, *Empires of the Indus: The Story of a River* (London: John Murray, 2008), 44.
8 This point has occurred to Wendy Doniger as well, and while she does not look at the rest of the quotation, she does examine Napier's own moral doubts as he expressed them elsewhere, and his anger over the new racial othering of the native officers by their European colleagues: Doniger, *The Hindus: An Alternative History* (New York: Penguin, 2009), 603.
9 Napier's journal, 7 October 1842, given in WN, 2:218.
10 James Outram, *The Conquest of Scinde: A Commentary* (Edinburgh and London: William Blackwood and Sons, 1846), 293.
11 Napier's Journal, 24 September 1842, given in WN, 2:196; Napier to Outram, 8 October 1842, 2:208–09.
12 Napier to Ellenborough, 20 October 1842, second letter, EP, TNA 30/12/62 [no folio number].
13 Napier to Ellenborough, 17 October 1842, quoted in WNCS, 122.
14 Outram to Napier, 18 October 1842, given in Great Britain, Parliament, *Accounts and Papers, 1843: Sinde*, No. 39 (1843), enclosure 35 in number 379, 411–13, paragraph 3.
15 Outram to Napier, 26 January 1843, PBC, BL Add. MS 40864, fols 37–44 at 37–38; substantial extract given in Outram, *Conquest*, 476–80.
16 *Perwanna* of Mir Nuseer Khan, given in Great Britain, Parliament, *Accounts and Papers, 1843: Sinde,* No. 39, item 360, 351–52; Lieutenant Brown to Napier, 5 October 1842,

item 368, 355–56; Napier to the Ameers of Hyderabad, 25 September 1842, item 372, 358–59.

17 Napier to Ellenborough, 17 October 1842, quoted in WNCS, 122; Outram, *Conquest*, 66–67.

18 Napier to Ellenborough, 17 October 1842, quoted in WNCS, 124.

19 Ibid, 125–27.

20 Napier to Ellenborough, 5 November 1842, EP, TNA 30/12/62 [no folio number]; Ellenborough to Napier, copy, 14 November 1842, PP, BL Add. MS 40522, fols 309–10.

21 Ellenborough to Peel, 15 November 1842, PP, BL Add. MS 40471, fols 255–58.

22 Fitzgerald to Peel, 11–12 January 1843; Peel to Fitzgerald, 12–13 January 1843; both given in Charles Stuart Parker (ed.), *Sir Robert Peel from His Private Papers*, 3 vols (London: John Murray, 1899), 3:2–4.

23 Ellenborough to Wellington, 22 March 1843, given in CEW, 355–59 at 356–57.

24 See C. U. Aitchison, *A Collection of Treaties, Engagements, and Sunnuds Relating to India and Neighbouring Countries*, vol. 6, *The Treaties, &c., Relating to the Punjab, Sind, and Beloochistan, and Central Asia*, rev. edn, A. C. Talbot (ed.) (Calcutta: Foreign Office Press, 1876), 6:294–98; Ellenborough to Napier, copy, 4 November 1842, PP, BL Add. MS 40522, fols 298–304, with a copy of the draft of the treaty, no date, fols 305–08.

25 Richard Grove, *Green Imperialism: Colonial Expansion, Tropical Island Edens, and the Origins of Environmentalism, 1600–1860* (Cambridge: Cambridge UP, 1995), 387, 456; Mahesh Rangarajan, 'Imperial Agendas and India's Forests: The Early History of Indian Forestry, 1800–1878', *Indian Economic and Social History Review* 31, 2 (1994), 147–67 at 151–52.

26 M. Postans, *Travels, Tales, and Encounters in Sindh and Balochistan, 1840–1843* (Oxford: Oxford UP, 2003), 4–7, 40; J. Burnes, *A Visit to the Court of Scinde* (1829; Karachi: Oxford UP, 1974), 103–04; Edward Delhoste, 'Narrative of a Journey from Mandvi to Hydrabad (Sind) and from Hydrabad to Khairpoor and Back (December 1831–May 1832)', in *Selections from the Pre-Mutiny Records of the Commissioner in Sind*, Selection 5 (Sind: Commissioner's Office, n.d.), 185–237 at 199, 230.

27 See Aitchison, *Treaties*, 6:294–98.

28 A. Burnes, *Travels*, 3:67–70, 73–74, 84–85, 223–24; 'Treaty with Meer Rustoom Khan, Chief of Kheirpore', 4 April 1832, given in Aitchison, *Treaties*, 6:274–75.

29 Outram to Napier, 30 October 1842, given in Great Britain, Parliament, *Accounts and Papers, 1843: Sinde*, No. 39 (1843), number 381, 430; Outram, *Conquest*, 104–05.

30 Napier to Ellenborough, 23 November 1842, first letter, EP, TNA 30/12/62 [no folio number]. See Lewis Pelly, 'Memoir on the Khrypoor State in Upper Sind' [1854], in Thomas (ed.), *Selections of the Records of the Bombay Government*, new series, 17 (Bombay: Printed for the Government at the Bombay Education Society's Press, 1855), 103–16; Sind Commissioner's Office, *History of Alienations in the Province of Sind*, 2 vols (Karachi: Commissioner's Press, 1886–1888), 2:142–46; Anonymous, 'Sindh Controversy: Napier and Outram', *Calcutta Review* 6 (July-December 1846), 569–614 at 595–96; LNS, 58, 72–73, 86–87.

31 Henry Lushington, *A Great Country's Little Wars; or, England, Affghanistan, and Sinde* (London: John W. Parker, 1844), 227–37, 285–91.

32 Copy of Napier to Outram, 15 January 1843, given as part of the eleventh appendix of documents that Napier sent to Ellenborough on one of the later occasions when he was asked to: Napier to Ellenborough, 26 August 1843, EP, TNA PRO 30/12/61 Part 1 [no folio number].

33 *Bath Chronicle and Weekly Gazette*, 10 November 1842, 4 col. a. But it is possible that the source that was not the Napier family, as the article suggested that the very presence of Napier's army made the Amirs reluctant to accept the new treaty – *Bath Chronicle and Weekly Gazette*, 9 February 1843, 1 col. a. In this the Bath newspaper reflected something of the view in the *Times*, critical of Ellenborough and expansionism – the *Times*, 7 February 1843, 4 cols a-b.

34 Napier's journal, 16 October 1842, given in WN, 2:222.

35 Napier to Ellenborough, 17 November 1842, EP, TNA PRO 30/12/62 [no folio number].

208   *The conquest of Sind*

36 Even turning against Napier and Ali Murad and embracing the cause of Mir Rustam, Outram continued to distrust Futeh Muhammed Ghoree as a schemer – Outram, *Conquest*, 34–35.
37 E. B. Eastwick, *A Glance at Sind before Napier, or Dry Leaves from Young Egypt*, 2nd edn, introduced by H. T. Lambrick (1851; Karachi: Oxford UP, 1973), 258–60, 265–67.
38 Napier to Ellenborough, 17 November, 18 November, 23 November 1842, EP, TNA PRO 30/12/62 [no folio number]; Napier's journal, 14 December, 17 December, and 18 December 1842, given in WN, 2:252–54.
39 LNS, 82–83.
40 18 November 1842, given in WN, 2:238.
41 Reports, 26 December 1839, given in Edward Paterson Delhoste, *Observing Sindh*, Matthew A. Cook (ed.) (Oxford: Oxford UP, 2008), 118, 129, 135.
42 Napier's journal, 18 November 1842, given in WN, 2:240.
43 Napier to Ellenborough, 30 November 1842, EP, TNA 30/12/62 [no folio number]; Napier to Emily Bunbury, 17 December 1842, NP, BL Add. MS 49109, fols 137–39.
44 LNS, 53; WNCS, 97–101; Outram, *Conquest*, 46–50.
45 Outram to Napier, 24 January 1843, copied and sent to Ripon, PBC, BL Add. MS 40864, fols 20–25, quotations at fol. 22; LNS, 118–19.
46 Napier to Outram, [?] January 1843, given in WN, 299–303 at 2:229.
47 Ibid, 2:299–300. See also Napier's journal, 23 January 1843, 2:160. Others too would trace the evil back to Auckland's unjust act: Lushington, *A Great Country's Little Wars*, 268.
48 Outram, *Conquest*, 317.
49 Ibid, 511–27.
50 Napier's report to Ellenborough, 17 October 1842, given in WN, 2:229–35 at 230. See also Yapp, *Strategies*, 491–92. The modern scholarly debate on 'Orientalism' in its different senses is too big to pursue here. Napier's position is close to that of John Stuart Mill, who as Alan Ryan explains, believed in governing India according to Western ideas of efficiency, but who had no interest in trying to displace Indian culture and religion – Ryan, *The Making of Modern Liberalism* (Princeton, NJ: Princeton UP, 2012), 371.
51 Napier to Richard Napier, 29 April 1843, NP, BL Add. MS 49111, fols 64–65* at 64*; Napier to George Arthur, [?] September 1843, given in WN, 2:440–41; Napier to Kennedy, 26 December 1846, 19 April 1843, NP, TNA PRO 30/64/6, fols 33–34.
52 Napier to Emily Bunbury, 16 March 1844, NP, BL Add. MS 49110, fols 5–7. Emphasis original.
53 WNAS, 7, 219–20.
54 Napier to Outram, [?] January 1843, given in WN, 2:297–303 at 300.
55 Outram to Napier, 26 January 1843, PBC, BL Add. MS 40864, fols 37–44 at 37.
56 Outram, *Conquest*, 33. See also 474–75.
57 Ibid, 170.
58 Napier's journal, 28 January 1843, given in WN, 2:307. Emphasis original.
59 Napier to Louisa Napier, 16 December 1842, Bodleian MS Eng. lett. c. 240, fols 138–39.
60 Napier's journal, 14 and 15 December 1842, given in WN, 2:263.
61 Napier to Ellenborough, 17 November 1842, EP, TNA 30/12/62 [no folio number].
62 See many passages from Napier's journal and letters as quoted in WN, such as 2:207–08, 225–26; Napier to Ellenborough, 3 November 1842, second letter, EP, TNA PRO 30/12/62 [no folio number]; Napier to Ellenborough, 20 November 1842, EP, TNA 30/12/62 [no folio number, and bound after the letter of 22 November].
63 Napier's journal, 17 October, 5 November 1842, given in WN, 2:223, 237; Napier to Louisa Napier, 16 December 1842, Bodleian MS Eng. lett. c. 240, fols 138–39.
64 John S. Galbraith, 'Some Reflections on the Profession of History', *Pacific Historical Review* 35, 1 (February 1966), 1–13 at 9, citing Huttenback, *British Relations with Sind*, 70–71.
65 Napier's Journal, 3 September, 19 and 21 December 1842, given in WN, 2:189, 264–66.
66 Napier's journal, 24, 26 November 1842, given in WN, 2:244, 246, quotation at 244.

16 To and from the battle of Miani

In his letter to Ellenborough on 17 October, Napier reported that troops belonging to the Amirs were increasingly well-coordinated and were arranged against his army.[1] Meanwhile, both General England at Quetta and Governor Arthur in Bombay (Arthur was Napier's superior) were led to conclude from various intelligence sources that the Amirs were spoiling for a fight.[2] James Outram had a different view. By the time of his long 1845 book on Sind – an indictment of Napier's behaviour in precipitating the war – Outram insisted that the body Sindhi troops had assembled together only because of internal squabbles among the Amirs themselves; and having been brought together in that way they could never be used against the British in the way both Napier and Ellenborough feared. Anyone who understood 'the Oriental character', Outram said, would recognize that eastern armies 'are little better than a multitudinous rabble' and could never pose a threat.[3]

Escalation continued and suspicion grew on both sides. In a secret Durbar in November, Mir Rustam suggested paying the British to leave, and failing that, driving them out. This is what Napier's spies told him. Another rumour the general heard was that the Amirs had discussed slitting the throats of their women and children in order to prepare for battle, and so Napier would understand the seriousness of their resolve.[4]

In response to all this, in early December Napier began writing to Mir Rustam more haughtily, demanding an immediate yes or no on the treaty and making threats if his camp were attacked. He said he knew that Rustam was trying to bribe his soldiers. And in a piece of Napierian humour that critics would seize upon (with some justification) as being impolite and inflammatory, Napier told the Mir that '[t]he Governor-General has occupied 'both sides of your Highness' river, because he had considered both sides of your Highness' argument'. Ellenborough had given his orders, Napier said he would carry them out. Did Mir Rustam accept the treaty or not?[5]

Mir Rustam wrote to Napier to plead his case. So did Mir Nasir Khan of Hyderabad, the man who had written to the Boogties. Both responses, translated for Napier by one of his officers, are models of clarity and restraint. There was no plan to attack Napier, the Amirs wrote, and Napier's allegations against them should be investigated and dismissed; until then, each man offered to

210   *The conquest of Sind*

put himself under Napier's power, saying they trusted in British justice.[6] But Napier would not listen. Events might have turned out differently if had done so – if he had distrusted the Amirs rather less and heard them out. But in the Sind, he neglected to pursue the policy of talking to all sides that he had followed in the north of England.

For a few days earlier, Napier had been told that some of the Amirs were demanding two years' worth of taxes from their peasants all at once before they lost control of the territory ceded in the treaty. Napier decided to 'protect these people [the peasants] if I can against an evil' by freeing them from the extra financial burden; and further he resolved to move against the Amirs before they could attack him. He now wanted to seize Rohri ahead of time – ahead of the approval of the treaty by which it would be ceded *de jure*. Napier told the Governor-General that he would hold off from taking this step until he could hear from him. But Napier issued an order forbidding the peasants of the area from paying their taxes to the Amirs beyond the coming January. And a week later he went ahead and occupied Rohri and the other disputed territories when he grew more frightened of the army massing against him.[7]

Mir Rustam now arranged to see Napier in person, yet when the time for the meeting came, Rustam did not appear. The Mir then tried to arrange another meeting with the general. He took the extraordinary step of asking for asylum, claiming that his family and his advisers had made him their plaything and that he wanted British protection. Napier was flabbergasted and refused to see Mir Rustam at all. He thought Mir Rustam was trying to manipulate him. This was on 20 December.[8] Napier and Rustam had never personally encountered one another, and each was a cipher in the other's eyes. Instead of agreeing to the old Mir's request to meet, Napier asked Mir Rustam to go instead to see his brother, Ali Murad, in whose favour he was to be deposed. (Years later, Ali Murad's supposed plots would lead the British to depose him in turn.[9])

This was when Napier recorded in his journal that dark night of the soul which we looked at not long ago, where he said 'Get thee behind me Satan!'. When the general was more wakeful, he explained to Ellenborough that sending Mir Rustam to Ali Murad in this way would remove the elderly Mir from the evil counsellors whom the man himself had complained about; it would make Ali Murad the real power in the land, which Napier wanted to do; and it would bring peace. All these benefits would flow without Napier himself having to take in Mir Rustam – and without Napier seeming to be the one who had deposed the Sindhi leader. And with his position strengthened, Ali Murad could begin to act as the chief policeman, keeping down the hill raiders who as it happened abutted his territory.[10]

In fact Mir Rustam did go to seek the protection of Ali Murad, but the transfer in power from older brother to younger took on a greater formality than Napier had expected. Mir Rustam resigned the turban of supremacy in favour of Ali Murad in a legal document written in several copies of the Koran. A board of Islamic scholars in Bombay would later rule that Mir Rustam's act of abdication was both lawful and irrevocable when recorded in the Koran in this way.[11]

There was yet another surprise. After resigning the turban, Mir Rustam fled to his brother's desert fortress of Dejee to reinforce the units there.[12] Napier found himself thwarted and he was suspicious:

> All my plans upset! These barbarians are not easily understood. It is decidedly in Ali Moorad's interest to be master in Scinde, yet he has let Roostum escape! This bothers me, but it is so far good that it gives me a more decided line to follow: there need be no delicacy now. [M]y information is, that all of the Ameers are assembling their forces at a place called *Dhingee*.[13]

Napier now began to suspect that Ali Murad had lied to his brother about British intentions, putting the 'old noodle' (as Napier referred to him) into a panic and sending him running off in open rebellion against British authority. Outram's interpretation at the time was that Rustam was now very far into senility and very confused.[14] Napier rejected this. He decided that Rustam could not *honestly* have feared capture at his hands only one day after trying to take refuge with him. The general wrote to Mir Rustam to make exactly this point.

After sending this letter, Napier no longer would have anything to do with Mir Rustam. Rustam seemed to be too devious – or otherwise too senile and too unstable to be the ally that Britain needed.[15] Meanwhile, Ali Murad began to take control of his brother's property.[16]

***

With Mir Rustam on the run, Napier took decisive action. For a variety of reasons – to make the point to everyone about who was in charge, to shore up the British flank, and if he could, to deliver the final peace that Mir Rustam's flight had snatched away – Napier set off on an expedition to take the fortress of Enum Ghur (later Imamgahr), which lay well out in the desert northeast of Hyderabad. Napier and his men were accompanied by Ali Murad himself and a body of his troops. By removing this native bolt-hole, Napier told himself that he was reducing the chances the Amirs would attack him. So he obtained Ali Murad's acquiescence on the theory that whoever held the turban was theoretically the overlord of the fort. Yet properly it was not Ali Murad's fort to dispose of.[17]

Napier carried out forced marches through the desert for eight nights without knowing exactly where he was going across the parallel ridges of sand. He found the fortress nonetheless. It seemed formidable but it was deserted. The men there had fled, so Napier decided to use the seven thousand pounds of gunpowder which they had left behind to blow it up. He did so on 15 January.[18]

The final breakdown

By now the Amirs had assembled a substantial army a few miles outside Hyderabad. Napier monitored it closely. At Ellenborough's suggestion in December, Napier had ordered the Amirs to disperse their forces.[19] They did not comply,

212   *The conquest of Sind*

and Napier became convinced they were prolonging the negotiations over the treaty until their army was large enough to attack him. So when he marched towards Imamghar, he sent the Amirs at Hyderabad another order. He made it clear that he and his army would arrive at Hyderabad very soon, and by then he expected a decision on whether they would sign. Then in late January Napier summoned the Amirs to a meeting with Outram at which everything could be hammered out. Almost none of them came. So Napier tried again, now summoning them to Hyderabad at Outram's insistence, and sending on to Hyderabad the three representatives whom some of the Amirs had deputized to talk to him directly.[20]

Outram would claim that assembling this large gathering at Hyderabad was a very bad decision and, further, that he was always against it. According to his later account, he wanted the aggrieved Amirs of the north kept far away from their Hyderabad cousins. If the northern party were to reach Hyderabad, then the Amirs of that city, as hosts, would be obliged to support the northerners through the principle of guest-friendship. While it is true that Outram did share this concern with Napier at the time, nonetheless the Hyderabad gathering was Outram's own idea. He thought that if he could travel to Hyderabad before the Northern Amirs arrived, then all would be well. His words could make everything right. But in fact Outram was unlucky and he was delayed in reaching the city. The Northern Amirs arrived first and they had their say.[21]

When Outram finally reached Hyderabad on 8 February, he found the assembled Amirs full of indignation over how Mir Rustam had been cheated by his brother. Yet in his letters to Napier over the succeeding days, Outram stressed that despite the ugly mood, he had been able to secure the seals of the princes on the document at hand – a promise that they would sign the treaty itself at some later date.

By now Napier believed – correctly – that for all the promises they might make, the Amirs were continuing to increase their army of tens of thousands, an army that he might have to face with his 2,800 men. He feared for the safety of his troops. One can quibble over how many enemy fighters there ultimately were, but there is no question that when the battle came a few days later, Napier's forces in the area were outnumbered by seven or eight to one.[22]

In letters on 10, 12, and 13 February, Outram kept imploring the general to keep his army as far away from the city as possible as a sign of good faith. Indeed, Napier did delay the latter stages of his progress south, although he did so for other reasons – the men and especially the camels had to rest from time to time, and there was an Islamic festival when the Amirs could not move their men against him and so his army was able to remain in one spot.[23] Meanwhile, Napier's men recovered letters showing that some of the Amirs had pledged to each other that they would attack him on or after 9 February. These letters were sent on the very day the Amirs wrote to Napier directly, asking as Outram kept doing that he should halt his march as a token of his good intentions.[24] But after seeing the intercepted correspondence discussing the plan to attack him, Napier rejected all the more strongly Outram's advice that he should trust the Amirs and advance to Hyderabad when and only when the Amirs asked him to do so.

On 11 February Outram could report that he had secured agreement to the treaty itself and the Amirs had signed it. So on 12 February he suggested that Napier should come alone to Hyderabad by steamer to remove any remaining doubts on the Amirs' part about his intentions. Napier commented that 'unquestionably, it would have removed all doubts and my head from my shoulders'.[25] He told Outram the Amirs had taken too long to sign. They knew he had stopped to rest his forces. All the while they had used the delay to continue to assemble their army. Their acceptance of the treaty was a ruse. The very Amirs who had agreed to it, Napier pointed out, were still receiving and helping to marshal the troops of those who did not. And he had their resolve to attack him in writing. He could wait no longer:

> The [British] troops have Lord Ellenborough's orders on their side, and I have delayed from first to last, at risk of their lives, and my own character as an officer, till *not the eleventh, but the twelfth hour*. If men die in consequence of my delay, their blood may be justly charged to my account.[26]

Napier did not want a repeat of the Kabul disaster of only a year before.

At the residency

On 14 February Outram himself finally became alarmed. He passed along to Napier the rumours of a planned attack on his own detachment in the city. So on 15 February, Napier told him to promise the Amirs nothing further. Napier said he fully intended to 'attack [the Amirs] instantly' when he came upon their army, which still had not dispersed.[27] '[I]t would be to betray the troops to delay another day. . . . I do hope, my dear friend that you will see the very perilous ground on which I stand.'[28]

Napier composed what he feared could be the final letters he would ever write to his family and John Kennedy. To Kennedy he said that with his small force he faced up to thirty thousand men; and he told Kennedy that he and William Napier would have the letter-books and journals they would need to defend him from the Indian press if after the battle 'my letter-writing [is] altogether interrupted'.[29]

The Amirs resolved for war on almost the same day as Napier did, if not well before.[30] On the morning of 15 February, with Napier and his army still two days' march away, Outram and the small garrison of 100 men in the British Residency in Hyderabad were assaulted by a force of 8,000 infantry and cavalry, with six heavy guns.[31] The British carried on a fighting retreat and managed to escape to a steamer on the Indus. Outram reached Napier's position on the following day, and the general called his actions in bringing his men to safety 'a brilliant example' of military technique.[32] But later on Outram himself minimized the seriousness of this attack on the Residency; he said the

214   *The conquest of Sind*

Beluchis and not the Talpurs with whom he had been negotiating were the attackers.[33] (The Talpur rulers were Beluchis as well, but they used other tribes of Beluchis as their army.)

The opening of hostilities in Hyderabad confirmed Napier in his determination to press on and attack before the forces amassed against him could grow any larger. Even the small Beluchi detachment attacking the Residency far outnumbered his own troops. Napier was now so focussed on the military details and saving his forces from annihilation that he did not bother to forward to Lord Ellenborough Outram's letters on the negotiations of the preceding week, although he had told Outram he would do so. Ellenborough would only hear of these letters in June, when Outram circulated them and they were thrown in the Governor-General's face by an indignant East India Company – demanding to know why Napier had started a war when a peace treaty had already been signed.[34]

***

Napier now moved his army quickly against the main body of the enemy amassed at Miani, six miles outside Hyderabad. The Battle of Miani, fought on 17 February 1843, became Napier's most famous victory. Napier found the Sindhis entrenched and waiting for him behind the dry ditch of the Fuleli River, parallel to his line of march. Turning to face them, he placed his army just outside of the range of their heavy guns. Because of the heavy Sindhi fire, the British could advance no closer to the edge of the ditch. From a high vantage point Napier was able to see across the Fuleli and make out what he thought was the main body of enemy troops and their camp beyond. With a village on one flank, forming cover that would be hard to storm, and with the other flank exposed to the Beluchi artillery (as reported to Napier by a cavalry party he sent out under John Jacob), there was no alternative left to him but a frontal assault.

So that is what he ordered. Napier used his own heavy guns to take out their Beluchi counterparts. The Beluchi guns did not have the effective range of the British pieces – mostly because the guns of the Beluchis were being fired by an apparently coerced *British* commander who was sabotaging the firing. Napier, having tried to neutralize the enemy artillery, ordered his men to advance. But what they saw as they reached the edge of the ditch was something their general could not see – for here in fact in this ditch was the main body of the enemy, thousands of men waiting for Napier's army with their swords drawn. Going down into the ditch seemed impossible. But as they paused, the British forces faced a line of gunmen aiming at them from the other bank. What is more, at one end the ditch itself turned ninety degrees, leading away from the battlefield – and as it stretched away, Napier's men could see that it too was full of a huge column of the enemy ready to rush forward to replace any who fell further up against the British line. So faced with all this, Napier's men naturally refused to plunge in. Instead they pulled back just out of the line of fire of the forces below, and they began employing their own weapons to pick off the enemy gunmen shooting at them from across the way. All the while Napier could not bring more than four of his own heavy guns into action. There was only so much space for the guns between a low wall and the edge of the precipice. While the four guns were firing again and again, Napier rode between his men and the edge of the ditch, screaming for an advance. So did his officers.

Strangely the general was not shot by either side. For some time he rode back and forth in front of the enemy and yet none of their shots hit him. Only three times did individual Beluchis charge at him with their swords. This reticence on their part he found strange; his men fended off the danger to their commander whenever it came.[35] Finally Napier ordered a cavalry charge on one flank and this is what saved the day for the British. The cavalry managed to get behind enough of the enemy to reach their reserve forces and begin to chase them, and the enemy line in the front began to break up. At just this time Napier's men broke through the low wall and brought a fifth gun into action. The rest of Napier's line now obeyed him and advanced to the edge of the ditch and even down into it. Hand-to-hand combat began in earnest as the enemy fell back in confusion (Figure 16.1).[36]

In this way Napier's 2,800 troops defeated the 20,000 troops of the Amirs in four hours. Napier had twelve pieces of artillery (only a few of which he could put in position during most of the battle, as we have seen) and the Amirs had fifteen. There were between 63 and 270 British killed – accounts vary. Most of Napier's officers died. They had the very dangerous task of trying to lead the advance into the ditch, and so they were in the midst of the hand-to-hand combat once their men raced down to attack the enemy swordsmen. In contrast to the light British casualties, certainly several thousand troops were dead on the Amirs' side. Throughout the battle, groups of Beluchis charged up into the British muskets or into the line of fire of the four British guns; many other Beluchi soldiers were cut down on the plain behind by the British cavalry, or they fell as they walked away in retreat (for they did not run) when the rest of the British heavy guns finally came into service.[37] The dead lay in heaps up to four deep – worse, as Napier would later recall, than anything he had seen in the Peninsular War.[38] The moral questions began at once. 'We beat them John at Meanee', Napier wrote a few days after. 'The battle was terrible. I rode over the horrid field and questioned my conscience. My dear Kennedy this blood is on the Ameers not on me.'[39]

At Miani Napier had gone up against huge odds. Before the battle he thought the other side had about the same number of heavy guns that he did.[40] But he knew that in terms of men he was heavily outnumbered. His army may indeed have had the technological advantage when it came to small arms, for they were armed with muskets and bayonets against the matchlocks and pistols of the Sindhis. But much of the killing was done with swords on the Sindhi side and bayonets on the British.[41]

And whatever one thinks of Napier's unsuccessful order to charge down into the ditch, he had ridden back and forth under fire to make sure that his

Figure 16.1 Miani, 17 February 1843, with Napier on horseback. After the painting by Edward Armitage, 1847.
The Battle of Miani, 1843 / Universal History Archive / UIG / Bridgeman Images

soldiers did their job in the face of the huge and impressive waves of Beluchis ranged against them; his soldiers had not broken when they saw what they were up against.[42] It was later alleged that Napier won the battle by sending agents ahead of time to buy off the commanders on the other side.[43] Be that as it may, he had prevailed against the large if not so well-coordinated army of the Amirs and he had saved the lives of his own troops.

It was a momentous day. Afterward Napier did not want his own courage and his strange escape from injury dwelt on or even talked of in public. '[I]t would savour of charlatanism' to assert that in all the fire he was not hit, as he told his sister, 'but such was the fact as the whole army here can tell you'.[44] That is, what happened was so unlikely that he did not see how he could discuss it without seeming pretentious or strange. Yet if he was uncomfortable thinking about his escape, he did not want the battle itself to be forgotten. He had a sense of the occasion. When peace came he erected a column on the site. Nor did he forget the men who fought under him. With Miani Napier became the first commander in British history to name the common soldiers in his dispatches and not merely the officers. And he named Indian soldiers well as British troops.[45] Here he was acting on his long-held belief (developed in his flogging book) that mere foot soldiers deserve honours and rewards as much as their colonels and generals do.

Was the war over? Napier expected the carnage of Miani to be repeated at Hyderabad if he should ever try to conquer the fort there. After Miani he *did* issue a demand that the Amirs should surrender their stronghold six miles away, but this hardly meant that they would do so. The Amirs might well have retained it and their independence in the subsequent negotiations.[46] Yet in short order Napier found himself accepting the huge, rich fort from their hands without another shot being fired (Figure 16.2). To his surprise, the Amirs (including Mir Rustam) came to him in his camp. They handed over their bejewelled ceremonial swords, worth several hundred pounds. Napier at once gave their swords back to them.[47]

And so the British flag went up in Hyderabad and the royal salute to Queen Victoria was given in the city on the 20th. Much of the Amirs' wealth now found its way into the hands of Napier's soldiers. But more of it found its way into the hands of the official Prize Agents. Once Napier appointed them, he refused to interfere with their work of apportioning what was taken. He told them to correspond with his superiors directly, without his involvement.[48] By May he was teasing his sister about what he was likely to get, perhaps – £50,000 – although he remained careful to save his military pay and now the pay from his civil duties. Napier earned £2,000 per year as commander and from now on the same amount again as governor, so he now had £4,000 a year in any case; and Ellenborough later gave him back pay as governor from the day he landed in Sind.[49] So his pay had returned to what it would have been had he remained in Poona, and it was soon raised to £7,000.[50]

***

Figure 16.2 'Hyderabad on the Indus', showing the fort. Drawn by William Purser and engraved by Edward Finden, from a sketch by Captain Robert Melville Grindlay, 1808. From Alexander Burnes, *Travels into Bokhara; Being the Account of a Journey from India to Cabool, Tartary and Persia; also, Narrative of a Voyage on the Indus*, 3 vols (John Murray, London, 1834), vol. 3, plate 5.

To and from the battle of Miani   219

Part of winning a war is defeating the enemy. Part is figuring out how to avoid future bloodshed once you have won. Having accepted the surrender of the fort from the Amirs, Napier at first sent his soldiers into it by stealth, establishing their authority a few at a time so the womenfolk would not be killed by their guards to keep them away from foreign defilement. The female relatives of the Amirs remained for three days in their *zenanas*, which were six strong buildings within the larger enclosure of the fort. Napier's men had strict orders not to enter the *zenanas*.[51] Indeed, no British guards could be deployed along the section of the wall running near the *zenanas* lest the soldiers be able to look down and see the women. If the soldiers could see them, the women would have to remain indoors in their individual buildings.[52] Yet while Napier's men had to stay away from the area, the ladies' servants (male and female) were able to come and go freely between the fort and the town, subject only to a search for treasure whenever they left the precincts. When the female servants left they were searched by an Indian ex-prostitute hired for the purpose.

The noblewomen themselves wanted to go out into the city to their family homes, where they would no longer be under the scandalous protection of infidels. After some discussion they were able to leave – in British army palanquins, so they could depart without ever being glimpsed by men or strangers. Nor were the noblewomen searched in any way when they did go. One of the ladies carried so much wealth that it would form the basis of the later political and military influence of her family. Yet in early May, Dr George Buist, editor of the *Bombay Times*, claimed the *zenanas* had been violated and the noblewomen carried off as the concubines of the British officers. When Napier's officers read this accusation, all one hundred four of them signed a statement of strong protest, with documentation and affidavits; Napier himself stressed that none of his men had ever seen even one lady of the *zenanas*.[53]

There were other rumours flying about. One story had it that the women in the *zenanas* were passing intelligence about the number, condition, and disposition of Napier's troops to the hostile forces that remained out in the countryside. It was also said that the Amirs were spying on Napier's army themselves. Napier had housed them in tents in a garden inside the fort, along with perhaps several hundred of their Beluchi guards.

Napier was concerned about intelligence leaks from the fort and he was also concerned about weapons being smuggled in, allowing the captive Amirs in the courtyard to turn themselves into a battle force. So before he fought the new army bearing down on him outside Hyderabad – which he had to do – Napier put the defeated Amirs temporarily onto steamers in the Indus. Thus he reduced his defensive lines in the city and freed for combat duty many of the four hundred soldiers guarding the mile-long perimeter of the fort.[54]

Outram, who left Sind for Bombay immediately after the Battle of Miani, would give a very different account of the events that played out in Hyderabad in his absence. For him, the women of the *zenanas* were turned out of their homes the moment he left the city, and they were despoiled of their jewellery

220   *The conquest of Sind*

and personal effects by the sepoys of the foreign army. And the Amirs were always held in squalor.[55]

Notes

1 Napier to Ellenborough, 17 October 1842, EP, TNA 30/12/62 [no folio number]; LNS, 87–88. For testimony to the large number of Beluchi troops massed under the Amirs' authority in the autumn, see Henry Lushington, *A Great Country's Little Wars; or, England, Affghanistan, and Sinde* (London: John W. Parker, 1844), 276–78. John Jacob, who came to hate Napier, strongly disagreed: H. T. Lambrick, *John Jacob of Jacobabad*, 2nd edn (Karachi: Oxford UP, 1975), 76–77.

2 Minute by Arthur, 2 September 1842, quoted in Great Britain, Parliament, *Accounts and Papers, 1843: Sinde*, No. 39 (1843), 352–53, number 362; England to Napier, 20 September 1842, quoted in Charles James Napier, *A Letter to the Right Hon. Sir J. Hobhouse, President of the Board of Control, on the Baggage of the Indian Army*, 4th edn (London: Edward Moxon, 1849), 24.

3 James Outram, *The Conquest of Scinde: A Commentary* (Edinburgh and London: William Blackwood and Sons, 1846), 96–98, quotation at 169–70; Napier to Ellenborough, 26 November 1842, EP, TNA 30/12/62 [no folio number].

4 Napier's journal, 30 November 1842, given in WN, 2:247; Napier to Emily Bunbury, 17 December 1842, NP, BL Add. MS 49109, fols 137–39. On the long tradition of government spy networks in India, see C. A. Bayly, *Empire and Information: Intelligence Gathering and Social Communication in India, 1780–1870* (Cambridge: Cambridge UP, 1996), 12–13, 32, 67–69, 133.

5 Sindh Controversy: Napier and Outram', 592; WNCS, 162–63; Napier to Ellenborough, 7 December, and 9 December 1842, second letter, with enclosed copy of Napier's letter to the Amirs, EP, TNA PRO 30/12/62 [no folio number]; Napier to Mir Rustam, 14 December 1842, given in WN, 2:262.

6 Mir Nazir Khan to Napier, Mir Rustam Khan to Napier, December 1842, enclosures in Napier to Ellenborough, 14 December 1842, EP, TNA 30/12/62 [no folio number].

7 Napier to Ellenborough, 9 December, first letter, and 14 December 1842, EP, TNA 30/12/62 [no folio number], quotation 7 December.

8 Napier to Ellenborough, 20 December 1842, NP, BL Add. MS 49105, fols 11–12. See also LNS, 96–99.

9 Robert A. Huttenback, *British Relations with Sind, 1799–1843: An Anatomy of Imperialism* (Berkeley and Los Angeles: University of California Press, 1962), 112; Sind Commissioner's Office, *History of Alienations in the Province of Sind*, 2 vols (Karachi: Commissioner's Press, 1886–1888), 2:146–47, 159; Michael H. Fisher, *Counterflows to Colonialism: Indian Travellers and Settlers in Britain, 1600–1857* (Delhi: Permanent Black, 2004), 405.

10 Napier to Ellenborough, 20 December 1842, BL Add. MS 37232, fols 131–34.

11 Their judgement is given in WNCS, 185–87. See also Mir Rustam Khan to Mir Muhammed Hussain, 20 December 1842, given in John Younghusband's translation in WNAS, 411–12. For the significance of the turban, see Bernard S. Cohn, *Colonialism and Its Forms of Knowledge: The British in India* (Princeton, NJ: Princeton UP, 1996), 115–16.

12 Algernon Law (ed.), *India under Lord Ellenborough, March 1842-June 1844: A Selection from the Hitherto Unpublished Papers and Secret Despatches of Edward Earl of Ellenborough* (London: John Murray, 1926), 186–87; Lushington, *A Great Country's Little Wars*, 238–47; LNS, 100; WNCS, 165–68.

13 Napier's journal, 28 December 1842, given in WN, 2:273.

14 Outram referred to the 'imbecility of Mir Rustam' from his 'old age and infirmities' – Outram to Napier, 26 January 1843, PBC, BL Add. MS 40864, fols 37–44 at 42.

15 WNCS, 181–82, 188–94, 233–34; LNS, 92, 102–03.

16 Outram, *Conquest*, 203–04.

To and from the battle of Miani 221

17 Napier's journal, 25 December, 31 December 1842, given in WN, 2:271–72, 274; Napier to Ellenborough, 27 December 1842, quoted in WNCS, 229–30; Napier to Henry Gee Roberts, 24 January 1843, Henry Gee Roberts Papers, BL A&AS MSS Eur F197/42, fols 5–6; Napier to Emily Bunbury, extract, 31 January [1843], NP, BL Add. MS 49109, fols 141–43; Law, *India under Ellenborough*, 187–88, 190; Albert H. Imlah, *Lord Ellenborough: A Biography of Edward Law, Earl of Ellenborough, Governor-General of India* (Cambridge, MA: Harvard UP, 1939), 137–38; T. Postans, *Personal Observations on Sindh* (London: Longman, Brown, Green, and Longmans, 1843), 327–29; Lushington, *A Great Country's Little Wars*, 253n–254n.

18 Napier to Ellenborough, 7, 13 January 1843, given in WN, 2:283–84, 286–87.

19 On 13 December. Kala Thairani, *British Political Missions to Sind: A Narrative of Negotiations from 1799 to 1843 Leading up to the State's Annexation* (New Delhi: Orient Longman, 1973), 160; Ellenborough to Napier, 20 December 1842, given in Great Britain, Parliament, *Accounts and Papers, 1843: Sinde*, No. 39, number 440, 533; Napier to Ellenborough, 15 February 1843, quoted in *Annual Register for 1843*, 353; LNS, 94–95.

20 Outram to Napier, 24 January 1843, copied and sent to Ripon, PBC, BL Add. MS 40864, fols 20–25 at 23–24; Napier to Outram, January 1842, given in WN, 2:297–303 at 303; Lushington, *A Great Country's Little Wars*, 254–55, Outram, *Conquest*, 284–92, 345.

21 Outram to Napier, 22 January 1843, extracts copied and sent to Ripon, PBC, BL Add. MS 40864, fols 18–19; Outram to Napier, 24 January 1843, copied and sent to Ripon, PBC, BL Add. MS 40864, fols 20–25 at 23–24; F. J. Goldsmid, *James Outram: A Biography*, 2nd edn, 2 vols (London: Smith, Elder & Co., 1881), 1:317; Napier to Richard Napier, [?] December 1843, given in WN, 3:25–27; Outram, *Conquest*, 290–91.

22 Napier to Ellenborough, 11 July 1843, NP, BL Add. MS 49105, fols 18–20; Law, *India under Ellenborough*, 189.

23 Outram, *Conquest*, 349–67; Napier's journal, 11, 12, 13 February 1843, given in WN, 2:317.

24 WNCS, 266–67, 276.

25 Imlah, *Ellenborough*, 134–35. He told Ellenborough 'my throat would have been cut of course' – Napier to Ellenborough, 11 July 1843, NP, BL Add. MS 49105, fols 18–20.

26 Napier to Outram, [?] February 1843, quoted in WNCS, 283.

27 Napier to Outram, 15 February 1843, copy, PBC, BL Add. MS 40865, fols 139–40; Law, *India under Ellenborough*, 189–90; WNCS, 292–95.

28 Napier to Outram, 13 February 1843, quoted in Lushington, *A Great Country's Little Wars*, 258.

29 Napier to Kennedy, 16 February 1843, NP, TNA PRO 30/64/6, fols 7–8.

30 Napier to Ellenborough, 17 February 1843, imperfect draft, NP, BL Add. MS 49105, fols 13–16; for the written resolution of some of the Amirs, see LNS, 132–33.

31 Outram to Napier, 15 February 1843, given in T. Postans, *Personal Observations*, 394–97.

32 Goldsmid, *Outram*, 1:319–25; Lionel J. Trotter, *The Bayard of India: A Life of General Sir James Outram, Bart.* (Edinburgh and London: William Blackwood and Sons, 1903), 114–17.

33 Outram, *Conquest*, 273n.

34 Napier to Ellenborough, 11 July 1843, NP, BL Add. MS 49105, fols 18–20; Law, *India under Ellenborough*, 189–91; Huttenback, *British Relations with Sind*, 104.

35 Napier to Louisa Napier, 16 March 1843, Bodleian MS Eng. lett. c. 240, fols 140–41.

36 Fortescue, *History of the British Army*, 13 vols (London: Macmillan, 1910–1930), 12:287–91; LNS, 137–47.

37 Napier to Ellenborough, 17 February 1843, imperfect draft, NP, BL Add. MS 49105, fols 13–17; Napier to Ellenborough, 18 February 1843, given in T. Postans, *Personal Observations*, 388–94; T. Postans, *Personal Observations*, 333, 388; WNCS, 313–14, 320; Lambrick, *John Jacob*, 87; Huttenback, *British Relations with Sind*, 103; Trotter, *The Bayard of India*, 118; Fortescue, *History of the British Army*, 12:290–92; LNS, 143–45.

38 Napier to W. Napier, 1845, given in WN, 3:288–89.

222 *The conquest of Sind*

39 Napier to Kennedy, 20 February 1843, NP, TNA PRO 30/64/6, fol. 8.

40 Napier to Kennedy, 15 February 1843, NP, TNA PRO 30/64/6, fols 7–8.

41 T. Postans, *Personal Observations*, 333; Napier to Ellenborough, 18 February 1843, given in Postans, 388–94 at 389–90; McMurdo (Napier's son-in-law) quoted in William Napier Bruce, *The Life of General Sir Charles Napier, G.C.B.* (London: John Murray, 1885), 205.

42 LNS, 144–45.

43 Isabel Burton, *The Life of Captain Sir Richard F. Burton*, 2 vols (London: Chapman and Hall, 1893), 1:141; Francis Hitchman, *Richard F. Burton, K.C.M.G.: His Early, Private, and Public Life, with an Account of His Travels and Explorations*, 2 vols (London: Sampson Low, Marston, Searle, and Rivington, 1887), 1:161.

44 Napier to Louisa Napier, 16 March 1843, Bodleian MS Eng. lett. c. 240, fols 140–41.

45 Johnny Torrens-Spence, *Historic Battlefields of Pakistan* (Karachi: Oxford UP, 2006), 42; WNCS, 324, 519–27; Byron Farwell, *Queen Victoria's Little Wars* (New York: W.W. Norton, 1972), 29.

46 Napier to Robertson, 23 October 1843, NP, BL Add. MS 49107, fols 74–78 at 75; Napier to Ripon, 7 February 1845, PBC, BL Add. MS 40871, fols 182–85.

47 Napier to Ellenborough, 18 February 1843, given in T. Postans, *Personal Observations*, 388–94 at 390; WN, 2:326; WNCS, 321; Napier to Emily Bunbury, [April 1844?], NP, BL Add. MS 49110, fol. 11, fragment.

48 Napier's journal, 20 February 1843, given in WN, 2:327; Napier to George Napier, letter on the battle of Miani, [no date], BL Add. MS 49168, fol. 22; LNS, 154–55.

49 Napier to Louisa Napier, 9 May 1843, Bodleian MS Eng. lett. c. 240, fols 145–45.

50 Napier to Emily Bunbury, 6 June 1844, NP, BL Add. MS 49110, fols 14–18 at 14.

51 General Order, 21 February 1843, given in Edward Green (ed.), *Compilation of the General Orders, &c., Issued in 1842–47, by Sir Charles Napier, G.C.B., Major-General Governor of Scinde, to the Army under His Command* (Bombay: James Chesson at the *Times* Press, 1850), 75.

52 Napier to George Arthur, [?] July 1843, quoted in WN, 2:401; Napier to Ripon, 7 August 1844, RP, BL Add. MS 40869, fols 61–71 at 68–69.

53 At this point there is no hint on Napier's side of any Orientalist fantasy about immorality within the *zenanas*, images of the kind that made their way into British literary works from the time of Byron – see Nancy L. Paxton, *Writing under the Raj: Gender, Race, and Rape in the British Colonial Imagination, 1830–1947* (New Brunswick, NJ: Rutgers UP, 1999), 40, 59–62, 74–75. But later on Napier would accuse one of the Amirs of having employed a brass-wire whip on the women in his *zenana* – Napier to W. Napier, 8 May 1843, given in WN, 3:378–81 at 378–79.

54 WNCS, 331–43, 412–15, 513–19; LNS, 153–55; Napier to Richard Napier, 14 September 1844, given in WN, 3:139–41.

55 Outram, *Conquest*, 429–38, 466.

17 The battle of Dubba

Within days Napier was securely in possession of Hyderabad, although he kept his men encamped outside the walls so they would remain confident about defending themselves without the need of a fort. Soon word came of the danger elsewhere. Before word of Miani could have reached the coast, threats had been made against the British forces at Karachi. The Hindu merchants began retreating onto ships in the harbour. A certain Captain Preedy then took control of the city, declaring it British territory (which technically in the British view it already was, according to one of the treaties from the period of the Afghan War). He put the Talpur officials into a camp, cut down the Talpur flag (alternating stripes of red and white), and hoisted the Union Jack.[1] So it seemed there indeed had been a coordinated plan to attack and drive out the British.

***

Not all of the Sindhi leaders had arrived in time to fight at Miani on the seventeenth. The most important of the latecomers was named Shere Muhammed. Or perhaps instead of arriving too late he had simply held his forces back, for his own reasons. But he was holding back no longer.

Soon after Napier's victory at Miani, Shere Mohammed sent Napier a message demanding his surrender and the evacuation of the British from the country, or Napier and his army would be exterminated. Napier did not respond well to this demand.[2] Shere Muhammed then assembled all the remaining native forces he could find. Napier bided his time, letting the lion, as he was called, gather so many soldiers that he depleted his treasury. Once Napier thought the time was ripe, he went out to meet the opposing army at Dubba, a few miles from Hyderabad. This was on 24 March 1843.

The enemy once again would number something over 20,000; there were perhaps 40,000 Sindhi troops in the area, but at any one time many of them were scattered about foraging off the land. Napier's own force in the wake of Miani numbered only 2,000 able-bodied men, and some of them would have to guard the Amirs on the steamers. (There were also the 30 men who came with the Aga Khan, who came from Persia to fight on the British side.[3]) Napier hoped for reinforcements but time was passing. Shere

224   *The conquest of Sind*

Muhammed was assembling more troops, and fighting weather was coming to an end. It was now typically 112° in the shade and it would get hotter yet.[4]

So at breakfast on the 23rd, Charles Napier ordered the attack for the next day, before Shere Muhammad's army could grow even larger than the 20,000 men he seemed to have at that moment. More Company troops arrived just in time from both upriver and downriver. Napier revised the order of battle to include these new men. Even setting aside the guards and the wounded, he now had 5,000 soldiers for the actual fighting. He still had only a very few officers, and hardly any of the officers whom he did have (either those who survived Miani or the new arrivals) were older than twenty-three.[5]

Napier's soldiers began the next day with a twelve-mile march. Reaching the battlefield, Napier found that there were woods, groves, and a village flanking it on either side, dictating as at Miani a frontal assault; and again as at Miani the Fuleli River ran through the middle of the battleground. But here the Fuleli was not entirely dry. There was impassable mud along part of its course, so on this occasion it worked even better as a Sindhi rampart.

Once again the Sindhis had chosen the field of battle. They had dug themselves in, taking full advantage of terrain and camouflage, making escarpments and loopholes to shoot from, ramps for escape from ditches, and so forth. The arrangement, both natural and artificial, was far more complex than at Miani. Leading up to the battlefield on the British side there was a natural defile between ravines, feeding Napier's troops in a particular direction if they were to attack. And beyond there were not one but *two* concealed ditches, each holding troops.

When the battle came, it was vicious, with no quarter asked or given in the 110° heat. The swords and the bayonets flew. Accounts of the actual course of the battle are confused, as the classic military historian John Fortescue pointed out more than once.[6] During the conflict both sides made their various sorties, and both sides fell back from time to time, so naturally there are conflicting stories about who was winning. This much is clear: There were four hours of close fighting. For a time the Sindhi cavalry dominated, but later they were chased across the field by Napier's own cavalry, British and sepoy. The British cavalry had charged (it would seem) against their orders, but their charge was a success. They began to cut down Shere Muhammed's foot soldiers, reversing the pattern set earlier in the day when the Sindhi cavalry had cut down the British.

This new British cavalry assault consisted of two uninterrupted hours of galloping. Napier for a time was at the head of it. He was nearly killed more than once, although in later years he claimed never to have personally fired a shot or injured a man at either Miani or Dubba. Yet Napier's troops could hardly miss his presence on the battlefield. They could not miss his flying whiskers, his extraordinary nose and glasses, his long hair and the neck flap of his self-designed sun hat trailing behind. He exhorted his troops to move where they needed to move and to do what needed to be done. He reacted to the unpredictable contingencies, in both the infantry and the cavalry phases of the battle.[7]

We may as well stop to remember once again that it was exceedingly hot. Napier was riding about for hours in the middle of a human maelstrom. He was sixty years old. He was never a robust man to begin with, and on top of that he had suffered from the pain in his face since the Battle of Busaco. Further his thigh had been opened up to the bone by a rocket seven months before. Because of this wound he could barely sit on his horse that day.[8]

***

In the end, the Battle of Dubba (soon renamed the Battle of Hyderabad when 'Dubba' proved to have unfortunate associations in Sindhi[9]) turned out to be another rout like Miani, except that Shere Muhammed escaped to join the hill raiders. Shere Mohammed's army numbered 25,000, as it turned out, with eleven heavy guns; Napier's forces killed between 2,000 and 5,000.[10] With no overwhelming advantage in the British weaponry, Napier's 5,000 troops killed perhaps 10 or 20 percent of the enemy. The British had the advantage when it came to centralized leadership, for the different Sindhi units did not fight together very well. Indeed their battle plan seems to have been confusing even to them, and there was occasional panic on their side. Napier's losses were 39 killed and 231 wounded.[11] These are amazingly small numbers, but the way the Sindhis dug themselves in on a prepared battlefield here and at Miani may have cancelled much of their numerical advantage. Many of their troops were held as reserves in the rear. At each battle, the tide turned when Napier's cavalry reached the reserves and scattered them. Perhaps the Sindhis would have done better to use their superior number of troops in mobile detachments, encircling Napier.

The success of Napier's forces against such a large foe was not supernatural, but it was impressive. Along with Miani, Napier's victory at Dubba was enough to seal his fame. Or it was enough to seal his infamy, depending on how you look at it.

The moral balance sheet

In the days leading up to Miani, if Napier had wanted to avoid battle he could have done so in only one way, by completely withdrawing from the area and leaving the Amirs in charge of the country. Indeed Outram would have had him do exactly this, marching east towards India.[12] Yet any such withdrawal would have moved the army away from its supply lines, and it would have placed Napier's men in between the main Sindhi army at Miani and the Sindhi garrison fort of Omercote (Umerkot). This would hardly have been prudent. Nor in any case would abandoning the country have comported with Napier's orders from Ellenborough or the wishes of Wellington as Commander-in-Chief of the Forces. The other option, which is what Napier chose, was to make his own attack before the various groups ranging themselves against him had joined together.

Even Outram's much-admiring biographer admitted in 1903 that Outram's own strongly held opinions – that the Amirs must be trusted, their army

226 *The conquest of Sind*

ignored, and the attack on the Residency discounted, with the lives of Napier's far outnumbered troops put at risk by standing down in the midst of the enemy – do not bear close scrutiny.[13] Napier did have opportunities to make peace, but they came much earlier.

Perhaps the most perceptive contemporary criticism of Napier's behaviour in Sind appeared not long after the British victory. It was written by Thomas Postans, Marianne's husband, who had been Henry Pottinger's deputy when Pottinger was Political Agent (this was before Outram's time in the country). Postans reviewed the Amirs' case with great clarity. As he explained the matter, the displacement of Mir Rustam by his younger brother Ali Murad while Mir Rustam was still living was unprecedented and impossible, especially alongside the other British demands. The Amirs negotiating at Hyderabad knew very well that they could never convince their own people to accept any settlement that the British might grant. In other words, the Beluchis were so angry at the British terms that the Amirs could not hope to control them. So in Hyderabad the Amirs temporized, and through Outram they asked Napier to halt because they were in an impossible situation. (Governor Arthur came to believe much the same thing.[14]) For their own part, they did not want a war. The Amirs had their families in Hyderabad and were hoping to avoid a fight.

To Postans, the attack on the Residency on 15 February was not what Outram, in his desire to exonerate the Amirs, claimed it had been. This attack was no *unorganized* movement by mere tribesmen, as Outram said. Instead, the attack with its heavy guns was the opening salvo of the war itself, carried out by the Amirs' own well-organized army – an attack that a good number of the Amirs with whom Outram was talking were unable to do anything about.

If we follow the line of reasoning suggested by Postans, any path to peace would have had to begin no later than the autumn. Sir Henry Pottinger, Outram's predecessor as Political Agent and Postans's mentor, can help us to clarify this view still further. He became an advocate for the imprisoned Amirs and a hostile critic of Napier.[15] But even he agreed that Napier was not a bad man. In Pottinger's view, Napier's attempts to impose the new arrangements were crippled by his own ignorance of Sind and how to handle its leaders, many of whom he had never met. Napier should have learned his way about.[16] Or he might have listened to the intriguing suggestion of his nominal superior, Governor Arthur in Bombay, who said that while the Amirs might be bad rulers, the Sindhis might prefer them to anyone else.[17]

The controversy

Perhaps the most piquant illustration of popular opinion at home came in 1844, when the newly founded *Punch* made its famous pun. *Punch* claimed that Napier's telegram to advise his superiors that he had won the war had been the single Latin word '*Peccavi*' – 'I have sinned'.[18] Some have taken the joke as Napier's own.[19] In reality the originator of the pun seems to have been a schoolgirl named Catherine Winkworth, whose teacher suggested to her that she ought send it to *Punch*.[20] But the fact that this joke was made at all shows something of the level of discomfort in England over what Napier had done.

Like *Punch* and the young Miss Winkworth, much of the British establishment distanced itself from the conquest. What about the idealism behind Napier's position, the universalism, the desire to spread freedom? His critics were having none of that:

> It is needless to say that we attach no value to the random statements of men like Sir Charles Napier, who, having made up their minds to have the country at any rate, are seized with a strong feeling of sympathy for the subjects of those termed by them oppressors, whose place they are anxious to take.[21]

Lord Ashley (Anthony Ashley-Cooper), the future Lord Shaftesbury, led the parliamentary campaign against Ellenborough and Napier. Ashley was to become a towering figure in nineteenth-century social legislation. He believed in the reform of the British nation at home and in reforming British behaviour abroad in the expectation of the eminent second coming of Jesus Christ. So Ashley, too, was a moral universalist, but of a different kind. The statue that commemorates his career, 'Eros' in Piccadilly Circus, stands not that far from Napier's statue in the southwestern corner of Trafalgar Square. And their busts sit next to each other in the National Portrait Gallery.

In the House of Commons, Ashley opened debate on 8 February 1844. He reviewed the history of the treaties, the bullying of the Amirs, the designs on their territory, and Napier's advance on Hyderabad, portraying the latter as the one provocation that led directly to the attack on the Residency and the gathering of the Sindhi army that would fight at Miani. All the while Ashley painted Napier more as Ellenborough's agent than as an independent force (and as we have seen there was much truth in this). Ashley then introduced his motion to free the Amirs, and if they could not safely be restored to their estates, to pay them off. Napier was treating them discourteously, and not at all as princes ought to be treated. The Amirs were accused having attacked and ruled an alien people, Ashley pointed out. This was exactly what Great Britain had done.[22]

Napier's defence was championed in Parliament by J. A. Roebuck, a radical M.P. of a very different stripe than the pious Ashley. One of J. S. Mill's philosophical radicals and an early associate of the Chartists, Roebuck as we have seen was M.P. for Bath and a friend of the Napiers.[23] He was known for his strong views and intemperate language. He gave what was said to be one of the longest and best speeches of his life (and he was known as a good speaker). Lord Auckland – 'the cause and origin of all the evils that followed' – had destabilized the region by invading Afghanistan, Roebuck said. Then Auckland imposed treaties on Sind which gave Great Britain a disproportionate influence there. Ellenborough and Napier were doing the best they could in this difficult situation. They had to respond to the machinations and falsehoods

228 *The conquest of Sind*

of the none-too-respectable government of the Amirs. Staying in the country was 'a fatal necessity, a direful evil'. And for his part, Napier had to preserve the army from another Kabul.[24] In the end there were sixty-eight votes for Ashley's motion and two hundred two against. Still, Ashley and some others thought he had won the moral case. As he noted in his diary:

> A Christian kingdom may refuse all intercourse with its neighbours, but if it open an intercourse and derive advantages, it cannot turn around when well satiated and exclaim, 'By-the-by, the thought strikes me, you are so abominably wicked that I really must exterminate you!'[25]

The case against interventionist universalism could not be put much better than this. But despite Ashley's undoubted eloquence in the House, in the end Roebuck's case persuaded more of the members.

Several days later, there were only seven votes against the motion to thank Napier and his army. One of the negative votes on this occasion (12 February) came from Lord Howick. Howick conceded that Napier would have got the army destroyed if he had listened to Outram in the days before Miani. But Howick was more troubled by Napier's behaviour over the preceding months. In his view it was Napier who had started bullying the Amirs and breaking the treaties, to which the Amirs had responded merely by preparing to defend themselves. Howick maintained that Napier in his ignorance of the country and of the people of Sind, and in his 'total want of sympathy' with the Amirs, was by himself the main cause of the war. And for Howick, Napier had been motivated mainly by the desire for personal glory and honour. In consequence, much blood had been shed – 'unnecessary and wanton bloodshed'. The House would share in the guilt if it thanked Napier.

Beyond the question of guilt, there was a question of policy. Howick did not want Napier thanked by the House because he did not want future commanders cutting their diplomacy short in a desire for conquest; he did not want to 'encourage for the future in India a system of unscrupulous aggrandisement' in which British commanders would be tempted wantonly to attack the Indians. Commanders had no right to act the way Napier had done. Howick explained: 'He certainly was not before aware that the eternal rules of right and wrong depended on place and varied with latitude and longitude.'[26] His version of universalism, too, was different from Napier's.

The key to how both of these votes came out – on Ashley's motion and on thanking the army – was the attitude of the Prime Minister. In August 1843 Robert Peel had expressed grave qualms over the fate of the former rulers of Sind:

> The treatment of the Ameers is really disgraceful to the Character of the Country. True policy would have counseled a course of conduct towards them liberal and indulgent so far as their personal treatment was in concern.

The battle of Dubba 229

In my opinion directions ought to be given to Sir George Arthur without loss of time to treat the Ameers with every degree of consideration.

We have taken their territories and despoiled them of their private property – surely we need not inflict further punishment and privations, from their wantonness, or a miserable parsimony.

It makes one ashamed of Indian policy.[27]

In December of that year, still two months before the debates in the Commons, the members of government were engaged in a sometimes rancorous dispute with Ellenborough over whether they would support him against the attacks now being made against his aggressiveness in India. Against that background the Prime Minister pondered Napier's role in the coming of the war. As he complained to Ripon,

Were we to take for granted that that discretionary power which [Ellenborough] entrusted to Sir Charles Napier, to decide on the guilt or the innocence of the Ameers – and on the fate of Scinde – *must necessarily* be soberly and wisely exercised – and that the natural tendencies of a military commander had no influence on his decisions?[28]

Peel had said in the House of Commons on 5 February 1839, during a debate on Afghanistan, that the empire seemed to have too much of a tendency to grow on its own. Imperial growth did *not* have to be helped along. Now four years later he had yet to change his mind. He wondered whether Lord Ellenborough thought the government could

overlook altogether the probable expense of defending our position in Scinde? The probable cost of life from the prevalence of sickness, the effects which our occupation of Scinde might have upon the Sikhs and other neighbouring nations. . . . Whatever Lord Ellenborough may think, there were and there *are* most grave considerations.[29]

And yet, Peel added (again, this was in December 1843), 'Time – distance – the course of events may have so fettered our discretion that we have no alternative but to maintain the annexation.' All he could do was to try to cover for his own government in Parliament, while privately he tried to convince his own party to swallow hard and accept what had happened. As the historian Sarah Ansari has shown, it was at about this point that the government decided to publish a set of doctored Blue Books, disguising the ways in which Whitehall had failed to instruct Lord Ellenborough more carefully and shifting any blame for the war to officials in India, the Amirs themselves, and the previous Whig government (Figure 17.1).[30] To the Prime Minister, omitting important documents about the involvement and lack of concern of the cabinet seemed far better than failing to publish anything at all; while publishing *everything*

Figure 17.1 Wellington and Peel attempting to guide or restrain Ellenborough in 1830: 'A Wild Elephant led Between Two Tame Ones'. Lithograph by John ('HB') Doyle, published by Thomas McLean, 16 February 1830. NPG Number D40982.

© National Portrait Gallery, London

The battle of Dubba 231

was impossible. Doing so would permanently injure the relationship between the Government and the Company.[31]

With the reputation of his own administration at stake in Ashley's debate (the debate of 8 February 1844), Peel naturally spoke against the motion to free the Amirs and repudiate the policies of his officials in India. And on 12 February it was the Prime Minister himself who proposed the motion of thanks to Napier and the army. Nonetheless he did not seem to like the annexation:

> With the policy of the measures in the execution of which, that army has been employed I have upon this occasion, nothing to do. Whether it were justifiable and politic to exact from the Ameers of Scinde penalties on account of the violation of their engagements – whether it were politic to demand the cession of territory in lieu of the tribute to which the Ameers were subject, are questions which, in my opinion, ought to be reserved altogether for separate consideration.[32]

Peel took care to distinguish between the policy which had led to annexing Sind – Ellenborough's policy, as the Prime Minister reminded everyone – and what Napier achieved on the battlefields of Miani and Hyderabad, which he found admirable. There was so formidable a concentration of hostile soldiers, the Prime Minister explained, that Napier had to act as he did – or find himself responsible for the destruction of another British army.

***

The parliamentary votes hardly settled the matter. Ashley and Howick had insisted upon a different kind of moral universalism, one which did not involve attacking and conquering people. Others thought the same way.

John Stuart Mill, notably – who had been so taken with the liberal imperialism on view in Napier's Cephalonia book – took a very different view in this case. In 1853 he had this to say about the behaviour of the East India Company's Court of Directors (his employers):

> That body who recalled Lord Ellenborough, who recorded an indignant condemnation of the greatest iniquity in modern Indian history – the seizure of Scinde (the joint act of their two bitterest enemies, Lord Ellenborough and Sir Charles Napier) . . . such a body is a power which no Indian Minister can despise. . . . These are the glorious pages in the recent history of the Court of Directors.[33]

East India Company officials did not like the way Sind had been annexed. One retired Indian officer, Mountstuart Elphinstone, wrote to another, Sir Charles Metcalfe:

> I do not know if you have time to think of India. Sindh was a sad scene of insolence and oppression. Coming after Afghanistan, it put one in mind of a bully who had been kicked in the streets, and went home to beat his

232　*The conquest of Sind*

wife in revenge. It was not so much Lord Ellenborough's act, however, as his General's.[34]

I do not agree with all of this assessment. As the naval officer Charles Ogilvy Hamley, writing in *Blackwood's* in 1857, pointed out: '[Ellenborough's] treaty was in fact a declaration of war, and the protest should have been made against that, and not the measures it necessitated.'[35]

***

Napier himself was incensed at the criticisms made against him in Parliament – especially Howick's allegation that he had started the war for his own selfish motives. Writing to Lord Ripon in 1844, Napier insisted: 'Were Lord Howick to read my private journal, which probably no one will ever do, he would see how unjust his speech was in accusing me of making a war for the sake of military glory.'[36] Later he told his sister Emily: '[T]hat malicious liar Lord Howick accused me of . . . making war for the sake of *prize money*! I could hardly sleep as soundly, as I do, amidst all these injured men loaded with the love of their countrymen, like a monster assassin stalking through the land.'[37]

In his journal he let himself rant:

> It is hard . . . for an honest man serving his country in the midst of dangers and trials, physical and moral, and acting from the honourable feeling of doing his duty in spite of any – I may say of every danger: it is hard for him to be exposed to the insolence, the falsehoods of men like Lord Howick. . . . To give him personal chastisement would give me pleasure, such as one feels at cutting a village cur dog with a whip, but I forgive all of them. After anger, contempt succeeds. I never feel angry in my heart against any one – beyond wishing to break their bones with a broomstick![38]

All was not bleak. Napier was pleased by what Peel, Wellington, Roebuck, Hardinge, and his cousin Admiral Charles Napier, M.P. (Black Charlie) said about him in the debates. He was reasonably satisfied by Ripon's contribution, too – Ripon had referred to 'the conduct of that gallant officer'. Yet Napier went told William that nonetheless Ripon was neither very wise nor very good at mastering detail.[39] For Lord Ripon was once Viscount Goderich, the Colonial Secretary who stopped responding to Napier over his Cephalonian complaints little more than a decade before.

Notes

1　Naomal Hotchand, *A Forgotten Chapter of Indian History as Described in the Memoirs of Seth Naomal Hotchand, C.S.I., of Karachi, 1804–1878*, (trans.) Alumal Trikamdas Bhojwani, H. Evan M. James (ed.) (Exeter: Printed for private circulation by W. Pollard, 1915), 124–29.

2　Napier's journal, 15 March 1843, given in WN, 2:348. As usual Outram argues that all violence was entirely Napier's fault; so in his huge tome he only once refers to Shere Muhammed's ultimatum, and then only obliquely – James Outram, *The Conquest of*

The battle of Dubba 233

Scinde: A Commentary (Edinburgh and London: William Blackwood and Sons, 1846), 452n. On the next page Outram entirely omits it – 453. See LNS, 158.

3 His fascinating story has nothing to do with Charles Napier – see Teena Purohit, *The Aga Khan Case: Religion and Identity in Colonial India* (Cambridge, MA: Harvard UP, 2012).

4 Copy of Napier to Ellenborough, 7 October 1843, RP, BL Add. MS 40877, fols 211–12; WNCS, 321, 327, 367–69.

5 WNCS, 370–72.

6 Fortescue, *History of the British Army*, 13 vols (London: Macmillan, 1910–1930), 12:296n, 298.

7 Napier to W. Napier, 16 April 1843, given in WN, 2:357–64 at 358; Napier to Richard Napier, 18 July 1843, 2:424–25; Fortescue, *History of the British Army*, 12:294–98; LNS, 161–67; Lieutenant H. Thomson to Napier, May 1844, given in Napier to W. Napier, July 1847, given in turn in WN, 4:110–15 at 114–15.

8 Napier's journal, 12 October 1848, given in WN, 4:109.

9 Napier to W. Napier, 24 October 1844, given in WN, 3:153–55.

10 T. Postans, *Personal Observations on Sindh* (London: Longman, Brown, Green, and Longmans, 1843), 336–38; Napier to Ellenborough, 24 March 1843, given in Postans, 397–401; WNCS, 385–92.

11 LNS, 167, citing John Jacob. Fortescue, *History of the British Army*, 12:298, has even lower figures: twenty-three dead, one hundred thirty-nine wounded.

12 Napier to Ellenborough, 11 July 1843, NP, BL Add. MS 49105, fols 18–20; Outram, *Conquest*, 380–85, 554n, 557–58.

13 Lionel J. Trotter, *The Bayard of India: A Life of General Sir James Outram, Bart.* (Edinburgh and London: William Blackwood and Sons, 1903), 139–40.

14 LNS, 215. Some British observers had already pointed out how the Amirs had trouble controlling their Beluchi troops: Delhoste's Report, 1832, given in Edward Paterson Delhoste, *Observing Sindh*, Matthew A. Cook (ed.) (Oxford: Oxford UP, 2008), 14.

15 Hardinge to Napier, 4 September 1844, BL Add. MS 54517, fols 85–90 at 86–87.

16 E. B. Eastwick, *A Glance at Sind before Napier, or Dry Leaves from Young Egypt*, 2nd edn, introduced by H. T. Lambrick (1851; Karachi: Oxford UP, 1973), 299–300.

17 A.G.L. Shaw, *Sir George Arthur, Bart, 1784–1854* (Melbourne: Melbourne UP, 1980), 244.

18 *Punch* 6 (1844), 209.

19 Stephen Jay Gould, *Bully for Brontosaurus: Reflections in Natural History* (New York: W.W. Norton & Co., 1991), 269; P. Napier, *I Have Sind: Sir Charles Napier in India, 1841–1844* (London: Michael Joseph, 1990), 160 – although in her next book, this author did admit some doubt about whether Napier said any such thing (P. Napier, *Raven Castle*, 6). For the career of the apocryphal telegram, see Doniger, *The Hindus: An Alternative History* (New York: Penguin, 2009), 600–03.

20 Billimoria, 'General Orders of Sir Charles Napier (1843–47)', 46–54 at 46.

21 [William Strachey], 'Conquest of Scinde', *Edinburgh Review*, 79, 160 (April 1844), 542.

22 HC Deb 8 February 1844 vol 72 cc342–64; Edwin Hodder, *The Life and Work of the Seventh Earl of Shaftesbury, K.G.*, 2 vols (London: Cassell, 1886), 2:5–12.

23 Napier to Roebuck, 27 April 1837, NP, BL Add. MS 49128, fols 20–22.

24 HC Deb 8 February 1844 vol 72 cc364–402.

25 10 February 1844, quoted in Hodder, *Shaftesbury*, 2:13. The idea that Ashley is rejecting – that of military intervention in the name of universal humanitarian values – seems to go back to Edmund Burke: Bernard Simms, ' "A False Principle in the Law of Nations": Burke, State Sovereignty, [German] Liberty, and Intervention in the Age of Westphalia', in Bernard Simms and D.J.B. Trim (eds), *Humanitarian Intervention: A History* (Cambridge: Cambridge UP, 2011), 89–110.

26 HC Deb 12 February 1844 vol 72 cc535–46.

27 Peel to Ripon, 17 August 1843, PP, BL Add. MS 40464, fols 447–48. Peel made similar points to Ripon on 2 December 1843 and 9 February 1844, PBC, BL Add. MS 40865, fols 110–11, 180–81.

28 Peel to Ripon, 9 December 1843, PBC, BL Add. MS 40866, fols 241–46 at fols 243–44.

234   *The conquest of Sind*

29 HC Deb 5 February 1839 vol 45 cc95–109 at cc95–97; Peel to Ripon, 9 December 1843, PBC, BL Add. MS 40866, fols 241–46 at fols 244–25.
30 Great Britain, Parliament, *Accounts and Papers, 1843: Sinde*, No. 39 (1843); and Sarah Ansari, 'Sind Blue Books of 1843 and 1844: The Political "Laundering" of Historical Evidence', *English Historical Review* 120, 485 (February 2005), 35–65.
31 Ansari, 'Sind Blue Books of 1843 and 1844', 44–49, 57, 60; Peel to Ripon, 2 May 1844, PP, BL Add. MS 40465, fols 257–58.
32 HC Deb 12 February 1844 vol 72 cc523–35.
33 John Stuart Mill, 'The India Bill', *Morning Chronicle* 5 July 1853, given in *Collected Works*, 25:1189.
34 Elphinstone to Metcalfe, 14 March 1844, given in John William Kaye, *Lives of Indian Officers*, 2 vols (London: Strahan and Co., 1869), 1:434–36.
35 [Charles Ogilvy Hamley], 'Life of Sir Charles J. Napier – Part II', *Blackwood's Edinburgh Magazine* 82 (August 1857), 241–64 at 256.
36 Napier to Ripon, 18 April 1844, PBC, BL Add. MS 40868, fols 84–87 at fol. 87.
37 Napier to Emily Bunbury, 29 November 1844, NP, BL Add. MS 49110, fols 31–34 at fol. 32.
38 Napier's journal, 6 June 1844, given in WN, 3:106.
39 HL Deb 12 February 1844 vol 72 c490; Napier to W. Napier, 13 April 1844, given in WN, 3:84–88.

Part V

'In Scinde as in Cephalonia . . .'

This completes the conquest of Scinde; every place is in my possession, and, thank God! I have done with war! Never again am I likely to see a shot fired in anger. Now I shall work in Scinde as in Cephalonia, to do good, to create, to improve, to end destruction and raise up order.[1]

No man in his senses would now [in the 1860s] propose to revert, even in the smallest province, to the most successful and despotic type of Indian government, that exercised by Sir Charles Napier in Sind, where all civil and military authority had been concentrated in a single hand.[2]

Notes

1 Napier's journal, 5 April 1843, given in WN, 2:356.
2 Eric Stokes, *The English Utilitarians and India* (Oxford: Oxford UP, 1959), 270.

18 Victory in the sun

Ellenborough formally proclaimed the annexation of Sind on 13 March. He made Napier governor of Sind while retaining him as military commander. To unite civil and military command was highly unusual in British Indian practice.[1] Napier waxed enthusiastic about all he might accomplish: 'My object now is to . . . make roads, buildings, open streets, to secure justice. O! how I long to begin thus to live, and to rest after the horrid carnage of these battles!'[2]

But in the aftermath of the Battle of Hyderabad, there was still the task of defeating Shere Muhammed and the forces with whom he had fled that day. To achieve this end, Napier led his troops into the field in the hottest part of the year. He knew that by doing so he would lose some of them to the heat,[3] but he hoped that by moving quickly he could save the lives of many more. His object was to defeat Shere Muhammed before the Amir and his forces could take refuge among the channels and thickets of the Indus delta, where the war could drag on indefinitely and with greater loss life. So Napier set forth. The army moved mostly at night. By day they kept to their tents with wet towels wrapped around their heads. Men died anyway as Napier executed a three-pronged pincer movement with himself as leader of the largest force.

***

At the end of this journey through the desert, as the pincer was about to close and the battle with Shere Muhammed neared, the mails came. Napier suddenly had hundreds of letters to respond to all at once in the terrible heat. Some of them demanded that he should find and send documents immediately; others that he should write long explanations for the questions which Outram was raising with officials in India and England over events in the run-up to the war. It may be no wonder that Napier's answers, as Outram would later anatomize them in multiple volumes of criticism, were hurried, self-justificatory, and filtered through Napier's own remembrances – giving Outram and his friends still further ammunition against the general in the years ahead.[4]

Over the next two years of continual military campaigning, Napier with almost every new bundle of mail would be called upon to re-examine and write at length about all that happened in the days and weeks before Miani. Sometimes there were dozens of substantial letters for him to answer on these

238 'In Scinde as in Cephalonia . . .'

and other matters. He would work in his tent after the soldiers had gone to sleep. There was no way around most of this work – long reports demanded by Bombay and even by the Governor-General. Napier did have secretaries who were able to copy passages from the official papers more or less accurately. (For 'between Scylla and Charybdis' one of his secretaries wrote 'between scythes and carabines', which Napier thought 'quite as good'.) But he had to draft everything himself.[5] As he explained to Outram (for they were still corresponding in friendly private letters, even while Outram's anti-Napier campaign was gathering steam in the press):

> You know the heat here, and that the operations I have carried on, both military and civil, since the capture of Hyderabad, preclude all work which is not absolutely necessary, but I nevertheless do mean to write the essay on the defence of the Residency when I *can*.
>
> I assure you that this business of defending my conduct has given me more pain and annoyance than anything that has happened to me in Scinde.[6]

Yet unlike Outram, Napier always carried a tablet in his pocket for recording conversations, and he travelled with all his notes.[7] So even on campaign in the desert, he was able to make at least some kind of case for himself. For example, he was able to demonstrate that indeed he had carefully weighed Outram's assertion that Ali Murad and not Mir Rustam was conspiring against him, and he was able to explain why he had found Mir Rustam's behaviour more suspicious than Ali Murad's.[8]

***

The sun never let up. As the pincer movement continued – and the paperwork too – Napier kept his favourite Arabian horse, Red Rover, in his tent. This was to keep the animal alive, although bringing a horse inside would hardly make things cooler for the human inhabitant.

The army tents had double roofs. Otherwise they were cooled only by 'tatties' – wet screens for the wind to blow through.[9] On the day that saw the final battle with the enemy – John Jacob in command of another arm of the pincer encountered and defeated the army of Shere Muhammed at Sahdadpur on 13 June – Napier and his own body of troops were encamped out of sight or sound of the fighting. The temperature in Napier's tent was 127°. The general, aged sixty-one, walked outside. The ambient temperature was 132°, and when he left the tent Napier was struck down at once with sunstroke. Thirty-one European soldiers and one European officer near him were struck down at about the same time. Most died within a few minutes. All but Napier himself were dead within three hours.

One might be tempted to say that naturally the general had the best of the medical care and the soldiers did not. Yet what the best of the care meant was that Napier was bled in both arms. He also recalled having his feet put in hot water and his head wrapped in towels. But it was at that moment that he was brought the news of Jacob's victory. 'I think it saved me', he said. 'I felt the life come back.' Yet he wrote to his brother five weeks later that 'I have never been right since. Such terrible weakness that I cannot write a letter without lying down; a sickening feeling comes over me that is quite undescribable'.[10]

It was time to make peace. In the aftermath of Jacob's success, one of Shere Muhammed's main lieutenants came to Napier to surrender. He and Napier had a pleasant conversation – Napier had recovered that much from his sunstroke. The General confirmed the Beluchi in his lands as an honoured and now defeated enemy. This decision was subject to Ellenborough's approval, and Napier protected the man until word came that Napier's will would indeed prevail in this matter – over Ellenborough's expressed desire to see the Beluchi punished.[11]

Napier again refused the offer of the Amirs' precious bejewelled swords. And in the expectation of the Hyderabad prize money, he bought a few swords at the prize auctions. He also wound up with a plainer sword given to him by one of his own men on the battlefield at Miani.

Shere Muhammed himself, along with one of Mir Rustam's sons, fled to the hills to join with Beebruck's tribe, the Boogties. Indeed, in the north these border tribes would still have to be dealt with, for they kept raiding the agricultural population.[12]

Meanwhile Napier's doctors ordered him to Karachi in August or September 1843. John Kennedy (still in Ireland) and all the medical men on the spot believed that Napier had to leave India at once if he wanted to live. But he would not go. He said that while other men were equally qualified to govern and reform Sind, he had a unique advantage. He could command everyone's respect as their conqueror. The Beluchis with their sense of honour would not accept the major reforms that he had in mind save at the hands of the general who had beaten them.[13]

Enter Hardinge

The combative Ellenborough was recalled by the irate Court of Directors of the East India Company in June 1844, so Napier no longer had the real author of Sindhi annexation to defend him against the constant criticism from Outram and the English civilian community in Bombay; one officer observed that Napier was 'the best-abused man of his day'.[14] But if Napier had lost one defender in India he gained another. The new Governor-General was Sir Henry Hardinge (soon to be created Viscount Hardinge of Lahore). He was Lord Ellenborough's brother-in-law, and he counted Ellenborough one of his earliest and closest friends. Hardinge had fought with Napier at La Coruña and defended him in the House of Commons over the conquest of Sind.[15] In London Hardinge watched Ellenborough's recall with horror. He genuinely believed the Amirs had behaved badly and deserved their fate. In his correspondence with Wellington and Ellenborough in the months before Ellenborough's unprecedented dismissal – and thus before anyone could have

240 *'In Scinde as in Cephalonia ...'*

imagined that Hardinge himself was about to be sent out as Ellenborough's successor – Hardinge also expressed his admiration for Napier's achievements on the battlefield. And he named his favourite horse 'Miani'.[16]

When Hardinge arrived in India, he found Napier 'an extraordinary man. . . . He has many Napier caprices but he is a fine fellow – able, resolute & original.' Napier 'gain[ed] the confidence & attach[men]t of those under his command, & I find him practicable, good-tempered, and considerate. He is a very superior man'.[17]

Hardinge would never change his mind about Napier's abilities (he wanted to see Napier ennobled[18]) but he began to change his mind about Napier's temperament. Watching Outram and his partisans in their continual sparring with William Napier in print over every detail regarding the coming of the war, and realizing that much of what William said about the matter was coming from Charles, Hardinge became convinced after a year or two that Napier was 'eccentric'.[19] Yet he continued to support the general's policies of reform in Sind. For its part, the Board of Control in London naturally felt aggrieved over the attacks that Napier kept making on the Company and its servants, but the Governor-General took care that the resentment of the Board was not allowed to touch the Governor of Sind. When a Bombay administrator took strong issue with Napier's disparagement of his colleagues and himself – Napier had called the administrators 'jackals driven by [Lord Ellenborough] from their prey', by which he meant the public treasury – Hardinge had the man reprimanded and made to apologize to Napier.[20]

The authorities in Bombay had real grounds for their resentment nonetheless. Napier was using their army to staff his civil as well as his military administration in Sind. Indeed, two-thirds of the forces of the Bombay Presidency were working for Napier rather than reporting to their proper commanders. The Bombay officials still had to pay the bills. And yet ever the follower of Cobbett, Napier kept abusing these very bureaucrats even as he demanded ever more resources from them for the Sindhi people under his care.[21] All the while Bombay pestered Napier with bureaucratic questions and complaints.

Despite the critics, and all the paperwork he had to do in defending himself over provoking the war – and even despite his own worsening health in the hot climate – under both Ellenborough and Hardinge Napier was given the political cover to carry out his reforms in Sind, and he was given a fair measure of material and staffing resources as well. So how did he govern his new Cephalonia?

The legal system and the police

Before Napier could hope to address any of the larger questions of social justice, he had to establish permanent control over town and countryside. He decided to base his administration upon the pre-existing institutions. Under the Talpurs, as Napier found, the *kardar* headmen had been responsible for keeping order in their villages. In this they had the assistance of small mounted units. There was also an efficient system of *puggees* (or trackers) for investigating crimes and apprehending criminals. Napier retained the *kardars* and their *puggees* and imposed his own structure of centralized control over them. The system he wound up with became influential throughout British India, where previously the police forces had been uncoordinated and sometimes underpaid and undisciplined.[22]

Napier divided the responsibility for law enforcement among four organizations: (1) the Regular Army, to secure the newly conquered country; (2) the Irregular Horse, which could move quickly and mix more familiarly with the people than the army could do; (3) the police themselves (divided into urban and rural branches), much closer to the people and thus more able to move among and learn from them; and (4) the civil administration, still less likely to be resented by the populace. The civil side, in turn, was divided into its own gradations ranging from the three 'Collectors' at the top (at Karachi, Hyderabad, and Sukkur and Rohri) down to the local level, integrating the *kardars* who collected taxes and kept order. Each of the four branches of administration and law enforcement had a chief who reported directly to Napier. The three Collectors reported to Napier's assistant, Lieutenant E. J. Brown, although Napier would often canvass their opinions directly.[23]

There were one hundred nine kardarates in 1847. In them the *puggees* continued with their work of preventing and detecting routine crime. The European civil authorities carried out the higher-level investigations and acted as judges. Serious crimes (those that might result in a sentence of over three months' imprisonment) were heard first by a magistrate, who sent a report up to the judge advocate and the governor. The governor would then order one or another kind of court martial, in which the judging and sentencing was done by the local Collector or his designee on the civil side – in Napier's time all of these men were military officers. In capital cases, the minutes and sentences then came back up to Napier for another review, and he would issue the order for the death sentence if necessary. Napier wished he had the choice of permanent banishment instead of death, but he did not have that power under military law. The only punishments available for the most serious crimes were death or temporary banishment, after which hardened criminals could come back into the country. In minor civil cases Napier retained the local juries or *Punchayet* of notables, which reminded him of the Greek *Veechiarde*; the one change he made was to pay the jurors. The Greek parallel was significant. Napier would tell Bartle Frere, who was one of his successors in Sind, that he had planned out the whole policing structure in his head when he was in Cephalonia. He gazed out one day towards the Greek mainland, wondering what he would do if he were called upon to govern such a country, plagued by organized bandits.

For Frere and other senior officials who knew Sind after Napier left, the organization of the police units was the best administrative innovation he made. They found the police honest and effective in their work, clear and simple in their organization. The policemen made more money than they

242   *'In Scinde as in Cephalonia . . .'*

could in the civil economy, and they were eager to make their arrests – just as the separately organized magistrates were zealous in the other direction, not wanting to condemn the accused too quickly or to be too harsh in the sentences they imposed. Each side, the police and the magistracy, made their official complaints about the other, and in that way a record was kept and any disagreements were fully documented and well aired. The only changes which later officials made to Napier's system would not affect the structure of policing per se – this was the creation of an independent judiciary.[24]

Napier enforced the same laws upon his own men as he did upon the conquered population. In his general orders, he insisted that officers should pay what was asked by the merchants, rather than simply paying what they wanted and demanding that the item be produced.[25] And when a private was convicted of the harassment of villagers, and the court-martial sentenced him to only two months' imprisonment, Napier refused to confirm the sentence. He found it shockingly lenient. Napier wanted the man sentenced to at least a year's imprisonment with hard labour. In his official decision, Napier said that in the interests of both the honour and the safety of the army he had to repress 'plunder' and 'marauding'. When it turned out that under military regulations the original sentence had to stand, Napier made it very clear that in the future he expected the sentences to be more severe and that plundering was not to be tolerated. If courts-martial would not pass adequate sentences, he said that as commander he would use the disciplinary powers which he had under statute and have the offending soldiers executed.[26]

In what might seem to be small matters, too, he felt honour bound to protect Sindhi interests. He even protected the Sindhi peacocks. But he explained that in fact this was no small matter. Napier did not want the Sindhis to be provoked into resistance by seeing their decorative fowl shot by British officers – who in any case had no right to shoot the birds at all. His order began this way:

> Officers must not shoot peacocks: if they do, the Beloochies will shoot officers, – at least so they have threatened, and Major-General Napier has not the slightest doubt but that they will keep their word. There are no wild peacocks in Scinde. They are all private property and sacred birds, and no man has any right whatever to shoot them. The Major-General is satisfied that, after this warning, no officer will again give such offense to the people, whose tranquil behaviour and extreme civility has been the subject of general remark and admiration.[27]

He concluded the order by reminding everyone what was at stake: 'If there be one evil which the Major-General has more strenuously endeavoured to avoid than any other, it is that of a Guerrilla war. If such a misfortune should arise, there is no saying where the sacrifice of life and treasure would end: every man who has common sense must see this.'

Victory in the sun   243

When an English officer acted disrespectfully towards a captain in the Indian Navy, and then threw an Indian in the water for obeying his captain's orders, Napier had the Englishman arrested: 'The Major-General has heard it said that the supremacy of the British over the Native must be maintained in India, and he entirely concurs in that opinion, but it must be maintained by justice.'[28]

Murder and liberal imperialism

Yet justice for the Sindhi population did not mean undue leniency. Napier grew incensed when he heard that Sindhis were receiving sentences of only two or three years for killing each other.[29]

In once case, a Beluchi man murdered someone whom he dismissed as a 'Sindhi slave' (the Sindhi owed him money). The Beluchi then tried to buy his way out of his punishment. Napier wanted to make his policy clear, so in response to this case he issued a proclamation that from then on all convicted murders should receive the death penalty: 'Whenever a man is murdered, I will hang the murderer. Society cannot exist if one man may slay another at his pleasure. The new law of Scinde is easily understood'.[30] The historian Sandria Freitag has argued that – as a 'rough model' – British officials usually failed to understand that in the South Asian tradition, private violence was a matter for the local community to address; violent crime did not call into question the central authority of the state and it was not punished by the state.[31] Certainly Napier took a different view.

What did not appear to be clear about Napier's proclamation was that he also wanted to punish murderers of women and not just murderers of men. And soon Napier began hearing more and more about *karo kiri*, or the honour killing of wives and female relations accused of sexual infidelity.[32] He now tried to make it abundantly clear that men convicted of killing women would be executed, too. The men of Sind, Napier wrote to his brother Richard,

> think that to kill a cat or a dog is wrong, but I have hanged at least six for killing women: on the slightest quarrel she is chopped to pieces. One was hanged this morning. Having had some words he drew his sword, the poor girl's father prayed in vain for her, and seeing it was no use turned his back while the fellow cut her to pieces, and then sending for a spade buried her. A chief came here yesterday to beg off another, a follower of his. I'll hang him said I. What! hang him! He only killed his wife! utter astonishment painted upon his face. Well, she did no wrong. Wrong! He was angry, why should he not kill her? Why then should I not kill him? I never saw anything like it. When there is jealousy or momentary erroneous suspicion there may be some excuse, but nothing more is required than anger at any trifle to bring out the sword. These two cases make eight, and I will hang 200 unless they stop.[33]

244   *'In Scinde as in Cephalonia . . .'*

On 6 August 1844, he issued another proclamation:

> Be it known to all the Mahomedan inhabitants of Scinde that I am the conqueror of Scinde, but I do not intend to interfere with your religion. I respect your religion, but it is necessary that you should also respect mine. We both worship one God, and that God has prohibited us to take away life, but notwithstanding this, you kill your wives without pity. I tell you plainly that I will not allow this. I am the ruler of the country, and if anyone here after kills his wife, I will have the matter investigated by a court of justice, and the offender shall be punished according to his crime.[34]

Furthermore, Napier urged his Collectors to hang the wife-murders without worrying overmuch about what he saw as the mere niceties of the laws of evidence. Justice must be done, however rough it might be – there must be no acquittals on technicalities. (Napier had long been impatient of military courts in which the undereducated officers would pretend to legal expertise rather than dispensing commonsense rulings given the facts of the case.[35]) Napier said that he was trying to stamp out a practice from society, not to observe empty legal forms.

Yet the practice that he was trying to stamp out was deeply rooted, and perhaps whipping his own officers into shape was not going to change that. Some of the Sindhi men preferred to avenge their honour on their womenfolk and then die for it, rather than changing their minds about what constituted honour. This fact did not soften Napier.[36]

If crusading for social justice, did he feel bound by the legal niceties to any degree at all? In one case Napier believed that two *jagirdars* (feudal landholders) had been robbing their people, so he had them deprived of their *jagir* lands and put in chains. One of their servants he had flogged and five more of their servants he hanged: 'I will break up their system of robbery and murder though it cost a hecatomb of merciless scoundrels'.[37] Nor was this the only time when he had chiefs or officials degraded and clapped into irons for robbing the people.[38] '*Kardars* and policemen I smash by dozens', he told William – although in writing down this *jeu de espirit* he was unlikely to have been striving for statistical accuracy.[39]

In Napier's mind, the point of his behaviour was to save the poor from oppression. But even he had to ask himself whether the poor people really looked to him for justice in the way he wanted to believe they did. He took comfort from how they came to him with their myriad complaints about hardships and the corrupt officials. And he always kept his door open in Sind so they could make their pleas. Further, he appointed extra officers in the collectorates so the poor could make their complaints closer to home. As he had done in Cephalonia, he made it a point to believe the poor over the rich. He wrote in his journal that he was 'most unjust: for against all evidence I side in favour of the poor'. He said his maxim was this: 'Punish the Government servants first, and inquire about the right and wrong when there is time. That is the way to prevent tyranny, and make the people happy, and render public servants honest.[40]

Napier was not so cavalier about everything. He wrote that when he had to overrule Keith Young, the Judge Advocate General, and order an execution on his own authority, he would brood over the case until his mind, his heart, and his soul ached.[41] He approved of capital punishment intellectually but he disliked it in practice, and more than once he considered resigning his position rather than having to pass death sentences. Yet he believed that in Sind some crimes were so horrible that they cried out for this ultimate sanction.[42] As usual, he read the transcripts of every case, some of them running to more than one hundred pages of foolscap. In one six-month period, Napier read four hundred criminal cases.[43]

Napier and *sati*

Napier's desire to punish those who killed women may have reflected the way British authorities in India traditionally had 'othered' Islamic men for the way they treated the female sex.[44]

Indeed, Napier was taking his place alongside the many officials of the East India Company who had worked to revolutionize gender relations in the subcontinent. Most notably, they had carried out an extended campaign against the burning of widows. The Company had banned *sati* in their Indian territories in 1829, partly in response to the reform campaign led by Ram Mohun Roy. And in more recent years the British had continued to fight *sati* in the native states where they did not have direct political control.[45]

And now it was Napier's turn. On one famous occasion, he faced a delegation of Sindhi Hindus who had come to tell him that *sati* was a time-honoured practice in their religion. 'Be it so', he said.

> This burning of widows is your custom, prepare the funeral pyre. But my nation also has a custom. When men burn women alive we hang them, and confiscate all their property. My carpenters shall therefore erect gibbets on which to hang all concerned when the widow is consumed. Let us all act according to national customs![46]

Napier's words (or some paraphrased version of them) are frequently cited by neoconservatives today. He is quoted when people make arguments for Western interventionism or for imposing a certain model of human rights on the rest of the world. And it is not only the neoconservatives who have taken note. What Napier said to the Hindu delegation on that day has been cited everywhere from science fiction novels to a book by the evolutionary psychologist Steven Pinker. Napier's words have become a touchstone in arguments for the at least notional right of the international community to uphold a universal standard of behaviour.[47]

246 *'In Scinde as in Cephalonia ...'*

One contemporary of Napier's asked whether *sati* even existed in the Islamic Sind.[48] But in reality many Hindus lived there, too. In some districts they numbered half the population – two-thirds in certain towns. In the city of Hyderabad the proportion was about one-third. In the upper Sind it was about one quarter.[49]

Certainly *sati* would have been unknown in the Islamic hill country in the extreme north. This is where John Jacob, chief of the Irregular Horse, ruled for years as a largely autonomous commander or marcher lord. (Jacob operated from a settlement that would be renamed 'Jacobabad' at the insistence of the Governor-General.[50]) Jacob insisted that there was never any *sati* for Napier to repress.[51] Yet travellers had left records of *sati* in Islamic-ruled northwestern India in the seventeenth century, and other records of it as late as the 1840s in the Sikh-ruled Punjab.[52] True, *sati* would have been highly unusual in Sind – but it was highly unusual everywhere in the subcontinent. The rite of *sati* was meant to be an exceedingly rare example of a certain kind of virtue, and it was only practised by (or 'on') a tiny fraction of widows. As the historian Anand Yang has shown, little more than one percent of widows ever underwent *sati*, and this was the extreme figure reached only in Bengal, and chiefly among certain social groups in the environs of Calcutta. Everywhere else the rate was a fraction of that. *Sati* did take place across India, but there were no more than a few isolated cases each year.[53] So whenever the British focused on *sati* outside of urban Bengal itself, they were looking at a rare practice. And yet a group of Hindus may well have come to Napier to discuss the possibility of a *sati*.

Even if the Hindus of Sind did not engage in *sati* themselves, nonetheless they *did* engage in the honour killing of their womenfolk, just as the Muslims did, a practice that some British magistrates in India had condoned.[54] Hindus and Muslims alike strangled women (when they wanted to pretend that a woman had hanged herself); or in the case of Muslims armed with swords, they simply beheaded their offending wives or sisters.[55] Because Napier reviewed all the court cases, he knew very well how infrequent *sati* was. He also knew how common it was for women to be strangled, hanged, beheaded – or left alive but without ears, lips, nose.[56] Napier worked hard to stamp out all of these practices.

But there was more to it than that. Like a number of other British observers in the first half of the nineteenth century, Napier used what he thought he knew of the mistreatment of Indian women to demonize and orientalize Indian society, and this formed part of his rationale-after-the-fact for extending British control.[57] For in the period *before* Miani he had not mentioned helping the women as a reason for the conquest; their plight became apparent to him later on.

In the last analysis, British officials who attacked *sati* were – as the cultural critic Gayatri Charavorty Spivak has pointed out – 'White men saving brown women from brown men'. Inherent in the behaviour of these officials was the idea that 'only imperialism can aggressively insist upon the universality' of modern Western capitalist norms. The voice of the women is obscured.[58] True, but in Napier's view their interests were not so obscure.

Tsar liberator

Napier also worked to abolish infanticide.[59] And he disarmed the population, although he refused to create unnecessary conflict by ordering a search for weapons.[60] Also, he freed the slaves at Ellenborough's behest.[61] But he freed them in his own way – all at once, at a stroke, with none of the deference to the property rights of the slave owners that Parliament had shown in emancipating the slaves of the British Empire only a few years before. The British government had bought the slaves of the Caribbean from their owners with money that came from British taxpayers, and they had freed the slaves over a period of years.[62] Napier did no such thing in Sind. He simply declared the slaves to be free. Richard Burton and other cynics in India (Outram among them) claimed that when the slaves were emancipated the act came so abruptly that they had nothing beside starvation to look forward to, as Napier had made no provision for them after they left their masters. Other authorities claim that there was food and work enough, so the freed slaves had hardly been left to starve.[63]

In any case, Napier set to work with a passion.[64] As he put it: 'My answers to the Beloochees, who argue their claims to slaves was well as if they were Professors of Brougham's London College, are handcuffs, the scourge, and working on the road.' On another occasion, he noted with all of the gruffness that he would affect when describing his own policies: 'Severity, injustice, violence, smite! smite! smite! if an oak is to be felled you must smite, and not reason with spectators. I listen to nothing and make prisoners of all accused, condemn without proof, punish without mercy.'[65]

***

In the modern world there may be a consensus among policymakers and pundits that certain behaviours cannot be tolerated even in another country – at least if world opinion acting through the agency of a multinational force or the great states can do anything about the situation.[66] But can one really go into another society and effect a revolution in social relations through repression? Could Napier revolutionize gender relations by hanging people?[67]

Certain Pakistani scholars, the two most recent of them professional policemen, point out that after Napier left Sind, his successors discovered that a sentence of transportation – that is, sending the convicted into exile across the seas – seemed to do more to deter honour killings than the death penalty had done. Napier himself noticed that the sentencing men to die for murdering women had led to a growth in the number of female 'suicides'. He saw through this at once and imposed a collective fine on any village where a 'suicide' took place. He fined the leading villagers more heavily yet, and the *kardar* headman of the village was dismissed. Finally, the dead woman's relatives were brought to Karachi for questioning.[68]

248   *'In Scinde as in Cephalonia . . .'*

It should be noted, too, that while Napier insisted on death sentences for men guilty of an honour killing, in the specific case of the murderous *husbands* he did not insist that the sentence should be carried out. Indeed, none of these husbands was executed when Napier was governor. The one murderous man who *might* have suffered death for killing his wife happened to escape. So with no executions, the gaols began to fill with condemned husbands.

Napier did not bother to announce that he was commuting these death sentences. Why should he? He was trying to discourage crime. And he did indeed execute the fathers, brothers, uncles, and so on who killed supposedly unfaithful women in the name of family honour.[69]

Notes

1　Napier to McMurdo, 3 April [1843], NP, NAM 2005–06–724, item 13; Sind Commissioner's Office, *History of Alienations in the Province of Sind*, 2 vols (Karachi: Commissioner's Press, 1886–1888), 1:17; George Nathaniel Curzon, *British Government in India: The Story of the Viceroys and Government House*, 2 vols (London: Cassell and Co., 1925), 92–93.

2　Napier's journal, 6 May 1843, given in WN, 3:378.

3　Napier to Richard Napier, 7 August 1843, given in ibid, 2:425–26.

4　WNCS, 422, 435–36; James Outram, *The Conquest of Scinde: A Commentary* (Edinburgh and London: William Blackwood and Sons, 1846), 118–19, 249–50, 258–59, 261–62 – where there is one brief acknowledgement in a footnote that Napier was ill when writing the answers demanded of him (343n). For an example of this charge against Napier – that by getting a date wrong he revealed his own sustained duplicity – see Robert A. Huttenback, *British Relations with Sind, 1799–1843: An Anatomy of Imperialism* (Berkeley and Los Angeles: University of California Press, 1962), 104.

5　Napier's journal, 30 July 1843, given in WN, 2:393; Napier to W. Napier, July 1843, 2:406–18 at 2:407; see also Keith Young, *Scinde in the Forties: Being the Journal and Letters of Colonel Keith Young, C.B.*, Arthur F. Scott (ed.) (London: Constable, 1912), 18.

6　Napier to Outram, 22 July 1843, given in WNCS, 493–97 at 497. Napier broke off communication with Outram three months later: Napier to Robertson, 23 October 1843, NP, BL Add. MS 49107, fols 74–78 at 76.

7　Outram, *Conquest*, 143.

8　Napier to Ellenborough, 13 July, 16 August 1843, and 29 September 1843, all given in WNCS, 476–80, 489–92.

9　Napier's journal, 14 April 1843, given in WN, 2:32.

10　Napier's journal, 15 June, 24 June 1843, given in ibid, 2:389–90; Napier to Kennedy, 18 July 1843, 2:402–04; Napier to Emily Bunbury, 11 July 1843, NP, BL Add. MS 49109, fols 149–50; Napier to W. Napier, 18 July 1843, given in WNCS, 527–30; Napier to Robertson, 10 August 1843, NP, BL Add. MS 49107, fols 70–73; Napier to Louisa Napier, 3 September 1843, Bodleian MS Eng. lett. c. 240, fols 148–50; WNCS, 437; H. T. Lambrick, *John Jacob of Jacobabad*, 2nd edn (Karachi: Oxford UP, 1975), 101.

11　Napier's journal, 4 May 1843, given in WN, 2:377.

12　Napier to Kennedy, 18 July 1843, given in ibid, 2:402–04; Napier to W. Napier, 21 December 1843, 3:20–25 at 21; WNCS, 440.

13　Kennedy to William Napier, 13 December 1843, Bodleian MS Eng. lett. d. 243, fols 1–2; Ellenborough to Wellington, 20 September 1843, given in CEW, 392–95; WNAS, 72, 79.

14　Lionel J. Trotter, *A Leader of Light Horse: Hobson of Hobson's Horse* (Edinburgh: William Blackwood, 1901), 122.

15　Hardinge to his wife, 23 June 1846, given in Bawa Satinder Singh (ed.), *The Letters of the First Viscount Hardinge Hardinge of Lahore to Lady Hardinge and Sir Walter and Lady James,*

1844–1847, Camden Fourth Series 32 (London: Royal Historical Society, 1986), 176–79; HC Deb 12 February 1844 vol 72 cc548–51.

16 Extracts of Hardinge to Ellenborough: 6 February 1843, 57; 6 June 1843, 82; 15 November 1843, 102–03; 5 January 1844, 117. Letter of Hardinge to Ellenborough, 6 May 1844, 157–60 – all given in Algernon Law, *India under Lord Ellenborough, March 1842-June 1844: A Selection from the Hitherto Unpublished Papers and Secret Despatches of Edward Earl of Ellenborough* (London: John Murray, 1926). For the name of the horse, see Bawa Satinder Singh (ed.), *My Indian Peregrinations: The Private Letters of Charles Stewart Hardinge, 1844–1847* (Lubbock, TX: Texas Tech UP, 2001), 8 at caption.

17 Hardinge to his wife, 21 March 1845, given in Singh (ed.), *Letters of Hardinge*, 59–61; Hardinge to James, 21 March 1845, given in ibid, 61–65 at 65.

18 Hardinge to his wife, 23 June 1846, given in ibid, 176–79.

19 Hardinge to James, 3 December 1847, given in ibid, 238–43 at 239. Wellington as Commander-in-Chief of the Forces once suggested ordering Napier never to write to his brother – Wilbur Devereux Jones, *'Prosperity' Robinson: The Life of Viscount Goderich, 1782–1859* (London: Macmillan, 1967), 260.

20 William Lee-Warner, *The Life of the Marquis of Dalhousie, K.T.*, 2 vols (1904; Shannon, Ireland: Irish UP, 1972), 1:306–07; C. Hardinge to his mother, 5 November 1845, given in Singh (ed.), *Indian Peregrinations*, 68–69; Napier to W. Napier, April 1843, quoted in WNCS, 195–96.

21 Arthur to Hardinge, 12 September 1844, RP, BL Add. MS 40869, fols 149–53 at 152; Arthur to Hardinge, 7 September 1844, in ibid, fols 167–72 at 170; A.G.L. Shaw, *Sir George Arthur, Bart, 1784–1854* (Melbourne: Melbourne UP, 1980), 247–51.

22 LNS, 183–84. Richard Hawkins makes a convincing argument that scholars are wrong to claim that Napier derived his policing system from Ireland: Napier's system differed from the Irish model. Hawkins gives Napier credit for developing his own system of policing out of what he learned in Cephalonia and the north of England: Hawkins, 'The "Irish Model" and the Empire: A Case for Reassessment', in David M. Anderson and David Killingray (eds), *Policing the Empire: Government, Authority, and Control, 1830–1940* (Manchester: Manchester UP, 1991), 18–32 at 21–22. The idea that Napier took his policing system from Ireland is repeated in S. A. Cook, *Imperial Affinities: Nineteenth Century Analogies and Exchanges between India and Ireland* (New Delhi: Sage, 1993), 31.

23 Napier to Ripon, 7 August 1844, RP, BL Add. MS 40869, fols 61–71 at 66–68. The centrality of the officials called 'Collectors' in British Indian administration originated with Warren Hastings – see Bernard S. Cohn, *Colonialism and Its Forms of Knowledge: The British in India* (Princeton, NJ: Princeton UP, 1996), 61–62.

24 Hamida Khuhro, *The Making of Modern Sind: British Policy and Social Change in the Nineteenth Century* (Karachi: Oxford UP, 1999), 3, 5–10, 18; Naomal Hotchand, *A Forgotten Chapter of Indian History as Described in the Memoirs of Seth Naomal Hotchand, C.S.I., of Karachi, 1804–1878*, (trans.) Alumal Trikamdas Bhojwani, H. Evan M. James (ed.) (Exeter: Printed for private circulation by W. Pollard, 1915), 141n; Edward Archer Langley, *Narrative of a Residence at the Court of Meer Ali Murad, with Wild Sports in the Valley of the Indus*, 2 vols (London: Hurst and Blackett, 1860), 1:119–20, and Frere quoted in Langley, 1:122–29 at 122–23; Charles Napier to Hobhouse, [?] 1846, given in WNAS, 301–20 at 308–11, 313; Pringle, 'Report', 11, 16–24; Napier to W. Napier, [15?] December 1843, given in WN, 3:18–20; Napier to John William Younghusband, 12 December 1850, Younghusband Papers, BL A&AS F197/42, fols 5-6; Rathbone to W. Napier, 15 January 1854, given in W. Napier, *Comments by Lieut.-General Sir William Napier, K.C.B., upon a Memorandum of the Duke of Wellington and other Documents Censuring Lieut.-General Charles James Napier, G.C.G., with a Defense of Sir C. Napier's Government of Scinde by Captain Rathbone, Collector of Scinde* (London: Charles Westerton, 1854), 63–97 at 74–75.

25 General Order, 22 April 1843, given in Edward Green (ed.), *Compilation of the General Orders, &c., Issued in 1842–47, by Sir Charles Napier, G.C.B., Major-General Governor of Scinde, to the Army under His Command* (Bombay: James Chesson at the *Times* Press, 1850), 79.

250 'In Scinde as in Cephalonia . . .'

26 General Orders, 22, 28 April 1843, quoted in Billimoria, 'General Orders of Sir Charles Napier (1843–47)', 49; Remarks on the Court Martial of 28 April 1843, given in Green (ed.), *General Orders*, 14.

27 General Order, 25 February 1844, given in Green (ed.), *General Orders*, 85.

28 General Order, 16 November 1842, given in ibid, 72–73. This kind of petty violence of European against Indians was widespread elsewhere in the subcontinent, as Eizabeth Kolsky has explored – Kolsky, *Colonial Justice and British India: White Violence and the Rule of Law* (Cambridge: Cambridge UP, 2010).

29 Remarks on Military Commissions held 25 April and 30 May 1844, given in ibid, 24–25.

30 LNS, 192; Khuhro, *Making of Modern Sind*, 10.

31 Sandria B. Freitag, 'Collective Crime and Authority in North India', in Anand A. Yang (ed.), *Crime and Criminality in British India* (Tucson: University of Arizona Press, 1985), 140–63 at 141–42.

32 A variety of stories had circulated about the killing of women, as well as female infants: Delhoste's Report, 1832, given in Edward Paterson Delhoste, *Observing Sindh*, Matthew A. Cook (ed.) (Oxford: Oxford UP, 2008), 15.

33 Napier to Richard Napier, [?] 1844, WN, 3:93–96. Napier wrote a similar account for John Kennedy: Napier to Kennedy, 27 July 1844, NP, TNA PRO 30/64/6, fols 12–17 at 15; and he also reported the matter to Ripon: Napier to Ripon, 7 August 1844, RP, BL Add. MS 40869, fols 61–71 at 68. Soon after the conquest, Marianne Postans herself referred to the practice of wife-murder – M. Postans, *Travels, Tales, and Encounters in Sindh and Balochistan, 1840–1843* (Oxford: Oxford UP, 2003), 66.

34 Aftab Nabi and Dost Ali Baloch, 'Early British Efforts to Crush Karo Kari in Colonial Sind', *Pakistan Journal of Criminology* 2, 2 (April 2010), 1–20.

35 Charles James Napier, *Remarks on Military Law and the Punishment of Flogging* (London: T. and W. Boone, 1837), 36.

36 Nabi and Baloch, 'Efforts to Crush Karo Kari', 4–9; Napier quoted in WNAS, 365–66.

37 Napier's journal, 4 April 1845, given in WN, 3:285–86.

38 Napier to Emily Bunbury, 20 October 1843, NP, BL Add. MS 49109, fols 163–66.

39 Napier to W. Napier, 30 September 1844, given in WN, 3:141–50 at 147.

40 LNS, 204; Napier to Emily Bunbury, 29 November 1844, NP, BL Add. MS 49110, fols 31–34; Napier's journal, 29 November 1844, given in WN, 3:184.

41 Young, *Scinde in the Forties*, 71–73; Napier to Emily Bunbury, 29 November 1844, NP, BL Add. MS 49110, fols 31–34; Napier to Hobhouse, [?] 1846, given in WNAS, 301–20 at 309–10; Napier to W. Napier, 24 March 1846, given in WN, 3:405–08; WNAS, 253.

42 Napier to General Hunter, 30 June 1844, given in WN, 3:121–23; Napier to W. Napier, 7 May 1845, 3:294–97; Napier to George Arthur, 7 August 1843, 2:426.

43 WNAS, 255; Napier to Emily Bunbury, 29 July 1844, NP, BL Add. MS 49110, fols 19–24 at 21.

44 Thomas R. Metcalf, *The New Cambridge History of India*, III.4, *Ideologies of the Raj* [1987] (New Delhi: Oxford UP, 1998), 7–8.

45 Lata Mani, *Contentious Traditions: The Debate on Sati in Colonial India* (Berkeley and Los Angeles: University of California Press, 1998); Sakuntala Narasimhan, *Sati: Widow Burning in India* (New York: Anchor Books, 1990), 66–72, 135–42; Jörg Fisch, *Immolating Women: A Global History of Widow Burning from Ancient Times to the Present*, (trans.) Rekha Kamath Rajan (Delhi: Permanent Black, 2005), 353–433; Andrea Major, *Sovereignty and Social Reform in India: British Colonialism and the Campaign Against Sati, 1830–60* (London: Routledge, 2011).

46 WNAS, 35.

47 S. M. Stirling, *Island in the Sea of Time: A Novel of the Change* (New York: Roc, New American Library, 1998), 526; Steven Pinker, *The Better Angels of Our Nature: Why Violence Has Declined* (New York: Viking, 2011), 136, quoting M. Gerson, 'Europe's Veiled Rage' (which Pinker gives as 'Europe's Burqa Rage'), *Washington Post*, 26 May 2010; Mark Steyn, *America Alone: The End of the World as We Know It* (Washington, DC: Regnery Publishing,

Victory in the sun 251

2006), 193–94; Paul Schneidereit, 'Confronting the Darkness that Drove Mohammed Shafia', *The Chronicle Herald* (Halifax, Nova Scotia), 31 January 2012;Yaqoob Khan Bangash, 'The Price of Humans', *The Express Tribune* (Karachi), 28 May 2012. And the story appears in display type in H. W. Crocker III, *The Politically Incorrect Guide to the British Empire* (Washington, DC: Regnery, 2011), 124 – within an eight-page, almost double-spaced account of Napier's life (117–26).

48 John William Kaye, *The Administration of the East India Company: A History of Indian Progress* (London: Richard Bentley, 1853), 440.

49 Lewis Pelly, 'Brief Notes Relative to the Khrypoor State in Upper Sind' [1854], in Thomas (ed.), *Selections of the Records of the Bombay Government*, new series, 17 (Bombay: Printed for the Government at the Bombay Education Society's Press, 1855), 117–23 at 121; Thomas Postans, 'Miscellaneous Information Relative to the Town of Shikarpoor' [1840–1], in Thomas (ed.), *Selections*, 85–102 at 89; T. G. Carless, 'Memoir of the Bay, Harbour, and Trade of Kurachee' [1838], also in Thomas (ed.), *Selections*, 188–208 at 196; Delhoste, 'Narrative', 201; Statement by Captain Preedy, Collector at Karachi, in Sind Commissioner's Office, 'Revenue Queries by Mr. R. K. Pringle, Commissioner in Sind to Collectors in Sind, and Replies Thereto', *Selections from the Pre-Mutiny Records of the Commissioner in Sind*, Selection 2 (Sind: Commissioner's Office, n.d.), 41–51 at 45, 47, 50; Statement by Captain Rathbone, Collector at Hyderabad, in ibid, 39–41.

50 Lambrick, *John Jacob*, 247.

51 John Jacob, *Notes on Sir W. Napier's Administration of Sinde* (privately printed, no date), 10, 13, for notes to W. Napier's pages 19, 30, 35.

52 P. Thomas, *Indian Women through the Ages* (New York: Asia Publishing House, 1964), 263–65, 271.

53 Anand A. Yang, 'Whose Sati?: Widow Burning in Early 19th Century India', *Journal of Women's History* 1, 2 (Fall 1989), 8–33, especially 13, 18–23; Tanika Sarkar, *Rebels, Wives, Saints: Designing Selves and Nations in Colonial Times* (London: Seagull, 2009), 43–50.

54 Radhika Singha, *A Despotism of Law: Crime and Justice in Early Colonial India* (Delhi: Oxford UP, 1998), 144–46.

55 Langley, *Narrative*, 1:157, 2:56–61.

56 Napier to Kennedy, 23 July 1844, NP, TNA PRO 30/64/6, fols 14–19 at 15; Napier to Emily Bunbury, 29 July 1844, NP, BL Add. MS 49110, fols 19–24 at 23.

57 Uma Chakravarti, 'What Happened to the Vedic *Dasi*: Orientalism, Nationalism, and a Script for the Past', in Kumkum Sangari and Sudesh Vaid (eds), *Recasting Women: Essays in Indian Colonial History* (1989; New Brunswick, NJ: Rutgers UP, 1990), 27–87 at 31–37.

58 Gayatri Chakravorty Spivak, 'Can the Subaltern Speak?' in Rosalind G. Morris (ed.), *Can the Subaltern Speak?: Reflections on the History of an Idea* (New York: Columbia UP, 2010), 21–78 at 49–52. Spivak's original essay was published in 1988; I have cited the revised and expanded version.

59 Napier to Richard Napier, 14 September 1844, given in WN, 3:139–41.

60 Bartle Frere quoted in Langley, *Narrative*, 1:123.

61 Ellenborough to the Secret Committee of the East India Company, 26 June 1843, given in Law, *India under Ellenborough*, 68–80; Ellenborough and the Council of India to the Secret Committee of the East India Company, 28 August 1843, 83–89.

62 For Napier, buying the slaves rather than freeing them had further overburdened 'the labouring class' of taxpayers, and it led to the cruelties of the apprenticeship system in the West Indies. He thought the slaves should be recognized as belonging chiefly to themselves, able to pay for their freedom through their own labour. See Napier's drafts on abolition, 1837, NP, BL Add. MS 54544, fols 157–62; and Napier to Emily Bunbury, 29 July 1844, NP, BL Add. MS 49110, fols 19–24 at 22.

63 Edward Rice, *Captain Sir Richard Francis Burton* (New York: Charles Scribner's Sons, 1990), 83. Slavery was common in Sind, with African slaves doing most of the labour in some areas: T. G. Carless, 'Memoir of the Province of Lus, and Narrative of a Journey to Beyla' [1838], in Thomas (ed.), *Selections of the Records of the Bombay Government*, 298–319

252 *'In Scinde as in Cephalonia . . .'*

at 305, 310; Outram, *Conquest*, 492–98. Richard Burton's story that Napier sent him to explore homosexual brothels has been disproven. See Jon R. Godsall, *The Tangled Web: A Life of Sir Richard Burton* (Leicester: Matador, 2008), 46–49, 52–54, 60–61, 64–65; Dane Kennedy, *The Highly Civilized Man: Richard Burton and the Victorian World* (Cambridge, MA: Harvard UP, 2005, 30, 53, 238.

64 Napier to Emily Bunbury, 29 November 1844, NP, BL Add. MS 49110, fols 31–35 at 32; WNAS, 151, 153–54; Ellenborough to Napier, 27 May 1843, given in Law, *India under Ellenborough*, 67–68; Napier to Ellenborough, 19 December 1844, quoted in WNAS, 353–60 at 356.

65 Napier's journal, 9 December 1844, given in W. Napier, 3:189; LNS, 314.

66 Fay Voshell, 'Tolerating Pederasty', American Thinker (25 September 2015), http://www.americanthinker.com/articles/2015/09/tolerating_pederasty.html, accessed 18 March 2016; Charles Chapman, 'The Only Appropriate Response to Honor Killings and Fatal Fatwas', Kurdish Women Action Against Honour Killing (12 March 2006), www.kwrw.org/kwahk/index.asp?id68, accessed 29 November 2013; Michael W. Doyle, *The Question of Intervention: John Stuart Mill and the Responsibility to Protect* (New Haven, CT: Yale UP, 2015), chapter 4; James D. Ingram, 'What is a "Right to Have Rights"?: Three Images of the Politics of Human Rights', *American Political Science Review* 102, 4 (November 2008), 401–16; Arthur Isak Applbaum, 'Forcing a People to be Free', *Philosophy & Public Affairs* 35, 4 (Autumn 2007), 359–400; International Commission on Intervention and State Sovereignty, *The Responsibility to Protect* (Ottawa: International Development Research Centre, 2001).

67 This question occurred to Napier's successor in Sind: Pringle, 'Report', 20–22.

68 Nabi and Baloch, 'Efforts to Crush Karo Kari', 10–12; Khuhro, *Making of Modern Sind*, 10–11. Such murders continued: Langley, *Narrative*, 2:56–59.

69 LNS, 329, 338; Young, *Scinde in the Forties*, 173–74.

19 'To protect the poor from Barbarian Tyranny!'[1]

So Napier worked to the best of his abilities to combat violence against women.[2] And he had freed the slaves. But if he were to go further – if he were to abolish usury and debt bondage and bring about a real social revolution in the countryside, then he needed to know rather more about how agricultural practices worked. To know about *sati* was to be against it. To know about abuses in rent did not mean abolishing rent, only tinkering with the details.

Napier did believe that he knew something about the matter: The Amirs had raised the price of grain when times were bad, he thought; and he would repeat the stories of how they had any *kardars* who would not participate in this profiteering hanged by the thumbs, with fiery-hot iron rods inserted in their rectums.[3]

But rumours like that would not do. He needed a finer-grained knowledge of how things worked in quotidian reality if he wanted to tinker with the class outcomes of complicated financial transactions. So he instructed the *kardars* to fill out questionnaires on agriculture, irrigation, commerce, population, and so forth, and he tried to use his other officials as a fact-gathering network, too, requiring a weekly report from each Collector and Deputy Collector. All of these reports were read aloud to him by his aide, Captain Brown.[4] (We might recall the questionnaires which he had sent out to the local commanders on taking over in the north of England.)

Besides the questionnaires, the main information on which Napier would rely during his modernization efforts came from the elaborate procedure which he had carried out for initially ascertaining and assigning landownership. Before the Battle of Hyderabad, Napier issued a proclamation securing the land tenure of the armed *jagirdars* – the higher level in the armies of the Amirs.[5] To further ensure their loyalty, at Lord Ellenborough's behest Napier invited all of them to a durbar held at Hyderabad on Queen Victoria's birthday, 24 May 1844. Those attending and giving their *salams* would be allowed to retain their landholdings (*jagirs*). Napier had little need for the military assistance which they had once owed to the Amirs in exchange for the land. Now, instead of fighting for the government they would pay taxes to it. Napier's intention was that they might earn the means to pay their taxes (usually collected in grain) by promoting agricultural and commercial improvement.

254 'In Scinde as in Cephalonia . . .'

So, by demanding rent-in-kind from the lords of an expanding agricultural sector – in place of the military tribute they used to owe – Napier thought he could revolutionize the countryside and pull Sind out of the feudatory system that robbed the poor.[6]

At the durbar it took fully three days to receive, greet, and give the appropriate paperwork to all the *jagirdars*. Each *jagirdar* was allowed to come lightly armed and accompanied by one retainer – coming alone would not have befitted their dignity. But with the two thousand *jagirdars* each bringing their one subordinate, there were four thousand armed Sindhis to be catered to. Napier paid careful attention to where they were camped and how they were treated. Yet to greet them, Napier characteristically wore corduroy trousers like a labourer, and his were none too clean for the occasion.[7]

While his dress may have been informal, the procedures which he devised bore all the old marks of care and detail, reminiscent of how he set down the way the currants of Cephalonia were to be weighed and paid for. So on making his *salam* each *jagirdar* was given an acknowledgement signed and sealed by Napier. The *jagirdar* would then take this to the Collector for the appropriate part of the country, along with the paperwork showing his grant from the Amirs. The Collector would compare the documents with the ample local records left by the Amirs where the British had come into possession of them.[8] The Collectors then wrote out orders to the appropriate *kardars*, who in turn would give the right paperwork to the local *jagirdars* in exchange for the orders that each *jagirdar* handed to them; the *jagirdars* were to be given only the land they controlled on the day of the Battle of Miani. These were the lands on which they could collect rent from their peasants, and for which they would pay their rent in grain to the government.[9]

***

Uncovering and standardizing the system of rent and rural taxation had also been a central task in the establishment of British power elsewhere in the Indian countryside. This was in the second half of the eighteenth century. But as Ranajit Guha shows in *A Rule of Property for Bengal*, when the officials of the East India Company fanned out over the land and attempted to collect the taxes or rent, they were interfering with complex arrangements that they did not understand. Without any real knowledge of the intricacies of local property law or even any mastery of the local languages, Company officers demanded that monies flow from one social group to another, or to the East India Company itself, in ways that only vaguely resembled how everything had worked before. And so they managed to disrupt the economic flows and incentives of rural life. In interfering in this way with the planting and distribution of food, they brought on a famine in which a third of the population of Bengal would die. This was in the 1770s. It took a struggle, but by Napier's time a new equilibrium had been reached in the British-ruled areas.[10]

Napier, too, had now put himself in the position of interfering with complex economic relationships about which he knew little. He did not produce

'To protect the poor from Barbarian Tyranny!' 255

a famine, but through his interference in the details of rural landholding he utterly transformed the social structure of Sind, and not in the way he wanted to.

How did this happen? Modern Pakistani historians have argued that in confirming the rights of the *jagirdars* so soon after conquering the country, Napier misunderstood the vital point that the state ultimately owned the land and the *jagirdars* did not. Most of the men who held *jagirs* had no personal stake in the lands they were given, and no tie of loyalty or affection to any territory assigned to them. Yes, under the Amirs they held the land as military feudatories, but they held each estate only temporarily. They had no continuing tie to it of the kind that Napier expected from all his knowledge of the European landed aristocracy. Yes, some few of the *jagirdars* might well have acted as the local rulers of their lands in fact as well as fiction – taking an active interest in their *jagirs*, dispensing justice to the local people, and so forth. But this happened only in the rare cases when they actually lived on the *jagir*. In fact most of the *jagirdars* were absentees, employing hereditary *zemindars* to collect what was due to them and the relevant Amir. These *zemindars* had the true local ties, for in many cases their ancestors had organized the settlement or reclamation of the land after one of the destructive floods of the Indus.[11] In Napier's time, the *zemindars* continued to coordinate the agricultural activities of each area – reclaiming land, sinking new wells, and paying their due to the government or to the *jagirdar*, where one had been appointed over them. The *zemindars* were the leaders of the stable local rural communities. The land under them could not be alienated; nor could it be transferred or assigned in any way to the Hindu merchants.

The key element of the system, economically, was neither the sale of cash crops nor the operation of any capitalist market in land, but the assignment and distribution of the *batai* – shares in the grain crop whose size varied wildly from year to year because of drought or flood. Because of this variability, the *batai* could not be converted into a fixed cash amount. The *jagirdars* were given a share of the *batai* from a number of *zemindar*-led communities to reward them for their services. That was all. But in trying to cement his control of the country, Napier assumed that the armed *jagirdars* were European feudal lords. He gave them permanent title to what he took to be their estates. In reality he created a class of great landowners where none had existed before.

And he did worse. Before Napier, the peasants had held the status of *ryots* – really farmer-proprietors whose efforts were coordinated by the *zemindar* middlemen who stood between the *ryots* and the *jagirdars*. The *ryots* were independent agents who, like the *zemindars*, could improve the land and buildings, subject to payments to the *zemindars* and *jagirdars*. But now under British rule – both at Napier's time and at an accelerated rate later on – the *ryots* of Sind were converted into something else. With the assignment of landownership to the *jagirdars* and (outside the *jagirs*) to the *zemindars*, the *ryot* was no longer a *ryot*, but a *hari*, who owed everything (even any improvements that he might make) to the landlord. Soon the *hari* was in debt-bondage to those who owned the land.[12] So the irony is that Napier had brought to Sind an impoverished,

256   *'In Scinde as in Cephalonia . . .'*

Irish-style rural peasantry. As in Ireland with its short leases, the Sindhi peasantry now had so little security of tenure and so few resources that they could no longer improve the land in any way or build anything. Rather than saving the Irish from the social system that afflicted them – as he had tried to do by spreading the word of Kennedy's reforms – Napier had spread the afflictions of the Irish people to another country.

It is true that under the Talpurs a few hereditary or long-term *jagirs* had been created, so perhaps the change that Napier promoted had already been under way. But it seems that in a stroke Napier had managed to convert and consolidate the *jagirdars* (and some *zemindars*) into the dominant landowning class of Sind; and he converted the Sindhi rural population into a pauperized agricultural proletariat.

Oddly, what happened in Sind seems to have mirrored a similar process under way in other parts of British India in the second quarter of the nineteenth century. Believing that they were rationalizing landownership, Company authorities attacked the complicated web of traditional communal land rights and tax exemptions which they had once recognized. Building on long-term shifts already under way in Indian society, in many regions the Company officials concentrated landownership into the hands of a local class of rich landlords – the *zemindars* themselves. This changed the position of the common people. Building on the work of C. A. Bayly and others, D. A. Washbrook has described the process as 'peasantisation'.[13]

But why would Napier the fiery leftist do any of this? It would seem that he simply was out of his depth. It is hard to go into someone else's country and know the finer-grained details of life – touching on land tenure and inheritance law and so forth – better than the natives do. Perhaps it was Napier's own special personality, his special pride that was at fault, and he simply would not listen. Or perhaps being a conqueror does something to your sense of self-confidence, even if you are not Charles Napier. As Linda Martin Alcoff points out:

> [W]e might also ask . . . what is the relationship between the project of conquest and the reliance on bad epistemic practices? Could it be that conquerors are in an epistemically poor cultural, intellectual, and political context for judgment, and are more likely to develop what Mills calls 'epistemologies of ignorance' that include substantive cognitive practices that obscure social realities?[14]

In Sind, Napier did not stop to inquire into – as he had done in Cephalonia – exactly how the rich inspected or warehoused the crop, or by what subtle (or not so subtle) means they might apportion a larger share to themselves. He did not get to know the on-the-ground details of the power relationships. He simply expressed a belief that on Sindhi government land a class of small independent farmers would develop who would counterbalance the social influence of the great former-*jagirdar* landowners.[15]

But it did not work out that way. The *jagirdars* now held all the cards; the peasants held nothing. And Napier's interference in land tenure may also have hurt the women he was trying to protect. By imposing a new regime of land-holding he had privileged male control over family property. He had fixed in place who the *male* landowners were and who their *male* tenants were. Beyond that point I have to speculate, because evidence about family life in Sind at the time is sketchy. But it seems possible that fixing land tenure in the men in this way may have produced a situation similar to what one researcher has found in neighbouring Punjab. There, as Veena Talwar Oldenburg has shown, a portion of the rural women used to have a say in family decisions because they retained a measure of control over their dowry property. Yet under the legal regime of the British the exaltation of the man as head-of-household led to an intensification of male power over women. And thus in Punjab there was an increase in the very kinds of male violence against women that we have seen Napier trying to fight in Sind.[16]

The Yeomen of young Sind

But what did Napier *think* he was doing in interfering with traditional land rights? His attempts to reform land tenure did not stop with the early guarantees to the *jagirdars*. Napier had still more ambitious plans for social reform.

As governor, Napier quickly decided that the *jagirdars* corresponded very closely to the great aristocrats of England. Meanwhile, the permanent, tax collecting *zemindars* who ranked underneath the *jagirdars* were like England's capitalist farmers – they were the parasitic 'class' he had identified some years before, a class of middlemen which in England he wanted to see removed from the scene. So now he had resolved that as a radical and anti-capitalist, he did not like the *zemindars*, who were just like English farmers. He went so far as to create a path – although it was a complicated one, hedged about with protections for those being dispossessed – by which the *jagirdars* could rid themselves of vested *zemindari* rights and reform agriculture in exactly the way he imagined the English aristocrats might someday do, creating the small farms that he and John Kennedy loved so much. Napier wanted the *jagirdars* to have the power to call into being a class of agricultural 'yeomen', a word that he used in Sind in the same way he had used it in the British Isles. He even thought of calling his beloved *jagirdars* 'Squire Magistrates.' In time he did put some limits on the size of *jagirs* and on who could inherit them. But otherwise the Squire Magistrates would have close to a free hand.[17]

And so Napier was trying to impose his class categories from England, and with them a much improved version of the English rural system. And he thought of going still further. He dreamt of abolishing primogeniture, as he said Napoleon had done. Further, he wanted to bring in the whole of the Code Napoleon. Through the Code's principle of equal inheritance, the landowning class would become democratized and uplifted. Yet on second thought,

258   'In Scinde as in Cephalonia . . .'

instituting the Code had to remain only a dream, as Napier explained, for the Sindhis would never accept the principle of equal inheritance *for women*. In that sense he knew that his vision of making Sind as democratic in its social structure as the rural France that he loved was not very likely to come to pass in its full glory.[18]

Napier soon had still more second thoughts about his programme of social engineering. Eventually seeing something of the permanence of the landed aristocracy that he had so quickly created, he tried to reclaim some lands for the *zemindars*. What he tried to do, as historian Hamida Khuhro has shown, was to ask his collectors to work out some mechanism by which the *jagirdars* who had inherited their land since the durbar could exchange part of what they held for a reduction in tax. And he worked to trim wastelands and underexploited lands from those *jagirs* that were not changing hands. Often the *jagirdars* themselves wanted to reassign to the state any land that could not produce the expected rent. In this way a good deal of territory was recovered from *jagir* status as one generation of *jagirdars* was succeeded by the next, for the new *jagirdars* took as much land as they thought they could pay the rent on.[19]

***

In the care that he showed for canals and wells, Napier was emulating the work of the Talpurs and especially the Kalhoras who came before them, and he seemed to understand the needs of the country. But as Khuhro argues, he did not comprehend why so many of his plans for reclaiming the land and reforming the *jagirs* seemed to prove fruitless. What he failed to understand is that the desert had its bad patches of soil intermixed with the good – and again these patches were intermixed, and so these were not stretches of the land that could be trimmed off the grant and returned to the government. Therefore not all the territory of a *jagir* would be viable. There was no decent survey of land quality; the survey that Napier commissioned would only establish the main latitudes, longitudes, and elevations for canal work.[20] Many of the *jagirs* did not have anything like the usable area available to them that Napier believed they did. So in fact their *jagirdars* did not enjoy the agricultural yields that would allow them to develop the land in the way they wanted and create the kind of independent peasantry that he was hoping for. Improvements were made, but not on the scale that Napier had hoped.

At least the canal department that he created made sense in theory. Perhaps he did something good there. But to follow the argument in Khuhro's extensive study of this topic: The canal department in Napier's time had too few trained officers. It therefore made mistakes in engineering in its new projects, and it lacked the expertise needed to oversee the cleaning and maintenance of the canals that already existed – the task of cleaning the canals which was inherited from the Talpurs. So the canal department did not prove itself, and later British authorities who had built their careers in wetter parts of India tended to ignore the irrigation needs of a desert. Napier's canal department was abolished soon after he left.[21]

Napier's ultimate goal

Whatever the real effects of his rule, in his own mind Napier was trying to lay the foundations for progress. And his idea of progress also included improving the character of the people.

Other officials doubted that the character of the Sindhis could be changed in any way, and they dismissed the idea that Sindhis could ever become modern. Outram once remarked snidely that Napier wanted 'to make Anglo-Saxons out of Hindoos'.[22] He was not far off. The sons of the *jagirdars* would grow up under British rule and in a time of peace, Napier predicted. They would learn to reclaim the land, to engage in trade ('mercantile pursuits'), and make the country fruitful. As for the *ryots*: He said they had been no better than 'slaves' to the *zemindars* and the *jagirdars*, but as 'civilization advances' under his powerful but soon to be progressive *jagirdars*, the *ryots* 'will be enfranchised and enabled to live in comfort if industrious'.[23]

So Napier did believe that in sufficient time – and from what he said it does not seem that he believed it would take very long – the rural peoples of Sind would become self-sufficient, self-respecting citizens of the modern world, participating in their own governance. There was no room for racial distinctions, however astonished Napier himself was about how slowly the Sindhis could work on occasion.[24] In keeping with his nonracialist liberal vision, he looked forward to the Indians and the English beginning to merge into one population:

> It is not by '*moderation* but by *victory*' that we must hold India and as victors mix up with *the people*, give them justice, give them riches, give them honours, give them a share of all things till we blend with them and are one nation and cannot be overset. When a half-caste or a native can be governor-general we shall not hold India as a colony but we shall be inhabitants, and as numerous as required to hold our own.[25]

This was his ultimate vision for what Sind might someday become.

And yet Napier saw that his own ideas about human mutability and the crossing of skin-colour categories were increasingly unpopular among the British community in the India of his day. On the rise was a new concept of immutable, physically inherited racial identities.[26] Napier tells us that his officers – all much younger than he was –

> doubt the native character, and perhaps they are right: yet much nonsense is talked about the 'native character'; it is the human character, modified by political and religious influences for centuries. In a living military life I have been intimately acquainted with many nations, English, Irish, Scotch, French, German, Spanish, Portuguese, Italians, Greeks, Turks, American negroes, and East Indians – Hindoo and Mussulman. The human character has therefore been to me as a much-read book. . . .

> If we look to causes for variety of character we can generally trace those varieties to government and climate, not to difference of race. Let children of many races be brought up together in a country foreign to all and they will all be as the men of that country are.[27]

The new racism of his subordinates had its real effects, and Napier did his best to combat them. He knew that if he allowed his officers to book travel on the government merchant steamers, they would take all the best cabins and beat up the traders, so he insisted that his men take only military transport.[28] But he could not keep his officers away from the Sindhis on land as easily as he could on the Indus, and he could not keep them from treating the natives suspiciously and contemptuously. As he said: 'My policy is so little understood that I have even had trouble to keep my highest officers from making Willie Chandia revolt; they class all natives alike, as rascals, but they are not so.'[29]

The administrative legacy

Napier once tried to describe to one of his sisters how little real power he had – despite appearances of Oriental splendour:

> Behind [me] came the Mogul guards, about 800 cavalry, in splendid Asiatic costume. Then I see in coruscations of light on their bright sword blades from front to rear of their long array. Behind them marched 300 infantry, the old sun-bronzed soldiers of the 13th Regiment. . . . The Lukkee hills now cast their long shades, and the Keerta range reflected from its mountain rocks the most beautiful lights, while [with] the rear of the troops came the baggage of Headquarters and troops. Hundreds of loaded camels with Guards and drivers and grotesque attendants, all slowly winding amongst the hills. Suddenly a small camp was seen among the jungle. . . . The old man dismounted. . . . [H]e goes to work, write! write! write!, and *despatches* after *dispatches*. . . . Such is royal life here, my Emily, for it is grand and kingly to ride through this land that we have conquered, and with the men who fought with me, yet what is it all? If I were a real king there would be something in it.[30]

The problem was that Napier was too drawn in by the romance of the campaign. His failure to delegate his military duties and leave the active work of command to others meant that not all of his initiatives as governor could receive the full measure of his attention. He commanded the army by day and tried to do his work as governor in the night. Left too much on their own, his Collectors arranged some rather expensive contracts, and not all the money that his government was spending would lead to any notable result.[31]

Napier's immediate successor in the position, R. K. Pringle, did not long remain in the country, and so there is no comparison to be made with him.[32] But Pringle was replaced by a man who went on to achieve great fame and the approval

'To protect the poor from Barbarian Tyranny!' 261

of the historians for his work in Sind, Sir Bartle Frere. Frere did not think Napier had done such a good job outside running the military and the police. In Frere's opinion, and many agreed with him, Napier had neglected to ensure uniformity among the Collectors and Deputy Collectors, so everything was done differently by each of them. And Napier had overburdened his officials because he would not make adequate use of the *zemindars* in local administration.[33]

***

It is important to remember that Napier was an Irish patriot for whom *laissez-faire* capitalism meant mass starvation. As he told his brother in Black '47, the worst year in Irish history:

> The Irish affairs are terrible. I should like to ask Roebuck, and Lord John Russell, who won't interfere with private trade to save the starving thousands of Ireland, why they won't allow a poor boatman on the Thames, or a cabman on his stand, to charge their own prices? Adam Smith was a shrewd man, but theories will not always apply to extreme cases; the food that trains one man in health, kills one that is sick.[34]

By this point Sind had its first-ever grain surplus, and the country was now exporting grain to England – for Napier was not as incompetent as all that. He reduced rural taxes or rents from one-third to one-quarter. He even set up a system of microgrants for the poor, so they could afford to buy farm animals or other means of getting on with their lives. Loans for seed grain were designed to free small cultivators from the overlordship of village lenders, and loans for the working poor were instituted to help people in case of accident or temporary setback. (The idea for these small loans came from a practice in the English countryside, Napier said.)[35] With these improvements in food production, Napier was able to offer eleven thousand tons of grain at one-third the English market price to help fight starvation in Ireland. In the previous year Ellenborough had rejoined the Cabinet as First Lord of the Admiralty, and he and the Duke of Wellington tried to arrange for the transportation of Sindhi grain. But ultimately the authorities do not seem to have taken Napier up on the offer of food.[36] The fruits of his promotion of agriculture in Sind did not in fact go towards easing the hunger of the Irish.

In the end I do not think that Napier was the 'Don Quixote' character that Khuhro claims he was.[37] For rather than being random reflections of whatever might catch his attention, his achievements in Sind show instead a definite pattern. He made some progress in creating civil order, for he was able to directly apply force to that end, hanging the wife-murderers and reorganizing law enforcement. But he made rather less progress reengineering the class system, where he wound up increasing rather than decreasing the level of inequality. That tends to be how it goes – the abuses of human rights which shocked the Westerners, motivating or justifying their conquest, may be repressed with some success, and a measure of economic growth might be achieved; but the

262 'In Scinde as in Cephalonia . . .'

more creative aspects of nation-building tend not to go so well, not for a long time.[38] It is hard enough to understand the economic and political factors for creating social justice in one's own country, much less someone else's. And this may be especially true for liberals like Napier. As Edgardo Lander has explained the matter, liberalism tends to focus on safeguarding autonomous individuals and their freedom as economic actors, and at the same time it de-emphasizes the communitarian element of socioeconomic life in colonized countries – as Napier himself did when he misunderstood the traditional land system of Sind and turned the *jagirdars* into sole owners.[39]

It seems that Napier did achieve something nonetheless. In discussing William Napier's book on the Sind campaign, the Pakistani academic and critic Tariq Rahman has this to say:

> While [William's] rhetoric about civilizing missions is obviously a device to rationalize conquest, the fact remains that the Amirs of Sindh governed despotically. They did not have even the semblance of a rule of law nor did they establish ports, printing houses, railways, hospitals and modern institutions of learning though they did endow *madrassas*. The British did all these things and these were beneficial for the people.[40]

Yet Rahman adds that the old feudal system continued at the lower level, and through it the British ruled.[41] And that started with Napier, too.

Notes

1 Napier to Kennedy, 21 April 1845, Napier NP, TNA PRO 30/64/6, fols 21–22.
2 They continued after he left. Edward Archer Langley, *Narrative of a Residence at the Court of Meer Ali Murad, with Wild Sports in the Valley of the Indus*, 2 vols (London: Hurst and Blackett, 1860), 2:56–61.
3 Napier to Hobhouse, [?] 1846, given in WNAS, 301–20 at 307.
4 Hamida Khuhro, *The Making of Modern Sind: British Policy and Social Change in the Nineteenth Century* (Karachi: Oxford UP, 1999), 7, 91; Charles Napier quoted in WNAS, 308; Sind Commissioner's Office, *History of Alienations in the Province of Sind*, 2 vols (Karachi: Commissioner's Press, 1886–1888), 1:61.
5 Napier's journal, 10 March 1843, given in WN, 2:357.
6 WNAS, 37, 100–02, 108–11; Pringle, 'Report ', 4–5; Napier to Somerset, 26 May 1844, given in WN, 3:103–06.
7 Napier's journal, 12 April, given in WN, 3:83–84; Napier to Somerset, 26 May 1844, 3:103–06.
8 Statement by Captain Rathbone, Collector at Hyderabad, given in Sind Commissioner's Office, 'Revenue Queries by Mr. R. K. Pringle', 88–89.
9 Naomal Hotchand, *A Forgotten Chapter of Indian History as Described in the Memoirs of Seth Naomal Hotchand, C.S.I., of Karachi, 1804–1878*, (trans.) Alumal Trikamdas Bhojwani, H. Evan M. James (ed.) (Exeter: Printed for private circulation by W. Pollard, 1915), 141; Khuhro, *Making of Modern Sind*, 37; Sind Commissioner's Office, *History of Alienations*, 2:6; LNS, 208–12.
10 Ranajit Guha, *A Rule of Property for Bengal: An Essay on the Idea of Permanent Settlement* (1963; Durham, NC: Duke UP, 1996), 5, 50, 163–64; Bernard S. Cohn, *Colonialism and Its Forms of Knowledge: The British in India* (Princeton, NJ: Princeton UP, 1996), 59–62.

'To protect the poor from Barbarian Tyranny!' 263

11 As the late-eighteenth-century official John Shore was careful enough to note, who the *zemindars* were and what class they represented varied across the subcontinent – Guha, *A Rule of Property for Bengal*, 206–07. See also Andrew Sartori, *Liberalism in Empire: An Alternative History* (Berkeley and Los Angeles: University of California Press, 2014), 39–45; and Rachel Sturman, *The Government of Social Life in Colonial India: Liberalism, Religious Law, and Women's Rights* (Cambridge: Cambridge UP, 2012), 46, 55.

12 For this and the previous paragraphs: Feroz Ahmad, 'Agrarian Change and Class Formation in Sindh', *Economical and Political Weekly* 19, 39 (29 September 1984), A153-A156; Suhail Zahir Lari, *History of Sind* (Karachi: Oxford UP, 1994), 171–73; Khuhro, *Making of Modern Sind*, xvii–xviii, 2, 31–37, 89–94, 103–05, 151; Sind Commissioner's Office, *History of Alienations*, 1:10–11; James McMurdo, *McMurdo's Account of Sind*, Sarah Ansari (ed.) [1834] (Karachi: Oxford UP, 2007), 42.

13 David Washbrook, 'Economic Depression and the Making of 'Traditional' Society in Colonial India, 1820–1855', *Transactions of the Royal Historical Society*, sixth series, 3 (1993), 237–63; C. A. Bayly, *The New Cambridge History of the British Empire*, 2, 1, *Indian Society and the Making of Empire* (Cambridge: Cambridge UP, 1988), 148–52, 205; Pradipta Chaudhury, 'Peasants and British Rule in Orissa', *Social Scientist* 1, 8/9 (August-September 1991), 28–56; Eric Stokes, *The Peasant and the Raj: Studies in Agrarian Society and Peasant Rebellion in Colonial India* (Cambridge: Cambridge UP, 1978), 7–8, 31–33, 46–54, 103–09.

14 Linda Martin Alcoff, 'Mignolo's Epistemology of Coloniality', *CR: The New Centennial Review* 7, 3 (Winter 2007), 79–101 at 82. She is referencing Charles Mills, *The Racial Contract* (Ithaca, NY: Cornell UP, 1994), 18.

15 Ahmad, 'Agrarian Change and Class Formation in Sindh', A-153; Napier quoted in WNAS, 336–37.

16 Veena Talwar Oldenburg, *Dowry Murder: The Imperial Origins of a Cultural Crime* (New York: Oxford UP, 2002). See also Anshu Malhotra, *Gender, Caste, and Religious Identities: Restructuring Class in Colonial Punjab* (New Delhi: Oxford UP, 2002), 65–66; and Sturman, *The Government of Social Life in Colonial India*, 52–61, 99–101. For a South Indian example of how the British constituted male authority and property rights: G. Arunima, *There Comes Papa: Colonialism and the Transformation of Matriliny in Kerala, Malabar, c. 1850–1940* (Hyderabad: Orient Longman, 2003).

17 Napier, 'Circular to Collectors', 10 September 1846, given in Sind Commissioner's Office, *History of Alienations*, 1: 61–63; on honorary magistrates, ibid, 1:108, and WNAS, 251; Napier to Hobhouse, 1846, 301–20 at 312–13; see also 304–05. For 'yeomen', see Napier to Ellenborough, 19 December 1844, quoted in ibid, 353–60 at 358; Khuhro, *Making of Modern Sind*, 46–53, 91–92; LNS, 185. Napier was not the first to disapprove of the *zemindars*: McMurdo, *Sind*, 25. C. A. Bayly connects Napier's fondness for an agricultural yeomanry to the views of Thomas Maitland and the example of the Scottish yeomen – C. A. Bayly, *Imperial Meridian: The British Empire and the World, 1780–1830* (London and New York: Longman, 1989), 156–57. Against this we might weigh the fact that at age sixty-eight Napier had never once set foot in Scotland – Napier to Lieut. McFarlane, 1849, given in WN, 4:207–08.

18 Napier, marginal notes in two letters from Captain Preedy, 9 July 1847, and Captain Goldney, 12 July 1847, given in Sind Commissioner's Office, *History of Alienations*, 1:83–85.

19 Sind Commissioner's Office, *History of Alienations*, 1:24–27, 54–56, 2:44–45; Ahmad, 'Agrarian Change and Class Formation in Sindh', A-153; Khuhro, *Making of Modern Sind*, 37–45.

20 Napier to Richard Napier, [April] 1844, given in WN, 3:93–97 at 96.

21 Pringle, 'Report', 14–15. For the canal issue I rely heavily on Khuhro, *Making of Modern Sind*, xvii, xxvii, 2, 41, 45, 88, 150–62. See also Sind Commissioner's Office, *History of Alienations*, 2:67.

22 Outram, *Conquest*, 507n.

23 WNAS, 336.

264 'In Scinde as in Cephalonia . . .'

24 Napier's journal, 27 October 1844, given in WN, 3:156.
25 Napier's journal, 18 October 1846, NP, BL Add. MS 49140, fols 204–05.
26 David Arnold, 'Race, Place and Bodily Difference in Early Nineteenth-Century British India', *Historical Research* 77, 196 (May 2004), 254–75; Erica Ward, *Vice in the Barracks: Medicine, the Military, and the Making of Colonial India, 1780–1868* (Basingstoke: Palgrave Macmillan, 2014), 34–36, 96, 100–02, 137, 196–97.
27 Napier's journal, 21 February 1845, given in WN, 3:254–55.
28 Napier to W. Napier, 15 November 1846, given in ibid, 3:471–77 at 473.
29 LNS, 314.
30 Napier to Emily Bunbury, 29 November 1844, NP, BL Add. MS 49110, fol. 31.
31 LNS, 349.
32 Khuhro, *Making of Modern Sind*, xxxii–xxxiii, 19–20.
33 Ibid, 16, 21.
34 Napier to W. Napier, 25 March 1847, given in WN, 4:44–46.
35 Napier to Emily Bunbury, 24 October 1845, NP, BL Add. MS 49110, fols 54–62 at 58; Napier to Ellenborough, 19 December 1844, quoted in WNAS, 353–60 at 357; Napier to Hobhouse, [?] 1846, 301–20 at 313; Napier, notes to W. Napier, 1846, given WN, 4:23–24; LNS, 327–28. The Collector in Karachi gave out these loans more freely than the other Collectors – see statements by Captain Rathbone, Major Goldney, and Captain Preedy (the Collectors at Hyderabad, Shikarpur, and Karachi), given in Sind Commissioner's Office, 'Revenue Queries by Mr. R. K. Pringle', 68–69.
36 Napier to Kennedy, 8 March, 19 April 1847, NP, TNA PRO 30/64/6, fols 27–28, 33–34; WNAS, 325; WN, 4:63; Napier to W. Napier, 14 August 1847, 4:73–74.
37 Khuhro, *Making of Modern Sind*, xxix.
38 The difficulty of success in rebuilding a country after an invasion can militate against the argument for invading in the first place: Gary J. Bass, 'Jus Post Bellum', *Philosophy & Public Affairs* 32, 4 (2004), 384–412.
39 Edgardo Lander, *Neoliberalismo, sociedad civil y democracia: ensayos sobre América Latina y Venezuela* (Caracas: Universidad Central de Venezuela, Consejo de Desarrollo Científico y Humanístico, 2000), 180–82.
40 Tarik Rahman, ' "Brother-in-Arms": Review of William Napier, *The History of Sir Charles James Napier's Conquest of the Scinde*', *News on Sunday* (Karachi), 30 September 2001.
41 Rahman is not the only recent Pakistani scholar to argue that Napier's reforms were a good idea, even if he did not have the time or the means to carry them out. See Sahib Khan Channa, 'Charles Napier in Sindh: Challenges and Achievements', in Mohammed Qasim Soomro and Ghulam Muhammed Lakho (eds), *Sindh: Glimpses into Modern History*, Proceedings of the PHRIC on History of Sindh 1843–1999 (Jamshoro, Pakistan: Department of General History, University of Sindh, 2008), 59–91 at 61–62 – although by the end of the chapter the picture is not so clear (see 78–80).

20 Conflict and decline

After one thousand raiding tribesmen sacked and burned a village seventeen miles from Shikarpur on 1 April 1844, killing forty people, Napier had to turn his attention back to the security of the country.[1]

As he explained to John Kennedy, the local population had been driven away from the harvest and would not go back. The offending chiefs must 'either [be] made peace with or *exterminated*' – a step that he said he would avoid if he could.[2] At first he planned to buy off the tribes, but the Indian government refused to spend the money.[3] Another possibility was hostage-taking.[4] But Napier preferred a different and a broader strategy. Beyond the farthest line of Sindhi villages he thought of filling in the wells and creating a buffer zone between the farms and the hill country. He also hoped to capture and hang the offending tribal leader, Bijar Khan, if he could get him. He planned to send his forces into the hills during the cold weather and get the offending tribes to fight among themselves. Napier wanted the exact form of this expedition to be decided by those who knew the area, which he admitted that he did not.[5]

Then on 16 June 1844 a group of labourers cutting grass in the countryside for the Irregular Horse were attacked by the raiders. Two hundred people were all killed along with their military escorts. Another twenty villages were attacked soon after, and several hundred villagers were murdered.[6] An officer named MacKenzie was able to intercept and defeat one of the raiding parties. But at the same time another group of his own men attacked a group of unarmed villagers whom they were supposed to be protecting – so difficult was it to tell villagers from hill tribesmen. Many innocent people died.

In the aftermath of this disaster Napier had the judge-advocate general establish a court of inquiry at which the surviving villagers could testify. Napier reluctantly accepted the verdict of the inquiry that the massacre could not be justified, and there were no extenuating circumstances by which it might be excused. So he ordered that in future operations against the hill raiders, the local people should never appear outside their villages under arms unless they were under the command of their *kardar* and flying a flag with the name of the village in English and Persian. More proactively, Napier also raised a local battalion and offered the land belonging to some of the hill tribes to other

266 *'In Scinde as in Cephalonia . . .'*

groups in order to create blood feuds. Meanwhile, the raids continued into the autumn.[7]

Napier now prepared an expedition into the hills, and led it himself. He overestimated the forces standing against him, and he planned a very large operation.

The tribesmen were committing atrocities, killing scores.[8] But would Napier meet an atrocity with an atrocity? The hill tribesmen were '[c]oming down without provocation on our unhappy villagers, killing every man and woman, and cutting off little children's hands' for their bracelets, he wanted 'to destroy the habitations of those mountaineers and force them to settle further back'. 'These hill villains must be terrified; but I think we may also find gentle means to civilize them in time'. He would send them word that if they would be good neighbours he would forgive them all they had done, but if they refused 'their country would be destroyed' when the cold weather came.[9]

The disturbances continued and Napier decided that he had to pursue the military option. Yet he wanted to stop well short of carrying out what might be called *'razzias'* – the term for the French campaigns that were famously bringing death and destruction to the Algerian countryside in the early 1840s. The French laid waste to North African villages and whole stretches of the countryside with no attempt to resettle the original inhabitants as Napier wanted to do, and indeed masses of women and children were being hunted down and killed. The French military was already notorious for these campaigns of murder.[10] Lord Hardinge, when he was on his way out to India to become Governor-General, had mentioned 'the infamous French system of *Razzias* in Algiers' in a letter to his wife.[11]

Napier found a more principled strategy. He planned an elaborate campaign of deception and encirclement. Before going into the hills he assembled his troops in a large camp on the plain. He chose a location that was rather further from the hill tribes than anyone might expect. Here Napier entertained diplomatic missions from the countries further north. Why the odd location, and why receive envoys from so far away? Napier was carrying out a feint, trying to make everyone believe that he was planning an invasion of central Asia and not the hills at all. The deception had to be a general one that would fool Europeans and natives alike, as he explained to his brother Henry, because the tribal chiefs read translations of the newspapers 'and get the pith of everything'.[12] In other words, he had to fool the European community, too, trading on his reputation as a warmonger – a reputation about which he protested before God[13] – so that everyone would believe that he was about to launch himself into an invasion of who knows where. Then when his troops were in place for their real aim, he sent letters saying his men were sick when they were not. He added that his forces would not be able to move for months. He had these letters sent along routes where he knew they would be intercepted by the tribesmen.[14]

Having established this element of surprise, Napier struck. He sent his forces up several entrances to the mountain country, not directly in pursuit of the enemy but outflanking them on either side. He tried to seal up all the entrances to the mountains, and then he and his forces took large guns up a few of the defiles. Napier wanted to concentrate the various feuding populations into an ever-smaller area while taking their cattle for his own men. Then he hoped the offending tribesmen would become ever more crowded together and ever hungrier, and they would be ever likelier to fall out with one another. When the time was right and the women and children were reasonably safe, Napier would move in to defeat some of the raiders and reach agreements with the others.[15]

During the ensuing campaign, Napier tried very hard *not* to attack the hill tribesmen when they were too close to their families. He worried that the enemy would kill the women and children rather than seeing them captured by the foreign infidel.[16] So if it seemed that there were any women and children in the area, Napier would refrain from fighting. Sometimes the women and children themselves were captured by his scouts. They were fed and housed, and their personal effects were never taken from them. Napier later told his sister that if he had been less interested in saving their lives he could have gone in with guns blazing and John Bull would have called him a hero.[17]

In the end his strategy proved a success and there was no major fighting. In late February 1845 Napier and his men stumbled upon their remaining opponents, secreted together in a valley surrounded by tall walls of rock in a place called Truckee (Figure 20.1). Soon Napier's forces and those of Ali Murad had the enemy position entirely surrounded. Early the next month the starving raiders surrendered. They were then resettled, many of them east of the Indus, where they became farmers. Rather than being executed, the leaders were given *jagirs*. Bijar (or 'Beja') Khan, chief of the raiders, was captured at the end of the campaign, and with less nobility Napier wanted to hang him. But Ali Murad intervened and finally Napier came round. Bijar Khan would live under observation in Ali Murad's territory for the rest of his life.[18]

For the most part, Napier's personal role in the hill campaign ended in the spring of 1845, save for promoting the feuds – Napier sent one chief a stock of gunpowder. John Jacob was left to do the fighting and alliance-building in this area for the next dozen years. Soon he persuaded Napier to support him in recruiting the Boogties themselves as a local force and in providing food and supplies to their families.[19]

The First Sikh War and the aftermath

The question of how far to go in fighting a guerrilla population was to be an important issue in Napier's future. But his next military campaign raised no such questions. The Sikhs had invaded British territory in force. In response, in February 1846 Napier was ordered to bring as much of his army as he could and rendezvous with Hardinge in Punjab. Yet on his way north, Napier received fresh orders. They required him to deviate from the most direct route.

Napier had now been directed to move his troops sideways (as it were) to Bahawalpur, instead of marching straight to the ancient fortress city of Multan. He was not happy about this diversion. He now began spending an

Figure 20.1 Napier at Truckee in 1845: 'Lieutenant General Sir Charles James Napier, G.C.B. Governor of Scinde. In the costume he wore during his campaign against the Hill Tribes. The rocky fastness of Truckee with walls 1000 feet high, where he forced them to surrender, forms the background.' By 'Smart', lithographed by Edward Morton, published by Paul and Dominic Colnaghi. British Museum Number 1863,1017.81.

© The Trustees of the British Museum. All rights reserved

Conflict and decline 269

inordinate amount of time writing in his journal, outlining again and again what *ought* to be happening rather than what really was happening. So many times, he described what he would do at Multan if only he were allowed to go there; and he outlined the various military and personal deficiencies of those in charge for not letting him do so. They did not have the right number of troops in the right places, he thought.[20]

There were problems with the command structure, too. Henry Hardinge as Governor-General was the civilian commander to whom General Gough, the Commander-in-Chief of India, had to report. But Hardinge was himself an accomplished general. So he decided to act as Gough's second-in-command in the field in Punjab while nonetheless continuing to overrule Gough on military matters whenever they might touch on the larger political or strategic questions remaining in his purview as Governor-General. In order to address this very problem – the obvious confusion over who was in charge of the British forces – Hardinge wanted Napier to break off from his troops and become Gough's deputy in his place. All the while Ellenborough, as First Lord of the Admiralty, was pushing hard for Napier to be appointed commander outright. He considered forcing Napier down the throats of the Court of Directors by act of Parliament, but the rest of the cabinet did not relish trying to pass a bill of that kind.[21]

Despite all these machinations, in fact Hardinge and Gough had won the war by the time Napier arrived in the Sikh capital at the beginning of March.

In Lahore, Napier and Hardinge now met for the first time. Despite all the complaining which he had been doing in his journal and the letters to William, Napier was impressed with the Governor-General when they met. There were substantial consultations. Napier and Gough both advised Hardinge against annexing Punjab and to restore a measure of Sikh independence, and this is what Hardinge did.[22]

Napier now went back to Sind. But for the next year he continued to review every inch of what might have been. He would write voluminously about every operational detail of the expedition to Multan that he had been ordered to abandon. And in the midst of these prolonged letters and journal entries, he also allowed himself to rehearse again and again all he had to say against Outram and his other critics. Covering that ground again and again, Napier now spent an amazing amount of time building a mountain of truly unbalanced private writing – over and above all the time he had to spend on his official reports and letters. He produced justification after justification for his military plans for Punjab, his conquest of Sind, and his use of the death penalty. He also began to write – constantly – about his own illnesses and presentiments of imminent death. Perhaps those presentiments help to explain something. The repetitiousness, the prolixity, and the self-pity of his letters and journals from the period after the end of the Punjab war, and indeed for the rest of 1846 and early 1847, are unlike anything else Napier ever wrote. The anti-Adam book was a far cleaner and saner production, and indeed it was full of interesting and powerful material – in comparison to this flood of repetitive complaints to friends and family.

270   'In Scinde as in Cephalonia . . .'

Napier wrote and wrote. Moreover, he was worn down as well by his rheumatism, the terrible heat, and the old war wound from Busaco, which had left him in some pain (it was worse when he had a cold) for thirty-six years.[23]

And griefs began to mount. In the summer of 1846 cholera came back to Karachi. It killed seven thousand people – over a third of the town and cantonment. Sixty thousand more died in the surrounding countryside. The dead included Napier's nephew John (George Napier's son), and John's small child. Napier was heartbroken, but for all his private sorrow the general visited every ill soldier twice each day, covering more than twenty miles in the intense heat to get between all the hospitals. There were the old deaths to grieve for as well. In 1846 and 1847 seemingly every anniversary of a death or a battle all the way back to the Napoleonic period sent Napier into still more hours of introspective writing. 'I think I am breaking up', he said in a letter to John Kennedy, 'I do not get thro [sic] work to my own satisfaction at all.'[24]

The gloom was lifted only slightly when he learned that he was made lieutenant-general in November (this was another promotion that was automatic because of his seniority).[25] He said he had little use for promotions and honours. 'You all set me up at much too high a value', he told his sister: 'You see the world agrees with me that I have done well, but nothing to brag of; and [I] have been very well paid, as all Indian officers are.' Not everyone at home thought even so highly of him as all that. Outram's book attacking him – and refuting much of what William had been publishing in his favour – had arrived in Sind in the autumn. Napier did not read it himself. He had his officers do so and point out the flaws.[26]

***

By mid-1847, Lady Napier's health too was very poor. It was clear for some time that the Napiers would have to leave Sind.[27] Napier had been thinking about resigning with every hot season, staying on for the last year only to finish out the five, and so he could see through the job of sending most of the extra regiments out of the country. That way he could show everyone that Sind would remain at peace when he did go.[28] Finally he wrote to his brother on 4 July 1847,

> I have resigned. My wife has nearly died. Seventeen days and nights I nursed her. She must not stay. Her danger has cured my ailings, my strength has returned; and there is need of it, for from Bombay comes every petty insult.[29]

Napier handed off to his successor on 30 September.

***

When Napier left India, Hardinge confessed having to 'manage [him] for 3 1/2 years'. 'I have done this', Hardinge wrote,

> by the most frank & friendly communications, defending him on all occasions when I could. . . . With gt. merit he is wild and *enteté*, and with

his temper soured by the Indian press he is at 65 a little crazy, still full of fire, & all his eccentricities are of an honourable character. . . . Dalhousie [the next Governor-General] will rejoice to find him out of his way. He has left Scinde in good-humour with this government & Hobhouse, his wrath being, how[eve]r, still unappeased agt. Outram.[30]

Wellington wanted to make Napier a Field Marshal; it seems Napier never learned of this. Hobhouse, an old Philhellene and friend of Byron, and now for the second time the President of the Board of Control, wanted to make Napier Commander-in-Chief of India. In spring 1847 Napier and Hardinge had already discussed this as a possibility, but Napier said he could not wait through the two more hot seasons before Lord Gough was due to leave in the latter part of 1848. Meanwhile most of the cabinet wanted nothing to do with either promoting Napier to Field Marshal or making him commander in India. They were afraid of offending the senior generals over whom he would have to be promoted if he were given a marshal's baton, and they knew the East India Company would have a hard time accepting Napier of all people – the scheming Ellenborough's choice for conquering Sind – as their Commander-in-Chief.[31]

So Napier did not become Commander-in-Chief – not yet. With bands playing, on 1 October 1847 he set sail from the Karachi Mole (which he had built). Earthly glory and its transitoriness were much on his mind as he left India. He wrote about how he could conquer an empire stretching from Constantinople to Peking, bringing free speech, economic equality, and prosperity if only he were thirty – and if only he had absolute power in India itself as his base. But when he laid out these fantastic scenarios he checked himself with a cry of 'Vanity'.[32]

Napier was never devoid of self-awareness regarding the strange position of the British in Sind. As he had told John Kennedy in 1844:

[P]eople thought I was of [the] opinion that we had *the love* of the Beloochis: we who are of a different religion, strangers and [who] have killed one or two members of every family in the land! *Love* I must have been a nice idiot if I had any such idea. No I trusted to their loving *themselves* and a shilling pay rather than three half-pence, and the latter paid in *grain, too,* for the Ameers never paid in *money* for any *thing in* Scinde.[33]

Notes

1　LNS, 277
2　Napier to Kennedy, 23 July 1844, NP, TNA PRO 30/64/6, fols 14–19, quotation at 14.
3　Napier to Ripon, 25 June 1844, PBC, BL Add. MS 40868, fols 378–85 at 381; also given in WN, 3:113–20 at 115.
4　Napier to George Arthur, [?] February 1844, given in WN, 3:38.
5　LNS, 277–78.
6　Napier to Emily Bunbury, 29 November 1844, NP, BL Add. MS 49110, fols 31–34.
7　Napier to W. Napier, November 1844, given in WN, 3:171–76 at 175; LNS, 283–85; H. T. Lambrick, *John Jacob of Jacobabad*, 2nd edn (Karachi: Oxford UP, 1975), 110–11; general

272   *'In Scinde as in Cephalonia . . .'*

order, 6 November 1844, given in Edward Green (ed.), *Compilation of the General Orders, &c., Issued in 1842–47, by Sir Charles Napier, G.C.B., Major-General Governor of Scinde, to the Army under His Command* (Bombay: James Chesson at the *Times* Press, 1850), 98–99.

8 Napier's nephew and aide-de-camp William Napier to Emily Cephalonia Napier, 5 January 1844, NP, BL Add. MS 49152, fols 15–17; quotations from Napier to W. Napier, [?] April 1844, given in WN, 3:88–90; Napier to Broadfoot, 2 January 1845, Broadfoot Papers, BL Add. MS 40127, fols 269–70; Napier to Ripon, 14 January 1845, PBC, BL Add. MS 40871, fols 143–46.

9 Napier to W. Napier, [?] April and 23 April 1844, given in WN, 3:88–91.

10 Jennifer Pitts (ed. and trans.), *Alexis de Tocqueville: Writings on Empire and Slavery* (Baltimore, MD: Johns Hopkins UP, 2001), xxii–xxiii, xxviii, 40.

11 Hardinge to his wife, 5 July 1844, given in Bawa Satinder Singh (ed.), *My Indian Peregrinations: The Private Letters of Charles Stewart Hardinge, 1844–1847* (Lubbock: Texas Tech UP, 2001), 26–27.

12 Napier to W. Napier, given in WN, 18 December 1844, 3:198–201; Napier to Henry Napier, December 1844, 3:201–04.

13 Napier's journal, 9 December 1844, given in WN, 3:191.

14 Napier's nephew and aide-de-camp William Napier to Emily Cephalonia Napier, 17 January 1845, NP, BL Add. MS 49152, fols 44–47; Napier to Jacob, 8 January 1845, printed in John Jacob's proof pages for 'Papers Regarding the First Campaign against the Predatory Tribes of Cutchee in 1839–40, and Affairs of the Sinde Frontier', H. T. Lambrick Papers, BL A&AS MSS Eur F208/99, 19–20.

15 WNAS, 176–77, 189, 194, 200–01, 209; Napier to W. Napier, 12 January 1845, given in WN, 3:212–14; WN, 3:211–12; Napier to Ripon, 14 January 1845, PBC, BL Add. MS 40871, fols 43–46; Hardinge to his wife, 20 February 1845, given in Singh (ed.), *Letters of Hardinge*, 52–55; C. Hardinge to James, 9 March 1845, given in Singh (ed.), *Indian Peregrinations*, 36–37. For other occasions when Napier insisted that women and children had to be saved even in the midst of battle, see Napier to Henry Gee Roberts, 6 March 1843, Henry Gee Roberts Papers, BL A&AS MSS Eur 265/2, fols 16–17; and Napier to John William Younghusband, Younghusband Papers, 13 July, 29 July 1847, BL A&AS MSS Eur F197/42, fols 1–2, 3–4.

16 Napier's nephew and aide-de-camp William Napier to Emily Cephalonia Napier, 3–5 March 1845, NP, BL Add. MS 49152, fols 126–31 at 130.

17 WNAS, 177–78, 195–97, 219, 225; Napier's journal, 13 January, 20 January, 23 January, 30 January, 1 March, 6 March 1845, given in WN, 3:214, 223–24, 227, 231, 264–66; Napier to Louisa Napier, 10 August 1846, Bodleian MS Eng. lett. c. 240, fols 207–09.

18 Napier to Emily Bunbury, 24 October 1845, NP, BL Add. MS 49110, fols 54–62 at 57; Laing's journal, various entries, March 1845, given in Eaton, 'Journal of Laing', 86–88; Napier's nephew and aide-de-camp William Napier to Emily Cephalonia Napier, 3–5 March 1845, NP, BL Add. MS 49152, fols 126–31, and 6–10 March, fols 132–38; Virendra Kumar, *India under Lord Hardinge* (New Delhi and Allahabad: Rajesh Publications, 1978), 123–25.

19 LNS, 297; Lambrick, *John Jacob*, 126–27, 136–45; Napier to W. Napier, 4 June 1845, given in WN, 3:300–01; John Martineau, *The Life and Correspondence of the Right Hon. Sir Bartle Frere*, 2nd edn, 2 vols (London: John Murray, 1895), 1:145, 150–52.

20 Napier's journal, 1, 6 January, 5 February 1846, NP, BL Add. MS 49140, fols 87–88, 93, 119–20.

21 Hardinge to Gough (copy), 26 January 1846. NP, B Add. MS 54517, fol. 216; Hardinge to Peel, 30 December 1845; given in Charles Stuart Parker (ed.), *Sir Robert Peel from His Private Papers*, 3 vols (London: John Murray, 1899), 3:296–300 at 299–300; Hardinge to Peel, 4 March 1846, 3:310.

22 Napier would come to favour the annexation of Punjab itself, to stabilize the situation and 'fix peace in India for 100 years', thereby crowning Hardinge's achievements. Hardinge

Conflict and decline 273

to James, 19 [January 1847], given in Singh (ed.), *Letters of Hardinge*, 203–04; Napier to Hardinge, 11 March 1847, NP, TNA PRO 30/64/6, fols 31–32.

23 Napier's journal, 27 September 1846, NP, BL Add. MS 49140, fol. 184.

24 Napier to W. Napier, given in WN, 9 May 1846, 3:422–29; Napier to Kennedy, 26 December 1846, NP, TNA PRO 30/64/6, fols 25a-25b.

25 *The Times*, 14 September 1846, 5 cols a-b; Napier to W. Napier, 8 January and 11 February 1847, given in WN, 4:31–32, 36–38; Napier's journal, 10 January, 32–33; *London Gazette*, 10 November 1846, 20660 p. 3987.

26 Napier to Louisa Napier, 10 August 1846, Bodleian MS Eng. lett. c. 240, fols 207–09; Napier to Henry Napier, August 1846, given in WN, 3:442–45.

27 Hardinge to his wife, 23 July 1847, given in Singh (ed.), *Letters of Hardinge*, 225–26; Emily Cephalonia Napier to Louisa Napier, 7 September 1846, 18 October/2 November 1846, NP, BL Add. MS 49158, fols 57–58 and fols 59–62.

28 Napier to W. Napier, 19 September 1843, given in WN, 2:431–36 at 432; [15?] December, 3:18–20; [?] June 1844, 3:106–10 at 108; Napier's journal, 10 January 1847, 4:33; Napier to W. Napier, 11 February, 8 March 1847, 4:36–40; Napier to Kennedy, 26 December 1846, NP, TNA PRO 30/64/6, fols 25a-25b.

29 Napier to W. Napier, 4 July 1847, given in WN, 4:73.

30 Hardinge to James, 3 December 1847, given in Singh (ed.), *Letters of Hardinge*, 238–43 at 239.

31 Robert E. Zegger, *John Cam Hobhouse: A Political Life, 1819–1852* (Columbia, MO: University of Missouri Press, 1973), 269–70; Napier to Hardinge, 11 March 1847, NP, TNA PRO 30/64/6, fols 31–32.

32 Napier's journal, 12 December 1846, NP, BL Add. MS 49140, fols 240–41; 29 August, 9 September 1849, given in WN, 3:463, 4:186, 188–89.

33 Napier to Kennedy, 23 July 1844, NP, TNA PRO 30/64/6, fols 14–19, quotation at 16.

Part VI

Commander-in-Chief

21 Home and back

On their way home from India on the eve of what would be a year of revolution, Napier and his family stopped for a time in Nice, which after 1814 was part of the Kingdom of Sardinia. There they spent the Christmas of 1847. George Napier was there, too. The English community of the city gave Charles a grand ball, and with his 'great nose and eagle eyes, and immense beard and mustachios' he was the star of the New Year's receptions and the Governor's *conversazione* (Figure 21.1).[1]

Danger loomed. After violence erupted in Paris in the new year, Charles Napier – still in Nice – wrote to John Kennedy:

> Great events have been succeeding each other like flashes of lightning. Tyranny has got such a shake as has taught our Rulers in this world that the people they have misgoverned will bear these things no longer. I am delighted at this tolerably broad hint. I think our own constitution can bear the momentary strain upon it without snapping and will be improved.

But as usual Napier was on the side of reform *and* order, and he was against bloodshed. He continued:

> I hope our government will teach . . . a lesson . . . that there are better ways to relieve a miserable people than that of deluging the land with their blood. Lord Edward Fitzgerald was sanctioned in his conduct, if rebellion ever was, by the atrocity of the Irish government. . . . There is now no cause for violence. The government *may err* but it seeks to do right if it can.[2]

Because Napier's daughter Emily had a serious lung complaint, the Napiers remained in Nice while she went with her husband to Pisa for treatment. Charles Napier said that if he rushed back to England now he would be leaving his wife and daughters with no protection on the Continent, with Italy as 'disturbed' as France. So as the first revolutions of the year gathered steam – the disturbances in France had begun in February, with outbreaks in Milan and Venice in March – Napier stayed where he was. He read the several volumes of Thier's history of the first French revolution, and he arranged his papers so he could rebut the criticisms levelled by Outram (Figure 21.2).

Figure 21.1 Self-representation: Napier's *carte de visite*. Printed by Henry Lenthall after a photograph by William Edward Kilburn, 1853 or before. NPG Number Ax17787.

© National Portrait Gallery, London

Figure 21.2 Self-representation represented: Napier writing. By Edwin Williams, 1849. NPG Number 1369.

© National Portrait Gallery, London

In his correspondence with his brother William, Napier discussed the possibility of a civil war breaking out in the United Kingdom. Each man would have to take sides, and his would be the side of order and good governance, he said.[3] Soon he began to wonder whether he might be sent for by the British government and put to work keeping the peace. Indeed, he even allowed himself the hope that he might be sent to the Ionian Islands in some capacity.[4] No such offer came.

***

280 Commander-in-Chief

In the middle of May 1848 Napier and family arrived at Portsmouth. The officers of the garrison and the marines in full uniform received him at the town hall, with the mayor and corporation in attendance. The *Times* carried a short account.[5] Apparently when he was in Sind he had become someone (Figure 21.3). In London there was a long round of receptions and speeches in his honour. Sir Robert Peel toasted him at a dinner at Lord Londonderry's house and said many flattering things.[6] Napier was exhausted by all the parties and politeness. He wrote in his journal on 25 May that he got no pleasure from the social round except for how it must have galled the East India Company to see him celebrated in this way. He also noted (inaccurately, as it turned out) that he would never make another entry in his journal after that one, for his active life was over.

The dinners continued into the autumn.[7] William Napier wrote that despite the glittering outward appearances, not one of the gatherings to honour Charles was good enough. Each had been tainted in some way by the old conspiracy to minimize all credit to the Napier family. Either that, or the gatherings were not

Figure 21.3 Representation by others: Napier's bust in a contemporary engraving. Engraving by William Henry Egleton after the posthumous bust by George Gammon Adams, taken from the death mask. Published by John Murray, 1857. NPG Number D38463.

© National Portrait Gallery, London

Home and back 281

reported widely enough in the newspapers – that was part of the conspiracy, too. When William looked back on the matter a few years later, he recalled that his own speech at the Junior United Service Club, detailing all the ways that his brother had been wronged, was to his amazement not even reported on at all.[8] By contrast here are Charles's observations of the very same occasion:

> Oct. 11. – A large public dinner. Lord Ellenborough's speech excellent; he told the Indian civilians, many of whom were present, that he did not like them: The Times would not insert any of the speeches, though their reporter was present.[9]

So not even Charles reported what William said.

In between all the dinners and addresses, Napier and his family spent part of the summer in Bath. From there he observed the unsettled events in Punjab very carefully.[10] By the end of the year of revolution, he had planted himself in the distinctly unrevolutionary environment of Cheltenham. He here settled into his retirement, leasing a house. The people of the town received him with another 'public feed' – 'how I hate these effusions of fish and folly', he said. He attended nonetheless. He did enjoy how the old soldiers would come and discuss their long-ago battles and how small their pensions were. How old they looked to him! And how old he looked to himself, he told his sister.[11]

***

Between all the dinners and the old soldiers and the horse-riding, which he enjoyed, Napier wrote a pamphlet on the way to handle baggage in the Indian army. The army baggage trains – a travelling bazaar with vendors, camel drivers, bearers and their families, and prostitutes – were huge affairs and they required protection in battle. In Sind, Napier reduced the personal effects which each officer might carry to three camel-loads. He also created an army baggage corps rather than continuing to allow the soldiers to hire their own bearers. The camels would have medallions hung around their necks to establish their weight class and the cargo they might carry without injuring themselves. Their drivers, now a part of the army, would be able to form up into defensive squares ready to shoot outward from the lines of kneeling animals, and so keep could themselves safe and out of the way when fighting came. In a poetic touch, Napier created a system of colour-coded lighthouses mounted on elephants and particular tom-tom rhythms that were played so the different units could find each other and mount up in the dust and darkness of the wee hours of the morning. Each unit in the baggage corps had its own colour of livery for its elephant which matched the colour of light from the lantern. By day or night, one followed one's elephant.

Moving the army required about 20,000 camels and a column fifty miles long, Napier explained; all the water for the men and animals had to be carried by the camel-load, and everything else besides, including a field hospital. The soldiers at the front of the column would be making camp before the rear

282   *Commander-in-Chief*

of the column carrying their supplies had left the previous campsite – for the
army could never travel anything like fifty miles in a day. Napier argued that
his soldiers, having walked perhaps thirty miles carrying weapon, bayonet, and a
pouch of heavy shot, should not have to wait so long for their water and basic
necessities. They were 'under a burning sun' for the latter part of the march, and
they were left in the sun for a time when they made camp so far in advance
of their tents. He said that what the soldiers of India suffer on foot the officers
on horseback forget. So reducing the size of the baggage train and increasing
efficiency in moving the army was of real importance.[12]

***

The attention that Napier paid to baggage is the more notable because this
pamphlet was the only material he would ever publish on his first period in the
east. He never wrote about the old quarrels with Outram. William could not
understood that. He would send Charles letter after letter on who might have
criticized him in the *Times*. Yet to William's consternation, Charles always
remained willing to talk to these supposed critics whenever he met them in
person. William was scandalized. Why would he not fight his enemies more
furiously?[13] On one of William's letters about the machinations of their supposed enemies, Napier simply noted that his brother did not understand the
politics involved.[14]

It is amusing to reflect on William when he came to write his multi-volume
life of Charles several years later. For all the slurs that he detected against Charles
in the press over the outbreak of the war or the question of the prize money,
which it took Charles some time to get,[15] Charles's own letters and journals from
this period never allude to the anti-Napier campaign in the press in any way. But
William never once stops to think about the contrast between Charles's own measured comments – as William himself so innocently presents them in the course
of his narrative – and the apocalyptic account of an organized conspiracy against
the Napiers and all they stand for that he describes in the same pages.[16]

***

And then William convinced himself that his brother was planning to fight
a duel with one of the Directors of the East India Company. He confessed
his suspicions to Charles's equally hot-headed son-in-law, William McMurdo,
who became convinced of it, too. So the two choleric Williams conferred
with each other about how to stop this affair of honour. On balance they did
not think that a duel would be the best thing for Charles's reputation. A duel
would give further ammunition (as it were) to the legions of anti-Charles con-
spirators, those who argued that Charles Napier was a violent man.

And *this* in the minds of the brother and the son-in-law was indeed the
main problem with Charles Napier duelling – that people might think him
violent. It was not a matter of life and death, but of public relations.

Yet there is no evidence that Charles was thinking of a duel at all. The last
time he had mentioned that he would like to challenge one of his critics to

mortal combat was four years in the past, in 1844, and on that occasion he only mentioned it – privately, in a letter to William – in order to say that he did *not* think he would have to fight the man (Sir Henry Pottinger). He stressed that he certainly did not want William or anyone else to fight the duel for him, either, or to get hurt.[17] Would a duel have crossed his mind even in 1844 if he did not have to calm his brother?

Now in January 1849, Charles directly challenged William. He denied that any conspiracy that might exist on the part of those disapproving of his behaviour in Sind – critics such as George Buist in the *Times* – needed to be worried about so very obsessively:

> I have always an idea of what you expect, viz., the directors trumping up some accusation against me. But they can do nothing because I have done nothing wrong. That you will say goes for nothing! But I am covered by Lord Ellenborough's and Lord Hardinge's orders: I was always a second fiddle, not a first. I am not afraid of them: let them do their worst.[18]

Napier was more interested in the recent military news coming out of India. The news was not good. As they discussed it back and forth, Charles and his brother made elaborate plans for what they might do if they were in charge. Charles fantasized about going back to India as Governor-General with William as his Commander-in-Chief. That is to say, he fantasized about this in concert with William but not with anyone else.[19]

Keeping his mind occupied was important. Sometimes he was in agonizing physical pain. The Busaco wound in his face and jaw could produce an almost unbearable feeling of suffocation. 'I am obliged to get up at night and light a candle', he told William. '[I]f I remained in the dark I should go mad; the light relieves me, yet I live in terror lest it should come on violently.'[20]

The return to India

Eventually the crisis in Punjab threatened to turn into a disaster.

After its defeat by the British under Lord Hardinge, the Punjab was allowed to remain an independent state. It was ruled by a changing set of Sikh military figures trying to keep the allegiance of their mercenary army. With thirteen million people, the country had nine times the population of the sparsely farmed Sind.[21] (So the population of Punjab was only about three million shy of that of England and Wales in the census of 1841.) As a defeated power, the Sikhs had been made to reduce their army, surrender territory, pay an indemnity, and accept a measure of British control, with their government placed under the influence of the British Resident, an East India Company army officer by the name of Henry Lawrence.

In 1848, Lawrence went on leave, and Lord Dalhousie, the new, thirty-five-year-old Governor-General of India who had succeeded Hardinge, appointed a civilian as Lawrence's temporary replacement. This man managed to provoke an anti-British rising in Multan which soon drew in the Afghans. The British-influenced government of Punjab made no effective response. Rebellions broke out elsewhere in Punjab and a general war was at hand between the Company and the Sikhs.

The British commander sent to Punjab was again Lord Gough, still the Commander-in-Chief of India as he had been during the First Sikh War. But Lord Dalhousie, with no military background and barely a year's experience in India, quickly joined Gough's army to supervise and indeed intervene in the conduct of the hostilities. In acting in this extraordinary way, inserting himself although he was a civilian into the operational conduct of the war, it seems that Dalhousie was trying to limit the power of a Commander-in-Chief who everyone told him was 'unfit' and 'uncontrollable' (and Dalhousie wanted to replace Gough). Writing to William some years before, Charles Napier had called Gough 'a brave idiot', though he would always praise Gough in public.[22]

With no effective leadership on the British side, the war with the Sikhs dragged on. Soon Wellington and the cabinet decided to change commanders. For several months Charles Napier's name was bandied about, but each time the Court of Directors quashed the idea. (The Court did not have the authority to name the Commander-in-Chief itself, but once the government made its selection, the Court had to appoint the new Commander-in-Chief a member of the Governor-General's Council.) Several other names were discussed without much enthusiasm — even that of Frederick Adam, who had put himself forward. Early in 1849 Charles Napier's brother George, former governor of the Cape, was proposed by the government and accepted by the Directors. George Napier would indeed have become the Indian Commander-in-Chief except that when he was finally heard from, for he was still living at Nice, he turned down the position, pleading bladder trouble. Next to be appointed, strangely, was the officer who had been Napier's (very short-term) successor in the Northern District, Sir William Gomm. Gomm was chosen for India despite his reputation as a very silly man. But Gomm was accepted by all concerned, and a letter of appointment was sent to him in Mauritius where he was serving as governor.

Then came word of the Battle of Chillianwalla, which had been fought in January. It was no better than a draw, and yet Gough's force suffered nearly 2,500 casualties, including more than 850 killed or missing. As Dalhousie commented, incurring that many casualties in one day showed 'total incompetence' on Gough's part, whether the result was a victory or not. Another such victory would be fatal.[23] A new commander was urgently required, a commander who knew what he was doing. The editor of the *Times*, John Thadeus Delane, told Hobhouse at the Board of Control that Napier ought to be sent instead of Gomm.

Delane predicted that Gomm would be vilified and mocked in the press.[24] And on this point Delane was as good as his word. He published a leading article on 5 March pointing out that Gomm had held no military post in thirty-five years. His appointments had all been civil or administrative. Meanwhile

General Gough was throwing soldiers at the enemy without much concern for strategy or the lives of his men – that was always the complaint about him. He attacked but he did not think. The *Times* demanded the appointment of Charles Napier as the one man most respected by the soldiers and most feared by enemy. The newspaper also told the Court of Directors that they needed to get over any pique they might feel about having to accept Napier – unpleasant though it would be for Directors themselves to have to employ a man who had criticized them so, and 'who possesses a tongue and a pen as sharp and as reckless as his sword'. 'He will have both his way and his say, and there is no holding him in,' said the *Times*, but he was worth five thousand soldiers, and 'his coolness, his skill, his science, and his success' made him indispensable if the East India Company wanted to retain hold on to the Indian Empire.[25]

There were caricatures of Napier as Cincinnatus at his plough approached by the chagrined Directors, or riding a chariot back into public life, pulled by the same embarrassed men. In *Punch*, William Makepeace Thackeray (who knew George Napier[26]) wrote a pastiche called the 'Story of Koompanee Jehan' (that is to say John Company, a familiar name for the East India Company and the British Raj). Koompanee Jehan had amassed an empire '[b]y picking endless quarrels, in which he somehow always *seemed* to be in the right'. Then news came to the city of Lundoon on the isle of Ingleez that Goof Bahawder (General Gough) had been beaten, and yet the men of the Hall of Lead (the headquarters of the East India Company were in Leadenhall Street) balked at sending out 'Napeer Singh', even though he was the best general of the land after Wellingtoon. Napeer Singh had once beaten 30,000 of the enemy with a force of 2,000. He 'had a beak like an eagle and a beard like a Cashmere goat':

> But this lion, though the bravest of animals, was the most quarrelsome that ever lashed his tail and roared in a jungle. After gaining several victories he became so insolent and contemptuous in his behaviour towards the King Koompanee Jehan, whom he insulted, whom he assailed, whom he called an old woman, that the offended monarch . . . vowed no more to employ him.[27]

But the Ingleez people would have no other commander.

***

A perhaps apocryphal story has grown up about Napier's appointment as Commander-in-Chief of India: the Duke of Wellington was asked to submit three possible names to the government. He chose 'Sir Charles Napier. Sir Charles Napier. Sir Charles Napier.'[28] We know that the Duke of Wellington certainly did back Napier for the position all the way through this period in late 1848 and early 1849, summoning him up from Cheltenham on 29 January – but telling him when he got to Apsley House that the Directors had balked at giving him the job after all. Meanwhile, whenever Napier tried to walk in the streets of London he was followed by crowds of strangers who wanted him to go and sort out Punjab; and when he and his wife sat in their carriage outside a

286 *Commander-in-Chief*

shop the crowds would gather around to cheer him – or so he tells us.[29] On or even before 5 March, the day of Delane's leading article, the government went ahead and made the decision to appoint Napier in preference to the already appointed Gomm, who was to be given command in Bombay instead.[30]

Napier was now sixty-six and increasingly he felt his age. His health had been bad and in February he began taking chloroform at night for the agony in his liver. He did not want to go to India. Wellington told him that if he did *not* go, then he, the Duke of Wellington, would have to go himself.[31] Napier asked to be made Governor-General as well as Commander-in-Chief, but he did not insist upon this, and nor did he bring the matter up again when nothing came of it. He then had to decide whether to accept the position of Commander by itself. He talked to his friends. Ellenborough advised him to hold out for extraordinary powers. Hardinge told Napier to ask for no such thing, and this was the advice that Napier took. After one day he accepted the appointment.[32]

The Prime Minister at the time was the same Lord John Russell who as Home Secretary had kept such a distance from Napier in the Chartist period. In their meeting now, he told Napier that the Court of Directors was looking for some reason, some precedent which they could use to give him the command *without* appointing him to the seat on the Supreme Council of India which was occupied by all previous Commanders-in-Chief. William had warned Charles that the Directors might try something of the kind. Charles Napier reported that he at once told the Prime Minister 'explicitly and peremptorily' – as we might well imagine him doing – that he would not go to India without being made a member of the Council.[33]

***

In the final analysis, the Directors of the East India Company were not the British government. The Prime Minister announced Napier's appointment in the House of Commons on 6 March even though the Court of Directors had yet to agree.[34] Lord John intimated to the Directors that continuing to resist the government in this matter would be bad for their interests in the House of Commons. The Directors bowed to official if not to popular pressure, and on 7 March they gave Napier his council seat with only three votes against. Hobhouse as President of the Board of Control wrote Napier the good news that afternoon.[35] John Kennedy was authorized to rejoin the army as a major and go out to India as Napier's secretary. Napier's aides-de-camp would include his son-in-law William McMurdo; his other son-in-law and nephew William C. E. Napier; and even a young man named Bunbury. (William C. E. Napier had also been Napier's aide-de-camp in the north of England.)[36]

A surprise

Charles Napier left England on 24 March 1849. It took him fourteen days to get to Alexandria, four days to get from there to Suez and re-embark, and over two weeks more to reach Calcutta, forty-three days after he left London.

Napier then journeyed through the terrible heat to reach Simla, where he had never been.[37] He describes the beautiful wooded mountains around and underneath the city, with the clouds floating in the deep valleys below. He noted how the clouds would sometimes pass through the room and dampen his beard, which he was growing out again. But the more troubling side effect of the altitude was that with his facial wound he had trouble breathing. He had to stop and draw a long breath every five minutes.[38]

He had a pleasant reception. As Lord Dalhousie wrote to a friend on 25 June:

> Sir Charles Napier has been living with me for a week. He has faced the terrible journey from Calcutta, in such a season as has rarely been known, without much harm, and I hope will remain here. He is a most agreeable inmate. We have had long and frequent conversations. I spoke to him very frankly on our relative positions,– he seems quite satisfied – so am I, and I do not anticipate any embarrassment from him, or any conflict between us in our respective jurisdictions.[39]

But why was Napier not at the front? There was one very good reason why he did not immediately take command in Punjab as he had been appointed to do. Gough had won a major battle and the war that Napier was sent out to fight was over before he arrived. Napier reached Calcutta just in time to attend the victory service. Dalhousie had already annexed Punjab, seized the Koh-i-nor Diamond for Queen Victoria, and accepted an advancement in the peerage, to become first Marquess.[40]

In a sense Napier was relieved, or at least his conscience was:

> It is a subject of gladness to me not to have commanded at Goojerat: I might not have been able to control that love of war which a certain consciousness of being able to wage it creates in me; and I know well what Goojerat and its results would have been in my hands.[41]

But war or no war, Napier was in India. He became Commander-in-Chief of India, and yes a member of the Council, on 7 May 1849. Under him were the Queen's Army in the country and the armies of the three Indian Presidencies of Bengal, Madras, and Bombay. All together he commanded 300,000 soldiers and controlled 400,000 pieces of mobile artillery.[42] He tells us that he agreed to go to India only because there was a war to be won, and because there was no war when he got there he had no free hand and faced a world of political intrigue.[43]

***

While Napier was worried about civilian interference with the military, for his part Dalhousie wondered whether Napier would interfere in civil matters. The Governor-General was determined to prevent any such thing. He told a friend that Napier would have complete authority over his own sphere, but

288 *Commander-in-Chief*

not a 'hair's breadth beyond'. And he said as much to Napier himself in their first interview.[44]

Serving under a Governor-General who was thirty years his junior and with no war to fight, Napier talked of going home by the following March if everything stayed quiet – although he never broached the subject of his departure with Dalhousie.[45]

Notes

1 C.J.F. Bunbury to his father H. E. Bunbury, 2 January 1848, given in Katherine M. Lyell (ed.), *The Life of Sir Charles J. F. Bunbury, Bart.*, 2 vols (London: John Murray, 1906), 1:269–70.

2 Napier to Kennedy, 29 March 1848, NP, TNA PRO 30/64/7, fols 1–2.

3 W. Napier to Napier, 5 June, 9 June 1848, NP, BL Add. MS 54525, fols 133–34, 136–37.

4 Napier to Henry Napier, 23 December 1847, 29 February 1848, given in WN, 4:92, 94; Napier's Journal, 30 March, 4:94–95; Napier to Kennedy, 29 March 1848, NP, TNA PRO 30/64/7, fols 1–2.

5 The *Times*, 17 May 1848, 6 col. f.

6 Napier to Emily Bunbury, 20 June 1848, NP, BL Add. MS 49110, fol. 70.

7 The *Times*, 7 October 1848, 5 col. f.

8 WN, 4:97–99; Napier's journal, 25 May 1848, 4:98.

9 Napier's journal, 11 October 1848, given in WN, 4:108.

10 Napier to Emily Bunbury, 3 October 1848, NP, BL Add. MS 49110, fols 72–74.

11 Napier to W. Napier, August 1848, 29 January 1849, given in WN, 4:104, 147–48; Napier to Emily Napier, 30 September 1848, 4:106–07.

12 Napier, *Baggage*. For the world of people who accompanied, provided for, and transported British troops – the camp-followers whom Napier was constantly trying to reduce in number – see C. A. Bayly, *Empire and Information: Intelligence Gathering and Social Communication in India, 1780–1870* (Cambridge: Cambridge UP, 1996), 288–89.

13 W. Napier to Napier, 1 June 1848, NP, BL Add. MS 54525, fols 130–31.

14 W. Napier to Napier, 25 November 1848, NP, BL Add. M 54526, fols 40–41.

15 The East India Company maintained that Napier should not get the traditional commander's one-eighth share because the real commander was Napier's superior officer, Governor Arthur in Bombay. But because Arthur had no role in conquering Sind, he should not get the commander's share, either. Wellington, Ellenborough, and Hardinge had to intervene for Napier, and even then he was not given the money until 1848. Napier to the Lords of the Treasury, 7 February 1845, PBC, BL Add. MS 40871, fol. 186; W. Napier to Napier, 26 May 1848, NP, BL Add. MS 54525, fols 128–29; Charles James Napier, *Defects, Civil and Military, of the Indian Government*, W.F.P. Napier (ed.) (London: Charles Westerton, 1853), 326–45.

16 WN, 4:116–21. William's letters to Charles in these months: NP, BL Add. MS 54526.

17 Napier to W. Napier, 7 August 1844, Bodleian MS Eng. lett. c. 243, fols 6–10 at 8.

18 Napier to W. Napier, 21 January 1849, given in WN, 4:144–45.

19 Napier to W. Napier, 18 December 1849, given in WN, 4:138–42; plan of Punjab campaign (with no room for William), 7 January 1849, NP, TNA PRO 30/64/7, fols 12–13.

20 Napier to W. Napier, 29 December 1848, given in WN, 4:142–43. See also Napier's Journal, 8 May 1848, 4:97.

21 Hamida Khuhro, *Making of Modern Sindh: British Policy and Social Change in the Nineteenth Century* (Karachi: Oxford UP, 1999), 89, 202.

22 Dalhousie to George Couper, 14 October 1848 and 22 December 1848, given in J.G.A. Baird (ed.), *Private Letters of the Marquess of Dalhousie* (Edinburgh: William Blackwood

and Sons, 1911), 35–36, 37–41, quotations at 35, 40; Dalhousie to Hobhouse, 25 July 1849, copy, BL A&AS MSS Eur F213/24, 218–19; Napier to W. Napier, 7 August 1844, Bodleian MS Eng. lett. c. 243, fols 6–10 at 6.

23 Dalhousie to Couper, 18 May 1849, given in BMD, 71–77.

24 Dalhousie to Couper, 8 May 1849, given in BMD, 71–77 at 74; Yapp, *Strategies*, 574–77, 579; The *Times*, 2 March 1849, 5 col. d.

25 The *Times*, 5 March 1849, 4 cols c–d; for Anglo-Indian happiness about Napier's employment, see Hugh Daly, *Henry Dermot Daly* (London: John Murray, 1905), 57–58.

26 Thackeray to Mrs. Brookfield, 13 September 1849, given in Gordon N. Ray (ed.), *The Letters and Private Papers of William Makepeace Thackeray*, 4 vols (Cambridge, MA: Harvard UP, 1946), 2:592–94.

27 [William Makepeace Thackeray], 'The Story of Kompanee Jehan', *Punch: or the London Charivari* 16 (17 March 1849), 105–06; Lewis Saul Benjamin, *William Makepeace Thackeray: A Biography Including Hitherto Uncollected Letters and Speeches and a Bibliography of 1300 Items*, 2 vols (London: John Lane, 1910), 2:247.

28 John Timbs (ed.), *Wellingtoniana: Anecdotes, Maxims, and Characteristics of the Duke of Wellington* (London: Ingram, Cooke, and Co., 1852), 73; W. Napier to Napier, 14 December 1848, NP, BL Add. MS 54526, fols 49–50.

29 Napier to W. Napier, 29 January 1849, given in WN, 4:147–48; Napier's journal, 3 September 1849, 4:187.

30 Anonymous, 'The Real Commander-in-Chief', *Punch: or the London Charivari*, 16 (1849), 136; Wellington to Dalhousie, 5 March 1849, NP, TNA PRO 30/64/8, fols 9–12 at fol. 11.

31 Napier to Emily Bunbury, 23 November, 1 December 1848, 1 January, 7 February 1849, NP, BL Add. MS 49110, fols 78–84, 90–91 at 81, 83, 91, 100; Napier to Louisa Napier, 11, 14, 14 (second letter), 16 February 1849, Bodleian MS Eng. lett. c. 241, fols 7–14; Napier, *Defects*, 7.

32 Charles C. F. Greville, *The Greville Memoirs (Second Part): A Journal of the Reign of Queen Victoria, 1837–1852*, Henry Reeve (ed.), 3 vols (London: Longmans, Green, and Co., 1885), 7, 25 March 1849, 3:274–76, 280.

33 William Napier to Napier, 12 December 1848, NP, BL Add. MS 54526, fols 47–48; Napier, *Defects*, 8.

34 HC Deb 6 March 1849 vol 103 cc252–53.

35 Evidence of M. Lewin, 18 April 1853, Great Britain, Parliament, *First Report from the Select Committee on Indian Territories*, (1852–1853), No. 426, 278; Hobhouse to Wellington, 7 March 1849, NP, TNA PRO 30/64/8, fol. 14.

36 John Mawson, *Records of the Indian Command of General Charles James Napier* (Calcutta: R. and C. Lepage, 1851), 4–7; Napier to Louisa Napier, 10 April 1839, Bodleian MS Eng. lett. c. 240, fols 48–49.

37 The railway would not approach the town for another twenty years – Dane Kennedy, *Magic Mountains: Hill Stations and the British Raj* (Berkeley and Los Angeles: University of California Press, 1996), 91.

38 Napier to Louisa Napier, 30 July 1849, Bodleian MS Eng. lett. c. 241, fols 23–24.

39 Dalhousie to Couper, 25 June 1849, given in BMD, 81; soon Dalhousie became if anything even more enthusiastic about how he and Napier seemed to agree on everything: Dalhousie to Couper, 10 July 1849, 81–85 at 84; Dalhousie to Hobhouse, 14 July 1849, BP, BL Add. MS 36477, fols 19–28 at 25–26. Eventually Napier's many criticisms of the civil governments in Sind and Punjab began to grate on the Governor-General: Dalhousie to Hobhouse, 22 September 1849, BP, BL Add. MS 36477 at 88–89.

40 Dalhousie to Couper, 30 March, 7 May 1849, given in BMD, 61–65, 68–70.

41 Napier's journal, 27 September 1849, given in WN, 4:193.

42 Napier, 'Memoir on the Defence of India, and the Military Occupation of the Punjaub', 27 November 1849, given in Napier, *Defects*, 362–98 at 368.

43 Napier, *Defects*, 6.

290 *Commander-in-Chief*

44 Copy of Dalhousie to Ellenborough, 8 May 1849, BP, BL Add. MS 36476, fols 550–53; Dalhousie to Couper, 30 March, 18 May 1849, with enclosures, given in BMD, 61–65, 71–77, quotation at 76; Napier, *Defects*, 229.
45 Colin Campbell's journal, 20 October 1849, given in Lawrence Shadwell, *The Life of Colin Campbell, Lord Clyde*, 2 vols (Edinburgh: William Blackwood and Sons, 1881), 1:239. Dalhousie kept picking up on the rumour: Dalhousie to Hobhouse, 26 August, 30 August, 6 October 1849, BP, BL Add. MS 36477, fols 47–58 at 56; fols 63–68 at 67; fols 91–96 at 95–96; Dalhousie to Couper, 18 September 1849 and 19 October 1849, given in BMD, 93–96 and 96–97.

22 Reforming the army

Meanwhile what would Napier do? Dalhousie suggested to Napier that he might try to reform the army. So the general set out on several tours of inspection. He wore his obviously dirty clothes, sported his huge beard, joked with the men, and abused the commissary officers who defrauded them. Napier demanded perfection in drill and on parade, and he praised the men for giving it to him (Figure 22.1).[1]

A number of army reforms suggested themselves.[2] Many officers lived in bungalows, each one set in a large individual compound. So a military cantonment in India in this period could stretch for up to seven miles, resembling a whole town of widely spaced villas. And beyond the officer's quarters lay still more bungalows for the civilian officials. Each building needed a

Figure 22.1 Napier as Commander-in-Chief of the Indian Army: *Illustrated London News*, 2 March 1850.

Commander-in-Chief Sir Charles Napier (engraving), English School, (19th century) / Private Collection / © Look and Learn / Illustrated Papers Collection / Bridgeman Images

twenty-four-hour guard, for as Napier explains, 'our Indian Government is so beloved, that after ruling above a century, magistrates cannot live out of the reach of bayonets'.[3] Therefore huge sets of guards existed, called Birkendauses and Chuprassees, to defend the homes of British personnel. The Birkendauses and the Chuprassees were proud and seasoned soldiers from good families. But many of the European officers and officials, who were made indolent by the heat and the high pay, had turned them into domestic servants; and so in their place regular troops had to be sent on permanent detachment to secure each house and do the work the guards could no longer do while they were waiting at table.

Meanwhile, more than ten thousand men each year served on detachments to move treasure around the country. In Napier's opinion, the troops of the line who had been taken away from their proper duties and were now ferrying treasure or guarding houses no longer maintained the discipline and camaraderie of the larger units to which they in theory belonged. Lord Ellenborough had attempted to form the Birkendauses and Chuprassees into a proper police militia so they would no longer be used as servants. Yet Ellenborough had left the country, Napier tells us, before he had created more than a few of the reformed units.

Napier's plan was to complete the conversion of these servants back into police guards and send the regular soldiers back to their units.[4] He wrote an overly didactic letter to Dalhousie on the matter, thinking (as he told William at the time) that if Dalhousie took offence at the tone he could resign as Commander-in-Chief and go home at once, which in any case he longed to do. But he also believed that the advice he was giving to the Governor-General – in this massive letter and others like it – was something the younger man needed to hear.[5] Napier pointed out that concentrating troops rather than spreading them out in small, easily overwhelmed detachments was the way to go when faced with a potentially hostile population. And in another echo of the north of England, he explained that except in cases of open rebellion, the civil authorities ought to be left to work out for themselves how to get along with the people they ruled. Officials needed to learn how to keep the peace themselves rather than living always under the protection of military guards and calling in the regular army on every occasion.[6]

The Commander-in-Chief wanted to take other steps, too, to keep the men of the Indian Army sharp. Because of what he learned from 'Abercrombie, Moore, Craufurd, Hope, [and] Wellington', Napier wanted to bring back strict military drill, and with it the army's ability to achieve 'great exploits'. He wanted to found special drilling camps both for officers and men. He also wanted the officer cadets sent to England for two years to learn their trade. Discipline was high in India, especially among sepoys, but not nearly high enough. If the level of discipline could be improved still further, then the Indian troops could be used in Europe in an emergency while the Gurkhas could be left to meet any need in India itself.[7]

Reforming the army 293

Napier did not remain in India long enough to organize the police units and the drill camps as he wished, but there were reforms that he could carry out more quickly. In putting them into effect he created a flurry of protest in the British Indian press. He insisted that the Bengal Army should retain its policy of promoting sepoys strictly according to seniority, as with British officers. So in an order that proved very unpopular he directed the Bengal army to retain its present system.[8] Napier stirred up another storm when he insisted that a haphazard knowledge of the local languages would no longer do. He required British officers to undertake intensive language study and pass a formal examination. '[A] subaltern's duties in the best native regiments' left plenty of free time to hit the books, learn Hindustani, and pass a written test on the language within one year. Many officers needed less time than this, he said. The resentment felt by the native troops at being put on guard or servant duty or at being passed over for promotions they believed their due was as nothing – in Napier's view – to having to shout their meaning to uncomprehending Englishmen who then had them put on trial for insolence. Worse, Napier feared that the officers did not know the language well enough to understand real insolence when they heard it.[9]

Another early area of concern originated with Dalhousie. The Governor-General wanted to reform the system of military pay. In a series of carefully deliberated measures, he had been trying to restrict the higher allowances the native soldiers received in certain theatres of service. For several years, sepoy troops who served outside the formal boundaries of British India had been paid slightly more than troops serving within British territory, to cover their extra expenses in being so far from home. Now that Dalhousie had formally annexed Punjab, the troops serving there were due for a reduction in this allowance, as they were no longer serving on foreign soil. Yet the annexation did not reduce the money they had to spend on food in the province, and it certainly did not reduce the distance from their families.

These lowered payments did not go down well with the soldiers. Word came to Napier by special messenger on 19 July 1849 – from Colin Campbell, who had served under him in the Chartist period[10] – that a number of sepoys at the Punjabi city of Rawalpindi had refused their pay rather than accept the reduction.[11] Then in December, soldiers elsewhere joined the protest and refused their pay.

Napier was never one for military disobedience. He did not sympathize with these soldiers in the slightest degree. Conceding to the sepoy demands and keeping the pay at the higher level *would cost us India*. And he told the Governor-General that preserving the obedience of 400,000 (as he quoted the number) was so important that it would be worth the 1,000 lives it might cost for the government to enforce the pay reduction. Out of indiscipline there might arise much greater bloodshed later on.[12]

In response to unfolding events, Napier decided to remain for a time at Simla to see how far the mutiny would spread. Dalhousie agreed that Napier had no business charging off to Rawalpindi and giving what Napier had called 'unadvisable importance' to the mutineers. Staying where he was, Napier sent two letters to Colin Campbell. One letter contained Campbell's official instructions: to reprimand or discharge the guilty while rewarding the soldiers who remained loyal. Napier's *private* letter advised Campbell to try to find some way of giving the men an opportunity to back down. But if trouble were to spread, Campbell should do whatever he thought necessary, 'for no special orders could be given from such a distance'.[13] Campbell for his part worked hard to avoid saying anything to offend the men while he waited for them to accept their lowered payments. They did so after six days. Campbell then separated units which he thought had been stationed together for too long, and he cashiered the ringleaders as Napier had ordered him to do.[14]

Meanwhile Napier went about his business. He left Simla for Delhi on a tour of inspection in early October. Dalhousie accompanied him part of the way.[15] Napier was investigating the old question of bad barracks. The mortality figures for newly arrived soldiers in India were horrible and everyone knew it. Nor was the survival rate much better among the soldiers who had been in the country for some time. Two regiments had been destroyed in their barracks since 1846; their colours and their uniforms remained, but by 1850 almost all of the men had died of disease. In one barracks, water stood on the floor. Roofs were low, there was little air, and there were swamps nearby – the same problems that Napier had found in Cephalonia and elsewhere. But Napier discovered that as Commander he was prevented from moving even a single soldier or fixing the worst barracks without two months delay for confirmation to come from various boards and commissions in Calcutta and Simla.[16]

One change that Napier wanted to make as soon as he could was to employ qualified engineers to design new barracks rather than leaving the work to infantry officers. In Loudiana, one new building was so poorly planned that it fell down in the wind, killing three hundred souls – soldiers and their families. Their deaths were due, Napier said, to the 'vile parsimony, selfish idleness, and ingratitude' for their military service of the Court of Directors and the Military Board. Napier wanted to see the Board abolished.[17]

Misunderstanding

On 20 November 1849, Napier set off on another tour of inspection. This time Dalhousie did not accompany him very far. By now the Governor-General was suffering from a number of ailments. Not the least of these was an abscess in his mouth that exposed the bone. Dalhousie's doctor confronted him one day with a long letter setting out why even the climate of Simla was unacceptable if he wanted to recover his health. The only hope, said the doctor, was a long sea voyage.

But Dalhousie did not want to resign and leave his work to others. He did not want to abandon the task of integrating Punjab into India. To resign before this work was done would be an admission of personal failure. Nor did Dalhousie think he could *afford* to resign, as he was already short of money before he became a Marquess, and now he needed an even greater income to support the new dignity.[18]

So Dalhousie went to sea – not the long voyage home but a cruise around the Indian Ocean. After travelling from Simla with Napier, he proceeded through Punjab itself, where he had spent so much time with the army during the recent war, and then down the Indus. The dissension over reduced pay which we noted above now began to spread beyond the soldiers of Rawalpindi, and so Napier wrote again to Dalhousie to press the seriousness of the disaffection. Yet for part of his journey Dalhousie was himself closer to the scene of the trouble than Napier was.

The trouble in Punjab did not seem as serious as the Commander-in-Chief kept telling him. Napier 'is a singular man, and is bothering me a little just now', Dalhousie wrote to his close friend George Couper on 17 November. Napier reported that army furloughs in the area had been withheld for more than a year; they should be granted to twenty-five men per company so the men could go and take care of family affairs. Dalhousie had agreed with this move. But then, as Dalhousie told his friend, Napier wrote two days later to say that Punjab was a volcano about to erupt. Dalhousie did not believe it, and he trusted his own information and his own reasoning rather than what Napier was saying. If things were so bad, why would Napier advise giving 'leave at one swoop to 19,500 men for four months?'

Here we see the first of several occasions when Dalhousie tried to read between the lines of what Napier was telling him. He would examine the minor details of the general's movements or his other initiatives, and then he would try to divine from these outward signs what Napier *really* had in mind. In the present instance, Dalhousie convinced himself that because Napier wanted to allow certain very disgruntled men to go on leave, the general did not think that the army as a whole could be out-of-sorts. Later, Dalhousie tried to judge from the location of Napier's travelling headquarters where the general thought the trouble truly lay – as though Napier would instantly transport to the centre of any disaffection the huge headquarters he had to maintain (he had reduced the Commander-in-Chief's entourage to a mere thirty elephants, three hundred thirty-four camels, and two hundred twenty-two tent-pitchers – it had been several times that size, with a travelling pavilion with glass doors[19]). Because Napier had not chosen to move his complex staff to one place or another, Dalhousie would decide that there could be no real trouble there, notwithstanding Napier's own testimony and that of the subordinate commanders of the great danger.[20]

At the present moment, because of what he saw in Lahore, Dalhousie concluded that Napier was 'either credulous or reckless' in his warnings about trouble at Rawalpindi – some one hundred sixty miles to the north of Dalhousie's own position. The Governor-General concluded:

> No more regiments are reported as grumbling on the reductions announced, and the 41st N.I. [the centre of the trouble so far] marched

296   *Commander-in-Chief*

on the day ordered without further ado. There never was a mutiny in this army except for our own injustice or ill-management. The Sepoy is a child in simplicity and biddableness, if you make him understand his orders, *and don't* pet him overmuch. This C.-in-C. is inclined to do so.[21]

Indeed, for Dalhousie, the idea

[t]hat Sepoys are as good as Britons (even if it were true) is just not the lesson to teach them while we are 25,000 and they are 200,000 disciplined men. But it is *not* true, and whenever it becomes true it will be time for us to be looking over our shoulders toward the Bay of Bengal and the outward bound.[22]

***

Sensing at about this time that he and the Governor-General had differing views about these larger questions of the nature of the sepoy army and the security of the military situation, Napier decided to explain his views to Dalhousie much, much more fully. He would write a sketch of the whole matter. It became a ten-thousand-word memorandum on where in India the various threats were and how serious they seemed to be.

Napier did not strive for diplomatic language in writing it. He stressed that the changes that Hardinge and Dalhousie himself had made to the military arrangements and administrative structures left by Lord Ellenborough had achieved nothing good. Sind had been pushed closer to the brink of rebellion. The Punjab too – Dalhousie's pride and joy – would also rebel because of the way the Governor-General had chosen to organize its government. Dalhousie did not find the report very gratifying.[23]

At this point Napier changed his plans, and rather than going back to Delhi he set off from Agra to visit the troubled Punjab himself. Here he crossed paths with Dalhousie, soon to embark on his sea voyage. And so in November the two men were again together for a short time. Napier used the opportunity to ask what extra powers he might have while the Governor-General was away. Dalhousie answered none, and nor did he need any. Dalhousie also left written instructions before he embarked that in his absence Napier was not to exceed his normal authority as Commander-in-Chief. He told his close friend that he expected Napier to try to defy him in some way, and that he would 'commit some escapade', although the Governor-General had to admit that so far not a word of disagreement had passed between them.[24]

Napier would require no special powers while the Governor-General was at sea because in Dalhousie's view there was nothing wrong; Napier put too much faith in his sources in Sind, and in any case the general could suggest no concrete steps to take against any imagined mutiny – no steps that Dalhousie had not already taken. Dalhousie told Couper that pay reductions were 'always ticklish', and he would be happy when they were over. Yet his own escort towards the mouth of the Indus would be the first to cross from the area of

Reforming the army 297

high pay to the area of low pay and to suffer the reduction, and he was not really worried about them. And then he would be aboard his ship, having seen his canal-building program in operation and trade reviving as he intended. All was going well in his eyes.[25]

Towards the end of January Dalhousie boarded his ship for two months of rest. He would be completely unreachable for much of this time. Over the course of his journey, he spent a week in Bombay, made brief stops for coal in Ceylon and elsewhere, and visited Singapore. He returned to Calcutta in March.[26]

Notes

1 See for example the contemporary Indian newspaper clippings given in John Mawson, *Records of the Indian Command of General Charles James Napier* (Calcutta: R. and C. Lepage, 1851), Appendix, v, x, and xvi–xvii.
2 Napier was not alone in this view. See G. W. Forrest, *Life of Field-Marshal Sir Neville Chamberlain* (Edinburgh: William Blackwood and Sons, 1909), 245–46.
3 Charles James Napier, *Defects, Civil and Military, of the Indian Government*, W.F.P. Napier (ed.) (London: Charles Westerton, 1853), 229.
4 Ibid, 229–34. For Ellenborough's intentions along these lines, to create better policing and 'alleviate the escort duties of the army', see Ellenborough to Wellington, 7 June 1842, given in CEW, 250–56 at 256.
5 Napier to W. Napier, 24 July 1849, Bodleian MS Eng. lett. c. 243, fols 160–63.
6 Copy of Napier to Dalhousie, 24 July 1849, Bodleian MS. Eng. lett. c. 241, fols 239–43, quotation at 241.
7 Napier, *Defects*, 240–42.
8 Ibid, 234–39; John Jacob, *Remarks on the Native Troops of the Indian Army* (London: no publisher, 1854), 18–19; H. T. Lambrick, *John Jacob of Jacobabad*, 2nd edn (Karachi: Oxford UP, 1975), 212–14.
9 Napier, *Defects*, 239–40; Lambrick, *John Jacob*, 192–93, 216.
10 Campbell still deeply admired Napier as a commander – Colin Campbell to Hope Grant, 20 June 1849, quoted in Lawrence Shadwell, *The Life of Colin Campbell, Lord Clyde*, 2 vols (Edinburgh: William Blackwood and Sons, 1881), 1:234–35.
11 Napier, *Defects*, 13.
12 Napier to Dalhousie, 5 January 1850, given in ibid, 181–84; 'General Order Disbanding the 66th Native Infantry', 27 February 1850, given in Mawson, *Records*, 101–06.
13 Napier, *Defects*, 13–18.
14 Colin Campbell to Napier, 26 July 1849, quoted in Shadwell, *Colin Campbell*, 1:230–33.
15 Dalhousie to Couper, 5 October 1849, given in BMD, 97–99.
16 Napier, *Defects*, 201–07; Napier to Emily Bunbury, 16 January 1850, NP, BL Add. MS 49110, fols 113–15.
17 Napier, *Defects*, 200–09, quotation at 209.
18 Dalhousie to Couper, 3 September 1849, given in BMD, 90–93; George Smith (ed.), *Physician and Friend, Alexander Grant, F.R.C.S: His Autobiography and his Letters from the Marquis of Dalhousie* (London: John Murray, 1902), 58–59.
19 Napier, *Defects*, 35–36.
20 Dalhousie to Couper, 17 November 1849, given in BMD, 99–102; Dalhousie to Hobhouse, 22 November 1849, BP, BL Add. MS 36477, fols 107–14 at 110–13.
21 Dalhousie to Couper, 17 November 1849, given in BMD, 101–02. Napier would assert that it was better to overpraise than underpraise potentially mutinous troops – Napier, *Defects*, 60.

298 *Commander-in-Chief*

22 Dalhousie to Couper, 17 November 1849, given in BMD, 99–102.
23 Napier, 'Memoir on the Defence of India', given in Napier, *Defects*, 366–67, 380. Drafts appear in NP, TNA PRO 30/64/14, and the memorandum itself (thirty-four pages of small handwriting) is at BL A&AS MSS Eur C 0123; Dalhousie to Hobhouse, 22 December 1849, BP, BL Add. MS 36477, fols 123–36 at 131–35.
24 Dalhousie to Couper, 15 December 1849, given in BMD, 104–07.
25 Dalhousie to Hobhouse, 22 December 1849, BP, BL Add. MS 36477, fols 123–36 at 126–29; Dalhousie to Couper, 2 December 1849, given in BMD, 102–04.
26 Dalhousie to Couper, 7 February, 4 March, and 16 March 1850, given in ibid, 110–15.

23 The Kohat expedition

By 30 November, Napier tells us, he had completed his seventeenth march across Punjab, a province which he said felt especially familiar to him because it was so much like Sind.

But in his view the British conquest of the country was not proceeding so smoothly as his own conquest had done in the south.[1] He recalled that in Sind he had been very careful over the reestablishment of public order. Napier's main complaint was that Dalhousie was nothing like so careful about how he established his authority in Punjab. The Governor-General had proclaimed the annexation of tribal areas in the hills without ever conquering them or having in any other way obtained the right to intervene in their territory. Dalhousie had proclaimed his rule there, but he might as well 'proclaim it over China!'[2]

And yet the recently embarked Governor-General, who ought in Napier's view to have limited his annexation to the eastern bank of the Indus, now wanted the hill tribes of the western bank broken for their disloyalty to his government. Dalhousie had despatched a military force to the area in early November 1849. Originally his plan was 'to make a severe example of the head-man of each village' for their failure to pay taxes.[3]

For Charles Napier, Dalhousie was unreasonable to expect any loyalty from these headmen in the first place − as though the proclamation of a line on a map could somehow form the basis for new native sentiments and allegiances. Worse, Dalhousie would not leave the hill tribes alone. He was interfering in their territory, buying the right-of-way for a road but failing to give the tribes the agreed-upon money. Instead, Dalhousie paid a set of middlemen who kept more than their fair share, while the tribes in question naturally expected the whole amount. These hill tribes, whom Napier called the Afreedees, found a road built through their land on a right-of-way that had not been paid for. And they were expected to pay a salt tax to a government they did not recognize. On top of that, Dalhousie multiplied the level of the tax seventeen-fold from what it had been under the Sikhs.

The result was that a party of Afreedees (or Afridis) came down from the hills and killed a dozen British soldiers in their tents. Napier resolved that the men who had carried out the raid must be handed over to face British justice.[4] But beyond that, a more permanent settlement should be worked out. Napier set down a several-stage programme for what he would do to build peace.

300   *Commander-in-Chief*

What then was Napier's not-to-be-realized plan for dealing with the Afridis? As he would explain a few years later, he wanted to begin by listening to the concerns of the chiefs about how they had not been paid. (So, unlike the situation when he was in Sind, Napier now wanted to listen.) He would listen also to any other complaints they had. Napier said he would then accept these complaints, apologize to the tribal leaders, and tell them that proper payments would be made in future – presuming that the men who had killed the British soldiers as they slept were handed over.[5]

Next, Napier would ask each tribe to appoint a negotiator. Whom the future payments should be directed to would then be worked out, and all subsequent payments would be made to those parties, in public and in Napier's presence in order to prevent graft. Moreover, the chiefs would be enrolled as agents of the police. Brigands would be apprehended and handed over by the locals, and the British would be able to travel the roads in peace.[6] Any tribes that refused to cooperate with all this would have their lands given to those who did. And Britain should contract with the Afridis themselves to build any future roads. (That this had not been tried before was only because 'English ignorance of Indian character is incredible.') The salt tax ought to be reduced. And finally on the list of Napier's recommendations, there should be frequent parades of troops in Peshawar, which was not far away. All who saw or heard of those parades would be able to understand their meaning: 'Justice – rupees – bayonets'.[7]

Irregular troops

Dalhousie's policy for addressing the problem of the hill tribes in Punjab was somewhat different from what Napier suggested. He had already ordered a certain Captain Bradshaw and his men, who were detached from the army and under the command of the Punjabi government, to go and pacify the hills. Napier was concerned about this entirely military solution. On 20 December 1849 he wrote to the Governor-General. He repeated that the salt tax was so high that it was leading to destabilization and conflict. And he asked how far to the northwest the military effort would have to be extended: '*Where will we stop?*' Either Bradshaw should be given extra support or he should be withdrawn. A true hill war, such as Napier's own in Sind, took six months to prepare and was a major undertaking. And Napier went so far as to remind the Governor-General that all wars are subject to 'accidents'. The Commander-in-Chief strongly recommended a less bellicose course of action.[8]

Dalhousie's response to Napier's comments – a response whose significance Napier did not seem to understand at the time – was to say that he thought Bradshaw's mission a success, and the 'severe punishment which appears to have been inflicted upon the refractory villages' (Dalhousie's words) would most likely prevent future conflict.

And yet, as Napier would argue later on, Bradshaw's mission *did not* prevent future conflict; the conflict continued.[9]

The Kohat expedition   301

In response, in the new year, Napier found that Dalhousie planned to send out more of these 'politicals' – troops detached from or raised separately from the regular army that Napier commanded. These had been placed under the command of Colin Campbell. They were to go into Afridi territory, where they were to traverse the mountain passes and fortify a town called Kohat.

Napier tells a story of what he found when he went to inspect these 'political' troops. Dalhousie and his minions and not the Indian Army had been responsible for their training and supplies:

> A fine, handsome soldier, six feet high, brawny and bronzed, a model Grenadier, his broad deep chest swelling with military pride, and his black brilliant eye sparking with a malicious twinkle, pretended to hold over his shoulder, between his fingers and them, a flint – his only arm! He was an epitome of political military arrangement – a powerful soldier rendered useless by ignorance![10]

Soon the order came for this ill-prepared, ill-equipped force to leave for the hills. Napier's response was a *coup-de-théâtre*. As Commander-in-Chief, he wanted to prevent another Kabul disaster. So he decided to go on this minor expedition to Kohat himself despite his high rank. He would use his own regular troops to protect these poorly led, abominably provisioned 'politicals' from slaughter. Napier could not prevent the mission, for it had been ordered by Dalhousie's political authorities in Punjab, but he could subsume the mission and use his own troops to protect the men so unwisely sent on it.[11]

There was also something else in Napier's mind. He wanted to go into the hill country and see for himself what was going on. For it seemed that some of Bradshaw's men were attacking civilians. In a letter to Colonel Campbell on 2 January 1850, Napier made very clear that he was horrified at the possibility that British troops could be behaving in this way. Was it indeed Bradshaw who had ordered the attacks on the property of non-combatants? Or was it the work of junior officers? Napier wanted an explanation as soon as possible. He wrote to Campbell:

> I am much annoyed to find in Bradshaw's report that *villages have been destroyed*. I cannot think he did this, but being resolved to know whose doing it was I send you an official memorandum through the Adjutant-General. What! British troops destroying villages and leaving poor women and young children to perish in the depth of winter? I can hardly believe this, but will take good care it never happens again under my command. A copy of my memorandum has gone to Lord Dalhousie to show him that this disobedience is not passed over, and that I am resolved to know who is at fault. Bradshaw is an excellent officer . . . and if he has done this I shall be vexed; yet who else could give any orders on the subject? However I care not who, if he was my own brother he should be shown up. I hope it has been the work of *politicals* not the soldiers.[12]

302   *Commander-in-Chief*

In the memorandum, Napier called the burning of villages 'at variance with humanity, and contrary to the uses of civilized warfare'. In fact this seems to have been Napier's own private interpretation of the laws of war. Emerich de Vattel, the eighteenth-century Swiss jurist whose book on international law was the main authority on such matters at the time, had suggested that moderation and the requirements of military necessity ought to limit the destruction of civilian property – but he did not rule out burning houses if necessary.[13] Nonetheless for his part Napier circulated a document making it very clear that in his view the practice must stop:

> Should the troops be again called up to act you will be pleased to issue orders that war is to be made upon men, not upon defenceless *women* and *children*, by destroying their habitations, and leaving them to perish without shelter from the inclemency of weather. I have heard of no outrage committed by these wild mountaineers that could call for conduct, so cruel, so unmilitary, and so impolitic.[14]

Bradshaw himself replied to Napier as soon as he could (the emphasis is in the original): '*The villages were destroyed by the orders and under the personal superintendence of the Deputy Commissioner of the Punjab*'. He added that the people of the villages were 'a race of mounted robbers'.[15] Bradshaw also claimed that the women and children had already left some weeks before. Napier was hardly mollified. Bradshaw's letter confirmed Napier's suspicion in his letter to Campbell that the 'politicals' were at fault.[16]

Meanwhile, Campbell told Napier that the soldiers were acting under orders given to them by – yes – the Punjab government.[17]

What all this really meant, Napier was about to see for himself.

***

The Kohat expedition set off as soon as Napier could get it fully organized and the troops properly equipped, which was on 9 February 1850.

There were skirmishes. Men shot at the British column in the mountain defiles. Lives were lost on both sides, positions rushed. The British were up against what may have been thousands of fighting men – they could not know the number.[18] In this atmosphere the British troops carried out certain actions that Napier believed might seem questionable to readers in England. When he published his book on the subject, he tried to explain these actions. There was the time when one Afridi stood atop a rock, waving his shield and gun, taunting the soldiers:

> A young artillery officer, – Maitre or Delane, – laid his gun with a shell and the flying death whizzing through the air burst as it struck the brave Afridi! His head, his legs, his arms flew like radii from a centre into the air, and a shout of exaltation burst from the troops! The amusements of a field of battle are grim. Condemn not that shout. Life was played for in the

rough game, and they who won naturally rejoiced. It is however a painful remembrance.[19]

A point of this story as Napier tells it in his book is to remind his reader, I think, that he himself was no pacifist but an experienced military man. His feelings would not be easily swayed. He was not soft.

***

And then the first village burned. Now what Dalhousie really meant when he described the 'severe punishment which appears to have been inflicted upon the refractory villages' began to dawn on Napier. Or it was only now that he finally allowed himself to fully understand it. What was taking place was not an attempt to defeat the men of each tribe in battle, or to capture the ringleaders, but to burn the homes of the women and children, and leave the people to wander in the cold of the mountains to die. Bradshaw and his men were not out of control, as Napier had feared. It was far worse. At last Napier allowed himself to fully take on board what was really happening: These men were only doing what someone well up the chain of command had – at least tacitly – ordered them to do.[20]

For his part, Dalhousie told Hobhouse in London that 'the particulars' about what Bradshaw had done had not yet reached him. But he knew the operations being undertaken there were 'a complete success'.[21]

Napier wanted no part of it. For one thing, he worried that he might receive the blame for these actions when word got home. Indeed, one of Bradshaw's gung-ho young officers, proud of the work of destruction, wrote a letter to his parents describing all that had been done to raze the villages and foul their water. The young man described the devastation in glowing terms and he gave Napier the credit for having been in command. This letter was printed in the *Times* and reprinted in the *Manchester Guardian*. No doubt it was reprinted elsewhere for all to read (the many dozens of provincial newspapers made it their practice of taking a great deal of their material from the *Times*).[22] 'It has been said in England, that the Afridi villages were burned by me', as Napier recalled later. 'That iniquity emanated entirely from the Punjab Administration, and my repudiation at the time was unmeasured.'[23]

Indeed, as we know, Napier had a temper, and when the first of the villages was set on fire he immediately sought out those responsible. It was the politicals. For Napier,

> this was [as] impolitic as it was dishonourable for the character of British soldiers; but no power was entrusted to me, and I had been sufficiently cautioned against interfering with the power of the Punjab Civil authorities. Entirely deprived of command over these troops, I was compelled to witness, and in some degree aid their abominable proceeding; for without the protection of my soldiers, those of the Board could not have executed their scandalous orders.[24]

304 *Commander-in-Chief*

Napier had given these troops his protection and they used that protection to commit war crimes. The boy from Celbridge, where all of five houses were burned more than fifty years before; the boy who grew up so close to the scenes of massacre on both sides in 1798 in County Kildare; that boy was now an old man. As a soldier he had been disgusted by the atrocities inflicted upon civilians at the hands of Marshal Masséna in the Peninsular War,[25] and again by the crimes committed by Franco-British forces in Hampton, Virginia. It is true that in the course of his own long career he had himself destroyed the property of civilian insurgents in the hills of the Sind border. He had done this in order to bring peace. But he had done it carefully. He had protected the women and children, and he had resettled the tribes on better land. And now under his protection British soldiers had destroyed six villages in his presence, leaving the civilian population to fend for themselves.

This was not the first time Napier had entertained moral qualms about attacking civilians in South Asia. In October 1842, he noted in his journal how troubled he was by the destruction of Afghan villages by the British forces leaving the country. He blamed the commander on the spot: 'Official accounts come of Nott's victory on the 8th of September, and of his destruction of Ghuznee. Why did he destroy it? I do not like this: he seems a harsh man'.[26] It was not that Napier was being particularly soft. General Pollock's destruction of a bazaar and two mosques had troubled the Duke of Wellington, too; he did not see how military orders could be issued for carrying out such acts.[27]

When Napier came to write his book on Dalhousie and Kohat, he tried his best to see both sides. He agonized over the matter. Why did he not interfere? While the orders were scandalous, '[t]he villages had however been entirely abandoned, save by fighting men, and the inhabitants had also carried away the contents of their dwellings, otherwise the orders to burn *should not have been executed!*'[28] But it was cold weather, and the villagers would have needed to come back to the homes fairly soon, when the British were gone.

Napier added other extenuating factors, not (I would argue) to justify what took place but more to excuse in his own conscience the behaviour of officers he respected, and whom he did not want to have to turn heart and mind against:

> The complete abandonment [of the villages] was not difficult, the villages are only occupied during the winter. . . . There were, however, other reasons for agreeing to the burning. On one hand little injury was done; on the other, the blame of the long frontier war was thus sure to be created, was thus sure to be attributed to my preventing the arson. It would have been said, burning was the way to force submission, and all the bloodshed and expense *which afterwards occurred* would have been laid on my Quixotic notions. But it was these and like shameful proceedings which did cause discontent and war, and Sir Colin Campbell has since been compelled to the contemplation of worse and more disgraceful scenes.[29]

The Kohat expedition 305

Napier goes on to praise Campbell, too, for leading his irregular troops so well in the several years that followed. Campbell deserved this praise, as Napier explained, because he had kept himself off the long list of commanders who had lost an army in those mountains. And as Bradshaw was dead by then, he too comes in for some kind words.[30]

But in the final analysis Napier could not stomach what happened. However many extenuating factors he might cite, however much he might want to minimize before the public the role of officers he respected in what turned into a many-year-long campaign of village burning, his initial shock comes through. Yet he seems to have felt far less disgust for the soldiers who carried the village burnings than for whoever it was, ultimately, who had ordered them. Napier had spent some time examining the question of command responsibility in his book on flogging and military law. In his view, the blame for any military atrocities accrued at the top. It belonged to the civilians responsible for the war.[31]

Indeed, at no time in his life would Charles Napier countenance the idea of common soldiers framing ethical or jurisprudential challenges to an illegal order. The possibility of the men having the right to disobey an order on moral grounds would arise only once (and only briefly at that). This was in the notes that Napier published in an edition of the works of the French military writer Vigny. Editing Vigny was a small writing project that Napier had taken on ten years before, and he joked at the time that he did very little work on it.[32] This question of disobeying orders for moral reasons only appeared in a revised edition that he brought out in 1850, after Kohat. In this 1850 volume, Napier explained that any truly horrible orders coming from a despotic monarch, orders that were not 'lawful', would not normally be obeyed by ordinary soldiers. But he made it clear that he was referring to orders that clearly violated a natural and not a human law, orders so extreme that soldiers could not *make themselves* obey them. And what he had in mind were orders so horrible that in his view no constitutional government would give them. His example is a superior officer ordering him to shoot one of his own daughters. Napier said he would shoot his superior officer instead.[33] Yet in less extraordinary situations, all that the officers and men of the military needed to concern themselves with was making sure they did not go beyond what was necessary. As he explained the matter in words that did indeed appear in both the first and second editions of his volume on Vigny: 'If we sailors and soldiers inflict more suffering upon individuals than the success of our operation demands, *then* we become responsible to God, to our sovereign, to our country, and we deserve condign punishment.'[34]

Again, Vattel was the most important legal authority here, and Vattel was very clear. The sovereign and only the sovereign who was responsible for the war was also responsible for any moral transgressions that he might order during the course of it. Napier had specifically referred to this chapter in Vattel in another context in Sind only a few years before, so it is clear that he read it.[35] The responsibility for what happened in a war resided in the ultimate commander.

306   *Commander-in-Chief*

But who was that in this case?

***

As we have seen, Captain Bradshaw and Colonel Campbell both told Napier that the village burning was ordered by the authorities in Punjab. And Bradshaw had specified the Deputy Commissioner of Punjab, John Lawrence. Who were these people?

John Lawrence was no lone wolf. He was part of the three-man Punjab Board that Dalhousie had set up to run the province after its annexation. The president of the Punjab Board was Lawrence's brother Henry; and their brother George, although he was not in fact the Board's third member, served as the Resident at Peshawar. George was the one Punjab official with whom Napier had at least some working relationship – Napier liked him, although he did not like taking advice from him.[36]

Although two of the Lawrences (Henry and George) were military officers, all three brothers held civil rather than military appointments; by quite some way they were the most important of the 'politicals' whom Napier loved to blame for the misrule in the province and for interfering with the military chain of command. And indeed it was the Lawrences whom Napier now blamed for the burning of the villages. He was entirely correct about this. In a book written years later, George Lawrence would recall having been – as the Resident of Peshawar – the very man to request that Campbell should set off on the expedition, put down the Afridis, and safeguard the building of the road. George Lawrence did not detail what 'punishment' he had advised against the tribesmen, but in fact he went on the expedition himself and took part in what was done. And he recorded that in his view the measures taken against the Afridis were never strong enough. He said very little about Napier, who would seem to have kept the major at a distance at this point.[37]

George's brother Henry, the head of the Punjab Board, would later recall how he worked with Dalhousie to frustrate Napier in this period. As Henry Lawrence and Lord Dalhousie both saw things, the Commander-in-Chief was attempting to impose military rule on the province in place of their own system.[38] After Napier's death it was Henry Lawrence too, who would respond to Napier's most impassioned criticisms. For Henry, there were no women and children who were left to die in the hills – the villages were empty.[39] He does not stop to consider that the villages *looked* empty because the population that did indeed live there had fled temporarily, hiding from the British troops. As winter set in, they would have no shelter unless others could take them in – all of them.

As support for this policy of laying waste to a countryside, Henry Lawrence also cites the precedent of Wellington's behaviour in the Peninsular War, when so much of Portugal was emptied of people and denuded of food.[40] But Punjab was not Portugal. When Wellington ordered the civilians whose country he was defending to retreat to Lisbon and take all their food with them on pain of death, he was trying to starve Masséna's army. At the same time, he worked to raise charitable donations in Britain for the displaced Portuguese. Atrocities took place during the Peninsular War over and above Wellington's strategic destruction of the Portuguese landscape – but these were atrocities that took place very definitely *against* Wellington's orders. Wellington strove to prevent these crimes and to punish those who carried them out – ruining the commanders and hanging the men.[41]

Henry Lawrence also brought up what Napier himself had done to the Boogties. Yet what had Napier done? He ordered the raiders shot. He depopulated a buffer zone behind which the raiders could fall back. And he chased them down and destroyed their army, while giving shelter to the non-combatants and settling everyone on farms later on, including the fighting men and their chiefs. All makes up a very different picture from what had been done on the way to Kohat.

***

In the report on the expedition that Napier sent to Dalhousie on the Governor-General's return, Napier said with some kindness that Dalhousie's own orders 'to avoid unnecessary harshness' had obviously been disobeyed.[42] Not a bit of it. For in writing to his friend Couper, Dalhousie expressed nothing but satisfaction over the village burnings. He was unhappy about only one detail: that Napier as Commander-in-Chief had invited himself along on the expedition, inflating the affair in the eyes of the enemy by his very presence, and making the staff worry that he might invade Kabul. Even the language of Napier's orders seemed unseemly; it was in Dalhousie's view a mixture of 'rodomontade and Billingsgate'.[43] Dalhousie ridiculed Napier's plan to bring peace to the Afridis without thoroughly mastering them first.[44] By now Dalhousie expected that the tribesmen would carry out their raids 'for years to come', as he told Hobhouse, and he did not like Napier referring to all this as though it had the seriousness of a war.[45]

At bottom, what bothered Napier about what was going on in these hills simply did not bother Dalhousie or the Lawrences. Morally the two sides could never come together. Looking back on the matter, John Lawrence, the youngest of the brothers (and later the Viceroy of India), said this of Napier's objections:

> It is certainly a difficult thing for a 'political' to advocate offensive measures while the commander-in-chief is for peace; but I much fear that they are necessary. We cannot exasperate the Afridis more than we have done, whereas, by punishing them well, we may make them fear us, which now they do not do.[46]

Neither Henry Lawrence nor his early biographers (two men who were both mid-nineteenth-century imperial officials) could find anything at all in Napier's objections besides peevishness, a peevishness that in their view Napier had probably worked up after the fact.[47]

308   *Commander-in-Chief*

Deep down, were the Lawrences at all sensitive to the moral qualms that Napier felt? Was anyone else at all sensitive to them, besides Napier himself and one or two other officers? The psychologist and historian Kathryn Tidrick points out that Henry Lawrence liked to say he and his brothers subdued Punjab without firing a shot; she adds that they burned villages instead. (In fact they fired shots, too.) But as Tidrick notes, Napier was around to point out the immorality of the village burning. He went on to point it out loudly and insistently, and the Lawrences were not pleased to hear it discussed in so critical a way.[48]

Tidrick's argument is right as far as it goes, in that Napier was indeed bringing publicity to the matter; but in fact the Lawrences did not seem at all embarrassed about what they were doing, whatever Napier said about it, and in any case what happened was no secret. We saw that a letter which lauded the burning of the villages appeared in the *Times* and was reprinted elsewhere. Even Charles Dickens' journal *Household Words* quoted from this letter: 'We burned all their villages, spoiled their crops, destroyed their water, and did all the harm we could.'[49] There were no words of condemnation in *Household Words*. The destruction did not seem to worry Dickens any more than it worried either Dalhousie or the men he employed to carry it out.

The policy of attacking civilians that began under Lord Dalhousie would remain a central part of British tactics in attempting to 'pacify' the hill tribes of India's north-western border until well into the twentieth century. In the 1940s George Orwell publicized the fact that in his day air strikes were being carried out against the villages in this region – and destroying the villages was called *'Pacification'*.[50] Now in the same general area, the West uses unmanned drones to do the work. Kohat is thirty miles south of Peshawar and it has not been the target of drones. But slightly farther from Peshawar, forty miles to the north of the city, lies Malakand, where the village burning of Orwell's day took place and where drones have recently fallen (although most of them fall well south of Kohat, in South Waziristan).

The case *for* village burning in the Peshawar area was made by Winston Churchill in *The Story of the Malakand Field Force* in 1898. He argued that

> in reality, throughout these regions, every inhabitant is a soldier from the first day he is old enough to hurl a stone, till the last day he has strength to pull a trigger, after which he is probably murdered as an encumbrance to the community.
>
> Equipped with these corrected facts, I invite the reader to examine the question of the legitimacy of village-burning for himself. . . . Of course, it is cruel and barbarous, as is everything else in war, but it is only an unphilosophic mind that will hold it legitimate to take a man's life, but illegitimate to destroy his property.[51]

Churchill seems to have elided the existence of the children, the old, and any other non-combatants who might have enjoyed the protections from the

The Kohat expedition 309

winter snows that an unburned village could provide. According to Churchill's 'corrected facts', the whole civilian population was a legitimate target.

It might be noted against even the authority of Winston Churchill that now after more than one hundred sixty years of having their villages burned, the peoples of this mountain region have not as yet become noticeably friendlier to the West.

***

While Napier was not personally involved in any more British attacks on the hill peoples, he kept himself informed about events in the area.[52] Two weeks after the Kohat expedition was over, the threat of further attacks by the Afridis led Napier to order his friend and subordinate Campbell to set out against the hill peoples again, if necessary, but on no account to burn crops as the civilians (George Lawrence among them) wanted him to do.

Then in March 1850, a British doctor working for the Punjab Board was attacked with his travelling party six miles from Kohat and died of his injuries. Afridi involvement was suspected, and the politicals sent out the cavalry under Captain Coke to round up the usual suspects. Whether the twenty or so men whom Coke apprehended had anything to do with the attack was by no means clear to Colonel Campbell.

In that month Campbell drafted for the Governor-General a substantial analysis of when the crops of different tribes would be ripe enough to destroy and when his troops would be in position to destroy them.[53] But at the same time, he strongly urged Dalhousie *not* to continue with this policy of sending out expeditions of destruction. He wanted Dalhousie to follow another path and seek reconciliation with the tribes. Over the subsequent months Campbell continued to press the idea of reaching a settlement upon the political authorities, from Lord Dalhousie and Henry and John Lawrence on down. For a time Campbell indeed prevailed upon the Governor-General to change his mind and substitute diplomatic engagement for a military offensive.[54] In response, the Lawrences held talks with the Afridis, who promised loyalty in exchange for an end to the salt tax. But no lasting agreement seems to have been reached.[55] Meanwhile Dalhousie counselled a surprise attack and as 'severe' a punishment as 'humanity' would allow on another tribe. Accounts differ on whether these attempts to treat with the Afridis under Colin Campbell and others bore any early fruit, or whether the Afridis continued to be a serious menace.[56]

What is clear is that in late October 1850 Dalhousie sent none other than Campbell himself on a new raid of destruction. The Governor-General told Campbell that he would 'relieve [him] of any personal responsibility as regarded the punishment he was about to inflict on the offending tribe' (in the words of Campbell's biographer). But Dalhousie also told him not to destroy property that might be useful later, when the area was resettled by groups more amenable to British rule.[57]

Between the accounts that Napier received directly from Campbell about all of this and certain orders that Dalhousie gave to George Lawrence to execute

310   *Commander-in-Chief*

at Kohat two months after Napier's own expedition, Napier finally had enough evidence to grasp the full truth. He finally came to understand that the policy of attacking the civilian population was ordered by Dalhousie himself.[58] It was Dalhousie who had inflamed and prolonged the war and who had committed crimes in doing so.

The politicals thought they were 'great generals', Napier said in looking back on the matter in his last book, and it was they who caused this war. Dalhousie 'and his *politicals* like many other men mistook *rigour with cruelty* for *vigour!*'[59] Looking back over the conflict, which still continued as he wrote, Napier reflected that

> [d]uring its progress, we have cruelly burned beautiful villages, and devastated the land, founding our claim to do so on a nominally assumed sovereignty of the Sikhs, who neither did nor could conquer the tribes in possession.
>
> Lord Dalhousie has saddled the government with a costly contest by bad administration.[60]

What Dalhousie had achieved was 'unjust, cruel warfare . . . for which to God he is responsible, and should be made so to man.'[61]

Notes

1 Charles James Napier, *Defects, Civil and Military, of the Indian Government*, W.F.P. Napier (ed.) (London: Charles Westerton, 1853), 72.
2 Dalhousie to Napier, 24 December 1849, given with interpolated comments in Napier, *Defects*, 160–64, quotation at 161.
3 Dalhousie to Hobhouse, [?] November 1849, BP, BL Add. MS 36477, fols 103–06.
4 Copy of Napier to Ellenborough, 26 February 1850, Bodleian MS. Eng. lett. c. 241, fols 229–32; Napier, *Defects*, 68–70.
5 Napier, *Defects*, 69–70.
6 Napier adds that *only* the British would be able to travel safely and freely on the roads, and only they would be protected under the new system. Non-British foreigners would still have to pay their blackmail in the time-honoured way to keep the rural economy going. Napier seems to remember the semi-respected Klepht brigands of Greece.
7 Napier, *Defects*, 72–78, quotation at 76.
8 Napier to Dalhousie, 20 December 1849, given in ibid, 111–13; and for Napier's belief, even as the expedition was about to set off, that the tribesmen would send a party to meet with him, leading to 'some arrangement' over the Kohat road and preventing bloodshed, see Napier to his daughter Emily, 8 February 1850, NP, BL Add. MS 49149, fols 103–04.
9 Dalhousie to Napier, 24 December 1849, given with interpolated comments in Napier, *Defects*, 160–64, quotation at 161. The original document (and Napier's original interpolations), Dalhousie to Napier, 24 December 1849, NP, BL Add. MS 49106, fols 57–59. Meanwhile, Dalhousie repeated to Hobhouse that 'the business . . . had been extremely well done by Col. Bradshaw. The villages, aided by the people of Swat (a valley beyond our position) have suffered heavy loss and been severely punished. A base will be established there, and I hope that . . . no further opposition will be offered.' – Dalhousie to Hobhouse, 5 January 1850, BP, BL Add. MS 36477, fols 137–43 at 138–39.
10 Napier, *Defects*, 85.

The Kohat expedition   311

11 Ibid, 83–86.

12 Napier to Campbell, 2 January 1850, given in ibid, 114–15.

13 Memorandum quoted in Napier, *Defects*, 115. Emerich de Vattel, *The Law of Nations: or, Principles of the Law of Nature, Applied to the Conduct and Affairs of Nations and Sovereigns* [1758] (London: G.G. and J. Robinson, 1797), book 3, chapter 9.

14 Napier, *Defects*, 115.

15 Bradshaw to Napier, 13 January 1850, given in ibid, 116–17.

16 Napier to Campbell, 2 January 1850, given in ibid, 114–15.

17 Lawrence Shadwell, *The Life of Colin Campbell, Lord Clyde*, 2 vols (Edinburgh: William Blackwood and Sons, 1881), 1:241.

18 Napier, *Defects*, 90–93, 95–97.

19 Ibid, 97. Delane's brother was the editor of the *Times* – Napier to Robertson, 25 February 1850, NP, BL Add. MS 49107, fols 97–100, imperfect.

20 W. H. Paget, *A Record on the Expeditions Against the North-West Frontier Tribes since the Annexation of the Punjab* [1873], revised edn, A. H. Mason (ed.) (London: Whiting & Co., [1884]), 319–24.

21 Dalhousie to Hobhouse, 22 December 1849, BP, BL Add. MS 36477, fols 123–36 at 125.

22 The *Times* 15 April 1850, 5 col. a; *Manchester Guardian*, 17 April 1850, 2.

23 Napier, *Defects*, 114.

24 Ibid, 91.

25 Napier's journal, 22, 23 March and 5 April 1810, given in WN, 1:159–61.

26 Napier's journal, 8 October 1842, given in WN, 2:218; see also Ellenborough to Wellington, 22 March 1843, given in CEW, 355–59 at 357–58.

27 Wellington to Ellenborough, 4 February 1843, copy for Ripon, PBC, BL Add. MS 40864, fols 26–33 at 27–28.

28 Napier, *Defects*, 91.

29 Ibid, 91–92.

30 Ibid, 113, 117. See also the less colourful praise of Campbell in Napier's General Order announcing the results of the Afridi Expedition, dated 16 February 1850, given in John Mawson, *Records of the Indian Command of General Charles James Napier* (Calcutta: R. and C. Lepage, 1851), 94–98.

31 Charles James Napier, *Remarks on Military Law and the Punishment of Flogging* (London: T. and W. Boone, 1837), ix–x.

32 Napier to Louisa Napier, 1 May 1840, Bodleian MS Eng. lett. c. 240, fols 66–68 at 68.

33 Napier, editor's note to Part 1, chapter 5, in Alfred Victor, comte de Vigny, *Lights and Shades of Military Life*, Charles James Napier (ed.), 2nd edn (London: Henry Colburn, 1850), 2nd edn, 85, 88.

34 Ibid, 16.

35 Vattel, *Law of Nations*, book 3, chapter 11. Napier to the Adjutant-General, 1842, quoted in WN, 2:180.

36 Herbert Benjamin Edwardes and Herman Merivale, *Life of Sir Henry Lawrence*, 2nd edn, 2 vols (London: Smith, Elder, & Co., 1872), 2:163.

37 George Lawrence, *Reminiscences of Forty-Three Years in India*, W. Edwards (ed.) (1874; Lahore, Pakistan: Sang-i-Meel Publications, 1981), 273–74.

38 Edwardes and Merivale, *Henry Lawrence*, 2:140–41.

39 Henry Lawrence, 'Sir Charles Napier's Posthumous Work', *Calcutta Review* 23 (1854), 208–90 at 256–59 and 259n.

40 Ibid.

41 Donald D. Horward, 'Wellington and the Defence of Portugal', *International History Review* 11, 1 (February 1989), 39–54 at 45–46, 49; Gordon to Aberdeen, 10 November 1810, given in Rory Muir (ed.), *At Wellington's Right Hand: The Letters of Lieutenant-Colonel Sir Alexander Gordon, 1808–1815*, Publications of the Army Records Society, 21 (Stroud, Gloucestershire: Sutton Publishing Company, 2003), 123–25; Wellington to Hill, 9 August 1810, Wellington to Lord Liverpool, 27 October 1810, given in Arthur

312 *Commander-in-Chief*

Wellesley, Duke of Wellington, *The Dispatches of Field Marshall the Duke of Wellington*, New edn, 13 vols. J. Gurwood (ed.) (London: John Murray, 1834–1839), 6:322–23, 6:519–20; and for Wellington's attempts to prevent and punish atrocities, Wellington to Burton, Wellington to Waters, Wellington to M'Kay, all 1 July 1813, 6:570–71.

42 Napier to Dalhousie, 25 February 1850, given in Napier, *Defects*, 118–20. Napier's public report was more discrete, but he insisted that the burnings had been carried out by the 'civil authorities' – Napier to Dalhousie, 16 February 1850, given in Mawson, *Records*, Appendix, xxvi–xxix, at paragraphs 4, 9, 12.

43 Dalhousie to Couper, 16 March 1850, given in BMD, 113–15.

44 Dalhousie to Couper, 23 March 1850, given in ibid, 115; Dalhousie to Hobhouse, 25 March, 8 April 1850, BP, BL Add. MS 36477, fols 173–83 at 180, and fols 185–90 at 187–88. The recent work of Hugh Beattie shows that Dalhousie would soon become even more of an advocate of making violent attacks against the tribes of this region than the Lawrences were: Beattie, *Imperial Frontier: Tribe and State in Waziristan* (Richmond, Surrey: Curzon Press, 2002), 33, 63–64.

45 Dalhousie to Hobhouse, 8 March 1850, BP, BL Add. MS 36477, fols 167–71 at 170. He did not think that Napier's dispatch on Kohat needed to be published, because he 'didn't think it expedient to publish every little thing.' – Dalhousie to Hobhouse, 25 May 1850, BP, BL Add. MS 36477, fols 218–21.

46 R. Boswell Smith, *Life of Lord Lawrence*, 2 vols (London: Smith, Elder, & Co., 1883), 1:352.

47 Edwardes and Merivale, *Henry Lawrence*, 2:160–61. Edwardes was a protégé of Lawrence – see 2:140. Merivale was permanent secretary at the Colonial Office and later at the India Office. He was not overly fond of native peoples. See Edward Beasley, *Mid-Victorian Imperialists: British Gentlemen and the Empire of the Mind* (London: Routledge, 2005), chapter 3.

48 Kathryn Tidrick, *Empire and the English Character* (London: I.B. Tauris, 1990), 10–11, 12.

49 *Household Words Narrative*, February 1850, 86–87. In an Indian newspaper another soldier, apparently not the one whose letter appeared in *Household Words*, also reported the burnings and destruction that he had taken part in with gusto and an utter lack of moral understanding. See Mawson, *Records*, Appendix, xxiii–xxvi, reprinted from the *Bengal Huruku* of 2 March 1850.

50 Geoffrey Fairbairn, *Revolutionary Guerrilla Warfare: The Countryside Version* (Harmondsworth, Middlesex: Penguin Books, 1974), 53–54; Arthur Swinson, *North-West Frontier: People and Events, 1839–1947* (New York: Frederick A. Praeger, 1967), 102, 106; George Orwell, 'Politics and the English Language' (1946), in *The Collected Essays, Journalism and Letters of George Orwell*, Sonia Orwell and Ian Angus (eds), 4 vols (New York: Harcourt, Brace, & World, 1968), 4:127–40 at 136.

51 Winston Churchill, *The Story of the Malakand Field Force: An Episode of Frontier War* [1898] (London: Thomas Nelson & Sons, 1916), 272–75, quotations at 273–74.

52 Napier to Emily Bunbury, 15 May 1850, 25 December 1851, NP, BL Add. MS 49110, fol. 116, fols 125–32 at 126.

53 See Campbell to Napier, copy, 5 March 1850, NP, TNA PRO 30/64/9, fols 15–16. Campbell pointed out that in time the women and children would be sheltered by other tribes who would become hostile in turn – so destroying the houses rather than reaching a settlement would leave the country up in arms all the way into the hot months when nothing could be done about it.

54 Shadwell, *Colin Campbell*, 1:246–61; Campbell to Napier, 11 May 1850, NP, BL Add. MS 49108, fols 13–15; Dalhousie to Hobhouse, 25 May 1850, BP, BL Add. MS 36477, fols 218–21; Campbell to Napier, 9 November 1850, NP, TNA PRO 30/64/9, fols 25–27.

55 Colin Campbell to Napier, 26 April 1850, NP, TNA PRO 30/64/9 [no folio number]; and Campbell to Napier, 12 June 1844, fols 32–36 at 33–34. To Napier's surprise and displeasure, the Lawrences did on one occasion accept from the Afridis an offer of safe conduct for a British regiment – Campbell to Napier, 2 April 1850, NP, TNA PRO 30/64/9 [no folio number], with Napier's comment at end.

The Kohat expedition 313

56 That the Afridis turned towards peace: Paget, *A Record on the Expeditions Against the North-West Frontier Tribes*, 325–26. That they did not: *The Times*, 16 April 1850, 5 col. d, 17 April 1850, 5 col. d, 6 May 1850, 4 cols c-e; *Manchester Guardian*, 20 April 1850, 5. For operational details: Intelligence Branch, Division of the Chief of Staff, Army Headquarters, India, *Frontier and Overland Expeditions from India*, 6 vols (Simla: Government Monotype Press, 1908), 2:131–44.

57 Campbell to Napier, 18 August 1850, NP, BL Add. MS 49108, fols 20–22; Shadwell, *Colin Campbell*, 1:264.

58 Napier, *Defects*, 117–18; Colin Campbell to Napier, 5 March 1850, extracts, quoted in ibid, 122–24; Napier to Colin Campbell, 11 March 1850, extracts, 124–26.

59 Napier's journal, 16 February 1850, extracts, quoted in Napier, *Defects*, 101; ibid, 118.

60 Napier, *Defects*, 71–72.

61 Ibid, 72.

24 The mutinies of Charles James Napier

We have seen that by early December 1849 Napier's warnings about widespread discontent over the reductions in army pay had led the Governor-General to set him down as a wild alarmist. Then at the end of that month Napier had to report that four sepoys who had refused their pay at Wuzzeerabad (the modern Wazirabad, between Lahore and Rawalpindi) were sentenced to hard labour, riveted into their chains on the parade ground for everyone to see, and sent off as felons. He hoped a court-martial would sentence them to death, 'for never was there a more distinct conspiracy to dictate to Government what pay the troops ought to receive.'[1] Whether or not Napier was an alarmist, certainly he was trying to sound the alarm here.

Yet as in the case of the murderous husbands of Sind, the fact that Napier wanted to see death sentences did not mean he wanted the condemned to die. In the end when the men were sentenced to death as he wished, he promptly commuted their sentences to transportation for life. The condemned would serve as 'living examples of the terrible fate which awaits traitors to their colours'.[2]

Napier feared general rebellion. There were 50,000 sepoys in the region, and he and his staff believed that 30,000 were on the brink of a rising that could extinguish the Indian Empire. So it was especially important to settle this pay dispute. Looking back on the matter, Napier explained that like most 'Easterns', the Sikh soldiers were very patriotic. But they were patriotic *towards* whoever controlled any Treasury that paid them regularly and paid them well. In the 1840s they had transferred their loyalties from leader to leader, leading to the downfall of the Sikh state and their loss of independence.[3] Now they could transfer their loyalties away from the British every bit as easily.

At Peshawar, Napier tried to gauge the mood of the troops. He had chosen the city because it lay a short distance *outside* the area where the pay was being cut. He could despatch a large and loyal force from the Peshawar garrison if there was trouble in the areas nearby where the pay reductions were being imposed.

Dalhousie would later use the visit that Napier made to Peshawar as evidence that the general expected no trouble from the pay reduction, or he would not have left the area where it was coming into effect. Things were more ambiguous up close. On their way to the city, Napier's officers still sensed 'a mutinous spirit', although all seemed quiet at the moment. Nor was the situation grave enough to warrant the opening of the soldiers' mail, Napier thought, although some of his officers had proposed doing so.[4]

***

Napier reached Peshawar on 30 December 1849. The Kohat expedition with the profound and disturbing questions that it would raise for Napier began a month later, and it unfolded over February. On 25 February, when Napier was still reeling from what he had seen, he received word that on the first of the month the 66th Native Infantry on the march to Lucknow had refused their pay and demanded their discharge, shouting at their officers and beginning to move toward them in an assembly. And then they crossed the line into open mutiny, attempting to take the fortress of Govindghur in the Sikh holy city of Amritsar. The fort sat next to the Sikh temple and the soldiers were Hindus, so the situation was very dangerous for British control of Punjab. The actions of these Hindu soldiers so close to the Golden Temple might spark unrest among the Sikh population.[5]

'*The crisis was come!*,' Napier thought. Mutiny had now spread to a city two hundred fifty miles from the first disturbances at Rawalpindi in July. At Govindghur, it was only by accident that a lieutenant-colonel named Bradford and his men saved the day for the British. They happened to be in camp outside the fort when they heard the cry of the mutiny. They ran to the gate as the sepoys tried to shut them out. After some hand-to-hand combat they were able to rush the gate and entered in force. British control was reestablished and the courts-martial began at once.[6]

Napier also had intelligence reports from Wazirabad, where the four now-transported soldiers had refused their pay in December. According to what he was now told, sepoys in a number of units across Punjab were waiting for news that rebellion had broken out in order to commence their own unrest.[7] Napier worried that Govindghur might trigger a general mutiny. On 27 February he wrote to Dalhousie, located somewhere on the high seas, that in the case of the mutinous troops at Govindghur he was taking the extraordinary step of disbanding the regiment. The native officers, NCOs, and sepoys were marched away and struck off; and then the colours of the 66th were presented to a unit of Gurkhas, who were thereby for the first time made British troops of the line – regular British forces. (Incorporating them in some way in the near future is something that Dalhousie and Napier had already discussed.) Napier did not technically have the power to disband the old 66th or to incorporate the Gurkhas as the new one,[8] but he did it anyway, and he hoped Dalhousie would approve, given the gravity of the situation. Serving with the Buddhist Gurkhas, Napier explained, should mortify the Brahmin soldiers and serve to remind them to remain loyal – for otherwise more Buddhists could be brought into the forces.[9]

Napier's actions and those of Bradford and others at Amritsar had shut down a mutiny. And when he first heard of these events, Dalhousie agreed that

316   *Commander-in-Chief*

indeed a mutiny had taken place at perhaps the most important fort in India; and he agreed that Napier was right in overstepping his authority and disbanding the 66th.[10] But Dalhousie would later argue that the quiet aftermath meant that there had never been a mutiny at all, and nor had there ever been any danger of one. In his later accounts, Dalhousie accused Napier of libelling the army in suggesting that even the possibility of a mutiny existed.

Napier's answer was this: Dalhousie had not commuted any of the prison sentences for the mutineers, and rather than reversing he had confirmed the disbanding of the old 66th and its reestablishment as a Ghurkha unit. So initially the Governor-General *did* seem to have accepted that a mutiny had taken place.[11]

The mutiny of Charles James Napier

Meanwhile there had been continuing trouble at Wazirabad. In early January, Brigadier Hearsey had informed Napier that the sepoys of the garrison were now on the edge of rebellion over another pay issue entirely, namely a change in the food allowances. Army practice had been to check the price of each major food item in the bazaar. Then the soldiers were given an appropriate allowance to buy what they needed. Now the army was shifting to a price index for the bazaar as a whole and deciding the food allowance based upon that, rather than looking at the prices of the main foods the soldiers bought. Hearsey said the change had come as a surprise to both himself and his men. It suddenly appeared as a technical revision in the pay regulations, buried within obscure language on other matters. But its application had real effects. The soldiers were already incensed over the cut in the foreign duty bonus, and they now stood to lose even more of their income.

Hearsey wrote a letter that set out the matter and this was duly passed up the chain of command to Sir Walter Gilbert, who agreed that something needed to be done, and countersigned the letter. It reached Napier as Commander-in-Chief about two weeks later, on 20 January, which was twelve days (as Napier reminds us in his later book) before the 66th mutinied at Amritsar. The countersigned letter was handed to Napier by the Adjutant-General of the Army, Colonel Patrick Grant, who made it clear that he agreed with it as well.[12] Grant explained how

> the regulation in question had been concocted by subordinates in office, merely to save trouble, and he did not believe the Governor-General or Commander-in-Chief of the time knew it bore hard on the Sepoy. That from its nature it only came into operation locally, and could be known but to a few regiments: to enforce it at Wuzzeerabad would be dangerous![13]

Napier tells us that Grant's account of where the regulation came from and what its enforcement could mean 'guided my conduct'. Nothing like the original regulation had existed in the army that he had commanded when he

The mutinies of Charles James Napier 317

was in Sind, so he asked the Adjutant to tell him more about its history. And then Napier had Grant write two letters, both dated that day, the 20th. One letter directed that the regulation should be suspended and that the higher rate of compensation should continue to be paid pending an appeal to the Governor-General-in-Council. (This was the Council of India, of which Napier was a member.) The other letter was the appeal itself. Along with it, Napier enclosed Colonel Hearsey's letter and the various endorsements added by the officers up the line. Napier's letter of appeal to the Council ended like this:

> [C]onfident of the support of Government, the Commander-in-Chief has directed that compensation shall be issued to the Native troops in the Punjaub, in accordance with the rules laid out in the old regulation; *as in the present state of transition from Scinde pay and allowances, to the regular pay of the troops, a transition which has produced a most unprovoked state of insubordination in some regiments, the Commander-in-Chief thinks that no cause of dissatisfaction should be given to the troops* [emphasis original].[14]

This letter, Napier says, reached Calcutta on 13 February, and the answer reached him on 26 February, at the end of the Kohat fighting.[15]

Both Napier and his Adjutant-General believed that the answer to their complaint, although it came from the Council, must have been written by one and the same subordinate who had framed the new regulation in the first place. For the answer they received ran to ten numbered paragraphs of legal justifications. These ten paragraphs set out how the new regulation had been reviewed and gazetted according to all the best bureaucratic procedures, and so everyone ought to have known all about it. Napier was also told that there had been no urgent need to review the new rule, and so he had no right to tamper with a matter of military pay that belonged to the purview of the overall government, and which was *not* a matter for the Commander-in-Chief. The issue would be brought to the attention of Lord Dalhousie on his return. The letter was drafted by a Major Wylie.[16]

In this way the Commander-in-Chief of India, who was a lieutenant-general, found himself upbraided by a major for defying the will of a small Council of which he was himself a member.[17] In this very substantial letter, the major had taken no notice of the military situation, or of the mutinies, or of Napier's larger, long-established support for Dalhousie's policy of reducing military pay; and nor did he take any account of all the officers in the chain of command underneath Napier who had agreed with Hearsey that applying the regulation with immediate effect was dangerous under the current circumstances. Wylie only mentioned the opinions of Hearsey and the other officers when he wanted to engage with them on the one and only subject that Wylie himself wanted to discuss: when the regulation had passed its bureaucratic hurdles at headquarters, and when therefore it had become known (ideally) to the men in the field.[18]

318   *Commander-in-Chief*

Napier did not fail to appreciate the tone of all this. He did not like having his arguments brushed off with so much 'laboured sophistry' by so junior an officer. And as he tells us, at the end of the Kohat campaign he was '[i]ll, and vexed with the loss of brave comrades, victims to ignorant governing'. Such was his frame of mind when he immediately sent off a response that he was later to admit was abrupt in its phrasing.[19] He told Wylie that he was not questioning the bureaucratic history of the regulation. Instead he was addressing the urgent situation on the ground. And Napier ended by saying that he was sure that Lord Dalhousie would agree with him when he got back.[20] For as Napier recalled, Dalhousie had more than once promised his 'unreservedly given' support for the care that – as Dalhousie had further detailed – Napier was 'very wise' in taking in order to make sure that any trouble over the pay cuts did not become more serious. Napier was now relying upon these promises of support.[21]

In the book that Napier wrote on all this, he added up the total of the cost of keeping the food allowances at the older, higher level for the three or four thousand Sikh soldiers involved: About £40 per month. He continues: 'Had an idea crossed my mind that Lord Dalhousie would regard this as a desperate attempt to usurp his supreme civil power, willingly would I have paid the Sepoys myself, to save bloodshed and vital mischief to the community.'[22]

But at the time, Napier did not suspect that Dalhousie would take Wylie's side, and in any case Napier was thinking about other things. He does not seem to have given the question of the food allowances another thought. After the Kohat expedition ended, he travelled back towards Simla. In late March, he was still writing confident and chatty letters to Dalhousie on a variety of matters, not suspecting the reception that awaited him when he reached the Governor-General.[23]

Napier, being difficult, and Dalhousie's response

Dalhousie sent his own views to Napier on 13 April 1850, no longer with the personal warmth and friendliness which had characterized their correspondence until that point. Indeed, his response was not in the form of a personal letter at all. It was signed by the same Major Wylie – although the Governor-General himself had written it, as he told his friend.[24]

This new letter stressed that the bureaucratic history of the new regulation 'left no room for doubt' about the change in pay. Napier was told that if there had been uncertainty about what the regulation meant and whether it applied in this case, he should have referred the matter to the Council and waited for a decision in the usual way. There was 'no call for haste'. However, because Napier had taken what this letter called the irrevocable step of cancelling the regulation (a step that as Napier would point out was for only one area, and hardly irrevocable[25]), his act to suspend it was reluctantly agreed to. Yet, Wylie and Dalhousie continued, Napier by overstepping his rights had permanently and with no hope of emendation thwarted the clearly articulated policy of

The mutinies of Charles James Napier   319

the government to bring the pay of Indian troops everywhere to a uniform standard. Therefore,

> the Governor-General, from a consideration of the papers before him, feels it necessary to intimate for the future guidance of his Excellency [Napier as Commander-in-Chief], that the Governor-General in Council will not again permit the Commander-in-Chief, *under any circumstances*, to issue orders which shall change the pay and allowances of the troops serving in India, and thus practically to exercise an authority which has been reserved, and most properly reserved for the Supreme Government alone.[26]

What Napier thought on reading this was that men at headquarters were intriguing against him. He believed Dalhousie was merely echoing his staff. In this Napier was mistaken – Dalhousie meant it, as he told the Board of Control as well as his friend Couper.[27] But as Napier went on to say, '[m]en of honest intentions are reluctant to accept the first aberration of a friend as a designed offence'. Because of 'Dalhousie's former cordiality', Napier wrote a private letter to him, as well as sending to the whole Council of India a short note on the trouble in Punjab.[28] In what he said to the Governor-General, he mentioned once again the other officers who had agreed with him about the dangers of the new regulation. Further, he wanted to clear up any idea that Dalhousie might have that he had anywhere criticized his administration. He had criticized *only* the government of Punjab, Napier said – mainly for massing troops ineffectively or for stationing them in unhealthy places. He had not criticized the supreme government, Lord Dalhousie's government.[29]

That Dalhousie might have identified himself with the very administrative system in Punjab that Napier was criticizing – a system that Dalhousie had set up only a year before – does not seem to have occurred to the general.

Napier's letter to Dalhousie seems moderate enough, designed perhaps to save a friendship. But Napier also took another step. For the conclusion of the letter from Dalhousie and Wylie had contained a stinger, and on reflection Napier felt himself much stung by it. Dalhousie had removed from Napier any power to suspend a pay regulation in the future. He could no longer change anyone's compensation. And for Napier, this meant that he would no longer have the power, even under the direst of circumstances, to take any step regarding pay or allowances that he might think necessary for the safety of the army. So having received Dalhousie's judgement, Napier after a time went ahead and took a step which he had been talking about ever since Kohat.[30] Acting according to protocol, he wrote to the Duke of Wellington through Lord Fitzroy Somerset at the Horse Guards, asking permission to petition Her Majesty the Queen to be allowed to resign his position as Commander-in-Chief of India.

Napier's letter to Somerset and the duke, dated 22 May 1850, explained the matter this way: He had come out to fight a war that Lord Gough had already won, and so he had focussed on improving the discipline of the army for his

320 *Commander-in-Chief*

successor. Napier stressed that he supported Dalhousie's pay reductions and he agreed that Dalhousie had the right to impose them. But in addition to supporting Dalhousie's policies, Napier also had to deal with a mutiny. And he had dealt with it successfully, putting an end to the fighting and restoring discipline. In return, he had received a reprimand and he had been forbidden from the free exercise of his judgement in the future. He continued:

> I have been treated as if I had assumed the powers of Government, which I had not done! I merely acted with decision in a dangerous crisis: So dangerous, that a few days after, the mutinous troops attempted to seize the strongest fortress in the Punjab. On that occasion, also, although the Governor-General publicly approved of what I did, in a private letter he regretted I had not consulted the Supreme Council at Calcutta. Such dangerous moments do not admit of slow and undecided counsels.[31]

Napier pointed out that he was almost seventy, and that he had been increasingly ill for the better part of a decade. The Indian climate was no good for his health.[32] He requested to be relieved by October, or as soon as possible.

***

Dalhousie told his friend Couper his side of things in mid-April, the day after sending the momentous order to Napier. In his account to Couper the Governor-General never once alluded to the opinions of the other officers (Hearsey, Gilbert, and Adjutant-General Grant) about how dangerous it would be to cut the food allowances at Wazirabad. As Dalhousie recounted the affair, Napier had found an apparent conflict in the regulations (and not a real one), and he had cancelled the new version simply because he thought he could get away with it, when Dalhousie was at sea. This trespassed on the power of the Governor-General, and it totally frustrated the pay regularization plans for India as a whole. Napier ought at least to have waited. If he had done so, then the technicality could have been cleared up in the normal way a month or two later. But now, Dalhousie wrote, he was 'obliged to give the C.-in-C. a punch in the head at last': 'He will be furious, I daresay, but I have him on the hip. He everywhere declares publicly that he goes to England in October: no one knows whether he will or not.'[33]

There are several points that we can take from this. For one thing, the order to Napier never again to change pay or benefits under any circumstances came when Dalhousie was speculating over just when Napier would finally leave. And Dalhousie deliberately framed the order to be 'a punch in the head at last'.

It may be remembered that the Governor-General had always looked over his shoulder for any interference from Napier, ever since their first meeting. And we saw that when Dalhousie set sail on his ocean voyage in January, he told Couper that he expected Napier to misbehave, and he left written instructions that the Commander-in-Chief should not exceed his normal powers in any way. As Dalhousie's biographer explains, the Governor-General put this

The mutinies of Charles James Napier 321

restriction upon Napier because someone repeated to him one of the general's flights of fancy. Napier once told his men that if he had three armies of fifty thousand in the right places, he would conquer Afghanistan and through it southern China, and divide China up among the soldiers.[34]

Was Dalhousie truly worried that Napier was insane and might start an adventure like this in the two months he was gone?

Perhaps there is another explanation, arising from Dalhousie's special concern over Punjabi affairs and his desire to keep Napier away from the province. For we should remember what Dalhousie was confronted with when he came back from his sea voyage and returned to work. He found waiting for him not only the correspondence regarding the pay regulation – the tempest in the teapot over the £40 extra money for the Sikh soldiers – but also Napier's excited letters about the policy of burning villages in the hills.[35] Both of these matters touched upon something that Dalhousie cared deeply about, the question of bringing order to the province he conquered, the province that was his own special project as Sind had been Napier's. After all, Dalhousie had cared so deeply about what was happening in Punjab that he stayed in India when doing so might have killed him. Napier had run a similar risk to remain in Sind in the 1840s and for a similar reason. Just as Napier had refused to resign after he almost died from heat stroke, Dalhousie refused to resign even when the bone was exposed in his mouth (and in an era before antibiotics this wound did not bode well).

Dalhousie had stayed on because he felt that he had a special mission. His style of governance in Punjab – it has been called 'The Punjab School' – was an ambitious Utilitarian programme of social reform and economic development. The Governor-General wanted to have the development of Punjab for his own special legacy.[36] And while he may have had to share credit with the Lawrence brothers, whom he appointed, he certainly did not want Napier interfering there as well. Now indeed Napier had interfered in Punjab in several ways. This could not be tolerated.

Last days in India

Meanwhile, even if his resignation were accepted by the authorities in London, Napier would not be leaving India for some time. As Commander-in-Chief he would still have to work with Dalhousie for a number of months. This did not go well. In July, Dalhousie told the general that in future he should communicate with the civilian authorities in Punjab only through official channels, in the normal way; and that he should write to them directly only in the case of an emergency. Napier responded that because the Governor-General would not accept his judgement about what constituted an emergency, he – Napier – would never again write directly to the authorities in Punjab no matter what the circumstances. Dalhousie responded that 'emergency' was a common enough word, and Napier could judge an emergency for himself and act accordingly.

322 *Commander-in-Chief*

Privately Dalhousie said that Napier was behaving with the petulance that would get a child whipped. He was probably right that Napier was abusing him to everyone within earshot and that in Napier he had made a 'mortal enemy'.[37] The Commander-in-Chief and the Governor-General now began a war of tit-for-tat memoranda, each trying to convince the authorities in London that he was right about the question of the pay.[38] Neither man behaved very well during all this.

In mid-May, Dalhousie promised Couper that he would use his pen to 'crucify' Napier should the Commander-in-Chief actually resign over the reprimand.[39] Over the next several months Dalhousie set out to do this very thing, as he began in earnest to press his side of things. Dalhousie's case ran something like this: Napier was an alarmist in his predictions of a general uprising. He did not need to suspend the pay regulation, for there was no mutiny in the army. There was no danger of one, and all was quiet after the disbanding of the 66th. If there had been any real danger, Napier would not have left Punjab to visit the garrison at Peshawar. So in saying that there was general unrest, Napier was running down the army that he commanded. And in not wanting to have his hands tied, Napier was trying to rule the government.

In laying out this argument, Dalhousie stressed that he did not want to quote any private papers in his public writings, for he was above doing that; but if he were to do so, he could 'tear [Napier] limb from limb'. Meanwhile he was worried that Napier would get the jump on him by writing to England first and twisting things in the press. It was by using the press that Napier had elevated himself into a position of eminence, wrote Dalhousie.[40]

While the Governor-General was worrying that the Commander-in-Chief might pick up his pen and win the battle of public opinion, in fact the irascible style that Napier would often use was beginning to annoy officials in London. As Sir John Hobhouse, President of the Board of Control, had told Dalhousie in March:

> I agree with you that the Commander in Chief ought to have replied speedily and precisely to your Punjaub Minute – but he is not like other men, and I can assure you that some of his orders and speeches make us at home stare not a little. As to when he is returning to England we do not hear a word of it now, so it is unnecessary to talk or think of his successor.[41]

In July Hobhouse wrote Napier personally to say that while he would do all he could to help him and to get him what he wanted for India, 'I should be acting very insincerely to you if I did not take this opportunity of telling you that I have been exceedingly annoyed by the tone of your correspondence on the military defences'. You have been 'overearnest with your Brutus', he told Napier. In June, Hobhouse told the Governor-General that the warnings and complaints which Napier was continuing to send home were 'so exceedingly objectionable' in 'tone and spirit' that he had passed them on to the Prime Minister and the Duke of Wellington.[42]

The mutinies of Charles James Napier 323

Indeed, Hobhouse was afraid that Napier might have shared his fears about a mutiny with Wellington, so the President of the Board of Control made sure that both Wellington and the Prime Minister saw all of Dalhousie's answers to Napier. That way they could 'compare the romance with the reality'.[43] Hobhouse told the Governor-General:

> It is certainly marvellous that such apprehensions [regarding mutiny] should enter into the head of such a man; credulity will scarcely account for them. Interest he can have none in misrepresenting so extravagantly the state of affairs; except, indeed, he may, by possibility, think it necessary to find some excuse for staying in India, after his friends had confidently given out that his immediate return to England was all but certain. This would not be quite worthy of his name, character, and brilliant career; but the best men are sometimes actuated by motives which they, hardly, themselves, recognize.[44]

Hobhouse said that even Hardinge agreed with him – Napier's views about a possible rebellion in Punjab in the near future were alarmist and unjustified.[45]

Against this background, Dalhousie had no trouble getting Hobhouse and the Secret Committee to agree with him about Kohat, too. In Hobhouse's words:

> No one here understands why the Commander in Chief thought it worth-while to make such a parade of General Orders, and what not, and to go himself to punish a few hundred marauders and assassins. . . . As for his project of paying there [*sic*] gentry instead of shooting them he might as well have thought of that before he marched to Kohat. Perhaps, however, you may make some arrangements with the heads of the mountain tribes which may give more security to your frontier.[46]

Yet despite these words of support, Dalhousie still did not know whether Napier's resignation would be approved. Hobhouse was not able to send Wellington's decision to the Governor-General until late in the summer. (The Duke wrote his memorandum on 30 July and Dalhousie received it on 18 September.) In Wellington's considered opinion, Napier had been in the wrong in countermanding the pay order, and he should not have resigned the high position with which he had been honoured; but as he had resigned his post, the resignation was accepted. And Wellington wrote directly to Dalhousie promising to back him up in Parliament should it come to that. Wellington's final verdict was that Napier was utterly mistaken: There had been no general mutiny over the pay issue (although in his memorandum itself, Wellington complained of not having been shown all the relevant papers). The Duke wrote that what Napier ought to have done was to delay the payday, give pay-day advances instead, and take any measures he could to avoid suspending the new pay regulation on his own authority.[47]

Attacks and counterattacks

When Napier had been dead for only a few years and the Indian Mutiny (or War of Independence) of 1857–1858 was raging, some people blamed Dalhousie and his policies for the carnage. The Mutiny erupted under Dalhousie's successor, but for many critics the real fault lay with Dalhousie's policies of modernization, annexation, and conquest during the eight years he ruled India (1848–1856). It was not hard to find support for this criticism of Dalhousie in the book that Napier would write at the close of his life.[48]

Bartle Frere was one of those who thought that if more attention had been paid to Napier's assessment of the mood of the native troops, the Mutiny might have been avoided or minimized.[49] Agreeing with Wellington that as a matter of military discipline Napier had been in the wrong in his behaviour over the pay cut, Frere told John Kaye:

> When you say that there is no blame to be recorded against the Governor-General for the conduct of his final dispute with Napier, do you not take a rather limited and official view of their differences? No doubt, technically and officially, the Governor-General was right and the Commander-in-Chief was wrong – there could be no question as to which the Ministry at home was bound to support – but will not history blame the statesman who refused to be warned by such a soldier as Napier? – who, as far as we can judge, shut his eyes to the danger Napier had clearly pointed out . . ., and who left the empire which he governed for so many years with the sincere conviction, as testified in his famous parting Minute, that the dangers which Napier, Jacob, and Henry Lawrence had been warning him had no existence?[50]

Kaye did not agree. He pointed out that when Napier was in Sind and again when he was Commander-in-Chief, he had many times praised the loyalty of sepoy units or the Indian Army as a whole. He said that in praising the troops in this way Napier must not have been afraid of them.[51]

Dalhousie would agree with this. When the Mutiny broke out, he began assembling a file of letters and clippings to illustrate how Napier had praised the soldiers who served under him in Sind and elsewhere. And so by proving to his own satisfaction that Charles Napier had expected no mutiny, Dalhousie tried to exonerate himself for not having foreseen what was to come. But perhaps all of Dalhousie's clippings could not erase the long memorandum that Napier had sent him on the various military threats in the subcontinent.

In any case, Dalhousie's failing health no longer permitted him to speak publicly on Indian affairs. By the time the Mutiny was over, Dalhousie had only two years to live.[52]

***

During his last months in India, Napier cut Dalhousie in Simla when he could – although he was pleasant to Lady Dalhousie when he saw her in the shops.[53] He rode out the public controversy over the death of a colonel who had been insulted by one of his own men. The insulted colonel had the man flogged. Napier then showed the soldier some mercy, refusing to send him into exile. In response the colonel killed himself, and many officers criticized Napier.[54] The Commander-in-Chief also continued dealing with the more routine aspects of running the army. And in the midst of all this, he brought out his new edition of the works of the military writer Vigny. One long passage which he let stand unmodified in his commentary, for apparently he had nothing to add to what he'd said ten years before, can serve as Charles Napier's final word on India *in India*:

> [T]he object of the English government was to enrich a parcel of shopkeepers; the 'shopocracy of England,' as it has been well termed; and a more base and cruel tyranny never wielded the power of a great nation. Our object in conquering India, the object of all our cruelties, was *money – lucre:* a thousand millions sterling are said to have been squeezed out of India in the last sixty years. Every shilling of this has been picked out of blood, wiped, and put into the murderers' pockets; but, wipe and wash the money as you will, the 'damned spot' will not 'out.' There it sticks for ever, and we shall yet suffer for the crime as sure as there is a God in heaven, where the 'commercial interests of the nation' find no place, or heaven is not what we hope and believe it to be![55]

And he railed against the complacent materialism of the new age:

> Justice and religion are mockeries in the eyes of 'a great manufacturing country,' for the true god of such a nation is Mammon. I may be singular, but, in truth, I prefer the despotic Napoleon to the despots of the East India Company. The man ambitious of universal power generally rules to do good to subdued nations. But the men ambitious of universal peculation rule only to make themselves rich, to the destruction of happiness among a hundred millions of people.[56]

So said the old liberal imperialist, now Commander-in-Chief of India.

Notes

1 Ibid, 57.
2 Napier's remarks on the sentences, 16 and 25 January 1850, given in John Mawson, *Records of the Indian Command of General Charles James Napier* (Calcutta: R. and C. Lepage, 1851), 88–91.
3 Charles James Napier, *Defects, Civil and Military, of the Indian Government,* W.F.P. Napier (ed.) (London: Charles Westerton, 1853), 60–61.
4 Ibid, 61–62, 66.
5 Ibid, 126–27; and the army headquarters copies of the following letters: Major General Gilbert, Commander in Punjab, to the Adjutant General of the Army, 2 February 1850,

326 *Commander-in-Chief*

     with enclosure from Major Troup, commander at Govindghur, of 1 and 2 February, NP, TNA PRO 30/64/13, fols 3–6; Bradford (now commanding at Govindghur) to Major General Gilbert, 2 February 1850, enclosed in Borroughs to the Adjutant General, 3 February 1850, fols 7–9; Bradford to the Adjutant General, 3 February 1850, fols 11–13.

6 Bradford to the Adjutant General, 3 February 1850, NP, TNA PRO 30/64/13, fols 11–13; Napier, *Defects*, 127–28.

7 Napier to Dalhousie, 5 January 1850, given in Napier, *Defects*, 181–84.

8 Supporting minute by an anonymous officer, 23 April 1850, given in ibid, 186–98 at 187.

9 'General Order Disbanding the 66th Native Infantry', 27 February 1850, given in Mawson, *Records*, 101–06.

10 Dalhousie to Couper, 16 March 1850, given in BMD, 113–15.

11 Copy of Napier to his wife, 24 June 1850, Bodleian MS. Eng. lett. c. 241, fols 132–35; Napier, *Defects*, 134.

12 Napier, *Defects*, 135–36.

13 Ibid, 136.

14 Ibid, 136–38.

15 Ibid.

16 Wylie to Napier, 14 February 1850, given in ibid, 139–43.

17 As Indian Commander-in-Chief Napier also had the brevet rank of full general while he was in the East – *London Gazette*, 9 March 1849, 20955 p. 816. But he always used his underlying permanent rank.

18 In twentieth-century literature, Wylie might be represented by Prostetnic Vogon Jeltz. Word reached Napier in 1853 that Wylie had become deranged – Robertson to Napier, 27 January 1853, NP, BL Add. MS 49107, fols 155–57.

19 Napier, *Defects*, 143–44.

20 Napier to the Council of India, [late February] 1850, quoted in ibid, 144–45.

21 Napier to Dalhousie, 18 January 1850, NP, BL Add MS 49106, fols 67–70; Dalhousie to Napier, 11 November 1849, given in Napier, *Defects*, 175–77; see also Dalhousie to Napier, 30 December 1849, 180–81.

22 Napier, *Defects*, 146.

23 Ibid, 147.

24 Dalhousie to Couper, 16 April 1850, 117–22 at 120–21.

25 Napier, *Defects*, 153.

26 Wylie to the Adjutant-General of the Army, 13 April 1850, given in ibid, 151–53.

27 Dalhousie to Hobhouse, 23 April 1850, BP, BL Add. MS 36477, fols 191–96 at 194–95.

28 Napier to the Council of India, 10 April 1850, given in Napier, *Defects*, 154–55.

29 Napier to Dalhousie, 26 April 1850, given in ibid, 155–57.

30 Dalhousie to Couper, 8 April 1850, given in BMD, 116–17; Dalhousie to Couper, 16 April 1850, 117–22 at 121.

31 Napier to Somerset, 22 May 1850, given in Napier, *Defects*, 157–59.

32 For what Napier's doctor told him about how he was killing himself with overwork, see Napier to Emily Bunbury, 16 August 1850, NP, BL Add. MS 49110, fols 117–19.

33 Dalhousie to Couper, 16 April 1850, given in BMD, 117–22.

34 William Lee-Warner, *The Life of the Marquis of Dalhousie, K.T.*, 2 vols (1904; Shannon, Ireland: Irish UP, 1972), 1:315. Part of the charge is echoed in Dalhousie to Hobhouse, 15 May 1850, BP, BL Add. MS 36477, fols 202–11 at 205.

35 Dalhousie to Couper, 16 April 1850, given in BMD, 117–22 at 119–20.

36 Eric Stokes, *The English Utilitarians and India* (Oxford: Oxford UP, 1959), 243, 248–52; R. Boswell Smith, *Life of Lord Lawrence*, 2 vols (London: Smith, Elder, & Co., 1883), 280–81, 304–12, 335, 341.

37 Dalhousie to Hobhouse, 11 July 1850, BP, BL Add. MS 36477, fols 238–47 at 245; copy of Dalhousie to Napier, 18 July 1850, NP, BL Add. MS 49106, fols 116–17; quotation in Dalhousie to Couper, 22 July 1850, given in BMD, 132–33.

The mutinies of Charles James Napier   327

38 For some of the memos and correspondence, see Great Britain, Parliament, *Accounts and Papers, 1854: Papers Relating to the Resignation of General Sir Charles Napier, G.C.B., of the Office of Commander in Chief in India*. No. 80.

39 Dalhousie to Couper, 16 May 1850, given in BMD, 123–25.

40 Dalhousie to Couper, 9 June 1850, given in ibid, 127–28.

41 Hobhouse to Dalhousie, 25 March 1850, copy, BL A&AS MSS Eur F213/27, 260–65 at 260–61.

42 Hobhouse to Napier, 5 July 1850, NP, TNA PRO 30/64/14, fols 35–36; Hobhouse to Dalhousie, 7 June 1850, copy, BL A&AS MSS Eur F213/27, 288–91.

43 Hobhouse to Dalhousie, 7 February 1850, copy, BL A&AS MSS Eur F213/27, 246–49.

44 Ibid, 246–47.

45 Hobhouse to Dalhousie, 20 April 1850, copy, BL A&AS MSS Eur F213/27, 271–73.

46 Hobhouse to Dalhousie, 20 April 1850, BL A&AS MSS Eur F213/27, 275–79 at 277–78.

47 Wellington's memorandum, 30 July 1850, given in Great Britain, *Papers Relating to the Resignation of General Sir Charles Napier*, 58–60; Dalhousie to Couper, 18 September, 7 October, 5 November 1850, given in BMD, 141–42, 144–45; Dalhousie to Hobhouse, 20 September 1850, BP, BL Add. MS 36477, fols 274–78 at 274–75.

48 Napier to W. Napier, 24 September 1845, given in WN, 333–42 at 336; Edward Archer Langley, *Narrative of a Residence at the Court of Meer Ali Murad, with Wild Sports in the Valley of the Indus*, 2 vols (London: Hurst and Blackett, 1860), 2:238–39; [G. B. Malleson], *The Mutiny of the Bengal Army: An Historical Narrative by One Who Served under Sir Charles Napier* (London: Bosworth and Harrison, 1857); John Bruce Norton, *The Rebellion in India, and How to Prevent Another* (London: Richardson Brothers, 1857); Anonymous, 'Sir Charles Napier in India', *Dublin University Magazine* 50, 196 (August 1857), 129–39; H. T. Tucker, *A Glance at the Past and the Future in Connection with the Indian Revolt*, 2nd edn (London: Effingham Wilson, 1857); John Malcolm Ludlow, *British India, Its Races, and Its History, Considered with Reference to the Mutinies of 1857: A Series of Lectures Addressed to the Students of the Working Men's College*, 2 vols (Cambridge: Macmillan and Co., 1858), 214–16. Richard Cobden noted that it was 'the fashion to praise' Napier's book on India: Cobden to Richard Hamilton, 18 September 1857, given in Anthony Howe and Simon Morgan (eds), *The Letters of Richard Cobden*, 3 vols (Oxford: Oxford UP, 2007), 3:343–44. Napier was not the only one to warn of a possible mutiny and to do so in strong language, as Governor Arthur reminded Hardinge in 1844: 7 September 1844, RP, BL Add. MS 40869, fols 167–72 at 171–72.

49 John Martineau, *The Life and Correspondence of the Right Hon. Sir Bartle Frere*, 2nd edn, 2 vols (London: John Murray, 1895), 1:81.

50 Frere to Kaye, 22 July 1865, given in Martineau, *Frere*, 1:174–75.

51 John William [Kaye], 'The Life and Opinions of Gen. Charles James Napier, G.C.B.', *Edinburgh Review* 106 (October 1857), 556–57.

52 Lee-Warner, *Dalhousie*, 2:343–50.

53 Dalhousie to Couper, 5 November 1850, given in BMD, 144–45.

54 Napier to W. Napier, 22 December 1849, Bodleian MS Eng. lett. c. 243, fols 170–73 at fol. 173; *Household Words Narrative*, September 1850, 207–08; Colonel King to Napier, 1850, quoted by William Napier in a letter to the *Times*, 13 September 1850, 5 col. c; *Allen's Indian Mail*, 8, 157 (24 September 1850), 541; Napier to W. Napier, 22 October 1850, Bodleian MS Eng. lett. c. 243, fols 185–86.

55 Napier, editor's note to Part 4, chapter 3 (a translation of Elzéar Blaze's *Military Life in Bivouac, Camp, Garrison, Barracks, etc.*), in Alfred Victor, comte de Vigny, *Lights and Shades of Military Life*, Charles James Napier (ed.), 2 vols in one (London: Henry Colburn, 1840), 2:323; 2nd edn, 297–98.

56 Ibid, Napier, 2:323–24; 2nd edn, 298.

Conclusion
Napier, liberalism, and imperialism

Final days and duties

When Napier left India for the second time, he did not stop in France but went directly home. When he got there he had an emotional and oddly happy reunion with the Duke of Wellington, despite everything, but otherwise all he wanted to do was get out of town and escape the great public dinners in his honour.[1] London, he said, turned him into a 'harness[ed] and 'driven beast'.[2] He did not like going to public dinners.

What he told his sister he was anxious to do, when his papers were finally released from the customs house, was to settle somewhere in the country and compose his answer to Lord Dalhousie. And in a house called Oaklands, near Portsmouth, that is exactly what he did. There were some distractions while he wrote the book, notably during the national panic over whether Napoleon III might invade England in 1852. Napier published a long essay about defending the nation should the invasion come, and on how the gentlemen of the countryside should arm themselves and their retainers. William Makepeace Thackeray read the work and admired its tone. 'I suppose old C. J. Napier's pamphlet can't come to you', the novelist wrote to a friend. 'You see a battle in reading it, and an immense gallant spirit writing and appealing to others'.[3]

There was a more fateful distraction. The Duke of Wellington, who had lived long enough to help to rally the country to defend itself from this latest French threat, died in September 1852. His funeral was one of the great state occasions in British history, and it took place on a very cold day in November. The procession was a long one and Napier was one of the Knights Grand Cross who attended the catafalque. There was a problem with the mechanism, and so Napier, his brother William, Lord Hardinge, and some others chose to remain in the cold for some time trying to get it moving. Then after catching a chill Napier sat through the funeral itself.[4]

It seems that he never got over the cold that he caught that day, although he would continue to travel when he could between London and Portsmouth over his anti-Dalhousie book and other matters. He admitted to John Kennedy that there were whole weeks when he was so ill he could not leave the house. Napier had also been ill the winter before. The liver disease of which he had long complained was rapidly worsening, and he was taking mercury.[5]

Conclusion 329

Yet he could hardly rest. He framed an indictment of every aspect of Dalhousie's rule, every area of economic policy, civil administration, and military affairs in India. And if that was not enough, he allowed himself to get worked up over new criticisms of his own Indian conquest. The *Quarterly Review* published an article called 'Sindh – Dry Leaves from Young Egypt'. It repeated all the old allegations that he had been motivated by greed and cruelty in his conquest of Sind and his subsequent treatment of the Amirs. The essay claimed that Napier had concealed documents and had lied in order to manipulate Ellenborough into the war.[6] Napier brought an action for criminal libel against the *Quarterly*. It failed on a legal technicality, and yet the judges who heard the case said they accepted Napier's version of the events completely. The *Times* urged Napier to reflect on his real position: If the English people truly believed that he had started this war and fought his battles for financial gain, he would not have had the honours he did. Nor would he have received his appointment as Commander-in-Chief in India.[7]

***

Charles Napier carried out one last public duty. The time had come for the every-twenty-year renewal of the charter of the East India Company. On 2 December 1852 Napier left his sickbed to testify before the parliamentary committee on Indian affairs.[8]

Lord Gough, whom Napier had replaced as Commander-in-Chief, turned out to be one of the more active questioners that day, but even Gough came a long way behind another committee member, none other than Lord Ellenborough. At times Ellenborough rather dominated the proceedings. (The chair of the committee was the Lord Privy Seal, the second Marquess of Salisbury.) Napier was asked several times about the state of the Indian Army and its equipment. In his responses he gave high praise to the army itself, while sharing his ideas for improvement – from lightening the muskets to creating a staff corps, so regiments would no longer have to be short-staffed when their officers were seconded to headquarters.

There is a good deal of colour in the transcript of this hearing: Napier with his unshakeable, fatal cold testifying in the London December about warm India and the camels of the desert. No, he explained, the camels cannot pull artillery in the hilly areas. Especially when it rains they have to get on their knees to go up a sharp incline, and they can't pull guns that way. And no, he explained, he did not have elephants with him to do the work: '[T]he elephant does not like going into action, being an exceedingly wise animal.'[9]

Soon he was able to turn to his more serious complaints – about the political officers and how they exerted their authority over senior commanders such as himself. The chairman, followed by Lords Gough and Elphinstone,[10] now began drawing him out on how in fact the junior officers could *not* countermand his orders. Napier explained that they were operating *outside* his orders, even in the middle of combat operations, and he could not tell them what to do.

330 *Conclusion*

And then he turned to his great example: How therefore he could not control the politicals when they burned villages during the Kohat expedition.

Ellenborough now began to prolong this line of questioning so that Napier could discuss the matter more fully. Charles Napier told the committee that he found a native soldier under George Lawrence's command setting a village on fire. Lawrence showed Napier the written order authorizing this action, and so Napier was not able to stop what was going on. He said he allowed the burning to continue because he had no authority to do otherwise, and the village was empty at the time.[11] He went on to discuss the irregular units commanded by Lawrence and Grant, and how they were ordered to go into the mountains and proceed against the Afridis without any reference to the military chain of command and without any word to Napier as Commander-in-Chief. Lord Canning noted that it was not in fact the political agents who were interfering with the military if the Supreme Council of India had ordered them to act in this way: It was the Supreme Council. Ellenborough retorted that the Supreme Council had made its determination based upon the information fed to it by the political agents, a point with which Napier heartily agreed.

And with that, the attention of the committee turned to Napier's views about the police and guard units, the height of barracks, and what could be done for the health of the men.[12]

***

Early in his testimony about Kohat, Napier mentioned that an officer had eventually resigned over the immorality of Dalhousie's military exploits against the hill tribes of Punjab. This was none other Colin Campbell.[13] Indeed, Campbell's letters to Napier were the source for much of his testimony about the more recent events on the Punjabi frontier.[14]

Several months after the hearing, Campbell went to stay with Napier, and he brought word of further acts of destruction. Campbell told him – as Napier recounted in a letter to Ellenborough – 'the shameful way in which whole districts have been devastated, and the most beautiful villages burned, without any apparent reason but the desire of the politicals to appear "vigorous" in the eyes of Lord Dalhousie!'[15] With fresh stories like this, Napier hurried to finish his anti-Dalhousie book while he still could, for as he said, 'such deeds disgrace our arms and ought not to be concealed'. British misrule was provoking the Indians to a great coordinated mutiny, he now said.[16]

Sometimes his mind ranged farther afield. In South Africa, too, British officers were carrying out colour-racist violence against non-combatants, as he told Ellenborough:

> [E]verywhere this vile barbarous spirit appears. I am told, but cannot prove, that the shooting of Kaffir women and children was encouraged, at least not punished by a distinguished officer. When the person who told me spoke to him of his men's misconduct, his answer was ' Oh! *damn them*

Conclusion 331

they are all wolves alike.' Yet the same person told me that this officer would not hurt a woman or a child himself, personally: – this I doubt.[17]

And it was now – now at last – that Charles Napier decided that there had been altogether too many British wars of conquest around the world. They provoked 'our neighbours' in Europe, and England was always 'meddling with other people's affairs'. Further, 'We have made a war with Burmah for £90.10.6*d.*! it will cost us far above a million!! and if we annex it we entail interminable warfare, as our folly has done at Peshawar on the Indus, and in Africa.'[18]

Here perhaps I might be guilty of one of the main sins of the biographer, at least as the sociologist and critic Mary Evans describes them – that of making the life I am writing fit the plot of countless novels.[19] So in the end, should I plead guilty to trying to twist the essential indeterminacy of Napier's life (Evans insists that all our lives are fragmented and multifaceted) into a journey towards redemption or awareness? Am I making Napier repent of conquest, even if he would not admit in so many words that his own act of conquest had been wrong?

I hope I am not being so determinist as all of that; and I do not think that I am creating for Napier any kind of deathbed conversion. For one thing, he had been able to see the ends of liberal imperialism many years before. If age and experience finally made him wiser – and why shouldn't they? – Napier had always been aware of the main underlying fact: That despite the supposed benefits of any act of conquest and the humanitarian ends which it might serve, conquest always means killing people and it always means oppression. He had made this point many years before when he was considering his options in Sind. It is a passage that we looked at some time ago:

> My position is difficult. If I thrash these chaps and take their land[,] abuse will follow; if I let them get the better in treating, it will be abandoning the only opportunity their poor subjects have of obtaining a little relief from grinding oppression.[20]

'Abuse will follow' – yes. Is it too much to see in Napier's critique of the imperial adventures of Lord Dalhousie something which the political scientist Karuna Mantena has described as 'high moral ambition followed by disillusionment, leading eventually to disavowal'? As Mantena demonstrates, this move from moral ambition to the disavowal of empire became rather common among liberal imperialists in the latter nineteenth century. Mantena also points to a similar disillusionment with the outcome of liberal imperialism in the aftermath of the Iraq War of the early twenty-first century; and she points out a similar reliance upon Western paternalism in the aftermath of that war, with a set of top-down policies having to be implemented in order to address the problems caused by the Western conquest itself.[21] In my view, Napier saw something of this liberal disillusion. While Evans might suggest

332 *Conclusion*

that this movement towards redemption which I am outlining (Napier's movement towards imperial scepticism) is something that I am imposing on the evidence, I adopt a plainer view: Liberal imperialism was an important ideological construct at the time, and its effects were visible even to the liberal conqueror of Sind.

***

Despite his illness, Charles Napier was able to finish most of the anti-Dalhousie book before his infirmity stopped him altogether. William took the manuscript to the printer. When Charles died, the book was already set to come out. He had been paid a partial advance of £42 for it in February 1853.[22] It was published several years before the Indian Mutiny that in its more pessimistic passages it seemed to predict.[23]

Napier took to his bed for the last time when he was in London in June. Ellenborough visited him and they discussed military policy.[24] In July he was moved, still in bed, to the train station and conveyed back to Oaklands. There he was carried into a ground floor room full of mementos arranged according to his rather sentimental specifications. He remained in bed in this room for the next month and a half; there he turned seventy-one on 10 August 1853. His was not an easy death. His mind wandered. He was in pain, not least from his old wounds. He died on 29 August at five in the morning. He had asked that his horse, Red Rover – the horse with whom he had shared his tent in Sind – should be brought to his bedside, but the animal was startled and would not come over for a final caress. But much of Napier's human family was around him.

After his last breath, his son-in-law William McMurdo improvised a ceremony by waving the regimental colours over the dead body. McMurdo and William Napier then set up an involved display of flags, shields, and swords.[25]

The funeral took place in Portsmouth on 8 September. Napier was buried outside the Garrison Church. Colin Campbell was one of the pall-bearers.[26] Lord Hardinge attended (after Wellington's death he was now Commander-in-Chief of the Forces). Also attending were Lord Ellenborough (who owed Napier that much) and Sir James Graham, the First Lord of the Admiralty; Graham had become Home Secretary just as Napier was leaving his command in the north of England. Another official in attendance was Sir Thomas Cochrane, who commanded the Portsmouth naval unit. He was the son of Napier's ultimate commanding officer in the Atlantic theatre in the war with America in 1812.

The men of the army and navy bases in Portsmouth also came in large numbers – three thousand army soldiers, according to one witness[27] – and they came voluntarily. They were not ordered to be there, nor did they come in any organized formation.

In total the mourners numbered sixty thousand, at least according to William. The *Illustrated London News* put it at fifty thousand and ran three engravings: The coffin and swords at the lying-in-state; Red Rover with his master's boots reversed; and the funeral procession itself. Most of the shops in the Portsmouth high street were closed for the day. The Masons headed the procession. The soldiers along the way fell in behind and formed the rear.[28] William tried to make a speech but he was crying so hard that he could say only a few words.

Napier as a liberal imperialist

In Bermuda in 1812, Napier wrote this:

> A great conquering nation should sacrifice all minor things to strength and magnanimity; which will not always square with honesty, because no generosity can afterwards wash out the first guilt of unprovoked conquest. Nevertheless, give riches and be poor; give plenty though at your monetary cost: let your chain be golden, or at last gilt, and you may rule the world.
>
> Such has been our conduct in Portugal. . . . [W]e might have done more on a sound system, but we always act on the confined basis of – present expediency. We might have regulated their whole civil government and founded a free nation, entirely and truly regenerating them as a people.[29]

He saw that empire leads to moral compromise, but still he had faith in the imperial mission. Nowhere here did he reflect that it is hard to give people freedom by conquering them. He did not stop to ask himself whether the Portuguese might do better making their own laws, however imperfect those laws might be.

I think that this last point is the key to liberal imperialism – at least as far as Napier's way of thinking illustrates it. He had his high ideals and he had great plans for improving the administration of nations and alleviating the plight of the poor, but he ignored the question of *agency*. Napier wanted good, liberal improvements that would help the impoverished, but he did not much care for the impoverished ruling themselves as the agents of their own liberation or progress. Within the United Kingdom, Napier certainly was in favour of universal male enfranchisement, yes, but he had a good idea about the kind of person he wanted the poor using their votes to elect. The people of the British Isles could enjoy all the blessings of liberty under the intelligent rule of men like himself. The peoples of the rest of the world needed freeing pure and simple, but after they were free they would still need tutelage from the West and not ballot boxes. This way of looking at the matter is not too far from what we can see in the writings of John Stuart Mill and to a lesser degree Alexis de Tocqueville – two giants of liberal imperialism whose thinking is explored in the political science literature discussed in the introduction to this book.[30]

The way in which Napier ignored agency on the part of those who were to be ruled has several implications. For one, he was not through and through a mainstream Chartist. For at bottom Chartism (or early Chartism in any case) meant constitutional change first and foremost. The Chartists looked forward

334   *Conclusion*

to a revolution in who ran the government, to be followed later by changes in particular policies. When the whole nation was properly represented in Parliament, rich and poor alike could come together and govern the country in a new way; and the unfairness of the Corn Law or any other element of British policy or custom could be addressed then.[31]

This was not Napier's vision. In that sense his domestic radicalism was more in line with the views of Joseph Rayner Stephens, a popular leader of the Chartist period known for his violent language and for his wish to combat poverty directly, but who did not care very much about the Charter itself. (Stephens and Napier would have parted company over Stephens's hope for a mass rising inspired by God.[32]) Napier was a supporter of the universal franchise, but there are hints that this is not where his heart was. His brand of radicalism, like that of Rayner Stephens, meant seeking economic change first and foremost, as Napier had revealed in his quarrel with O'Connell. Napier had some points in common with the critics of Chartism, too. He shared something of Carlyle's disdain for the Chartist leaders – believing that while the poor talked of the franchise, what they really meant was to make themselves more comfortable (Carlyle), or to get out from under the poverty imposed by their corrupt rulers (Napier). That the poor were making an articulate case about agency rather than a *cri de coeur* about economic suffering could not be admitted even by an aristocratic radical like Charles Napier, who otherwise agreed with most of the demands the Chartists were making – such as a universal franchise, annual parliaments, and the secret ballot, as he told the political committee in Oldham – and who agreed with almost everything in the Chartist speeches he heard, sharing much of the Chartist understanding of poverty and privilege.

***

But there are more implications to explore, for still this picture is a little too neat. There was more to Napier than his desire to patronize the poor rather than empowering them. For we have seen that in his more mature years, long after Bermuda, on occasion he would acknowledge their agency and autonomy in some way. When he was in the north of England, Napier did the leg work of empowerment. He may not have incorporated the idea of an autonomous realm of action for the poor into his dreams of reform, but in practice – in order to keep the peace – he strove for the daily detailed back-and-forth accommodations between interests and classes that we might define as nose-to-the-grindstone politics. And this too is a form of acknowledging the agency of the parties concerned. It is something like what Uday Singh Mehta has argued for – having an open-ended conversation when two cultures come into contact, a conversation where each side accepts the richness and irreducibility of the mental life of the other.[33] As I mentioned above, the sociologist Edgardo Lander has discussed something along these lines, as well. So has the philosopher Duncan Ivison in his *Post-Colonial Liberalism*. I am not saying that we should retreat from the liberal idea of universal humanity and adopt the condescending view that other cultures are childlike in comparison

Conclusion 335

with our own. But as Ivison puts it (not I admit in the context of Sind, but in regard to indigenous communities within a Westernized country), what is needed is 'a space within liberal democracies and liberal thought in which these Aboriginal perspectives and philosophies can not only be heard, but given equal opportunity to shape (and reshape) the forms of power and government acting on them'.[34]

Napier's tragedy was that he did not go about really listening to people in this way when he was in Sind, after he had done something of this very kind in the north of England.

Yet even there Napier *did* expect that fairly soon, and perhaps in only a few generations, Europeans and Sindhis would unite and step up to the task of governing themselves. This was not so far from Thomas Babington Macaulay's vision, too, along the lines of Lord, make the Indians independent, but not yet. Macaulay famously said that when India finally grew up and demanded 'European institutions', it would be 'the proudest day in English history'. But it does not seem that Macaulay expected that day to come for some time.[35] Napier's South Asians would have their independent agency much sooner than Macaulay had in mind – but still *not yet*.

We should take stock: All the varieties of nineteenth-century liberalism with which we are concerned seem to have had certain features in common – favouring the emancipation of the common people; working to give them the material conditions for self-development; knowing better than they did themselves what was good for them; conceiving of history as moving forward towards liberty; conceiving of liberty and civilization as universal values applicable to everyone; and yet thinking of these apparently universal values as moving outward from northwestern Europe.[36] (Pure *laissez faire* liberalism I am less interested in.) Napier's radical views on these questions made up an extreme form of this liberal programme. His was the liberalism of a less patient man – less patient than Macaulay at any rate.

And Napier's was a more extreme liberal imperialism than what we would expect to see if we were to examine the subject in the decades before the First World War – the period when the word 'imperialism' was in familiar use and the phrase 'liberal imperialism' was coined. By then, the liberal imperialists had retreated from their key belief in universal humanity. As Mantena has demonstrated, the more common belief in Britain in the late nineteenth century, even among thinkers of a liberal tendency, was that other cultures were simple-minded and unready for modern freedom. And so the traditional institutions of a conquered people ought to be respected, their traditional rulers kept in place – because nothing better could be expected of them. This is something like what James Outram had maintained in his argument with Napier over the morality of conquering Sind. By contrast, Napier thought the Sindhis deserved better than their traditional rulers were giving them. He had always doubted the legitimacy of traditional Muslim governance, whether in Greece, Egypt, or Sind. We have seen that ever since his Greek period he had shared the traditional Western suspicions about the tyranny and cruelty of

336 *Conclusion*

Islamic rulership. And he was sure that as a practically trained British officer who had weighed the currants in Cephalonia, he could do a better job governing the people and moving them forward to where they deserved to be than any native ruler in South Asia could do.[37] That is one measure of his liberal imperialism.

Yet to be fully accurate in characterizing him, we ought to stop and remember something else – for indeed, besides Napier's universalism and his impatience, there was another factor that pushed him towards imperial conquest: In the moment when he attacked the Amirs he was worried about his own security. He was worried about an attack by the dangerous Easterners.

So there we have our liberal imperialism, I think: The desire to make another people free seems to be put into effect in an invasion not so much because one is ignorant of the agency and autonomy of the people one is invading, but because in the moment it seems more convenient to forget for a while about any of these things, to forget for a time about any rights that other peoples may have to independence and self-government. And it seems especially convenient to forget all this chiefly when going ahead and conquering another country is in one's own security interest. Of course the need to defend oneself might be the result of projecting the power of the imperial state in the first place – Auckland's invasion of Afghanistan and Dalhousie's interference with the hill tribes of Punjab. As historian Antoinette Burton argues, having an empire means that there will always be troubles of this kind.[38]

When faced with danger on the fringes of empire it may seem better to conquer and rule the people in question rather than to continuing to talk to them – or to put it another way, continuing to talk to them *again and again* as they exercise their frustratingly autonomous role in the development of events. What we have seen in the case of Napier is that it is *most* tempting to forget the irreducible autonomy of others and take over their country when one is frightened for one's own safety. Clearly, he was worried about the possible destruction of his army in the aftermath of events in Afghanistan. Confronting dangers like this, it may be that the choice of intervention over negotiation, and of fighting rather than trying to engage in retail politics, will seem all the more compelling. The cultural strangeness of the Orientalized Easterners whom one needs to talk with – the Chartists had been so much easier for Napier to understand – might also contribute to a decision to opt for conquest.

From time to time in his later years Napier admitted to having qualms about the bloodshed in which, as he said, 'I am steeped'. He insisted that he tried to avoid spilling blood, and he sometimes expressed a fatalism about human affairs.[39] After he took charge of Sind he tried to make the best of the matter by governing according to his own inclinations. Other officials at the time also suggested that good government at the hands of the British might help to atone for the original act of conquest.[40] But as governor, Napier did not listen carefully enough to the governed. So he could not accomplish what he set out to do, at least in reengineering the class system. In his ignorance, he wound up entrenching the feudal oppressors instead of getting rid of them.

Domestic policy

Some attention should also be given to the domestic side of Napier's liberalism and to what he thought about the state. Napoleon, Cobbett, and Sismondi were Napier's main touchstones as he developed his own vision of the future liberal order. What Napier wanted was a government that could engineer for the poor a proper standard of living as independent farmers. And there should not be too much social change, too fast. Any lack of political agency by the poor in the near term would not bother Napier in the way something else did: the ever-growing political domination of the Haves, and with it the class interest of the legislation that the Haves imposed. A universal manhood franchise would help to control this, while governance remained in the hands of men like himself, men who could lay out the roads of Cephalonia.

Was this anything like the core of modern liberalism as it would develop by the middle of the nineteenth century, especially in the English context? As historian Jonathan Parry has explored the matter,[41] liberalism in that period was no longer focussed on removing the influence of the Old Corruption and the dead hand of church and state, as it had been in Cobbett's day. The new goal was to help the common people enjoy and profit from their autonomy. The masses needed the schools, the ports, the railways, the decent water, the sewer systems, on top of all of which (fairly literally) they could build their new autonomous lives. The world needed to be made safe for the autonomous capitalist actor, in one's own country and in other people's countries. We have seen that Napier wanted to improve Cephalonian agriculture and agriculture elsewhere; and that he gave some passing thought to pushing steamships up the Indus.

But Napier's vision was that economic development should unfold in the fullness of time and not too quickly. For all his radicalism, perhaps not so surprisingly Napier was an early- and not a mid- to late-Victorian liberal. He was a Sismondian and not a member of Gladstone's Liberal party. The mid-century Liberals were to show more fondness for the free market and for rapid change than Napier ever did. For him, the new urban world was (in England) a world of corruption, finance, Whig hypocrisy, Cobbett's Thing. And at bottom, this Thing was grounded upon selfishness, inefficiency, and incompetence.

Yet it makes sense to talk about Charles Napier as a liberal and a universalist, even if he was no Gladstonian. Liberalism, in the sense of a desire to rationalize government and to free and uplift the people, had existed for a long time all across the political spectrum. Opinions such as these had been associated with the Pittite Tories during the Napoleonic period, and liberal views would become associated with the Tories once again in the 1820s. But equally liberal views were characteristic of the radicals – at the opposite end of the spectrum from William Pitt the Younger and the Tories he led. Napier's liberalism was of the radical kind; he damned all Tories (and the Whigs as well) for sustaining the Old Corruption. And he damned them for their repressive tendencies when faced with popular revolt.

338   *Conclusion*

But what of his relationship with those in the middle – the Foxite Whigs with whom Napier had his family connection? We have seen that, like the Whig grandees (at least as historian Peter Mandler discusses them), Napier had his suspicions about the dry, materialistic political economists, those thinkers whom he described in his Australia book as putting profit before traditional life. And like the Whigs, as well, Napier believed that dedicated, educated governors ought to rule *for* the common people, *de haut en bas*. But unlike the Whigs of this period Napier wanted every man to have a vote.[42] Moreover, for the repressiveness of their governments in the 1830s the Whigs would earn his special hatred. So while elements of liberalism could be found across the political spectrum (as Mandler and others have shown), Napier's version as we have explored it was of the radical and not the Tory kind; nor did his desire for fundamental social change and his desire for the universal application of the principles of good governance bear much resemblance to the more measured reform efforts of the Whig party.

By no means was Charles Napier measured, certainly not in his emotional reactions. Anger welled up within him, especially in his two most troubled periods: when he came home from Cephalonia and wrote up his resentments against Frederick Adam; and in the period before he left Sind, when he was constantly sending his brother such long complaints about what Outram and others had said of him. As Napier himself admitted at the farewell dinner when he left India in 1851,

> I have never felt real anger with anybody, sometimes indeed I have felt anger for a moment, and I have often wished for a good broomstick, and to have been within three yards of the object of them [*sic*]. Every one has his little peculiarities and I'll not hide mine.[43]

He finally came to regret some of his animosities, at least as he had expressed them in the anti-Adam book. As he wrote in his journal in 1851: '[T]aking a retrospect of my adventurous and strange life, [I] repent of whatever I have done amiss and in anger. The worst was my book against Adam – and yet he deserved it.'[44] But too often he would let the anger fester. A few years after his death, one journalist explained Napier's emotional state rather well, and I will paraphrase: Charles Napier was a very honest and very competent man, and he was shocked by the compromises that are inseparable from professional life. He was too sensitive about being criticized or being thwarted, and so he got angry and condemned anyone who got in his way.[45] He was not the most even-tempered of men.

Napier's anger certainly bothered his contemporaries. As *Household Words* put the matter on the occasion of his resignation as Commander-in-Chief of India:

> It may . . . not be inconsistent with a high admiration for the great quali-ties of all the Napiers, to express a wish that this remarkable family were

better provided with what the world commonly agrees to call discretion and prudence; and that they could bring themselves, when out of office, to be something less of the democrat, and, when in office, something less of the tyrant.[46]

Napier now stands in Trafalgar Square. Ellenborough helped raise the funds for the statue in a public campaign. The idea was to put it on Pall Mall, at the lower end of Waterloo Place, but this site was later withdrawn by the Board of Works. (There was an abortive plan to connect Waterloo Place and The Mall, and the statue would have been in the way.) When the original site was withdrawn, Ellenborough offhandedly suggested Trafalgar Square instead, and his suggestion was accepted.[47] The bronze has been called one of the worst statues in London.[48] Yet the fact that Napier stands in Trafalgar Square in some form is fitting in many ways. He gazes out upon the centre of a welfare state that would fulfil many of his liberal dreams – a state that in the early twenty-first century participated in a war of conquest in the Islamic world, a war so like his own.

Notes

1　Napier to W. Napier, March 1851, given in WN, 4:193.
2　Napier to Louisa Napier, April 1851, NP, Bodleian MS Eng. lett. c. 241, fols 38–41.
3　Charles James Napier, *A Letter on the Defense of England by Corps of Volunteers and Militia, Addressed to Parliament* (London: Edward Moxon, 1852); Thackeray to Mrs. Carmichael-Smyth, 16 February 1852, given in Gordon N. Ray (ed.), *The Letters and Private Papers of William Makepeace Thackeray*, 4 vols (Cambridge, MA: Harvard UP, 1946), 3:15–18.
4　*London Gazette*, 6 December 1852, 21388 p. 3559; Napier to Kennedy, [?] November 1852, NP, TNA PRO 30/64/16 fols 36–37; *The Times*, 19 November 1852, 5 cols c and f.
5　Napier to Louisa Napier, 6 September 1851, Bodleian MS Eng. lett. c. 241, fols 33–34; Napier to Emily Bunbury, 11 January 1853, NP, BL Add. MS 49110, fols 148–50; Napier to Kennedy, 25 February 1852, 19 February 1853, NP, TNA PRO 30/64/16, fols 28–29, 38–39. Mercury: Napier to Louisa, 19 February 1852, Bodleian MS Eng. lett. c. 241, fols 55–57.
6　[Henry Thoby Prinsep and E. B. Eastwick], 'Scinde – Dry Leaves from Young Egypt', *Quarterly Review* 91, 182 (September 1852), 379–401.
7　*The Times*, 24 November 1852, 5 cols a-c.
8　Napier to Robertson, 3 November 1852, NP, BL Add. MS 49107, fols 153–54; Great Britain, Parliament, *First Report from the Select Committee of the House of Lords appointed to Inquire into the Operation of the Act 3 & 4 Will, 4, c. 85, for the Better Government of Her Majesty's Indian Territories* (1852–1853), No. 627, 75–95.
9　Great Britain, *First Report . . . Indian Territories*, 77.
10　The latter a former regional governor in India.
11　Great Britain, *First Report . . . Indian Territories*, 88.
12　Ibid, 89–90. He wrote a substantial report on barracks while in India, a report to which Dalhousie and the East India Company would frame their rebuttals – Court of Proprietors of the East India Company, *Discussions between the Marquis of Dalhousie and Lieut.-General Sir C. J. Napier, G.C.B., also Proceedings Regarding the Construction of Barracks for the European Troops* (London: Court of Proprietors of the East India Company, 1854).
13　Great Britain, *First Report . . . Indian Territories*, 87; Campbell to Napier, 18 August 1852, NP, BL Add. MS 49108, fols 43–44; Dalhousie to Couper, 13 June 1852, 6 January 1856,

340 *Conclusion*

given in BMD, 205–07, 366–68. Dalhousie revelled in the village-burning being carried out at this time: Dalhousie to Couper, 15 January 1853, 238–42 at 242.

14 Napier to Kennedy, 29 October 1851, NP, TNA PRO 30/64/16, fols 6–9.

15 Napier to Ellenborough, extracts, April 1853, given in WN, 4:390.

16 Napier to Ellenborough, 5 March 1853, given in ibid, 4:386–87.

17 Napier to Ellenborough, extracts, April 1853, given in ibid, 4:390–91; see also Napier to Robertson, 30 May 1853, NP, BL Add. MS 49107, fols 175–76.

18 Napier to Mr Turner, Chairman of the Manchester Commercial Association, 22 January 1853, extracts, given in WN, 4:381.

19 Mary Evans, *Missing Persons: The Impossibility of Auto/Biography* (London: Routledge, 1999), 24, 135.

20 Napier's journal, 18 November 1842, given in ibid, 2:240.

21 Karuna Mantena, *Alibis of Empire: Henry Maine and the Ends of Liberal Imperialism* (Princeton, NJ: Princeton UP, 2010), 180. As Mantena discusses (186), her work is informed on this point by Thomas R. Metcalf, *The New Cambridge History of India*, III.4, *Ideologies of the Raj* [1987] (New Delhi: Oxford UP, 1998), chapters 5 and 6.

22 Emily Bunbury to Napier, [13/14 March], 22 March 1853, NP, BL Ad. MS 49110, fols 165–69; Caroline Napier to Napier, 13 February 1853, NP, BL Add. MS 49111, fol. 42; WN, 4:385n.

23 Charles James Napier, *Defects, Civil and Military, of the Indian Government*, W.F.P. Napier (ed.) (London: Charles Westerton, 1853), 256.

24 Napier to Emily Bunbury, 21 June 1853, BL Add. MS 49110, fols 174–75.

25 WN, 4:396–98.

26 *Household Words Narrative*, September 1853, 208.

27 C.J.F. Bunbury to Mrs Henry (Katharine) Lyell, 13 September 1853, given in Lyell (ed.), *Bunbury*, 1:368–69.

28 WN, 4:399–400; *Illustrated London News*, 17 September 1853, 229–30.

29 Napier's journal in Bermuda, 1812, given in WN, 1:237–38.

30 Boesche, 'The Dark Side of Tocqueville', 740, 744–46; Mantena, 'Mill and the Imperial Predicament'; Uday Singh Mehta, *Liberalism and Empire: A Study in Nineteenth-Century British Liberal Thought* (Chicago: University of Chicago Press, 1999), Chapter 3.

31 William Lovett and John Collins, *Chartism: A New Organization of the People* (1840; New York: Humanities Press, 1969), 5, 11–13, 57–60; Gareth Stedman Jones, 'Rethinking Chartism', in Stedman Jones (ed.), *Languages of Class: Studies in English Working-Class History, 1832–1982* (Cambridge: Cambridge UP, 1983), 90–178; Dorothy Thompson, *Outsiders: Class, Gender, and Nation* (London: Verso, 1993), 22.

32 Michael S. Edwards, *Purge This Realm: A Life of Joseph Rayner Stephens* (London: Epworth Press, 1994), 54–57, 65, 71–74.

33 Mehta, *Liberalism and Empire*, 40–44, 192, 216–17. See also Thomas McCarthy, *Race, Empire, and the Idea of Human Development* (Cambridge: Cambridge UP, 2009), 36–38.

34 Duncan Ivison, *Post-Colonial Liberalism* (Cambridge: Cambridge UP, 2002), 1.

35 HC Deb 10 July 1833 vol 19 c536. See Catherine Hall, 'Macaulay's Nation', *Victorian Studies* 51, 3 (Spring 2009), 505–23 at 513–17. Macaulay never objected to Napier's conquests, although he detested the man for his salty language and choleric temperament: Macaulay's journal, 17 March 1849, 26 February 1857, William Thomas (ed.), *The Journals of Thomas Babington Macaulay*, 5 vols (London: Pickering & Chatto, 2008), 2:55, 5:15.

36 Napier to W. Napier, 3 June 1847, WN, 4:70–72. For thoughts on the difficulty of defining the liberalism of nineteenth-century imperialists, see Matthew Fitzpatrick, Jennifer Pitts, and Uday Singh Mehta, 'Conclusion: Liberalism and Empire Reconsidered: A Dialogue', in Fitzpatrick (ed.), *Liberal Imperialism in Europe* (New York: Palgrave Macmillan, 2012), 241–66 at 244–47, 251–52.

37 For 'imperialism' and related terms, see Richard Koebner and Helmut Dan Schmidt. *Imperialism: The Story and Significance of a Political Word, 1840–1960* (Cambridge: Cambridge

UP, 1964). For the imperialist embrace of local elites later on, see Mantena, *Alibis of Empire*.

38 Antoinette Burton, *The Trouble with Empire* (Cambridge, MA: Harvard UP, 2015), 1.

39 Napier to Emily Bunbury, 16 August 1850, NP, BL Add. MS 49110, fols 117–19.

40 Mantena, *Alibis of Empire*, 29, 195n39, 196n42.

41 J. P. Parry, *The Rise and Fall of Liberal Government in Victorian Britain* (New Haven, CT: Yale UP, 1993); and Parry, 'The Decline of Institutional Reform in Nineteenth-Century Britain', in David Feldman and John Lawrence (eds), *Structures and Transformations in Modern British History* (Cambridge: Cambridge UP, 2011), 164–86, especially 170.

42 Peter Mandler, *Aristocratic Government in the Age of Reform: Whigs and Liberals, 1830–1852* (Oxford: Clarendon Press, 1990), chapter 1.

43 31 January 1851, given in John Mawson, *Records of the Indian Command of General Charles James Napier* (Calcutta: R. and C. Lepage, 1851), Appendix, liii.

44 Napier's journal, 6 April 1851, given in W. Napier, *Life*, 4:323. Kennedy had advised Napier to take out the 'personal irritation' if he wanted the Adam book to really convince people. With its overly strong language it would do more harm than good: Kennedy to Napier, 26 June, [1 July] 1832, NP, BL Add. MS 54535, fols 92–95 (quotation from second letter, fol. 95).

45 John Skelton, 'Charles James Napier: A Study of Character', *Fraser's Magazine* 57 (February 1858), 254–68 at 256.

46 *Household Words Narrative*, September 1850, 207.

47 Ellenborough to Molesworth, 25 July 1854; Pennefather memorandum to Molesworth, 13 July 1855 [no folio number]; Molesworth to Ellenborough, 20 July 1855 [no folio number]; Ellenborough to Molesworth, 31 May 1856 [no folio number]; Molesworth to Ellenborough, 5 June 1856 – all in TNA WORKS 20/32.

48 In a letter of 23 May 1855, TNA WORKS 20/3, Kennedy agreed with William Napier that a sculptor named Park (Patric Park, perhaps) captured Napier looking especially animated; while George Gammon Adams produced a lesser piece of art but did a better job of rendering Napier's usual expression. Adams's work was chosen. For later, mostly negative opinions about the artistic quality of the piece, see Rodney Mace, *Trafalgar Square: Emblem of an Empire* (London: Lawrence and Wishart, 1976), 129.

Bibliography

Abbreviations

BL	British Library
BP	Broughton Papers
BMD	J.G.A. Baird (ed.), *Private Letters of the Marquess of Dalhousie*
CEW	Lord Colchester, *History of the Indian Administration of Lord Ellenborough in his Correspondence with the Duke of Wellington*
EP	Ellenborough Papers
ISSL	Countess of Ilchester and Lord Stavordale, *The Life and Letters of Lady Sarah Lennox, 1745–1826*
LNS	H. T. Lambrick, *Sir Charles Napier and Sind*
NAM	National Army Museum
NLB	Napier's letter book, Napier Papers, British Library Additional Manuscript 49129
NP	Napier Papers
PBC	Correspondence with successive Presidents of the Board of Control and the Prime Minister
PP	Peel Papers
TNA	The National Archives
WNAS	William Napier, *The History of General Sir Charles Napier's Administration of Scinde and Campaign in the Cutchee Hills*
WNCS	William Napier, *The History of General Sir Charles Napier's Conquest of Scinde*
WN	William Napier, *The Life and Opinions of General Sir Charles James Napier, G.C.B.*

Archival sources

Bodleian Library, Oxford

Napier Papers

British Library, Bloomsbury

Broughton Papers

344   *Bibliography*

Correspondence with successive Presidents of the Board of Control and the
  Prime Minister
Napier Papers
Peel Papers
Ripon Papers

British Library, Bloomsbury, Asian and African Studies

Papers of John Cam Hobhouse as President of the Board of Control, 1846–52
H. T. Lambrick Papers
Henry Gee Roberts Papers
Younghusband Papers

The National Archives, Kew

Board of Works Papers, WORKS 20/32
Colonial Office Papers, CO 136
Ellenborough Papers, PRO 30/12
Home Office Papers, HO 41/14, HO 41/15, HO 45/41
Home Office Papers, Online ('Digital Microfilm'), HO 40, HO 52
Napier Papers, PRO 30/64

National Army Museum, Chelsea

Napier Papers

Parliamentary Debates

Hansard's Parliamentary Debates (HC Deb, House of Commons; HL Deb, House of Lords).
  Online at hansard.millbanksystems.com.

Parliamentary Papers (Blue Books)

Great Britain. Parliament. *Accounts and Papers, 1843: Sinde.* No. 39.
Great Britain. Parliament. *Accounts and Papers, 1854: Papers Relating to the Resignation of General
  Sir Charles Napier, G.C.B., of the Office of Commander in Chief in India.* No. 80.
Great Britain. Parliament. *An Account, Specifying the Names of the Governors, Lieutenant Gov-
  ernors, and General Officers, upon the Staff of the Several Foreign Colonies, Settlements, and
  Governments, Now Belonging to His Majesty. . . .* (1814–1815), No. 353.
Great Britain. Parliament. *Copies of any Correspondence in the Colonial Department Relative
  to the Establishment of the Settlement of South Australia, since the Year 1831, and its Present
  Financial Difficulties.* (1841 session 1), No. 129.
Great Britain, Parliament, *Copies of the Special Reports of the Indian Law Commissioners*
  (1847), No. 14.
Great Britain. Parliament. *First Report from the Select Committee of the House of Lords appointed
  to Inquire into the Operation of the Act 3 & 4 Will, 4, c. 85, for the Better Government of Her
  Majesty's Indian Territories* (1852–1853), No. 627.

Great Britain. Parliament. *First Report from the Select Committee on Indian Territories.* (1852–1853), No. 426.

Great Britain. Parliament. *Return of the Names of the Officers in the Army Who Receive Pensions for the Loss of Limbs, or for Wounds. . . .* (1818), No. 294.

Printed East India Company or Indian Government records

Aitchison, C. U. *A Collection of Treaties, Engagements, and Sunnuds Relating to India and Neighbouring Countries,* vol. 6, *The Treaties, &c., Relating to the Punjab, Sind, and Beloochistan, and Central Asia,* rev. edn, A.C. Talbot (ed.) (Calcutta: Foreign Office Press, 1876).

Carless, T. G. 'Memoir of the Bay, Harbour, and Trade of Kurachee' [1838]. In R. Hughes Thomas (ed.), *Selections of the Records of the Bombay Government,* new series, 17 (Bombay: Printed for the Government at the Bombay Education Society's Press, 1855), 188–208.

Carless, T. G. 'Memoir of the Province of Lus, and Narrative of a Journey to Beyla' [1838]. In R. Hughes Thomas (ed.), *Selections of the Records of the Bombay Government,* new series, 17 (Bombay: Printed for the Government at the Bombay Education Society's Press, 1855), 298–319.

Court of Proprietors of the East India Company, *Discussions between the Marquis of Dalhousie and Lieut.-General Sir C.J. Napier, G.C.B., Also Proceedings Regarding the Construction of Barracks for the European Troops* (London: Court of Proprietors of the East India Company, 1854).

Delhoste, Edward. 'Narrative of a Journey from Mandvi to Hydrabad (Sind) and from Hydrabad to Khairpoor and Back (December 1831-May 1832)'. In *Selections from the Pre-Mutiny Records of the Commissioner in Sind,* Selection 5 (Sind: Commissioner's Office, n.d.), 185–237.

Hart, S.V.W. 'Report on the Town and Port of Kurachee' [1840]. In R. Hughes Thomas (ed.), *Selections of the Records of the Bombay Government,* new series, 17 (Bombay: Printed for the Government at the Bombay Education Society's Press, 1855), 209–45.

Intelligence Branch, Division of the Chief of Staff, Army Headquarters, India. *Frontier and Overland Expeditions from India,* 6 vols (Simla: Government Monotype Press, 1908).

Pelly, Lewis. 'Brief Notes Relative to the Khrypoor State in Upper Sind' [1854]. In R. Hughes Thomas (ed.), *Selections of the Records of the Bombay Government,* new series, 17 (Bombay: Printed for the Government at the Bombay Education Society's Press, 1855), 117–23.

Pelly, Lewis. 'Memoir on the Khrypoor State in Upper Sind' [1854]. In R. Hughes Thomas (ed.), *Selections of the Records of the Bombay Government,* new series, 17 (Bombay: Printed for the Government at the Bombay Education Society's Press, 1855), 103–16.

Postans, Thomas. 'Miscellaneous Information Relative to the Town of Shikarpoor' [1840–1841]. In R. Hughes Thomas (ed.), *Selections of the Records of the Bombay Government,* new series, 17 (Bombay: Printed for the Government at the Bombay Education Society's Press, 1855), 85–102.

Pringle, R. K. 'Report on the Condition and Mode of Administration in Sind', 31 December 1847. In *Selections from the Pre-Mutiny Records of the Commissioner in Sind,* Selection 1 (Sind: Commissioner's Office, n.d.), 1–35.

Sind Commissioner's Office. *History of Alienations in the Province of Sind,* 2 vols (Karachi: Commissioner's Press, 1886–1888).

Sind Commissioner's Office. 'Revenue Queries by Mr. R.K. Pringle, Commissioner in Sind to Collectors in Sind, and Replies Thereto', in *Selections from the Pre-Mutiny Records of the Commissioner in Sind,* Selection 2 (Sind: Commissioner's Office, n.d.), 41–51.

346 *Bibliography*

Published works of Lieutenant-General Sir Charles James Napier

Billimoria, N. M. 'General Orders of Sir Charles Napier (1843–47)', *Journal of the Sind Historical Society* 3, 4 (1938), 46–54.

Green, Edward (ed.). *Compilation of the General Orders, &c., Issued in 1842–47, by Sir Charles Napier, G.C.B., Major-General Governor of Scinde, to the Army Under His Command* (Bombay: James Chesson at the *Times* Press, 1850).

[Napier, Charles James]. *War in Greece.* (London: James Ridgway, 1821).

[Napier, Charles James]. *Greece in 1824.* (London: James Ridgway, 1824).

Napier, Charles James. *Memoir on the Roads of Cephalonia.* (London: James Ridgway, 1825).

Napier, Charles James. *The Colonies: Treating of their Value Generally – Of the Ionian Islands in Particular; The Importance of the Latter in War and Commerce – As Regards Russian Policy – Their Finances – Why an Expense to Great Britain – Detailed Proofs that they need not be so – Turkish Government – Battle of Navarino – Ali Pacha – Sir Thomas Maitland – Strictures on the Administration of Sir Frederick Adam* (London: Thomas and William Boone, 1833).

Napier, Charles James. *Colonization, Particularly in Southern Australia, with some Remarks on Small Farms and Overpopulation* (London: T. and W. Boone, 1835; NY, Augustus M. Kelly, 1969).

Napier, Charles James. *Remarks on Military Law and the Punishment of Flogging* (London: T. and W. Boone, 1837).

Napier, Charles James. *An Essay on the Present State of Ireland, Showing the Chief Cause of, and the Remedy for, the Existing Distress of that Country* (London: Ridgway, 1839).

Napier, Charles James. *A Letter to the Right Hon. Sir J. Hobhouse, President of the Board of Control, on the Baggage of the Indian Army*, 4th edn (London: Edward Moxon, 1849).

Napier, Charles James. Editor's notes in Alfred Victor, comte de Vigny, *Lights and Shades of Military Life*, Charles James Napier (ed.), 2 vols in one (London: Henry Colburn, 1840).

Napier, Charles James. Editor's notes in Alfred Victor, comte de Vigny, *Lights and Shades of Military Life*, Charles James Napier (ed.), 2nd edn (London: Henry Colburn, 1850).

Napier, Charles James. *A Letter on the Defense of England by Corps of Volunteers and Militia, Addressed to Parliament* (London: Edward Moxon, 1852).

Napier, Charles James. *Defects, Civil and Military, of the Indian Government*, W.F.P. Napier (ed.) (London: Charles Westerton, 1853).

Napier, Charles James. *William the Conqueror: A Historical Romance*, William Napier (ed.) (London: G. Routledge & Co., 1858).

Newspapers and news periodicals cited

Allen's Indian Mail
Annual Register
Bath Chronicle and Weekly Gazette
Express Tribune (Karachi)
Household Words
Household Words Narrative
Illustrated London News
London Gazette
Manchester Guardian
Manchester Mercury
Northern Star
The Times (London)

Bibliography 347

Other eighteenth- and nineteenth-century sources (including post-1900 editions of nineteenth-century primary sources)

Adams, Henry. *History of the United States of America during the Second Administration of James Madison*, 3 vols (New York: Charles Scribner's Sons, 1890).

Allen, I. N. *Diary of a March through Sinde and Affghanistan* (London: J. Hatchard and Son, 1843).

Anonymous. 'Sons of Glory!: Recruiting at Birmingham', *Punch: Or, the London Charivari* 7 (1844), 233.

Anonymous. 'The Real Commander-in-Chief', *Punch: or the London Charivari* 16 (1849), 136.

Anonymous. 'Opium', *Household Words* 384 (1 August 1857), 104–08.

Anonymous. 'Sir Charles Napier in India', *Dublin University Magazine* 50, 196 (August 1857), 129–39.

Anonymous. 'John Pitt Kennedy', *Minutes of the Proceedings of the Institution of Civil Engineers* 59, 1 (1879–80), 293–98.

Aspinall, A. (ed.). *The Later Correspondence of George III*, 5 vols (Cambridge: Cambridge UP, 1966).

Baird, J.G.A. (ed.). *Private Letters of the Marquess of Dalhousie* (Edinburgh: William Blackwood and Sons, 1911).

Bruce, H. A. *Life of General Sir William Napier, G.C.B.*, 2 vols (London: John Murray, 1864).

Bruce, William Napier. *The Life of General Sir Charles Napier, G.C.B.* (London: John Murray, 1885).

[Buller, Charles.] 'Napier on the Ionian Islands', *London Review* 25 (July 1835), 295–316.

Burnes, Alexander. *Travels into Bokhara: Being an Account of a Journey from India to Cabool, Tartary, and Persia; also, a Narrative of a Voyage on the Indus, from the Sea to Lahore*, 3 vols (London: John Murray, 1834).

Burnes, James. *A Visit to the Court of Scinde* (1829; Karachi: Oxford UP, 1974).

Burton, Isabel. *The Life of Captain Sir Richard Burton, K.C.M.G., F.R.C.S.*, 2 vols (London: Chapman and Hall, 1893).

Butler, William F. *Sir Charles Napier* (London: Macmillan, 1890).

Byron, George Gordon Noel, Lord. *Letters and Journals*, vol. 6. Rowland E. Prothero (ed.) (London: John Murray, 1901).

Byron, George Gordon Noel, Lord. *The Complete Poetical Works of Lord Byron*. Leslie Stephen (ed.) (London: Macmillan, 1909).

Churchill, Winston. *The Story of the Malakand Field Force: An Episode of Frontier War* [1898] (London: Thomas Nelson & Sons, 1916).

Colchester, Lord. *History of the Indian Administration of Lord Ellenborough in His Correspondence with the Duke of Wellington* (London: Richard Bentley and Son, 1874).

Comstock, John L. *History of the Greek Revolution* (New York: William W. Reed, 1828).

Connolly, T.W.J. *The History of the Corps of Royal Sappers and Miners*, 2 vols (London: Longman, Brown, Green, and Longmans, 1855).

Craufurd, Alexander H. *General Craufurd and His Light Division* (London: Griffith, Farran, Okeden, and Welsh, 1891).

Davenport, R. A. *The Life of Ali Pasha, of Tepelini, Vizier of Epirus: Surnamed Aslan, or the Lion* (London: Thomas Tegg and Son, 1837).

Delhoste, Edward Paterson. *Observing Sindh*. Matthew A. Cook (ed.) (Oxford: Oxford UP, 2008).

Dickens, Charles. *The Posthumous Papers of the Pickwick Club* [1836–1837] (London: Penguin, 1999).

348 *Bibliography*

Eastwick, E. B. *A Glance at Sind before Napier, or Dry Leaves from Young Egypt*, 2nd edn, introduced by H.T. Lambrick (1851; Karachi: Oxford UP, 1973).

Edwardes, Herbert Benjamin, and Herman Merivale. *Life of Sir Henry Lawrence*, 2nd edn, 2 vols (London: Smith, Elder, & Co., 1872).

Finlay, George. *History of the Greek Revolution and the Reign of King Otho*, 2 vols (Edinburgh: William Blackwood and Sons, 1861).

Fitzgerald, Brian (ed.). *Correspondence of Emily, Duchess of Leinster (1731–1814)*, 3 vols (Dublin: Stationery Office, 1953).

Gamba, Count Peter. *A Narrative of Lord Byron's Journey to Greece* (London: John Murray, 1825).

Gammage, R. C. *History of the Chartist Movement, 1837–1854* [1854] (1894; reprint, London: Merlin Press, 1969).

Goldsmid, F. J. *James Outram: A Biography*, 2nd edn, 2 vols (London: Smith, Elder & Co., 1881).

Gordon, Thomas. *History of the Greek Revolution*, 2nd edn, 2 vols (Edinburgh: William Blackwood; London: T. Cadell, 1844).

Greville, Charles C. F. *The Greville Memoirs (Second Part), a Journal of the Reign of Queen Victoria, 1837–1852*. Henry Reeve (ed.), 3 vols (London: Longmans, Green, and Co., 1885).

[Hamley, Charles Ogilvy.] 'Life of Sir Charles J. Napier – Part II', *Blackwood's Edinburgh Magazine* 82 (August 1857), 241–64.

Herold, J. Christopher (ed. and trans.). *The Mind of Napoleon: A Selection from His Written and Spoken Words* (1955; New York: Columbia UP, 1961).

Hitchman, Francis. *Richard F. Burton, K.C.M.G.: His Early, Private, and Public Life, with an Account of His Travels and Explorations*, 2 vols (London: Sampson Low, Marston, Searle, and Rivington, 1887).

Hodder, Edwin. *The Life and Work of the Seventh Earl of Shaftesbury, K.G.*, 2 vols (London: Cassell, 1886).

Holmes, Thomas Rice. *Four Famous Soldiers: Sir Charles Napier; Hodson of Hodson's Horse; Sir William Napier, Sir Herbert Edwardes* (London: W.H. Allen, 1889).

Hotchand, Naomal. *A Forgotten Chapter of Indian History as Described in the Memoirs of Seth Naomal Hotchand, C.S.I., of Karachi, 1804–1878*, (trans.) Alumal Trikamdas Bhojwani., H. Evan M. James (ed.) (Exeter: Printed for private circulation by W. Pollard, 1915).

Howe, Anthony, and Simon Morgan (eds). *The Letters of Richard Cobden*, 3 vols (Oxford: Oxford UP, 2007).

Howe, Samuel Gridley. *An Historical Sketch of the Greek Revolution* [1828], revised and edited by George Georgiades Arnakis (Austin, TX: Center for Neo-Hellenic Studies, 1966).

Ilchester, Countess of, and Lord Stavordale. *The Life and Letters of Lady Sarah Lennox, 1745–1826*, 2 vols (London: John Murray, 1901).

Jacob, John. *Notes on Sir W. Napier's Administration of Sinde* (privately printed, no date).

Jacob, John. *Remarks on the Native Troops of the Indian Army* (London: [no publisher named], 1854).

[Kaye, John William.] *The Administration of the East India Company: A History of Indian Progress* (London: Richard Bentley, 1853).

Kaye, John William. 'The Life and Opinions of Gen. Charles James Napier, G.C.B.', *Edinburgh Review* 106 (October 1857), 322–55.

Kaye, John William. *Lives of Indian Officers*, 2 vols (London: Strahan and Co., 1869).

Kirkwall, Viscount [George William Hamilton Fitzmaurice Orkney]. *Four Years in the Ionian Islands*, 2 vols (London: Chapman and Hall, 1864).

Laing, Samuel. *The Autobiography of Samuel Laing of Papdale, 1780–1868*. R.P. Fereday (ed.) (Kirkwall, Orkney: Bellavista Publications, 2000).

Bibliography 349

Lane-Poole, Stanley. *The Life of the Right-Honourable Stratford Canning, Viscount Stratford de Redcliffe*, 2 vols (London: Longmans, Green, and Co., 1888).

Langley, Edward Archer. *Narrative of a Residence at the Court of Meer Ali Murad, with Wild Sports in the Valley of the Indus*, 2 vols (London: Hurst and Blackett, 1860).

Lauzun, Armand Louis de Gontaut, duc de, duc de Biron. *Memoirs of the duc de Lauzun (Armand Louis de Gontaut, duc de Biron), 1747–1783*, (trans.) E. Jules Méras (New York: Sturgis & Walton, 1912).

Law, Algernon (ed.). *India under Lord Ellenborough, March 1842-June 1844: A Selection from the Hitherto Unpublished Papers and Secret Despatches of Edward Earl of Ellenborough* (London: John Murray, 1926).

Lawrence, George. *Reminiscences of Forty-Three Years in India.* W. Edwards (ed.) (1874; Lahore, Pakistan: Sang-i-Meel Publications, 1981).

Lawrence, Henry. 'Sir Charles Napier's Posthumous Work', *Calcutta Review* 23 (1854), 208–90.

Leader, Robert Eadon. *Life and Letters of John Arthur Roebuck, P.C., Q.C., M.P., with Chapters of Autobiography* (London: Edward Arnold, 1897).

Liddell Hart, B. H. (ed.). *The Letters of Private Wheeler* (Boston: Houghton Mifflin, 1952).

Lord, Walter Frewen. *Sir Thomas Maitland: The Mastery of the Mediterranean* (London: T. Fisher Unwin, 1897).

Lovett, William. *The Life and Struggles of William Lovett in His Pursuit of Bread, Knowledge, and Freedom* [1876] (London: MacGibbon & Kee, 1967).

Lovett, William, and John Collins. *Chartism: A New Organization of the People* (1840; New York: Humanities Press, 1969).

Ludlow, John Malcolm. *British India, Its Races, and Its History, Considered with Reference to the Mutinies of 1857: A Series of Lectures Addressed to the Students of the Working Men's College*, 2 vols (Cambridge: Macmillan and Co., 1858).

Lushington, Henry. *A Great Country's Little Wars; or, England, Affghanistan, and Sinde* (London: John W. Parker, 1844).

McMurdo, James. *McMurdo's Account of Sind.* Sarah Ansari (ed.) [1834] (Karachi: Oxford UP, 2007).

[Malleson, G. B.] *The Mutiny of the Bengal Army: An Historical Narrative by One Who Served under Sir Charles Napier* (London: Bosworth and Harrison, 1857).

Manningham, Coote. *Military Lectures Delivered to the Officers of the 95th (Rifle) Regiment at Shorn-Cliff Barracks, Kent, during the Spring of 1803* (London: T. Egerton, 1803; reprinted, no publisher, 1897).

Martineau, John. *The Life and Correspondence of the Right Hon. Sir Bartle Frere*, 2nd edn, 2 vols (London: John Murray, 1895).

Maurice, J. F. (ed.). *The Diary of Sir John Moore*, 2 vols (London: Edward Arnold, 1904).

Mawson, John. *Records of the Indian Command of General Charles James Napier* (Calcutta: R. and C. Lepage, 1851).

Mill, John Stuart. *Collected Works*, 33 vols. Ann M. Robson and John Robson (eds) (Toronto: University of Toronto Press, 1963–1991).

Millingen, Julius. *Memoirs of the Affairs of Greece* (London: John Rodwell, 1831).

Moore, Thomas, and Martin MacDermott. *The Memoirs of Lord Edward Fitzgerald* (London: Downey and Co., 1897).

Muir, Rory (ed.). *At Wellington's Right Hand: The Letters of Lieutenant-Colonel Sir Alexander Gordon, 1808–1815*, Publications of the Army Records Society, 21 (Stroud, Gloucestershire: Sutton Publishing Company, 2003).

Napier, Elizabeth. *The Nursery Governess* (London: T. & W. Boone, 1834).

Napier, George Thomas. *Passages in the Early Military Life of General George T. Napier, K.C.B., Written by Himself.* W.C.E. Napier (ed.) (London: John Murray, 1884).

350   *Bibliography*

Napier, Richard. *Remarks on Lieut.-Colonel Outram's Work, Entitled 'The Conquest of Sindh, a Commentary'* (London: James Ridgway, 1847).

Napier, William. *History of the War in the Peninsula and in the South of France, from the Year 1807 to the Year 1814*, 6 vols (London: Thomas and William Boone, 1828–1840).

Napier, William. *The History of General Sir Charles Napier's Conquest of Scinde* (London: T. & W. Boone, 1845).

Napier, William. *The History of General Sir Charles Napier's Administration of Scinde and Campaign in the Cutchee Hills* (London: Chapman and Hall, 1851).

Napier, William. *Comments by Lieut.-General Sir William Napier, K.C.B., upon a Memorandum of the Duke of Wellington and other Documents Censuring Lieut.-General Charles James Napier, G.C.G., with a Defense of Sir C. Napier's Government of Scinde by Captain Rathbone, Collector of Scinde* (London: Charles Westerton, 1854).

Napier, William. *The Life and Opinions of General Sir Charles James Napier, G.C.B.*, 2nd edn, 4 vols (London: John Murray, 1857).

Napier, William. *The History of General Sir Charles Napier's Conquest of Scinde.* Edited and introduced by Hamida Khuhro (London: Charles Westerson, 1845; Karachi: Oxford UP, 2001).

Norton, John Bruce. *The Rebellion in India, and How to Prevent another* (London: Richardson Brothers, 1857).

Orlich, Leopold von. *Travels in India, Including Sinde and the Punjab*, (trans.) H. Evans Lloyd, 2 vols (London: Longman, Brown, Green, and Longmans, 1845).

Outram, James. *The Conquest of Scinde: A Commentary* (Edinburgh and London: William Blackwood and Sons, 1846).

Paget, W. H. *A Record on the Expeditions against the North-West Frontier Tribes since the Annexation of the Punjab* [1873]. Revised edn, A.H. Mason (ed.) (London: Whiting & Co., 1884).

Parker, Charles Stuart (ed.). *Sir Robert Peel from His Private Papers*, 3 vols (London: John Murray, 1899).

Parry, William. *The Last Days of Lord Byron* (Paris: A. and W. Galignani, 1826).

Postans, Marianne. *Travels, Tales, and Encounters in Sindh and Balochistan, 1840–1843* (Oxford: Oxford UP, 2003).

Postans, Thomas. *Personal Observations on Sindh* (London: Longman, Brown, Green, and Longmans, 1843).

Prentice, Archibald. *History of the Anti-Corn Law League*, 2nd edn, 2 vols (1st edn 1853; London: Frank Cass; New York: Augustus M. Kelley, 1968).

Prevelakis, E., and K. Kalliataki Merticopoulou (eds). *Epirus, Ali Pasha, and the Greek Revolution: Consular Reports of William Meyer from Preveza*, 2 vols, Academy of Athens Monuments of Greek History 12 (Athens: Research Centre for the Study of Modern Greek History, 1996).

[Prinsep, Henry Thoby, and E. B. Eastwick.] 'Scinde – Dry Leaves from Young Egypt', *Quarterly Review* 91, 182 (September 1852), 379–401.

Ray, Gordon N. (ed.). *The Letters and Private Papers of William Makepeace Thackeray*, 4 vols (Cambridge, MA: Harvard UP, 1946).

Ricardo, David. *On Protection to Agriculture* (London: John Murray, 1822).

[Scrope, G. Poulett.] 'Jones on the Doctrine of Rents', *Quarterly Review* 46 (November 1831), 81–117.

Sedgwick, Romney (ed.). *Letters from George III to Lord Bute* (London: Macmillan, 1939).

Senior, Nassau William. *Three Lectures on the Rate of Wages*, 2nd edn (London: John Murray 1831; New York: Augustus M. Kelley, 1966).

Shadwell, Lawrence. *The Life of Colin Campbell, Lord Clyde*, 2 vols (Edinburgh: William Blackwood and Sons, 1881).

Bibliography   351

Shaw, Charles. *Personal Memoirs and Correspondence of Colonel Charles Shaw of the Portuguese Service*, 2 vols (London: Henry Coulburn, 1837).

Singh, Bawa Satinder (ed.). *The Letters of the First Viscount Hardinge of Lahore to Lady Hardinge and Sir Walter and Lady James, 1844–1847*, Camden Fourth Series 32 (London: Royal Historical Society, 1986).

Singh, Bawa Satinder (ed.). *My Indian Peregrinations: The Private Letters of Charles Stewart Hardinge, 1844–1847* (Lubbock: Texas Tech UP, 2001).

Sismondi, Jean-Charles Léonard Simonde de. *Political Economy and the Philosophy of Government: A Series of Essays Selected from the Works of M. de Sismondi* (London: John Chapman, 1847; New York: Augustus M. Kelley, 1966).

[Skelton, John.] 'Charles James Napier: A Study of Character', *Fraser's Magazine* 57 (February 1858), 254–68.

Smith, George (ed.), *Physician and Friend, Alexander Grant, F.R.C.S: His Autobiography and his Letters from the Marquis of Dalhousie* (London: John Murray, 1902).

Smith, R. Boswell. *Life of Lord Lawrence*, 2 vols (London: Smith, Elder, & Co., 1883).

South Australian Literary and Scientific Association. *Laws of the South Australian Literary and Scientific Association* (London: Privately printed, 1834).

Stanhope, Leicester. *Greece in 1823 and 1824* (Philadelphia: A. Small, E. Parker, Marot & Walter, and E. Littell, 1825).

[Strachey, William.] 'Conquest of Scinde', *Edinburgh Review* 79, 160 (April 1844), 476–544.

[Thackeray, William Makepeace.] 'The Story of Kompanee Jehan', *Punch: Or the London Charivari* 16 (17 March 1849), 105–06.

Thomas, William (ed.). *The Journals of Thomas Babington Macaulay*, 5 vols (London: Pickering & Chatto, 2008).

Timbs, John (ed.). *Wellingtoniana: Anecdotes, Maxims, and Characteristics of the Duke of Wellington* (London: Ingram, Cooke, and Co., 1852).

Tocqueville, Alexis de. *The Old Régime and the French Revolution, Vol. 1: The Complete Text*. François Furet and Françoise Mélonio (eds) (trans.) Alan S. Kahan (Chicago: University of Chicago Press, 1998).

Trelawny, Edward John. *Recollections of the Last Days of Shelley and Byron* (London: Edward Moxon, 1858).

Tucker, H. T. *A Glance at the Past and the Future in Connection with the Indian Revolt*, 2nd edn (London: Effingham Wilson, 1857).

Vattel, Emerich de. *The Law of Nations: Or, Principles of the Law of Nature, Applied to the Conduct and Affairs of Nations and Sovereigns* [1758] (London: G.G. and J. Robinson, 1797).

[Wakefield, Edward Gibbon.] 'A Letter from Sydney, the Principal Town of Australasia [1829]'. In *A Letter from Sydney and Other Writings* (London: J.M. Dent, 1929), 3–106.

Wellesley, Arthur, Duke of Wellington. *The Dispatches of Field Marshall the Duke of Wellington*, New edn, 13 vols. J. Gurwood (ed.) (London: John Murray, 1834–1839).

Whately, E. Jane. *Life and Correspondence of Richard Whately, D.D., Late Archbishop of Dublin*, 2 vols (London: Longman's, Green, and Co., 1866).

Wilson, Edward. *Rambles at the Antipodes: A Series of Sketches of Moreton Bay, New Zealand, the Murray River, and South Australia, and the Overland Route* (London: W.H. Smith and Son, 1859).

Wolff, Joseph. *Travels and Adventures of the Rev. Joseph Wolff, D.D., L.L.D.* (London: Saunders, Otley, and Co., 1861).

Young, Keith. *Scinde in the Forties: Being the Journal and Letters of Colonel Keith Young, C.B.* Arthur F. Scott (ed.) (London: Constable, 1912).

352   *Bibliography*

References, 1901 and After

Ahmad, Feroz. 'Agrarian Change and Class Formation in Sindh', *Economical and Political Weekly* 19, 39 (29 September 1984), A149–64.

Akenson, Donald H. *The Irish Education Experiment: The National System of Education in the Nineteenth Century* (London: Routledge & Kegan Paul, 1970).

Albinia, Alice. *Empires of the Indus: The Story of a River* (London: John Murray, 2008).

Alcoff, Linda Martin. 'Mignolo's Epistemology of Coloniality', *CR: The New Centennial Review* 7, 3 (Winter 2007), 79–101.

Anderson, Patricia. *The Printed Image and the Transformation of Popular Culture, 1790–1860* (Oxford: Clarendon Press, 1991).

Ansari, Sarah. 'The Sind Blue Books of 1843 and 1844': The Political "Laundering" of Historical Evidence', *English Historical Review* 120, 485 (February 2005), 35–65.

Applbaum, Arthur Isak. 'Forcing a People to Be Free', *Philosophy & Public Affairs* 35, 4 (Autumn 2007), 359–400.

Arafat, K. W. 'A Legacy of Islam in Greece: Ali Pasha and Ioannina', *Bulletin (British Society for Middle Eastern Studies)* 14, 2 (1987), 172–82.

Arnold, David. *Colonizing the Body: State Medicine and Epidemic Disease in Nineteenth-Century India* (Berkeley and Los Angeles: University of California Press, 1993).

Arnold, David. 'Race, Place and Bodily Difference in Early Nineteenth-Century British India', *Historical Research* 77, 196 (May 2004), 254–75.

Arunima, G. *There Comes Papa: Colonialism and the Transformation of Matriliny in Kerala, Malabar, c. 1850–1940* (Hyderabad: Orient Longman, 2003).

Asad, Talal. 'Two European Images of Non-European Rule'. In Asad (ed.), *Anthropology and the Colonial Encounter* (Atlantic Highlands, NJ: Humanities Press International; Reading, UK: Ithaca Press, 1973), 103–18.

Ayling, Stanley. *Fox: The Life of Charles James Fox* (London: John Murray, 1991).

Baggally, John W. *Ali Pasha and Great Britain* (Oxford: Basil Blackwell, 1938).

Bangash, Yaqoob Khan. 'The Price of Humans', *The Express Tribune* (Karachi), 28 May 2012.

Barkawi, Tarak. 'Globalization, Culture, and War: On the Popular Mediation of "Small Wars" ', *Cultural Critique* 58 (Autumn 2004), 115–47.

Bartlett, C. J., and G. A Smith. 'A "Species of Milito-Nautico-Guerilla-Plundering Warfare": Admiral Alexander Cochrane's Naval Campaign against the United States, 1814–1815'. In Julie Flavell and Stephen Conway (eds), *Britain and America Go to War: The Impact of War and Warfare in Anglo-America, 1754–1815* (Gainesville, FL: UP of Florida, 2004), 174–204.

Bass, Gary J. 'Jus Post Bellum', *Philosophy & Public Affairs* 32, 4 (2004), 384–412.

Bass, Gary J. *Freedom's Battle: The Origins of Humanitarian Intervention* (New York: Alfred A. Knopf, 2008).

Bayly, C. A. *The New Cambridge History of the British Empire*, 2, 1, *Indian Society and the Making of Empire* (Cambridge: Cambridge UP, 1988).

Bayly, C. A. *Imperial Meridian: The British Empire and the World, 1780–1830* (London and New York: Longman, 1989).

Bayly, C. A. *Empire and Information: Intelligence Gathering and Social Communication in India, 1780–1870* (Cambridge: Cambridge UP, 1996).

Bayly, C. A. *Recovering Liberties: Indian Thought in the Age of Liberalism and Empire* (Cambridge: Cambridge UP, 2012).

Beasley, Edward. *Mid-Victorian Imperialists: British Gentlemen and the Empire of the Mind* (London: Routledge, 2005).

Beasley, Edward. *The Victorian Reinvention of Race: New Racisms and the Problem of Grouping in the Human Sciences* (New York: Routledge, 2010).

Bibliography 353

Beaton, Roderick. *Byron's War: Romantic Rebellion, Greek Revolution* (Cambridge: Cambridge UP, 2013).

Beattie, Hugh. *Imperial Frontier: Tribe and State in Waziristan* (Richmond, Surrey: Curzon Press, 2002).

Belchem, John. *'Orator' Hunt: Henry Hunt and English Working-Class Radicalism* (Oxford: Clarendon Press, 1985).

Bell, Duncan. 'Victorian Visions of Global Order: An Introduction'. In idem (ed.), *Victorian Visions of Global Order: Empire and International Relations in Nineteenth-century Political Thought* (Cambridge: Cambridge UP, 2007), 1–25.

Benjamin, Lewis Saul. *William Makepeace Thackeray: A Biography Including Hitherto Uncollected Letters and Speeches and a Bibliography of 1300 Items*, 2 vols (London: John Lane, 1910).

Beresford, Kathryn. ' "Witnesses for the Defence": The Yeomen of Old England and the Land Question, *c*. 1815–1837'. In Matthew Cragoe and Paul Readman (eds), *The Land Question in Britain, 1750–1850* (Basingstoke: Palgrave Macmillan, 2010), 37–56.

Black, Jeremy. *The War of 1812 in the Age of Napoleon* (Norman, OK: University of Oklahoma Press, 2009).

Blake-Hill, Phillip V. 'The Napier Papers', *British Library Journal* 1 (1975), 25–31.

Bloomfield, Paul. *Edward Gibbon Wakefield: Builder of the British Commonwealth* (London: Longmans, Green, & Co., 1961).

Boesche, Roger. 'The Dark Side of Tocqueville: On War and Empire', *Review of Politics* 67, 4 (Fall 2005), 737–52.

Bowden, Brett. *The Empire of Civilization: The Evolution of an Imperial Idea* (Chicago: University of Chicago Press, 2009).

Bradley, Ian. *The Call to Seriousness: The Evangelical Impact on the Victorians* (New York: Macmillan, 1976).

Brantlinger, Patrick. *Dark Vanishings: Discourse on the Extinction of Primitive Races, 1800–1930* (Ithaca, NY: Cornell UP, 2003).

Brendon, Piers. *The Decline and Fall of the British Empire, 1783–1997* (2007; New York: Alfred A. Knopf, 2008).

Brewer, David. *Greece, the Hidden Centuries: Turkish Rule from the Fall of Constantinople to Greek Independence* (London: I.B. Tauris, 2010).

Burroughs, Peter. 'Crime and Punishment in the British Army, 1815–1870', *English Historical Review* 100, 396 (July 1985), 545–71.

Burton, Antoinette. *The Trouble with Empire* (Cambridge, MA: Harvard UP, 2015).

Cannon, John. 'New Lamps for Old: The End of Hanoverian England'. In John Cannon (ed.), *The Whig Ascendancy: Colloquies on Hanoverian England* (New York: St. Martin's), 100–18.

Cassell, Frank A. 'Slaves of the Chesapeake Bay Area and the War of 1812', *Journal of Negro History* 57, 2 (April 1972), 144–55.

Chablani, S. P. *Economic Conditions in Sind, 1592–1843* (Bombay: Orient Longman, 1951).

Chadwick, Owen. *The Victorian Church*, 2 vols (New York: Oxford UP, 1970).

Chakravarti, Uma. 'What Happened to the Vedic *Dasi*: Orientalism, Nationalism, and a Script for the Past'. In Kumkum Sangari and Sudesh Vaid (eds), *Recasting Women: Essays in Indian Colonial History* (1989; New Brunswick, NJ: Rutgers UP, 1990), 27–87.

Channa, Sahib Khan. 'Charles Napier in Sindh: Challenges and Achievements'. In Mohammed Qasim Soomro and Ghulam Muhammed Lakho (eds), *Sindh: Glimpses into Modern History*, Proceedings of the PHRIC on History of Sindh 1843–1999 (Jamshoro, Pakistan: Department of General History, University of Sindh, 2008), 59–91.

Chapman, Charles. 'The Only Appropriate Response to Honor Killings and Fatal Fatwas', Kurdish Women Action Against Honour Killing (12 March 2006), www.kwrw.org/kwahk/index.asp?id68, accessed 29 November 2013.

354   Bibliography

Chase, Malcolm. *Chartism: A New History* (Manchester: Manchester UP, 2007).

Chaudhury, Pradipta. 'Peasants and British Rule in Orissa', *Social Scientist* 1, 8/9 (August–September 1991), 28–56.

Chichester, H. M. 'Maitland, Sir Thomas (1760–1824)'. Revised by Roger T. Stearn. In H.C.G. Matthew and Brian Harrison (eds), *Oxford Dictionary of National Biography* (Oxford: Oxford UP, 2004). Online edn, edited by Lawrence Goldman, May 2006. http://www.oxforddnb.com/view/article/17835, accessed 25 April 2016.

Church, Roy A. *Economic Change in a Midland Town: Victorian Nottingham, 1815–1900* (London: Frank Cass, 1966).

Clark, J.C.D. 'Religion and the Origins of Radicalism in Nineteenth-Century Britain'. In Glenn Burgess and Matthew Festenstein (eds), *English Radicalism 1550–1850* (Cambridge: Cambridge UP, 2007), 241–84.

Clifford, James. ' "Hanging up Looking Glasses at Odd Corners" '. In Daniel Aaron (ed.), *Studies in Biography* (Cambridge, MA: Harvard UP, 1978), 41–56.

Cohn, Bernard S. *Colonialism and Its Forms of Knowledge: The British in India* (Princeton, NJ: Princeton UP, 1996).

Commager, Henry Steele. *The Empire of Reason: How Europe Imagined and America Realized the Enlightenment* (London: Weidenfeld and Nicolson, 1978).

Cook, S. A. *Imperial Affinities: Nineteenth Century Analogies and Exchanges between India and Ireland* (New Delhi: Sage, 1993).

Crocker, H. W., III. *The Politically Incorrect Guide to the British Empire* (Washington, DC: Regnery, 2011).

Crook, Tom, and Glen O'Hara (eds). *Statistics in the Public Sphere: Numbers and the People in Modern Britain, c. 1800–2000* (London: Routledge, 2011).

Cullen, Michael J. *The Statistical Movement in Early Victorian Britain: The Foundations of Empirical Social Research* (Hassocks, Sussex: Harvester, 1975).

Curzon, George Nathaniel. *British Government in India: The Story of the Viceroys and Government House*, 2 vols (London: Cassell and Co., 1925).

Dakin, Douglas. *British and American Philhellenes during the War of Greek Independence, 1821–1833* (Thessaloniki: Society for Macedonian Studies, 1955).

Daly, Hugh. *Memoirs of Sir Henry Dermot Daly* (London: John Murray, 1905).

Daniel, Norman. *Islam, Europe, and Empire* (Edinburgh: Edinburgh UP, 1966).

Davies, Godfrey. *Wellington and His Army* (Oxford: Basil Blackwell, 1954).

Davies, Huw W. *Wellington's Wars: The Making of a Military Genius* (New Haven, CT and London: Yale UP, 2012).

de Beer, E. S., and Walter Seton. 'Byroniana: The Archives of the London Greek Committee', *Nineteenth Century* 100 (September 1926), 396–412.

Desch, Michael C. 'America's Illiberal Liberalism: The Ideological Origins of Overreaction in U.S. Foreign Policy', *International Security* 32, 3 (Winter 2007/8), 7–43.

Dickson, David. 'Smoke without Fire?: Munster and the 1798 Rebellion'. In Thomas Bartlett, David Dickson, Dáire Keogh, and Kevin Whelan (eds), *1798: A Bicentenary Perspective* (Dublin: Four Courts Press, 2003), 147–73.

Dinwiddy, J. R. 'The Early Nineteenth-Century Campaign against Flogging in the Army', *English Historical Review* 97, 383 (April 1982), 308–31.

Dixon, C. Willis. *The Colonial Administrations of Sir Thomas Maitland* (London: Longmans, Green, and Co., 1939).

Doniger, Wendy. *The Hindus: An Alternative History* (New York: Penguin, 2009).

Dooley, Allan C. *Author and Printer in Victorian England* (Charlottesville, VA: University Press of Virginia, 1992).

Doyle, Michael W. *The Question of Intervention: John Stuart Mill and the Responsibility to Protect* (New Haven, CT: Yale UP, 2015).

Driault, Édouard. *Histoire Diplomatique de la Grèce de 1821 a nos Jours*, vol. 1, *L'Insurrection et l'Independence (1821–1830)* (Paris: Les Presses Universitaires de France, 1925).

Duarte, Adrian. *A History of British Relations with Sind, 1613–1843* (Karachi: National Book Foundation, 1976).

Durey, Michael. *The Return of the Plague: British Society and Cholera, 1831–2* (Dublin: Gill and Macmillan, 1979).

Durrell, Lawrence. *The Greek Islands* (New York: Viking Press, 1978).

Dyson, Ketaki Kushari. *A Various Universe: A Study of the Journals and Memoirs of British Men and Women in the Indian Subcontinent, 1765–1856* (New Delhi: Oxford UP, 1978).

Edgerton-Tarpley, Kathryn. *Tears from Iron: Cultural Responses to Famine in Nineteenth-Century China* (Berkeley and Los Angeles: University of California Press, 2008).

Edsall, Nicholas C. *Richard Cobden: Independent and Radical* (Cambridge, Massachusetts: Harvard UP, 1986).

Edwards, Michael S. *Purge this Realm: A Life of Joseph Rayner Stephens* (London: Epworth Press, 1994).

Epstein, James. *The Lion of Freedom: Fergus O'Connor and the Chartist Movement* (London & Canberra: Croom Helm, 1982).

Epstein, James. *Radical Expression: Political Language, Ritual, and Symbol in England, 1790–1850* (New York: Oxford UP, 1994).

Evans, Mary. *Missing Persons: The Impossibility of Auto/Biography* (London: Routledge, 1999).

Fairbairn, Geoffrey. *Revolutionary Guerrilla Warfare: The Countryside Version* (Harmondsworth, Middlesex: Penguin Books, 1974).

Farooqui, Amar. *Colonialism as Subversion: Colonialism, Indian Merchants, and the Politics of Opium, 1790–1843* (Lanham, MD: Lexington Books, 2005).

Farwell, Byron. *Queen Victoria's Little Wars* (New York: W.W. Norton, 1972).

Farwell, Byron. *Eminent Victorian Soldiers* (New York: Norton, 1985).

Fisch, Jörg. *Immolating Women: A Global History of Widow Burning from Ancient Times to the Present*, (trans.) Rekha Kamath Rajan (Delhi: Permanent Black, 2005).

Fisher, Michael H. *Counterflows to Colonialism: Indian Travellers and Settlers in Britain, 1600–1857* (Delhi: Permanent Black, 2004).

Fitzgerald, Brian. *Lady Louisa Conolly, 1743–1821: An Anglo-Irish Biography* (London: Staples Press, 1950).

Fitzpatrick, Matthew P., Jennifer Pitts, and Uday Singh Mehta. 'Conclusion: Liberalism and Empire Reconsidered: A Dialogue'. In Fitzpatrick (ed.), *Liberal Imperialism in Europe* (New York: Palgrave Macmillan, 2012), 241–66.

Fleming, K. E. *The Muslim Bonaparte: Diplomacy and Orientalism in Ali Pasha's Greece* (Princeton, NJ: Princeton UP, 1999).

Forrest, G. W. *Life of Field-Marshal Sir Neville Chamberlain* (Edinburgh: William Blackwood and Sons, 1909).

Fortescue, J. W. *A History of the British Army*, 13 vols (London: Macmillan, 1910–1930).

Fortescue, J. W. *Historical and Military Essays* (London: Macmillan, 1928).

Foster, David. *The Rural Constabulary Act 1839: National Legislation and Problems of Enforcement* (London: Bedford Square Press, 1982).

Fredungbeg, Mirza Kalichbeg (trans.). *History of Sind*, 2 vols, 2 parts (Karachi: Commissioner's Press, 1902).

Freitag, Sandria B. 'Collective Crime and Authority in North India'. In Anand A. Yang (ed.), *Crime and Criminality in British India* (Tucson, AZ: University of Arizona Press, 1985), 140–63.

356   *Bibliography*

Gahan, Daniel. *The People's Rising: Wexford, 1798* (Dublin: Gill & Macmillan, 1995).

Galbraith, John S. 'Some Reflections on the Profession of History', *Pacific Historical Review* 35, 1 (February 1966), 1–13.

Gallant, Thomas W. *Experiencing Dominion: Culture, Identity, and Power in the British Mediterranean* (Notre Dame, IN: University of Notre Dame Press, 2002).

Gates, David. *The British Light Infantry Arm, c. 1790–1815: Its Creation, Training, and Operational Role* (London: B.T. Batsford, 1987).

Gaynor, Tony. 'The Abercromby Affair'. In Thomas Bartlett, David Dickson, Dáire Keogh, and Kevin Whelan (eds), *1798: A Bicentenary Perspective* (Dublin: Four Courts Press, 2003), 394–405.

George, Christopher T. *Terror on the Chesapeake: The War of 1812 on the Bay* (Shippensburg, PA: White Mane Books, 2000).

Glover, Michael. *The Peninsular War, 1807–1814: A Concise Military History* (Newton Abbot: David and Charles, 1974).

Glover, Richard. *Peninsular Preparation: The Reform of the British Army, 1795–1809* (Cambridge: Cambridge UP, 1963).

Godsall, Jon R. *The Tangled Web: A Life of Sir Richard Burton* (Leicester: Matador, 2008).

Gould, Stephen Jay. *Bully for Brontosaurus: Reflections in Natural History* (New York: W.W. Norton & Co., 1991).

Griffin, Carl J. *The Rural War: Captain Swing and the Politics of Protest* (Manchester and New York: Manchester UP, 2012).

Grove, Richard. *Green Imperialism: Colonial Expansion, Tropical Island Edens, and the Origins of Environmentalism, 1600–1860* (Cambridge: Cambridge UP, 1995).

Guha, Ranajit. *A Rule of Property for Bengal: An Essay on the Idea of Permanent Settlement* (1963; Durham, NC: Duke UP, 1996).

Habibi, Don A. 'The Moral Dimensions of J. S. Mill's Colonialism', *Journal of Social Philosophy* 30, 1 (Spring 1999), 125–46.

Hall, Catherine. 'The Nation Within and Without'. In Catherine Hall, Keith McClelland, and Jane Rendall (eds), *Defining the Victorian Nation: Class, Race, Gender, and the Reform Act of 1867* (Cambridge: Cambridge UP, 2000), 179–233.

Hall, Catherine. *Civilising Subjects: Metropole and Colony in the English Imagination, 1830–1867* (Chicago: University of Chicago Press, 2002).

Hall, Catherine. 'Macaulay's Nation', *Victorian Studies* 51, 3 (Spring 2009), 505–23.

Hammond, J. L., and Barbara Hammond. *The Age of the Chartists, 1832–1854: A Study of Discontent* (London: Longmans, Green, and Co., 1930).

Hannell, David. 'The Ionian Islands under the British Protectorate: Social and Economic Problems', *Journal of Modern Greek Studies* 7, 1 (May 1989), 105–32.

Harling, Philip. *The Waning of 'Old Corruption': The Politics of Economical Reform in Britain, 1779–1846* (Oxford: Clarendon Press, 1996).

Harrison, Mark. *Climates and Constitutions: Health, Race, Environment, and British Imperialism in India, 1600–1850* (Oxford: Oxford UP, 1999).

Hawkins, Richard. 'The "Irish Model" and the Empire: A Case for Reassessment'. In David M. Anderson and David Killingray (eds), *Policing the Empire: Government, Authority, and Control, 1830–1940* (Manchester: Manchester UP, 1991), 18–32.

Hickey, Donald R. *The War of 1812: A Forgotten Conflict. Bicentennial Edition* (Urbana, Chicago, and Springfield, IL: University of Illinois Press, 2012).

Hinde, Wendy. *Richard Cobden: A Victorian Outsider* (New Haven: Yale UP, 1987).

Hitsman, J. Mackay, and Alice Sorby. 'Independent Foreigners or Canadian Chasseurs', *Military Affairs* 25, 1 (Spring 1961), 11–17.

Bibliography   357

Hobsbawm, Eric, and Georges Rudé. *Captain Swing: A Social History of the Great English Agricultural Uprising of 1830* (New York: W.W. Norton, 1968).

Hollis, Patricia. *The Pauper Press: A Study in Working-Class Radicalism of the 1830s* (Oxford: Oxford UP, 1970).

Holmes, Thomas Rice. *Sir Charles Napier* (Cambridge: Cambridge UP, 1925).

Horward, Donald D. 'Wellington and the Defence of Portugal', *International History Review* 11, 1 (February 1989), 39–54.

Hovell, Mark. *The Chartist Movement*. T. F. Tout (ed.) 2nd edn (Manchester: Manchester UP, 1925).

Huttenback, Robert A. *British Relations with Sind, 1799–1843: An Anatomy of Imperialism* (Berkeley and Los Angeles: University of California Press, 1962).

Imlah, Albert H. *Lord Ellenborough: A Biography of Edward Law, Earl of Ellenborough, Governor-General of India* (Cambridge, MA: Harvard UP, 1939).

Ingram, James D. 'What Is a "Right to Have Rights"?: Three Images of the Politics of Human Rights', *American Political Science Review* 102, 4 (November 2008), 401–16.

International Commission on Intervention and State Sovereignty. *The Responsibility to Protect* (Ottawa: International Development Research Centre, 2001).

Ivison, Duncan. *Post-Colonial Liberalism* (Cambridge: Cambridge UP, 2002).

James, H. and, Evan M. 'Introduction in Naomal Hotchand'. In (trans.) Alumal Trikamdas Bhojwani, H. Evan, and M. James (ed.), *A Forgotten Chapter of Indian History as Described in the Memoirs of Seth Naomal Hotchand, C.S.I., of Karachi, 1804–1878* (Exeter: Printed for private circulation by W. Pollard, 1915).

Jay, Elizabeth. *The Religion of the Heart: Anglican Evangelicalism and the Nineteenth-Century Novel* (Oxford: Clarendon Press, 1979).

Jayapalan, N. *History of India*, vol. 3, *From 1773 to Lord Minto, Including Constitutional Development* (New Delhi: Atlantic Publishers and Distributors, 2001).

Jones, David J. V. *The Last Rising: The Newport Insurrection of 1839* (Oxford: Clarendon Press, 1985).

Jones, Wilbur Devereux. *'Prosperity' Robinson: The Life of Viscount Goderich, 1782–1859* (London: Macmillan, 1967).

Kafka, Ben. *The Demon of Writing: Powers and Failures of Paperwork* (New York: Zone Books, 2012).

Kealy, Máire M. *Dominican Education in Ireland, 1820–1830* (Dublin: Irish Academic Press, 2007).

Kennedy, Dane. *Magic Mountains: Hill Stations and the British Raj* (Berkeley and Los Angeles: University of California Press, 1996).

Kennedy, Dane. *The Highly Civilized Man: Richard Burton and the Victorian World* (Cambridge, MA: Harvard UP, 2005).

Kerrigan, Paul M. 'General John Moore in Ireland in 1798', *Irish Sword* 3, 94 (2003), 401–08.

Khera, P. N. *British Policy towards Sindh up to the Annexation, 1843* (1941; Delhi: Ranjit Printers & Publishers, 1963).

Khristof, Nicholas D. 'Odysseus Lies Here?', *New York Times*, 11 March 2012, SR11.

Khuhro, Hamida. *The Making of Modern Sind: British Policy and Social Change in the Nineteenth Century* (Karachi: Oxford UP, 1999).

Koebner, Richard, and Helmut Dan Schmidt. *Imperialism: The Story and Significance of a Political Word, 1840–1960* (Cambridge: Cambridge UP, 1964).

Kolsky, Elizabeth. *Colonial Justice and British India: White Violence and the Rule of Law* (Cambridge: Cambridge UP, 2010).

Kriegel, Abraham D. 'Whiggery in the Age of Reform', *Journal of British Studies* 32, 3 (July 1993), 290–98.

358   *Bibliography*

Kumar, Virendra. *India under Lord Hardinge* (New Delhi and Allahabad: Rajesh Publications, 1978).

Laidlaw, Zöe. *Colonial Connections, 1815–1845: Patronage, the Information Revolution, and Colonial Government* (Manchester: Manchester UP, 2005).

Laidlaw, Zöe. 'Richard Bourke: Irish Liberalism Tempered by Empire'. In David Lambert and Alan Lester (eds), *Colonial Lives across the British Empire: Imperial Careering in the Long Nineteenth Century* (Cambridge: Cambridge UP, 2006), 113–44.

Lambert, David, and Alan Lester. 'Introduction: Imperial Spaces, Imperial Subjects'. In idem (eds), *Colonial Lives Across the British Empire: Imperial Careering in the Long Nineteenth Century* (Cambridge: Cambridge UP, 2006), 1–31.

Lambrick, H. T. *Sir Charles Napier and Sind* (Oxford: Clarendon Press, 1952).

Lambrick, H. T. *John Jacob of Jacobabad*, 2nd edn (Karachi: Oxford UP, 1975).

Lander, Edgardo. *Neoliberalismo, sociedad civil y democracia: ensayos sobre América Latina y Venezuela* (Caracas: Universidad Central de Venezuela, Consejo de Desarrollo Científico y Humanístico, 2000).

Lari, Suhail Zahir. *A History of Sindh* (Karachi: Oxford UP, 1994).

Larkin, Emmet. 'Introduction'. In Emmet Larkin (ed. and trans.), *Alexis de Tocqueville, Alexis de Tocqueville's Journey to Ireland, July-August, 1835* (Washington, DC: Catholic University of America Press, 1990), 1–15.

Latimer, John. *1812: War with America* (Cambridge, MA: Harvard UP, 2007).

Lawrence, Rosamund. *Charles Napier: Friend and Fighter* (London: John Murray, 1952).

Lee-Warner, William. *The Life of the Marquis of Dalhousie, K.T.*, 2 vols (1904; Shannon, Ireland: Irish UP, 1972).

Lorimer, Douglas A. *Colour, Class, and the Victorians: English Attitudes to the Negro in the Mid-Nineteenth Century* (Leicester: Leicester UP, 1978).

Low, Sidney, and Lloyd C. Saunders. *The History of England during the Reign of Queen Victoria (1837–1901)* (1907; New York: Haskell House, 1969).

Luvaas, Jay. *The Education of an Army: British Military Thought, 1815–1940* (Chicago: University of Chicago Press, 1964).

Lyell, Katherine M. (ed.). *The Life of Sir Charles J.F. Bunbury, Bart.*, 2 vols (London: John Murray, 1906).

McCarthy, Thomas. *Race, Empire, and the Idea of Human Development* (Cambridge: Cambridge UP, 2009).

McCord, Norman. *The Anti-Corn Law League, 1838–1846* (London: George Allen & Unwin, 1958).

McDowell, R. B. *Ireland in the Age of Imperialism and Revolution, 1760–1801* (Oxford: Clarendon Press, 1979).

Mace, Rodney. *Trafalgar Square: Emblem of an Empire* (London: Lawrence and Wishart, 1976).

Major, Andrea. *Sovereignty and Social Reform in India: British Colonialism and the Campaign against Sati, 1830–60* (London: Routledge, 2011).

Malhotra, Anshu. *Gender, Caste, and Religious Identities: Restructuring Class in Colonial Punjab* (New Delhi: Oxford UP, 2002).

Mandler, Peter. *Aristocratic Government in the Age of Reform: Whigs and Liberals, 1830–1852* (Oxford: Clarendon Press, 1990).

Mandler, Peter. *The English National Character: The History of an Idea from Edmund Burke to Tony Blair* (New Haven and London: Yale University Press, 2006).

Mani, Lata. *Contentious Traditions: The Debate on Sati in Colonial India* (Berkeley and Los Angeles: University of California Press, 1998).

Mantena, Karuna. 'Mill and Imperial Predicament'. In Nadia Urbananti and Alex Zakarias (eds), *J. S. Mill's Political Thought: A Bicentennial Reassessment* (Cambridge: Cambridge UP, 2007), 298–318.

Mantena, Karuna. *Alibis of Empire: Henry Maine and the Ends of Liberal Imperialism* (Princeton, NJ: Princeton UP, 2010).

Markovits, Claude. 'The Political Economy of Opium Smuggling in Early Nineteenth Century India: Leakage or Resistance?', *Modern Asian Studies* 43, 1 (2009), 89–111.

Martin, John E. ' "A Small Nation on the Move": Wakefield's Theory of Colonisation and Relationship between State and Labour in the Mid-Nineteenth Century'. In Friends of the Turnbull Library (eds), *Edward Gibbon Wakefield and the Colonial Dream: A Reconsideration* (Wellington, New Zealand: GP Publications, 1997), 106–22.

Mather, F. C. *Public Order in the Age of the Chartists* (1959; New York: Augustus M. Kelley, 1967).

Meacham, Standish. 'The Evangelical Inheritance', *Journal of British Studies* 3, 1 (November 1963), 88–104.

Mehta, Uday Singh. *Liberalism and Empire: A Study in Nineteenth-Century British Liberal Thought* (Chicago: University of Chicago Press, 1999).

Metcalf, Thomas R. *The New Cambridge History of India*, III.4, *Ideologies of the Raj* [1987] (New Delhi: Oxford UP, 1998).

Miller, William. *The Ottoman Empire and Its Successors, 1801–1827, with an Appendix, 1927–1936* (Cambridge: Cambridge UP, 1936).

Millett, Nathaniel. 'Britain's 1814 Occupation of Pensacola and America's Response: An Episode in the War of 1812 in the Southeastern Borderlands', *Florida Historical Quarterly* 84, 2 (Fall 2005), 229–55.

Mills, Charles. *The Racial Contract* (Ithaca, NY: Cornell UP, 1994).

Mills, Lennox A. *Ceylon under British Rule, 1795–1932* [1933] (London: Frank Cass, 1964).

Mitchell, L. G. *Charles James Fox* (Oxford: Oxford UP, 1992).

Morris, Jan. *Heaven's Command: An Imperial Progress* (1972; New York: Harcourt, Brace, Jovanovich, 1974).

Nabi, Aftab, and Dost Ali Baloch. 'Early British Efforts to Crush Karo Kari in Colonial Sind', *Pakistan Journal of Criminology* 2, 2 (April 2010), 1–20.

Napier, Priscilla. *The Sword Dance: Lady Sarah Lennox and the Napiers* (London: Michael Joseph, 1971).

Napier, Priscilla. *Revolution and the Napier Brothers, 1820–1840* (London: Michael Joseph, 1973).

Napier, Priscilla. *I Have Sind: Sir Charles Napier in India, 1841–1844* (London: Michael Joseph, 1990).

Napier, Priscilla. *Raven Castle: Sir Charles Napier in India, 1844–1851* (London: Michael Joseph, 1991).

Narasimhan, Sakuntala. *Sati: Widow Burning in India* (New York: Anchor Books, 1990).

Navickas, Katrina. *Protest and the Politics of Space and Place, 1789–1848* (Manchester: Manchester UP, 2016).

Norris, J. A. *The First Afghan War, 1838–1842* (Cambridge: Cambridge UP, 1967).

O'Brien, Michael. *Conjectures of Order: Intellectual Life in the American South, 1810–1860*, 2 vols (Chapel Hill: University of North Carolina Press, 2004).

O'Donnell, Rúan. *Aftermath: Post-Rebellion Insurgency in Wicklow, 1799–1803* (Dublin: Irish Academic Press, 2000).

O'Donnell, Rúan. *Robert Emmet and the Rising of 1803* (Dublin: Irish Academic Press, 2003).

360   *Bibliography*

Oldenburg, Veena Talwar. *Dowry Murder: The Imperial Origins of a Cultural Crime* (New York: Oxford UP, 2002).

Oldstone-Moore, Christopher. 'The Beard Movement in Victorian Britain', *Victorian Studies* 48, 1 (Autumn 2005), 7–34.

Olson, Alison Gilbert. *The Radical Duke: Career and Correspondence of Charles Lennox, Third Duke of Richmond* (London: Oxford UP, 1961).

Oman, Carola. *Sir John Moore* (London: Hodder and Stoughton, 1953).

Oman, Charles. *A History of the Peninsular War*, 6 vols (Oxford: Oxford University Press, 1902–1930).

O'Neill, Kevin. ' "Woe to the Oppressor of the Poor": Post-rebellion Violence in Ballitore, County Kildare'. In Thomas Bartlett, David Dickson, Dáire Keogh, and Kevin Whelan (eds), *1798: A Bicentenary Perspective* (Dublin: Four Courts Press, 2003), 363–77.

Orwell, George. *The Collected Essays, Journalism and Letters of George Orwell*. Sonia Orwell and Ian Angus (eds), 4 vols (New York: Harcourt, Brace, & World, 1968).

Osborne, John W. *The Silent Revolution: The Industrial Revolution in England as a Source of Cultural Change* (New York: Charles Scribner's Sons, 1970).

Pagden, Anthony. 'Human Rights, Natural Rights, and Europe's Imperial Legacy', *Political Theory* 31, 2 (April 2003), 171–99.

Page, Anthony. *John Jebb and the Enlightenment Origins of British Radicalism* (Westport, CT: Praeger, 2003).

Pakenham, Thomas. *The Year of Liberty: The Story of the Great Irish Rebellion of 1798* (1969; Englewood Cliffs, NJ: Prentice-Hall, 1970).

Palmer, Stanley H. 'Charles Napier: Irishman, Chartist, and Commander of the Northern District in England, 1839–41', *The Irish Sword: The Journal of the Military History Society of Ireland* 15 (1982), 89–100.

Palmer, Stanley H. *Police and Protest in England and Ireland, 1780–1850* (Cambridge: Cambridge UP, 1988).

Parry, J. P. *The Rise and Fall of Liberal Government in Victorian Britain* (New Haven, CT: Yale UP, 1993).

Parry, J. P. 'The Decline of Institutional Reform in Nineteenth-Century Britain'. In David Feldman and John Lawrence (eds), *Structures and Transformations in Modern British History* (Cambridge: Cambridge UP, 2011), 164–86.

Paxton, Nancy L. *Writing under the Raj: Gender, Race, and Rape in the British Colonial Imagination, 1830–1947* (New Brunswick, NJ: Rutgers UP, 1999).

Peers, Douglas M. 'Sepoys, Soldiers, and the Lash: Race, Caste, and Army Discipline in India, 1820–1850', *Journal of Imperial and Commonwealth History* 23, 2 (1995), 211–47.

Pickering, Paul A. *Chartism and the Chartists in Manchester and Salford* (Basingstoke: Macmillan, 1995).

Pickering, Paul A. *Feargus O' Connor: A Political Life* (Monmouth: Merlin Press, 2008).

Pickering, Paul A., and Alex Tyrell. *The People's Bread: A History of the Anti-Corn Law League* (London: Leicester UP, 2000).

Pike, Douglas. *Paradise of Dissent* (London: Longmans, Green, and Co., 1957).

Pinker, Steven. *The Better Angels of Our Nature: Why Violence Has Declined* (New York: Viking, 2011).

Pitts, Jennifer (ed. and trans). *Alexis de Tocqueville: Writings on Empire and Slavery* (Baltimore, MD: Johns Hopkins UP, 2001).

Pitts, Jennifer. *A Turn to Empire: The Rise of Imperial Liberalism in Britain and France* (Princeton, NJ: Princeton UP, 2005).

Potts, Jim. *The Ionian Islands and Epirus: A Cultural History* (Oxford: Oxford UP, 2010).

Powell, Geoffrey. *The Kandyan Wars: The British Army in Ceylon, 1803–1818* (London: Leo Cooper, 1973).

Prineas, Peter. *Britain's Greek Islands: Kythera and the Ionian Islands, 1809–1864* (Darlington, New South Wales: Plateia, 2009).

Pugh, R. B. 'Chartism in Somerset and Wiltshire'. In Asa Briggs (ed.), *Chartist Studies* (London: Macmillan, 1959), 174–219.

Purohit, Teena. *The Aga Khan Case: Religion and Identity in Colonial India* (Cambridge, MA: Harvard UP, 2012).

Pye, Neil. *The Home Office and the Chartists, 1838–1848: Protest and Repression in the West Riding of Yorkshire* (Pontypool, Wales: Merlin Press, 2013).

Rahman, Tarik. ' "Brother-in-Arms": Review of William Napier, *The History of Sir Charles James Napier's Conquest of the Scinde'*, *News on Sunday* (Karachi), 30 September 2001.

Rangarajan, Mahesh. 'Imperial Agendas and India's Forests: The Early History of Indian Forestry, 1800–1878', *Indian Economic and Social History Review* 31, 2 (1994), 147–67.

Reus-Smit, Christian. 'Human Rights in a Global Ecumene', *International Affairs* 87, 5 (2011), 1205–18.

Rice, Edward. *Captain Sir Richard Francis Burton* (New York: Charles Scribner's Sons, 1990).

Richards, J. F. 'The Indian Empire and Peasant Production of Opium in the Nineteenth Century', *Modern Asian Studies* 15, 1 (1981), 59–82.

Rosen, F. *Bentham, Byron, and Greece: Constitutionalism, Nationalism, and Early Liberal Political Thought* (Oxford: Clarendon Press, 1992).

Rubinstein, W. D. *Elites and the Wealthy in Modern British History: Essays in Social and Economic History* (Brighton: Harvester; New York: St. Martin's, 1987).

Ryan, Alan. *The Making of Modern Liberalism* (Princeton, NJ: Princeton UP, 2012).

St. Clair, William. *That Greece Might Still Be Free: The Philhellenes in the War of Independence* (London: Oxford UP, 1972).

Sarkar, Tanika. *Rebels, Wives, Saints: Designing Selves and Nations in Colonial Times* (London: Seagull, 2009).

Sartori, Andrew. 'The British Empire and Its Liberal Mission', *Journal of Modern History* 78, 3 (September 2006), 623–42.

Sartori, Andrew. *Liberalism in Empire: An Alternative History* (Berkeley and Los Angeles: University of California Press, 2014).

Schneidereit, Paul. 'Confronting the Darkness the Drove Mohammed Shafia', *The Chronicle Herald* (Halifax, Nova Scotia), 31 January 2012.

Schor, Naomi. 'The Crisis of French Universalism', *Yale French Studies* 100 (2001), 43–64.

Schulz, Bart, and Georgios Varouxakis (eds). *Utilitarianism and Empire* (Lanham, MD: Lexington Books, 2005).

Semmel, Stuart. 'English Radicals and "Legitimacy": Napoleon in the Mirror of History', *Past & Present* 167 (May 2000), 140–75.

Sen, Sudipta. 'Liberal Empire and Illiberal Trade: The Political Economy of "Responsible Government" in Early British India'. In Kathleen Wilson (ed.), *A New Imperial History: Culture, Identity, and Modernity in Britain and the Empire, 1660–1840* (Cambridge: Cambridge UP, 2004), 136–54.

Seymour, Miranda. 'Shaping the Truth'. In Peter France and William St. Clair (eds), *Mapping Lives: The Uses of Biography* (Oxford: Oxford UP, 2002), 253–66.

Seymour, Richard. *The Liberal Defence of Murder* (London: Verso, 2008).

Sharma, Sanjay. *Famine, Philanthropy, and the Colonial State: North India in the Early Nineteenth Century* (New Delhi: Oxford UP, 2001).

Shaw, A.G.L. *Sir George Arthur, Bart, 1784–1854* (Melbourne: Melbourne UP, 1980).

362 Bibliography

Simms, Bernard. ' "A False Principle in the Law of Nations": Burke, State Sovereignty, [German] Liberty, and Intervention in the Age of Westphalia'. In Bernard Simms and D.J.B. Trim (eds), *Humanitarian Intervention: A History* (Cambridge: Cambridge UP, 2011), 89–110.

Singha, Radhika. *A Despotism of Law: Crime and Justice in Early Colonial India* (Delhi: Oxford UP, 1998).

Singham, Shanti. 'From Cosmopolitan Anticolonialism to Liberal Imperialism: French Intellectuals and Muslim North Africa in the Late Eighteenth and Early Nineteenth Centuries'. In Charles Walton (ed.), *Into Print: Essays in Honor of Robert Darnton* (University Park: Pennsylvania State UP, 2011), 198–215.

Skiotis, Dennis N. 'From Bandit to Pasha: First Steps in the Rise to Power of Ali of Tepelen, 1750–1784', *International Journal of Middle East Studies* 2, 3 (July 1971), 219–44.

Skiotis, Dennis N. 'The Greek Revolution: Ali Pasha's Last Gamble'. In Nikiforos P. Diamandouros, John P. Anton, John A. Petropulos, and Peter Topping (eds), *Hellenism and the First Greek War of Liberation (1821–1830), Continuity and Change* (Thessaloniki: Institute for Balkan Studies, 1976), 98–109.

Smith, Vincent A. *The Oxford History of India*, 4th edn. Percival Spear (ed.) (Delhi: Oxford UP, 1981).

Sørenson, Georg. *A Liberal World Order in Crisis: Choosing between Imposition and Restraint* (Ithaca and London: Cornell UP, 2011).

Southall, Humphrey. 'Agitate! Agitate! Organize! Political Travellers and the Construction of a National Politics, 1839–1880', *Transactions of the Institute of British Geographers*, n.s., 21, 1 (1996), 177–93.

Spater, George. *William Cobbett: The Poor Man's Friend*, 2 vols (Cambridge: Cambridge UP, 1982).

Spivak, Gayatri Chakravorty. 'Can the Subaltern Speak?' In Rosalind G. Morris (ed.), *Can the Subaltern Speak?: Reflections on the History of an Idea* (New York: Columbia UP, 2010), 21–78.

Staum, Martin S. *Labeling People: French Scholars on Society, Race, and Empire, 1815–1848* (Montreal and Kingston: McGill-Queen's University Press, 2003).

Stedman Jones, Gareth. *An End to Poverty?: An Historical Debate* (New York: Columbia UP, 2004).

Stedman Jones, Gareth. 'Rethinking Chartism'. In idem (ed.), *Languages of Class: Studies in English Working-Class History, 1832–1982* (Cambridge: Cambridge UP, 1983), 90–178.

Stepan, Nancy. *The Idea of Race in Science: Great Britain, 1800–1960* (Hamden, CT: Archon Books, 1982).

Steyn, Mark. *America Alone: The End of the World as We Know It* (Washington, DC: Regnery Publishing, 2006).

Stirling, S. M. *Island in the Sea of Time: A Novel of the Change* (New York: Roc, New American Library, 1998).

Stocking, George. 'Introduction to James Cowles Prichard'. In George Stocking (ed.), *Researches into the Physical History of Man* [1813] (Chicago: University of Chicago Press, 1973), ix–cx.

Stokes, Eric. *The English Utilitarians and India* (Oxford: Oxford UP, 1959).

Stokes, Eric. *The Peasant and the Raj: Studies in Agrarian Society and Peasant Rebellion in Colonial India* (Cambridge: Cambridge UP, 1978).

Stone, Lawrence. *The Family, Sex, and Marriage in England, 1500–1800* (New York: Harper & Row, 1977).

Sturman, Rachel. *The Government of Social Life in Colonial India: Liberalism, Religious Law, and Women's Rights* (Cambridge: Cambridge UP, 2012).

Bibliography   363

Sutherland, Gillian (ed.). *Studies in the Growth of Nineteenth-Century Government* (Totowa, NJ: Rowman and Littlefeld, 1972).

Swinson, Arthur. *North-West Frontier: People and Events, 1939–1947* (New York: Frederick A. Praeger, 1967).

Temple, Philip. *A Sort of Conscience: The Wakefields* (Auckland, New Zealand: Auckland UP, 2002).

Thairani, Kala. *British Political Missions to Sind: A Narrative of Negotiations from 1799 to 1843 Leading up to the State's Annexation* (New Delhi: Orient Longman, 1973).

Thomas, P. *Indian Women through the Ages* (New York: Asia Publishing House, 1964).

Thomas, William. *The Philosophic Radicals: Nine Studies in Theory and Practice, 1817–1841* (Oxford: Clarendon Press, 1979).

Thomis, Malcolm I. *Politics and Society in Nottingham, 1785–1835* (New York: Augustus M. Kelly, 1969).

Thompson, Dorothy. *The Chartists: Popular Politics in the Industrial Revolution* (New York: Pantheon, 1984).

Thompson, Dorothy. *Outsiders: Class, Gender, and Nation* (London: Verso, 1993).

Thompson, E. P. *The Making of the English Working Class* (1963; New York: Vintage Books, 1966).

Thompson, Noel. *The People's Science: The Popular Political Economy of Exploitation and Crisis, 1816–34* (Cambridge: Cambridge UP, 1984).

Tidrick, Kathryn. *Empire and the English Character* (London: I.B. Tauris, 1990).

Tillyard, Stella. *Aristocrats: Caroline, Emily, Louisa, and Sarah Lennox, 1740–1832* (New York: Farrar, Straus, and Giroux, 1994).

Tillyard, Stella. *Citizen Lord: The Life of Edward Fitzgerald, Irish Revolutionary* (New York: Farrar, Straus and Giroux, 1997).

Todorov, Tzvetan. *On Human Diversity: Nationalism, Racism, and Exoticism in French Thought.* Catherine Porter (trans.) (Cambridge, MA: Harvard UP, 1993).

Torrens-Spence, Johnny. *Historic Battlefields of Pakistan* (Karachi: Oxford UP, 2006).

Trevelyan, G. M. *British History in the Nineteenth Century (1782–1901)* (London: Longmans, Green, and Co., 1922).

Trotter, Lionel J. *A Leader of Light Horse: Hobson of Hobson's Horse* (Edinburgh: William Blackwood, 1901).

Trotter, Lionel J. *The Bayard of India: A Life of General Sir James Outram, Bart.* (Edinburgh and London: William Blackwood and Sons, 1903).

Tuan, Mao-Lan. *Simonde de Sismondi as an Economist*, Columbia University Studies in the Social Sciences 298 (New York: Columbia UP, 1927; New York: AMS Press, 1968).

Tzoref-Ashkenazi, Chen. 'Romantic Attitudes toward Oriental Despotism', *Journal of Modern History* 85, 2 (June 2013), 280–320.

Vance, Norman. 'Improving Ireland: Richard Whately, Theology, and Political Economy'. In Stefan Collini, Richard Whatmore, and Brian Young (eds), *Economy, Polity, and Society: British Intellectual History, 1750–1950* (Cambridge: Cambridge UP, 2000), 181–202.

Vetch, R. H. 'Kennedy, John Pitt (1796–1879)'. Revised by Roger T. Stearn. In H.C.G. Matthew and Brian Harrison (eds), *Oxford Dictionary of National Biography* (Oxford: Oxford UP, 2004). Online edn, edited by Lawrence Goldman, May 2010. http://www.oxforddnb.com/view/article/15387, accessed 25 April 2016.

Voshell, Fay. 'Tolerating Pederasty', American Thinker (25 September 2015), http://www.americanthinker.com/articles/2015/09/tolerating_pederasty.html, accessed 18 March 2016.

Waller, John H. *Beyond the Khyber Pass: The Road to British Disaster in the First Afghan War* (Austin, TX: University of Texas Press, 1990).

364   *Bibliography*

Walter, James. ' "The Solace of Doubt"?: Biographical Writing after the Short Twentieth Century'. In Peter France and William St. Clair (eds), *Mapping Lives: The Uses of Biography* (Oxford: Oxford UP, 2002), 321–35.

Ward, Erica. *Vice in the Barracks: Medicine, the Military, and the Making of Colonial India, 1780–1868* (Basingstoke: Palgrave Macmillan, 2014).

Ward, J. T. *Chartism* (London: B.T. Batsford, 1973).

Washbrook, David. 'Economic Depression and the Making of "Traditional" Society in Colonial India, 1820–1855', *Transactions of the Royal Historical Society*, sixth series, 3 (1993), 237–63.

Weaver, Stewart Angas. *John Fielden and the Politics of Popular Radicalism, 1832–1847* (Oxford: Clarendon Press, 1987).

Welch, Cheryl B. 'Colonial Violence and the Rhetoric of Evasion: Tocqueville on Algeria', *Political Theory* 31, 2 (April 2003), 235–64.

Wiener, Joel H. *The War of the Unstamped* (Ithaca, NY: Cornell UP, 1969).

Wiener, Martin J. *An Empire on Trial: Race, Murder, and Justice under British Rule, 1870–1935* (Cambridge: Cambridge UP, 2009).

Wilks, Ivor. *South Wales and the Rising of 1839: Class Struggle as Armed Struggle* (London: Croom Helm, 1984).

Will, Pierre-Étienne, and R. Bin Wong (eds). *Nourish the People: The State Granary System in China*, Michigan Monographs in Chinese Studies 60 (Ann Arbor: Center for Chinese Studies Publications, University of Michigan, 1991).

Williams, William Appleman. *Empire as a Way of Life: An Essay on the Causes and Character of America's Present Predicament, along with a Few Thoughts about an Alternative* (New York: Oxford UP, 1980).

Wolpert, Stanley. *A New History of India*, 3rd edn (New York: Oxford UP, 1989).

Wolpert, Stanley. *Zulfi Bhutto of Pakistan: His Life and Times* (New York: Oxford UP, 1993).

Wong, J. Y. 'British Annexation of the Sind in 1843: An Economic Perspective', *Modern Asian Studies* 31, 2 (May 1997), 225–44.

Wong, J. Y. *Deadly Dreams: Opium, Imperialism, and the Arrow War (1856–1860) in China* (Cambridge: Cambridge UP, 1998).

Woodhouse, C. M. *The Philhellenes* (London: Hodder and Stoughten, 1969).

Woodhouse, C. M. *Capodistria: The Founder of Greek Independence* (London: Oxford UP, 1973).

Wrigley, W. D. 'Dissension in the Ionian Islands: Colonel Charles James Napier and the Commissioners (1819–1833)', *Balkan Studies* 16, 2 (1975), 11–22.

Wrigley, W. D. *The Diplomatic Significance of Ionian Neutrality, 1821–1831*. American University Studies 9, *History*, vol. 41 (New York: Peter Lang, 1988).

Yang, Anand A. 'Whose Sati?: Widow Burning in Early 19th Century India', *Journal of Women's History* 1, 2 (Fall 1989), 8–33.

Yapp, M. E. *Strategies of British India: Britain, Ireland, and Afghanistan, 1798–1850* (Oxford: Clarendon Press, 1980).

Young, G. M. *Early Victorian England: 1830–1865*, 2 vols (Oxford: Clarendon Press, 1934).

Zastoupil, Lynn. *John Stuart Mill and India* (Stanford: Stanford UP, 1994).

Zegger, Robert E. *John Cam Hobhouse: A Political Life, 1819–1852* (Columbia, MO: University of Missouri Press, 1973).

Unpublished thesis

Rodger, Thomas. '*The Life and Opinions of General Sir Charles James Napier, G.C.B.* and Chartism'. B.A. thesis, School of History, University of Leeds, 2009.

Index

Abercromby, Ralph (army commander in Ireland) 20, 180, 292

Aborigines, Australian 111–12

Acre 167–8

Adam, Frederick: criticises Napier 83, 97; Maitland's deputy in Ionian Islands 64, 70, 83; Napier's poor opinion of 78–9, 84, 86, 88, 98, 105; possible command in India 284; removes Napier 93–5; succeeds Maitland and governs Ionian Islands 74, 76, 78, 82–4; use of gallows 78

Afghanistan 7, 186, 205, 284, 321

Afghan War 181–4, 186, 189, 195, 224, 336; opinions about 182–3, 227, 229, 231, 304

Afridis (hill tribe in Punjab) 184, 299–303, 306–7, 309, 330

agricultural reform: Cephalonian 86–7, 94, 337; English 19, 109–10; Irish 20, 106–20, 122–3, 129, 162; Sindhi 188, 253–7, 261

Alcoff, Linda Martin (philosopher) 256

Alexandria 168, 179–80, 286

Ali Murad (Mir in Sind and *rais* in upper Sind) 199, 201, 210–11, 226, 238, 267

Ali Pasha of Joannina (or Ioannina) 56, 59, 201; death of 61, 76

Amirs of Sind: British views of 188, 200–1, 226–8, 239; captivity of 219–20, 227–9, 329; early British relations with 187, 189; families of 219, 226; James Outram's views of 196, 199, 202–4, 209, 212, 225–6; Napier's views of 186–8, 194–7, 200–6, 209, 213, 239; relations with Napier 199–200, 206–11; rule by 187–8, 194, 240–1, 253–5, 258, 262; statements by 209–10, 227–9, 329; treaties with 189, 196–200, 213–14;

see also Ali Murad; Dubba, Battle of; Miani, Battle of; Nasir Khan; Rustam Ali; Shere Muhammed

Amritsar 315–16

Anastasia (mother of Napier's children) 67–9, 82

annexation (opinions about): as a general policy 7, 331; in South Asia 184, 184–5, 188–90, 229–31, 324; *see also* Burma, annexation of; Punjab, annexation of; Sind, annexation of

Anti-Corn Law League 130, 169

Argostoli 65, 69–70, 81, 84, 87, 116

army career, Napier's views of 28, 179, 205

Arthur, George (Governor of Bombay) 180–1, 209, 226, 229, 288n15

Asad, Talal (anthropologist) 63n33

Ashley, Lord (Anthony Ashley Cooper 7th Earl of Shaftesbury) 227–8, 231

Athens 57, 72

atrocities: in Afghanistan 182, 304; in Algeria 266; in Australia 111; by British in Sind 265; by British in the Kohat Valley 301–10, 323, 330; in Hampton, Virginia 42–3; by hill tribes in Northern Sind 265–6; in Ireland (1798) 20–2, 26, 277

atrocities, allegations of (Sind) 219, 253

Auckland, George Eden 1st Earl of (Governor-General of India) 181–4, 198, 227; Napier's opinions about 183–4, 202–3

Australia 103–5, 110–11, 147

baggage (in moving an army) 44, 260, 281–2

bakery (Cephalonia) 86, 94–5

ballot, secret 55–6, 117, 120–1, 130–1, 157, 334

Barnsley 164

366   *Index*

barracks, construction, siting, and defense of 53; in north of England 139–40, 143–5, 155, 164, 167; in South Asia 186, 294, 330
Bartlett, C. J. (historian) 46
batai (rent payment in share of crop) 255
Bath 98, 105, 119–22, 200, 227, 281
Bathurst, Henry 3rd Earl Bathurst (Colonial Secretary) 73
Bayly, C. A. (historian) 19–20, 256
Beckwith, Sydney (general) 40–4, 46
Beirut 167
Belgium 47
Beluchis 187, 213–15, 217, 219, 236, 233n14, 239, 243
Bengal 184, 246, 254, 287
Bermuda 40, 44, 116, 333
Bijar (or 'Beja') Khan (hill raider) 265, 267
biography, validity of 331
Birmingham 132, 155, 159n20
Blackburn 142
'Black Charlie' *see* Napier, Charles, Admiral
Blackwood's Edinburgh Magazine 232
Blatchington Barracks (Sussex) 26–7
Board of Control 184, 187, 240, 319; *see also* Presidents of the Board of Control
Bolan Pass 189
Bombay 168, 179, 182, 186, 190, 210, 219, 238–40, 270, 297
Bombay Presidency (division of British-run India) 96, 179–81, 240, 286–7
Bombay Times 219
Boogties (hill tribe in northern Sind) 200, 209, 239, 267, 307
Bradford 160–1, 163–4, 168, 173n32
Bradford (army officer at Amritsar) 315
Bradshaw, Captain (army officer in Punjab) 300–3, 305–6
British Empire, Napier's opinions about 41, 45–6, 103–6, 111–12, 271, 325, 331
British relations with Sind: early period 186–90; Ellenborough's revised treaties 195–200, 209, 213–14; *see also* Sind, annexation of
Buist, George (editor of *Bombay Times*) 219, 283
Bukkur (Sind) 197–8
Bunbury, Charles: marries and divorces Lady Sarah Lennox 15
Bunbury, Emily *see* Napier, Emily
Bunbury, Henry (Napier's brother-in-law) 160, 170
Bunbury, Louisa (Napier's half-sister) 15, 18
Burma, annexation of 331

Burnes, Alexander (early visitor to Sind) 187–8, 199
Burnes, James (early visitor to Sind) 187–8
Burnley 146, 155
Burton, Antoinette (historian) 336
Burton, Richard Francis (as army officer in Sind) 247, 252n63
Busaco, Battle of (1810) 34–5
Byron, George Gordon Noel 6th Baron 57, 61, 69–73, 82, 271

Caen 99, 110, 121
Cairo 179–80
Calcutta (capital of India) 180, 246, 286–7, 294, 297, 317, 320
camels 212, 260, 281, 295, 329
Campbell, Colin 1st Baron Clyde (later Commander-in-Chief of India): burns villages 304–6; destroys crops 309; opposes destruction 309; pall-bearer 332; in Punjab 293–4, 301–2, 306; resigns and briefs Napier 330
canals 29, 60, 82, 194, 258, 297
Canning, Charles John, Earl Canning (later Governor-General and Viceroy of India) 330
cantonments 196, 198
Capodistrias, John (Ioannis Antonios Kapodistrias) (Russian Foreign Minister and Greek head of state) 76
Captain Swing 133, 146
Carlisle 146
Carton House (seat of the Leinsters) 18, 20
Castletown House (seat of the Conollys) 16, 18, 20–1
categorization, imperial *see* imperial categorization
Celbridge (County Kildare) 18–20, 22, 27, 304
Cephalonia: description 64–7; Napier's rule over 77–88
Ceylon 55, 297
charity, opinions about 90, 162–3; Napier's opinions about 87–90, 108, 162–3
Chartism: beliefs and goals 130–3, 333–4; course of 151–6, 160–70; fears regarding 133, 143, 146; Napier's views of 138–9, 146–7, 153, 169–70; threats of violence 132, 141–2, 151–4, 160–1, 163–4
Chase, Malcolm (historian) 3, 132, 160
Chatham 27, 29, 37n12
Cheltenham 168, 179, 281, 285
Chester 141, 146, 166–8

child labour, Napier's comments on 1, 111, 117
Chillianwallah, Battle of (1849) 284
China 90, 168, 179, 190, 299, 321
cholera 99, 181, 186, 270
Church, R. W. (Greek Commander) 76
Churchill, Winston 2, 308–9
civil conflict, Napier's views on 22, 110, 117–19, 138–9, 279
civilians, attacks on: Afghanistan 304; Chesapeake Bay 42–4; Copenhagen 30; Egypt 167; general problem of 115–16; Ireland 20–2; Punjab 301–10, 330; Sind 265
Coa, Battle of (1810) 34
Cobbett, William (radical writer and MP) 6, 36, 47–8, 73, 130, 240, 337
Cochrane, George (admiral) 45
Cockburn, George (admiral) 41–4
Cockermouth 157
Code Napoléon 257–8
Coercian Bills 80, 119, 122, 129
Coke, Captain (army officer in Punjab) 309
Collectors (Sind) 241, 244, 249n23, 353–4, 258, 260–1
Colne (Lancashire) 166–7
Colonial Reform (Wakefieldian) 103–5, 107, 109
Colonial Secretaries (Secretaries of State for War and the Colonies) see Bathurst; Ripon
colonization, Napier's views of 105–6, 109, 111–12
Commanders-in-Chief of India see Campbell; Gomm; Gough; Napier, Charles James, Lieutenant-General
Commanders-in-Chief of the Forces see Dundas; Hardinge; Hill, Rowland 1st Viscount; Wellington; York and Albany
command responsibility 117, 305
concentration of troops, importance of: in India 292; in the north of England 144–5, 149n36
Conolly, Lady Louisa, née Lennox (Napier's aunt) 16
Conolly, Tom (Irish landowner and Napier's uncle) 16, 18, 30
conquest, arguments against 184, 204, 227–9, 256, 331
conquest, defensive reasons for 183, 202, 212–13
conquest, economic reasons for 180, 189–90, 325

conquest, humanitarian reasons for 45–6, 60–1, 168, 194–7, 201–3, 205–6, 265–6; see also liberal imperialism
conquest, Orientalist reasons for 60–1, 70, 168, 179–80, 271
conquest, strategic reasons for 61, 182–3
conquest as a civilizing mission 41, 180, 196, 200, 333
Constantinople 56, 60–1, 70, 72, 271
Copenhagen, Battle of (1807) 29–30
Corfu 56, 64, 67, 82, 84, 88, 93, 98
Corinth 60, 64
Cornwallis, Charles 1st Marquess (as Lord Lieutenant of Ireland) 20, 22
correspondence, excessive 95, 97–8, 237–8, 269
Coruña see La Coruña
Council of India 286, 317, 319, 330
Couper, George (confidant of Dalhousie) 295–6, 307, 319–20, 322
Court of Directors (East India Company) 231, 239, 269, 283–6, 294
Craney Island (Virginia) 42
Craufurd, Robert (general) 34, 292
crop destruction 308–10
crop rotation 87, 123
currants 65, 67, 86, 254, 336

Dalhousie, James Andrew Broun Ramsay 10th Earl and 1st Marquess of Dalhousie (Governor-General of India): in 2nd Sikh War 283–4; accompanies Napier on tours 294, 296; annexes Punjab 287, 293; and burning villages 300, 303, 309–10; changing views on army pay mutinies 293–6, 314–16, 322; complaints about Napier 296–7, 307, 318, 320–2; considers alternatives to village burning 309; greets Napier 287; ill health and sea voyage 294–7; interferes with hill tribes 299–300, 336; mentioned by Hardinge 270; reforms army pay 293, 296; relations with Colin Campbell 309; relations with Punjab Board 306, 321; reputation during Indian Mutiny 324; restricts Napier's authority 96, 296, 318–21; suggests army reforms 291
danger to army, Napier's fears over 204–5, 209, 213–13; referred to by others 226, 228, 231
De Bosset, Major (official in Cephalonia) 65
debt bondage 253, 255
Delane, John Thadeus (editor of the Times) 284, 286

368   *Index*

Delane (army officer in India, brother John Thadeaus Delane) 302
despotism: concepts of 5–6, 53, 77, 188, 200, 235, 262; Napier's idea about 3, 5, 53, 55–6, 77, 117, 122, 180, 305, 325
Dewsbury 164
Dickens, Charles 121, 308
disfigurement and disability (Napier) 35, 64, 169, 283
disfigurement of women (Sind) 246
Dost Mohammed Khan (Emir of Afghanistan) 182
Doyle, Michael W. (political scientist and diplomat) 5
drones 2, 308
Dubba (or Hyderabad), Battle of (1843) 223–5, 237, 253
Dublin 18, 27, 120, 122–3, 136–7
duelling 282–3
Dundas, David (Commander-in-Chief of the Forces) 33–4, 36
Durham 157

East India Company: finances 189–90, 240; structure and governance 284–6, 317, 319, 330; *see also* Board of Control; Court of Directors; Presidencies
economic imperialism 184–6, 189–90, 198, 325
Egypt 167–8, 179–80
elephants 281, 295, 329
Ellenborough, Edward Law 1st Earl of: at 1848 dinner 281; at 1852 India hearing 329–30; dismissal 231, 239; First Lord of the Admiralty 261, 269; Governor-General of India 182–3, 202, 211, 214, 217, 237, 239, 247, 253, 292, 296; and Napier's death 332; on Napier's return to India 286; and Napier's statue 339; opinions on annexing Sind 183–7, 189–90, 197–8; President of the Board of Control 187; relationship with Napier 183, 192, 197, 227, 229–31, 240
Elphinstone, Lord, John Elphinstone 13th Lord Elphinstone and 1st Baron Elphinstone (Indian official) 239
Elphinstone, Mountstuart (Indian official) 231
emancipation in Sind 247
Emmet's Rebellion (1803) 27
England, Richard (general in Afghanistan) 209
Epirus 56, 59, 61
erosion 81–2, 188

Evans, Mary (cultural critic) 331
execution 61, 77, 245, 248, 261; of military personnel 44, 242, 307; Napier's views regarding 77, 164, 166, 243

Factory Acts 111
factory owners, inhumanity of 111, 121, 165–6
famine: Bengal 254; Cephalonia 86–90; England 121; Ireland 89–90, 261
Farnham (military college) 47
Farwell, Byron (historian) 19
feudal social order, alleged: in Cephalonia 55, 77–80, 85; in Sind 254–5, 262, 336
Fielden, John (MP) 130, 141
Fitzgerald, Lord, William Vesey-Fitzgerald 2nd Baron Fitzgerald and Vesey and 1st Baron Fitzgerald (President of the Board of Control) 198
Fitzgerald, Lord Edward (Napier's older cousin) 16, 20; Napier's views of 277
flogging 114–17, 244, 325
Fortescue, John (historian) 224
Foulkesmills, Battle of (1798) 22
Fox, Charles James (Napier's older cousin): entertains Napier 27; intervenes for Napier 29; Napier's opinion 30; political views of 1, 29–30, 338; youth 17
Fox, Henry Edward (Napier's older cousin and commander) 27, 29
Fox, Lady Caroline *see* Holland, Baroness
France 41, 57, 179; Napier's opinions about 110, 121, 258; Napier's periods of residence in 47–8, 99–100; *see also* Napoleon I
France, history of: 1848 revolution 277; First Empire 53, 65; French Revolution 277; the Hundred Days 47; reign of Charles X 110, 121
franchise: in England 16, 119–20, 129–33, 157, 333–4, 337–8; in Sind 259; *see also* suffrage; voting
Freitag, Sandria (historian) 243
Frere, Bartle (later Commissioner for Sind) 241, 261, 324

Gallant, Thomas (historian) 79–80, 84
George III 15–16, 33
George IV 94, 187
Ghent 47
Ghoree, Futeh Muhammed (minister of Mir Rustam) 201
Gibbet Rath, atrocities at (1798) 22
gibbets 78, 245

Index 369

Gilbert, Walter (army officer in India) 316, 320

Goderich *see* Ripon

Gomm, William (general; Napier's successor in the north of England and as Commander-in-Chief of India) 284, 286

Gordon, Lord William 15

Gordon, Thomas (Philhellene and historian of Greece) 100

Gough, Hugh 1st Viscount: 271; at 1852 India hearing 329; in 2nd Sikh War 284–5; commander in 1st Sikh War 269; defeats Sikhs 287, 319; Napier's view of 284

government, role of, Napier's views on 87–90, 108, 118, 155

Governor of Bombay *see* Arthur, George

Governors-General of India *see* Auckland; Canning; Dalhousie; Ellenborough; Hardinge

Govindghur, Fort of (Amritsar) 315

Graham, James (Home Secretary, later First Lord of the Admiralty) 332

Grant, Patrick (army officer in India) 316–17, 320

Greece: kingdom 85, 100; revolutionary period 56–61, 64, 69–73, 76, 80; *see also* Cephalonia; Septinsular Republic

Greek Committee *see* London Greek Committee

Guernsey 29, 36, 40, 116

Guha, Ranajit (historian) 254

Guibert (French drummer) 31–2

Gurkhas 292, 315

Habibi, Don (philosopher) 5

Haiti 55

Halifax 141–2, 144

Halifax, Nova Scotia 46

Hammond, J. L. and Barbara (historians) 170

Hardinge, Henry 1st Viscount Hardinge of Lahore (Governor-General of India): and First Sikh War 267–9, 283; against French razzias 266; as Governor-General 117, 271, 296; at Napier's funeral 332; on Napier's return to India 286; opinions about Napier 232, 240, 270, 323; sent to India 239–40; at Wellington's funeral 328

hari (landless peasant) 255

Hearsey, Brigadier (army officer in India) 316–17, 320

heat prostration 227, 238–9

Heywood (Lancashire) 141

Hill, Rowland (founder of Penny Post) 104–5

Hill, Rowland 1st Viscount (Commander-in-Chief of the Forces) 136–7, 154–5, 184

hill tribes: Punjab 299–300, 302, 306–9, 330; Sind 200, 225, 210, 239, 265–7; *see also* Afridis; Boogties

Hobhouse, John Cam 1st Baron Broughton (Philhellene and President of the Board of Control) 183–4, 271, 284, 286, 303, 317, 322–3

Holland, Baroness, née Lady Caroline Lennox (Napier's aunt) 17

Homer 93

Home Secretaries *see* Graham, James; Normanby; Russell

Hope, John (officer at the Battle of La Coruña) 31

Horse Guards (headquarters of British Army) 34, 36, 47, 122, 136, 145, 154, 319; *see also* Somerset

Household Words 190, 308, 338–9

Hovell, Mark 170

Howick, Lord, Henry George Grey 3rd Earl Grey 228, 231–2

Huband, George (army officer in north of England) 160–1

Huddersfield 151

Hull 141, 146, 155

humanitarian conquest; *see also* conquest, humanitarian reasons for

Hyderabad, Battle of *see* Dubba, Battle of

Hyderabad (Sind) 194, 196, 200, 209, 211–14, 217, 223, 226–7, 241, 246, 253

Hyderabad Fort 217–19

Hythe 29–30, 68

ignorance: British ignorance in South Asia 254, 301; of conditions in the north of England 139–42; in empire-building 6, 256, 334–5; Napier's ignorance in Sind 226, 228, 253–6, 262, 334–6

illegal orders 304–5

Imamgahr (Emun Ghur) (Sind fort) 211

imperial categorization: in 18th-century Bengal 254; Napier's 256–7; *see also* Orientalism

imperial overstretch: Ellenborough on 184–5; Napier on 331; Peel on 229

Indian Army, Napier's opinions about 292–3, 324, 329

Indian Government *see* East India Company

370   *Index*

Indus River 180, 194, 200–1, 203, 213, 219, 295–6; British plans for 183–6, 189, 195–8, 299, 331; erosion and flood control 188, 255
Indus River delta 237
information-gathering 137; *see also* questionnaires; spying
Ionian Islands 48, 53, 64–5, 70, 77–81, 84–5; *see also* Cephalonia; Corfu; Ithaca; Septinsular Republic; Zante
Ionian Islands, Lord High Commissioners of the *see* Adam; Maitland; Nugent
Ireland: agriculture in 19–20, 106, 122–3, 137, 162, 204, 256; badly governed 80, 123; education system 123; hunger in 86, 89–90, 261; Napier's childhood in 18–19; policing in 249n22; poor law for 90, 106, 120–1, 130, 141; unrest in 20–2, 27, 123, 146
Irish troops: limitations on 30; troop reinforcements from 145–7
Islamic rulership, Napier's views on 56–61, 167–8, 179–80, 188, 194–7, 200–1, 203, 253
Italy 53, 67, 106, 277; *see also* Venetian Republic; Venice
Ithaca 65, 70
Ivison, Duncan (philosopher) 334–5

Jackson, Richard (general in England) 136–7, 139, 144, 170
Jacob, John (army officer in Sind) 8, 214, 238–9, 246, 267, 324
jagirdars (land grantees) 244, 253–9, 262
jagirs (land grants) 244, 253, 255–8, 267
Jericho 72
jury trials 10n16, 78, 241

Kabul 182–3, 213, 218, 301, 307
Kafka, Ben (historian and psychoanalyst) 98
Kalhoras (earlier rulers of Sind) 187, 202, 258
Karachi 103, 190–6, 198, 200, 223, 341, 247, 270–1; Napier in 186, 239, 271
kardars (village headmen in Sind) 240–1, 244, 247, 253–4, 245
Kaye, John (Indian army officer and writer) 324
Kelly, Elizabeth *see* Napier, Elizabeth
Kennedy, James Shaw (army officer in England) 146
Kennedy, John Pitt (army engineer and Napier's friend): complains in London 97–8; counsels Napier to leave Sind 239; Irish agricultural and educational

reformer 122–3, 256–7; mentioned 100, 137, 188, 204, 213, 215, 265, 270–1, 277, 328; Napier's deputy and engineer in Cephalonia 82–5; re-enters army and acccompanies Napier to India 286; refuses positions in England and India 162, 168; relationship with Frederick Adam 83, 94–5
Kersal Moor (Manchester) 151–3
Khuhro, Hamida (historian and Pakistan Minister of Education) 189, 258, 261
Khyber Pass 182, 184, 189
Khyrpore (or Khairpur) (Sind) 199
Kildare 18, 21–2, 304
Kirkwall, Viscount, George William Hamilton Fitzmaurice Orkney 85
Kohat expedition 2, 301–10, 315, 317–18, 323, 330

labour strife 165–6, 168–70
La Coruña, Battle of (1809) 31–3, 239
Lahore 269
Laidlaw, Zoë (historian) 137
laissez-faire 36, 107–8, 261
Lambrick, H. T. (historian and 20th-century British official in Sind) 2, 8, 201
Lander, Edgardo (sociologist) 6–7, 262, 334
land reclamation: Cephalonia 81–2; Ireland 106, 122–3; Sind 188, 255, 258
land reform: England 109–10; Ireland 123; Sind 253–8
Lawrence, George St. Patrick (Indian army officer and Resident at Peshawar) 306, 309, 330
Lawrence, Henry Montgomery (Indian army officer and President of Punjab Board) 283, 306–9, 321, 324
Lawrence, John Laird Mair 1st Baron (member of Punjab Board, later Viceroy of India) 306–9, 321
laws of war 44, 46, 302, 304–5
Leeds 132, 142–4, 146
Leinster, Duchess of, née Lady Emilia Lennox (Napier's aunt) 16, 18
Lennox, Charles 3rd Duke of Richmond and Lennox, and duc d'Aubigny (Napier's uncle) 16, 18, 29
Lennox sisters *see* Conolly, Lady Louisa; Holland, Baroness; Leinster, Duchess of; Napier, Lady Sarah
liberal imperialism 5–8, 41, 112, 177, 333–6; *see also* conquest, humanitarian reasons for

Index 371

liberalism 5–8, 262, 333–5, 337–8
lighthouse (Cephalonia) 84
light troops 27, 34
Lisbon 31, 35, 306
Liverpool 146, 180
Lixouri (Cephalonia) 65, 84
loans for the poor 87–90, 261
London, Napier's views of 27, 328
London Greek Committee 70, 72–3, 100, 104
Loudiana (or Ludhiana) (Punjab) 294
Lough Ash (County Tyrone) 122, 162
Lovett, William (author of People's Charter) 131–2

Macaulay, Thomas Babington: disagreement with Napier over travel reimbursements 166; imperial liberalism of 235; poor opinion of Napier personally 340n35
MacDonald, James (appointed High Commissioner of Ionian Islands) 98
Mackenzie (army officer in Sind) 265
M'Mahon, Thomas (army commander in Bombay Presidency) 181
McMurdo, William: marries Sarah Susan Napier 67; Napier's aide-de-camp in India (1849–50) 286; at Napier's deathbed 332; worried about a duel 282
Macnaghten, William (Political Agent at Kabul) 182
Madras Presidency (division of British-run India) 96, 180, 182–3, 287
magistrates: in Cephalonia 77, 88; in England 115, 118–19; in north of England 4, 127, 141–2, 144–5, 151, 153–6, 160–1, 163–6, 170; in South Asia 242, 246, 292; see also 'Squire Magistrates'
Mahabaleshwar (Bombay Presidency) 181
Maitland, Thomas (army officer and colonial governor): advises Napier on Cephalonian justice system 77–8; British Commander in the Mediterranean and Lord High Commissioner of the Ionian Islands 53, 64, 70, 83, 100; despotic tendencies 55, 65; dies 78; radicalism of 53; support of Ali Pasha 56
Malakand Valley (Punjab) 2, 308
Malcolm, John (earlier Indian official) 203
Malthus, Thomas 106–7
Malwa opium 189–90
Manchester 132, 146, 151–3, 161, 165, 167
Manchester Guardian 303
Manningham, Coote (army officer in England) 27

Mantena, Karuna (political scientist) 5, 331, 335
markets (Cephalonia) 84–6
martial law 77, 118–19
Martineau, Harriet 106–7
Masséna, André (Marshal of France) 35, 304, 306
Mavrocordatos, Alexandros (Greek leader) 77
Mehmet Ali (Muhammed Ali Pasha) (Khedive of Egypt) 167–8, 179–80
Mehta, Uday Singh (political scientist) 5, 177, 334
Metaxata (Cephalonia) 70, 72, 82
Metcalfe, Charles (Indian official) 231
Methodism 70
Miani, Battle of (1843) 214–17, 223–5, 227–8, 231, 237, 239, 254
microgrants 261
military discipline 40–1, 69; Napier's views regarding 44–6, 114–18, 242–3, 292–3; see also execution; flogging
military occupation, rules for 44–5
military prizes 44, 46, 183, 205, 217, 232, 239, 282
military strategies and tactics of Napier: in 1st Sikh War 267–9; after Afghan defeat 183; in conquest of Sind 205, 211, 214, 237; defence of India 292, 296; in north of England 144–7, 153–4, 163, 167; against Punjabi hill tribes 300; against Sindhi hill tribes 265–7
Mill, James 5, 84
Mill, John Stuart 5–6, 78–9, 208n50, 227, 231, 333
Mir Rustam *see* Rustam
Molesworth, William (MP) 120
Moore, John (general): and Battle of La Coruña 31; commands in England and Denmark 26, 29; in Ireland 22, 26; personality of 26–7, 34
Morea (the Peloponnesian Peninsula) 64, 71, 73
Muhammed Ali Pasha *see* Mehmet Ali
Multan (Punjab) 200, 267–9, 284
murder 22, 41–3, 116, 163; in Cephalonia 77; by colonists 111; by factory owners and capitalists 1, 117, 325; in French Algeria 266; in Sind 179, 203, 243–4, 247–8, 261, 265
mutiny 40, 293, 296, 315–16, 320, 322–3, 330
Mutiny, Indian (or War of Independence) (1857–8) 324, 332

372   *Index*

Nafplion (Greece) 71–3, 76
Napier, Caroline (Napier's sister) 30, 35
Napier, Charles, Admiral (Napier's cousin, 'Black Charlie'): Carlist War 161; on China coast 179; defeat of Egypt 167–8, 180; Napier in Parliament 232; Peninsular War 31, 34–5
Napier, Charles James, Lieutenant-General, assessments of (19th century): by Bartle Frere 241–2, 261, 324; discussed in Parliament 228, 231; by former Indian officials 226, 231–2; by Frederick Adam 95; by James Outram 8, 195, 204, 225–6, 335; by J. S. Mill 79, 231; by Lord Ashley 227–8; Thomas Gordon 100
Napier, Charles James, Lieutenant-General: assessments of (20th century) 2–3, 170, 258, 261–2
Napier, Charles James, Lieutenant-General, career of: as aide-de-camp 34; appointed Commander-in-Chief of India 284–6; appointed Governor of Sind 217, 237; appointed Resident of Cephalonia 64; army command in north of England 139–70; Australian project 103–4; Bath politics 119–22; Battle of Busaco 34–5; Battle of Dubba 223–5; Battle of La Coruña 31–2; Battle of Miani 214–17; in Belgium and France 47; in Bermuda 40–1; consults with British Government 139; in England 280; enters military 19, 26; goes to Sind 186; governs Cephalonia 77–93; governs Sind 240–8, 253–62; hill war 265–7; Indian appointment 168; in India 287–8, 291–7, 299–305, 314–18; Inspector of Militia in Ionian Islands 48, 56; leaves Sind 270; military college 47–8; missions to Ali Pasha 56; Peninsular War 31–6; at Poona 180–1; raiding Virginia 41–6; regiment in Guernsey 36, 40; resignation 319–20; return to England 328; rifle corps 26; seeks employment 122; selected for command in England 136–7; staff corps 28; testifies on India 329–30; trains as engineer 29; visits London Greek Committee 73
Napier, Charles James, Lieutenant-General, family of 15–18; Anastasia as mistress 67–9; childhood 18–19, 29; on Continent 277; educates children 99–100; Elizabeth's illnesses and death 93, 99; has children with Anastasia 67–8; illness

of 2nd wife 270; in India 181; marries Elizabeth Kelly 68; marries Frances Alcock 105; meets Elizabeth Kelly 30; in north of England 166–9; on voyage to India 179
Napier, Charles James, Lieutenant-General, finances of 30, 46, 98, 130, 166–9, 179, 181, 183, 217, 239
Napier, Charles James, Lieutenant-General, illnesses and wounds of: battle wounds 31–2, 35, 169, 225, 270, 283; broken leg 29; cholera 99; final years 328, 332; heat prostration 238–9; rheumatism 169, 270; rocket injury 186; shingles 137
Napier, Charles James, Lieutenant-General, liberalism of 3–7, 107–9, 119, 333–8
Napier, Charles James, Lieutenant-General, military promotions: brevet Major 29; Captain 28; First Lieutenant 37n10; Lieutenent-Colonel 36, 40, 46; Lieutenant-General 270; Major-General 137
Napier, Charles James, Lieutenant-General, periods of mental disturbance: after death of 1st wife 99; his comments on 28, 270, 338; after leaving Cephalonia 96–9; in Sind 269–70; in youth 27–8
Napier, Charles James, Lieutenant-General, postings: American coast 41–6; Bermuda 40–1; Blatchington 26–7; Bognor 29; Cephalonia 64–70, 77–89; Chatham 27, 29; Chester 166–70; Dublin 27; Farnham 47; Guernsey 29–30, 36, 40; Hythe 29; India 287–325; Ionian Islands 48, 53–6; Limerick 26; London 27–8; Nottingham 139–66; Peninsular War 31–5; Poona 181; Shorncliffe 27; Sind 186–271, 281–2
Napier, Charles James, Lieutenant-General, radicalism of 36–7, 47–8, 106, 120–4, 335
Napier, Charles James, Lieutenant-General, residences of: Bath 98–9, 105, 115–22; Caen 99–100, 110, 121; Cheltenham 179, 281, 285; in childhood 18–22; Portsmouth 328, 332; St. Omer 47
Napier, Charles James, Lieutenant-General, statue of (Trafalgar Square) 227, 339
Napier, Charles James, Lieutenant-General, views and beliefs of see Adam, Frederick; Amirs of Sind; army career; Auckland; British Empire; Burma, annexation of; charity; Chartism; child labour; civil conflict; colonization; command

responsibility; danger to army; despotism; Egypt; execution; factory owners; Fitzgerald, Lord Edward; flogging; Fox, Charles James; France; Gough; government, role of; imperial overstretch; Indian Army; Islamic rulership; land reform; London; Malthus; Martineau; military discipline; murder (by colonists); murder (by factory owners and capitalists); Napier, William Francis Patrick; Napoleon I; Orientalism; policing; Poor Law Amendment Act; Rustam; secret ballot; Sind; Sismondi; slavery; small farms; suffrage; Tories; Turks; universalism; village-burning; Whigs; yeomen; *zemindars*

Napier, Charles James, Lieutenant-General, works of: *The Colonies. . . . Strictures on the Administration of Sir Frederick Adam* (1833) 78–80, 84, 88–9, 93, 98–100, 108, 269, 338; *Colonization, Particularly in Southern Australia . . .* (1835) 104–7, 109–12, 122; *Defects, Civil and Military, of the Indian Government* (1853) 304, 310, 328, 330–2; editor's notes in Alfred Victor, comte de Vigny, *Lights and Shades of Military Life* (1840, new edn 1850) 305, 325; *An Essay on the Present State of Ireland . . .* (1839) 123; *Greece in 1824* (1824) 61; *A Letter on the Defense of England by Corps of Volunteers and Militia . . .* (1852) 328; *A Letter to the Right Hon. Sir J. Hobhouse . . . on the Baggage of the Indian Army* (London: 1849) 281–2; *Memoir on the Roads of Cephalonia* (1825) 81–2; *Remarks on Military Law and the Punishment of Flogging* (1837) 114–19, 305; *War in Greece* (1821) 57–61; *William the Conqueror: A Historical Romance* (1858) 119

Napier, Elizabeth, formerly Mrs. Elizabeth Kelly, née Oakley (Napier's first wife): book on child-rearing 100; illnesses and death 93, 99; marries Napier 68; relationship with Napier 30–3

Napier, Emily, later Emily Bunbury (Mrs Henry Bunbury) (Napier's sister) 16, 33, 38n24, 203, 232, 260

Napier, Emily Cephalonia (Napier's younger daughter) 67–9, 103, 181, 277

Napier, Frances, formerly Mrs Frances Alcock, née Foley (Napier's 2nd wife) 105, 168, 181, 183, 270, 277, 285

Napier, George (Napier's brother): Governor of the Cape 182; knew Charles Shaw 161; knew William Makepeace Thackeray 285; in Nice 277; in the Peninsular War 31–5; refuses appointment as Command-in-Chief of India 284

Napier, Henry (Napier's brother) 30, 169, 266

Napier, Lady Sarah, formerly Lady Sarah Bunbury, née Lennox (Napier's mother): blind widow in London 32–3, 47, 122; closeness to nephew Charles James Fox 17; death 68; divorced by Charles Bunbury 15; on Irish unrest 21–2; marriage to Hon. George Napier 16; as a mother 29; Napier's letters to 27, 29–30, 47–8, 64; obtains Napier's commission 19; possible marriage to George III 15

Napier, Louisa (Napier's half-sister) 18, 33, 38n24, 68, 123, 166, 169–70

Napier, Priscilla, née Hayter (popular biographer in 20th century) 10n11, 12n34

Napier, Sarah Susan (Napier's elder daughter; later Susan McMurdo) 67–8, 103, 181

Napier, the Hon. George (Napier's father) 16–19

Napier, William C. E. (Napier's nephew, son-in-law, and aide-de-camp) 286

Napier, William Francis Patrick (Napier's brother): in Bath 119; conspiracy theorist 95–6, 98, 280–3, 286; defender of Napier 200, 213, 240, 262, 270, 282; mass of Charles' correspondence with 95, 269; at Napier's funeral 332–3; Napier's opinion of 96, 138, 281, 283; in the Napoleonic Wars 28–30, 34–5, 47; untrustworthy but prolific author 8–9, 21–2, 101n14

Napoleon I 27, 31, 34, 56, 64; imperial theories of 7; Napier's views on 29–30, 41, 47, 53, 100, 257–8, 325; Sismondi's views on 107–8

Napoleon III 328

Nasir Khan (Nasir Khan Talpur Baloch of Hyderabad) (Mir in Sind) 196, 200, 209

Newcastle 146, 157

New Poor Law *see* Poor Law Amendment Act of 1834; Poor Law Guardians

Newport Rising (1839) 160–1, 164

Ney, Michel (Marshal of France) 32

374   *Index*

noncombatants, protection of 205, 267
Normanby, Constantine Henry Phipps 1st
    Marquess of (Home Secretary) 163
Northern Star 132, 161
Nott, William (general in Afghanistan)
    304
Nova Scotia 46
Nugent, Lord, George Grenville 2nd
    Baron (Lord High Commissioner of the
    Ionian Islands) 84

O'Connell, Daniel ('the Liberator') 120–2,
    334
O'Connor, Feargus 130, 132, 138–9, 141–2,
    151, 161
Ocracoke (Virginia) 43, 46
Old Corruption 36, 57, 337
Oldenburg, Veena Talwar (historian) 257
Oldham 129–32, 141, 334
Omercote (or Umerkot) (Sind) 225
opium 189–90, 194
Orangemen 20, 22
Orientalism: of officials in India 203–4,
    296, 308–9; of travellers in Sind 187–8;
    of Napier 57, 59–61, 203, 208n50,
    222n53, 245–7, 254–60; *see also* Islamic
    rulership
Orwell, George 2, 308
Otho (King of Greece) 100
Ottoman Empire 56, 59–61, 64–5, 70, 80
Outram, James (Political Agent in Sind):
    campaign against Napier 209, 214,
    219–20, 237–40, 247, 270; defends
    residency in Hyderabad 213–14; military
    plans of 225; negotiates with Amirs
    202, 212; Orientalism of 203–4, 259; on
    shortcomings of native rule 196–7, 199,
    202, 209; turns against Napier 202

Paris 47, 110, 277
Parry, Jonathan (historian) 337
'peasantisation' (Washbrook) 256
'*peccavi*', 226–7
Peel, Robert (Prime Minister) 170, 184,
    197; toasts Napier (1848) 280; views of
    annexation of Sind 198, 228–30; views
    of Napier 230
Peloponnesian Peninsula *see* Morea
Peninsular War 30–6, 40, 56, 215, 304,
    306–7
Penn, William 105
Penny Magazine 105, 109
People's Charter 131

Peshawar 2, 300, 306, 308, 314–15, 322,
    331
petition (Chartist) 132–3, 142, 151, 157
Philhellenes 69–72, 271
Phillipps, Samuel March (Undersecretary
    of State at the Home Office) 145
Pinker, Steven (psychologist) 245
Pitts, Jennifer (political scientist) 5–6
policing, Napier's views on: in Australia
    105; in north of England 151–2, 157–8,
    166; in South Asia 240–2, 292, 300
Pollock, George (general in Afghanistan)
    184, 304
Poor Law Amendment Act of 1834
    (England) 103, 129, 155, 165; Napier's
    opposition to 120, 123–4, 130, 139, 141,
    157, 162
Poor Law Guardians 117, 139, 141, 162–3,
    172n18
poor people, Napier's opinions about 3–4,
    47–8, 106, 121; in Cephalonia 55, 77–8,
    85–6, 123–4; in the north of England
    147, 162–4; in Sind 194–5, 205–6, 244
Portland, William Bentinck 4th Duke of
    (landowner) 143–4, 163
Portsmouth 29, 280, 328, 332
Portugal 30–1, 35, 306–7; possible British
    rule of 41, 180, 333
Postans, Marianne (writer in India and
    Sind) 188
Postans, Thomas (earlier official in Sind)
    188, 226
Potato Famine 261
Pottinger, Henry (earlier official in Sind
    and later colonial governor) 189, 204,
    226, 283
Preedy, Captain (army officer in Sind) 223,
    264n35
Presidencies (India) 179–81, 240
Presidents of the Board of Control
    see Ellenborough; Fitzgerald, Lord;
    Hobhouse; Ripon
Prichard, James Cowles (anthropologist) 58
Prime Ministers *see* Peel; Ripon; Russell;
    Wellington
Pringle, R. K. (later Commissioner for
    Sind) 260
Prize Agents 217
prize money 44, 46, 183, 205, 232, 239, 282
puggees (trackers) 241
Punch 114, 226–7, 285
Punjab 179–80, 184, 200, 246, 257; unrest
    in garrison 293, 295–7, 315, 319–20, 322;

unrest in hills 2, 299–300, 309; *see also* Kohat expedition

Punjab, annexation of: carried out 287, 293, 299; considered 183, 186, 189, 269, 272–3n22

Punjab, history of: 1st Sikh War 267–9; 2nd Sikh War 284–7; British Resident 283–4; Ranjit Singh 187; restored independence 269, 281; rule by Punjab Board 306–8, 320–1

Pye, Neil (historian), alternative interpretation of Napier 149n36

Quarterly Review 329

questionnaires 4, 139, 253

race: environmental theories of 57–8; Napier on new ideas of race 203, 259–60; Napier on races 58, 80–1, 111–12

racist violence 249n28, 330–1

radicalism: appropriateness of term in early 19th century 36; and mid-19th century liberalism 334–5, 337–8; Napier's identification with 4, 36, 47–8, 111, 119, 139; popular radicalism before Chartism 129

Rahman, Tariq (historian and critic) 262

rais (headship) of upper Sind 198–9, 220n11; *see also* Ali Murad; Rustam

Rawalpindi 293–5, 315

razzias (Algeria) 266

Reform Act (1832) 119–20, 129

regime change *see* conquest, humanitarian reasons for

resettlement 266–7, 304, 309

Revolt of the United Irishmen (1798) 7, 16, 20, 22, 26, 145–6, 304

Rifle Corps 26–7, 154

Riot Act, operation of 118, 156

Ripon, Frederick Robinson 1st Viscount Goderich and 1st Earl of Ripon (Prime Minster, Colonial Secretary, and President of the Board of Control) 95–7, 229, 232

Robertson, Frederick (clergyman and Napier's friend) 168

Rochdale 140–1, 146, 156

Rodger, Thomas (historian) 12n37

Roebuck, John (MP) 120, 227–8, 232, 261

Rohri (Sind) 198, 210, 241

Ross, Hew (army officer in north of England) 146, 156

Rousseau, Jean-Jacques 16

Roworth, William (Nottingham Mayor) 162

Roy, Ram Mohun 245

Russell, Lord John 1st Earl Russell (Home Secretary and Prime Minister): distant relationship with Napier 145–6; as Home Secretary 122, 145, 154, 156–7; meeting with Napier over Chartism 139; meeting with Napier over command of Indian Army 286; as Prime Minister 261–86; rejection of Chartist demands 133

Russia 56, 59–61, 65, 77, 182–3

Rustam Ali Khan Talpur (Mir of Khyrpore and *rais* of upper Sind) 199–201, 212, 217, 226; Napier's opinions about 209–11, 238

ryots (tenant farmers) 255, 259

salt tax (Punjab) 299–300, 309

Sami (Cephalonia) 65, 67

Sartori, Andrew (historian) 6

sati 245–6

Scotland 107, 132; Napier family in 17, 31; Napier never visits 263n17

secret ballot, Napier's support for 117, 120–1, 334

sepoy soldiers 180, 186, 220, 224, 293, 315–16, 318; Dalhousie's views of 296, 324; Napier's views of 292–3, 314, 324

Septinsular Republic 53, 55, 64–5; *see also* Ionian Islands

Shaftesbury, Lord *see* Ashley

Shaw, Charles (Manchester police official) 161–2

Sheffield 141, 164

Shere Muhammed (Sher Muhammed Talpur) (Mir in Sind) 223–5

shikargahs (forest preserves in Sind) 188, 194, 198

Shorncliffe (Kent) 27, 29

Shuja Shah Durrani (Emir of Afghanistan) 182

Simla (summer capital of India) 287, 293–5, 318, 324–5

Sind, annexation of: carried out 210, 237; considered 185, 194–7, 200, 229–31

Sind, history of: British rule after Napier 241–2, 258, 260–1; Kalhora rule 187, 202, 258; Napier's rule 235–71; Talpur rule 187–8, 194, 240–1, 253–5, 258, 262

Sind, Napier's opinions about 188, 194–7, 202–3, 237, 257–60, 269, 271

376   *Index*

Sismondi, Jean Charles Léonard Simonde de 106–8; Napier's reliance upon 110–11, 157, 337

slavery: in America 45–6, 60, 80; metaphorical 58–60, 80, 88, 147, 168, 243, 259; in Sind 186, 247

small farms, Napier views of 109–10, 123, 257

Smith, G. A. (historian) 46

Somerset, Lord Fitzroy 1st Baron Raglan (Military Secretary at the Horse Guards) 122, 136–7, 168, 181, 319

Soult, Jean-de-Dieu (Marshal General of France) 31–2

South Australia Company 103–5

Spain, war in *see* Peninsular War

Spivak, Gayatri Chakravorty (literary theorist) 246–7

spying 132, 143–4, 165, 209, 219

'Squire Magistrates', 297

Stanhope, Charles (officer at La Coruña) 31

Stanhope, Leicester (Philhellene) 72

Stanhope, Lord, Philip Henry Stanhope 4th Earl Stanhope 124

statue of Napier (Trafalgar Square) 227, 339

steamers on Indus 185, 194–5, 198, 213, 219, 223, 260

Stephens, Joseph Rayner (radical) 334

Stone, Lawrence (historian) 29

stoning 118, 156, 167, 308

suffrage, universal: for men 16, 131, 133, 156–7; Napier's support for 117, 120, 130, 147, 157–8, 333–4, 337; for women 134n12; *see also* franchise; voting

'suicides' of women killed by men 247

Sukkur (Sind) 186, 189, 194, 197–8, 241

Sunderland 146

Sutlej River 184

Talpur Amirs of Sind *see* Amirs of Sind

Tatah (Sind) 198

Thackeray, William Makepeace 285, 238

Thier, Adolphe (historian and politician) 277

Tidrick, Kathryn (historian and psychologist) 308

Times (London) 121, 200, 280–5, 303, 308, 329

Tippoo Sultan 53

Tocqueville, Alexis de 5–6, 20, 333

torch-lit meetings 132, 141, 157

Tories, Napier's opinions of 64, 132, 144, 158, 170, 180, 337

troops, concentration of *see* concentration of troops

troops, discipline of *see* military discipline

Turks 56, 64–5, 69, 70, 100; Napier's opinions of 59–61, 72, 80, 259

United Irishmen 16, 20, 26

United States, war with (1812–15) 40–6

universalism 5–7, 177, 204, 227–8, 246–7, 334–8; in Napier's thought 6, 58, 60, 79, 112, 204, 245, 325

universal suffrage *see* suffrage

unstamped press movement 129–31

Vattel, Emerich de (18th-century legal theorist) 302, 305

Venetian Republic 64–5, 80

Venice 227

Victoria (Queen) 217, 253, 287

Vigny, Alfred Victor, comte de (Romantic poet, novelist, and military writer) 305, 325

village-burning, Napier's opinion of 2, 301–4, 306–8, 310, 321, 330

Vinegar Hill, Battle of (1798) 22

Virginia 41–6

Virgin Islands 46

Vitoria, Francisco de (16th-century theologian and jurist) 5

voting (examples of): in Cephalonia 55–6; in England 121; in English clubs 55–6; in France 121; *see also* franchise; suffrage

Wakefield, Edward Gibbon 103–5, 107, 109, 129

Washbrook, D. A. (historian) 256

Waterloo, aftermath of battle 47

Wazirabad (Punjab) 314–16, 320

Wellington, Arthur Wellesley 1st Duke of: Commander-in-Chief of the Forces 136, 184; on illegal orders 304; Irish Potato Famine 261; and Napier's resignation as Commander-in-Chief 319, 322–3; Peninsular War 34–5, 306–7; plans for keeping Sind 184, 189, 225; reconciliation with Napier and funeral 328; recruits Napier as Commander-in-Chief of India 284–6; relationship with Ellenborough 189, 198, 239; wants to promote Napier 271; at Waterloo 47

Wemyss, Thomas (army officer in north of England): dislike of factory owners and local officials 165; Napier's subordinate 146–7, 155–6, 161, 169; Tory beliefs of 153

Wexford 22, 26
Whately, Richard (Archbishop of Dublin) 123
Whigs, Napier's opinions of 110–11, 117, 120, 122, 138, 144, 147, 155, 158, 337–8
Wigan 146
William IV 94
Winkworth, Catherine (schoolgirl) 226–7
Wong, J. Y. (historian) 189–90
Wylie, Major (army officer in India) 317–19

Yang, Anand (historian) 246
Yapp, M. E. (historian) 2

yeomen class, Napier's ideas about 110, 257
York and Albany, Prince Frederick, Duke of (Commander-in-Chief of the Forces) 27, 33, 36
Young, G. M. (historian) 3
Young, Keith (army officer and judge in India) 245, 265

Zante 65, 78, 84, 97
Zastoupil, Lynn (historian) 5
zemindars (land officers) 255–6, 261; Napier's opinions about 257–9
zenanas (women's quarters) 219